July 13–17, 2016
Halifax, Nova Scotia, Canada

Association for Computing Machinery

Advancing Computing as a Science & Profession

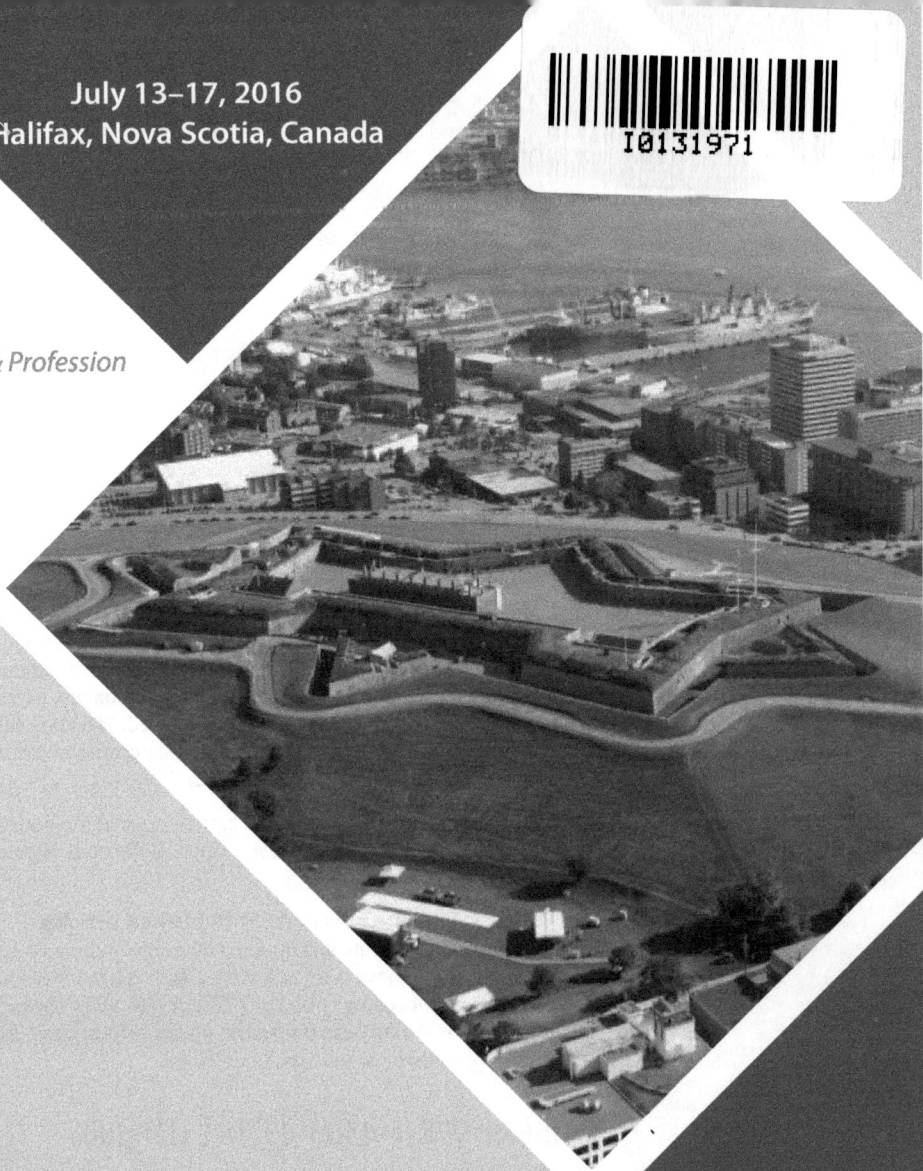

UMAP'16

Proceedings of the 2016 Conference on
User Modeling Adaptation and Personalization

Sponsored by:
ACM SIGCHI & ACM SIGWEB

Supported by:
User Modeling Inc., National Science Foundation, Microsoft, Dalhousie University, Springer, & Google

**Association for
Computing Machinery**

Advancing Computing as a Science & Profession

The Association for Computing Machinery
2 Penn Plaza, Suite 701
New York, New York 10121-0701

Notice to Past Authors of ACM-Published Articles
ACM intends to create a complete electronic archive of all articles and/or other material previously published by ACM. If you have written a work that has been previously published by ACM in any journal or conference proceedings prior to 1978, or any SIG Newsletter at any time, and you do NOT want this work to appear in the ACM Digital Library, please inform permissions@acm.org, stating the title of the work, the author(s), and where and when published.

ISBN: 978-1-4503-4370-1 (Digital)

ISBN: 978-1-4503-4612-2 (Print)

Additional copies may be ordered prepaid from:

ACM Order Department
PO Box 30777
New York, NY 10087-0777, USA

Phone: 1-800-342-6626 (USA and Canada)
+1-212-626-0500 (Global)
Fax: +1-212-944-1318
E-mail: acmhelp@acm.org
Hours of Operation: 8:30 am – 4:30 pm ET

Printed in the USA

Chairs' Welcome

Welcome to the 24th ACM International Conference on User Modeling, Adaptation, and Personalization (UMAP 2016) in Halifax, Canada, July 13-16, 2016. UMAP is the premier international conference for researchers and practitioners working on systems that adapt to individual users or to groups of users. UMAP is the successor of the biennial User Modeling (UM) and Adaptive Hypermedia and Adaptive Web-based Systems (AH) conferences that were merged in 2009. It has traditionally been organized under the auspices of User Modeling Inc. This year (2016) UMAP became an ACM conference, sponsored by ACM SIG CHI and SIG WEB.

The conference spans a wide scope of topics related to user modeling, adaptation, and personalization. UMAP 2016 is focused on bringing together cutting-edge research from user interaction and modeling, adaptive technologies, and delivery platforms. It includes high-quality peer-reviewed papers featuring substantive new research in one of **five research areas**, each chaired by leaders in the field:

- *User Modeling for Recommender Systems* (chairs: Alexander Felfernig & Pasquale Lops)

- *Adaptive & Personalized Educational Systems* (chairs: Antonija Mitrovic & Kalina Yacef)

- *Personalization in the Social Web & Crowdsourcing Era* (chairs: Alessandro Bozzon & Harith Alani)

- *Adaptive, Intelligent, & Multimodal User Interfaces* (chairs: Julien Epps & Hatice Gunes)

- *Architectures, Techniques, & Methodologies for UMAP* (chairs: Stephan Weibelzahl & Mihaela Cocea)

This year we received 123 submissions. In keeping with UMAPs rigorous standards, each paper was carefully reviewed by members of the Program Committee (PC) while the Area Chairs (ACs) coordinated the reviews and provided recommendations to the Program Chairs. The international Program Committee (PC) consisted of 132 members who were assisted by 49 subreviewers. These were leading researchers as well as highly promising young researchers.

Papers were assigned to at least 4 members of the PC and to 1 AC member based on their expertise, interests, and other factors. Each paper received at least 3 reviews, and 95% received 4 reviews. After the initial reviews were submitted, the designated AC facilitated discussion amongst reviewers in order to resolve differences and correct misunderstandings. The AC then provided a summative meta-review and a recommendation to the Program Chairs. The final decisions were based on these recommendations, the meta-reviews, and reviewer scores.

We accepted 21 long papers (23.9% acceptance rate) and 13 short papers (27.6% acceptance rate) for oral presentation and an additional 17 extended abstracts for poster presentation and inclusion in the proceedings. The program also features posters, demos, and late breaking results, which collectively showcase the wide spectrum of novel ideas and latest results in user modeling, adaptation and personalization.

We also invited three distinguished **keynote speakers**, each illustrating significant issues and prospective directions for the field.

- *Hossein Derakhshan* (shared keynote speaker with Hypertext 2016) is an Iranian-Canadian blogger who was imprisoned in Tehran from November 2008 to November 2014. He has been called the "father of Persian blogging" and has helped promote podcasting in Iran. His talk,

"Killing the Hyperlink, Killing the Web: the Shift from Library-Internet to Television-Internet," reflects his views on the Internet today.

- *Lada Adamic* leads the Product Science group within Facebook's Data Science Team. She is also an adjunct associate professor at the University of Michigan's School of Information and Center for the Study of Complex Systems. Her talk *"The Life and Times of Information in Networks"* focuses on cascades of information-sharing and resharing within social media.

- *Sandra Carberry* was one of the founders of the User Modeling research area at the first workshop in Maria Laach in 1986. As appropriate for the 30th anniversary, her talk *"User Modeling: The Past, The Present and The Future"* discusses how the field evolved, insights into where the field is headed, and the hottest topics for exploration.

The conference includes a **doctoral consortium** that provides an opportunity for doctoral students to explore and develop their research interests under the guidance of distinguished scholars. This track received 18 submissions of which nine were accepted as full papers and eight as posters.

A set of seven **workshops** and two **tutorials** round out the program.

- *(Workshop) IFUP: Workshop on Multi-dimension Information Fusion for Modeling and Personalisation* (half-day) organized by Robin Burke (DePaul University, USA), Feida Zhu (Singapore Management University, Singapore), Neil Yorke-Smith (American University of Beirut, Lebanon), and Guibing Guo (Northeastern University, China)

- *(Workshop) INRA: News Recommendation and Analytics* (half-day) organized by Jon Atle Gulla (Norwegian University of Science and Technology Trondheim, Norway), Luc Martens (Minds-UGent-WiCa Ghent, Belgium), Özlem Özgöbek (Norwegian University of Science and Technology Trondheim, Norway), and Nafiseh Shabib (TNS Gallup, Oslo, Norway)

- *(Workshop) SOAP: Workshop on Surprise, Opposition, and Obstruction in Adaptive and Personalized Systems* (half-day) organized by Peter Knees (Johannes Kepler University Linz, Austria), Kristina Andersen (Studio for Electro Instrumental Music, Amsterdam, the Netherlands), Alan Said (Recorded Future, Gothenburg, Sweden), and Marko Tkalcic (Free University of Bozen-Bolzano, Italy)

- *(Workshop) HAAPIE: Human Aspects in Adaptive and Personalised Interactive Environments* (half-day) organized by Panagiotis Germanakos (SAP SE, Germany), Marios Belk (Department of Computer Science, University of Cyprus), George Samaras (Department of Computer Science, University of Cyprus), and Vania Dimitrova (University of Leeds, UK)

- *(Workshop) EvalUMAP: Towards comparative evaluation in the user modelling, adaptation and personalization space* (full-day) organized by Owen Conlan (Trinity College Dublin, Ireland), Liadh Kelly (Trinity College Dublin, Ireland), Kevin Koidl (Trinity College Dublin, Ireland), Séamus Lawless (Trinity College Dublin, Ireland), Killian Levacher (Trinity College Dublin, Ireland), and Athanasios Staikopoulos (Trinity College Dublin, Ireland)

- *(Workshop) FuturePD: The future of personal data: envisioning new personalized services enabled by Quantified Self technologies* (half-day) organized by Amon Rapp (University of Torino, Italy), Federica Cena (University of Torino, Italy), Judy Kay (University of Sidney, Australia), Bob Kummerfeld (University of Sydney, Australia), Frank Hopfgartner (University Gardens Glasgow, UK), Jakob Eg Larsen (Technical University of Denmark, Denmark), and Elise van den Hoven (University of Technology Sydney, Australia).

- *(Workshop) PALE: Personalization Approaches in Learning Environments* (full-day) organized by Milos Kravcik (RWTH Aachen University, Germany), Olga C. Santos (UNED, Spain), Jesus G. Boticario (UNED, Spain), and Maria Bielikova (FIIT STUBA, Slovakia)

- *(Tutorial) Semantics-Aware Techniques for Social Media Analysis, User Modeling, and Recommender Systems* (half-day) by Pasquale Lops and Cataldo Musto (University of Bari Aldo Moro, Italy)

- *(Tutorial) Games, Gamification and Personalization* (half-day) by Amon Rapp (University of Torino, Italy).

We would like to acknowledge the excellent work and help from the UMAP 2016 Organizing Committee including:

- *Area chairs, Program Committee, and Subreviewers*

- *Workshop and Tutorial chairs*: Jie Zhang (NTU, Singapore) and Federica Cena (University of Torino, Italy)

- *Doctoral Consortium chairs*: Vania Dimitrova (University of Leeds, UK) and Maria Bielikova (Slovak University of Technology, Slovakia)

- *Poster, Demos, and Late-breaking Results chairs:* Darina Dicheva (Winston Salem University, USA) and Michel Desmarais (Polytechnique Montreal, Canada)

- *Publicity*: Christoph Trattner (University of Graz, Austria)

- *Student Funding Committee*: Cristina Gena (University of Torino, Italy), Vania Dimitrova (University of Leeds, UK), Bamshad Mobasher (DePaul University, USA), and Sidney D'Mello (University of Notre Dame, USA).

- *Website Design and Maintenance:* Eelco Herder (University of Hannover, Germany), Emmanuel Kaku and Julita Vassileva (University of Saskatchewan, Canada)

- We would like to acknowledge the use of EasyChair for management of the submissions and review process.

Finally, thanks to the authors for sending us their best work and to all the attendees who bring UMAP 2016 to life.

Lora Aroyo
UMAP 2016 Program Chair
VU Amsterdam, the Netherlands

Sidney D'Mello
UMAP 2016 Program Chair
University of Notre Dame, USA

Julita Vassileva
UMAP 2016 General Chair
University of Saskatchewan, Canada

James Blustein
UMAP 2016 General Chair
Dalhousie University, Canada

Table of Contents

Session: Adaptive & Personalized Education and Recommender Systems

Session: Recommender Systems I

Session: Recommender Systems II

Session: Extended Abstracts

UMAP 2016 Conference Organization

General Chairs: Julita Vassileva (University of Saskatchewan, Canada)
James Blustein (Dalhousie University, Canada)

Program Chairs: Lora Aroyo (VU Amsterdam, the Netherlands)
Sidney D'Mello (University of Notre Dame, USA)

Workshop and Tutorials Chairs: Federica Cena (University of Torino, Italy)
Jie Zhang (Nanyang Technological University, Singapore)

Doctoral Consortium Chairs: Vania Dimitrova (University of Leeds, UK)
Maria Bielikova (Slovak University of Technology in Bratislava, Slovakia)

Poster, Demo and Late-Breaking Results chairs: Darina Dicheva (Winston Salem University, USA)
Michel Desmarais (Polytechnique Montreal, Canada)

Area Chairs: Harith Alani (KMi, The Open University, UK)
Alessandro Bozzon (Delft University of Technology, Netherlands)
Mihaela Cocea (School of Computing, University of Portsmouth, UK)
Julien Epps (UNSW Australia and Data61 CSIRO, Australia)
Alexander Felfernig (Graz University of Technology, Austria)
Hatice Gunes (University of Cambridge, UK)
Pasquale Lops (University of Bari, Italy)
Antonija Mitrovic (University of Canterbury, Christchurch, New Zealand)
Stephan Weibelzahl (PFH Private University of Applied Sciences Göttingen, Germany)
Kalina Yacef (The University of Sydney, Australia)

Publicity Chair: Christoph Trattner (Graz University of Technology, Austria)

Student Funding Committee: Cristina Gena (University of Torino, Italy)
Vania Dimitrova (University of Leeds, UK)
Bamshad Mobasher (DePaul University, USA)
Sidney D'Mello (University of Notre Dame, USA)

Program Committee: Kenro Aihara (National Institute of Informatics, Japan)
Omar Alonso (Microsoft, USA)
Liliana Ardissono (University of Torino, Italy)
Ivon Arroyo (Worcester Polytechnic Institute, USA)
Martin Atzmueller (University of Kassel, Germany)
Nilufar Baghaei (UNITEC, New Zealand)
Ryan Baker (Teachers College, Columbia University, USA)
Mathias Bauer (mineway GmbH, Germany)
Shlomo Berkovsky (CSIRO, Australia)

Program Committee (continued):	Nadia Berthouze (University College London, UK)
Maria Bielikova (Slovak University of Technology in Bratislava, Slovakia)
Gautam Biswas (Vanderbilt University, USA)
Pradipta Biswas (Indian Institute of Science, UK)
Kalina Bontcheva (University of Sheffield, UK)
Derek Bridge (University College Cork, Ireland)
Paul Brna (University of Leeds, UK)
Joost Broekens (TU Delft, Netherlands)
Peter Brusilovsky (University of Pittsburgh, USA)
Grégoire Burel (The Open University, UK)
Iván Cantador (Universidad Autónoma de Madrid, Spain)
Rosa M. Carro (Universidad Autonoma de Madrid, Spain)
Federica Cena (University of Torino, Italy)
Eva Cerezo (Universidad de Zaragoza, Spain)
Li Chen (Hong Kong Baptist University, Hong Kong)
Keith Cheverst (Lancaster University, UK)
Min Chi (North Carolina State University, USA)
David Chin (University of Hawaii, USA)
Cristina Conati (University of British Columbia, Canada)
Paolo Cremonesi (Politecnico di Milano, Italy)
Alexandra Cristea (University of Warwick, UK)
Elizabeth M. Daly (IBM Research, Ireland)
Munmun De Choudhury (Georgia Institute of Technology, USA)
Marco De Gemmis (University of Bari, Italy)
Pasquale De Meo (VU University, Amsterdam, Netherlands)
Michel Desmarais (Ecole Polytechnique de Montreal, Canada)
Ernesto Diaz-Aviles (IBM Research, Ireland)
Chris Dijkshoorn (VU University Amsterdam, Netherlands)
Vania Dimitrova (School of Computing, University of Leeds, UK)
Peter Dolog (Aalborg University, Denmark)
Benedict du Boulay (University of Sussex, UK)
Casey Dugan (IBM T.J. Watson Research, USA)
Bruce Ferwerda (Johannes Kepler University Linz, Austria)
Davide Fossati (Emory University, USA)
Jill Freyne (CSIRO, Australia)
Ujwal Gadiraju (L3S Research Center, Germany)
Fabio Gasparetti (Roma Tre University, Italy)
Mouzhi Ge (Universitaet der Bundeswehr Munich, Germany)
Cristina Gena (University of Torino, Italy)
Rosella Gennari (Free U. of Bozen-Bolzano, Italy)
Panagiotis Germanakos (University of Cyprus, Cyprus)
Werner Geyer (IBM T.J. Watson Research, USA)
Bradley Goodman (The MITRE Corporation, USA)
Ido Guy (Yahoo Research, Israel)

Program Committee (continued):

Program Committee (continued):   Denis Parra (Pontificia Universidad Catolica de Chile, Chile)
Christopher Peters (KTH Royal Institute of Technology, Sweden, Sweden)
Paolo Petta (Austrian Research Institute for Artificial Intelligence, Austria)
Luiz Pizzato (Commonwealth Bank of Australia, Australia)
Kaska Porayska-Pomsta (London Knowledge Lab, UK)
Judith Redi (Delft University of Technology, Netherlands)
Francesco Ricci (Free University of Bozen-Bolzano, Italy)
Ma. Mercedes T. Rodrigo (Ateneo de Manila University, Philippines)
Ido Roll (University of British Columbia, Canada)
Cristobal Romero (University of Cordoba, Spain)
Domenico Rosaci (University Mediterranea of Reggio Calabria, Italy)
Matthew Rowe (Lancaster University, UK)
Giancarlo Ruffo (Universita' di Torino, Italy)
Alan Said (University of Skövde, Sweden)
George Samaras (University of Cyprus, Cyprus)
Olga C. Santos (aDeNu Research Group (UNED), Spain)
Markus Schedl (Johannes Kepler University Linz, Austria)
Giovanni Semeraro (University of Bari, Italy)
Elena Simperl (University of Southampton, UK)
Barry Smyth (University College Dublin, Ireland)
Mohammad Soleymani (University of Geneva, Switzerland)
Marcus Specht (Open University of the Nethderlands, Netherlands)
Ben Steichen (Santa Clara University, Canada)
Markus Strohmaier (University of Koblenz-Landau, Germany)
Andrea Tagarelli (University of Calabria, Italy)
Loren Terveen (University of Minnesota, USA)
Dhavalkumar Thakker (University of Bradford, UK)
Nava Tintarev (Bournemouth University, UK)
Marko Tkalcic (Free University of Bozen-Bolzano, Austria)
Christoph Trattner (Know-Center, Austria)
Khiet Truong (University of Twente, Netherlands)
Amali Weerasinghe (The University of Adelaide, Australia)
Martijn Willemsen (Eindhoven University of Technology, Netherlands)
Joseph Jay Williams (Harvard University, USA)
Michael Yudelson (Carnegie Mellon University, USA)
Massimo Zancanaro (FBK, Italy)
Jie Zhang (Nanyang Technological University, Singapore)
Yong Zheng (DePaul University, USA)
Ingrid Zukerman (Monash University, Australia)

Additional reviewers:

Marwan Al-Tawil
Alessia Amelio
Satabdi Basu
Marios Belk
Claudio Biancalana
Veronica Bogina
Annalina Caputo
Matt Dennis
Rafael Dias Araújo
Yi Dong
Mehdi Elahi
Fabian Flöck
Shuguang Han
Matthias Hirth
Yun Huang
Roberto Interdonato
Shamya Karumbaiah
Ondrej Kaššák
Georgios Katsimpras
Michal Kompan
Mark Kröll
Lydia Lau
Chen Lin
Peter Looms
Brian Metzger

Fedelucio Narducci
Terry Peckham
Diego Perna
Dimitris Pierrakos
Alicja Piotrkowicz
Amon Rapp
Tuukka Ruotsalo
Márius Šajgalík
Giuseppe Sansonetti
Daniel Schlör
Sarah Schultz
Jennifer Seaton
Shitian Shen
Jakub Simko
Marcella Tambuscio
Chun-Hua Tsai
Dimitrios Vogiatzis
Katrin Weller
Naomi Wixon
Beverly Woolf
Peng Xu
Yuan Zhang
Guojing Zhou
Daniel Zoller

UMAP 2016 Sponsors & Supporters

Sponsors:

Supporters:

Killing the Hyperlink, Killing the Web:
The Shift from Library-Internet to Television-Internet

Hossein Derakhshan
New Media Society
Tehran, Iran
hodertemp@gmail.com

ABSTRACT

The Web, as envisaged by its inventors, was founded on the idea of *hyperlinks*. Derived from the notion of hypertext in literary theory, a hyperlink is a relation rather than an object. It is a system of connections that connects distant pieces of text, resulting in a non-linear, open, active, decentralized, and diverse space we called the World Wide Web.

But in the past few years, and with the rise of closed social networks, as well as mobile apps, the hyperlink — and thereby the Web — are in serious trouble. Most social networks have created a closed, linear, centralized, sequential, passive, and homogeneous space, where users are encouraged to stay in all the time — a space that is more like television. The Web was imagined as an intellectual project that promoted knowledge, debate, and tolerance; as something I call *library-internet*. Now it has become more about entertainment and commerce; I call this *tv-internet*.

This topic is extensively articulated in "The Web We Have to Save," published in July 2015 by Matter magazine[1].

[1]https://medium.com/matter/the-web-we-have-to-save-2eb1fe15a426#.nh8n86sqw

Used with permission in the UMAP'16 Proceedings.

HT'16, July 10–13, 2016, Halifax, Nova Scotia, Canada
ACM ISBN 978-1-4503-4247-6/16/07.
DOI: http://dx.doi.org/10.1145/2914586.2914605

The Life and Times of Information in Networks

Lada A. Adamic
Facebook Inc.
1 Facebook Way
Menlo Park, CA 94025, USA
ladamic@fb.com

ABSTRACT

Cascades of information-sharing are a primary mechanism by which content reaches its audience on social media. In this talk, I will describe three large-scale analyses of reshare cascades on Facebook, which were performed in aggregate using de-identified data. The first study aims to understand how predictable the growth of cascades is. We formulate the problem as one of predicting whether a cascade will double in size, and find that the prediction accuracy increases the longer a cascade has been observed. Furthermore, temporal and structural features of the cascade, as well as properties of its origin and content, along with the characteristics of those participating, are all useful in predicting how much more a cascade will grow.

If we examine these cascades over significantly longer time scales, we find that many large cascades recur, exhibiting multiple bursts of popularity with periods of quiescence in between. We characterize recurrence by measuring the time elapsed between bursts, their overlap and proximity in the social network, and the diversity in the demographics of individuals participating in each peak. We discover that content virality, as revealed by its initial popularity, is a main driver of recurrence, with the availability of multiple copies of that content helping to spark new bursts. Still, beyond a certain popularity of content, the rate of recurrence drops as cascades start exhausting the population of interested individuals. We reproduce these observed patterns in a simple model of content recurrence simulated on a real social network. Using only characteristics of a cascade's initial burst, we demonstrate strong performance in predicting whether it will recur in the future.

Finally, I will discuss not just how information is transmitted perfectly, but how it evolves as changes are made as it is copied. Using a dataset of thousands of memes collectively replicated hundreds of millions of times, we find that the information undergoes an evolutionary process that exhibits several regularities. A meme's mutation rate characterizes the population distribution of its variants, in accordance with the Yule process. Variants further apart in the diffusion cascade have greater edit distance, as would be expected in an iterative, imperfect replication process. Some text sequences can confer a replicative advantage; these sequences are abundant and transfer "laterally" between different memes. Subpopulations of the social network can preferentially transmit a specific variant of a meme if the variant matches their beliefs or culture. Understanding the mechanism driving change in diffusing information has important implications for how we interpret and harness the information that reaches us through our social networks.

Keywords
Social networks; cascades

BIO

Lada Adamic leads the Product Science group within Facebook's Data Science Team. She is also an adjunct associate professor at the University of Michigan's School of Information and Center for the Study of Complex Systems. Her research interests center on information dynamics in networks: how information diffuses, how it can be found, and how it influences the evolution of a network's structure. Her projects have included identifying expertise in online question and answer forums, studying the dynamics of viral marketing, and characterizing the structural and communication patterns in online social media. She has received an NSF CAREER award, a University of Michigan Henry Russell award, the 2012 Lagrange Prize in Complex Systems.

REFERENCES

[1] Cheng, J., Adamic, L. A., Dow, P. A., Kleinberg, J., and Leskovec, J. 2014. Can cascades be predicted? *WWW'14.*

[2] Cheng, J., Adamic, L. A., Kleinberg, J., Leskovec, J., 2016. Do cascades recur? *WWW'16.*

[3] Adamic, L.A., Lento, T.M., Adar, E., Ng, P.C., 2016. Information evolution in social networks, *WSDM'16.*

UMAP '16, July 13-17, 2016, Halifax, NS, Canada
ACM 978-1-4503-4370-1/16/07.
DOI: http://dx.doi.org/10.1145/2930238.2930292

The Past, the Present, and the Future

Sandra Carberry
Department of Computer Science
University of Delaware
Newark, Delaware 19716
carberry@udel.edu

ABSTRACT

User modeling and adaptation had its inception as a field at a workshop in Maria Laach, Germany in 1986. Most of the work at that time focused on applications in natural language processing, such as adapting explanations to the user's level of expertise. Since then, the field has grown tremendously and new applications are arising each year. As appropriate for the 30th anniversary of the first workshop, this talk will discuss how the field has evolved, novel work that we are pursuing on applying user modeling and adaptation to information retrieval, insights into where the field is headed and the hottest topics for exploration, and some thoughts on the conflict between the benefits of user modeling and its intrusion on people's lives.

Keywords

user modeling, adaptation, graph retrieval, ethics

Bio

Sandra Carberry has been a Professor of Computer Science at the University of Delaware and served as Department Chair. She is one of the founders of the User Modeling research area at the first workshop in Maria Laach, 1986. Her areas of research are natural language understanding, response generation, user modelling, summarization, graph retrieval, intelligent interfaces, and plan recognition. She has twice served as program chair of the user modeling conference, has been editorial board member of UMUAI since its inception, co-edited special issues, co-chaired many workshops, doctoral consortiums, and has served on the board of directors of UM Inc. Many of her papers have received best-paper awards, and she has received two excellence in teaching awards. She has served also as Associate Editor for the International Journal of Human-Computer Studies, on the editorial board of the Computational Linguistics Journal, and on the executive board of ACL.

UMAP '16 July 13-17, 2016, Halifax, NS, Canada

© 2016 Copyright held by the owner/author(s).

ACM ISBN 978-1-4503-4370-1/16/07.

DOI: http://dx.doi.org/10.1145/2930238.2930807

Analyzing and Predicting Task Reminders

David Graus[*]
University of Amsterdam
Science Park 904, Amsterdam, The Netherlands
d.p.graus@uva.nl

Paul N. Bennett, Ryen W. White, Eric Horvitz
Microsoft Research
One Microsoft Way, Redmond, WA USA
{pauben, ryenw, horvitz} @microsoft.com

ABSTRACT

Automated personal assistants such as Siri, Cortana, and Google Now provide services to help users accomplish tasks, including tools to set reminders. We study how people specify and use reminders. Our study analyzes a sample of six months of logs of user-specified reminders from Cortana (Microsoft's intelligent personal assistant), the first large-scale analysis of such reminders. We focus our analyses on time-based reminders, the most common type of reminder found in the logs. We perform a data-driven analysis to identify common categories of tasks that give rise to these reminders across a large number of users, and we arrange these tasks into a taxonomy. We identify temporal patterns linked to the type of task, time of creation, and terms in the reminder text. Finally, we show that these patterns generalize by addressing a prediction task. Specifically, we show that a reminder's creation time is a strong feature in predicting the notification time, and that including the reminder text further improves prediction accuracy. The results have implications for the design of systems aimed at helping people to complete tasks and to plan future activities.

Keywords

Reminders, prospective memory, intelligent assistant, log studies.

1. INTRODUCTION

Automated personal assistants such as Siri, Cortana, Google Now, Echo, and M support a range of reactive and proactive scenarios, ranging from question answering to alerting about plane flights and traffic. Several of these personal assistants provide reminder services aimed at helping people to remember future tasks that they may otherwise forget. We perform an exploratory analysis of a large-scale log of user-created reminders within Microsoft Cortana aimed at understanding users' needs and enhancing the system's reminding services.

Table 1 presents an example of the types of reminder dialogs recorded in the dataset. These logs offer insights about the reminder generation process, including the types of tasks for which people formulate reminders, task descriptions, the times that reminders of different types are created, and the periods of time between the creation of reminders and notifications. Beyond analysis of the nature and timing of reminders, we demonstrate how information about patterns of reminder usage and general trends seen across users can be harnessed to assist people with setting reminders. We focus primarily on reminders for tasks planned for a future time. We make the following contributions in this paper:

Table 1. Example interaction sequence for setting a reminder.

Turn	Who	Text
1	User	Remind me to do the laundry.
2	System	When would you like to be reminded?
3	User	Sunday at noon.
4	System	Alright, remind you to do the laundry at 12:00PM on Sunday, is that right?
5	User	Yes.
6	System	Great, I'll remind you! {success chime}

- Study the creation of time-based reminders at scale in natural settings, revealing common reminders specified across users.
- Develop a taxonomy of task types for these common reminders.
- Study temporal patterns in reminder setting and notification, demonstrating noteworthy patterns.
- Build models that predict the desired timing of reminders, demonstrating a direction in harnessing the patterns.

The findings provide insights about the tasks and goals of users in the real world and about the behaviors and needs of people with regards to memory and reminding. They also support efforts on modeling the tasks and goals of users.

2. RELATED WORK

Several areas of research are relevant to our research on tasks and reminders. We focus largely on research on memory and completing planned tasks. We review research in the following areas: (i) reminders, (ii) memory aids, (iii) prospective memory, and (iv) mining and modeling human behavior at scale.

2.1 Reminders

Several systems have been developed to help remind people about future actions [8,9,21,24,30], many of which leverage contextual signals for more accurate reminding. These systems can help generate reminders associated with a range of future actions, including location, events, activities, people, and time. Two of the most commonly supported types of reminders are location- and time-based (and combinations thereof [8,28]). Location-based reminders fire when people are at or near locations of interest [26,36]. Time-based reminders are set and triggered based on time [14,18], including those based on elapsed time-on-task [6]. While time-based reminders can provide value to many users, particular groups may especially benefit from time-based reminders. These include the elderly [29], those with memory impairments [22], and people seeking to comply with prescribed medications [17]. In this paper, we study time-based reminders in the Cortana reminder service. We omit location- and person-based reminders, as they are less common in our data, and more challenging to study across users per their reliance on personal context and relationships between the user and the locations and persons to trigger the reminders.

[*] Work performed during an internship at Microsoft Research.

UMAP '16, July 13-17, 2016, Halifax, NS, Canada
© 2016 ACM. ISBN 978-1-4503-4370-1/16/07...$15.00
DOI: http://dx.doi.org/10.1145/2930238.2930239

2.2 Memory Aids

Memory aids help people to remember past events and information. Studies have shown that people leverage both their own memories via recall strategies and the use of external memory aids to increase the likelihood of recall [19]. Aids can assume different forms, including paper [27] to electronic alternatives [3,15,33]. One example of a computer-based memory aid is the Remembrance Agent [33], which uses context information, e.g., words typed into a text processor to retrieve similar documents. People have been shown to use standard computer facilities to support future reminding (e.g., positioning documents in noticeable places on the computer desktop) [3]. Such uses can be inadequate for a number of reasons, including the lack of alerting [14]. Other work has focused on the use of machine learning to predict forgetting, and the need for reminding about events [21]. Cortana is an example of an interactive and intelligent external memory aid. Studying usage patterns and user behavior enables us to better understand users' needs, develop improved methods for system-user interaction and collaboration, and more generally, enhance our understanding of the types of tasks where memory aids provide value.

2.3 Prospective Memory

Prospective memory (PM) refers to the ability to remember actions to be performed at a future time [5,11]. Beyond simply remembering, successful prospective memory requires recall at the appropriate moment. PM failures have been an area of study [13,35], and studies have shown that failures can be linked to external factors such as interruptions [7,31]. Prospective tasks are usually divided into time-based tasks and event-based tasks [11]. Time-based tasks are tasks targeted for execution at a specific future time, while event-based tasks are performed when a particular situation or event occurs, triggered by external cues, e.g., person, location, or object [12]. Laboratory studies of PM have largely focused on retention and retrieval performance of event-based PM as this is straightforward to operationalize in an experimental setting. Time-based PM is a largely overlooked type in PM studies [10], as this type of self-generated PM is difficult to model in a laboratory setting. The Cortana reminder logs that we study represent a rich resource of real-life time-based PM instances. They provide insights in the type and nature of tasks that users are likely to forget to execute.

2.4 Mining and Modeling User Activity

Large-scale user logs from many users have been used for a range of different purposes to improve online services and advance our understanding of how people use systems. Search engine queries and search-result clicks have been used to understand how people seek information online [37], train search engine ranking algorithms to better serve user needs [1,20], and more generally, teach us about how humans behave in the world [34]. Although large-scale log analysis of online behavior has focused largely on search and browsing activity, recent work has targeted the large-scale usage of communication tools such as email [23] and instant messaging [25]. In the case of intelligent agents, analyzing user logs may support inferring users' intents [2] or current activities [32]. Where previous work addressed modeling users' long-term goals [4], Cortana reminder logs can help us to understand short term goals.

2.5 Contributions

We extend previous studies in several ways. We present the first study of the creation of common time-based reminders at scale in natural settings. Second, we develop a taxonomy of types of time-based reminders, facilitated by the data we have about the reminders created by a large populations of users. Third, we characterize important aspects of the reminder generation process, including their nature (e.g., reminding about ongoing versus planned activities), and the relationship between the reminder text and the time of setting the reminder and alerting to remind. Finally, to show that the patterns that we uncover represent general trends, we build predictive models of when reminders should fire.

3. REMINDER TYPES

We first investigate user behavior around reminder creation by studying common tasks linked to setting reminders. We focus on the question: *"Is there a body of common tasks that underlie the reminder creation process?"* To answer this question, we extract reminders that are observed frequently and across multiple users. Then, we categorize the reminders in a task taxonomy to better understand the task types associated with the reminders.

3.1 Reminder Composition

In the left column of Table 2, we present three examples of common reminders. The examples show a structure that is frequently observed in the logged reminders. Reminders are typically composed as predicate sentences. They contain a phrase related to an action that the user would like to perform (typically a verb phrase) and a referenced object that is the target of the action to be performed.

Table 2. Example reminders as predicates.

Reminder	Predicate
"Remind me to take out the trash"	Take out (me, the trash)
"Remind me to put my clothes in dryer"	Put (me, clothes in dryer)
"Remind me to get cash from the bank"	Get (me, cash from the bank)

3.2 Data

A session for setting a reminder consists of a dialog, where the user and the intelligent assistant interact in multiple turns. Typically, the user starts by issuing the command for setting a reminder, and dictates the reminder. Optionally, the user specifies the reminder's notification time. Next, the assistant requests to specify the time (if the user has not yet specified it), or provides a summary of the reminder, i.e., the task description and notification time, asking the user to confirm or change the proposed reminder (see Table 1).

We analyze a sample of two months of Cortana reminder logs, spanning all of January and February 2015. We pre-process this set of reminders by including only reminders from the United States market (the only market which had Cortana enabled on mobile devices at that time). To narrow the scope of our analysis, we focus on time-based reminders and remove location (e.g., *"remind me to do X when I am at Y"*) and person-based reminders (e.g., *"remind me to give X when I see Y"*), which are less common and more challenging to study across users due to their personal nature. Finally, we retain only reminders that are confirmed by the user (turn 6 in Table 1). The resulting sample contains 576,080 reminders from 92,264 users. For each reminder, we extract the reminder task description and notification time from Cortana's summary (turn 4 in Table 1). We also extract the creation time based on the local time of the user's device. Each reminder is represented by:

r_{task}: The reminder's textual *task description*; i.e., the phrase which encodes the future task or action to be taken, as dictated by the user. We extract the text from Cortana's final summary response (*"do the laundry"* from turn 4 in Table 1).

r_{CT}: The reminder's *creation time*. This represents the time at which the user *encodes* the reminder. We represent r_{CT} as a discretized time-value; Section 4.1 defines the discretization process. We extract this timestamp from the client's device.

r_{NT}: The *notification time* set for the reminder to fire an alert. This data represents the time at which the user wishes to be reminded about a future task or action. We represent r_{NT} in the same discretized manner as r_{CT}. We extract the notification time from Cortana's summary response (turn 4 in Table 1).

r_{AT}: Subtracting the creation time from the notification time yields the *time delta*, the delay between the reminder's creation and notification time. Intuitively, reminders with smaller time deltas represent short-term or immediate tasks ("*remind me to take the pizza out of the oven*"), whereas reminders with larger time deltas represent tasks planned further ahead in time ("*remind me to make a doctor's appointment*").

3.3 Identifying Common Tasks

To understand the common needs that underlie the creation of reminders, we first identify common reminders, i.e., reminders that are frequently observed across multiple users. Studying common reminders can aid system designers in understanding broad usage patterns, and steer the design and implementation of features to better support this usage. We employ a mixed methods approach, comprising data-driven and qualitative methodologies, to extract and identify common task types.

Frequent task description extraction. First, we extract common task descriptions, by leveraging the predicate (verb+object) structure described at the start of this section. To ensure that the underlying task descriptions represent broad tasks, we filter to retain only descriptions that start with a verb (or a multi-word phrasal verb) that occurs at least 500 times, across at least ten users, with at least five objects. This yields a set of 52 frequent verbs,[1] which covers 60.9% of the reminders in our sample. The relatively small number of verbs which cover the majority of reminders in our log indicates that there are likely many common task types that give rise to reminder creation. To analyze the underlying tasks, we include the most common objects, by pruning objects observed less than five times with a verb. This yields a set of 2,484 unique task descriptions (i.e., verb+object), covering 21.7% of our sample log.

Manual labeling. Next, we aim to identify common tasks which underlie the frequent task descriptions, and categorize them into a broader task type taxonomy. Specifically, by manual inspection, we identified several key dimensions that separate tasks. In particular, dimensions that commonly separate tasks are: whether the task represents an interruption or continuation of a user's activity, the context in which the task is to be executed (i.e., at home, at work), and the (expected) duration of the task. This enabled us to label the frequent task descriptions as belonging to one of six broad task types with several subclasses.

3.4 Task Type Taxonomy

In this section we describe each of the six task types in turn, and provide examples of the associated verb+object patterns. The example objects are shown in decreasing order of frequency, starting with the most common. Note that verbs are not uniquely associated with a single task type, but the verb+object-pair may determine the task type (compare, e.g., "*start dishwasher*" to "*start cooking*").

1. Go somewhere (33.0%): One third of the frequent tasks refer to the user moving from one place to another. We distinguish between two subtypes: the first subtype is running an errand (83.2%), where

the reminder refers to executing a task at some location (e.g., "*pick up milk*"). Running an errand represents an interruption of the user's activity, but a task of a relatively small scale, i.e., it represents a task that briefly takes up the user's availability. The second subtype is more comprehensive, and represents tasks which are characterized by a switch of context (16.8%), e.g., moving from one context or activity to another ("*go to work*", "*leave for office*"), which has a larger impact on the user's availability.

Run errand	
grab [something]	laundry, lunch, headphones
get [something]	batteries
pick up [something/someone]	laundry, person, pizza
buy [something]	milk, flowers, coffee, pizza
bring [something]	laptop, lunch, phone charger
drop off [something]	car, dry cleaning, prescription
return [something]	library books
Switch context	
leave (for) [some place]	house, work, airport
come [somewhere]	home, back to work, in
be [somewhere]	be at work, at home
go (to) [somewhere]	gym, work, home, appointment,
stop by [some place]	the bank, at Walmart
have (to) [something]	work, appointment

2. Chores (23.8%): The second most common type of reminders represent daily chores. We distinguish two subtypes: recurring (66.5%) and standalone chores (33.5%). Both types represent smaller-scale tasks which briefly interrupt the user's activity.

Recurring	
take out [something]	trash, bins
feed [something]	dogs, meter, cats, baby
clean [something]	room, house, bathroom
wash [something]	clothes, hair, dishes, car
charge [something]	phone, fitbit, batteries
do [something]	laundry, homework, taxes, yoga
pay [something]	pay rent, bills, phone bill
set [something]	alarm, reminder
Standalone	
write [something]	a check, letter, thank you note
change [something]	laundry, oil, air filter
cancel [something]	amazon prime, netflix
order [something]	pizza, flowers
renew [something]	books, driver's license, passport
book [something]	hotel, flight
mail [something]	letter, package, check
submit [something]	timesheet, timecard, expenses
fill out [something]	application, timesheet, form
print [something]	tickets, paper, boarding pass
pack [something]	lunch, gym clothes, clothes

3. Communicate (21.1%): Next, a common task is to remind to contact ("*call,*" "*phone,*" "*text*") another individual, either a person (e.g., "*mom,*" "*jack,*" "*jane*"), organization/company ("*AT&T*"), or other ("*hair dresser,*" "*doctor's office*"). We identify two subtypes: the majority reflects general, unspecified communication (94.7%)

---

[1] be, book, bring, buy, call, cancel, change, charge, check, clean, come, do, drop off, eat, email, feed, fill out, finish, get, get ready, go (to), grab, have, have to, leave, mail, make, order, pack, pay, pick up, play, print, put, renew, return, schedule, send, set, start, stop, stop by, submit, take, take out, tell, text, turn on, turn off, wash, watch, write.

(e.g., "*call mom*"), and a smaller part (5.3%) represents coordination or planning tasks (e.g., "*make doctor's appointment*"). Both subtypes represent tasks which briefly interrupt the user's activity.

General	
send [something]	email, text, report
email [someone]	dad, mom
text [someone]	mom, dad
call [someone]	mom, dad
tell [someone] [something]	my wife I love her, happy birthday mom

Coordinate	
set [an appointment]	doctors appointment
make [an appointment]	doctors appointment, reservation
schedule [an appointment]	haircut, doctors appointment

4. Manage ongoing external process (12.9%): These reminders represent manipulation of an ongoing, external process, i.e., tasks where the user monitors or interacts with something, e.g., the laundry or oven. These tasks briefly interrupt a user's activity and are less comprehensive than performing a chore.

turn [on/off] [something]	water, oven, stove, heater
check [something]	email, oven, laundry, food
start [something]	dishwasher, laundry
put [something] in [something]	pizza in oven, clothes in dryer
take [something] out	pizza, chicken, laundry

5. Manage ongoing user activity (6.3%): This class of reminders is similar to the previous class. However, as opposed to the user interacting with an external process, they reflect a change in the user's own activity. These tasks incur a higher cost on the user's availability and cognitive load. We distinguish three subtypes: preparing (31.4%), starting (61.4%), and stopping an activity (7.2%).

Activity/Prepare	
get ready [to/for]	work, home

Activity/Start	
start [some activity]	dinner, cooking, studying
make [something]	food, breakfast, grocery list
take [something]	a shower, a break
play [something]	game, xbox, basketball
watch [something]	tv, the walking dead, seahawks game

Activity/Stop	
stop [some activity]	reading, playing
finish [something]	homework, laundry, taxes

6. Eat/consume (2.8%): Another frequent reminder type refers to consuming something, most often food ("*have lunch*") or medicine ("*take medicine*"). These tasks are small and range from brief interruptions ("*take pills*") to longer interruptions ("*have dinner*").

take [something]	Medicine
eat [something]	lunch, dinner, breakfast, pizza
have [something]	lunch, a snack, breakfast

In summary, we performed a data-driven qualitative analysis and manually labeled frequently occurring task descriptions to identify a set of common underlying tasks. We find that the majority of reminders reflect a plan to travel to a destination, communicate with others, or perform daily chores.

4. REMINDER PATTERNS

Next, we study the temporal patterns of reminders. We seek to understand when people create reminders, when reminders are set to notify users, and the average delay between creation and notification time for different reminders. Such knowledge could prove useful in providing new competencies to reminder services, such as providing likelihoods about when certain tasks tend to happen, suggesting notification times (slot filling), predicting (follow-up) tasks, or proactively blocking out time on people's calendars. In this section we focus on the research question: *"Can we identify patterns in the times at which people create reminders, and, via notification times, when the associated tasks are to be executed?"*

We study reminders on several levels of granularity. In Section 4.2 we look at global patterns and trends across all reminders. Next, we study temporal patterns per task type in Section 4.3. In Section 4.4, we perform a temporal analysis of task description terms. Finally, we study the relation between reminder creation and notification times in Section 4.5. First, we explain how we represent the reminder's creation and notification time to enable our analyses.

4.1 Method

To study common temporal patterns of reminders, we discretize time by dividing each day into the following six four-hour buckets: (i) late night [00:00-04:00], (ii) early morning [04:00-08:00], (iii) morning [08:00-12:00], (iv) afternoon [12:00-16:00], (v) evening [16:00-20:00], and (vi) night [20:00-00:00]. By combining this time-of-day division with the days of week we yield a 7 by 6 matrix M, whose columns represent days, and rows times. Each r_{CT} and r_{NT} can be represented as a cell in matrix M, i.e., $M_{i,j}$ where i corresponds to the day of week, and j to the time of day. Furthermore, we distinguish between M^{CT} and M^{NT}, the matrices whose cells contain reminders that are created, or respectively set to notify, at a particular day and time. We represent each reminder as an object $r \in M$, with the attributes described in Section 3.2: the reminder's task description (r_{task}), creation time (r_{CT}), notification time (r_{NT}), and time delta ($r_{\Delta T}$). To study the temporal patterns, we look at the number of reminders that are created, or whose notifications are set, per cell. We compute conditional probabilities over the cells in M^{CT} and M^{NT}, where the reminder's creation or notification time is conditioned on the task type, time, or the terms in the task description.

$$P(r_{CT} = X \mid w) = \frac{|\, r \in R : w \in r_{task} \wedge r_{CT} = X \,|}{|\, w \in r_{task}, r \in M^{CT} \,|} \quad \textbf{Eq. 1}$$

$$P(r_{NT} = X \mid w) = \frac{|\, r \in R : w \in r_{task} \wedge r_{NT} = X \,|}{|\, w \in r_{task}, r \in M^{NT} \,|} \quad \textbf{Eq. 2}$$

To estimate the conditional probability of a notification or creation time, given a term from the task description, we take the set of reminders containing term w, that are created or whose notification is set at time X, over the total number of reminders which contain the word (see Eq.1 and Eq.2). By computing this probability for each cell in M^{NT} or M^{CT}, (i.e., $\sum_{i,j \in M} P(r_{NT} = i, j \mid w)$) we generate a probability distribution over matrix M.

$$P(r_{NT} = X \mid r_{CT} = i, j\,) = \sum_{i,j \in M^{CT}} \frac{|\, r \in M_{i,j}^{CT} : r_{NT} = X \,|}{|\, r \in M_{i,j}^{CT} \,|} \quad \textbf{Eq. 3}$$

To study the common patterns of the periods of time between the creation of reminders and notifications, we estimate a probability distribution for a reminder's notification time given a creation time (see Eq. 3). We compute this probability by taking the reminders in each cell of M^{CT} that have their notifications set to fire at time X, over all the reminders in that cell.

Finally, we study the delays between setting and executing reminders, by collecting counts and plotting histograms of $r_{\Delta T}$ of reminders for a given subset, e.g., $|\, r_{CT} \in R : w \in r \,|$ or $|\, r_{CT} \in R : r_{CT} = X \,|$.

4.2 Global Patterns

We now describe broad patterns of usage, and answer the following questions: *"At which times during the day do people plan (i.e. create reminders), and at which times do they execute tasks (i.e. reminder notification trigger)?"* and *"How far in advance do people plan tasks?"* To answer these questions, we examine the temporal patterns in our log data over the aggregate of all reminders in the two-month sample (576,080 reminders).

Figure 1 shows the prior probability of a reminder's creation time, $P(r_{CT})$, and notification time, $P(r_{NT})$, in each cell in M^{CT} and M^{NT}. Looking at Figure 1, we see that in our sample, planning (reminder creation) most frequently happens later in the day, more so than during office hours (morning and midday). This observation could be explained by the user's availability; users may have more time to interact with their mobile devices in the evenings. Additionally, the end of the day is a natural period of time to "wrap up the day," i.e., looking backward and forward to completed and future tasks.

Turning our attention to notification times, the right plot of Figure 1 shows a slightly different pattern: people execute tasks (i.e. notifications trigger) throughout the day, from morning to evening. This shows that users want to be reminded of tasks throughout the day, in different contexts (e.g., both at home and at work). This is reflected in our task-type taxonomy, where tasks are related to both contexts. We also note how slightly more notifications trigger on weekdays than in weekends, and more notifications trigger at the start and end of the workweek. This observation may be attributed to the same phenomenon for reminder creation; users may tend to employ reminders for activities that switch between week and weekend contexts. Finally, comparing the two plots shows the notification times are slightly less uniformly distributed than creation times, e.g., users create reminders late at night, when it is relatively unlikely for notifications to fire.

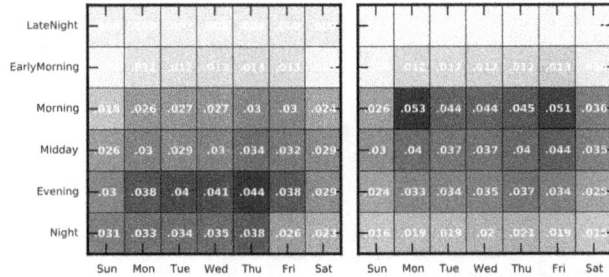

Figure 1. Distribution of reminder creation times (left plot) and reminder notification times (right plot) for all reminders in two-month sample (*n*=576,080).

Next, to determine how far in advance users typically plan, we look at the delays between reminder creation and notification in Figure 2. The top plot shows distinct spikes around five-minute intervals, which are due to reminders with a relative time indication (e.g.: *"remind me to take out the pizza in 5 minutes"*). These intervals are more likely to come to mind than more obscure time horizons (e.g., *"remind me to take out the pizza at 6.34pm"*). The second and third plots clearly illustrate that the majority of reminders have a short delay: around 25% of the reminders are set to notify within the same hour (second plot), and around 80% of the reminders are set to notify within 24 hours (third plot). Interestingly, there is a small hump around 8-9 hours in the second plot, which may be explained by reminders that span a night, e.g., created at the end of the day, to notify early the next day), or a 'working day' (creation in the morning, notification at the end of the day).

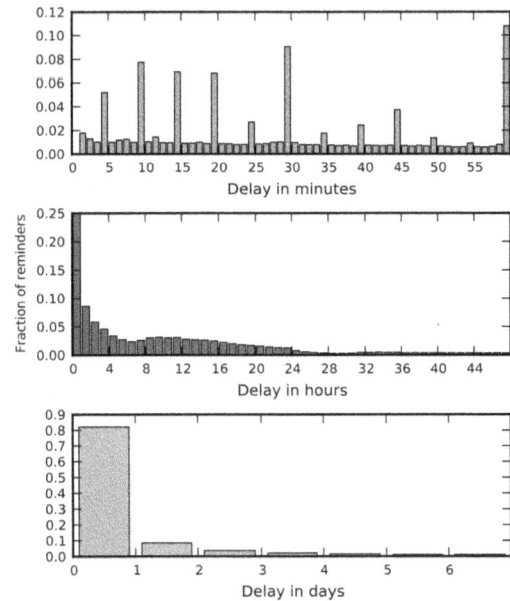

Figure 2. Histograms of delays (in minutes, hours, and days) between reminder creation and notification times.

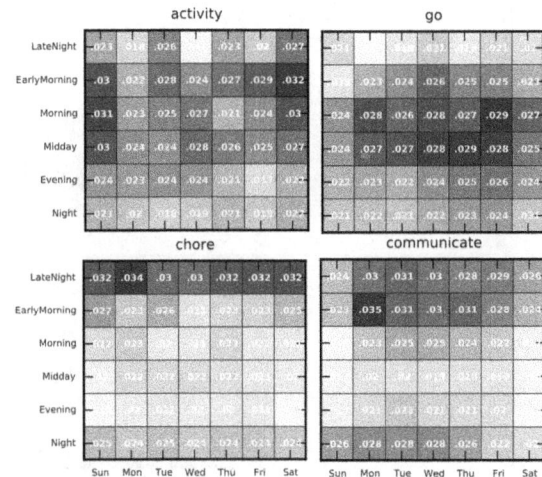

Figure 3. Creation times for different task types.

In summary, we find that on average people tend to set plans in the evening, and execute them throughout the day. Furthermore, most tasks that drive reminder setting are for short-term tasks to be executed in the next 24 hours.

4.3 Task Type

We now explore whether different task *types* are characterized by distinct temporal patterns that differ from the global patterns seen in the previous section. To do so, we use the set of 2,484 frequent reminders to label the two-month sample of reminders. This yields a subset of 125,376 reminders with task type-labels that we use for analysis. We aim to answer the same questions raised in the previous section, but on the level of task type, as opposed to a characterization of the global aggregate.

Creation and Notification Times. First we look at the probability distribution of reminder creation times per task type, i.e., $P(r_{CT} \mid tasktype)$. Looking at the distributions for each task type, we discover two broader groups: per task type, reminders are either created mostly in morning and midday blocks (roughly corresponding to office hours), or outside these blocks. Figure 3 shows examples of both types: "*Activity*" and "*Going somewhere*" reminders are mostly created during office hours, while e.g., "*Communicate*" and "*Chore*" reminders are more prone to be created in evenings. Another interesting observation is that activity-related reminders are comparatively frequent on weekends.

Next, we study reminder notification times per task type, i.e., $P(r_{NT} \mid tasktype)$. Here, a similar pattern emerges. Broadly speaking there are two types of tasks: those set to notify during office hours, and those that trigger outside these hours. See Figure 4 for examples. "*Communicate*" and "*Go*" fall under the former type, whereas "*Chore*" and "*Manage ongoing process*" fall under the latter. The nature of the tasks explains this distinction: the former relate to work-related tasks (communication, work-related errands), whilst the majority of the latter represent activities that are more common in a home setting (cooking, cleaning).

Taking a closer look at the *Communicate* task subclasses in Figure 5, we show how "*Communicate/General*" and "*Communicate/Coordinate*" differ: the former is more uniformly distributed, whilst the latter is denser around office hours. The general subtask too has comparatively more reminders trigger in weekends, whereas coordinate is more strongly centered on weekdays. The distinct patterns suggest these subclasses indeed represent different types of tasks.

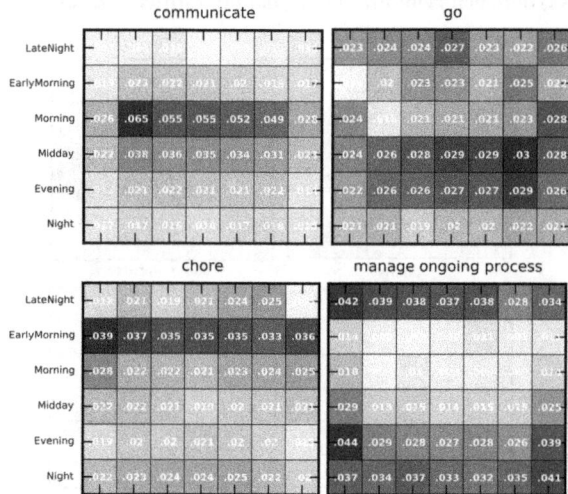

Figure 4. Reminder notification time probability distributions over time, for different task types.

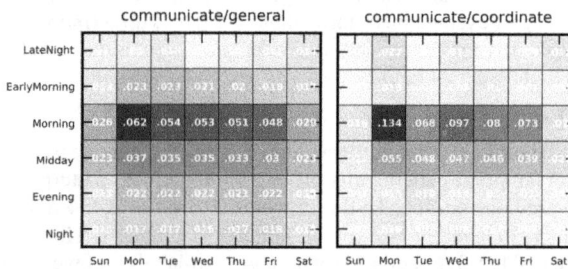

Figure 5. Reminder notification time probability distributions for the *Communicate* subclasses.

Reminder Creation and Notification Delay. To better understand differences in the lead times between reminder creation and notification, we present an overview of the distribution of reminder delays per task type in Figure 6. In general, the lower the boxplot lies on the *y*-axis, the lower the lead time, i.e., the shorter the delay be-

tween creating the reminder and executing the task. It is worth comparing, e.g., the plot of "*Manage ongoing process*," to both "*Go*" or "*Communicate*" task types: execution of managing ongoing processes tasks seem to be planned with a much shorter lead time than the other types of task. Considering the nature of the tasks, where ongoing processes often represent the close monitoring or checking of a process (e.g., cooking or cleaning tasks), it is understandable that the delays are on the order of a few minutes, rather than hours. "*Communicate/Coordinate*" has the largest delay on average, i.e., it is the task type people plan furthest in advance.

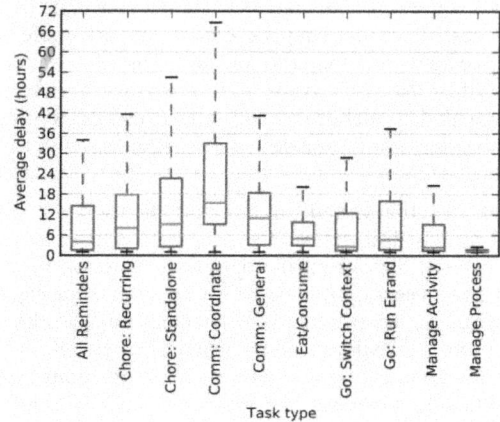

Figure 6. Boxplots showing delay between reminder creation and notification times (*n* = 125,376).

A more detailed examination of the differences between the "Communicate" subtasks, illustrated in Figure 7, we see that "*Communicate/General*" subtasks are more likely to be executed with lower lead time, as noted by the peak at hour 0 in the top plot. The "*Communicate/Coordinate*" subtask is about as likely to be executed the next day, as seen by the high peak around the 12 hour mark in the bottom plot. Much like the observations made in the previous section, the difference in the patterns between both "*Communicate*" subtasks suggests that the distinction between the subtypes is meaningful. Differences are not only found on a semantic level through our qualitative analysis, but also in temporal patterns.

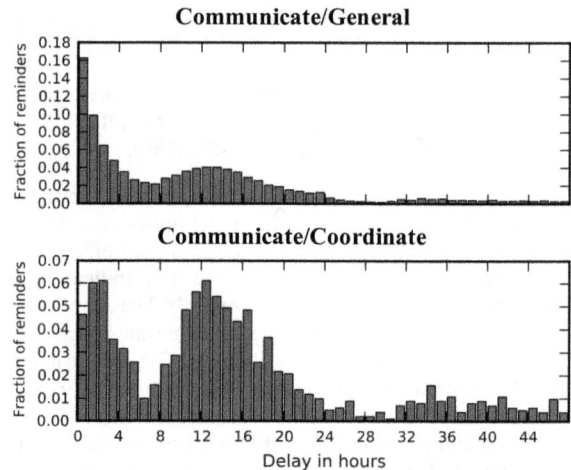

Figure 7. Delay (lead time) between reminder creation and notification for "Communicate" subtasks.

In summary, we have clearly shown how task type-specific temporal patterns differ from the aggregate patterns in Section 4.2.

4.4 Terms

One can hypothesize that the terms in task descriptions show distinct temporal patterns, i.e., reminders that contain the term *"pizza"* are likely to trigger around dinner time. Presence of these temporal patterns may be leveraged for reminder creation or notification time prediction. To study this, we manually inspected the temporal distribution of task descriptions' terms of the 500 most frequent terms. More specifically, we compute conditional probabilities for a cell in M^{CT} or M^{NT} given a term w (see Eq. 1 and Eq. 2). We found several intuitive patterns, which we illustrate below with examples. These patterns provide intuition behind the terms we use as features in predictive modeling, discussed in Section 5.

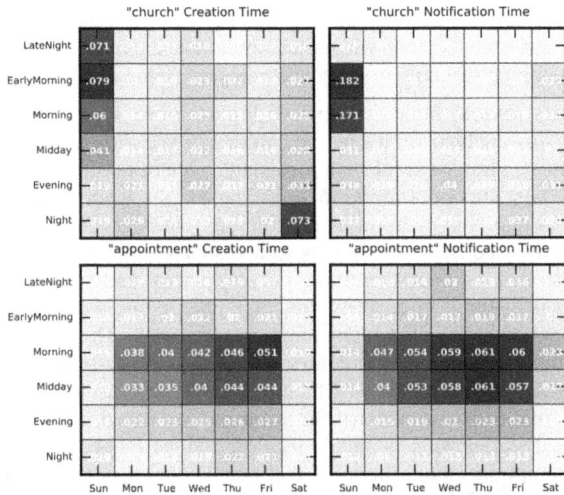

Figure 8. Creation & Notification times for reminders with the terms "church" (top) & "appointment" (bottom).

Figure 8 shows creation and notification times of task descriptions which contain the terms "church" or "appointment." The "appointment" plot shows a strong pattern around the morning and midday blocks, representing office hours. Reminders that contain "church" show a clear pattern too; they are largely created from Saturday night through Sunday morning, and are set to notify on Sunday early morning and mornings. When we examine the delays between reminder creation and notification, clear patterns emerge.

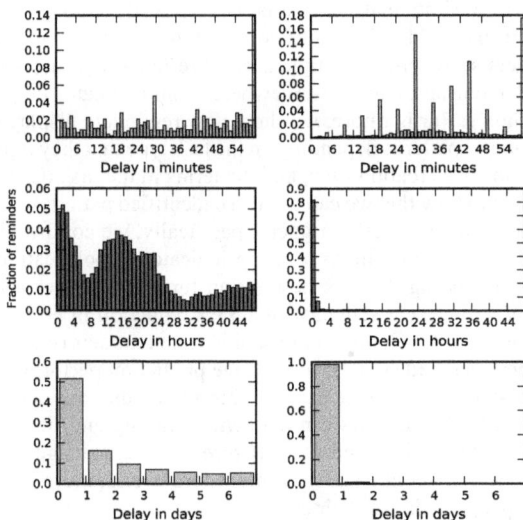

Figure 9. Delays between reminder creation and notification for reminder task descriptions containing the terms "appointment" (left) and "laundry" (right).

In Figure 9, we compare the average delays of reminders containing the term "appointment" to "laundry." Clearly, on average, "appointment" reminders have longer delays, reflected by the nature of the task (which may involve other individuals and hence require more planning), whereas "laundry" reminders are more likely to reflect short-term tasks (which may be performed individually). In summary, we see distinct temporal patterns in task descriptions' terms. In Section 5, we study the generalizability of these patterns.

4.5 Time

Finally, we look at correlations between reminders' creation and notification times. Motivated by the observations that most reminders are set to notify shortly after they are created, we study the probability of a reminder's notification time given its creation time, $P(r_{NT} \mid r_{CT})$. See Figure 10 for examples. Looking at the plots in detail, we see how reminders across different creation times appear similar: they are most likely to have their notification fire within the same cell or the next, confirming earlier observations that the majority of reminders are short-term (i.e., same cell). However, upon closer inspection, we see that as the reminder's creation time moves towards later during the day, reminders are more likely to be set to notify the next day. Furthermore, in the third plot from the left, we see how reminders created on Friday evenings have a small but substantial probability of having their notification fire on Monday morning (i.e., the reminder spans the weekend). These patterns show how delay between reminder creation and notification time is low on average, but the length of delay is not independent from the creation time.

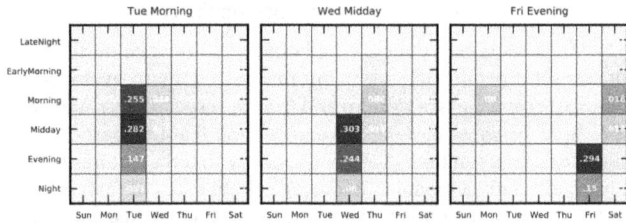

Figure 10. $P(r_{NT} \mid r_{CT})$ for three different r_{CT}.

In summary, we have shown distinct temporal patterns of reminders of different task types, and of the terms in task descriptions. Finally, we have shown that a reminder's notification time is most likely set shortly after creation time, but the later in the day a reminder is created, the more likely the notification time is further in the future.

5. PREDICTING NOTIFICATION TIME

In the previous section we have shown temporal patterns in reminder creation and notification time of four types: aggregate patterns, task type-related, term-based, and time-based. To study whether these patterns can be harnessed for aiding users in reminder setting, we address a prediction task. Specifically, we turn to the task of predicting the day of the week in which a task is most likely to happen (i.e., predicting r_{NT}). Motivated by our observation that the majority of the reminders are set to trigger soon after being set (Section 4.2 and 4.5), and by the patterns we observed of the terms from task descriptions (Section 4.4), we aim to answer the following research questions: *"Is the reminder's creation time indicative of its notification time?"* and *"Do term-based features yield an increase in predictive power?"* Rather than seeking to harness a predictive model about timing, the primary aim of the experiments is to study whether the patterns discussed earlier generalize, as demonstrated by their contribution to predictive performance.

We cast the task of predicting the day of week a reminder is set to notify as multiclass classification, where each day of the week corresponds to a class. The input to our predictive model is the reminder's task description (r_{task}), creation time (r_{CT}), and the target class is the notification time (r_{NT}) day of week. We measure the predictive power of the patterns identified in the previous sections via term-based and (creation) time-based features. Specifically, for term-based features, we extract unigram bag of word features, and our time-based features correspond to R_{CT}'s time of day (row) and day of week (column), and the minutes since the start of week.

5.1 Experimental Setup

We use Gradient Boosted Decision Trees for classification. This method has proven to be robust and efficient in large-scale learning problems [16]. The ability of this method to deal with non-linearity in the feature space and heterogeneous features make it a natural choice. To address the multiclass nature of our problem, we employ a one vs. all classification strategy, where we train seven binary classifiers and output the prediction with the highest confidence as final prediction. We compare the accuracy to randomly picking a day of the week (with accuracy of $1/7 \approx 0.1429$) and to a more competitive baseline which predicts the notification will be for the same day that the notification was created (BL-SameDay).

For the experiments, we sample six months of data (January through June 2015). All data were filtered according to the process described in Section 3.2, resulting in a total of 1,509,340 reminders. We split this data sequentially: the first 70% (approx. January 1 to May 7) forms the training set and the last 30% (approx. May 8 to June 30) forms the test set. We use the first two months of the training set for the analysis described in Sections 3 and 4 as well as for parameter tuning before we retrained on the entire training set.

In the next section, we report predictive performance on the held-out test set. Specifically, we report macro and micro-averaged accuracy over the classes (Macro and Micro, respectively). We compare three systems: one that leverages time features based on the reminder's creation time (Time only), one with term features (Terms only), and finally a model that leverages both types of features (Full model). We test for statistical significance using t-tests, comparing our predictive models against BL-SameDay. The symbols ▲ and ▼ denote statistically significant differences (greater than the baseline and worse than the baseline, respectively) at $\alpha = 0.01$.

6. RESULTS

Table 4 shows the results of our prediction task. First we note that the baseline of predicting the notification time to be the same day as the creation time performs much better than random (at 0.1429). This indicates users mostly set reminders to plan for events in the short-term. Next, we see that the *Time only* model significantly improves over the baseline, indicating that the reminder creation time helps further improve prediction accuracy. As noted earlier, tasks planned late at night are more likely to be executed on a different day, and the use of creation time helps leverage this and more general patterns. Finally, the model that uses only features based on the task description (*Terms only*) performs better than random, but does not outperform the baseline. However, when combined with the time model (*Full model*) we see an increase of 8.2% relative to the time only model. We conclude that the creation time provides the most information for predicting when a task will be performed, the task description provides significant additional information, primarily when the description is used in combination with the reminder's creation time.

7. DISCUSSION AND IMPLICATIONS

Through log analyses we have shown common reminders and made an attempt at identifying and categorizing the types of tasks that underlie them. We identified that the majority of reminders in our

Table 4. Average accuracy of the day-of-week prediction task.

Run	Micro	Macro	Error reduction
Full model	**0.6788**▲	**0.6761**▲	**+0.3381**
Time only	0.6279▲	0.6258▲	+0.2333
Terms only	0.1777▼	0.1772▼	−0.6944
BL-SameDay	0.5147	0.5165	

sample refer to either daily household chores, running errands, or switching contexts. We have shown there are distinct temporal patterns across reminders and reminder types. Finally, we demonstrated that we can leverage these patterns to predict the day of the week that a reminder is most likely to trigger, i.e., the day the task is most likely to be executed. The findings have implications for designing systems to help with task completion, and more generally for developing technology to reduce prospective memory failures.

There are several limitations in our log analyses. First, we performed this analysis on a specific subset of reminders: reminders from one geographic locale and for a single type of reminder: time-based. There are opportunities to understand cultural and linguistic factors in reminder creation by considering reminders from multiple regions. We additionally seek to investigate other types of reminders, such as those involving people, places, and events. Second, it is difficult to quantify the comprehensiveness of the task type taxonomy, which covers common reminders. The ontology may therefore not cover more intricate, personal, specific, or complex reminders, the nature of which needs to be better understood. Finally, our approach and analysis is entirely log based. The taxonomy's categories were manually labeled, and we make inferences and assumptions about the tasks that people are engaged in. User studies are needed to better understand the reminder process, including the generation and value of reminders, including how people behave when they are notified.

We explored a potential use of predictions about the day of the week that a reminder will trigger. Understanding when people tend to perform tasks is useful more generally, e.g., for effective resource scheduling or tailored advertising purposes. Understanding task durations could be useful in developing systems to automatically terminate ongoing tasks or allocate time for task completion.

8. CONCLUSIONS AND FUTURE WORK

We performed an analysis of a large corpus of reminder data collected in the wild. We identified common task types in frequent reminders seen across multiple users. We found that users largely remind themselves to go somewhere, communicate, or perform daily chores. Furthermore, we show how reminders display different temporal patterns depending on the task type that they represent, the reminder's creation time, and the terms in the task description. Finally, we show that we can use these identified patterns to predict when a reminder is set to trigger. Specifically, we confirm that the reminder's creation time is a strong indicator of notification time, but that including the task description further improves accuracy over the strongest baseline, with a 33% reduction in error. Future work includes developing more sophisticated models (e.g., considering personalized signals) to improve prediction performance. In the long-term, we believe that insights and predictions about tasks and the use of reminders can help with building and fielding systems with the ability to proactively reserve time, manage conflicts, remind people about tasks they might forget, and, more generally, to help people achieve their goals.

Acknowledgements The first author is supported by the Netherlands Organisation for Scientific Research (NWO) under project nr 727.011.005.

REFERENCES

1. Agichtein, E., Brill, E., and Dumais, S. (2006). Improving web search ranking by incorporating user behavior information. *Proc. SIGIR* (pp. 19–26).

2. Armentano, M.G. and Amandi, A.A. (2009). Recognition of User Intentions for Interface Agents with Variable Order Markov Models. *Proc. UMAP '09* (pp. 173-184).

3. Barreau, D. and Nardi, B.A. (1995). Finding and reminding: File organization from the desktop. *ACM SIGCHI Bulletin*, 27(3), 39–43.

4. Barua, D., Kay, J., Kummerfeld, B., Paris, C. (2014). Modelling Long Term Goals. *Proc. UMAP 2014.* pp 1-12.

5. Brandimonte, M.A., Einstein, G.O., and McDaniel, M.A. (2014). *Prospective Memory: Theory and applications.* Psychology Press.

6. Chaurasia, P., McClean, S.D., Nugent, C., and Scotney, B. (2014). A duration-based online reminder system. *Int. J. of Pervasive Computing and Communications*, 10(3), 337–366.

7. Czerwinski, M., Horvitz, E., and Wilhite, S. (2004). A diary study of task switching and interruptions. *Proc. SIGCHI* (pp. 175–182).

8. DeVaul, R., Clarkson, B., and Pentland, A. (2000). The Memory Glasses: Towards a wearable context aware, situation-appropriate reminder system. *Proc. SIGCHI Workshop on Situated Interaction in Ubiquitous Computing.*

9. Dey, A.K. and Abowd, G.D. (2000). Cybreminder: A context-aware system for supporting reminders. In *Handheld and Ubiquitous Computing* (pp. 172-186).

10. Dismukes, R. K. (2012). Prospective Memory in Workplace and Everyday Situations. In *Current Directions in Psychological Science*, 21 (4): 215--220.

11. Einstein, G.O. and McDaniel, M.A. (1990). Normal aging and prospective memory. *J. of Experimental Psychology: Learning, Memory, and Cognition*, 16(4), 717.

12. Ellis, J. (1996). Prospective memory or the realization of delayed intentions: A conceptual framework for research. *Prospective memory: Theory and applications*, 1–22.

13. Ellis, J. and Kvavilashvili, L. (2000). Prospective memory in 2000: Past, present and future directions. *Applied Cognitive Psychology*, 14, 1–9.

14. Fertig, Scott, Freeman, E., and Gelernter, D. (1996). "Finding and reminding" reconsidered. *SIGCHI Bulletin*, 28(1), 66–69.

15. Fertig, S., Freeman, E., and Gelernter, D. (1996). Lifestreams: An alternative to the desktop metaphor. *Proc. SIGCHI Conference Companion* (pp. 410–411).

16. Friedman, J.H. (2002). Stochastic gradient boosting. *Comput. Stat. Data Anal.* 38(4), 367–378.

17. Hanauer, D.A., Wentzell, K., Laffel, N., and Laffel, L.M. (2009). Computerized Automated Reminder Diabetes System (CARDS): E-mail and SMS cell phone text messaging reminders to support diabetes management. *Diabetes Technology and Therapeutics*, 11(2), 99–106.

18. Hicks, J.L., Marsh, R.L., and Cook, G.I. (2005). Task interference in time-based, event-based, and dual intention prospective memory conditions. *J. Memory and Language*, 53(3), 430–444.

19. Intons-Peterson, M.J. and Fournier, J. (1986). External and internal memory aids: When and how often do we use them? *Journal of Experimental Psychology: General* 115(3), 267.

20. Joachims, T. (2002). Optimizing search engines using click-through data. *Proc. SIGKDD* (pp. 133–142).

21. Kamar, E. and Horvitz, E. (2011). Jogger: Models for context-sensitive reminding. *Proc. AAMS* (pp. 1089–1090).

22. Kapur, N., Glisky, E.L., and Wilson, B.A. (2004). Technological memory aids for people with memory deficits. *Neuropsychological Rehabilitation*, 14(1-2), 41–60.

23. Koren, Y., Liberty, E., Maarek, Y., and Sandler, R. (2011). Automatically tagging email by leveraging other users' folders. *Proc. SIGKDD* (pp. 913–921).

24. Lamming, M. and Flynn, M. (1994). Forget-me-not: Intimate computing in support of human memory. *Proc. FRIEND21* (pp. 2–4).

25. Leskovec, J. and Horvitz, E. (2008). Planetary-scale views on a large instant-messaging network. *Proc. WWW* (pp. 915–924).

26. Ludford, P.J., Frankowski, D., Reily, K., Wilms, K., and Terveen, L. (2006). Because i carry my cell phone anyway: Functional location-based reminder applications. *Proc. SIGCHI* (pp. 889–898).

27. Malone, T.W. (1983). How do people organize their desks? Implications for the design of office information systems. *ACM TOIS*, 1(1), 99–112.

28. Marmasse, N. and Schmandt, C. (2000). Location-aware information delivery with commotion. *Proc. Handheld and Ubiquitous Computing* (pp. 157–171).

29. McGee-Lennon, M.R., Wolters, M.K., and Brewster, S. (2011). User-centred multimodal reminders for assistive living. *Proc. SIGCHI* (pp. 2105–2114).

30. McGee-Lennon, M., Wolters, M., McLachlan, R., Brewster, S., and Hall, C. (2011). Name that tune: Musicons as reminders in the home. *Proc. SIGCHI* (pp. 2803–2806).

31. O'Connail, B. and Frohlich, D. (1995). Timespace in the workplace: Dealing with interruptions. *Proc. SIGCHI Conference Companion* (pp. 262–263).

32. Partridge, K. and Price, R (2009). Enhancing mobile recommender systems with activity prediction. *Proc. UMAP '09.* 307-318.

33. Rhodes, B. and Starner, T. (1996). Remembrance Agent: A continuously running automated information retrieval system. *Proc. Practical Application of Intelligent Agents and Multi Agent Technology* (pp. 487–495).

34. Richardson, M. (2008). Learning about the world through long-term query logs. *ACM TWEB*, 2(4), 21.

35. Sellen, A.J., Louie, G, Harris, J.E., and Wilkins, A.J. (1996). What brings intentions to mind? An in situ study of prospective memory. *Memory*, 5(4), 483–507.

36. Tu, Y., Chen, L., Lv, M., Ye, Y., Huang, W., and Chen, G. (2013). ireminder: An intuitive location-based reminder that knows where you are going. *IJHCI*, 29(12), 838–850.

37. White, R.W. and Drucker, S.M. (2007). Investigating behavioral variability in web search. *Proc. WWW* (pp. 21–30).

Identifying Grey Sheep Users in Collaborative Filtering: a Distribution-Based Technique

Benjamin Gras
Loria - Université de Lorraine
Campus Scientifique
Vandœuvre-lès-nancy, France
benjamin.gras@loria.fr

Armelle Brun
Loria - Université de Lorraine
Campus Scientifique
Vandœuvre-lès-nancy, France
armelle.brun@loria.fr

Anne Boyer
Loria - Université de Lorraine
Campus Scientifique
Vandœuvre-lès-nancy, France
anne.boyer@loria.fr

ABSTRACT

The collaborative filtering (CF) approach in recommender systems assumes that users' preferences are consistent among users. Although accurate, this approach fails on some users. We presume that some of these users belong to a small community of users who have unusual preferences, such users are not compliant with the CF underlying assumption. They are *grey sheep users*. This paper aims at accurately identifying grey sheep users. We introduce a new distribution-based grey sheep users identification technique, that borrows from outlier detection and from information retrieval, while taking into account the specificities of preference data on which CF relies: extreme sparsity, imprecision and users' bias. The experimental evaluation conducted on a state-of-the-art dataset shows that this new distribution-based technique outperforms state-of-the-art grey sheep users identification techniques.

Keywords

Recommender systems, Collaborative filtering, Grey sheep users, Outlier detection

1. INTRODUCTION

Recommender systems (RS) [16] are becoming an everyday part of our lives. They aim at assisting users (of a service or on the Web) during their activities, by recommending them relevant resources. RS are a way to avoid users to be overwhelmed by the large amount of resources they can access. RS rely on the knowledge they have collected about users. They are used in many application domains, including e-commerce [25], e-learning [38], tourism [39], etc.

RS have been extensively studied these last twenty years. The most prevalent approach is collaborative filtering (CF). CF assumes that users' preferences are consistent among users, so it relies on the preferences of a group of users to infer the preferences of a given user [31].

Providing users with accurate recommendations (that satisfy them) is of the highest importance. In e-commerce it

UMAP '16, July 13-17, 2016, Halifax, NS, Canada

© 2016 ACM. ISBN 978-1-4503-4370-1/16/07...$15.00

DOI: http://dx.doi.org/10.1145/2930238.2930242

increases customer retention; in e-learning it improves learners' learning process; etc. While the quality of CF-based recommenders is now considered on average as acceptable [7], some users receive inaccurate recommendations (the RMSE on these users is high). The main reason of this failure is the lack of preferences the system has collected about them: it is referred to as the cold-start problem [32]. Recently, the literature has emphasized that the unusual preferences of some users, in comparison to those of the others, may explain why they get inaccurate recommendations [14]. As their preferences do not consistently agree or disagree with any community of users, collaborative filtering does not provide them with high quality recommendations [10]. These users are referred to as a *grey sheep users* [10, 14].

The problem addressed in this paper is the automatic identification of grey sheep users (for simplicity, they will be referred to as GSU), prior to the recommendation process, so by relying only on their preferences, not on their feedback following recommendations. We make this choice to avoid providing these users with inaccurate recommendations. Indeed, such recommendations may result in critical consequences: unsatisfied users, user defection, failure among learners, etc. Once GSU are identified, the system may either not provide them with any recommendation, or rely on an other recommendation approach [15]. In addition, the literature has shown that GSU affect the recommendation quality of the whole community, so they are often discarded from the set of users when learning the preferences of the whole community [15]. We consider that identifying GSU upstream the recommendation process is a crucial issue, in order to discard them. We also consider of the highest importance that the GSU identification techniques do not identify normal users as GSU (false positive). Indeed, such users may either receive no recommendation, or some recommendations computed through other recommendation techniques (and that may be less accurate recommendations), whereas their recommendations would be accurate if they were identified as normal users.

The issue we are facing is thus: given a set of users associated with their preferences, how to identify those who are GSU, *i.e.* who have preferences that differ from those of others, and who will get inaccurate recommendations. We view this problem as closely related to the well-known outlier detection problem in data mining. Surprisingly, both tasks have been rarely linked up in the literature. Some characteristics of preference data may however make traditional outlier detection techniques fail. First, the preferences expressed by users are imprecise [4], this characteristic is not managed by traditional outlier detection techniques. Second, each user (also referred to as an instance) has his/her own preferences. Outlier detection techniques assume that a unique (or few) mechanism(s) have generated the instances, so these techniques may not be adequate to manage preference data. Last, standard preference datasets are extremely sparse (less than 4% of known data). Recent outlier detection methods can manage sparse datasets [3], but the extreme sparsity of preference datasets probably impacts their accuracy.

In this paper, we show that several GSU identification techniques from the literature are similar to some outlier detection techniques. Our main contribution is the introduction of a new distribution-based GSU identification technique that belongs to the distribution-based class of outlier detection and that borrows from the information retrieval domain. It does not assume that all resources have the same distribution. Moreover, it is designed to cope with the characteristics of preference data: extreme sparsity, imprecision and users' bias. Last, it has the advantage of identifying GSU prior to the computation of any recommendation, so GSU can, in a second phase, be easily managed aside from other users.

Section 2 presents an overview of recommender systems, of outlier detection and of GSU identification techniques. Section 3 introduces the GSU identification technique we propose. Then, Section 4 focuses on the experiments conducted. Finally, we discuss and conclude our work.

2. RELATED WORKS

2.1 Collaborative Filtering

Collaborative Filtering (CF) relies on the preferences of users on resources to provide a user u, referred to as the *active user*, with some personalized recommendations. The preference of u on a resource r is denoted by $n_{u,r}$, with $n_{u,r} \in V$, V being the set of possible preference values (often some ratings). The ratings of the set of users U on the set of resources M are generally represented in the form of a rating matrix.

Two main approaches are used in CF: memory-based and model-based approaches. Memory-based approaches [31] directly exploit users' preferences, without pre-processing. One of the most commonly used technique is the user-based KNN (K Nearest Neighbors) that computes the similarity of preferences between each pair of users. The missing preference of the active user u on r is estimated by relying on the preferences of his/her K nearest neighbors. This technique is easy to implement and takes into account each new preference dynamically in the recommendation process. However, it hardly scales due to the computation cost of the similarities [30] and it suffers from the extreme sparsity of the preference dataset (the similarity of two users may not be computable, or two similarity values may not be comparable) [19, 18].

Model-based approaches learn a model of preferences. Clustering, Bayesian networks and data mining-based techniques have been studied for many years [1]. The matrix factorization technique has recently proved to be very successful in collaborative filtering [28, 36] and is now the most commonly used technique. The matrix of user preferences is factorized into two sub-matrices where one matrix represents the users and the other one the items, both in a common sub-space

of latent features. These approaches do not suffer so much from the scalability problem nor from sparsity. However, they do not easily allow dynamic changes in the model, especially if it has to be updated each time a new preference is provided.

2.2 Outlier Detection

Outlier detection is an important task in data mining, which has been the focus of many works for a long time [22, 24]. It finds use in a large variety of applications, ranging from fraud detection to medical analysis through weather prediction. An outlier is commonly defined as "an observation which deviates so much from the other observations as to arouse suspicions that it was generated by a different mechanism" [22]. According to the application domain, outliers are also referred to as anomalies, exceptions, noise, errors, novelty, damage, faults, aberrations, etc. [8] and they are opposed to "normal" observations.

Several scenarios may occur for outlier detection: supervised, unsupervised, or semi-supervised [24]. In this paper, we focus on unsupervised outlier detection: the label of each learning instance (normal or outlier) is unknown. In that frame, a parameter that represents the number or the percentage of outliers to detect has to be fixed by hand. As, by definition, outliers are rare instances, the possible values of this parameter are rather limited.

Various techniques have been proposed for discovering outliers in an unsupervised scenario: distance-based, clustering-based, deviation-based, density-based, distribution-based [21, 5]. The choice of the technique mainly depends on the structure, nature, size and sparsity of data [5].

The distance-based technique exploits the distance between each pair of instances (local distances). The KNN technique assumes that normal instances have a close neighborhood (its K nearest neighbors), so if an instance is significantly distant from its neighbors, it is considered as an outlier [29]. One advantage of this technique is that it is non-parametric, so no prior assumption is made about the distribution of the instances. However, its complexity is linked to the number of instances, as well as to the dimension of the data and it requires a predefined distance threshold.

The cluster-based technique forms clusters of instances, that characterize the local distribution of data. Small-size clusters are generally considered as clusters of outliers. One drawback lies in the criteria that determine why an instance is labelled as an outlier, which are hidden.

The deviation-based technique assumes that outliers are instances that are the outermost instances of the entire dataset (they deviate from other instances).

The density-based technique exploits the density around an instance, in comparison to the density of its neighbors. An instance with a density significantly lower than that of its neighbors is considered as an outlier.

Finally, the distribution-based technique assumes that normal instances follow a predefined (that may be estimated) distribution, which is referred to as the model of the data. Outliers are instances that deviate from this model: it is unlikely they have been generated by it. This technique is parametric and generally uses standard distributions (*e.g.* gaussian). Its main drawback lies in the fact that it requires to know the data distribution, which may be either unknown or expensive to compute.

2.3 Grey Sheep Users Identification in Recommender Systems

Grey sheep users (GSU) is a term commonly used in recommender systems. They are also referred to as deviant users, abnormal users, atypical users, unusual users, etc. [12, 14]. They refer to the users whose opinions do not consistently agree or disagree with any community of people [10], or to users with completely different opinions from every other user of the system [35].

Many techniques used to perform GSU identification in RS come from the field of statistics and they are usually based on distribution properties of the variables (the resources). From the outlier detection point of view, they can be classified as distribution-based techniques. The most commonly used technique forms a basic model of the data (preference data), represented by the average preference on each resource. Given this model, the *Abnormality* measure [12] (see equation (1)) evaluates to what extent a user u is distant from the model. It computes the average difference between the ratings of u on the resources he/she rated and the average rating on these resources (the model).

$$Abnormality(u) = \frac{\sum_{r \in R_u} |n_{u,r} - \overline{n_r}|}{\|R_u\|}, \qquad (1)$$

where $\overline{n_r}$ is the average rating on resource r, R_u is the set of resources rated by u and $\|R_u\|$ is their number. This measure has the advantage of not being complex, but it does not take into account any characteristics or users' bias, nor more specific characteristics of the resources.

We have recently proposed the *AbnormalityCRU* measure [17], an improved version of *Abnormality*. *AbnormalityCRU* not only takes into account the bias of each user, by centering the ratings around each user's average rating, but also takes into account the characteristics of the resources, by weighting the resources according to the variance of their ratings (see equation (2)).

$$Abnormality_{CRU}(u) = \frac{\sum_{r \in R_u} [(|n_{u,r} - \overline{n_u} - \overline{n_{C_r}}|) * C(r)]^2}{\|R_u\|}, \qquad (2)$$

where $\overline{n_u}$ is the average rating of u (the bias), $\overline{n_{C_r}}$ represents the average centered rating on resource r, $C(r)$ is the controversy associated with resource r. The controversy of a resource is based on the normalized variance of this resource. Both measures assume that the distribution along the resources is gaussian. *AbnormalityCRU* has shown to significantly outperform *Abnormality*.

Although being distribution-based techniques, the information on which they rely is minimal: the average rating on each resource and each user, and the variance on the resources.

Clustering is also a technique used to perform GSU identification. [23] identifies, among the set of clusters, a specific cluster made up of users with a high *Abnormality* and who get inaccurate recommendations as well: a cluster of GSU. We are convinced that, in the specific context of CF-based RS, clustering fails to build a cluster of GSU. Indeed, a GSU, in the sense of CF, has preferences that are not close to those of other users. Thus, if a user belongs to a cluster, it means that his/her preferences are similar to those of users in the same cluster. So, he/she is not a GSU. Although this work relies on clustering, it cannot be classified as a cluster-based technique from the outlier detection point of view, as the way it identifies GSU does not match the cluster-based approach of outlier detection. Indeed, in outlier detection, the instances that belong to very small clusters are considered as outliers, which means that they have few similar other instances, which is closer to the definition of grey sheep users on which we rely.

To the best of our knowledge, few works perform GSU identification through a distance-based technique. We think that the main reason for this is the extreme sparsity of preference datasets. Indeed, a distance-based technique relies on the distance between instances, which may be, in the case of extreme sparsity, either not computable or not comparable if two distances are computed on different sets of resources. The work presented in [15] can still be considered as a distance-based technique from the outlier detection domain. Authors assume that GSU have a low correlation with almost all users. So, to identify GSU they group users into clusters and the similarity between each pair of users is evaluated within a cluster. Users who have a low similarity with others are identified as GSU.

Some works, motivated by performance prediction of RS [20], investigate the link between users' characteristics (number of ratings, number and quality of neighbors, etc.) and the recommendation error. While not designed to detect GSU, they provide an overview of which characteristics can determine which users are grey sheeps. However, it has been shown that, used alone, these characteristics are not a good performance estimator, especially those related to nearest neighbors [20, 17].

[6] has proposed to take into account the specific preferences of users, in the evaluation of the similarity between two users. This new measure is based on the singularity of ratings. A rating on a resource is considered as singular if it does not correspond to the majority rating on this resource. When computing the similarity between two users, the more a rating is singular, the greater its importance. The use of the singularity can be associated to a distribution-based technique for GSU identification.

3. DISTRIBUTION-BASED TECHNIQUE FOR GSU IDENTIFICATION

As previously mentioned, distance-based outlier detection techniques are not adequate for GSU identification due to the extreme sparsity of preference datasets.

Distribution-based techniques, which rely on the distribution of the variables, are traditionally used. In this frame, both outlier detection and GSU identification presume that "normal" data (in opposition to outlier data) follow a unique (or few) distributions, which are often assumed to be gaussian [2]. The specificity of GSU identification techniques is that one distribution is managed for each variable (resource). The generally used measures only rely on the mean and sometimes on the standard deviation of the variables (resources). However, some (or all) variables may not follow such a distribution. We assume that it is the case of preference data. For example, a movie may have been disliked by 40% of the population, highly appreciated by 40%, the remaining 20% being spread over other appreciations. The corresponding ditribution is obviously not gaussian.

Although other parametric families of distributions can be considered (Zipf, Poisson, etc.), estimating the fitting and the parameters for each of them is costly, and may not produce satisfactory results. To avoid this difficulty, we propose to not infer any standard distribution from data, but perform a simple non-parametric density estimation for each resource. This choice is the one also commonly made in information retrieval, more specifically in statistical language modeling [11]. The main difference here is that the density estimation is performed for each resource (variable), whereas a single density estimation is performed in information retrieval. As preference data is discrete, estimating the probability density function comes down to estimating a set of probabilities: one for each possible rating value ($v \in V$) for each resource r. These probabilities, computed from the estimator $f(r, v)$ (see equation (3)), form the model θ.

$$f(r, v) = \frac{\sum_u \delta(u, r, v)}{\sum_v \sum_u \delta(u, r, v)}, \tag{3}$$

where $\delta(u, r, v) = 1$ when $n_{u,r} = v$ and $\delta(u, r, v) = 0$ otherwise. Since $\sum_u \delta(u, r, v)$ is memorized when loading the data, the estimation of θ is not complex, it is in $O(m)$, where m is the number of resources in the dataset.

To determine if a user u is a GSU (if his/her preferences are different from those of others), we rely on the model θ, that represents the distribution of the preferences of the entire population. We propose to exploit $Likelihood$ [13], a function that evaluates to which extent an instance has been generated by a model. In information retrieval, it is traditionally used to determine if a query or a document is likely to have been generated by a model. In CF-based RS, $Likelihood$ evaluates to which extent a user's preferences (ratings) have been generated by θ, the model of preferences of the entire population. Concretely, $Likelihood$ evaluates the probability of a user's preferences given θ.

Due to the extreme sparsity of preference data, the likelihood of two users may not be evaluated on the same number of resources, so may not be comparable. We thus modify the traditional likelihood measure to take into account this number of terms, by exploiting the $||R_u||^{th}$ root of the traditional likelihood (see equation (4)).

$$Likelihood(u, \theta) = \sqrt[||R_u||]{\prod_{r \in R_u} f(r, n_{u,r})} \tag{4}$$

Notice that some users may have a null likelihood, as some terms in the product may be null. To cope with this problem, we use smoothing in equation (3) to give some probability mass to unseen ratings on some resources, as made in traditional language models [11]. We choose the Kneser and Ney smoothing [27], as suggested in [9]. The complexity of this measure is then in $O(nm)$, with n the number of users.

One limitation of f lies in the fact that it does not take into account users' bias. Indeed, the ratings of strict users should not be considered the same way as those of tolerant users. Taking into account users' bias has often shown to improve performance in RS, such as in $AbnormalityCRU$ for GSU identification. To take into account this bias, we center the ratings of each user u around his/her average rating. The resulting equation, the User-Bias-Free Likelihood ($UBFLikelihood$), is presented in equation (5). Let us notice that the term bias is deviated from its original statistical meaning, it is however the term classically used in collaborative filtering.

$$UBFLikelihood(u, \theta) = \sqrt[||R_u||]{\prod_{r \in R_u} f'(r, (n_{u,r} - \overline{n_u}))}, \tag{5}$$

where $(n_{u,r} - \overline{n_u})$ is referred to as a user-bias-free rating. The complexity of this measure is similar to the one of $Likelihood$, $O(nm)$. As the resulting user-bias-free ratings are continuous, the estimator f, which was designed for discrete variables, can no more be used as it is. It is replaced by the estimator f', a histogram density estimator [34]. With the purpose of ensuring comparability, f' manages a number of bins equal to the one of the possible discrete values, all bins having an equal size. One main drawback of the histograms lies the choice of the position of the first bin, which may impact the resulting estimations. We choose to make the first bin start with the lowest value and the last one end with the highest value.

A second limitation of equations (4) and (5) lies in the fact that they do not manage the well known imprecision of ratings [4]. For example, when a user is asked to rate an item twice (at two different moments), he/she may rate it differently, although coherently. This difference is not only due to the context of notation, but also to the existence of a discrete rating scale, which forces users to make a choice when the preference he/she has in mind is between two rating values.

Equations (4) and (5) only exploit the probability of the interval (the bin) the rating (or the user-bias-free rating) belongs to. When a user-bias-free rating is at the limit of an interval, it may in fact belong to the interval beside it, due to the imprecision. As the histogram estimator f' does not take into account the link between two different intervals, the probability used may not actually reflect the rating. We propose to form, for each user-bias-free rating, an interval where the rating is at the center of the interval, thus freeing the estimator (histogram) from a particular choice of the bin positions. The corresponding estimator is referred to as the naive estimator [34]. Let h represent the imprecision of ratings. The resulting intervals are thus not fixed prior to the estimation, only their width. We assume they model each rating better than through the use of predefined intervals, as in equations (4) and (5). The resulting likelihood, with dynamic intervals ($DILikelihood$), is defined in equation (6).

$$DILikelihood(u) = \sqrt[||R_u||]{\prod_{r \in R_u} f''(n_{u,r} - \overline{n_u}, h)}, \tag{6}$$

where the estimator f'' represents the naive estimator, that manages the centered ratings. $f''(n_{u,r} - \overline{n_u}, h)$ estimates the probability that a user-bias-free rating $(n_{u,r} - \overline{n_u})$ is in the interval $[n_{u,r} - \overline{n_u} - h; n_{u,r} - \overline{n_u} + h]$. Once more, we compute the distribution of user's preferences on each resources among the GSU identification process. The complexity of $DILikelihood$ remains in $O(nm)$. Notice that the use of dynamic intervals is related to the choice of a non-parametric density estimation. It would not have been necessary to use them if we had chosen to exploit predefined laws.

4. EXPERIMENTS

In this section, we present the experiments we conduct to assess the pertinence of using a distribution-based technique in the context of grey sheep users (GSU) identification. We evaluate the three likelihood-based measures introduced in the previous section, as well as some measures from the state-of-the-art.

4.1 Dataset

The experiments are conducted on the *MovieLens* 20*M* dataset[1], made up of 20 million ratings from 138,493 users on 27,278 movies (resources). The rating scale ranges from 0.5 to 5.0 stars, with half-star increments. This dataset was published in april 2015 and is the current standard dataset for the evaluation of CF recommenders.

To not bias the evaluation, we choose to discard users who may be associated with the cold-start problem: those with less than 20 ratings in the dataset [33]. The set of users is then reduced to 123,053 users (88.8% of the original set of users) and is made up of 19.6 million ratings (98% of the original set of ratings). In the resulting dataset, users have provided up to 8,400 ratings, with an average number of 159 ratings per user. The sparsity of this dataset is higher than 99%, it is thus extremely sparse.

We use a five-fold cross-validation. The dataset is randomly split into 5 subsets, each of them contains 20% of the ratings of each user. At each fold, one subset is used for test and the 80% remaining ratings are used for learning.

4.2 Evaluation Protocol

We implement the well-known matrix factorization recommendation technique. The ALS factorization technique with regularization is used, with 20 features, a learning rate equal to 0.01 and a regularization parameter set to 0.05.

Regarding the imprecision of users' ratings, the literature has shown that on the *MovieLens* 100*K* dataset (where ratings are also on a 5 points rating scale), the imprecision is equal to 1 point [26]. We thus set h to 1 in equation (6).

We evaluate the accuracy of a recommendation provided to a user through the RMSE (Root Mean Squared Error) measure. It evaluates the discrepancy between the rating this user assigned to the recommended resource and the rating estimated by the recommender. We specifically exploit the per-user RMSE ($RMSE(u)$), computed by equation (7).

$$RMSE(u) = \sqrt{\frac{\sum_{r \in R_u}(n_{u,r} - n^*_{u,r})^2}{||R_u||}}, \qquad (7)$$

where $n^*_{u,r}$ is the estimated rating of user u on resource r.

We have defined a GSU as a user who has preferences that differ from those of others, and who also gets inaccurate recommendations. We thus propose to study a GSU identification measure through its ability to identify users who get inaccurate recommendations.

The experimental protocol we design to evaluate and compare various GSU measures is divided into three steps. First, we evaluate the correlation between each measure and the recommendation error (RMSE). The correlation used is the Pearson correlation coefficient. This correlation will be a first indicator of the ability of each measure to estimate the

[1]http://grouplens.org/datasets/movielens/

Measure	per-user RMSE
$500^{th}NN$	-0.06
$AbnormalityCRU$	0.58
$Likelihood$	-0.55
$UBFLikelihood$	-0.64
$DILikelihood$	**-0.68**

Table 1: Correlations between identification measures and RMSE with a MF recommendation technique

quality of the recommendations provided to a user.

Second, we focus on the ability of the measures to accurately identify GSU, through their precision. The precision of a measure, in our context, represents the ratio between the number of users it identifies as GSU and who have a high RMSE (number of good detections), and the total number of users identified as GSU by this measure (number of detections).

Third, we focus on the ability of the measures to identify the users with the highest RMSE, through the dispersion of the RMSE values of the GSU they identified (minimum, 1st quartile, median, 3rd quartile and maximum values).

We compare the accuracy of the three likelihood-based measures introduced in this paper, and two state-of-the-art techniques from both outlier detection and GSU identification. First, we implement a distance-based technique from outlier detection: the Kth $NearestNeighbor$ [37]. This technique considers a user as an outlier if he/she is far from his/her K^{th} nearest neighbor. We set K to 500. Second, we implement the distribution-based $AbnormalityCRU$ [17] from grey sheep users identification, which outperforms the state-of-the-art $Abnormality$ measure.

4.3 Correlation between GSU Identification Measures and RMSE

We focus here on the correlation between each GSU identification measure and the associated recommendation error (per-user RMSE). The correlations are presented in Table 1.

The $K^{th}NN$ measure from the state-of-the-art is the one that has the lowest correlation with the per-user RMSE: -0.06, which is not a significant correlation. It means that their is no explicit link between the similarity of a user's K^{th} Nearest Neighbor and the quality of the recommendations provided to this user. This distance-based measure is thus not a good candidate. This tends to confirm what is reported in the literature: distance-based techniques, such as $K^{th}NN$, are not designed to handle extremely sparse datasets. Notice that on a less sparse dataset (*MovieLens 100K*, with 96% sparsity), this correlation has shown to be higher, even though it was not significant either [17].

The correlation associated with $AbnormalityCRU$, from the state-of-the-art, is 0.58. It is significant and confirms the existence of a link between the value of $AbnormalityCRU$ of a user and the accuracy of the recommendation he/she gets: the higher the value of $AbnormalityCRU$ of a user, the lower the accuracy of the recommendations he/she receives. At the opposite, the lower the value of $AbnormalityCRU$, the higher the accuracy. This tends to mean that distribution-based measures, contrary to distance-based measures, are more adequate to identify GSU on extremely sparse datasets.

The three following measures are also distribution-based

measures. *Likelihood*, which is classically used in information retrieval, and that we propose to use in this paper, has a correlation with RMSE of -0.55. A user with a low *Likelihood* value tends to receive inaccurate recommendations (a high RMSE). Although significant, this correlation is slightly lower than the one of *AbnormalityCRU*. This lower accuracy was expected due to the limits of *Likelihood*, that we pushed in the two new likelihood-based measures.

The correlation between *UBFLikelihood* and the per-user RMSE reaches -0.64. It increases the one of *Likelihood* by 16%. It tends to confirm that managing users' bias improves the quality of the estimation of the accuracy of the recommendations provided to users.

The last measure proposed, *DILikelihood*, has a correlation equal to -0.68. It slightly improves the one of *UBFLikelihood* by 6%, which means that managing dynamic intervals improves the quality of the estimation of the accuracy of the recommendations provided to users. The correlations of *UBFLikelihood* and *DILikelihood* tend to suggest that these measures may outperform the state-of-the-art reference for GSU identification.

The correlations of *Likelihood*, *AbnormalityCRU*, *UBFLikelihood* and *DILikelihood* are significant. So, these four measures will be studied in further experiments.

Recall that a correlation reflects the relationship between two variables, in the entire range of their observations. However, there may be a strong relationship on only a subset of the observations of these variables. In that case, the correlation may not allow to accurately identify this relationship. Therefore, in the following experiments we will no more focus on the correlation between identification measures and RMSE, we will specifically focus on the RMSE values of the users identified as GSU.

4.4 Precision of Identification Measures

As mentioned previously, we consider of the highest importance that a GSU identification measure does not identify a grey sheep user as a user who is actually a normal user and who will get accurate recommendations.

So, to evaluate the ability of some measures to accurately identify GSU, we study their precision. The higher the precision of a measure, the more accurate it is.

As we are in an unsupervised scenario, the number, as well as the set of GSU, are unknown. However, to evaluate the precision of a measure, the set of GSU has to be known. Recall that we have defined a GSU as a user who receives inaccurate recommendations (in addition to having preferences different from others), *i.e.* a user with a high per-user RMSE. We propose to define the meaning of "high" through a threshold. In the following experiments, we study two thresholds: (i) the median RMSE of the entire set of users. This means that we consider that the 50% of users of the entire set who have a RMSE higher than this value, have a high RMSE. On the *MovieLens* 20M dataset, the median RMSE is equal to 0.82. The associated precision will be denoted by $p_{0.82}$. (ii) the 3rd quartile of the RMSE values of the entire set of users. This means that we consider that the 25% of users of the entire set who have a RMSE higher than this value, have a high RMSE. On the *MovieLens* 20M dataset, the 3rd quartile of the RMSE is equal to 1.0. The associated precision will be denoted by $p_{1.0}$.

Let us precise that, due to the context of an unsupervised scenario, we cannot evaluate the recall of the various mea-

sures. Indeed, some users may get inaccurate recommendations (high RMSE), without being GSU (due to a lack of information about them for example).

Figure 1 presents the precision values of the identification measures chosen from the previous section, according to the number of GSU selected. This number ranges from 0.1% (about 120 users) to 8% users (about 9,800 users). We have decided to not study larger numbers of GSU as GSU are, by definition, rare.

In Figure 1(a), that depicts precision $p_{0.82}$, we can first see that *Likelihood* has a precision significantly lower (by between 8% and 14%) than other measures. It is in accordance with the correlation values presented in the previous section. However, the difference in the correlation between *Likelihood* and *AbnormalityCRU* is smaller (about 5%). *AbnormalityCRU* has a precision slightly lower (between 2% and 3.5%) than *UBFLikelihood* and *DILikelihood*, whereas the difference in their correlations is larger (about 17%). *DILikelihood* and *UBFLikelihood* are the two most accurate measures, they have similar precisions whatever is the number of users selected. Between 1% and 8% of users selected, the precision of *Likelihood* only decreases by about 2%, whereas it decreases by 5% on other measures.

If the number of users selected as GSU is set to 1% (1,200 users), using *AbnormalityCRU* guarantees to select users with a RMSE higher than the median RMSE, with a precision of 96%, whereas *DILikelihood* and *UBFLikelihood* guarantee to selected these 1% of users with a precision of 98%.

We can notice that, surprisingly, the precision of *Likelihood* increases between 0.1% and 1% of users selected (about $1,200$ users), whereas on other measures, it decreases. The first 0.1% of users selected by *Likelihood* have a very low precision: the users with the lowest likelihood have a low RSME. When studying the number of ratings provided by these users, they do not tend to be associated with coldstart users. This increase can be explained by the fact that *Likelihood* is the only measure that does not manage any user bias, so one explanation can be that there is a bias on the users with the lowest *Likelihood* values.

To analyze further Figure 1(a), we choose to consider four precision thresholds for $p_{0.82}$: 90%, 92.5%, 95% and 97.5% (*i.e.* 10%, 7.5%, 5% and 2.5% of false positive detections respectively) and we study the number of GSU identified by the measures (see Table 2, left part). *Likelihood* is not presented as it never reaches such precision thresholds.

If we want to guarantee 90% of precision with *AbnormalityCRU*, the number of users to select has to be at most 10% (value not displayed on Figure 1(a)). It can be 15.4% and 17.9% with *UBFLikelihood* and *DILikelihood*, which corresponds to an increase of more than 50% of the number of selected users, with a similar precision. Let us recall that the increase in the precision was only at most 3.5%.

Being more strict and guaranteeing 92.5% of precision, results in a decrease of the number of users selected (only 5.4% of users for *AbnormalityCRU*). The number of users that can be selected, with the same 92.5% of precision, is twice larger with *UBFLikelihood* and *DILikelihood*.

When considering even more strict precisions (95% or 97.5%), the difference in the number of users that can be selected is increased. With a precision of 97.5%, *DILikelihood* allows to select 10 times more users than *AbnormalityCRU*: 1.90% of users (more than 2,000 users) can be selected.

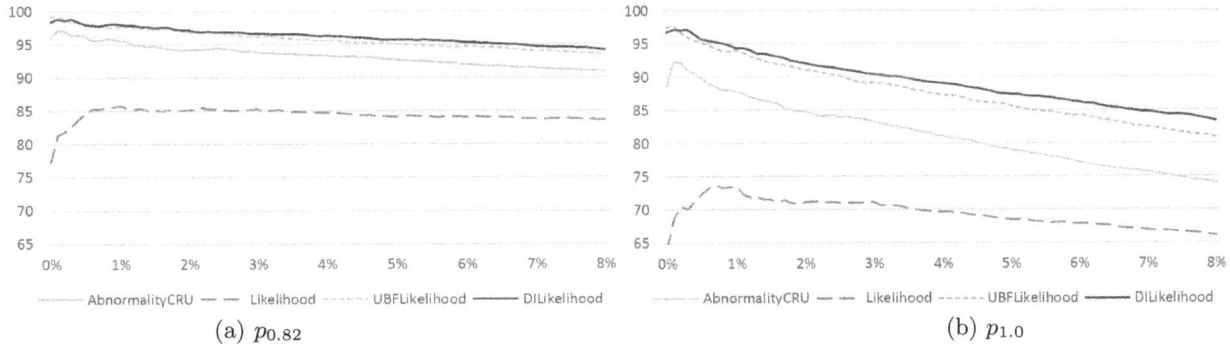

| | (a) $p_{0.82}$ | | (b) $p_{1.0}$ |

AbnormalityCRU —— Likelihood ---- UBFLikelihood —— DILikelihood

Figure 1: Precision values (a) $p_{0.82}$ and (b) $p_{1.0}$ of identification measures according to the number of users selected

	$p_{0.82}$				$p_{1.0}$			
	90%	92.50%	95%	97.50%	90%	92.50%	95%	97.50%
AbnCRU	10.00%	5.40%	1.30%	0.20%	0.60%	//	//	//
UBFLikd	15.40%	10.30%	5.20%	1%	2.70%	1.50%	0.60%	//
DILikd	17.90%	11.50%	**6.70%**	**1.90%**	3.50%	1.90%	**1%**	//

Table 2: Number of GSU selected (in %) according to the precision thresholds

When focusing on Figure 1(b), where the threshold managed by the precision is the 3rd quartile of the RMSE, we can first see that the ranking of the four measures is preserved, compared to Figure 1(a): *Likelihood* remains the less accurate measure. However, its difference in precision with other measures is larger, it is on average 29% lower than *DILikelihood*. Contrary to $p_{0.82}$, *DILikelihood* and *UBFLikelihood* show differences in their precision, especially when the number of users selected is larger than 1%. *DILikelihood* outperforms *UBFLikelihood* by 3% when 8% of users are selected. It is in accordance with the conclusions drawn from the correlations.

As with $p_{0.82}$, the precision of *Likelihood* increases until 1% of users are selected. This means that the users with the highest *Likelihood* value have a really low RMSE.

From Table 2, right part, we can see, as expected, that the number of users selected is quite smaller. *AbnormalityCRU*, from the state-of-the-art, cannot guarantee to select users with a RMSE greater than the 3rd quartile, with a precision greater or equal to 92.5%. However, *DILikelihood* guarantees a precision of 95% when it selects 1% of the users (about 1,200), which is quite high. None of the measures can select users while guaranteeing a precision of 97.5%.

In addition to these figures, we studied to what extent these measures, although highly precise, still identify some users with very low RMSE (below the 1st quartile of the RMSE of the entire set). Among the 1% of users (1,200 users) selected by *UBFLikelihood* and *DILikelihood*, only about 1% of users (11 users, see Table 3) have a RMSE below the 1st quartile, whereas 2% of these users are selected by *AbnormalityCRU*. It confirms that these measures are accurate.

We can conclude that *UBFLikelihood* and *DILikelihood* are the two most accurate measures, in terms of precision. *DILikelihood* even slightly outperforms *UBFLikelihood*. On the *MovieLens* 20M dataset, when 1% of users are selected by *UBFLikelihood*, these users are among the 25% of users with the highest RMSE, with a precision of 95%.

AbnCRU	*UBFLikhd*	*DILikhd*
22	13	**11**

Table 3: Number of well-recommended users selected depending on the measure, with a selection of 1% of users.

Moreover, to ensure a high accuracy of GSU identification (*i.e.* a precision higher than 90% based on the third quartile), the number of selected users should not exceed 3%.

4.5 Dispersion of the RMSE of GSU

In the previous section, we concluded that *AbnormalityCRU*, *UBFLikelihood* and *DILikelihood* are the most accurate measures. To thoroughly analyze their accuracy, we propose to compare the dispersion of the RMSE of the GSU they identify, in terms of minimum, 1st quartile, median, 3rd quartile and maximum values. The higher these values, the more accurate the identification measure. From the analysis of the precision, we concluded that selecting up to 3% of users (up to 3,690 users) guarantees a high precision of the GSU selected. We will study the dispersion of the RMSE when 1%, 2% and 3% of users are selected. Values are presented in Table 4, which also presents the dispersion values on the entire set of users, for comparison sakes.

Table 4 (column 1%) presents the dispersion of the RMSE values of each identification measure when 1% users are selected. We can first see that the measures do not differ in their maximum RMSE, which even corresponds to the maximum RMSE values in the entire set of users. The analysis of the minimum RMSE shows that the one of *AbnormalityCRU* (0.43) is higher than that of both likelihood-based measures (0.11), whereas *AbnormalityCRU* has the less accurate precision. This can be explained by the fact that the minimum value depends on only one RMSE value. Therefore, the selection of only one well-recommended user by both likelihood-based measures can explain this result. Table

	Entire	1%			2%			3%		
		AbnCRU	UBFLikhd	DILikhd	AbnCRU	UBFLikhd	DILikhd	AbnCRU	UBFLikhd	DILikhd
Min.	0.06	**0.43**	0.11	0.11	0.35	0.11	0.11	**0.11**	0.11	0.11
1st Q.	0.67	1.16	1.31	**1.34**	1.11	1.21	**1.24**	1.08	1.17	**1.20**
Med.	0.82	1.37	1.49	**1.51**	1.30	1.40	**1.42**	1.27	1.34	**1.37**
3rd Q.	1.00	1.59	1.68	**1.70**	1.52	1.58	**1.59**	1.48	1.52	**1.54**
Max.	**3.01**	**3.01**	**3.01**	**3.01**	3.01	3.01	3.01	3.01	3.01	3.01

Table 4: Dispersion of the RMSE values when 1%, 2% and 3% of users are selected, according to the identification measures. The dispersion of the entire set of users is also presented.

3 confirms this fact: $AbnormalityCRU$ selects more users with accurate recommendations (with a RMSE below the 1st quartile of the entire set of users), it is actually less accurate.

$UBFLikelihood$ and $DILikelihood$ have similar precision values when selecting this number of users (see Figure 1). Their minimum and maximum RMSE values are also similar. However, they differ in terms of their 1st quartile, median and 3rd quartile, where $DILikelihood$ outperforms $UBFLikelihood$ (by between 1.1% and 2.5%): it tends to select users with higher RMSE, so it is more accurate.

Table 4 (column 2%) and (column 3%) present the same indicators of dispersion, when 2% and 3% of users are selected respectively. The minimum and maximum values tend to remain unchanged, whatever is the number of users selected. So, the same conclusions can be drawn than from Table 4 (column 1%).

When focusing on 1st quartile, median and 3rd quartile when 2% and 3% of users are selected, $DILikelihood$ outperforms $UBFLikelihood$ by between 1.3% and 2.5%, which is similar to when 1% of users are selected. The improvement of $DILikelihood$ over $UBFLikelihood$ in terms of dispersion is thus independent of the number of users selected, whereas it is in terms of precision (see Figure 1). Beyond 3% of selected users, this difference increases.

When focusing on the quartile values between 1% and 3% of users selected, they decrease as the number of users selected increases. This was expected as the precision of these measures also decreases (between 5% and 7%) when the number of users selected increases. However, the decrease in terms of quartiles is higher (between 7.5% and 11.5%). $AbnormalityCRU$ is more stable than $DILikelihood$ and $UBFLikelihood$. This fact has to be viewed cautiously as $AbnormalityCRU$ is the less accurate measure.

One important information that we would like to highlight is that when 3% of users are selected, the 1st quartile of $DILikelihood$ (1.20) corresponds to the 9th decile of the entire set of users: 75% of selected users (2,769 users) have a RMSE comparable to the 10% worse RMSE of the entire dataset. Even more significant, when 1% of users are selected, 75% of selected users (922 users) have a RMSE comparable to the 5% worse RMSE of the entire dataset.

Given the 3 steps of the evaluation protocol, we can conclude that whatever is the evaluation criterion (correlation, precision or dispersion), $UBFLikelihood$ and $DILikelihood$, introduced in this paper, significantly outperform the best state-of the-art measure ($AbnormalityCRU$). This conclusion stands whatever is the number of GSU selected. The accuracy of $UBFLikelihood$ and $DILikelihood$ are quite close, but most of the time, $DILikelihood$, which has a similar complexity than $UBFLikelihood$ and $AbnormalityCRU$,

slightly outperforms $UBFLikelihood$ whatever is the evaluation criterion. When up to 1% of users are selected, they have a similar precision: more than 95% of the users they select have a RMSE greater than the 3rd quartile of the RMSE of the entire set of users. When the number of users increases (up to 3%), $DILikelihood$ is the most accurate measure, and still guarantees a precision greater than 90%.

Thus, managing users' rating bias as well as a dynamic interval (of width h) leads to the best GSU identification accuracy.

5. CONCLUSION AND PERSPECTIVES

In this work we focused on the identification of grey sheep users (GSU) in the frame of CF-based recommender systems. We have noted that the well-known outlier detection task has similar goals and comparable techniques than the grey sheep users identification task, although they have both been rarely views as close. We have proposed to inspire from techniques developed for outlier detection, especially from distribution-based techniques, while managing the specificities of preference data managed by recommender systems: imprecision of data, users' bias and extreme sparsity, that are not the focus of outlier detection techniques. We also rely on the works conducting in information retrieval.

The measures we proposed do not assume that data variables (resources) follow a unique law, nor a standard distribution and they rely on a model of data that copes with sparsity. One of them takes into account users' bias, by centering ratings. Another one manages, in addition, the imprecision of ratings by exploiting dynamic intervals.

Experimental evaluation shows that the measures that manage users' bias significantly improve measures from the state-of-the-art, while they have similar complexities. The measure that manages in addition the imprecision of ratings through dynamic intervals has an accuracy slightly higher, especially when a larger number of GSU is selected. For example, when this last measure selects 1% of users, it guarantees with a confidence of 95%, that they will get inaccurate recommendations (their RMSE will be in the set of the 25% worse RMSE in the entire set of users). In addition, 75% of these users are in the 5% of users who get the worse recommendations. Such an accurate identification is a reliable step towards even more accurate recommender systems.

In a future work, we will focus on multivariate grey sheep users identification to increase the accuracy of the measures. The challenge will, once more, lie in the management of data sparsity, which will be even worse in this context. We will also investigate the other possible reasons why some users do actually get inaccurate recommendations, while being normal users. Last, we will focus on the design of alternative recommendation techniques, dedicated to grey sheep users.

6. REFERENCES

[1] G. Adomavicius and A. Tuzhilin. Toward the next generation of recommender systems: A survey of the state-of-the-art. *IEEE transactions on knowledge and data engineering*, 17(6):734–749, 2005.

[2] C. Aggarwal. An introduction to outlier analysis. In *Outlier Analysis*, pages 1–40. Springer New York, 2013.

[3] C. Aggarwal and S. Yu. An effective and efficient algorithm for high-dimensional outlier detection. *The VLDB Journal*, 14:211–221, 2005.

[4] X. Amatriain, J. M. Pujol, and N. Oliver. I like it... i like it not: Evaluating user ratings noise in recommender systems. In *Proceedings of the User Modeling, Adaptation, and Personalization (UMAP'09)*, 2009.

[5] I. Ben-Gal. *Data Mining and Knowledge Discovery Handbook: A Complete Guide for Practitioners and Researchers*, chapter Outlier Detection. Kluwer Academic Publishers, 2005.

[6] J. Bobadilla, F. Ortega, and A. Hernando. A collaborative filtering similarity measure based on singularities. *Inf. Process. Manage.*, 48(2):204–217, Mar. 2012.

[7] S. Castagnos, A. Brun, and A. Boyer. When diversity is needed... but not expected! In *IMMM 2013, The Third Int. Conf. on Advances in Information Mining and Management*, 2013.

[8] V. Chandola, A. Banerjee, and V. Kumar. Anomaly detection: a survey. *ACM CSUR*, 41(3), 2009.

[9] S. Chen and J. Goodman. An empirical study of smoothing techniques for language modeling. Technical Report TR-10-98, Harvard University, 1998.

[10] M. Claypool, A. Gokhale, and T. Miranda. Combining content-based and collaborative filters in an online newspaper. In *Proceedings of the SIGIR Workshop on Recommender Systems: Algorithms and Evaluation*, 1999.

[11] B. Croft. *Language modeling for information retrieval*. Springer, 2003.

[12] L. Del Prete and L. Capra. differs: A mobile recommender service. In *Proc. of the 2010 Eleventh Int. Conf. on Mobile Data Management*, MDM '10, pages 21–26, Washington, USA, 2010. IEEE Computer Society.

[13] A. Edwards. *Likelihood*. Cambridge University Press, 1972.

[14] M. Ghazanfar and A. Prugel-Bennett. Fulfilling the needs of gray-sheep users in recommender systems, a clustering solution. In *2011 Int. Conf. on Information Systems and Computational Intelligence*, January 2011.

[15] M. A. Ghazanfar and P.-B. A. Leveraging clustering approaches to solve the gray-sheep users problem in recommender systems. *Expert Systems with Applications*, 41:3261–3275, 2014.

[16] D. Goldberg, D. Nichols, B. Oki, and D. Terry. Using collaborative filtering to weave an information tapestry. *Communications of the ACM*, 35(12):61–70, 1992.

[17] B. Gras, A. Brun, and A. Boyer. Identifying users with atypical preferences to anticipate inaccurate recommendations. In *Proceedings of the 11th International Conference on Web Information Systems and Technologies*, 2015.

[18] M. Grcar, D. Mladenic, B. Fortuna, and M. Grobelnik. *Advances in Web Mining and Web Usage Analysis*, volume 4198, chapter Data Sparsity Issues in the Collaborative Filtering Framework, pages 58–76. Springer, 2005.

[19] M. Grcar, D. Mladenic, and M. Grobelnik. Data quality issues in collaborative filtering. In *Proc. of ESWC-2005 Workshop on End User Aspects of the Semantic Web*, 2005.

[20] J. Griffith, C. O'Riordan, and H. Sorensen. Investigations into user rating information and predictive accuracy in a collaborative filtering domain. In *Proc. of the 27th ACM Symposium on Applied Computing*, 2012.

[21] J. Han and M. Kamber. *Data Mining: Concepts and Techniques*. Morgan Kaufmann, 2006.

[22] D. M. Hawkins. *Identification of outliers*, volume 11. Springer, 1980.

[23] C. Haydar, A. Roussanaly, and A. Boyer. Clustering users to explain recommender systems' performance fluctuation. In *Foundations of Intelligent Systems*, volume 7661 of *LNCS*, pages 357–366. Springer, 2012.

[24] V. Hodge and J. Austin. A survey of outlier detection methodologies. *Artificial Intelligence Review*, 22:85–126, 2004.

[25] S. Huang. Designing utility-based recommender systems for e-commerce: Evaluation of preference-elicitation methods. *Electronic Commerce Research and Applications*, 10(4), 2011.

[26] N. Jones, A. Brun, and A. Boyer. Comparisons instead of ratings: Towards more stable preferences. In *IEEE/WIC/ACM WI-IAT*, pages 451–456, 2011.

[27] R. Kneser and R. Ney. Improved backing-off for m-gram language modeling. In *Proceedings of the IEEE International Conference on Acoustics Speech and Signal Processing (ICASSP)*, volume 1, pages 181–184, 1995.

[28] Y. Koren, R. Bell, and C. Volinsky. Matrix factorization techniques for recommender systems. *Computer*, 42(8):30–37, 2009.

[29] S. Ramaswamy, R. Rastogi, and K. Shim. Efficient algorithms for mining outliers from large data sets. In *Proceedings of the ACM SIGMOD International Conference on Management of Data*, 2000.

[30] A. Rashid, S. Lam, A. LaPitz, G. Karypis, and J. Riedl. *Web Mining and Web Usage Analysis*, chapter Towards a Scalable kNN CF Algorithm: Exploring Effective Applications of Clustering. Springer, 2008.

[31] P. Resnick, N. Iacovou, M. Suchak, P. Bergstrom, and J. Riedl. Grouplens: An open architecture for collaborative filtering of netnews. In *Proc. of the 1994 ACM Conf. on Computer Supported Cooperative Work*, CSCW'94, 1994.

[32] A. I. Schein, A. Popescul, L. H. Ungar, and D. Pennock. Generative models for cold-start recommendations. In *Proc. of the 2001 SIGIR workshop on recommender systems*, 2001.

[33] V. Schickel-Zuber and B. Faltings. Overcoming incomplete user models in recommendation systems via an ontology. In *Proc. of the 7th Int. Conf. on Knowledge Discovery on the Web*, WebKDD'05, pages 39–57, Berlin, 2006. Springer.

[34] B. Silverman. *Density estimation for statistics and data analysis*. Chapman and Hall, London, 1986.

[35] X. Su and T. M. Khoshgoftaar. A survey of collaborative filtering techniques. *Adv. in Artif. Intell.*, 2009:4:2–4:2, Jan. 2009.

[36] G. Takacs, I. Pilaszy, B. Nemeth, and D. Tikk. Scalable collaborative filtering approaches for large recommender systems. *Journal of Machine Learning Research*, 10:623–656, 2009.

[37] C. H. Teixeira, G. H. Orair, W. Meira Jr, and S. Parthasarathy. An efficient algorithm for outlier detection in high dimensional real databases. Technical report, Technical report, Universidade Federal de Minas Gerais, Belo Horizonte, MG, Brazil, 2008.

[38] K. Verbert, N. Manouselis, X. Ochoa, and M. Wolpers. Context-aware recommender systems for learning: A survey and future challenges. *IEEE Transactions on Learning Technologies*, 5(4), 2012.

[39] M. Zanker, M. Fuchs, W. Hăűpken, M. Tuta, and N. Muller. *Information and communication technologies in tourism*, chapter Evaluating recommender systems in tourism a case study from austria. Springer, 2008.

On the Value of Reminders within E-Commerce Recommendations

Lukas Lerche
TU Dortmund University
Dortmund, Germany
lukas.lerche@
tu-dortmund.de

Dietmar Jannach
TU Dortmund University
Dortmund, Germany
dietmar.jannach@
tu-dortmund.de

Malte Ludewig
TU Dortmund University
Dortmund, Germany
malte.ludewig@
tu-dortmund.de

ABSTRACT

Most research in recommender systems is focused on the problem of identifying and ranking items that are relevant for the individual users but *unknown* to them. The potential value of such systems is to help users discover new items, e.g., in e-commerce settings. Many real-world systems however also utilize recommendation lists for a different goal, namely to *remind* users of items that they have viewed or consumed in the past. In this work, we aim to quantify the value of such reminders in recommendation lists ("reminders"), which has to our knowledge not been done in the past. We first report the results of a live experiment in which we applied a naive reminding strategy on an online platform and compare them with results obtained through different offline analyses. We then propose more elaborate reminding techniques, which aim to avoid reminders of too obvious or of already outdated items. Overall, our results show that although reminders do not lead to new item discoveries, they can be valuable both for users and service providers.

Keywords

Recommender systems; e-commerce; reminders

1. INTRODUCTION

Recommender systems (RS) have become a common feature of modern e-commerce platforms. Many major web sites implement techniques to continuously suggest additional items to their customers when they navigate the website based on the customers' past profiles and their current navigation and item viewing behavior. The research literature often considers the main value of recommenders to be their ability to point users to potentially relevant items which the users are not aware of, thereby creating additional sales or activity on the site. In practice, however, a typical strategy of websites like Amazon.com is that some presented recommendation lists include almost exclusively items that the user has viewed in the past. In this case, the intended goal of the recommender is not item discovery or catalog exploration but to remind users of items that were of (recent) interest to them. Generally, recommending items that the user already knows can serve different purposes.

(1) Reminders as Shortlists: Before making a purchase decision, customers often browse the catalog to explore the set of alternatives. Reminders of recently visited items can serve as automated decision "shortlists" and thereby help to reduce the cognitive effort in online shopping [17, 22]. Similarly, customers might return to the site after having slept on a decision and reminders for items that were viewed in a previous session might be particularly valuable [12].

(2) Familiarity Aspects: Recommending familiar items can generally help to increase the customers' trust and willingness to purchase. Amazon.com, for example, relied on familiar items as recommendations for a long time [24].

(3) User Cold-Start: In cold-start situations, where little is known about the user, reminders can serve as a fallback before switching to more elaborate algorithms.

(4) Repeated Recommendations: Finally, in some domains like music or video recommendation, reminders help encourage users to revisit items that they have purchased or consumed in the past but may have forgotten [3, 16]. Such "repeated recommendations" can be based on long-term user profiles. In contrast, the focus of our work is on recommending items that the user knows (has viewed), but has not necessarily purchased so far. These reminders are in our view particularly helpful in scenarios where the user focuses on a smaller set of candidate items before making a decision.

In our previous work, we have explored – among other aspects – the usefulness of a naive "reversed history" reminding strategy using navigation logs of an online retailer [12]. The results showed that recommendations worked best in terms of information retrieval measures when they contain both reminders from the user's recent navigation history and collaborative filtering (CF) recommendations.

In this work, we first provide empirical evidence from deployed applications that show that (a) many online customers "accept" reminders in recommendation lists ("reminders") and (b) that reminders can help to generate business value. As our main contribution, we propose and empirically evaluate novel algorithmic approaches of reminding, which aim to avoid too obvious as well as outdated item recommendations and at the same time focus on reminders that are relevant for the user's current shopping context.

UMAP '16, July 13-17, 2016, Halifax, NS, Canada
© 2016 ACM. ISBN 978-1-4503-4370-1/16/07...$15.00
DOI: http://dx.doi.org/10.1145/2930238.2930244

2. ANALYSIS OF RECOMINDERS IN DEPLOYED SYSTEMS

We evaluated the use and effectiveness of reminders in recommendations in the context of two real e-commerce sites.

2.1 User Acceptance of Recominders on an E-Commerce Site

First, we analyzed a dataset containing recommendation and user navigation logs provided to us by Zalando, a European online fashion retailer. From the comparably large dataset – more details in Section 4.3 – we sampled 3,000 "heavy users", for which we expect more reliable insights regarding their behavior than from one-time or infrequent visitors. The log file subset contains about 106,000 purchases and over 3.1 million *view actions* for over 188,000 different items[1]. An average shopping session of a user comprised about 9 item views and a purchase was made in about every third session.

The most important aspect for our analysis is that the item view actions in the log are usually accompanied by a three-element subset of recommendations that were displayed to the user when viewing the item. The click events on these recommended items were recorded in the log. Our log analysis revealed the following.

1. About every tenth of all *displayed* recommendations were reminders of already seen items, i.e., where a *view event* occurred before the recommendation was displayed. About one quarter of all recommendation lists contained at least one reminder.

2. More than 40% of all *successful* recommendations, i.e., where the click on a recommended item led to a purchase in the same session, were reminders. Therefore, users often knew the recommended item they eventually purchase from a previous visit of its detail page.

3. For those items that were "purchased from a recommendation list", we observed that customers often had inspected this item several times (over the course of several days) before the purchase. This suggests that the recommendations served at least partially as navigation shortcuts. Figure 1 shows when and how often users viewed an item before they purchased it based on a suggestion in a recommendation list.

4. In general, in each session customers on average only look at items from about 2.7 different product categories (of 334 existing ones). This indicates that they have often very specific shopping goals when arriving at the site. In such situations, reminders could be particularly helpful as *shortlists* [17, 22] during the decision making process.

Overall, our analysis reveals that reminders occur in the recommendation lists of the examined transaction logs and that customers in practice use these reminders as a starting point for subsequent purchase actions. Clearly, we cannot infer with certainty whether these purchases would not have been made if there were no reminders. At least, however, we see that customers seem to rely on recommendation lists even if they contain items which they already know.

[1] The data was preprocessed by Zalando in a way that no conclusions about the real proportions in Zalando's live traffic can be drawn.

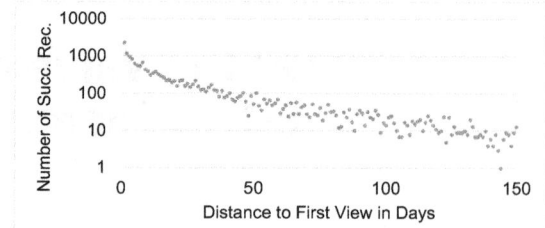

(a) Distance in days between first view event for an item and its successful recommendation.

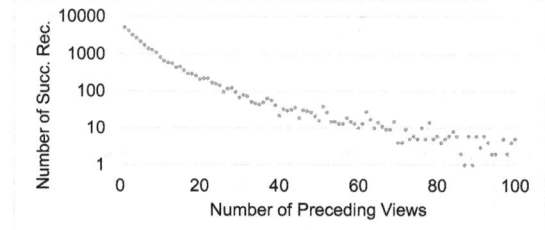

(b) Number of preceding view events for an item before its successful recommendation.

Figure 1: Distribution statistics for successful recommendations (Zalando *heavy* subset; Y-axes in base-10 log scale.)

2.2 Effectiveness Analysis on an Electronics and Gadgets Website

Our second analysis is based on an A/B test performed on the website of China-Gadgets, a German platform for consumer goods and electronics from Chinese wholesale sites. On China-Gadgets, items are presented as blog articles, sometimes with a textual review. We implemented different strategies to generate four-item recommendation lists that were shown both below the first (most recent) article on the site's landing page and on each item's detail page. Besides a popularity-based baseline, the techniques included Bayesian Personalized Ranking (*BPR*) [20], two content-based strategies, as well as a "Recently Viewed" [12] strategy.

The user interactions after implementing the different recommenders were recorded over the course of three months. On average, there were about 1.8 sessions per user and 80% of the users only visited the shop once. In our subsequent analyses we focus only on the remaining 20% of the users who have visited the shop at least twice during the monitoring period. The resulting subset contains 287,000 item view events by 49,000 users for 4,100 products. About 2.6% of the views were induced by a recommendation.

To estimate the business value of the recommendations, we measure their *success rate*. For each recommended item that was displayed to the user we call the recommendation "successful" if the item was clicked and the user subsequently visited the external Chinese site. Similar to the analysis in the previous section, a substantial fraction (38%) of the successful recommendations were not new to the users. Including reminders in recommendations can therefore represent a promising strategy.

Figure 2 shows the average success rates of the different strategies. The reminding strategy actually worked best in this domain. The success rate is at 0.34% which is signifi-

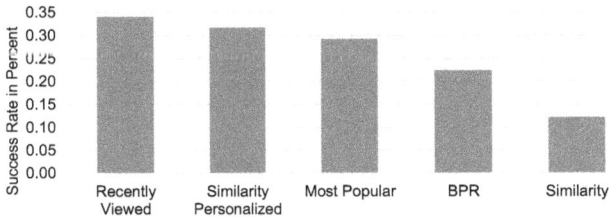

Figure 2: Success rate of the different recommendation strategies in the China-Gadgets live experiment.

cantly better[2] than the next best strategy *Similarity Personalized*, which recommends items similar to the user's history based on the TF-IDF representations of the textual item descriptions. Recommending the most popular items generally seems to be a reasonable strategy in this domain since we observe a comparably skewed popularity distribution of the items, as will be discussed later on in Section 4.3. The *BPR* method – whose model was re-trained every 30 minutes and whose parameters were optimized in an offline process – in contrast is less effective, presumably because there are only very few implicit ratings per user that can be used for learning. Finally, a *Similarity* recommender, which suggests items similar to the currently viewed item, led to the weakest performance.

All tested algorithms were "allowed" to recommend items that the user had viewed in the past. The *Similarity Personalized* method – without being designed for reminders – in fact produced lists in which about 75% of the items were already known by the users. The results therefore not only suggest that reminding can be beneficial also in this domain, but that other techniques of reminding can be successful.

3. ADAPTIVE REMINDERS

Our analyses so far show that placing (some) reminders in the recommendation lists can be an effective strategy. However, the simple "Recently Viewed" technique can easily lead to suggestions that are too obvious or already outdated. In the subsequent sections we will therefore design and evaluate different "adaptive" reminding strategies that can help to avoid some of these problems.

The general approach of all proposed strategies is to first determine a set of candidate items that the user has interacted with in the past and which can be used as reminders. The specific task is then to filter and rank these items with the goal to improve the recommendation accuracy and, if desired, to avoid too obvious suggestions. As the candidate set is usually only a small part of the whole item catalog, the reminders can be computed efficiently at runtime.

This set of candidate items H_u^I is taken from the user's recent history H_u which consists of a limited window of the user's previous sessions[3]. The choice of H_u will be discussed in more detail in Section 4.1. Each session is a set of interaction tuples of the form $\langle item, action, timestamp \rangle$. Possible actions for example include an item view, a purchase, or a shopping cart event. In this work, we will focus on past

item *view* actions and use H_u^V to denote the set of all tuples describing the view actions in all sessions of H_u.

3.1 Ranking Strategies

All proposed ranking strategies rely on assigning personalized scores to the recommendation candidates H_u^I based on heuristics. Items with a score of zero are not recommended[4].

Interaction Recency (IRec): This baseline recommends items depending on the time point of the last interaction of the user with an item, e.g., an item view event, a purchase or a shopping cart event. *IRec* therefore corresponds to a generalized "Recently Viewed" strategy as used in the previous section and in [12]. To make our results comparable with previous works, we only use the timestamps of the view events to compute a ranking score$_{ui}^{IRec}$ for a user u and an item i. Let $H_u^V(i)$ be the set of interaction tuples in H_u^V concerning item i and $time()$ be a function that returns the timestamp of a past interaction tuple t, then

$$\text{score}_{ui}^{IRec} = \max_{t \in H_u^V(i)} (time(t)) \qquad (1)$$

As we only include reminders in our recommendations, the "distance" between timestamps of the recommendations is not relevant. If reminders are mixed with novel recommendations, more weight could be given to the more recent interactions by applying an exponential decay function [3].

Interaction Intensity (IInt): If a user interacts longer or more frequently with an item, this *interaction intensity* indicates increased interest in the item. Here, we use the frequency of item view events in the interaction history, i.e.,

$$\text{score}_{ui}^{IInt} = |H_u^V(i)|. \qquad (2)$$

If two items have the same score, the *IRec* strategy can be used as a fallback to determine the ranking order.

Item Similarity (ISim): Assume a user was searching for shoes two weeks ago, but did not purchase a pair in the end. One week ago, the user browsed for scarves and today, she searches again for shoes. The idea of the proposed *ISim* strategy is to find elements in the past interaction history that match the current shopping goal.

This proposed approach corresponds to a content-based hybrid technique. We first determine the similarity of the items in H_u^I to the items viewed in the current session of user u. Let C_u be the set of items appearing in the current session of u, then

$$\text{sim}_{item}(u, i) = \frac{\sum_{j \in C_u} \text{sim}_{cos}(i, j)}{|C_u|}. \qquad (3)$$

In our experiments we use the cosine similarity sim_{cos} as a distance measure. The used feature vectors are TF-IDF representations of item descriptions or are created from additional item information like category and brand identifiers.

We then pick the k most similar items from H_u^I according to Equation 3, denoted as $\text{top}_k^I(u)$. To determine the final score score$_{ui}^{ISim}$, we re-sort these items by their view frequency according to the *IInt* heuristic, i.e.,

$$\text{score}_{ui}^{ISim} = \text{score}_{ui}^{IInt} \cdot \mathbf{1}_{\text{top}_k^I(u)}(i). \qquad (4)$$

---

[2]According to a four field χ-squared test ($p < 0.05$) with Bonferroni correction to compare the number of successful and unsuccessful recommendations between two strategies.

[3]A session represents a sequence of user actions within a particular time period identified by a session ID.

[4]In our work we focus on determining relevance scores and the ranking of *already known items*. Combining the reminding strategies with other algorithms is possible and might lead to mixed recommendations of known and new items. In these cases, the reminding techniques can provide (additional) relevance scores for the already known items.

The indicator function in Equation 4 leads to a score of zero for items not appearing in the top list. Other scoring techniques are possible that, e.g., use the similarity score in a weighted approach.

Session Similarity (SSim): Continuing the example from above, assume that two weeks ago the user also searched for belts that go well with the shoes. Once we observe that the user is again browsing for shoes, the previous *ISim* approach however would not remind the user of the belts.

To find good complementary items, like belts, from the user's past, we propose the *SSim* strategy that aims to find past sessions of a given user that had the same shopping intent as the current session. In contrast to the *ISim* technique, we rather look for similar sessions than for similar individual items. Let s be a past session of u and V_s the set of the viewed items of session s, then

$$\text{sim}_{session}(u, s) = \frac{\sum_{i \in V_s} \sum_{j \in C_u} \text{sim}_{cos}(i, j)}{|V_s| \cdot |C_u|}. \quad (5)$$

Let $\text{top}_k^S(u)$ be the k most similar sessions when compared with the current session according to Equation 5. Also, let $Items(\text{top}_k^S(u))$ be the set of items appearing in these sessions. Like in the *IInt* method, we re-rank the items that appear in the top k sessions based on their view frequency.

$$\text{score}_{ui}^{SSim} = \text{score}_{ui}^{IInt} \cdot \mathbf{1}_{Items(\text{top}_k^S(u))}(i) \quad (6)$$

Note that both the *SSim* and *ISim* strategies are still useful when multiple users share an account, because the items are selected based on the most recent user actions and therefore fit the interests of the currently active user.

3.2 Feature-based Category Filtering

In certain e-commerce domains repeated purchases for some item categories can be uncommon. Therefore, at least for some time, no items should be recommended that belong to a category in which a user has recently made a purchase. The proposed ***Feature Filter (FF)*** technique removes items from the list of reminder candidates that are not relevant anymore, i.e., belong to the *same category* as a recently purchased item. We therefore propose to maintain a *blacklist* of "outdated" categories based on the purchases made in the user's previous sessions. If a user however continues to view items from such a presumably outdated category, we remove the category from the *blacklist* again.

Generally, the *FF* technique can be used in combination with any of the previously discussed ranking strategies that provide a score$_{ui}^*$. If the category of an item i is on the blacklist, the filter sets its score to zero. In case the filter leads to too few remaining items, a popularity-based baseline technique can be used to fill up the recommendation list.

Note that in principle various combinations (hybrids) of the ranking strategies like *ISim* and *SSim* themselves are possible as well. In this work, we however focus on analyzing the effects of the individual ranking techniques in combination with the feature filtering method.

4. EXPERIMENTAL EVALUATION

The goal of our experimental analysis is to explore the effectiveness of different reminding strategies in terms of their capability to find relevant items. Other potential quality factors like diversity are not in the focus of our current work.

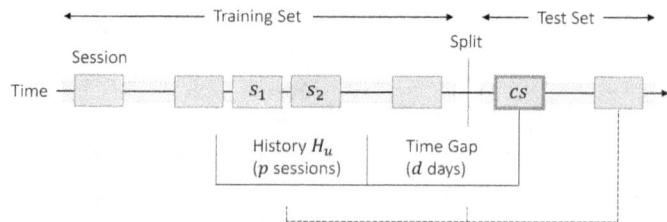

Figure 3: Evaluation scheme. The *training* and *test set* are determined per user. For each purchase that has to be predicted, p previous sessions before a time gap of d days represent the considered *history* H_u of a user, e.g., if cs is the *current session* for which purchases have to be predicted, the sessions $H_u = \{s_1, s_2\}$ are the user's relevant history before the time gap.

4.1 Evaluation protocol

An extension of the protocol proposed in [12] was used for the comparative evaluation of the proposed techniques and is shown in Figure 3.

Creating Training and Test Sets.

For each user the log entries are organized in sessions and split into a *training* set and hidden *test set*. In the experiments the splitting was done in a way that the test sessions comprise the last 20% of the purchases of a user. The recommendation task consists of predicting each purchase action in the sessions of the *test set* individually. To account for random effects, we use a 5-fold user-wise cross-validation by randomly assigning the users into five bins and executing the experiments five times without including the users of one bin each time.

Defining The Short-Term History.

Size of the history: Similar to [12] we assume that it is important to consider the most recent user behavior – the history H_u – to adapt the recommendations to the user's current shopping intents. The history H_u consists of p sessions that precede the currently evaluated test session plus those item view events of the currently evaluated test session that happened before the purchase that we want to predict. The choice of p depends on the domain. Too large values might lead to the inclusion of already outdated items; too small values might make the set of reminder candidates too small. We report the results for $p = 6$ in Section 5 as this value led to good results for all the used datasets.

Adding an "Obviousness Gap": As stated above, reminders should not be too obvious. To be able to vary and analyze the *degree of obviousness*, we introduce a time gap of d days between the user's history and the purchase that has to be predicted. Items that the user has interacted with in this time gap should not be used as reminder candidates. This also means that no actions from the current session are used as candidate items for reminders if $d > 0$. For example, for $d = 1$, items that were viewed within the last day of the current session would be considered too obvious and of too little value for the user as a reminder, see Figure 3. By varying d, we can therefore measure the performance of our reminding strategies when avoiding recommendations that are too obvious. Alternatively, the time gap could also be defined in terms of sessions instead of days.

Evaluation Measures.

As evaluation measures we use the *Hitrate@N* (Recall) and Mean Reciprocal Rank *MRR@N* for the computed *top-N* recommendation lists. Since we predict each purchase individually, there can only be one relevant item per recommendation list. Precision is therefore proportional to Recall.

4.2 Baselines Techniques

Although the focus of this work is on the adaptive reminding strategies, we are also interested in the effects of recommending known items using (a) standard CF techniques and (b) special context-aware schemes from the literature. We selected three implicit feedback techniques that have shown good predictive performance in the past.

(1) Bayesian Personalized Ranking (BPR): A learning-to-rank technique for implicit feedback [20]. To create a personalized ranking of all items for each user, *BPR* optimizes a generic optimization criterion that is the maximum posterior estimator for a Bayesian analysis of the ranking task. The model is trained with a bootstrapped, stochastic gradient descent method. *BPR* was the best-performing individual CF method in the analysis in [12]. In contrast to the usual setup, we allow *BPR* to include items in the recommendation lists that the user already knows as done in our A/B test on the China-Gadgets platform[5].

(2) Context-KNN (C-KNN): A *k*-nearest-neighbor recommendation technique using those sessions of all users in the *training set* that are most similar to the items in the history H_u^I of the current user u. This technique has been successfully used for contextualized playlist generation in [10] or [13]. Let V_s again be the set of items viewed in a session s. To calculate the similarity $\text{sim}_{binary}(u, s)$ between a user u and a session s from the *training set*, we use the cosine similarity $\text{sim}_{cos}(\vec{H_u^I}, \vec{V_s})$ between bit vectors that indicate for each item whether it is included in each set or not.

$$\text{sim}_{binary}(u, s) = \text{sim}_{cos}(\vec{H_u^I}, \vec{V_s}) \quad (7)$$

Let $\text{top}_k^T(u)$ be the k most similar sessions to u from all sessions in the *training set* T according to $\text{sim}_{binary}(u, s)$. The recommendation score for item i and user u is the sum of similarities for sessions in $\text{top}_k^T(u)$ where item i was viewed.

$$\text{score}_{ui}^{C-KNN} = \sum_{s \in \text{top}_k^T(u)} \text{sim}_{binary}(u, s) \cdot \mathbf{1}_{V_s}(i) \quad (8)$$

(3) Co-occurrence patterns (CO): A technique based on association rule mining used in [12] for e-commerce data and for the contextualized recommendation of workflow elements in [11]. This method learns size-two association rules of the form "Users who viewed A, also viewed B" from the training data. The recommendation score of an item i is the sum of the *confidence* values for the associations $j \rightarrow i$ by applying the rules to the items in the users current history H_u^I.

$$\text{score}_{ui}^{CO} = \sum_{j \in H_u^I} \text{confidence}(j \rightarrow i) \quad (9)$$

As we are interested in how many of the recommendations made by the CF baselines are actually known items, we furthermore report a metric *RepeatRate@N* for them which

---

[5]We made additional experiments with other techniques including in particular Factorization Machines [19] or Funk's SVD [1]. As these methods perform worse than *BPR*, we do not report the results here.

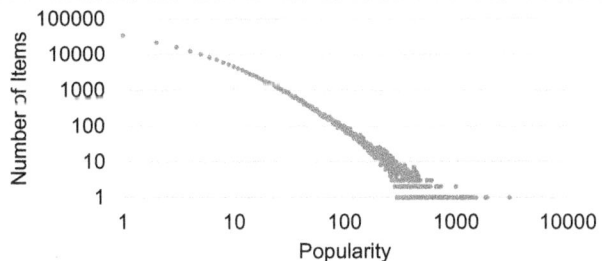

Figure 4: Popularity distribution for the Zalando *heavy* subset. X-axis: Item popularity (view and purchase actions per item). Y-axis: Number of items. Both in base-10 log scale.

calculates the percentage of items in the *top-N* lists that the user has already viewed in a previous session. The *RepeatRate@N* for the proposed reminding strategies is of course 100%.

4.3 Datasets

We use log data from Zalando, China-Gadgets and a public dataset from TMall [12]. For Zalando, we created subsets of *heavy* and *random* users. For the *heavy* users, we observe at least 80 site visits (sessions) during one year. The average number of sessions for *random* users is 28. For the smaller logs of China-Gadgets, we selected 10,000 users that are not one-time visitors. For TMall we selected 5,000 random users.

The Zalando and China-Gadgets log data files contain a few user events that can be attributed to the already deployed recommendation components on the sites. We removed those user actions from the logs that were induced by the recommenders, i.e., we removed item views that resulted from a click on recommendation lists. A small bias can still remain as users might have noticed the recommendations without having clicked on them. The detailed statistics of the datasets are shown in Table 1. In addition, Figure 4 shows the popularity distribution for the Zalando *heavy* subset. As is typical for RS datasets, the distribution is skewed with few highly popular and many unpopular items from the long-tail. The Zalando *random* and TMall datasets have similar characteristics, but the Zalando *heavy* subset contains more items with high popularity. The China-Gadgets subset has an overall smaller item catalog.

5. RESULTS

We first report the results of the CF baselines and then discuss the performance of the reminding strategies.

5.1 Effects of Recommending Known Items in Baseline Algorithms

In our first measurement, we compared the best-performing "standard" CF method from [12], *BPR*, with the context-aware baselines *C-KNN* and *CO*. We manually tuned the algorithm parameters for *BPR* and *C-KNN* ($k = 5$) to optimize the hit rate and tested two configurations: (a) without repeated recommendations, (b) with repeated recommendations[6]. Table 2 shows the results for the Zalando *heavy*

---

[6]Remember that we do not call these repeated recommendations "reminders" as the selection of items is not limited to items in the recent user history.

Table 1: Characteristics of the Zalando, China-Gadgets and TMall datasets.

	Zalando			China-Gadgets		TMall	
	complete	*heavy* subset	*random* subset	complete	subset	complete	subset
Users	3.5M	3k	3k	466k	10k	424k	5k
Items	460k	188k	121k	4.4k	3.7k	1M	195k
Views	200M	3.1M	906k	1.1M	192k	49M	660k
Purchases	3.9M	106k	47k	804k	142k	3.2M	50k
Sessions	3.5M	338k	89k	859k	123k	7.1M	96k

subset with the configuration parameters $d = 0$ and $p = 6$, i.e., the contextualized strategies use six previous sessions before the user's current session cs as the history H_u.

The results show that considering recent navigation actions from previous sessions – as done by the *C-KNN* and *CO* methods – leads to significant (Student's t-test, $p < 0.01$) accuracy improvements when compared to a "context-agnostic" learning-to-rank method like *BPR* as was discussed in [12][7]. Also, *BPR* tends to recommend many already known items and *C-KNN* is significantly more accurate than *CO*. Second, including repeated recommendations in all settings proved to be important and strongly increased the accuracy. Similar observations were also made for the other datasets and are omitted due to space constraints.

In the live experiment for China-Gadgets (Section 2.2), repeated recommendations were allowed for *BPR*. Preliminary online tests also indicated that the success rate of *BPR* is significantly lower when repeated recommendations are forbidden, which corroborates our offline results.

5.2 Results of the Reminding Strategies

In the next series of experiments, we benchmarked the simple "reverse history" strategy *IRec*, which was also used in [12], against the recominder strategies proposed in Section 3. The choice of p depends on the indented goal of the reminders and used techniques, e.g. increasing p can improve the accuracy of *ISim* due to more candidates but decrease the accuracy of *IInt* due to noise from older items. We take $p = 6$ sessions for the history H_u (from which the reminders will be selected) as an overall acceptable setting to show the general characteristics of all techniques. Fine-tuning of p is not in the scope of this work. To show the influence of reminding obvious items on the accuracy metrics, we also report the results for different time gap values $d = 0$ and $d = 3$ and a special case $d = 0^*$. In that last case we exclude the events from the user's current sessions in the history that were views of the item that should be predicted. This way, we can show the impact of not recommending the most obvious item. The results are given in Table 3 for the Zalando data and in Table 4 for the China-Gadgets and TMall data.

Including Obvious Reminders.

First, consider the situation $d = 0$, i.e., where users can be reminded of items they have just looked at. Both in the Zalando *heavy* and *random* user subset, the basic reminding strategy *IRec* works comparably well as users naturally often view items right before they purchase them. The hit rate is however not 1, since the purchased item does not necessarily need to be among the last 10 viewed items. Putting more

weight on frequently viewed items (*IInt*) or reminding the user of similar items (*ISim*) leads to worse results.

In contrast, our content-based *SSim* strategy, which looks for similar shopping sessions in the past, works significantly ($p < 0.01$) better than the simple *IRec* strategy on the *heavy* user subset both in terms of the hit rate and the MRR. This indicates that it is not unusual that users abandon an unsuccessful shopping or browsing session, look for different items, and eventually continue the previous search to finally make a purchase. As a result, the *SSim* strategy shows that *adapting reminders* to the current user goals can be beneficial. However, for the *random* user dataset the *IRec* baseline cannot be beaten by *SSim*, since there are often not enough similar past sessions available for new users that can be used to predict the continuation of the current session.

If the time gap is zero ($d = 0$), actions from the current session are part of the history, including view actions for the item that was eventually purchased and that we want to predict. In the additional experiment labeled with $d = 0^*$ we did not include these actions in the history. As can be seen from Table 3, excluding this item results in a strong accuracy decrease, especially for the *IRec* strategy. Under this configuration, reminding frequently viewed items (*IInt*) performs best. Still, the hit rate of *IRec* is comparably high which indicates that users often browse items in previous sessions and sleep on their decisions before the purchase.

Avoiding the Obvious: Long-Term Reminders.

To avoid obvious recommendations, we do not remind users of what they have looked at during the last few days by increasing the time gap; here we report $d = 3$ days. Generally, when increasing d, the absolute values for the hit rate and the MRR decrease, which is however expected, given that some of these less obvious reminders may already be outdated. How to set d for "long-term reminders" depends on the application domain. In e-commerce, a few days might be appropriate [3]. In the domain of music streaming, it might in contrast be plausible to remind users of what they liked and listened to a few weeks or months ago.

The results in Table 3 show that the simple *IRec* strategy seems to include too many already outdated reminders under the $d = 3$ configuration. All other techniques proposed in our work mostly lead to better results than *IRec* in terms of the rate and MRR. By far the best results are obtained when using the content-based *ISim* method in combination with the feature filter (*FF*), i.e., when we remove reminders that relate to item categories in which the user has already purchased in the meantime. The *SSim* and *ISim* methods show a similar performance when the feature filter is not applied. The results however suggest that *SSim* includes too many item view events for products that the user eventually lost interest in and did not purchase in the end.

---

[7] As the recommendations are generated from a fairly large pool of items, the resulting values for the hit rate and the MRR are expected to be generally small [14].

Table 2: *Hitrate@10* (HR), *MRR@10* and *RepeatRate@10* (RR) results for the CF techniques for the Zalando *heavy* subset with/without the ability to recommend known items. History $p = 6$, time gap $d = 0$. The best values are highlighted in grey.

Dataset	Zalando – *heavy* subset								
Technique	C-KNN			CO			BPR		
Metric@10	HR	MRR	RR	HR	MRR	RR	HR	MRR	RR
No repeated recomm.	0.051	0.032	0	0.013	0.005	0	0.001	0.001	0
Repeated recomm.	0.156	0.072	0.375	0.123	0.046	0.343	0.066	0.024	0.830

Table 3: *Hitrate@10* (HR) and *MRR@10* results for the Zalando *heavy* subset and the Zalando *random* subset. History $p = 6$, time gap $d = 0$, $d = 0^*$, $d = 3$. The best values are highlighted in grey.

Dataset	Zalando – *heavy* subset						Zalando – *random* subset					
Configuration	$p = 6, d = 0$		$p = 6, d = 0^*$		$p = 6, d = 3$		$p = 6, d = 0$		$p = 6, d = 0^*$		$p = 6, d = 3$	
Metric@10	HR	MRR	HR	MRR	HR	MRR	HR	MRR	HR	MRR	HR	MRR
FF (SSim)	0.681	0.296	0.293	0.139	0.193	0.110	0.642	0.268	0.237	0.109	0.136	0.077
FF (ISim)	0.561	0.219	0.353	0.146	0.521	0.200	0.561	0.217	0.266	0.112	0.504	0.191
SSim (k = 2)	0.697	0.327	0.210	0.111	0.167	0.093	0.678	0.294	0.176	0.088	0.117	0.062
ISim (k = 20)	0.588	0.241	0.319	0.137	0.170	0.077	0.600	0.236	0.240	0.105	0.135	0.060
IInt	0.561	0.217	0.363	0.147	0.162	0.071	0.545	0.205	0.271	0.111	0.129	0.054
IRec	0.653	0.309	0.230	0.069	0.136	0.058	0.697	0.295	0.174	0.052	0.120	0.054

Results for the China-Gadgets and TMall Datasets.

Table 4 shows the results obtained with the same protocol configurations for the China-Gadgets and TMall datasets. The results are mostly in line with those from the previous experiment, which shows that the proposed reminder strategies may generalize to other datasets.

Specifically, when applying a time gap of $d = 3$, the feature filter method in combination with the content-based *ISim* method works consistently better than any other tested strategy. For the TMall subset with $d = 0$, the *SSim* method is again better than *IRec* in terms of hit rate and MRR, similar to Zalando *heavy*. However, this is not the case for China-Gadgets where – like Zalando *random* – there are not enough similar past sessions available for some users. A possible explanation that the *IRec* method works particularly well for the blog-style China-Gadgets platform can be that the entries on this site are time-ordered and the most recent additions appear on the top of the page. The order of the items may therefore often be directly related to their general attractiveness. Thus, the recommendations made by the *IRec* strategy can be used as navigation shortcuts for users to repeatedly inspect these most recent items.

Lastly, when removing the item that should be predicted from the history ($d = 0^*$), the *IInt* strategy works best for TMall, as was the case for the Zalando subsets. However, for China-Gadgets none of the reminding strategies stands out in particular regarding the hit rate and MRR.

Discussion.

A comparison of the absolute values obtained for the reminding strategies and the baseline techniques in Table 2 shows that reminders lead to substantially higher accuracy values. The results of our offline experiments therefore confirm the results obtained from our analyses of real-world systems in Section 2 and emphasize the potential value of including known items into recommendation lists. Furthermore, the experiments indicate that more elaborate reminding strategies can be more effective than a "reverse history" approach. To which extent combinations of these reminding strategies with long-term CF models can help to further increase the accuracy is part of our ongoing work.

Finally, all our reminding strategies needed less than 10 ms to compute one reminder list using a current generation Intel Xeon CPU. On the same hardware, the baseline techniques (*BPR*, *C-KNN*, *CO*) needed significantly more time (up to one second) to compute one list. Combining personalization methods with adaptive reminders will therefore not significantly increase the run-time complexity.

6. RELATED WORK

The systematic inclusion of reminders in recommendation lists has, to our knowledge, not been discussed or analyzed to a large extent in the RS research literature. Some exceptions exist, which, for example, mention the use of reminders in "check-out" situations in online shops ("Don't forget to buy") [18] or report of a mobile shopping assistant that displays similar known items while browsing for new products ("Similar to what you liked in the past") [17]. Both mentioned works however do not propose algorithmic solutions.

Recommendations for repeated consumption were investigated, e.g., in [3] and [15]. In contrast to repeated recommendations of already purchased or consumed items, our work focuses on reminders, i.e., items that the user knows, but that were not necessarily consumed so far. The analysis in [3] showed that the recency of interactions is the strongest predictor of repeated consumption and that there is an exponential decay factor. The authors propose a model to recommend known items with a probability that is proportional to the time of its last consumption. Such an exponential decay function can be integrated into our *IRec* reminding strategy, in particular when it should be combined with a CF model. In [15] the listening behavior of users when browsing for music tracks was investigated and the authors propose an approach to automatically derive whether the user is currently looking for something new or not. Their approach could be combined with our work to decide if reminders should be generally included in the current user session or not.

In the online shopping scenario, this question of "When to remind?" translates to determining whether the user currently is in a catalog exploration phase or in the phase of re-inspecting the choice set before making a decision. Based

Table 4: *Hitrate@10* (HR) and *MRR@10* results for the China-Gadgets and TMall subsets. History $p = 6$, time gap $d = 0$, $d = 0^*$, $d = 3$. The best values are again highlighted in grey.

Dataset	China-Gadgets – subset						TMall – subset					
Configuration	$p=6, d=0$		$p=6, d=0^*$		$p=6, d=3$		$p=6, d=0$		$p=6, d=0^*$		$p=6, d=3$	
Metric@10	HR	MRR	HR	MRR	HR	MRR	HR	MRR	HR	MRR	HR	MRR
FF (SSim)	0.577	0.344	0.219	0.128	0.206	0.121	0.482	0.220	0.228	0.101	0.142	0.078
FF (ISim)	0.532	0.276	0.172	0.116	0.481	0.225	0.415	0.185	0.239	0.096	0.405	0.176
SSim (k = 2)	0.616	0.376	0.223	0.136	0.212	0.121	0.483	0.214	0.173	0.082	0.135	0.067
ISim (k = 20)	0.541	0.254	0.223	0.134	0.189	0.109	0.415	0.185	0.195	0.082	0.140	0.067
IInt	0.539	0.254	0.223	0.134	0.188	0.106	0.429	0.181	0.241	0.094	0.138	0.063
IRec	0.615	0.586	0.220	0.126	0.186	0.099	0.463	0.191	0.125	0.032	0.117	0.049

on the context of the user, there might be situations where reminding is particularly useful as discussed in [18] and the problem of finding the best time for repeated recommendations has also been mentioned for commercial systems like eBay [23, 26] or Netflix [8]. In our work, we focus on the problem of selecting the right items and we consider the problem of determining whether we should present reminders at all as a related but complementary problem.

Our reminding strategies can also be seen as context-aware recommendation approaches, where the context to which the recommendations are adapted is the user's short-term shopping goal. In particular the *ISim* and *SSim* techniques try to rank those items from the user's navigation history higher that are presumably a good match for the items that the user has most recently inspected.

In practice, one would probably not implement a "pure" reminding strategy – which only includes items that the user already knows – but rather create one or multiple lists that contain a mix of items that match the long-term user model and a number of reminders. Some of these strategies that combine assumed short-term shopping intents with long-term collaborative filtering models were discussed in our previous work [12]. The results showed that the combined models which implemented a "contextual post-filtering" strategy [2] worked best in the tested configurations, but already the most simple reminders had a significant impact on the recommendation accuracy. Our current work continues this research and shows that there are more effective reminding strategies than the "reverse history" approach from [12].

Research on short-term adaptation for collaborative filtering approaches is comparably scarce in the recommender systems literature[8]. Recent exceptions include [10], [21], or [25]. These works propose different strategies of understanding the user's shopping intents, but do not explicitly include reminders in their recommendations. From an algorithmic perspective, our *Session Similarity* reminding method is related to nearest-neighbor approaches used in music playlist generation techniques as described in [9], where the goal is to find past listening sessions or playlists that are similar to the user's most recent listening behavior. Our *Feature Filter* method on the other hand implements a similar idea to the post-purchase product recommendation technique described in [26] where the goal was to avoid the recommendation of items on eBay that are too similar to recent purchases.

The ranking of the reminders in our approaches is often based on a time-based criterion. Our work is therefore related to "time-aware recommender systems" as a special case of context-aware systems. Campos et al. review time-aware systems with a focus on evaluation aspects in [5]. According to their classification, our protocol represents a time-dependent cross-validation procedure with user resampling. In addition, our protocol implements a session-wise evaluation procedure as done in similar form in [4]. We however use the hit rate and the MRR as standard evaluation measures.

As discussed in the introduction, one possible value of automatically generated reminders as recommendations is that they can be used as navigation shortcuts by users. In [22], Schnabel et al. conduct a user study to assess the value of providing online customers with a web shop feature to create their own shortlists. Their study shows that many participants used these shortlists to organize their shopping sessions and remind themselves of recently inspected items. In addition, shortlists were shown to be helpful by reducing the cognitive effort for the users. An earlier study from the business literature [7] revealed that some online users – in absence of a shortlist functionality – use their shopping baskets to keep track of their candidate items, i.e., they misuse the cart as a shortlist with a reminder functionality. In contrast to these works, the discussed reminding strategies populate such shortlists automatically and in particular our results obtained from the logs of the deployed systems indicate that customers actually use these shortlists.

7. SUMMARY AND FUTURE WORKS

In this paper, we have analyzed the value of including reminders in recommendations, which is a common strategy in real-world systems, through offline and online experiments. We have furthermore proposed and successfully evaluated novel strategies which avoid the recommendation of unrelated or too obvious items. In practice, recommending only reminders might in many cases not be the most effective strategy. While reminders might increase familiarity and trust, they are by design unsuited to help users discover new items. Measuring the true value or obviousness of recommendations in offline settings is however challenging [18].

In our future work we will thus explore strategies that combine novel recommendations and reminders in a balanced way to increase diversity and plan to investigate techniques to better assess the *right time* for reminding, e.g., taking product consumption cycles into consideration. Furthermore, we will try to estimate their perceived value through user studies and measure their effect in real world scenarios.

---

[8]In conversational and critiquing based systems [6] usually only short-term goals are relevant and the item filtering process is based on explicit user constraints. In our work we are however interested in learning-based, adaptive recommendation approaches.

8. REFERENCES

[1] http://sifter.org/~simon/journal/20061211.html (last accessed: 02/2016), 2006.

[2] Gediminas Adomavicius and Alexander Tuzhilin. Context-aware recommender systems. In *Recommender Systems Handbook*, pages 217–253. Springer, 2011.

[3] Ashton Anderson, Ravi Kumar, Andrew Tomkins, and Sergei Vassilvitskii. The dynamics of repeat consumption. In *Prof. WWW '14*, pages 419–430, 2014.

[4] David Ben-Shimon, Alexander Tsikinovsky, Michael Friedmann, Bracha Shapira, Lior Rokach, and Johannes Hoerle. RecSys challenge 2015 and the YOOCHOOSE dataset. In *Proc. RecSys '15*, pages 357–358, 2015.

[5] Pedro G. Campos, Fernando Díez, and Iván Cantador. Time-aware recommender systems: A comprehensive survey and analysis of existing evaluation protocols. *UMUAI*, 24(1-2):67–119, 2014.

[6] Li Chen and Pearl Pu. Critiquing-based recommenders: Survey and emerging trends. *UMUAI*, 22(1):125–150, 2011.

[7] Angeline G. Close and Monika Kukar-Kinney. Beyond buying: Motivations behind consumers' online shopping cart use. *Journal of Business Research: Advances in Internet Consumer Behavior & Marketing Strategy*, 63(9–10):986–992, 2010.

[8] Carlos A. Gomez-Uribe and Neil Hunt. The Netflix recommender system: Algorithms, business value, and innovation. *ACM TMIS*, 6(4):13, 2015.

[9] Negar Hariri, Bamshad Mobasher, and Robin Burke. Context-aware music recommendation based on latenttopic sequential patterns. In *Proc. RecSys '12*, pages 131–138, 2012.

[10] Negar Hariri, Bamshad Mobasher, and Robin Burke. Adapting to user preference changes in interactive recommendation. In *Proc. IJCAI '15*, pages 4268–4274, 2015.

[11] Dietmar Jannach, Michael Jugovac, and Lukas Lerche. Adaptive recommendation-based modeling support for data analysis workflows. In *Proc. IUI '15*, pages 252–262, 2015.

[12] Dietmar Jannach, Lukas Lerche, and Michael Jugovac. Adaptation and evaluation of recommendations for short-term shopping goals. In *Proc. RecSys '15*, pages 211–218, 2015.

[13] Dietmar Jannach, Lukas Lerche, and Iman Kamehkhosch. Beyond "hitting the hits" – generating coherent music playlist continuations with the right tracks. In *Proc. RecSys '15*, pages 187–194, 2015.

[14] Dietmar Jannach, Lukas Lerche, Iman Kamehkhosh, and Michael Jugovac. What recommenders recommend: An analysis of recommendation biases and possible countermeasures. *User Modeling and User-Adapted Interaction*, 25(5):427–491, 2015.

[15] Komal Kapoor, Vikas Kumar, Loren Terveen, Joseph A. Konstan, and Paul Schrater. "I like to explore sometimes": Adapting to dynamic user novelty preferences. In *Proc. RecSys '15*, pages 19–26, 2015.

[16] Elizabeth Hellmuth Margulis. *On Repeat: How Music Plays the Mind*. Oxford University Press, 2014.

[17] Carolin Plate, Nathalie Basselin, Alexander Kröner, Michael Schneider, Stephan Baldes, Vania Dimitrova, and Anthony Jameson. Recomindation: New functions for augmented memories. In *Adaptive Hypermedia and Adaptive Web-Based Systems*, pages 141–150, 2006.

[18] George Prassas, Katherine C. Pramataris, Olga Papaemmanouil, and Georgios J. Doukidis. A recommender system for online shopping based on past customer behaviour. In *Proc. 14th Bled eConference*, pages 766–782, 2001.

[19] Steffen Rendle. Factorization machines with libFM. *ACM TIST*, 3(3):57:1–57:22, 2012.

[20] Steffen Rendle, Christoph Freudenthaler, Zeno Gantner, and Lars Schmidt-Thieme. BPR: Bayesian personalized ranking from implicit feedback. In *Proc. UAI '09*, pages 452–461, 2009.

[21] Steffen Rendle, Christoph Freudenthaler, and Lars Schmidt-Thieme. Factorizing personalized markov chains for next-basket recommendation. In *Proc. WWW '10*, pages 811–820, 2010.

[22] Tobias Schnabel, Paul N. Bennett, Susan T. Dumais, and Thorsten Joachims. Using shortlists to support decision making and improve recommender system performance. *CoRR*, abs/1510.07545, 2015.

[23] Neel Sundaresan. Recommender systems at the long tail. In *Proc. RecSys '11*, pages 1–6, 2011.

[24] Kirsten Swearingen and Rashmi Sinha. Interaction design for recommender systems. In *Proc. DIS' 02*, pages 312–334, 2002.

[25] Maryam Tavakol and Ulf Brefeld. Factored MDPs for detecting topics of user sessions. In *Proc. RecSys '14*, pages 33–40, 2014.

[26] Jian Wang, Badrul Sarwar, and Neel Sundaresan. Utilizing related products for post-purchase recommendation in e-commerce. In *Proc. RecSys '11*, pages 329–332, 2011.

Reinforcement Learning:
the Sooner the Better, or the Later the Better?

Shitian Shen
Department of Computer Science
North Carolina State University
Raleigh, NC 27695
sshen@ncsu.edu

Min Chi
Department of Computer Science
North Carolina State University
Raleigh, NC 27695
mchi@ncsu.edu

ABSTRACT

Reinforcement Learning (RL) is one of the best machine learning approaches for decision making in interactive environments. RL focuses on inducing effective decision making policies with the goal of maximizing the agent's cumulative reward. In this study, we investigated the impact of both immediate and delayed reward functions on RL-induced policies and empirically evaluated the effectiveness of induced policies within an Intelligent Tutoring System called Deep Thought. Moreover, we divided students into *Fast* and *Slow* learners based on their incoming competence as measured by their average response time on the initial tutorial level. Our results show that there was a significant interaction effect between the induced policies and the students' incoming competence. More specifically, Fast learners are less sensitive to learning environments in that they can learn equally well regardless of the pedagogical strategies employed by the tutor, but Slow learners benefit significantly more from effective pedagogical strategies than from ineffective ones. In fact, with effective pedagogical strategies the slow learners learned as much as their faster peers, but with ineffective pedagogical strategies the former learned significantly less than the latter.

Keywords

Reinforcement learning, Pedagogical strategy, Immediate Reward, Delayed Reward, Worked Example, Problem Solving

1 Introduction

Optimal decision making in complex interactive environments is challenging. In Intelligent Tutoring Systems (ITSs), for example, the system's behaviors can be viewed as a sequential decision process where at each step the system chooses an appropriate action from a set of options. *Pedagogical strategies* are policies that are used to decide what action to take next in the face of alternatives. Each of these

UMAP '16, July 13-17, 2016, Halifax, NS, Canada

© 2016 ACM. ISBN 978-1-4503-4370-1/16/07. . . $15.00

DOI: http://dx.doi.org/10.1145/2930238.2930247

system decisions will affect the user's subsequent actions and performance. Its impact on outcomes cannot be observed immediately and the effectiveness of each decision is dependent upon the effectiveness of subsequent decisions.

Reinforcement Learning (RL) is one of the best machine learning approaches for decision making in interactive environments. RL focuses on inducing effective decision making policies for an agent with the goal of maximizing the agent's cumulative reward. In many domains RL is applied with immediate reward functions. In an automatic call center system, for example, the agent can receive an immediate reward for every question it asks because the impact of each question can be assessed instantaneously [27]. Immediate rewards are generally more effective than delayed rewards for RL-based policy induction. This is because it is easier to assign appropriate credit or blame when the feedback is tied to a single decision. The more we delay the rewards or punishments, the harder it becomes to assign credit or blame properly.

On the other hand, the most appropriate reward to use in an ITSs is student learning gains which are typically unavailable until the entire training process is complete. This is due to the complex nature of the learning process which makes it difficult to assess students' learning moment by moment and more importantly, many instructional interventions that boost short-term performance may not be effective over the long-term. Therefore, in this study, we explored both immediate and delayed rewards in our policy induction and empirically evaluated the impact of the induced policies on student learning.

Prior research has shown that some learners are less sensitive to the learning environment and can always learn; while others are more sensitive to variations in learning environments and may fail to do so [4]. We refer to the former as high learners and the latter as low learners. It is not fully understood why such differences exist. One hypothesis is that low learners lack crucial skills such as general problem-solving strategies and meta-cognition. In order to be effective and to honor the promises of learning environments, a system should support both high and low learners effectively, especially the low learners. It is our hypothesis that our induced pedagogical strategies may have different impacts on students with different learning competence. More specifically, in this study, we divide students into *Fast* and *Slow* groups based upon their average response time and we found that the RL-induced pedagogical strategies had significantly more impact on Slow learners than on their Fast peers. That is, Slow learners in this study behave more like low learners in that they are more sensitive to effectiveness of the RL-induced pedagogical strategies while Fast learners are more like high learners in that they can learn equally effectively regardless of the pedagogical strategies employed.

We applied RL to induce two sets of policies: Immediate and Delayed. We focused on one important tutorial decision: whether to provide students with a Worked Example (WE) or to require them to engage in a Problem Solving (PS). Our primary research questions are: 1) would our induced policies improve students' learning, especially for Slow learners? 2) which policy, Immediate or Delayed, would be more effective?

2 Related Work

2.1 Applying RL to ITSs

Beck et al [2] investigated application of RL to induce pedagogical policies that would minimize the time students take to complete each problem on AnimalWatch, an ITS that teaches arithmetic to grade school students. In the training phase of their study, they used simulated students. Given that student time can be assessed at each step, they used an immediate reward function. In the test phase, the induced policies were added to AnimalWatch and the new system was empirically compared with the original version of AnimalWatch. They found that the policy group spent significantly less time per problem than their no-policy peers.

Iglesias and her colleagues [6, 7, 8], on the other hand, focused on applying RL to improve the effectiveness of an Intelligent Educational System that teaches students Database Design. They applied Q-learning and used immediate rewards. Their goal when inducing the policy was to provide students with direct navigation support through the system's content with the expectation that this would help students learn more efficiently. Iglesias and her colleagues used simulated students in their training phase much like Beck et al. In the test phase, they evaluated the induced policy empirically with real students. Their results showed that while the policy led to more effective system usage behaviors from students, the students using a system equipped with a policy did not outperform their no-policy peers in terms of learning outcomes.

Martin and Arroyo [10] applied a model-based RL method, Policy Iteration, to induce pedagogical policies that would increase the efficiency of hint sequencing on Wayang Outpost web-based ITS. During the training phase, the authors used a student model to generate the training data for inducing the policies and they used delayed rewards. Here the student model was similar to the simulated students used in Beck et al and Iglesias et al. In the test phase, the induced policies were tested on simulated student model rather than human students.

Tetreault et al [23] used an Intelligent Spoken Tutoring System, ITSPOKE, which teaches students college-level physics [9]. In their work, they used a previously collected set of physics tutorial dialogues as a training corpus and investigated the application of Policy Iteration to induce pedagogical policies from it. The focus of their work was on introducing a novel method for evaluating state representations. Thus they did not measure students' learning gains nor did they compare the policy-equipped system to a prior version. Additionally, note that because the training corpus used in

this work was not collected with the goal of exploring the full range of tutorial decisions, the tutor often executed only one type of action for many dialogue states. In this study, they used a delayed reward function.

Finally, Chi et al [16] applied model-based RL to induce pedagogical policies to improve the effectiveness to an Intelligent Natural Language Tutoring System, Cordillera, which teaches students college physics. In that study, they collected an exploratory corpus by training human students on the ITS that makes random decisions and then applied RL to induce pedagogical policies from the corpus they used an exploratory training corpus. Their empirical evaluation showed the induced policies were significantly more effective than the previous ones. In that study, they explored two types of reward functions but both are delayed.

Although there have been other studies on application of RL to ITSs, they mostly involved inducing domain models rather than pedagogical policies. For example, Barnes and Stamper [1, 21] have applied Markov Decision Processes (MDP) to construct problem solutions from existing students' solutions for an ITS called Proofs Tutorial, which teaches college-level discrete mathematics. They used a form of the model-based RL method Value Iteration and the resulting problem solutions were then used to generate hints for new students. They found that the extracted solutions and the proposed hint-generating functions were able to provide hints over 80% of the time for the new students.

In short, RL has been applied to induce pedagogical policies in ITSs but previous research explored either delayed or immediate reward but not both. Moreover, previous research has investigated whether all students' learning performance were improved by the induced RL policies while we hypothesized that certain learners are more likely to be affected by the effectiveness of the induced pedagogical strategies than others. The type of the decision we focused on is: PS vs. WE.

2.2 Problem Solving vs. Worked Example

A great deal of research has investigated the differing impacts of worked examples (WE) and problem solving (PS) on student learning [11, 13, 15, 18]. During PS students are given a training problem which they must solve independently or with partial assistance while during WE students are shown a detailed solution to the problem. McLaren and colleagues compared WE-PS pairs with PS-only [12]. Every student was given total of 10 training problems. Students in the PS-only condition were required to solve every problem while students in the WE-PS condition were given 5 example-problem pairs. Each pair consists of an initial worked example problem followed by tutored problem solving. They found no significant difference in learning performance between the two conditions, however the WE-PS group spent significantly less time than the PS group.

McLaren and his colleagues found similar results in two subsequent studies [11, 13]. In the former, the authors compared three conditions: WE, PS and WE-PS pairs, in the domain of high school chemistry. All students were given 10 identical problems. As before, the authors found no significant differences among the three groups in terms of learning gains but the WE group spent significantly less time than the other two conditions; and no significant time on task difference was found between the PS and WE-PS conditions.

In a follow-up study, conducted in the domain of high school stoichiometry, McLaren and colleagues compared four conditions: WE, tutored PS, untutored PS, and Erroneous Examples (EE) [13]. Students in the EE condition were given *incorrect* worked examples containing between 1 and 4 errors and were tasked with correcting them. Again the authors found no significant differences among the conditions in terms of learning gains, and as before the WE students spent significantly less time than the other groups. More specifically, for time on task they found that: *WE < EE < untutored PS < tutored PS*. In fact, the WE students took only 30% of the total time that the tutored PS students did.

The advantages of worked examples were also demonstrated in another study in the domain of electrical circuits [26]. The authors of that study compared four conditions: WE, WE-PS pairs, PS-WE pairs (problem-solving followed by an example problem), and PS only. They found that the WE and WE-PS students significantly outperformed the other two groups, and found no significant differences was found among four conditions in terms of time on task.

In short, prior research has shown that problem-level worked examples can be as or more effective than problem solving or alternating problems with examples, and the former can take significantly less time than the latter two [13, 17, 11].

2.3 Fast vs. Slow Learners

We hypothesized that certain learners, specifically low learners, are more sensitive to the effectiveness of pedagogical strategies than high learners. Therefore, we need to first distinguish high and low learners based upon some measurement of incoming competence. One way to measure students' incoming competence is to use their prior performance. In this study while all students received the same initial training on level 1, we cannot use their performance alone as a measure of competence as the material is novel and the data would be noisy. This is because: 1) students may make early errors due to their unfamiliarity with the system; 2) students may refer to external resources for information given that all students get the same training problems on level 1. Thus using their performance alone at Level 1 may obscure the student's true incoming competence.

On the other hand, ever since the mid-1950s, response time has been used as a preferred dependent variable in cognitive psychology [25]. It has primarily been used to assess student learning because response time can indicate how active and accessible student knowledge is. For example, it is shown that response time reveals student proficiency [19] and there was a significant negative correlation between the students' average response time and their final exam scores taken at the end of the semester [5]. With the advent of computerized testing, more and more researchers have begun to use response-time as a learning performance measurement [19]. Therefore in this work we used response time as the measure of initial incoming competence.

More specifically, we used the students' average response time on level 1 to split students into fast and slow groups. We compared the students' average response time on level 1 to the median of all average response times on level 1. Students below the median are classified as fast learners while students above the median are classified as slow learners.

3 Inducing Pedagogical Strategies

Prior RL research has typically used Markov Decision Processes (MDPs) [22] to model user-system interactions. The central idea behind this approach is to transform the problem of inducing effective pedagogical strategies on what action the agent should take at any state into computing an optimal policy in an MDP.

3.1 Markov Decision Process

An MDP is a mathematical framework for representing a RL task. It is defined by a tuple $\langle S, A, T, R \rangle$. $S = \{S_1, S_2, ..., S_n\}$ denotes the state space; $A = \{A_1, A_2, ..., A_m\}$ represents a set of agent's possible actions; $T : S \times A \times S \to [0, 1]$ is a transition probability table, where each element is $T_{S_i S_j}^a = p(S_j | S_i, a)$ which indicates the probability of transiting from state S_i to state S_j by taking an action a; $R : S \times A \times S \to \mathbb{R}$ assigns rewards to state transitions given actions. And $\pi : S \to A$ is defined as a policy, mapping state S into action A with the purpose of maximizing expected reward.

After defining the MDP, we can transfer student-system interaction dialog into the trajectory which can be represented as follows:

$$S_1 \xrightarrow{A_1, R_1} S_2 \xrightarrow{A_2, R_2} S_3 \xrightarrow{A_3, R_3} ... \to S_N$$

Where $S_i \xrightarrow{A_i, R_i} S_{i+1}$ means that the tutor executed action A_i and received reward R_i under state S_i and then transferred to the next state S_{i+1}. In general, the reward can be divided into immediate and delayed rewards, where immediate reward exists during the state transition process while delayed reward follows terminal state.

3.2 Training Datasets

Our dataset was collected from the Deep Thought (DT) tutoring system [14]. It included a total of 303 undergraduate CS students who used DT as part of class assignment in Fall 2014 and Spring 2015. The average amount of time spent in the tutor was 416.60 minutes. When the students start each new training problem, DT will make a simple decision: should it ask the student to solve the next problem (**PS**), or should it provide them with a worked example (**WE**). In order to model the students' learning process, we extracted a total of 134 state feature variables, which can be grouped into the following five categories:

1. **Autonomy (AM):** the amount of work done by the student: such as the number of problems solved so far *PSCount* or the number of hints requested *hintCount*.

2. **Temporal Situation (TS):** the time related information about the work process: such as the average time taken per problem *avgTime*, or the total time for solving a problem *TotalPSTime*.

3. **Problem Solving (PS):** information about the current problem solving context, such as the difficulty of the current problem *probDiff*, or whether the student changes the difficulty level *NewLevel*.

4. **Performance (PM):** information about the student's performance during problem solving: such as the number of right application of rules *RightApp*.

5. **Student Action (SA):** the statistical measurement of student's behavior: such as the number of non-empty-click actions that students take *actionCount*, or the number of clicks for derivation *AppCount*.

3.3 Immediate vs. Delayed Policies

The reward function in DT datasets is calculated based upon the level score $LevelScore_i$ where $i \in [1,6]$, which is calculated based upon the students' performance on the last problem in each level without receiving any formative feedback from system. As described below, students were trained either on high track or low track on each level (except on level 1) so it is hard to compare their performance directly. Therefore, a student's level score at level i is calculated based on *rank* of the student performance score at level i relative to whole population performance scores at the same level.

Our experimental results indicate that there exists a significant correlation between students' performance on last level ($LevelScore_6$) and their final test score taken at the end of the semester: $R^2 = 0.396$, p-value =1.433e-11. This suggests that the students' level score indeed reflects their knowledge level.

We designed two types of reward: immediate and delayed reward with the goal of measuring the students' learning gains. The immediate reward is defined as $R_i = LevelScore_i - LevelScore_{i-1}$ where $i \in [1,6]$, $R_1 = LevelScore_1$, it reflects the change in students' performance level by level. The delayed reward is defined as $R_{delay} = LevelScore_6 - LevelScore_1$, which determines the change in students' performance across levels. For convenience, we denote the DT datasets with immediate reward as *DT-Immed* and that with delayed reward as *DT-Delay*. Note that the sum of each student's immediate rewards will equal their final delayed reward. Apart from the reward functions, both two datasets are identical.

Both Immediate and delayed policies were induced using the same general procedure. We apply the ensemble feature selection method to the corresponding dataset. In order to extract the state feature set that can represent learning context compactly and accurately, we set the maximum number of state feature size to be 8. The ensemble method comprises 6 correlation-based methods and 4 RL-based methods and more details are described in [20]. Based upon the extracted feature set, we induce our policy using the toolkit developed by Tetreault and Litman[24]. The effectiveness of policy is valuated by Expected Cumulative Reward (ECR)[3] defined as:

$$ECR = \sum_i \frac{N_i}{N} \times V^\pi(S_i)$$

where N denotes the number of initial states in training corpus, N_i means the number of state S_i as initial states. The higher the ECR value of a policy, the better the policy is supposed to perform. Our best Immediate policy has a feature size of 7 and our best Delayed policy has a feature size of 6, as shown in Section 5.

Our primary goal is to empirically evaluate the effectiveness of the RL induced policies. In order to do so, we incorporated them back into the DT tutor and empirically compared them against a baseline policy that makes random decisions. Thus, we have three conditions: Immediate, Delayed and Random. Apart from the differing policies, the remaining components of the system, including the GUI interface, the same training problems, and the tutorial scripts,

were the same for all three conditions. Next, we will describe our experiment into details.

4 Experiment

The purpose of this experiment is to compare the student performance on DT using Immediate, Delayed, and Random policies respectively.

4.1 Participants

The study was conducted in "Discrete Mathematics for Computer Science" a course offered at North Carolina State University in the Spring of 2016. 106 undergraduate students were assigned to complete the task as one of their regular homework assignments.

4.2 Conditions

The participants were randomly distributed into three conditions. The group sizes were as follows: $N = 30$ for Random, $N = 38$ for Delayed, and $N = 38$ for Immediate condition[1]. A total of 98 students completed the experiment and were distributed as follows: $N = 28$ for Random, $N = 37$ for Delayed, and $N = 33$ for Immediate. We performed a χ^2 test of independence to examine the relationship between completion rate and condition. We found no significant differences among three groups: $\chi^2(2, N = 106) = 1.40, p = 0.496$.

4.3 DT Tutor & Procedure

Deep Thought (DT) is a data-driven ITS that teaches logic proofs and it was used as part of an assignment in undergraduate discrete mathematics course. DT is based upon a data-driven mastery learning system, consisting of 6 strictly ordered levels of proof problems [14]. Each level can be split into two proficiency tracks. The high proficiency track has a smaller number of complex problems, while the low proficiency track contains a larger number of simple problems. The students were required to complete 1-4 problems per level and a total of 7–24 problems overall. All of the students received the same set of problems in level 1. Their initial proficiency is calculated based upon the number of mistakes made on the final problem of level 1. The proficiency reflects how well they understand the knowledge and can apply the logic rules in the proof process. In each sequential level, DT firstly estimate the students' proficiency and then assign them to the high or low track.

4.4 Performance Measure

When inducing both the Immediate and Delayed policies, we calculated our reward function based upon the students' level scores $LevelScore_i$ where $i \in [1,6]$. Both Immediate and Delayed policies are induced to maximize the students' improvement from level 1 to level 6. This can be calculated as: $levelScore_6 - levelScore_1$. Here we treat $levelScore_6$ as the posttest score, $levelScore_1$ as pretest score, and calculate each student's learning gain as $levelScore_6 - levelScore_1$. In addition to raw learning gains, we also used the normalized learning gain (NLG) as the reward value. This measures students' learning gain by considering *their incoming competence* and has been widely used for mearsuring student learning performance in the field of ITS. The NLG is

---

[1]Note that a slightly smaller portion of students were assigned to the baseline Random condition.

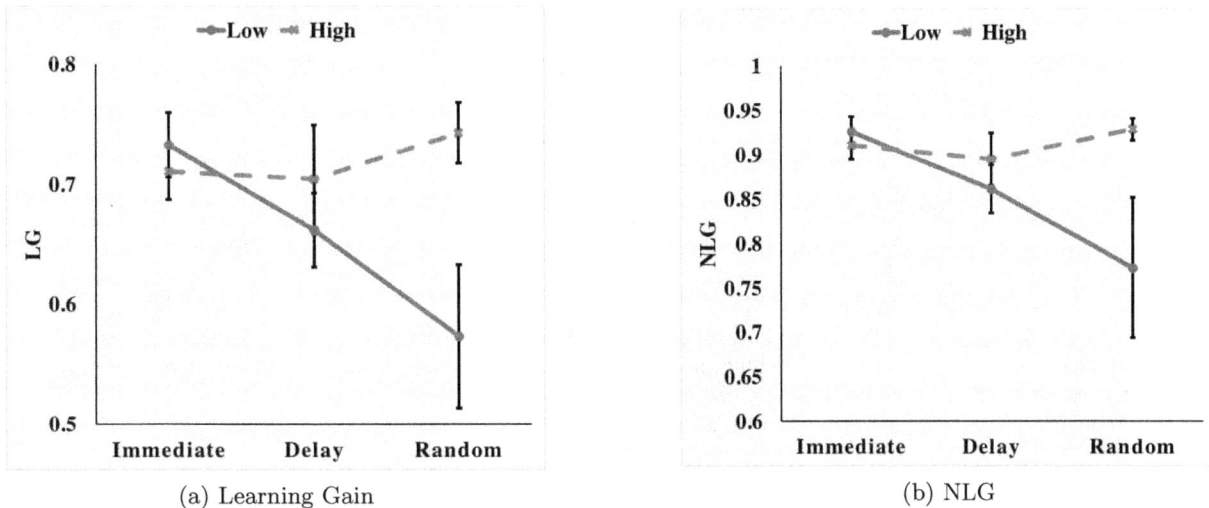

(a) Learning Gain

(b) NLG

Figure 1: Learning Performance across Three Groups

defined as: $NLG = \frac{posttest-pretest}{Max-pretest}$, that is, how much did the student learn given how much he/she can learn. In this study, we calculated NLG as: $NLG = \frac{levelScore_6-levelScore_1}{MaximumScore-levelScore_1}$. Here $MaximumScore$ is the maximum score a student can get. We will report our students' performance using both the raw learning gain and the NLG. Both scores were normalized to [0,1].

5 Results

We found no significant difference among the three groups in terms of their level 1 score: $F(2,97) = 0.037, p = 0.964$. As described in Section 2, we subdivided the groups into Fast ($n = 49$) and Slow ($n = 49$) groups based upon their average response time on Level 1. As expected, there was a significant difference between the Fast and Slow students on $LevelScore_1$: $F(1,98) = 10.05, p = 0.002$. We then partitioned the students into six groups based upon their incoming competence and condition: Immediate-Fast (n = 16), Immediate-Slow (n = 17), Delayed-Fast (n = 17), Delayed-Slow (n = 20), Random-Fast (n = 16), and Random-Slow (n = 12). Again, we find no significant difference among the Slow groups on their level 1 score: $F(2,46) = 0.56, p = 0.58$. Nor did we find any significant difference among the Fast groups on the same score: $F(2,46) = 0.64, p = 0.53$.

A two-way ANOVA based upon Condition {Immediate, Delayed, Random} and Incoming Competence {Fast, Slow} showed no significant differences among the three conditions on overall training time: $F(1,98) = 0.131, p = .877$. However there was a significant Incoming Competence effect: the fast learners spent less time on task than the slow learners: $M = 387, SD = 81$ for fast learners and $M = 662, SD = 83$ for the slow learners and the difference was significant: $F(1,98) = 5.54, p = .021$. In addition there was no interaction effect. Therefore, we can conclude that the fast learners spend less time on task than the slow learners across all three conditions.

Next we will report the impact of RL policies on students' performance and then discuss the characteristics of the induced policies.

5.1 Learning Performance

We performed two one-way ANOVAs using condition as the factor and the student's raw learning gain or NLG as the dependent measure respectively. We found no significant difference among the three groups: $F(2,97) = 1.54$, $p = 0.22$ for raw learning gains and $F(2,97) = 2.15$, $p = 0.12$ for NLG scores. While no significant difference was found, the comparatively large SD suggests that both fast and slow students may benefit differently from the induced policies. For example, on the raw learning gain scores, $M = 0.72, SD = 0.10$ for the Immediate group, $M = 0.68, SD = 0.16$ for the Delayed group, and $M = 0.67, SD = 0.17$ for the Random group. The same pattern was repeated for NLG.

A two-way ANOVA using Condition {Immediate, Delayed, Random} and Incoming Competence {Fast, Slow} as two factors and the student's raw learning gain or NLG as the dependent measure showed an significant interaction effect, $F(2,97) = 3.43$, $p = 0.037$ for the raw learning gain and $F(2,97) = 3.48$, $p = 0.035$ for NLG. Additionally, we also found a significant main effect from the *Incoming Competence*: $F(1,98) = 4.68$, $p = 0.033$ for the raw learning gain and $F(1,98) = 4.90$, $p = 0.029$ for the NLG. Therefore the fast learners learned significantly more than the slow learners: $M = 0.719, SD = 0.14$ for the fast learners vs. $M = 0.656, SD = 0.145$ for the slow learners on the raw learning gain. In other words, this results confirmed our assumption that Fast learners can be seen as the high learners while Slow learners can be seen as the low learners. Finally, the main effect of Condition was not significant: $F(1,98) = 1.54$, $p > 0.05$.

Figure 1 shows that the raw learning gain and NLG results are consistent with our hypothesis: no significant difference was found among the three fast groups on either the raw learning gain or NLG: $F(2,46) = 0.377$, $p = 0.69$ for the raw learning gain and $F(2,46) = 0.64$, $p = 0.53$ for NLG respectively.

On the other hand, Figure 1 shows a significant difference among the three slow groups: $F(2,46) = 3.99$, $p = 0.025$ for the raw learning gain and $F(2,46) = 3.22$, $p = 0.049$ for NLG. Pairwise t-tests showed that the Immediate-Slow group significantly outperformed the Random-Slow group on

Feature	Definition	Category
TotalPSTime (f_{I1})	Total time for solving a problem	Temporal Situation
NewLevel (f_{I2})	Whether current solved problem is in the new level	Problem Solving
WrongApp (f_{I3})	Number of wrong application of rules	Performance
TotalWETime (f_{I4})	Total time for working on an example	Temporal Situation
UseCount (f_{I5})	Number of different types of applied rules in Use category	Problem Solving
AppCount (f_{I6})	Number of clicks for derivation	Student Action
NumProbRule (f_{I7})	Number of expected distinct rules for a solved problem	Problem Solving
stepTimeDev (f_{D1})	Step time deviation	Temporal Situation
probDiff (f_{D2})	Difficulty of current solved problem	Problem Solving
symbolicRCount (f_{D3})	Number of whole problems for symbolic representation	Problem Solving
actionCount (f_{D4})	Number of non-empty-click actions that students take	Student Action
SInfoHintCount (f_{D5})	Number of System Information Hint	Student Action
NSClickCountWE (f_{D6})	Number of next step click in Work Example	Student Action

both measures: $t(27) = 2.69$, $p = 0.012$ for the raw learning gain and $t(27) = 2.23$, $p = 0.034$ for NLG. The Immediate-Slow group outperformed the Delayed-Slow group on both measures. However these differences were only marginally significant: $t(35) = 1.67$, $p = 0.098$ for the raw learning gain and $t(35) = 1.94$, $p = 0.060$ for NLG respectively. Furthermore, we found no significant differences between the Delayed-Slow and the Random-Slow groups. Thus, our results suggest that all three Fast groups learned equally well after training on DT while the Slow learners are indeed more sensitive to induced policies. For three slow groups, Immediate policies significantly outperforms Random ones and there is a trend that the Immediate policies beat the Delayed ones while no significant difference between Delayed and Random.

Finally, we compared the fast and slow groups across all three conditions. For the Immediate condition, we found no significant differences among the Immediate-Fast and Immediate-Slow groups on either the raw learning gain or NLG: $F(1, 33) = 0.38$, $p = 0.55$ for the raw learning gain and $F(1, 33) = 0.45$, $p = 0.51$ for NLG. Likewise, for the Delayed condition, no significant difference was found between the Fast and Slow groups: $F(1, 37) = 0.622$, $p = 0.435$ for the raw learning gain and $F(1, 37) = 0.708$, $p = 0.41$ for NLG. Therefore, both fast and slow groups learned equally well when following the RL induced policies.

For Random group, however, the Random-Slow students learned significantly less than their Random-Fast peers: $F(1, 27) = 8.18$, $p = 0.008$ for the raw learning gain and $F(1, 27) = 5.03$, $p = 0.034$ for NLG respectively.

Overall, our results suggest that the Fast learners are not sensitive to the effectiveness of the pedagogical strategy while the Slow learners will learn more with the effective pedagogical strategy. We found that for the Slow learners the Immediate policy is more effective than a Random policy, and is marginally more effective than the Delayed policy.

5.2 Induced Pedagogical Strategy

Immediate Policy. The Immediate policy used seven features f_{I*}, which are listed in Table 1. It's interesting to note that the Immediate policy contained features from every category except Autonomy. Table 2 shows this policy. Each row of table represents one combination of the first four features and each column represents the combination of final three. The black cells indicate that the tutorial ac-

tion that is associated with the state is PS, while the white

Table 2: Immediate Policy

Last three features $f_{I5}{:}f_{I6}{:}f_{I7}$
First four features $f_{I1}{:}f_{I2}{:}f_{I3}{:}f_{I4}$

Table 3: Delayed Policy

Last three features $f_{D4}{:}f_{D5}{:}f_{D6}$
First three features $f_{D1}{:}f_{D2}{:}f_{D3}$

Table 4: Statistical measurement of several features among three groups

Feature	Immediate	Delay	Random	Significance	
TotalCount	19.42(2.07)	20.73(2.08)	19.81(2.09)	$F(2,98) = 3.67,$	$p = 0.03$
PSCount	8.09(1.37)	13.41(1.38)	12.34(1.39)	$F(2,98) = 140.14,$	$p = 0.00$
diffPSCount	4.21(1.90)	7.83(1.91)	6.74(1.92)	$F(2,98) = 32.60,$	$p = 0.00$
WECount	11.33(1.32)	7.32(1.32)	7.47(1.33)	$F(2,98) = 97.11,$	$p = 0.00$
diffWECount	7.78(1.69)	4.38(1.70)	5.50(1.71)	$F(2,98) = 35.78,$	$p = 0.00$

cells indicate the action is WE. The gray cells indicate that no rule was learned for the state. There are a total of 86 rules for the Immediate policy, of which 21 are associated with PS and 65 are associated with WE. More specifically, we found that the states in the row 0:0:1:0 almost always associate with PS; while the states in rows 0:0:0:0, 0:0:0:1, 1:1:1:0 almost always relate to WE; the rules in rows 0:1:0:0, 0:1:0:1, 0:1:1:0, 1:1:0:0, 1:1:1:1 do not contain PS; there are no rules for row 0:1:1:1. In general, the Immediate policy favors WE.

Delayed Policy. The Delayed policy used six features f_{D*}, which are listed in Table 1. They are drawn from the Temporal Situation, Problem Solving and Student Action categories. No features are drawn from the Autonomy and Performance categories. Table 3 shows the Delayed policy, where each row represents one combination of the first three features and each column represents one combination of last three. Each cell has the same meaning as described above. There are a total of 68 rules for the Delayed policy, of which 48 are associated with PS and 20 are associated with WE. More specifically, states in row 1:1:0 only associate with PS; states in rows 0:0:1, 0:1:1, 1:1:1 almost always correspond to PS; while the rules in row 1:0:1 only contain WE. Therefore the Delayed policy is more likely to take PS.

Immediate Policy vs. Delayed Policy. The ECR of the best Immediate policy was 137.97 while the ECR of the best Delayed policy was 14.06. This is likely due to the credit assignment problem. The more we delay success measures from a series of sequential decisions, the more difficult it becomes to identify which of the decision(s) in the sequence are responsible for our final performance. Furthermore, this may explain why, for the slow learners, the low-Immediate students learned more than the low-Random and the low-Delayed students. The former difference was statistically significant while the latter was marginal. We found no significant difference between the low-Random and low-Delayed students.

5.3 Log Analysis

Having compared the individual student's learning performance and the characteristics of the induced policies, this subsection will compare the log file variations across the conditions. More specifically, we focused on the total number of problems that students encountered (TotalCount); the total number of problems that the students solved (PSCount); the total number of WEs reviewed (WSCount); the total number of difficult problems that the students solved (DiffPSCount); and the total number of difficult WEs (DiffWECount).

Table 4 shows comparisons of the different counts across the conditions. A two-way ANOVA using Condition {Immediate, Delayed, Random} and Incoming Competence: {High, Low} on all behavior counts showed a significant main effect for the Condition on all measures. Both the main effect of Incoming Competence and the interaction effect were not significant.

Table 4 summarizes one-way ANOVA comparisons on the different counts among the three conditions. Columns 2-4 list the three groups in comparison and their corresponding mean and SD scores. The last column lists the statistical results of the one-way ANOVA comparisons. Table 4 shows that the Immediate group solved significantly fewer total problems than the Delayed group. The former solved significantly fewer difficult problems than the other two groups. On the other hand, the Immediate group studied significantly more worked examples on both total and difficult problems than the other two groups.

6 Conclusion

In this study, we investigated the impact of different reward functions (Immediate vs. Delayed) on the effectiveness of the induced RL policies. Our results show that the two policies include substantially different state features and that the policies generate different patterns of decisions. The Immediate policies are more likely to give worked examples while the Delayed polices are more likely to require problem-solving. Additionally, the Expected Cumulative Reward (ECR) for our immediate polices was an order of magnitude higher than the delayed ECR.

We also investigated the impact of RL-induced polices on different groups of learners. We divided students into fast and slow learners based upon their average response time in the first level. Our results confirm our hypothesis that the fast learners in all three conditions learned more than their slow peers and that there was no meaningful differences among them across three conditions; the slow learners, on the other hand, were more sensitive to the learning environment. The Random-Slow students learn the least while the Immediate-Slow group learned the most and in fact, it learned as much as their Immediate-Fast peers. Indeed, the Immediate-Slow students learned significantly more than the Random-Slow students, and marginally more than the Delayed-Slow students. Therefore, the Immediate polices appear to be more effective than the Delayed polices and are significantly better than the Random policy.

Finally, our preliminary log analysis showed that students using the Immediate policies studied significantly more worked examples, in terms of both total and difficult problems, than the other two groups. And more importantly, they solved significantly fewer problems, especially difficult problems. Previous research on WE versus PS has primarily relied on fixed or hand-coded adaptive rules to decide whether to present the next question as a WE or PS, this is the first study in which we applied RL to induce adaptive pedagogical strategies directly from students' logs to decide whether to present the next question as a WE or PS. We showed that the induced policies are indeed effective at improving students' learning especially for Slow learners.

7 Acknowledgements

This research was supported by the NSF Grant 1432156 "Educational Data Mining for Individualized Instruction in STEM Learning Environments".

8 References

[1] T. Barnes and J. C. Stamper. Toward automatic hint generation for logic proof tutoring using historical student data. In *Intelligent Tutoring Systems*, pages 373–382, 2008.

[2] J. Beck, B. P. Woolf, and C. R. Beal. Advisor: A machine learning architecture for intelligent tutor construction. In *AAAI/IAAI*, pages 552–557, 2000.

[3] M. Chi, K. VanLehn, D. Litman, and P. Jordan. Empirically evaluating the application of reinforcement learning to the induction of effective and adaptive pedagogical strategies. *User Modeling and User-Adapted Interaction*, 21(1-2):137–180, 2011.

[4] L. J. Cronbach and R. E. Snow. *Aptitudes and instructional methods: A handbook for research on interactions.* New York: Irvington, 1977.

[5] W. J. González-Espada and D. W. Bullock. Innovative applications of classroom response systems: Investigating students' item response times in relation to final course grade, gender, general point average, and high school act scores. *Electronic Journal for the Integration of Technology in Education*, 6:97–108.

[6] A. Iglesias, P. Martínez, R. Aler, and F. Fernández. Learning teaching strategies in an adaptive and intelligent educational system through reinforcement learning. *Applied Intelligence*, 31:89–106, 2009. 10.1007/s10489-008-0115-1.

[7] A. Iglesias, P. Martínez, R. Aler, and F. Fernández. Reinforcement learning of pedagogical policies in adaptive and intelligent educational systems. *Knowledge-Based Systems*, 22(4):266–270, 2009. Artificial Intelligence (AI) in Blended Learning.

[8] A. Iglesias, P. Martínez, and F. Fernández. An experience applying reinforcement learning in a web-based adaptive and intelligent educational system. *Informatics in Education*, 2(2):223–240, 2003.

[9] D. J. Litman and S. Silliman. Itspoke: an intelligent tutoring spoken dialogue system. In *Demonstration Papers at HLT-NAACL 2004*, pages 5–8. Association for Computational Linguistics, 2004.

[10] K. N. Martin and I. Arroyo. Agentx: Using reinforcement learning to improve the effectiveness of intelligent tutoring systems. pages 564–572.

[11] B. M. McLaren and S. Isotani. When is it best to learn with all worked examples? In *Artificial Intelligence in Education*, pages 222–229. Springer, 2011.

[12] B. M. McLaren, S.-J. Lim, and K. R. Koedinger. When and how often should worked examples be given to students? new results and a summary of the current state of research. In *Proceedings of the 30th annual conference of the cognitive science society*, pages 2176–2181, 2008.

[13] B. M. McLaren, T. van Gog, C. Ganoe, D. Yaron, and M. Karabinos. Exploring the assistance dilemma: Comparing instructional support in examples and problems. In *Intelligent Tutoring Systems*, pages 354–361. Springer, 2014.

[14] Z. L. Mostafavi Behrooz and T. Barnes. Data-driven proficiency profiling. In *Proc. of the 8th International Conference on Educational Data Mining*, 2015.

[15] A. S. Najar, A. Mitrovic, and B. M. McLaren. Adaptive support versus alternating worked examples and tutored problems: Which leads to better learning? In *User Modeling, Adaptation, and Personalization*, pages 171–182. Springer, 2014.

[16] M. Chi, K. VanLehn, D. J. Litman, and P. W. Jordan. Empirically evaluating the application of reinforcement learning to the induction of effective and adaptive pedagogical strategies. *User Model. User-Adapt. Interact.*, 21(1-2):137–180, 2011.

[17] A. Renkl, R. K. Atkinson, U. H. Maier, and R. Staley. From example study to problem solving: Smooth transitions help learning. *The Journal of Experimental Education*, 70(4):293–315, 2002.

[18] R. J. Salden, V. Aleven, R. Schwonke, and A. Renkl. The expertise reversal effect and worked examples in tutored problem solving. *Instructional Science*, 38(3):289–307, 2010.

[19] D. L. Schnipke and D. J. Scrams. Exploring issues of examinee behavior: Insights gained from response-time analyses. *Computer-based testing: Building the foundation for future assessments*, pages 237–266, 2002.

[20] S. Shen and M. Chi. Aim low: Correlation-based feature selection for model-based reinforcement learning. 2016.

[21] J. C. Stamper, T. Barnes, and M. J. Croy. Extracting student models for intelligent tutoring systems. pages 1900–1901.

[22] R. S. Sutton and A. G. Barto. *Reinforcement Learning.* MIT Press Bradford Books, 1998.

[23] J. R. Tetreault, D. Bohus, and D. J. Litman. Estimating the reliability of mdp policies: a confidence interval approach. In *HLT-NAACL*, pages 276–283, 2007.

[24] J. R. Tetreault and D. J. Litman. A reinforcement learning approach to evaluating state representations in spoken dialogue systems. *Speech Communication*, 50(8):683–696, 2008.

[25] R. D. L. V. S. Thomas et al. *Response Times: Their Role in Inferring Elementary Mental Organization: Their Role in Inferring Elementary Mental Organization.* Oxford University Press, USA, 1986.

[26] T. Van Gog, L. Kester, and F. Paas. Effects of worked examples, example-problem, and problem-example pairs on novices' learning. *Contemporary Educational Psychology*, 36(3):212–218, 2011.

[27] J. D. Williams. The best of both worlds: unifying conventional dialog systems and pomdps. In *INTERSPEECH*, pages 1173–1176, 2008.

Automatic Teacher Modeling from
Live Classroom Audio

Patrick Donnelly[1], Nathan Blanchard[1], Borhan Samei[2], Andrew M. Olney[2],
Xiaoyi Sun[3], Brooke Ward[3], Sean Kelly[4], Martin Nystrand[3], and Sidney K. D'Mello[1]
[1]University of Notre Dame; [2]University of Memphis
[3]University of Wisconsin, Madison; [4]University of Pittsburgh
118 Haggar Hall, Notre Dame, IN, 46556, USA
pdonnel4@nd.edu

ABSTRACT

We investigate automatic analysis of teachers' instructional strategies from audio recordings collected in live classrooms. We collected a data set of teacher audio and human-coded instructional activities (e.g., lecture, question and answer, group work) in 76 middle school literature, language arts, and civics classes from eleven teachers across six schools. We automatically segment teacher audio to analyze speech vs. rest patterns, generate automatic transcripts of the teachers' speech to extract natural language features, and compute low-level acoustic features. We train supervised machine learning models to identify occurrences of five key instructional segments (Question & Answer, Procedures and Directions, Supervised Seatwork, Small Group Work, and Lecture) that collectively comprise 76% of the data. Models are validated independently of teacher in order to increase generalizability to new teachers from the same sample. We were able to identify the five instructional segments above chance levels with F_1 scores ranging from 0.64 to 0.78. We discuss key findings in the context of teacher modeling for formative assessment and professional development.

Keywords

classroom discourse; dialogic instruction; speech recognition; automatic feedback; educational data mining

1. INTRODUCTION

Dialogic instruction is a form of classroom discourse that is characterized by thought-provoking discussions between teachers and students with the goal of facilitating a meaningful exchange of ideas intended to elicit deeper student thought and analysis. The dialogic approach to classroom instruction positively correlates with student engagement [16] and achievement [2, 24]. For example, in a two year, large-scale study of dialogic instruction, Nystrand et al. coded classroom activities for 256 class sessions, covering 2,141 students across 25 schools [23]. After controlling for gender, race/ethnicity, socioeconomic status, school type (e.g., urban/rural, public/private), grade level, and prior achievement, a dialogic-oriented instructional style had positive effects on achievement. In particular, the proportion of time spent on discussion, open-ended questions with no scripted response, and instances of uptake (e.g., follow-up questions) correlated with

UMAP '16, July 13-17, 2016, Halifax, NS, Canada
© 2016 ACM. ISBN 978-1-4503-4370-1/16/07...$15.00
DOI: http://dx.doi.org/10.1145/2930238.2930250

student achievement [16, 22, 24]. These findings were replicated by another large-scale study of 974 students from 19 different schools across five states [2].

Despite these pedagogical benefits of dialogic instruction, classroom instruction continues to be dominated by traditional teacher-centric instructional techniques such as lecture, recitation, and seatwork [4]. But it need not be this way. Research has demonstrated that the quality of classroom instruction can be enhanced with teacher training programs [6], suggesting that dialogic instruction can be formatively assessed by classroom observations and improved via teacher professional development programs [15]. For example, research has demonstrated that discussing data-driven analysis of classroom practices with teachers correlates with student achievement [17].

The ability to provide teachers with qualitative and formative feedback on their instruction is paramount to improving and refining their teaching strategies over time. Regrettably, current efforts to assess the quality of classroom discourse rely on manual coding by trained observers, a labor and cost intensive endeavor that cannot be deployed practically, broadly, nor uniformly.

To address this critical bottleneck, this study is part of a large multi-disciplinary project that analyzes classroom instructional practices towards the goal of automatic analysis of classroom discourse. The automation of such analysis would lead to the development of a *teacher model*, for use in personalized assessment and professional development. In line with this, we present an approach to automatically identify key instructional segments (e.g., Question & Answer or Lecture) in live classrooms based solely on audio of teachers' speech.

1.1 Related Work

The automatic analysis of text and discourse is a frequently studied research problem in education, such as in automatic essay analysis [12], evaluation of online discussions [20], plagiarism detection [3], or dialog-based intelligent tutoring systems [26]. The focus, however, has been on the student not on the teacher. There is a long research history on the use of audio (and video) to study instructional practices and student behaviors in live classrooms [1, 11] - most notably see [10]. However, the recorded signals are typically processed by humans; automatic analyses of classroom video and audio are few and far between. Thus, while there is an active field of automatic student modeling (or learner modeling) [29], the complementary field of teacher modeling is just beginning to emerge.

The initial attempt at the automatic identification of components of instructional discourse from audio recordings appeared in 2013 by Wang et al. [30, 31]. The authors adapted the Language ENvironment Analysis (LENA) system [9], an expensive proprietary microphone intended to be worn by preschool age children, to analyze teacher instruction. They recorded 608 hours of classroom audio from 12 teachers in 1st to 4th grade mathematics classes. They divided the recorded audio into 30 second segments. Two trained coders listened to each segment and annotated the dominant classroom activity: teacher lecture, class discussion, or student group work. They also provided a level of confidence for their annotations. Working independently, the coders achieved an agreement level of 83% (Cohen's kappa, $\kappa = 0.72$). The authors trained a random forest classifier to identify the dominant class activity of each 30 second segment, reporting an overall accuracy of 84% when compared to the human annotations.

Although this result is an important first step in automated teacher activity analysis, some methodological concerns are warranted. In particular, the authors trained their classification model using the segments with highest confidence of one coder (62% of the data) and tested on the annotations on all segments of the second coder. Therefore, the same audio segments appeared in both the training and testing sets, albeit using different but highly correlated (83% similar) annotations. Second, the authors did not validate their model independently of the teacher, permitting examples from each teacher to appear in both the training and test sets. Therefore, it is difficult to ascertain if their model was successful in identifying components of the classroom activity or merely adjusting to patterns of speech of specific teachers. Third, all coding was completed offline solely based on the audio recording, thereby losing important visual contextual clues that would be available during a live-coding session. Finally, the authors consider only three types of classroom activity, seemingly forcing each 30 second segment into one of these broad categories and perhaps overlooking more subtle differences (e.g., individual work vs. group work).

1.2 Current Contributions

In this paper we describe a low-cost, non-invasive approach to analyze teacher instructional activities in live class sessions. As a proof-of-concept, we previously explored the automatic detection of Question & Answer segments on a dataset of 21 class sessions obtained from three teachers [5]. Using only recordings of teacher audio, we extracted 11 features pertaining to the timing of speech and rest patterns. We achieved an overall accuracy of 67% (AU-ROC of 0.78) validated in a teacher-independent fashion.

Since the eventual goal of this research is to enable wide-scale deployment across many teachers and schools, we design our system with the following design criteria: practicality, generalizability, and scalability [7]. In terms of practicality, the system must be usable by researchers and teachers with minimal training, and non-invasive as to not interfere with the teacher's instruction nor distract students in any way. For this reason, we focus on recording the teachers, unlike approaches that record individual students [9]. It must be economically affordable so that a typical school can afford the system. Additionally, it must not have a human labor cost in that it should run autonomously without human monitoring. Second, the system must be able to generalize to new teachers, classrooms, and domains, hence, we must avoid heavily tuning to the specific teachers or classrooms when training the models. Finally, the system should be flexible enough to operate in a variety of classroom setups and should scale to larger classrooms with minimum loss in fidelity.

The present study advances previous work (see above) and this proof-of-concept in several novel ways. First, we collected the largest dataset in this domain to date, drawn from recordings of multiple teachers across different schools coupled with annotations

coded live during each class session. We explore features not previously used in this domain, including analysis of automatic speech transcriptions and acoustic features. We then train supervised classification models to identify five different key instructional segments based on audio recordings of the teacher, validated independently of the teacher and intended to generalize to new teachers.

2. DATA COLLECTION
Data was collected from U.S. middle school literature, language arts, and civics classes. Over the course of three semesters, data was collected from 76 class sessions, covering eleven different teachers (three male, eight female) across six schools. The teachers were not coached in the practice of dialogic instruction and were asked to carry out their normal lesson plan, allowing the capture of an unbiased real-world sample of teachers' instructional practices.

Each teacher wore a wireless microphone to capture their speech. Based on previous work [7], a Samson 77 Airline wireless microphone was chosen for its portability, noise-canceling abilities, and low-cost. The teacher's speech was captured and saved as a 16 kHz, 16-bit single channel audio file.

Each class session lasted between 30 minutes to 90 minutes, depending on the school, with an average class length of 60:25 minutes. These recordings, totaling over 76 hours, capture the gamut of events typical in a classroom, from focused instruction to distracting interruptions.

2.1 Coding Classroom Discourse
The Nystrand and Gamoran classroom coding scheme [21] considers a hierarchy of classroom events, ranging from general to more specific: (1) episodes refer to the general topic being addressed in the class (e.g., *the Civil War*); (2) instructional segments represent one the 17 possible instructional activities used to implement the episode (e.g., Lecture, Discussion), and (3) individual questions asked by teachers or students during some instructional segments. We focus on the second level of this coding scheme, the automatic identification of instructional segments.

An observer who was trained in the Nystrand and Gamoran scheme was present during each recorded class session. The observer used software specifically developed for live coding of classroom discourse to mark episodes, instructional segments, and teacher's dialogic questions as they occurred. Live coding allowed the observer to utilize visual information, which ostensibly yields additional information to contextualize the coding. For example, the coder may observe that students are working on a task in small groups rather than individually, an assessment that may be difficult to determine from the audio recording alone.

There were three trained observers in this study. Each class session was coded by one observer, whose coding was subsequently verified by a second trained observer at a later time. Disagreements were discussed and the coding refined until both observers reached complete agreement. The instructional segments noted by the coders form the ground truth used to evaluate our classification models.

2.2 Analysis of Instructional Segments
We focus on detecting the five most frequent segments that individually comprised at least 10% of the data: Question & Answer (21%), Procedures and Directions (20%), Supervised Seatwork (12%), Small Group Work (11%), and Lecture (11%). Ironically, Discussion, an instructional segment important to student success,

represents only 1% of the dataset. Since Discussion is related to Question & Answer (both feature whole-class, interactive discourse), we combined the two segments in this study, leading to a Question & Answer occurrence of 22%.

There are eleven additional types of instructional segments that occur less frequently, such as an occasional distraction, the discipline of a student, a test or quiz, or students engaging in silent reading. Individually, these segments are rare, but together they comprise 24% of the dataset. Although we do not build models for these segments, we retain them in our dataset as a Miscellaneous category.

We refer to [21] for a full description of each of the five key segments. Briefly, in a *Question & Answer* segment, the teacher asks a question, one or more students may respond, and the teacher evaluates the response. These segments may feature pre-scripted test questions by the teacher or they may be open-ended, providing the opportunity to transition into a more in-depth Discussion segment. In *Procedures and Directions*, the teacher mainly communicates instructions, often as a transition to another instructional segment. *Small Group Work* divides the class into groups of two or more students to collaborate on a task. During *Supervised Seatwork* segments, students work independently on tasks while the teacher walks around and answers individual questions that arise. *Lectures* involve the delivery of pre-scripted material, occasionally supplemented with video.

Error! Reference source not found. shows the class time spent on each of the five key instructional segments by each teacher. The individual teachers divide time differently, a reflection of their unique style. For example, two teachers did not assign any Small Group Work and three teachers did not spend any lesson time on Supervised Seatwork. There was also considerable variation over the different class sessions, even within each teacher, which reflects differences in lesson plans each day. In general, an individual teacher or class session may not contain all five instructional segments, a challenge we discuss in our results.

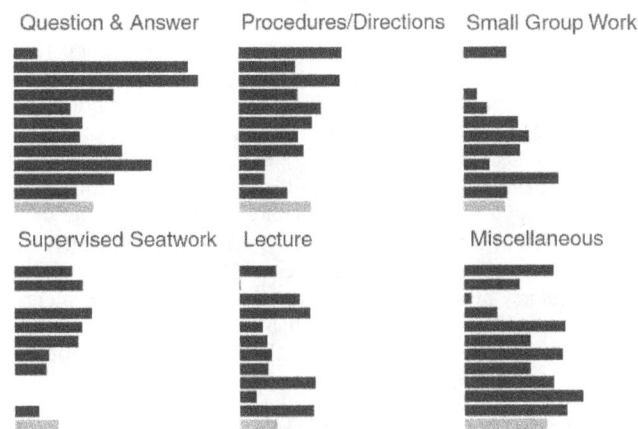

Figure 1. Proportion of time spent by each of the eleven teachers on each of the instructional segments. For each teacher (each row), the total time across the six segments sums to 1.0. The proportion of total time spent on the segment within the dataset is shown last in gray.

3. MODEL BUILDING

In this section, we discuss our approach to building classification models for the identification of the key instructional segments. We present our approach to segmenting the teacher's audio channel and generating automatic speech recognition transcripts, followed by discussion of our approach to partitioning the classroom recordings into windowed instances for classification. Finally, we present our feature extraction scheme and present our classification models.

3.1 Partitioning Audio into Windows

A system that is to be deployed in classrooms will not have the benefit of human coders present and we will be unable to determine the boundaries of the instructional segments. Although we could potentially build detectors to automatically infer segment boundaries, this itself is an unsolved research problem beyond the scope of this study. Therefore, we divided the recording of each class session into consecutive non-overlapping windows of time for classification. We examined non-overlapping windows to consider each moment of class time only within a single windowed instance as to not bias our results through classification of particularly easy or difficult segments multiple times in the dataset. Each window was assigned a label of the classroom activity using the segment annotations provided by the classroom coders. This label corresponds to the ground-truth for training and validation of the models.

For the cases in which a particular window spans more than one annotation, the dominant classroom activity (in terms of time) was chosen as the segment annotation. An example of this process for a 60-second window is illustrated in Figure 2. This approach, although an imperfect generalization, allows tracking the broader picture of the teacher's time. In particular, the average segment is 2.9 minutes long, which we use to inform our selection of possible window sizes. Specifically, we explored windows sizes ranging from 30 seconds to 5 minutes.

Figure 2. Example of the windowing scheme for a sample of five minutes of class time considering a 60 second window.

3.2 Utterance Segmentation

Each recording represents an uninterrupted channel of teacher audio lasting the duration of the class session. In order to analyze teachers' instructional practices, we must subdivide the audio signal into smaller audio chunks, each of which ideally represents an utterance spoken by the teacher. We adopted a method developed in [7] for teacher utterance extraction.

Patterns of speech and rest differ between teachers as do unintentional noises such as breathing or coughing. Therefore, we employed a general method to segment utterances to avoid overfitting to specific teachers, potentially increasing the ability to generalize to new teachers. First, we analyzed the amplitude envelope of the audio to identify moments of silence in which the amplitude of the signal dropped below a predefined noise threshold, which was empirically tuned in previous work [5]. Whenever the amplitude remained below the threshold for at least one second, we identified this as a moment of silence in the recording and used this silence as a breakpoint from which to partition the recording into the smaller utterances (called *potential utterances*). This approach is not without limitations, as each utterance may contain multiple ideas, or a single idea may be spread across several utterances.

Next, we analyzed this set of potential utterances in order to retain those that contain the teachers' speech and discard others (e.g., background noise, heavy breathing). To identify the utterances containing speech, we passed each through the Microsoft Bing automatic speech recognition (ASR) system [7]. If the ASR identified any speech within the potential utterance, we retained it as a speech utterance, otherwise we discarded it. In a validation study using 1000 randomly-sampled potential utterances, we achieved high levels of both precision (96.3%) and recall (98.6%) using this method. This resulted in an F_1 score of 97.4% [7], which we deemed sufficiently accurate for the purposes of this study.

Using this process on our dataset of 76 classroom recordings yielded 40,138 candidate utterances, 23,610 (59%) of which were retained as containing speech. The average length of these speech utterances is 5.24 seconds (SD = 8.17), however 2% of the utterances last over thirty seconds in length; for example, when the teacher makes a long statement without pausing.

3.3 Feature Extraction

We extracted features from each of the windows (see Figure 2 above) to create the instances used to train and test our classification models. We explored three different types of features, two of which have not yet been explored for this task. Specifically, timing features capturing patterns of the teacher speaking and pausing have been previously considered [5, 31]. We complimented these with novel features generated from natural language processing of speech transcriptions of the teacher, no small task due to the noisy nature of the classroom. These features allow consideration of the specific words a teacher speaks, beyond the mere timing of speech. We also added acoustic features generated from the recording of the teacher. We chose these features to potentially help differentiate between speaking and silence, for example, or between the difference in classroom noise generated by a single speaker and the louder moments when many voices speak simultaneously, such as occurs during Small Group Work.

Utterances Timing Features: We analyzed the timing of the extracted teacher utterances described in Section 3.2. For each partitioned window of time, we identified any speech utterances present within the windows. If any utterance straddled the boundary of the partitioned window, only the portion of the utterance contained within the window was considered. Using the timing of the utterances and considering any time between utterances as rest, we constructed a sequence of speech and rest. We then extracted six features from the speech-rest sequences: the number of occurrences, the total length of all utterances, the mean and standard deviation of utterance duration, and the durations of the longest and shortest utterance. In a similar manner, we extracted the same six features from the timing of the rest patterns. We added in one more feature representing the normalized temporal position of the window proportionate to the total length of the classroom recording, resulting in a total of 13 features.

Natural Language Features: In prior work, we evaluated several different ASR engines on data recorded in the noisy classroom environment [4, 7]. We considered two metrics: word error rate (WER), a word level edit distance comparing the ASR and human transcripts, and simple word overlap (SWO), a measurement of proportion of words found in both transcripts. Bing ASR achieved a WER of 0.52 and a SWO score of 0.62. Although outperformed by the Google ASR engine, we selected Bing given its ability to freely transcribe large volumes of audio, an important consideration for broader deployment.

Given an ASR transcript generated for each teacher speech utterance, we must extract meaningful language features that ostensibly capture differences in instructional segment. For this task, we employed a natural language feature tagger [25] that was specifically designed to classify questions and has been validated in studies of classroom discourse [27, 28]. We considered a set of high-level NLP features because the topics covered vary between class sessions and a bag-of-words analysis may not generalize since the course material is not likely to repeat between teachers. We extracted 37 natural language features, including counts of parts of speech (e.g., adjectives, nouns) and counts of particular words (e.g., *what, how, why*). Because the ASR transcriptions are time-stamped at the utterance level rather than the word level, we analyzed the entire utterance even if it overlapped with the time window.

We include both the sum and mean of the 37 natural language features to attempt to capture differences of use within the window, for a total of 74 features. Although potentially correlated, the sum of the feature counts the number of times the feature occurred within the time window whereas the mean tracks the use of the feature averaged by number of utterances in the windows. For example, consider the question word "*why.*" The word may appear multiple times in a single long utterance, such as during a Lecture, or it may appear across of sequence of speech and rest by teacher, potentially signally a Question & Answer segment in which the teacher's speech alternates with student responses.

Acoustic Features: Lastly, we extracted a set of features based on the acoustic properties of the audio signal using the Music Information Retrieval toolbox for Matlab [18]. Unlike the other aforementioned modalities, these features were not extracted from segmented teacher utterances but directly from the window of audio. We did not calibrate the features by individual teacher to encourage generalization to new teachers in the future. These features include common descriptors that characterize volume, spectra, and the frequency curve of the signal. We include the following features: seven statistical moments describing the spectral distribution (*centroid, flatness, spread, skew, kurtosis,* and *entropy*); *brightness,* a measure of high energy (above 1500 Hz); *zero crossing,* a measure of noisiness counting the times the signal changes sign; two measures of *roll-off,* the frequency cutoff such that 85% and 95% of the total energy is below the cutoff; *root-mean-square energy,* a global measure of the energy of the signal; *low energy,* the proportion of 50 millisecond frames with below average energy; and 13 *Mel-frequency cepstral coefficients,* a representation of the short-term power spectrum. Additionally, we included measures of voiced frequencies [8], including the *global mean* frequency and *standard deviation* of all voiced frequencies, the *number of blocks* of voiced syllables, and the *average* and *standard deviation* of these blocks. In all, we extracted 30 acoustic features from each time window.

3.4 Supervised Classification

We generated 117 features in total for each windowed partition of the audio recording. These features were used to train supervised classification models to identify instructional segments. As noted in Section 2.2, there was considerable data imbalance due to an infrequent occurrence of some segments and the high variance in use between different teachers and class sessions. Therefore, we prioritized the five most common segments, and trained an individual binary classifier to differentiate each segment from all others. For example, the Lecture classifier determines if each instance in the dataset is an example of a Lecture segment or one of the other potential segments, whether another common segment or one of the 11 infrequently occurring Miscellaneous segments.

We considered the Naïve Bayes classifier using the WEKA machine learning toolbox [14]. Naïve Bayes was chosen based on preliminary experiments with several other standard classifiers (e.g., logistic regression, support vector machine, k-nearest neighbor, decision tree, random forest) and because of its popular and successful use as a baseline classifier in many domains [19].

4. EXPERIMENTS AND RESULTS

All experiments were conducted with a leave-one-teacher-out cross validation. For each of the 11 teachers, all instances stemming from that teacher's class sessions were added to the test set and the training set was formed from instances of the other ten teachers. This process was repeated for each teacher such that each teacher appeared in the test set only once, and the results were calculated as the average of the 11 folds. This approach allows better generalization to new teachers, preventing the classification models from overfitting based on characteristics of individual teachers.

In terms of metrics, accuracy, or recognition rate, is not an ideal measure when base rates between class labels are highly skewed, as they are in our data. Therefore, we evaluated the efficacy of our binary target segment vs. all others classifier models by examining the F_1 score, a balance of precision and recall, for the class label of interest (i.e. the target segment such as Question & Answer). This ensures that we focus on the model's ability to detect the segments of interest, which was always the minority label, rather than prioritizing the dominant class label (i.e. the other category).

4.1 Comparing Window Time

The size of an analysis window is an important design choice as it determines the temporal resolution of our predictions. While a shorter window will yield more fine-grained predictions, a longer window allows the consideration of more information for each prediction. In this experiment, we varied the window size ranging from 30 seconds to 300 seconds in increments of 30 seconds. The F_1 scores for each target segment are shown in Figure 3.

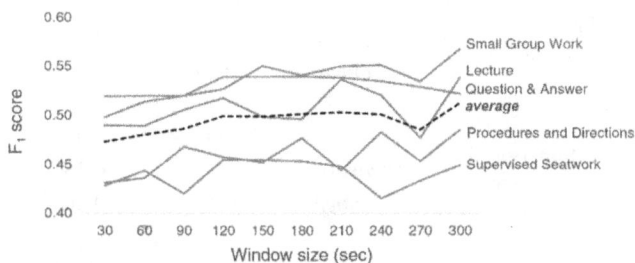

Figure 3. The F_1 score of the target segment label for each window size. The average score of the five classifiers is represented as a dashed line.

The results indicated that all five classifiers had lower performance on short window times, such as 30 seconds. Although performance generally increased with window size, longer windows resulted in fewer instances per class session. Furthermore, given the majority takes-all segment labeling approach described in Section 3.1, longer windows risk masking short occurrences of instructional segments. This effect is undesirable because it loses information about the use of class time.

The results indicated that the optimal classification window might need to be varied between classification models for different

segments. In future work, we will explore tuning the window size depending on the type of instructional segment to be classified. For the reminder of the experiments, we focused on a window size of 120 seconds, which showed improved performance for all classifiers over shorter window sizes while not exceeding the average length of segments (176 seconds). A window size of 120 seconds yielded 2,254 instances for classification across the 76 class sessions.

4.2 Comparing Feature Types

In our second experiment, we explore the relative effectiveness of the different feature types described in Section 3.3 in the classification of instructional segments. We trained a separate Naïve Bayes classifier for each of the three feature types (timing, NLP, or acoustic), and a fourth model which fused all three sets of features. The results are shown as Figure 4.

We observe that NLP features were most successful in detecting Procedures and Directions, perhaps unsurprisingly as these segments feature common patterns of imperative instructions provided by the teacher. Timing of teacher's speech and rest patterns aided in the classification of Question & Answer segments. The acoustic features were notably less useful in the classification of Small Group Work and Supervised Seatwork. As the present work only considers a recording of the teacher, it is likely that not enough information is available during these student-focused segments. Furthermore, the acoustic features may have difficulty in generalizing between male and female teachers as our current dataset contains more examples of female teachers.

We compared the average F_1 score across segments by feature type: timing (0.49), NLP (0.53), and acoustic (0.36) to the average score using all features (0.52). Although the average score of NLP features trivially exceeds the score of all features, we observe that the boost only comes from the Procedures and Directions classifier. Therefore, we consider all the features in the remaining experiments, although we will investigate additional feature engineering in future work.

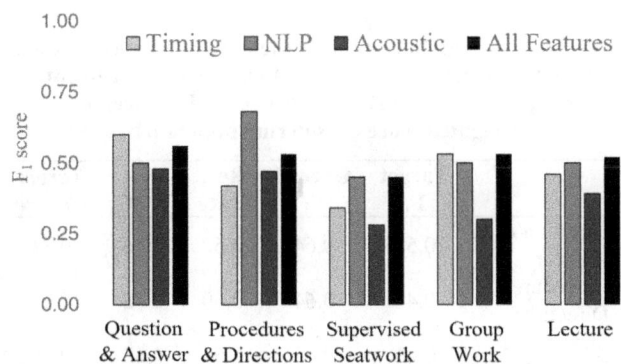

Figure 4. The F_1 score of the target segment label for each of the three feature types and the combination of all features.

4.3 Individual Feature Analysis

Following the analysis of feature category in the previous section, we explored the utility of each of the 117 individual features. In this experiment, we trained a binary classifier for each single feature and for each instructional segment. We ranked the features by the F_1 score for the target segment to explore the contribution of individual features. There was no clear pattern of features that worked best across the different segments. Overall, no single feature achieved an F_1 score greater than 0.25. This is unsurprising as we did not expect a single feature to dominate over the combination of many features.

For Question & Answer segments, the ten most useful features were all NLP features and included features such as the number of occurrences of certain question words (e.g., "*why*", "*what*") and the number of proper nouns. This is an encouraging result, demonstrating the utility of our NLP features despite the noise introduced by the imperfect ASR transcription. Furthermore, this demonstrates the timing features that capture teacher speech-rest patterns, used in previous work [5, 31], should be supplemented with additional feature modalities. Procedures and Directions also benefited most from NLP features, although these features differed from those useful to detect Question & Answer. For Supervised Seatwork, we note that acoustic features account for seven of the top ten features. This is an encouraging result and support our hypothesis that student-focused segments may be difficult to identify based on the teacher's speech, as the teacher may be silent for extended periods of time. No single feature alone achieved success in identifying Small Group Work from the other segments. However, since we are able to classify Small Group Work above chance levels using all features, this result underscores the utility of combinations of different features. The Lecture classifier best benefited from timing features, particularly those that described the length of moments of rest, which may necessary to determine non-Lecture segments in which the teacher is silent for extended periods of time.

4.4 Final Classification Results

Informed by the previous experiments, we trained a set of Naïve Bayes classifiers, considering a window of 120 seconds and using all 117 features to generate 2,254 windowed instances for classification. In Table 1, we report the overall F_1 score to provide a measure of the binary classifiers' performance across both the class labels. The target F_1 score tracks the performance of the classifier only on the target label of interest (e.g., Lecture). We include recognition rate (accuracy) and AU-ROC for comparison to other studies.

Table 1. Classification results for each of the five instructional segments. Target F_1 refers to the F_1 score of the segment of interest, listed in each row, while overall F_1 represents the weighted score considering both labels.

	Target F_1	Overall F_1	Rec. Rate	AU-ROC	*Target chance*
Question & Answer	0.55	0.64	0.60	0.76	*0.31*
Procedures/ Directions	0.47	0.64	0.60	0.72	*0.27*
Supervised Seatwork	0.45	0.67	0.59	0.65	*0.19*
Group Work	0.53	0.65	0.56	0.70	*0.19*
Lecture	0.52	0.78	0.71	0.58	*0.16*
Average	0.50	0.68	0.61	0.68	*0.23*

For a binary dataset that contains an equal distribution of labels, an F_1 score of 0.50 represents chance, and reflects a random assignment of the two labels. However, for datasets containing a large imbalance in the dataset, such as ours, the level of chance prediction is not as straightforward. For comparison to our target F_1

score, we calculated chance levels as follows. We considered chance-level precision as the precision of a classifier that always selects the target segment, which yields a precision that matches that proportion of the target segment in the dataset (see Section 2.2). We considered chance-level recall as prediction rate of the target label (e.g., Lecture) for each segment classifier. Using these values, we calculated an F_1 baseline for chance prediction of the target segment, shown in Table 1. We define chance in this manner to emulate classification with the same prediction rate as our models on a dataset reflecting the same distribution as our data.

The target F_1 score reveals the efficacy of predicting the minority class labels, which correspond to each of our key instructional segments. For all segments, we were able to predict at levels well above our target F_1 chance baseline. However, we were more successful predicting Question & Answer, Small Group Work, or Lecture compared to Procedures and Directions or Supervised Seatwork.

Table 2 presents the confusion matrix for each binary classifier as a proportion of the total instances. We most readily correctly identified true cases of Question & Answer segments (72% of the time), compared to the target class of the other classifiers. We note that all five classifiers were able to identify their respective segment at levels well above chance, but do suffer from misclassifications. In particular, the classifiers had high false positive rates, in which, for example, a non-Seatwork segment was identified as a Supervised Seatwork segment. This too is likely a consequence of the frequency of occurrence of certain segment types for certain teachers.

Table 2. Confusion matrices of each of the five classifiers. The column headers represent the predicted segment, while the row header denotes the actual segment.

	Actual	**Predicted**	
Question & Answer		*Q&A*	*Other*
	Q&A	0.72	0.28
	Other	0.44	0.56
Procedures and Directions		*Directions*	*Other*
	Directions	0.70	0.30
	Other	0.42	0.58
Supervised Seatwork		*Seatwork*	*Other*
	Seatwork	0.63	0.38
	Other	0.44	0.56
Small Group Work		*Group*	*Other*
	Group	0.67	0.34
	Other	0.45	0.55
Lecture		*Lecture*	*Other*
	Lecture	0.59	0.41
	Other	0.27	0.73

The confusion matrices are generally symmetric, with the exception of the Lecture classifier. Here, it appears that we are more successful at detecting non-Lecture than the Lecture segments themselves. This might be because Lecture segments are much more variable as they pertain to the general subject matter of the day, topics unlikely to be visited in other class sessions.

Furthermore, Lecture segments may contain supplementary video or other aspects that add unique challenges to classify based solely on audio recordings.

4.5 Comparison with Previous Work

A direct comparison with previous work is not possible because our dataset, preprocessing steps, feature extraction, and classifiers differ substantially. Nevertheless, we discuss our work in the context of the previous two studies in this domain. On the surface, our Question & Answer segment results are comparable to [5], which considered only Question & Answer segments from a small set of three teachers, reporting an AU-ROC of 0.78. This study reported results from a logistic regression classifier, a classifier which we also considered in our preliminary experiments but discarded as it had a tendency to overfit to the dominant class label and did not scale well to larger sets of features. Furthermore, in our work, we considered Question & Answer and Discussion segments together, rendering it a harder problem while [5] simply discarded Discussion segments altogether.

Wang et al. reported 84% accuracy across a limited set of three possible instructional segments [31]. As we reviewed in Section 1.1, the authors re-used their training examples in their test set, albeit with testing the label given by the other human coder, achieving an accuracy of 84%. Since two coders had an 83% agreement in their annotations, this resulted in highly correlated training and test sets. In comparison, our approach used separate training and test sets validated independently of the teacher. The differences between our results and [31] underscore the need to validate classification models in a manner independent of the teacher or the class session in order to generalize to new teachers and class sessions.

5. DISCUSSION

We considered the task of automatically identifying instructional segments from live classrooms using only an audio recording of the teacher's speech. This is quite a challenging task as we are drawing from a single uninterrupted channel of classroom audio in order to make high-level predications on instructional activities at specific moments during the class session. Although our classification models are not perfect, we are able to detect five individual instructional segments well above chance levels. Despite the fact that the instructional content discussed in classrooms represents high-level discourse, our system did not have the benefit of an accurate text transcript or recordings of individual students. Instead, it used only low-level features derived solely from teacher audio.

5.1 Contributions

Our system fulfills our design goals of practicality, generalizability, and scalability. First, we described a non-invasive method of recording the teacher using a low-cost and portable microphone that does not interfere with the teacher's regular teaching routine. All data processing tasks, including audio capture, automatic speech recognition, feature extraction, and classification can be performed on a standard personal laptop. By prioritizing a simple and affordable technical setup, we will more easily be able to facilitate practical deployment in classrooms. This is a significant advantage over the approach used in [31] which requires expensive and propriety recording equipment and analysis software.

Second, we evaluated our system on the largest and most diverse dataset thus far considered for this task, covering multiple teachers, schools, and course subjects. We considered all class recordings, despite the potential absence of certain instructional segments in

several class sessions. We also had to handle the difficulties of undesirable noise, such as the persistent heavy breathing of one teacher or distracting background noise from the classroom, in others. Additionally, we focused on the identification of five key instructional segments, extending beyond previous attempts at automatic classification of instructional activities, which considered only a single activity [5] or a limited set of only three activities [31]. Of the five instructional segments considered in this work, Question & Answer segments are the most important component of dialogic instruction as certain types of questions and in-depth discussion sections correlate to increased student achievement [16, 22, 24]. Therefore, it is encouraging that we can more readily identify these Question & Answer segments, although further refinement is needed to reduce the false positive rate.

Third, we studied the influence of three diverse features types for the detection of instructional segments. We considered features derived from natural language processing of ASR transcriptions and non-verbal acoustic features extracted from noisy classroom audio recordings. It is encouraging that the NLP features were successful in identifying certain segments, despite the fact that they are generated from ASR transcriptions, an imperfect process hindered by mumbled speech or ambient background noise.

Most importantly, we built and validated our models in a teacher-independent manner which increases confidence that our approach generalizes to new teachers, schools, or class sessions. We have found our results scale across the set of eleven teachers with no indication that our approach overfits to specific teachers.

5.2 Limitations and Future Work

Our study is not without limitations. One limitation is that our data was collected from within a single U.S. state and does not capture larger geographic differences, such as regional accents and phrasing [13] or state-wide curriculum requirements that guide the teacher's lesson plans. We anticipate that different regional accents may not be a significant issue given the wide-spread use of ASR, but this requires empirical confirmation. We have also only tested our system in English language classrooms. Given the proliferation of ASR for many languages, we anticipate our approach will largely extend to other languages, provided an adaption be made to the natural language processing features to suit other languages. Lastly, we note that the differences between curricula across different states and countries may affect the distribution of certain instructional segments, a potential issue we will consider in the future.

Although this work demonstrates encouraging progress towards the goal of automatic analysis of class instruction, significant refinement is necessary to improve the efficacy of our predictions. In particular, our classifier will likely benefit if given additional data apart from the teacher's speech. Recording individual students is impractical with regards to both cost and privacy concerns. Presently, additional data collection is underway which includes a pressure zone microphone to capture general classroom activity. Although the additional microphone is still subjective to the same challenges as the teacher channel, such as classroom noise or imprecise speech transcriptions, this second channel of audio, coupled with the recording of the teacher, would allow modeling teacher-student interactions, potentially yielding stronger insight to the classroom activity in progress.

We also considered only a single classification model (Naïve Bayes) to facilitate comparison of results across experiments. In further experiments, we will explore the use of different classifiers for each of the five segments, as different classifiers likely have different strengths and weaknesses depending on the instructional segment at hand. Furthermore, as we continue to refine our approach and improve our results, we will explore combining the binary models into a multi-class approach to classification.

Furthermore, we observed that we are better able to identify an instructional segment if it occurred frequently during the class session. There was, however, a tendency to overpredict when a segment did not occur in a classroom session. To address this limitation, we will explore models that consider the instructional segments in the larger context of the class session. For example, we will attempt to first predict if examples of the segment exist in a particular class session, before classifying the individual windowed segments. Although we validated our approach across teachers, we did not explicitly consider the order of the windowed instances within a class session. As future work, we will explore the use of temporal models, such as a hidden Markov models or conditional random fields, which can incorporate information that occurred earlier in the class session when making predictions. This approach enables the inclusion of additional contextual information when making predictions, a potentially important benefit for the present task.

A major difficulty of our task stems from the imbalance of segments of interest across the entire dataset. In order to work towards the goal of achieving a deployable system, we must overcome the challenge of class label imbalance as it reflects the reality of real-world classes. The collection of additional classroom recording is ongoing and this will provide more examples of the various instructional segments and additional teachers.

5.3 Concluding Remarks
We took steps towards automated teacher modeling by identifying teachers' instructional activities from audio data collected in live classrooms. The teacher model will be used to generate personalized formative feedback, which will afford reflection and improvement of their pedagogy, ultimately leading to increased student engagement and achievement.

6. ACKNOWLEDGMENTS
This research was supported by the Institute of Education Sciences (IES) (R305A130030). Any opinions, findings and conclusions, or recommendations expressed in this paper are those of the author and do not represent the views of the IES.

7. REFERENCES
[1] Alibali, M.W., Nathan, M.J., Wolfgram, M.S., Church, R.B., Jacobs, S.A., Johnson Martinez, C. and Knuth, E.J. 2014. How teachers link ideas in mathematics instruction using speech and gesture: A corpus analysis. *Cognition and Instruction*. 32, 1 (2014), 65–100.

[2] Applebee, A.N., Langer, J.A., Nystrand, M. and Gamoran, A. 2003. Discussion-based approaches to developing understanding: Classroom instruction and student performance in middle and high school English. *American Educational Research Journal*. 40, 3 (2003), 685–730.

[3] Barrón-Cedeño, A., Vila, M., Martí, M.A. and Rosso, P. 2013. Plagiarism meets paraphrasing: Insights for the next generation in automatic plagiarism detection. *Computational Linguistics*. 39, 4 (2013), 917–947.

[4] Blanchard, N., Brady, M., Olney, A.M., Glaus, M., Sun, X., Nystrand, M., Samei, B., Kelly, S. and D'Mello, S. 2015. A Study of Automatic Speech Recognition in Noisy Classroom Environments for Automated Dialog Analysis.

Artificial Intelligence in Education. Springer International Publishing. 23–33.

[5] Blanchard, N., D'Mello, S., Nystrand, M. and Olney, A.M. 2015. Automatic Classification of Question & Answer Discourse Segments from Teacher's Speech in Classrooms. *Proceedings of the 8th International Conference on Educational Data Mining (EDM 2015), International Educational Data Mining Society* (2015).

[6] Caughlan, S., Juzwik, M.M., Borsheim-Black, C., Kelly, S. and Fine, J.G. 2013. English teacher candidates developing dialogically organized instructional practices. *Research in the Teaching of English*. 47, 3 (2013), 212.

[7] D'Mello, S.K., Olney, A.M., Blanchard, N., Samei, B., Sun, X., Ward, B. and Kelly, S. 2015. Multimodal Capture of Teacher-Student Interactions for Automated Dialogic Analysis in Live Classrooms. *Proceedings of the 2015 ACM on International Conference on Multimodal Interaction* (2015), 557–566.

[8] Drugman, T. and Stylianou, Y. 2014. Maximum voiced frequency estimation: Exploiting amplitude and phase spectra. *Signal Processing Letters, IEEE*. 21, 10 (2014), 1230–1234.

[9] Ford, M., Baer, C., Xu, D., Yapanel, U. and Gray, S. 2008. *The LENA language environment analysis system*. LENA Foundation Technical Report LTR-03-02.

[10] Gates Foundation 2013. *Ensuring fair and reliable measures of effective teaching: Culminating findings from the MET project's three-year study—Policy and practitioner brief*. Bill & Melinda Gates Foundation Seattle, WA.

[11] Goldman, R., Pea, R., Barron, B. and Derry, S.J. 2014. *Video research in the learning sciences*. Routledge.

[12] Graesser, A.C. and McNamara, D.S. 2012. Automated analysis of essays and open-ended verbal responses. *APA handbook of research methods in psychology. Washington, DC: American Psychological Association*. (2012).

[13] Hall, J.K. 2008. Language education and culture. *Encyclopedia of language and education*. Springer. 45–55.

[14] Hall, M., Frank, E., Holmes, G., Pfahringer, B., Reutemann, P. and Witten, I.H. 2009. The WEKA data mining software: an update. *ACM SIGKDD explorations newsletter*. 11, 1 (2009), 10–18.

[15] Juzwik, M.M., Borsheim-Black, C., Caughlan, S. and Heintz, A. 2013. *Inspiring dialogue: Talking to learn in the English classroom*. Teachers College Press.

[16] Kelly, S. 2007. Classroom discourse and the distribution of student engagement. *Social Psychology of Education*. 10, 3 (2007), 331–352.

[17] Lai, M.K. and McNaughton, S. 2013. Analysis and discussion of classroom and achievement data to raise student achievement. *Data-based decision making in education*. Springer. 23–47.

[18] Lartillot, O., Toiviainen, P. and Eerola, T. 2008. A matlab toolbox for music information retrieval. *Data analysis, machine learning and applications*. Springer. 261–268.

[19] Lewis, D.D. 1998. Naive (Bayes) at forty: The independence assumption in information retrieval. *Machine learning: ECML-98*. Springer. 4–15.

[20] Mu, J., Stegmann, K., Mayfield, E., Rosé, C. and Fischer, F. 2012. The ACODEA framework: Developing segmentation and classification schemes for fully automatic analysis of online discussions. *International Journal of Computer-Supported Collaborative Learning*. 7, 2 (2012), 285–305.

[21] Nystrand, M. 2004. CLASS 4.0 user's manual. *The National Research Center on.* (2004).

[22] Nystrand, M. 2006. Research on the role of classroom discourse as it affects reading comprehension. *Research in the Teaching of English.* (2006), 392–412.

[23] Nystrand, M., Gamoran, A., Kachur, R. and Prendergast, C. 1997. *Opening dialogue: Understanding the Dynamics of Language and Learning in the English Classroom. Language and Literacy Series.*

[24] Nystrand, M., Wu, L.L., Gamoran, A., Zeiser, S. and Long, D.A. 2003. Questions in time: Investigating the structure and dynamics of unfolding classroom discourse. *Discourse processes.* 35, 2 (2003), 135–198.

[25] Olney, A., Louwerse, M., Matthews, E., Marineau, J., Hite-Mitchell, H. and Graesser, A. 2003. Utterance classification in AutoTutor. *Proceedings of the HLT-NAACL 03 workshop on Building educational applications using natural language processing-Volume 2* (2003), 1–8.

[26] Rus, V., D'Mello, S., Hu, X. and Graesser, A. 2013. Recent advances in conversational intelligent tutoring systems. *AI magazine.* 34, 3 (2013), 42–54.

[27] Samei, B., Olney, A., Kelly, S., Nystrand, M., D'Mello, S., Blanchard, N., Sun, X., Glaus, M. and Graesser, A. 2014. Domain independent assessment of dialogic properties of classroom discourse. *Proceedings of the 7th International Conference on Educational Data Mining (EDM 2014) International Educational Data Mining Society* (2014).

[28] Samei, B., Olney, A.M., Kelly, S., Nystrand, M., Blanchard, S.D.N. and Graesser, A. Modeling Classroom Discourse: Do Models that Predict Dialogic Instruction Properties Generalize across Populations?

[29] Sottilare, R.A., Graesser, A., Hu, X. and Holden, H. 2013. *Design Recommendations for Intelligent Tutoring Systems: Volume 1-Learner Modeling.* US Army Research Laboratory.

[30] Wang, Z., Miller, K. and Cortina, K. 2013. Using the LENA in Teacher Training: Promoting Student Involvement through automated feedback. *Unterrichtswissenschaft.* 4, (2013), 290–305.

[31] Wang, Z., Pan, X., Miller, K.F. and Cortina, K.S. 2014. Automatic classification of activities in classroom discourse. *Computers & Education.* 78, (2014), 115–123.

Predicting Individual Differences for Learner Modeling in Intelligent Tutors from Previous Learner Activities

Michael Eagle[1], Albert Corbett[1], John Stamper[1], Bruce M. McLaren[1], Ryan Baker[3],

Angela Wagner[1], Benjamin MacLaren[1], and Aaron Mitchell[2]

[1]Human-Computer Interaction Institute, [2]Department of Biological Sciences, Carnegie Mellon University
{meagle, ac21, jstamper, bmclaren, awagner, maclaren, apm1}@andrew.cmu.edu
[3]Teacher's College, Columbia University
ryanbaker@gmail.com

ABSTRACT

This study examines how accurately individual student differences in learning can be predicted from prior student learning activities. Bayesian Knowledge Tracing (BKT) predicts learner performance well and has often been employed to implement cognitive mastery. Standard BKT individualizes parameter estimates for knowledge components, but not for learners. Studies have shown that individualizing parameters for learners improves the quality of BKT fits and can lead to very different (and potentially better) practice recommendations. These studies typically derive best-fitting individualized learner parameters from learner performance in existing data logs, making the methods difficult to deploy in actual tutor use. In this work, we examine how well BKT parameters in a tutor lesson can be individualized based on learners' prior performance in reading instructional text, taking a pretest, and completing an earlier tutor lesson. We find that best-fitting individual difference estimates do not directly transfer well from one tutor lesson to another, but that predictive models incorporating variables extracted from prior reading, pretest and tutor activities perform well, when compared to a standard BKT model and a model with best-fitting individualized parameter estimates.

Keywords
BKT; Genetics; Machine Learning; Student Modeling

1. INTRODUCTION
Intelligent tutoring systems have employed learner models to improve learning outcomes for over two decades. Learner models have been used both to individualize curriculum sequencing [1, 2, 3] and/or to individualize hint messages [4, 5]. Each of the five successful modeling frameworks cited here employs a Bayesian method to infer learner knowledge from learner response accuracy, and Bayesian modeling systems have been shown to accurately predict students' tutor and/or posttest performance [1, 3, 6, 7].

Bayesian models generally individualize model parameters for different reasoning skills, or *knowledge components*, (KCs), but not for different students. Several studies have shown that individualizing parameters for students, as well as for KCs, improves the quality of the models [1, 8, 9, 10].

These modeling studies of individual differences among students have employed data sets consisting of tens of KCs, or even many

hundreds of KCs [10]. These studies have analyzed students' performance on a set of KCs retroactively, deriving the individualized student parameters for that set of KCs from existing tutor log files. These methods successfully address the research question, but are complicated to use for actual student modeling in ITSs, since the concurrent estimation and use of individualized parameters within a tutor lesson can be quite challenging at best.

In this paper we examine whether parameter estimates can be individualized for students prior to embarking on a tutor module, based on student performance in earlier activities. First, we examine whether parameter estimates can be individualized based on performance in two activities that naturally precede tutor use: reading on-line instructional text and taking a conceptual knowledge pretest.

Second, we examine whether, once a student begins using an ITS, parameter estimates in a prior tutor module can be individualized based on student performance in a prior module. In particular, how well do individualized student parameters directly transfer from one tutor module to the next? If not well, what measures of student performance in a tutor lesson can be used to predict individual student parameters in a following lesson?

We explore this issue in the Bayesian Knowledge Tracing modeling framework [1] and in a unit of the Genetics Cognitive Tutor [6]. In the following sections we describe Knowledge Tracing, the on-line student activities, and the predictors derived from students' reading, pretest, and prior tutor activities. Finally, we report our success in using these predictors to model individual differences in student learning and performance in the tutor.

2. MODELING FRAMEWORK
Bayesian Knowledge Tracing (BKT) [1] employs a two-state Bayesian learning model for each knowledge component (KC) in a tutor curriculum: at any time a student either has learned or not learned a given KC. BKT employs four parameters to estimate the probability that a student has learned each KC:

pL_0 *initial knowledge* the probability a student has learned how to apply a KC prior to the first opportunity to apply it in the ITS

pT *learning rate* the probability a student learns a KC at each opportunity to apply it

pG *guessing* the probability a student will guess correctly if the KC is not learned

pS *slips* the probability a student will make an error when the KC has been learned

Cognitive Tutors employ BKT to implement cognitive mastery, in which the curriculum is individualized to afford each student just the number of practice opportunities needed to enable the student to "master" each of the KCs. Mastery is generally operationalized as a 0.95 probability that the student has learned the KC.

2.1 Individual Differences

Knowledge Tracing generally employs best-fitting estimates of each of the four parameters for each KC but not for individual students. In this work, we incorporate individual differences among students into the model in the form of individual difference weights. Following Corbett & Anderson [1], four best-fitting weights are estimated for each student, one weight for each of the four parameter types, wL_0, wT, wG, wS. In estimating and employing these *individual difference weights* (IDWs), each of the four probability estimates for each rule is converted to odds form ($p/(1-p)$), multiplied by the corresponding student-specific weight and the resulting odds form is converted back to a probability. Let i represent the parameter type, (i.e., pL_0, pT, pG, pS), r represent the reasoning rule (KC) and s the student, then the individually weighted parameter for each rule and student, p_{irs}, is given by the equation:

$$p_{irs} = p_{ir} * w_{is} / (p_{ir} * w_{is} + (1 - p_{ir})) \quad (1)$$

where p_{ir} is a best fitting parameter estimate for the rule across all students and w_{is} is the corresponding individual difference weight for the students.

2.2 Related Work

Several previous studies have employed tutor log files to retroactively examine the impact of individualizing BKT parameters for students. Corbett and Anderson [1] individualized all four BKT parameters for students, as described in Section 2.2, and found that the resulting model predicted individual differences in posttest performance better than the standard, non-individualized BKT model. Lee & Brunskill [8] employed a different method to derive four individual difference parameters and examined the impact on another property of the models – the number of practice opportunities that would be required to reach mastery. They found that the individualized model recommended substantially greater practice for some students and substantially less practice for others than the standard, non-individualized model. Two other studies focused on individualizing just the learning parameters, pL_0 and pT and obtained somewhat different results. Pardos and Heffernan [9], individualized the *initial knowledge* parameter, pL_0, alone, based on either the student's first attempt at each KC or on all attempts at each KC – and found that either individualized method yielded reliably better fits than the standard, non-individualized BKT model. Finally, Yudelson, Koedinger and Gordon [10] individualized both the learning parameters, and found that individualizing the *learning rate* parameter pT yielded reliably better fits than the standard, non-individualized BKT model. However, unlike Pardos and Heffernan [9], they found that individualizing pL_0, alone or along with pT, did not reliably improve the goodness of fit. Finally, in an alternative approach to modeling student differences, a variety of student modeling frameworks grounded in Item-Response Theory have employed a single individual difference parameter as a basic component of the model [11,12,13].

All of these studies model student differences with log files after the students have completed the tutor activities. In this paper, we examine whether individual student differences can be estimated before students start using a tutor lesson, based on student performance in prior activities that are natural components of on-line learning activities.

3. GENETICS TUTOR

This study employed the Genetics Cognitive Tutor [6]. This tutor consists of over 25 lessons that support problem solving across a wide range of topics in genetics, including Mendelian transmission, pedigree analysis, gene mapping, population genetics and genetic pathways analysis. Various subsets of the modules have been piloted at 15 universities and four high schools in the U.S.

The genetics topic in this study is gene interaction, which examines how two genes can interact in controlling a single phenotypic trait (an observable trait, e.g., hair color). When two genes, each with a dominant and recessive allele, control a single trait, e.g., bell pepper color, there can be up to four different resulting phenotypes (four colors). However, there are many ways the two genes can interact that result in only two or three different phenotypes.

The study employs two gene interaction lessons, which require that students reason about the topic in two different ways. In the first, forward reasoning or *process modeling* lesson, each problem provides a description of how two genes interact and students determine the phenotype that is associated with each genotype and the offspring phenotype rates that will result from various parental crosses. In the second, *abductive reasoning* lesson, students analyze offspring phenotype rates that result from various parental crosses, and reason backwards to infer the genotypes of the parents and the offspring, and ultimately, how the two genotypes interact to determine phenotype.

This study focuses on four on-line activities that students completed in succession: reading the gene interaction instructional text online, taking a gene interaction pretest, and finally using both the Genetics Cognitive Tutor Gene Interaction process modeling and abductive reasoning modules.

On-Line Instructional Text. The online instructional text consisted of 23 screens, structured like pages in a book. Students could move forward and backward through the text, one screen at a time. After a student touched each page at least once, a "done" button appeared on the final (23rd) screen and the student could then continue reading (e.g., back up to re-read pages), or exit at any time.

Conceptual Knowledge Pretest. Students completed a pretest with nine conceptual questions divided into three topics. The first three questions focused on general knowledge of basic Mendelian transmission with 2 genes, the second three questions focused on process modeling, and the last three questions focused on abductive (backward) reasoning. This was not a problem-solving pretest; the last six questions are not similar to the Cognitive Tutor problems. Instead, they required students to reason about genetics processes and abductive reasoning more abstractly.

Genetics Cognitive Tutor: Gene Interaction Process Modeling. This lesson consisted of 5 problems. In each problem, students were given a description of how two genes interact to determine a phenotype, e.g., bell pepper color. Students (a) mapped the description onto one of seven gene interaction templates with 3 menus, (b) identified the phenotypes of the four true-breeding genotypes. (c) modeled the offspring genotypes and phenotypes resulting from two different parental crosses, and finally (e) summarized the phenotypes associated with all possible individual genotypes and how the phenotypes arise.

Genetics Cognitive Tutor: Gene Interaction Abductive Reasoning. This lesson consisted of 6 problems. Each problem, displayed the offspring phenotype rates that result from 3 parental crosses. Students inferred the genotypes of the parents and offspring in each of the three crosses and how the two genes interact to determine genotypes

The Cognitive Model for the Two Lessons. There was an average of 45 steps in each of the process modeling problems and 25 steps in each of the abduction problems. Some of the KCs governing the steps in a problem were unique to the problem, while others were applicable in multiple problems. In this analysis we excluded KCs that occurred only once or twice across the problems in a lesson, leaving 31 KCs in the process modeling lesson and 22 KCs in the abduction lesson.

3.1 Predictor Variables

In this study, we examine the effectiveness of four categories of student performance variables in predicting Lesson 2 (abduction) IDWs: (1) reading the instructional text, (2) pretest performance, (3) Lesson 1 IDWs and (4) features of student performance in completing Lesson 1.

In a prior paper [14] we derived 12 predictor variables for the students in this in this study, based on their gene interaction reading and pretest activities – 6 reading variables and 6 pretest variables, as described in this section. In that paper these 12 measures were used to predict best fitting IDWs for tutor Lesson 1 (process modeling), as summarized in section 3.2 below.

3.1.1 Predictors Derived from Instructional Text and Reading Performance

We derived two types of measures of student reading performance: reading time and revisiting pages in the text. Between these two measures we derived a total of 6 predictor variables, as follows.

Reading Time (4 variables): No prior ITS research employs reading rates to individualize parameters in a learning environment, but there is substantial evidence that reading time may prove sensitive to individual differences in comprehension difficulty. Harvey and Anderson [15] showed that reading times for on-line declarative instruction in the ACT Programming Tutor are sensitive to differences in processing time necessary to encode familiar versus novel material. More generally, an extensive research literature demonstrates that, reading time is sensitive to relative comprehension difficulty [16].

We performed a factor analysis on log reading times for the 23 individual pages to reduce the number of predictors. The factor analysis yielded a total of four factors (see RTF1, RTF2, RTF3, RTF4 in Table 1), which align with subtopics in the text, as summarized in Table 1.

Text Pages Revisited (2 variables): Students can read through the declarative instruction as they would pages in a book. Some students may choose to strictly read forward through the text, while others may choose to revisit earlier pages in the text. We calculated two measures of student behavior in revisiting text pages: the number of pages re-read and number of intervening pages traversed in re-reading text pages.

3.1.2 Predictors Derived from a Conceptual Knowledge Pretest

Some prior projects have employed pretest accuracy to initialize ITS student models [3, 17]. We derived three types of measures of student pretest performance: accuracy, answer changes and time on task. Between these three measures, we derived a total of 6 predictor variables, as follows.

Pretest Accuracy (3 variables): We calculated students' average pretest accuracy on each of the three types of pretest questions, general knowledge, process modeling and abductive reasoning.

Pretest Answer Changes (2 variables): We calculated the number of times students changed their answers in the pretest from a correct initial answer to an incorrect final answer, or vice versa.

Time on Task (1 variable): Finally we calculated students' total time to complete the pretest.

3.1.3 Lesson 1 Individual Difference Weights

In the prior study [14] we derived four best-fitting individual difference weights in the first tutor lesson for each of the students in this study. In this study we examine both how well these Lesson 1 IDWs directly apply to Lesson 2, and whether they can be used to improve the predictive model for Lesson 2 IDWs.

3.1.4 Lesson 1 Performance Features

Finally, we derived six features of student performance in solving the Lesson 1 tutor problems.

Error Rate: Corbett and Anderson [1] found that students' raw error rate within a tutor lesson is strongly correlated with the logarithm of students' IDWs for that lesson. In this study we calculated students' raw error rate in completing the Lesson 1 problems and examine whether Lesson 1 error rate predicts Lesson 2 IDWs.

Average response time: We calculated students' average response time for their first problem-solving action at each opportunity to apply one of the 22 KCs in tutor Lesson 2.

3.1.4.1 Performance Features that Predict Transfer and Preparation for Future Learning

Predicting individual differences in students' initial knowledge, pL_0, in a tutor lesson from their performance in a prior tutor lesson is closely related to examining the direct *transfer* of knowledge from the first lesson to the second lesson. Similarly, predicting individual differences in students' learning rate, pT, in a lesson from their performance in a prior tutor lesson is closely related to examining students' *preparation for future learning* [18] after completing the first lesson.

Prior research [19] has identified features of students' performance in a Genetics Cognitive Tutor lesson that predict transfer and preparation for future learning, which are both manifestations of deep or "robust" student understanding [20]. Conversely, features that predict shallow learning have also been identified [21]. In this study we examine four performance features that correlate with at least two of these three constructs.

Help Avoidance: The proportion of problem-solving steps in which the probability that the student knows the relevant KC is low and the first action is an error instead of a hint request.

Bug Message Long Pause: The proportion of a student's actions in which a bug message (error messages given when the student's behavior indicates a known misconception) is followed by a long pause before a subsequent action.

Hint Long Pause: The proportion of a student's actions in which a hint request is followed by a long pause before the next action.

Hint Correct Long Pause: The proportion of a student's actions in which a hint request is followed by a correct action and then a long pause before the next action.

3.2 Prior Gene Interaction Lesson 1 Results

Eagle, et al, [14] examined the feasibility of setting individual difference weights for the first lesson in this tutor curriculum sequence, before students begin work in the lesson. That study derived best-fitting standard BKT parameters for each of the 31 KCs in the first gene interaction lesson, as described in Section 2 above, calculated best-fitting IDWs for each of the students, as described in Section 2.1, then examined how well each student's best-fitting IDWs could be predicted from the 12 reading and pretest variables described in sections 3.1.1 and 3.1.2.

The BKT model with *best-fitting* IDWs (FIDW-31) improved the goodness of fit of the standard non-individualized BKT model by 8.7%, reducing the RMSE from 0.306 to 0.279. The BKT model with *predicted* IDWs (PIDW-31) was about 40% as successful as the best-fitting model. It improved the goodness of fit of the standard non-individualized BKT model by 3.6%, reducing RMSE from 0.306 to 0.295.

As Koedinger, et al [22] observed, even small differences in model fits can have large effects on the amount of recommended work assigned to the student. To compare the practical impact of the individualized best-fitting FIDW-31 and predicted PIDW-31 models for Lesson 1, we calculated the number of practice opportunities that would be needed for students to reach mastery under the standard non-individualized BKT model (SBKT), and under the FIDW-31 and PIDW-31 models – that is the number of opportunities that would be required for *pL* (the probability the students has learned a KC) to reach the mastery criterion (0.95). While students completed a fixed curriculum in this study, most students had in fact reached the mastery criterion for most of the KCs.

Under the FIDW-31 individualized model, 56 students required less practice to reach mastery than under the SBKT non-individualized model and these students required 17 fewer opportunities on average. Under the FIDW-31 model, 27 students needed more practice than under the SBKT model to reach mastery. These students required an average of 27 fewer opportunities.

There was substantial, but not perfect agreement between the predicted PIDW-31 and best-fitting FIDW-31 models on the amount of practice individual students needed to achieve mastery. The PIDW-31 model recommended less practice then the SBKT model for 54 students, vs. 56 for FIDW-31, and the two models agreed on 46 of these students. The PIDW-31 model recommended less practice to reach mastery for 27 students, and the two models agreed on 19 of these students. However, the PIDW-31 only recommended 11 fewer opportunities for the first group (vs. 17 for the FIDW-31 model) and only 14 more opportunities for the latter group (vs. 27 for the PIDW-31 model).

Given this moderate level of success in predicting IDWs from prior activities before students embark on the first tutor lesson, in the current study we examine two questions. (1) Should IDWs be estimated separately for successive lessons in a tutor curriculum? (2) Can we predict IDWs in the second lesson more accurately if we employ predictor variables from student performance in the first tutor lesson, as well as from reading and pretest activities?

4. METHODS AND MATERIALS
The data analyzed in this study come from 83 CMU undergraduates enrolled in either genetics or introductory biology courses who were recruited to participate in this study for pay. Students participated in two 2.5-hour sessions on consecutive days in a campus computer lab. In this study, the first session focused on gene interaction and students read the on-line gene interaction instructional text, took the on-line pretest, and used the gene interaction process modeling tutor module and the abductive reasoning tutor module as the first four activities in this session. The study focuses on modeling the 83 students' first actions on 10,309 problem-solving steps in the abduction module.

4.1 Fitting Procedures
We first found best-fitting group parameter estimates for each of the 4 parameters (*pL0*, *pT*, *pG*, *pS*) in the standard BKT model for each of the 22 KCs in Lesson 2, with nonlinear optimization. The objective function takes the observed opportunities for a single skill and a set of group parameters as input and returns the negative log-likelihood (-LogLik). Optimization ultimately returns the set of group parameters that best fit the skill. Both pG and pS were bounded to be less than 0.5, as in [23] to avoid paradoxical results that arise when these performance parameters exceed 0.5 (e.g., a student with a higher probability of knowing a KC is less likely to apply it correctly.)

Second, we re-fit the lesson 2 tutor data with an individualized BKT model: We obtained four best-fitting Individual Difference Weights (IDWs) for each of the 83 students, one weight for each of the four parameter types, *wL0*, *wT*, *wG*, *wS*. As described in Section 2.1 equation 1, each student's four weights are mapped across the best-fitting group learning and performance parameter estimates for each of the 22 KCs in the lesson to individualize these parameter estimates. The objective function takes the fixed group parameters, the observed opportunities for a student, and a set of IDWs (*wL0*, *wT*, *wG*, *wS*) and returns the -LogLik. Optimization ultimately returns the set of IDWs that maximize the fit.

Table 1. 22 Predictor variables employed in this study.

Reading Predictors (from Eagle, et al [14])	
1. **RTF1**	Reading: Time for a 5-page intro with familiar content on basic Mendelian genetics
2. **RTF2**	Reading: Time for 6 pages with charts of various ways 2 genes can interact
3. **RTF3**	Reading: Time for 3 pages on parental crosses with offspring genotypes & traits
4. **RTF4**	Reading: Time for 2 pages with full-page diagrams of dominant & recessive alleles
5. **RRNP**	Reading: Total number of previous pages re-read
6. **RRTD**	Reading: Total distance traversed (intervening pages) in re-reading text pages

Pretest Predictors (from Eagle, et al [14])	
1. **PACC1**	Pretest: % Correct for 3 general knowledge questions
2. **PACC2**	Pretest: % Correct for 3 process modeling questions
3. **PACC3**	Pretest: % Correct for 3 abductive reasoning questions
4. **PCCI**	Pretest: Number of answers initially correct changed to incorrect
5. **PCIC**	Pretest: Number of answers initially incorrect changed to correct
6. **Ptime**	Pretest: Total time to complete the pretest

Tutor Lesson 1 Individual Difference Weights	
1. **L1wL0**	Lesson 1 Initial Learning IDWs
2. **L1wT**	Lesson 1 Learning Rate IDWs
3. **L1wG**	Lesson 1 Guessing IDWs
4. **L1wS**	Lesson 1 Slip IDWs

Tutor Lesson 1 Predictors	
1. **TErr**	Lesson 1 proportion of errors
2. **TTime**	Lesson 1 average response time
3. **HELPA**	Not requesting help on poorly learned skills
4. **BugLP**	Bug message followed by a long pause
5. **HNLP**	Hint message followed by a long pause
6. **HNLPC**	Hint message followed by a correct action then a long pause

Third, we derived 6 features from student performance in Lesson 1, as described in section 3.1.4. Along with the 12 reading and pretest features and 4 best-fitting individual difference weights derived in [14], this yields a total set of 22 predictor variables, displayed in Table 1.

Fourth, we employed these variables to independently predict the four Lesson 2 IDWs: wL_0, wT, wG, wS. We generated three predictions for each of the IDWs with successively larger subsets of features: (1) the 12 reading and pretest features; (2) the 12 reading and pretest features and 4 Lesson 1 IDWs; (3) the 12 reading and pretest features, the 4 Lesson 1 IDWs, and the 6 Lesson 1 performance features. Since we are predicting multiplicative weights, we fit a transformation of the weights $w/(1+w)$. This transformation has the property that the neutral weight 1.0 (which does not modify the corresponding best-fitting group parameter), is the midpoint of the transformed scale.

4.2 Model and Feature Selection

In order to reduce the number of features, and to compare to the previous work in [14] we used Least Angle Regression (LAR) [24] a variant of Lasso. For each of the four Lesson 2 IDWs we use LAR to select the best 12 predictors (out of 22.) Lasso performs both variable selection and regularization, and restricts the size of the coefficients making some of the values be zero (not included in the model.)

We then built a robust regression model with the 12 predictors for each of the IDWs. Robust regression is less sensitive to outliers, variable normality, and other violations of standard linear regression assumptions [25].

Finally, we employed the various sets of predictors to calculate 5 new IDW BKT models, yielding a total of six BKT model variants displayed in Table 2. Analysis work was performed using R [26], Optimx [27], rlm [28], and lars [24].

Table 2. Six Lesson 2 BKT models calculated in this analysis

1. **SBKT**: Standard BKT non-individualized model with best-fitting group parameter estimates.
2. **FIDW-22** Individualized BKT model with Fitted Individualized Difference Weights from Lesson 2
3. **FIDW-31**: Individualized BKT model with Fitted Individualized Difference Weights from Lesson 1
4. **PIDW-RP**: Individualized BKT model with predicted IDWs from reading and pretest features.
5. **PIDW-RPW**: Individualized BKT model with IDWs predicted from 12 reading and pretest features and 4 Lesson 1 IDWs
6. **PIDW-RPWF**: Individualized BKT model with IDWs predicted from 12 reading and pretest features, 4 Lesson 1 IDWs and 6 Lesson 1 performance features.

5. RESULTS

This section examines three main questions:

- How well do best-fitting IDWs transfer from one tutor lesson to a following tutor lesson?

- Do features of reading and pretest performance still predict best-fitting IDWs in a tutor lesson following an intervening tutor lesson?

- Do performance features from a prior tutor lesson further improve predicted IDWs in a subsequent tutor lesson?

5.1 Best-Fitting Models and Generalizability of Individual Difference Weights

Table 3 displays the overall fit to student performance in tutor Lesson 2 of three best-fitting BKT models. Column 2 displays root mean squared error (RMSE) and column 3 displays accuracy (the probability a model correctly predicts whether a student response will be correct or incorrect, with a 0.5 threshold on predicted accuracy.) The first row in the table displays the standard BKT model (SBKT) with no individualization for students as a baseline.

Table 3. Goodness of fit of 3 models for Lesson 2 tutor data: The standard BKT model & 2 BKT models with lesson-specific IDWs

Model	RMSE	Accuracy
SBKT 22 KCs	0.413	0.749
Lesson 2 FIDW-22 KCs	0.385	0.784
Lesson 1 FIDW-31 KCs	0.415	0.756

The last two rows in Table 3 display the goodness of fit of two BKT models that incorporate best-fitting IDWs. The second row displays the BKT model with IDWs trained on the 22 KCs in Lesson 2 (FIDW-22). As can be seen, this model improves the goodness of fit compared to the SBKT model, reducing RMSE by about 6.8% (RMSE 0.385 vs. 0.413) and increasing accuracy by about 4.7% (Accuracy 0.784 vs. 0.749).

The last row examines the generalizability of IDWs across the two tutor lessons. This row displays the BKT model for lesson 2 with the IDWs that were previously trained on the 31 IDWs in lesson 1 in [14]. As can be seen, the IDWs trained on lesson 1 KCs do not transfer well to lesson 2. The overall RMSE for this individualized model is slightly worse than for the non-individualized SBKT model, while the Accuracy is somewhat better. Even for these two highly related tutor lessons, which require students to reason differently about the same genetics knowledge, simply propagating IDWs from one lesson to another is not successful.

5.2 Predicting Lesson 2 IDWs

In this section we evaluate three methods for predicting Lesson 2 IDWs from student performance with three activities that precede Lesson 2: reading instructional text, a pretest, and tutor Lesson 1. We employ the FIDW-22 model with best-fitting lesson-specific IDWs as our gold standard for evaluating model fits with predicted IDWs. Table 4 displays the overall goodness of fit of these three models. (The first two rows display the fit of the standard non-individualized SBKT model, and best fitting BKT model with lesson-specific IDWS, FIDW-22, for comparison.)

Table 4. Goodness of fit of 5 models for lesson 2 tutor data: The standard BKT model, 4 BKT models with lesson-specific IDWs.

Model	RMSE	Accuracy
Lesson 2 SBKT	0.413	0.749
Lesson 2 FIDW-22	0.385	0.784
Lesson 2 PIDW-RP	0.399	0.764
Lesson 2 PIDW-RPW	0.397	0.769
Lesson 2 PIDW-RPWF	0.396	0.769

5.2.1 Predicting Lesson 2 IDWs with Reading and Pretest Variables

We first employed the six reading measures and six pretest measures derived previously [14] to predict Lesson-2 specific IDWs, as described in Section 4.1. The overall goodness of fit for this model PIDW-RP is displayed in row 3 of Table 4. This model with predicted Lesson 2 IDWs is 50% as successful as the best-fitting FIDW-22 model in reducing RMSE: The new model reduces RMSE by 3.4% compared to the non-individualized SBKT model, 0.399 vs. 0.413, vs. a 6.8% improvement for the best-fitting FIDW-22 model). The FIDW model is also about 2.0% more accurate than the SBKT model, 0.764 vs. 0.749, (vs. a 4.7% improvement for the best-fitting FIDW-22 model).

Table 5. Differences in practice needed to reach mastery.

Model	# Stus. needing less	# Fewer Opps. Needed	# Stus. needing more	# More Opps. Needed
FIDW-22	49	16.69	33	12.21
PIDW-RP	57 (40)	4.73	22 (14)	7.21
PIDW-RPW	54 (38)	4.35	23 (15)	8.28
PIDW-RPWF	56 (40)	4.65	29 (16)	8.96

As discussed earlier, small differences in model fits can have large effects on the amount of recommended work assigned to the student [22]. To compare the practical impact of the best-fitting FIDW-22 model and the three predicted IDWs, we calculated the number of practice opportunities that were necessary for students to reach mastery under each of the models - that is, the number of opportunities required for pL (the probability the student has learned a rule) to reach 0.95. While students completed a fixed curriculum in this lesson, this analysis is possible because most students reached mastery for most of the KCS in the available number of opportunities under all three models. Across all students and skills, students mastered 75% of the skills under the SBKT model, 77% under the FIDW model, and 77% under the PIDW-RP model. If a student did not reach mastery on a KC under one model, we conservatively estimated that the student would reach mastery on the next opportunity. This means that the number of *More Opps* is a lower bound and interpreted as the minimum number of opportunities the model would recommend.

The practice recommendations are displayed in Table 5. The second column displays how many students would need less practice under the individualized model than under the non-individualized SBKT model. The third column displays how many fewer practice opportunities these students would need on average. The fourth column displays how many students would need more practice under the individualized model than under the non-individualized SBKT model. The fifth column displays how many more opportunities would be needed on average.

Both the best-fitting FIDW-22 model in row 2 and the predicted PIDW-RP model in row 3 substantially modify the amount of practice students need to reach mastery compared to the SBKT model. Under the best-fitting FIDW model, 49 students needed less practice to master all the KCs than under the non-individualized SBKT model and on average these students re-

quired 16.69 fewer practice opportunities to reach mastery under FIDW than under SBKT. Under the predicted PIDW-RP model, 57 students needed an average of 4.73 fewer opportunities to master all the KCS than under the SBKT model. The two individualized model agree on a set of 40 students who need fewer practice opportunities to reach mastery, but again the FIDW model requires less practice (16.69 opportunities) of these students than the PIDW-RP model (4.73 opportunities).

Under the best-fitting FIDW model, 33 students needed more practice to master all the KCs than under the non-individualized SBKT model and on average these students required 12.21 fewer practice opportunities to reach mastery under FIDW than under SBKT. Under the predicted PIDW-RP model, 22 students needed an average of 7.21 fewer opportunities to master all the KCS than under the SBKT model. The two individualized model agree on a set of 14 students who need fewer practice opportunities to reach mastery, but again the FIDW model requires less practice (18.38 opportunities) of these students than the PIDW-RP model (7.58 opportunities).

Overall, the FIDW and PIDW-RP models were in 65% agreement on which students needed fewer or more opportunities to master all the KCs than under the SBKT model, but the new predicted PIDW-RP model is not realizing all the learning efficiency gains identified by the best-fitting FIDW model.

5.2.1.1 Models with Reading and Pretest Variables.

Table 6 displays the coefficients for each of the 12 predictors in the regression models for each of the four Lesson 2 IDWs. The predictors that enter reliably into the robust regression models are highlighted with asterisks.

Both reading time variables and pretest variables continue to be reliable predictors of individual difference weights in gene interaction tutor lesson 2, even after students have completed an intervening tutor lesson. All four reading time factors each reliably predicted at least one of the four individual differences weights. Both variables that measure the extent to which students revisit text pages also marginally predict wG.

Not surprisingly, pretest accuracy variables reliably entered into the four IDW models. Differences in student accuracy on general knowledge (PACC1) and on process-modeling (PACC2) each reliably predict three of the four IDWs. Surprisingly, student accuracy on abductive reasoning questions (PACC3), the type of reasoning employed in this second tutor lesson did not reliably predict any lesson 2 IDWs. Pretest reasoning about process modeling is a better predictor of students acquiring abductive reasoning skills than a pretest measure of abductive reasoning. Finally, the number of answer changes students made and total time did not reliably predict any of the four IDWs.

5.2.2 Predicting Lesson 2 IDWs from Student Reading, Pretests and Lesson 1 IDWs

While the best-fitting Lesson 1 IDWs fit the Lesson 2 data poorly, our next predictive model includes them along with the 12 reading and pretest variables. The overall goodness of fit for this model PIDW-RPW is displayed in row 4 of Table 4. This PIDW-RPW model improves upon the predictive accuracy of the earlier PIDW-RP model. The PIDW-RPW model is 57% as successful as the best-fitting FIDW-22 model both in reducing RMSE (vs. 50% for the earlier PIDW-RP model) and in increasing Accuracy (vs. 43% for the earlier PIDW-RP model). The new model reduces RMSE by 3.9% compared to the non-individualized SBKT model, (0.397 vs. 0.413) and increases accuracy by 2.7% compared to the SBKT model (0.769 vs. 0.749).

The practice recommendations for this PIDW-RPW model are displayed in row 3 of Table 5. Like the earlier individualized BKT fits, this fit substantially modifies the amount of practice students need to reach mastery compared to the SBKT model. While this new PIDW-RPW predictive model fits the tutor data better than the earlier PIDW-RP model, the practice recommendations of the two predictive models are very similar. Overall, the best-fitting FIDW and PIDW-RPW models were in 64% agreement on which students needed fewer or more opportunities to master all the KCs than under the non-individualized SBKT model, but the new predicted PIDW-RP model is not realizing all the learning efficiency gains identified by the best-fitting FIDW model.

Table 6. Coefficient Summary Table (*<0.10, **<0.05, ***<0.01)

	wL0	wT	wG	wS
(Intercept)	0.501***	0.559***	0.511***	0.509***
RTF1	-0.027	-0.047	-0.013	0.037***
RTF2	-0.016	0.076**	-0.005	-0.048***
RTF3	-0.052**	-0.025	0.023	-0.017
RTF4	0.04*	-0.017	0.03	-0.013
RRTD	-0.021	0.072	-0.105*	-0.025
RRNP	0.032	-0.088	0.115*	0.039
PACC1	0.06**	0.012	0.074**	-0.054***
PACC2	0.093***	0.084**	0.051	-0.046***
PACC3	0.017	-0.015	-0.002	0.005
PCCI	-0.001	-0.039	-0.046	0.006
PCIC	-0.032	0.022	-0.005	0.003
Ptime	-0.012	0.001	-0.008	0.021
RMSE	0.186	0.217	0.233	0.109

5.2.2.1 The Predictive Models with Reading and Pretest Variables and Lesson 1 IDWs.

Table 7 displays the coefficients for each of the 16 predictors in the regression models for each of the four Lesson 2 IDWs. As described in Section 4.1, Lasso was used to identify the best 12 predictors for each of the four IDWs. The predictors that enter reliably into the four robust regression models are highlighted with asterisks. All four Lesson 1 IDWs enter into at least two of the models. Each of the two learning weights, L1wL0, and L1wT reliably predicts the corresponding weight in Lesson 2, but the two Lesson 1 performance weights do not reliably predict the performance weights in Lesson 2. The pattern of reading predictor variables that reliably predict each of the four weights is very similar between the first and second predictive models. But with the inclusion of the Lesson 1 IDWs, the first two pretest variables no longer enter reliably into the predictive models for the two learning weights, wL0, and wT, nor into the guessing weight, wG, although they continue to predict the slip weight, wG, reliably. Thus, overall, information on individual differences in students' Lesson 1 learning and performance largely replaces pretest assessments of student knowledge in predicting Lesson 2 IDWs.

5.2.3 Predicting Lesson 2 IDWs from Reading, Pretests, Lesson 1 IDWs, and performance features

Our final model examines whether predictive model accuracy is further improved by including the six features of student performance in Lesson 1, along with the reading and pretest features and Lesson 1 IDWs. The overall goodness of fit for this model PIDW-

RPWF is displayed in row 5 of Table 4. This PIDW-RPWF does not markedly improve the overall goodness of fit, compared to the prior PIDW-RPW model. This PIDW-RPWF is 60% as successful as the best-fitting FIDW-22 model in reducing RMSE (vs. 57% for the earlier PIDW-RP model) and 57% as successful in increasing Accuracy (vs. 57% for the earlier PIDW-RP model). The new model reduces RMSE by 4.1% compared to the SBKT model, (0.396 vs. 0.413) and increases accuracy by 2.7% compared to the SBKT model (0.769 vs. 0.749).

Table 7. Coefficient Summary Table (*< 0.10, ** < 0.05, ***<0.01)

	wL0	wT	wG	wS
(Intercept)	0.497***	0.558***	0.51***	0.509***
RTF1	-0.035*	-0.036		0.021
RTF2	-0.02	0.052*		-0.043***
RTF3	-0.049**		0.009	
RTF4	0.029		0.021	
RRTD		0.075	-0.1*	
RRNP	0.011	-0.088	0.092*	0.019
PACC1		0.008	0.045	-0.038**
PACC2	0.029	0.041	0.036	-0.048**
PACC3	0.002	-0.025	-0.024	0.022
PCCI	-0.007	-0.023	-0.04	0
PCIC	-0.022			0
Ptime		-0.021		0.024*
L1wL0	0.075***		0.021	
L1wT		0.074**	0.083**	-0.035**
L1wG	0.012	0.08**	0.013	0.021
L1wS	-0.106***	0.014	-0.005	0.028
RMSE	0.153	0.205	0.222	0.100

The practice recommendations for this PIDW-RPWF model are displayed in row 4 of Table 5. Like the earlier individualized BKT fits, this model again substantially modifies the amount of practice students need to reach mastery compared to the SBKT but, again, the practice recommendations for the FIDW-RPWF model are similar to the two prior predictive models. Overall, the FIDW and PIDW-RP models were in 67% agreement on which students needed fewer or more opportunities to master all the KCs than under the SBKT model, but the new predicted PIDW-RP model is not realizing all the learning efficiency gains identified by the best-fitting FIDW model.

5.2.3.1 The Models with Reading, Pretest Variables, and Lesson 1 IDWs and performance features.

Table 8 displays the coefficients for each of the 22 predictors in the regression models for each of the four Lesson 2 IDWs. As described in Section 4.1, Lasso was used to identify the best 12 predictors for each of the four IDWs. The predictors that enter reliably into the four robust regression models are highlighted with asterisks. As can be seen, among the 22 predictors, only help avoidance did not enter into any of the four predictive IDW models, although another 8 predictors were not even marginally significant in any of the four models. With the introduction of both four lesson 1 IDW weights and 6 lesson 1 performance features as predictive variables, five of the six reading time variables still reliably predict at least one of the four lesson 2 IDWs. However, only two of the six pretest variables enter even marginally into predicting a single lesson 2 IDW. Each of the lesson 1 IDWs reliably predicts a single lesson 2 IDW, but lesson 1 L1wT no longer reliably predicts three of the four lesson 2 IDWs. Among the six Lesson 1 performance variables, raw error rate and mean response time did not enter reliably into any of the four IDW models. Long pauses after bugs (and help avoidance) also did not reliably enter into any of the models. Each of the hint response-related variables entered at least marginally into predicting two of the four lesson 2 IDWs, so student responses to hints in lesson 1 provide information about individual differences in lesson 2 learning and performance over and above measures of student reading and pretest performance and students' lesson 1 IDWs.

Table 8. Coefficient Summary Table (* < 0.10, ** < 0.05, **<0.01)

	wL0	wT	wG	wS
(Intercept)	0.496***	0.564***	0.509***	0.508***
RTF1	-0.026	-0.031	0.018	0.015
RTF2	-0.022	0.034		-0.035**
RTF3	-0.042**		0.017	
RTF4	0.032*		0.018	
RRTD			-0.117**	
RRNP		-0.022	0.11**	
PACC1			0.03	-0.033*
PACC2	0.024	0.024	0.027	-0.041**
PACC3		-0.046		
PCCI			-0.047	
PCIC	-0.023			
Ptime				0.019
L1wL0	0.064**		-0.004	
L1wT		0.035	0.088**	-0.028
L1wG	0.011	0.069**		0.023
L1wS	-0.07**			0.022
TErr	-0.042	-0.059	-0.011	0.005
TTime		-0.04		0.01
HELPA				
BugLP	-0.018	0.015		
HNLP		0.056*	-0.077**	0.005
HNLPC	-0.033*	-0.058**		0.006
RMSE	0.146	0.198	0.214	0.101

6. CONCLUSIONS
We have examined four methods of incorporating individual student differences into a traditional Bayesian Knowledge Tracing model in an intelligent tutor lesson based on student performance in earlier on-line activities. The simplest method, of directly employing best-fitting individual difference weights (IDWs) from the preceding tutor lesson on a closely related topic, was unsuccessful. The fit of this individualized model was no better overall than the standard non-individualized BKT model.

The other three methods employed measures of student performance in reading instructional text, taking a pretest, and completing the prior tutor lesson to predict individual difference weights in the following lesson. We found that the predictive model, which only employs measures of students' performance in reading an instructional text and in taking a pretest, was quite successful. The goodness of fit of this predictive model falls midway between the non-individualized standard BKT model and the model with actual best fitting IDWs. The individualized practice recommendations for this predictive model are similar to the practice recommendations for the model with best fitting IDWs, , although this predictive model does not identify all the opportunities to decrease the amount of practice for some students, nor the need to increase the amount practice for other students, that are identified in the best-fitting model. A second predictive model which incorporates these reading and pretest variables along with the four individual weights from the prior lesson appreciably improves the goodness of fit. However, a third predictive model which includes all of these predictor variables and another six measures of student performance in the prior tutor lesson did not appreciably improve the goodness of fit of the second predictive model.

An important conclusion of this study is that student performance in reading on-line instructional text is a useful predictor of learning and performance in an intelligent tutor. In the second model, five of six reading variables entered at least marginally into the prediction of at least one IDW, even though students had completed an intervening tutor lesson and the students' IDWs from the prior lesson were incorporated into the predictive models. Not surprisingly, in the first model, several conceptual pretest variables also reliably predicted individual differences in learning and performance in the second lesson. However, when IDWs from the first lesson are incorporated into the second model, pretest measures become much less important in predicting IDWs. A final intriguing conclusion is that in the third model, students' responses to hint messages in the first lesson were a reliable predictor of individual differences in learning and performance in the second lesson.

Predicting individual student differences in a tutor lesson from prior activities is important since incorporating individual differences into a lesson is easier if they can be assigned before students starting working with the tutor. We anticipate that the quality of predicted individual differences will further increase with additional research. And, while the lesson 1 IDWs and performance features are specific to an ITS environment, we believe that reading data, as well as pretest data, could be used to predict individual difference parameters in other types of learning environments.

7. ACKNOWLEDGMENTS
This research was supported by the National Science Foundation via the grant "Knowing What Students Know: Using Education Data Mining to Predict Robust STEM Learning", award number DRL1420609.

8. REFERENCES
1. Corbett, A.T., Anderson, J.R.: Knowledge tracing: Modeling the acquisition of procedural knowledge. User modeling and user-adapted interaction, 4, 253-278. (1995)
2. Mayo, M., Mitrovic, A. Optimising ITS behaviour with Bayesian networks and decision theory. International Journal of Artificial Intelligence in Education, 12, 124-153 (2001).

3. Shute, V.: Smart: Student Modeling Approach for Responsive Tutoring. User Modeling and User Adapted Interaction, 5 (1), 1-44. (1995)

4. Ganeshan, R., Johnson, L., Shaw, E., Wood, B.: Tutoring diagnostic problem solving. In G. Gauthier, C. Frasson, K. VanLehn (eds.) ITS2000 Intelligent Tutoring Systems, LNCS vol. 1839, pp. 33-42. Springer, Heidelberg. (2000)

5. Conati, C., Gertner, A., VanLehn, K. Using Bayesian networks to manage uncertainty in student modeling. User Modeling and User-Adapted Interaction, 12, 371-417. (2002)

6. Corbett, A.T., MacLaren, B., Kauffman, L., Wagner, A., Jones, E. A.: Cognitive Tutor for Genetics Problem Solving: Learning Gains and Student Modeling. Journal of Educational Computing Research, 42 (2), 219-239. (2010)

7. Gong, Y., Beck, J., Heffernan, N.: Comparing knowledge tracing and performance factor analysis by using multiple model fitting. In V. Aleven, J. Kay, J. Mostow (eds.) ITS2010 Intelligent Tutoring Systems. LNCS vol. 6094, pp. 35-44. Springer, Heidelberg. (2010)

8. Lee, J., Brunskill, E.: The impact of individualizing student models on necessary practice opportunities. In: Yacef, K., Zaiane, O., Hershkovitz, A., Yudelson, M., Stamper, J. (eds.) EDM2012 Proceedings of the 5th International Conference on International Educational Data Mining Society, 118-125. (2012)

9. Pardos, Z. Heffernan, N.: Modeling individualization in a Bayesian networks implementation of Knowledge Tracing. In De Bra, P., Kobsa, A., Chin, D. (eds.) UMAP2010 Proceedings of the 18th International Conference on User Modeling, Adaptation, and Personalization, LNCS vol. 6075, pp. 255-266. Springer, Heidelberg (2010)

10. Yudelson, M., Koedinger, K., Gordon, G.: Individualized Bayesian knowledge tracing models. In: Lane, C., Yacef, K., Mostow, J., Pavlik, P. (eds.) AIED2013 Artificial Intelligence in Education, LNCS vol. 7926, pp. 171-180, Springer, Heidelberg. (2013)

11. Pirolli, P., Wilson, M: A theory of the measurement of knowledge content, access, and learning. Psychological Review, 105(1), 58-82. (1998)

12. Cen, H., Koedinger, K., Junker, B.: Comparing two IRT models for conjunctive skills. In B. Woolf, E. Atmour, R. Nkambou, S. Lajoie (eds.) ITS2008 Intelligent Tutoring Systems LNCS vol. 5091, pp. 796-798. Springer, Heidelberg. (2008)

13. Pavlik, P., Yudelson, M., Koedinger, K.: Using contextual factors analysis to explain transfer of least common multiple skills. In G. Biswas, S. Bull, J. Kay, A. Mitrovic (eds.) AIED2011 Artificial Intelligence in Education, LNCS vol. 6738, pp. 256-263. Springer, Heidelberg. (2011)

14. Eagle, M., Corbett, A., Stamper, J., McLaren, B.M., Wagner, A., MacLaren, B., Mitchell, A.: Estimating individual differences for student modeling in intelligent tutors from reading and pretest data. ITS2016 Intelligent Tutoring Systems. (in press)

15. Harvey, L., Anderson, J.: Transfer of declarative knowledge in complex information processing domains. Human-Computer Interaction, 11 (1), 69-96. (1996)

16. Zwann, R., Singer, M.: Text comprehension. In A. Graesser, M. Gernsbacher, S. Goldman (eds.) Handbook of discourse processes, pp. 83-121. Mahwah, NJ: Erlbaum. (2003)

17. Arroyo, I., Beck, J., Woolf, B., Beal, C., Schultz, K.: Macroadapting Animalwatch to gender and cognitive differences with respect to hint interactivity and symbolism. In G. Gauthier, C. Frasson, K. VanLehn (eds.) ITS2000 Intelligent Tutoring Systems, LNCS vol. 1839, pp. 574-583. Springer, Heidelberg. (2000)

18. Bransford, J. D., & Schwartz, D. (1999). Rethinking transfer: A simple proposal with multiple implications. In A. Iran-Nejad & P. D. Pearson (Eds.), Review of Research in Education (Vol. 24). Washington, DC: American Educational Research Association.

19. Baker, R.S.J.d., Corbett, A.T., Gowda, S.M. (2013). Generalizing automated detection of the robustness of student learning in an intelligent tutor for genetics. Journal of Educational Psychology. 105, 946-956.

20. Koedinger, K.R., Corbett, A.T. and Perfetti, C. (2012). The Knowledge-Learning-Instruction (KLI) Framework: Bridging the Science-Practice Chasm to Enhance Robust Student Learning. Cognitive Science, 36, 757-798.

21. Baker, R.S.J.d., Gowda, S.M., Corbett, A.T., Ocumpaugh, J.: Towards automatically detecting whether student learning is shallow. In S. Cerri, W. Clancey, G. Papadourakis, K. Panourgia (eds.) ITS2012 Intelligent Tutoring Systems LNCS vol. 7315, pp. 444-453. Springer, Heidelberg. (2012)

22. Koedinger, K., Stamper, J., McLaughlin, E., Nixon,T.: Using data-driven discovery of better student models to improve student learning. In: Lane, C., Yacef, K., Mostow, J., Pavlik, P. (eds.) AIED2013 Artificial Intelligence in Education, LNCS vol. 7926, pp. 421-430, Springer, Heidelberg. (2013)

23. Baker, R., Corbett, A., Aleven, V.: More Accurate Student Modeling Through Contextual Estimation of Slip and Guess Probabilities in Bayesian Knowledge Tracing. In B. Woolf, E. Aimeur, R. Nkambou, S. Lajoie (eds.) ITS2008 Intelligent Tutoring Systems. LNCS vol. 5091, pp. 406-415. Springer, Heidelberg. (2008)

24. Efron, B., Hastie, T., Johnstone, I., & Tibshirani, R. Least angle regression. The Annals of statistics, 32(2), 407-499. (2004).

25. Andersen, Robert. Modern methods for robust regression. Sage, 2008.

26. Ihaka, Ross, and Robert Gentleman. "R: a language for data analysis and graphics." Journal of computational and graphical statistics 5.3, 299-314. (1996)

27. Nash, John C., and Ravi Varadhan. "Unifying optimization algorithms to aid software system users: optimx for R." Journal of Statistical Software 43.9, 1-14. (2011)

28. Venables, W. N., Ripley, B.D., Modern Applied Statistics with S. Forth Edition. Springer, New York. (2013)

Gender Differences in Facial Expressions of Affect During Learning

Alexandria K. Vail
Department of Computer
Science
North Carolina State University
Raleigh, North Carolina
akvail@ncsu.edu

Joseph F. Grafsgaard
Department of Psychology
North Carolina State University
Raleigh, North Carolina
jfgrafsg@ncsu.edu

Kristy Elizabeth Boyer
Department of Computer &
Information Science &
Engineering
University of Florida
Gainesville, Florida
keboyer@ufl.edu

Eric N. Wiebe
Department of STEM
Education
North Carolina State University
Raleigh, North Carolina
wiebe@ncsu.edu

James C. Lester
Department of Computer
Science
North Carolina State University
Raleigh, North Carolina
lester@ncsu.edu

ABSTRACT

Affective support is crucial during learning, with recent evidence suggesting it is particularly important for female students. Facial expression is a rich channel for affect detection, but a key open question is how facial displays of affect differ by gender during learning. This paper presents an analysis suggesting that facial expressions for women and men differ systematically during learning. Using facial video automatically tagged with facial action units, we find that despite no differences between genders in incoming knowledge, self-efficacy, or personality profile, women displayed one lower facial action unit significantly more than men, while men displayed brow lowering and lip fidgeting more than women. However, numerous facial actions including brow raising and nose wrinkling were strongly correlated with learning in women, whereas only one facial action unit, eyelid raiser, was associated with learning for men. These results suggest that the entire affect adaptation pipeline, from detection to response, may benefit from gender-specific models in order to support students more effectively.

Keywords

Affect, facial expression, gender effects, learning, intelligent tutoring systems.

1. INTRODUCTION

Modeling and adapting to users during learning has long been a central goal of the user modeling community [15, 38,

UMAP '16, July 13-17, 2016, Halifax, NS, Canada

© 2016 ACM. ISBN 978-1-4503-4370-1/16/07. . . $15.00

DOI: http://dx.doi.org/10.1145/2930238.2930257

42]. These models of users frequently focus on cognitive aspects of learning, by modeling domain knowledge with techniques such as constraint-based modeling [38], knowledge tracing [15], and strategy learning for tutoring [9, 27].

Building on a rich history of modeling the cognitive aspects of learning, there is increasing awareness that the affective aspects of learning are perhaps equally important (e.g., [12, 39]). For example, adapting to students' uncertainty [9] and confusion [14] have been shown to significantly improve the effectiveness of tutoring. Recent years have thus seen increasing attention to assessing students' affective states while interacting with learning environments, including through self-reports [43] and through affect detectors that utilize log data [10].

Of all of these mechanisms for sensing or detecting affect, facial expressions are among the most useful channels because of their rich expressiveness and relative ease of automatic collection and analysis [13, 7]. Facial expressions have long been studied in psychology, where the findings have established the importance of the face in expressing emotion [20]. In contrast to the "basic emotions" that have been identified as central in everyday life—such as anger, fear, and happiness—there is growing consensus that, during learning, a subset of these emotions, along with learning-centric emotions such as boredom and confusion are highly prominent and influential [17, 4]. Empirical results have found that important facial expression differences emerge between students who find a learning experience frustrating versus those who find it engaging [25], and preliminary findings point to different patterns of facial expression depending on learners' age [24].

Complementing research on affect in learning, a host of studies have established that females and males express emotion differently on the face, and also exhibit differing levels of capability to recognize facial expressions of emotion. For example, women respond with more pronounced facial expression when viewing the facial expressions of others [16], and women can more accurately identify multiple emotions from facial expression even in the presence of minimal information to identify an emotion [30]. In light of these results, a central open question emerges for user modeling during learning: *In what ways do females and males differ in their facial expression of emotion during learning?*

This paper investigates that question in the context of one-on-one tutoring for introductory computer programming. These results suggest that women and men display systematically different facial expressions during learning, and that modeling these facial expressions may lead to deeper understanding of affective learning processes.

2. RELATED WORK

2.1 Gender and Facial Expression

Research in psychology, biology, and physiology has long examined facial expressions and uncovered differences based on gender. Women are more facially expressive than men; for example, when viewing another person's facial expression, women show more pronounced facial reactions [16]. Men and women both show differences in emotion expression based on context: for example, while a smile is generally a genuine indicator of positive emotions, it may sometimes be contrived to meet social expectations. Gender plays a role in this difference, particularly when there is a power differential between two conversational partners [33]. In addition to differences in expression, there may also be important differences in emotion recognition between females and males. For example, when asked to identify multiple emotions from the facial expression of another person, women were significantly better at emotion identification than men [30]. Women also seem to be substantially better at decoding verbal cues than men [29]. Given these many differences, there is reason to believe that when it comes to facial expression, women express affect during learning differently than men and that gender differences may be important to consider in models of affect.

2.2 Facial Expression in Learning

Facial expression is one of the foremost channels with which to infer learning-centric emotion [18]. In a longstanding line of work involving Wayang Outpost, a mathematics tutoring system, researchers have categorized facial expression according to the affective state it suggests [44] and have attempted to predict interest and confidence using multimodal features including facial expression [2]. In studies with AutoTutor, a tutoring system with a conversational dialogue agent, students' emotions as evidenced by "emoting aloud" were modeled using facial expressions [11] and affect-adaptive versions of the system have been built that respond to emotions such as boredom, frustration, and confusion [19]. Facial expression as tutoring unfolds has also been shown to predict frustration and engagement that students self-report at the end of the tutoring session [26]. It is clear that analyses of facial expression can provide insight into affective processes that significantly influence learning.

2.3 Gender and Learning From Tutoring

Tutoring, both human-human tutoring and tutoring with intelligent systems, have been shown to be very effective means of support learning [41]. Recent results have suggested that women and men benefit from different approaches to tutoring. When different versions of an intelligent tutoring system for computer science were compared, women

reported significantly more engagement and less frustration with the version that offered affective support than with other versions of the system [40]. In another comparison of different intelligent tutoring systems for mathematics, women benefited from having choice within an intelligent tutoring system while men did not show a significant difference [27]. Previous studies have also demonstrated that embodied agents [1] and motivational scaffolding [3] are particularly beneficial for female students, and that females are more sensitive to the coordination between an agent's verbal and nonverbal behaviors [6]. Because women and men appear to benefit from different tutoring strategies, and because models of affect are highly informative for tutorial strategy choice, it is important for the field to devise affective models for learning that take gender into account.

3. HUMAN-HUMAN TUTORING STUDY

The data examined in the present analysis consists of a set of computer-mediated human-human interactions through a tutorial interface during a set of lessons in introductory computer science [28, 37]. The tutorial interface, displayed below in Figure 1, consists of four panes: the task description, the students source code, the compilation and execution output from the student's program, and the textual dialogue messages exchanged between the tutor and the student. Tutors' interactions with the student were limited to the exchange of textual messages and progressing between tasks. For an example of the dialogue exchanged between the tutor and student, see Table 1.

3.1 Participants

Student users ($N = 67$) were university students in the United States recruited from an introductory engineering course. There were 24 female students and 43 male students, with an average age of 18.5 years ($s = 1.5$ years). Most (58) of the students were college freshmen. Nearly all (59) of the students were majors in an engineering discipline, with 10 from computer science, 6 each from aerospace engineering and electrical and computer engineering, 5 each from mechanical and electrical, and the remaining students from disciplines such as civil, industrial, and nuclear engineering, as well as mathematics or physics. The human tutors ($N = 5$) were primarily graduate students with previous experience in tutoring introductory computer science.

3.2 Learning Outcomes

The students completed a series of six 40-minute lessons over the course of four weeks. The present analysis focuses on data from the first lesson. Immediately prior to and immediately following the completion of each session, students were administered a content-based pretest and an identical posttest. The average raw learning gain for the first lesson was 22.15% ($s = 17.7\%$); for female students the average was 23.65% ($s = 15.13\%$) and for males 21.29% ($s = 19.14\%$). Normalized learning gain was calculated according to Equation 1.

$$norm\_gain = \begin{cases} \dfrac{post - pre}{1 - pre} & post > pre \\ \dfrac{post - pre}{pre} & post \leq pre \end{cases} \quad (1)$$

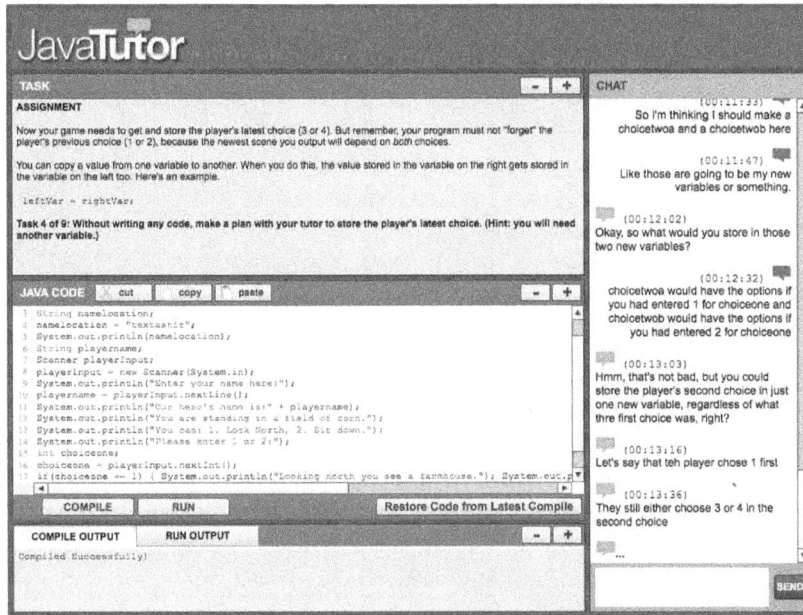

Figure 1: The tutorial interface for introductory Java programming.

3.3 Facial Expression Data Collection

Interaction data was collected through a set of multi-modal sensors, including a Kinect depth camera, an integrated webcam, and a skin conductance bracelet, as seen in Figure 2. Facial expression features were automatically extracted using a state-of-the-art facial expression recognition and analysis software known as FACET (commercial software previously released under the research-focused Computer Emotion Recognition Toolbox, CERT) [35]. This software provides frame-by-frame tracking of nineteen facial action units according to the Facial Action Coding System [34, 21]. These action units include expressions such as AU4 BROW LOWERER, AU15 LIP CORNER DEPRESSOR, AU18 LIP PUCKERER, and AU24 LIP PRESSOR (see Figure 5 for illustration). For each of these nineteen action units, the FACET software provides an *Evidence* measure, suggesting the chance that the target expression is present, as opposed to not present.

4. ANALYSIS AND RESULTS

The objective of the present analysis is to investigate how men and women express affect (particularly through facial expression) differently during learning. In order to identify these differences, we first examine the presence of each facial action unit in the set of female students versus the presence of each expression in the set of male students, and discuss the differences that emerge. We explore the possibility that these differences exist as a result of incoming student characteristics, but find no significant differences across genders. Finally, we examine the hypothesis that learning gain can be predicted differently by different affective features for male and female students.

4.1 Facial Expression Differences by Gender

The statistical comparisons were conducted using standard Student's t-tests. Additionally, a Bonferroni correction $p \leq \alpha/n$ was applied to control the familywise error rate,

where $n = 19$ is the number of statistical tests conducted (one for each facial action unit detected). The FACET Evidence measure for each action unit (see Section 3.3) was averaged across each student's session, giving $n = 67$ ratings per action unit. The results, displayed in Table 2 and illustrated in Figure 4, suggest some key differences.

In particular, female students tended to express AU15 LIP CORNER DEPRESSOR (Figure 3b) more frequently than male students ($t = -3.852$, $p = 0.008$). On the other hand, male students were more likely to express AU4 BROW LOWERER (Figure 3a, $t = +3.296$, $p = 0.015$), AU18 LIP PUCKERER (Figure 3c, $t = +4.374$, $p < 0.001$), and AU24 LIP PRESSOR (Figure 3d, $t = +3.208$, $p = 0.023$).

In order to examine whether these differences across genders may have arisen from other incoming student characteristics, we examined results from the surveys and tests administered the students prior to any interaction with the system. We detail each of these instruments below.

First, we considered the possibility that students with more incoming knowledge in computer science may be more comfortable with the material presented than those with less, and therefore may express affect differently throughout the session. We therefore examined incoming knowledge via pretest score to determine whether females and males in our study had different incoming knowledge. Prior to every lesson, students were given a content pretest on the content covered in the upcoming lesson. There was no significant difference between pretest scores between male and female students ($p > 0.99$).

Next we investigated whether the facial expression differences could have arisen from differences in self-efficacy, or how confident students are in their own ability to complete tasks and reach their goals. The higher a student's self-efficacy, the more she believes that she can succeed academically. Prior to any interaction with the tutoring environment, students completed the eight-item New General Self-

67

TUTOR	hang on :)	
TUTOR	When we show you example code, it is not the code you need to write.	
TUTOR	Look at the task again.	
	Student writes programming code.	
TUTOR	YUP	
TUTOR	Perfect	
TUTOR	OK. Go ahead and test.	
STUDENT	And I don't need anything in the parentheses?	
TUTOR	Line 9 is correct. You do NOT need anything inside the parentheses.	
STUDENT	Ok	
	Student compiles and runs code successfully.	
TUTOR	Good.	
TUTOR	Moving on.	
	Tutor advances to the next task.	
	Student writes programming code.	
TUTOR	Syntactically correct. But there is a logic error	
TUTOR	When will the output statement display your request to the player?	
STUDENT	AFTER they put in their name	
TUTOR	Exactly	

Table 1: Sample dialogue between a tutor and a student occurring in the tutorial corpus.

	Females	Males
AU4 BROW LOWERER	-0.536 ± 0.418	-0.133 ± 0.566
AU15 LIP DEPRESSOR	-0.499 ± 0.296	-0.786 ± 0.281
AU18 LIP PUCKERER	-0.510 ± 0.590	0.136 ± 0.556
AU24 LIP PRESSOR	-0.353 ± 0.358	-0.051 ± 0.386

Table 2: Summary statistics (mean $\pm$ standard deviation) for significantly different facial expressions across gender.

Efficacy scale [8]. There was no significant difference in self-efficacy scores between male and female students ($p > 0.56$)

Finally, we considered the possibility that personality traits may be influential in facial expression. We measured personality with the Big Five Factor model of personality, one of the standard frameworks for identifying personality traits [22]. Prior to any interaction with the system, students completed the 44-item Big Five Factor Inventory survey, which included items to identify Openness, Conscientiousness, Extraversion, Agreeableness, and Neuroticism. We hypothesized that two of these factors may have had an impact on affective expression: Extraversion and Neuroticism. Extraversion is defined as the part of the Big Five Factors that identifies gregariousness, activity, positive emotions, and warmth, whereas Neuroticism is defined as the part that identifies anxiety, impulsiveness, and negative emotions [31]. However, there was no significant difference in either Extraversion or Neuroticism scores between male and female students ($p > 0.91$).

4.2 Predicting Learning from Facial Expression

The comparative analyses described above provide evidence that men and women's facial expressions differ significantly during learning, even when incoming knowledge,

self-efficacy levels, and personality do not significantly differ across genders. Next, we examine the question of whether different facial action units are predictive of learning gains in male and female students. In order to answer this question, we built two predictive models for learning gain: one for female students and one for male students. Each feature described in Section 3.3 was standardized by subtracting the mean and dividing by the standard deviation. All of these features were then provided to a stepwise regression modeling procedure that optimizes the leave-one-student-out cross-validated R^2 value (that is, the coefficient of determination) while at the same time applying a strict $p < 0.05$ cut-off value for significance. The models are presented in Tables 3 and 4.

Table 3: Predictive model for standardized normalized learning gain in female students.

Normalized Learning Gain =	R^2	p
+0.6508 * AU2 OUTER BROW RAISER	0.2209	0.009
+1.2120 * AU9 NOSE WRINKLER	0.1109	0.003
+1.7156 * AU12 LIP CORNER PULLER	0.1591	0.006
−0.7100 * AU20 LIP STRETCHER	0.0908	0.005
−0.9414 (Intercept)		1.000
Leave-One-Out Cross-Validated R^2 = 0.5817		

Four facial expressions are significantly predictive of learning gain in female students, three of which are positively predictive (Table 3). The more present that AU2 OUTER BROW RAISER (Figure 5a) is during the session, the more likely that the student will achieve a high learning gain at the end of the session. Similarly, the more that AU9 NOSE WRINKLER (Figure 5c) and AU12 LIP CORNER PULLER (Figure 5d) are present, the more the student tends to learn. Finally, the

Figure 2: Multimodal instrumented tutoring session, including a Kinect depth camera to detect posture and gesture, a webcam to detect facial expression changes, and a skin conductance bracelet to detect electrodermal activity.

more present AU20 LIP STRETCHER (Figure 5e) during the session, the *less* likely that the student will achieve a high learning gain.

Table 4: Predictive model for standardized normalized learning gain in male students.

Normalized Learning Gain =	R^2	p
−0.6628 * AU5 UPPER LID RAISER	0.1199	0.010
+0.1747 (Intercept)		1.000
Leave-One-Out Cross-Validated $R^2 = 0.1199$		

Only a single facial action unit was found to be significantly predictive of learning gain in male students (Table 4). The more present AU5 UPPER LID RAISER (Figure 5b) during the session, the more likely the student is to achieve a high learning gain at the end of the session.

4.3 Contrast Between Predictive Models of Learning

A widely known limitation of the type of stepwise regression procedure utilized here is that there can be some variation in the features selected depending on factors such as the order of addition of the predictors. In order to investigate the extent to which the two predictive models of learning differ in meaningful ways (rather than in subtle feature selection outcomes) we tested the predictive power of the female model on the data from male students, and vice versa. First, we created a comparison model for male students by providing it only the features that were significant in the female model. We then trained this comparison model on the male data. In leave-one-student-out cross-validation, the model showed no predictive power, with an R^2 of −0.29. Similarly, when a model was trained on female data but forced to use

the predictor that had performed best on male data, the R^2 was −0.04. In both comparison models, none of the facial action unit features for the other gender was significantly correlated with the learning outcome: no p-value for any feature was lower than 0.62 (p-values greater than 0.05 are not significant in the regression model).

5. DISCUSSION

A large body of evidence suggests that emotional experience, nonverbal displays of affect, and societal norms differ significantly across genders [5]. The present study has demonstrated differences in facial expression of female and male students during tutoring, as well as differing facial expression predictors of learning across genders. These results have important implications in how learning environments may adapt and personalize to students of each gender. We discuss each result and suggest specific directions for follow-up analyses.

These results reveal particular differences in lower face fidgeting of female and male students. The female students exhibited facial movements of the corners of the lips that may have been associated with moments of negative affect or uncertainty. Male students, on the other hand, exhibited more facial actions involving the lips themselves—specifically lip puckering and lip pressing. These facial movements may also have co-occurred during moments of mental effort or negative affect. Interestingly, while research on basic emotions would indicate these movements indicate negative affect [21], there is very little empirical evidence regarding these lip movements in learning contexts. Therefore, a cautious interpretation is that these results provide differential evidence of how female and male students express moments of mental effort or uncertainty during learning.

An additional facial action unit, brow lowering, was displayed more frequently by male students. This facial move-

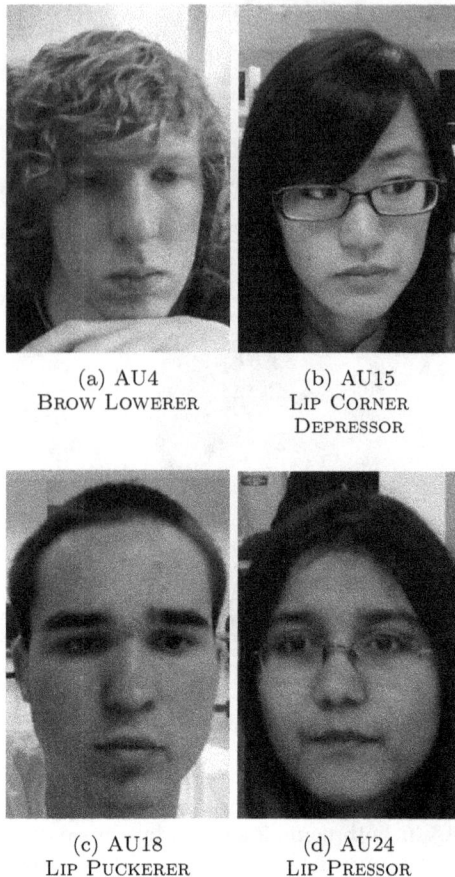

(a) AU4
BROW LOWERER

(b) AU15
LIP CORNER
DEPRESSOR

(c) AU18
LIP PUCKERER

(d) AU24
LIP PRESSOR

Figure 3: Sample frames from the student webcam illustrating the facial action unit features appearing significantly differently in male and female students, as identified by FACET.

ment has been acknowledged as a key indicator of mental effort or confusion in learning contexts [17, 36, 23]. This result provides evidence that male students displayed this facial movement more frequently, though it is unclear whether this corresponds to greater affective experience of confusion.

The predictive model of normalized learning gain for female students provides both positive and negative indicators of learning. Two of the positive predictors, outer brow raising (AU2) and nose wrinkling (AU9), have typically been interpreted as indicating negative facial expressions. However, as noted above, these facial movements may have distinctly different meanings in the context of learning. As a component of empirically identified anxiety, outer brow raising may occur when students are feeling overwhelmed. However, the student's subsequent progress on the learning task determines learning outcomes. Similarly, nose wrinkling moves the eyebrows in a similar way to brow lowering and has been associated with negative affect, such as anger. Again, in the context of learning, this is more likely an indicator of mental effort at salient moments of tutoring. Thus, facial movements that may naively be interpreted as negative affect are identified here as positive predictors of learning.

The remaining predictors in the model of learning for female students provide a more straightforward contrast. Both are highly social displays of emotion, with smiling

(AU12) associated with enjoyment [21] and lip stretching (AU20) identified as a component of embarrassment [32]. The evidence shows that these facial movements follow the presumed directions: smiling is predictive of higher learning gain and the component of embarrassment, lip stretching, is predictive of lower learning gain. That these socially oriented facial expressions are predictive of female students' learning seems to be consistent with the notion that females more openly and richly express emotion.

Male students, on the other hand, had a single predictor, eyelid opening (AU5), associated with lower learning gain. There are several competing interpretations for this predictor: 1) that male students opened eyes wide while being overwhelmed with the learning task, resulting in lower learning gains; 2) that widened eyes corresponded to a greater amount of reading, but this was in turn associated with extraneous cognitive processing that resulted in less efficient learning; or 3) that eye widening was performed in an attempt to stave off boredom, which has been found to be a negative affective state coinciding with lower learning gain. These competing interpretations offer the possibility of follow-up studies to determine the specific ways in which facial expressions co-occur with impactful moments during tutoring.

Notably, the predictive models of learning included facial movements that were entirely separate from the comparisons of facial expression frequency across the genders. Female students were found to more frequently display lip corner fidgeting, while male students puckered and pressed their lips more frequently. Additionally, male students lowered their brows more frequently, which has been noted as a prominent indicator of mental effort in past research. As these facial action units were not predictive of learning for each gender, they appear to indicate more subtle nuances of facial expression across female and male students. It is unclear whether societal gender roles would produce these differences, but automated facial expression recognition provides a tool to explore how these occur within the context of learning. These results have highlighted gender differences in facial expression that are both predictive of learning and show how nonverbal behavior associated with internal states relevant to learning (e.g., mental effort) may be expressed differently across genders.

6. CONCLUSION

Modeling users' affect during learning is one of the central challenges for user-adapted systems. Of all the channels through which affect can be detected, facial expression offers one of the richest. However, there is significant evidence that the expression of emotions through facial expression differs substantially across genders, with women typically expressing in a somewhat more pronounced way. However, the ways in which facial expressions during learning differ between genders is an open question.

We have presented an analysis of a data set of one-on-one computer-mediated human tutoring in which we collected students' facial expressions, automatically tagged them with facial expression analysis software, and compared the occurrence of all facial action units across genders. We found significant differences, with females displaying one lower face movement around the mouth more frequently than men, while men displayed more brow lowering and different lower face movements. These findings suggest that women and

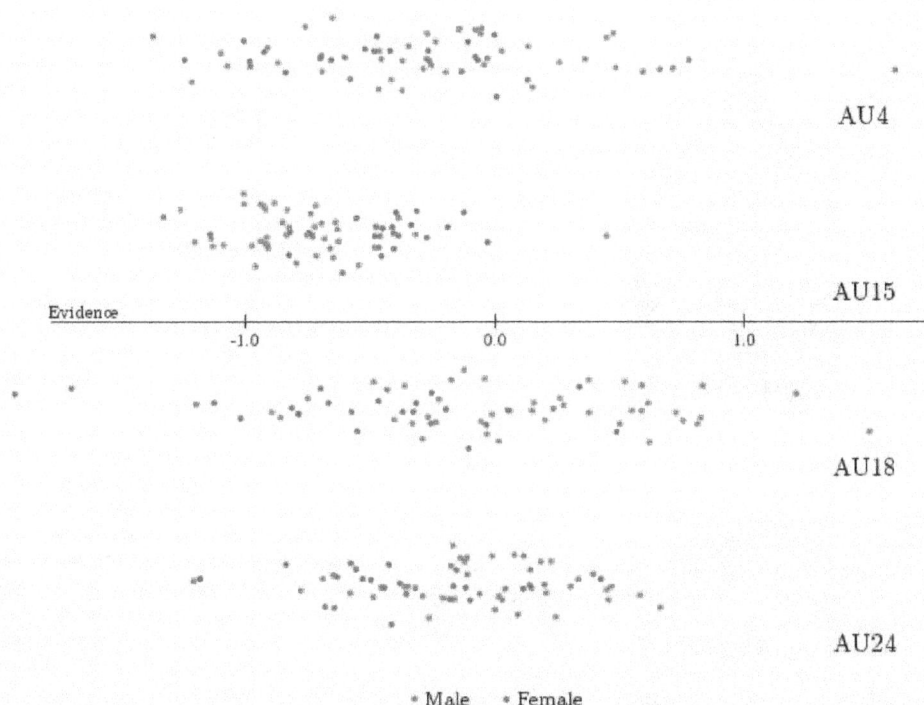

Figure 4: Distribution of average Evidence measure of each of the facial expressions found to be expressed differently between male and female students

men express moments of mental effort or uncertainty differently during tutoring. We also found that indicators of effort and components of embarrassment were predictive of women's learning outcomes, while eyelid opening negatively predicted men's learning outcomes. We suggest three potential explanations as to why this finding would have emerged, which in future work should be explored to elucidate the causes.

These results point to several important directions for future work. First, it is important to gain a deeper understanding of the affective processes that underlie the observations reported here. Triangulating different modalities in order to understand how the facial expressions displayed by learners co-occur with physiological indicators of emotion will shed light on the affective processes themselves. Second, it is important to investigate adaptive strategies that respond to detected affective states, via either facial expression or other channels. It is hoped that this line of investigation will lead to a more complete understanding of learning-centered affective processes, reveal how they differ across genders, and lead to gender-sensitive user-adaptive learning support.

Acknowledgments

The authors wish to thank the members of the LearnDialogue and Intellimedia groups at North Carolina State University for their helpful input. This work is supported in part by the Department of Computer Science at North Carolina State University and the National Science Foundation through Grants DRL-1007962, IIS-1409639, CNS-1042468, CNS-1453520, and a Graduate Research Fellowship. Any opinions, findings, conclusions, or recommendations expressed in this report are those of the participants, and do not necessarily represent the official views, opinions, or policy of the National Science Foundation.

7. REFERENCES

[1] I. Arroyo, W. Burleson, T. Minghui, M. K, and B. P. Woolf. Gender Differences in the Use and Benefit of Advanced Learning Technologies for Mathematics. *Journal of Educational Psychology*, 105(4):957–969, 2013.

[2] I. Arroyo, D. G. Cooper, W. Burleson, B. P. Woolf, M. K, and R. M. Christopherson. Emotion Sensors Go To School. In *Proceedings of the 14th International Conference on Artificial Intelligence in Education*, pages 17–24, 2009.

[3] I. Arroyo, B. P. Woolf, D. G. Cooper, W. Burleson, and K. Muldner. The impact of animated pedagogical agents on girls' and boys' emotions, attitudes, behaviors and learning. In *Proceedings of the 11th International Conference on Advanced Learning Technologies*, pages 506–510, 2011.

(a) AU2
OUTER BROW RAISER

(b) AU5
UPPER LID RAISER

(c) AU9
NOSE WRINKLER

(d) AU12
LIP CORNER PULLER

(e) AU20
LIP STRETCHER

Figure 5: Sample frames from the student webcam illustrating the facial action unit features appearing significantly in predictive models of learning gain in male and female students, as identified by FACET.

[4] R. S. J. d. Baker, S. K. D'Mello, M. T. Rodrigo, and A. C. Graesser. Better to be frustrated than bored: The incidence, persistence, and impact of learners' cognitive-affective states during interactions with three different computer-based learning environments. *International Journal of Human-Computer Studies*, 68(4):223–241, 2010.

[5] L. R. Brody and J. A. Hall. Gender and emotion in context. *Handbook of emotions*, 3:395–408, 2008.

[6] W. Burleson and R. W. Picard. Gender-specific approaches to developing emotionally intelligent learning companions. *IEEE Intelligent Systems*, 22(4):62–69, 2007.

[7] R. A. Calvo and S. K. D'Mello. *New Perspectives on Affect and Learning Technologies*. Springer Science & Business Media, 2011.

[8] G. Chen, S. M. Gully, and D. Eden. Validation of a new general self-efficacy scale. *Organizational Research Methods*, 4(1):62–83, 2001.

[9] M. Chi, K. VanLehn, D. J. Litman, and P. W. Jordan. Empirically evaluating the application of reinforcement learning to the induction of effective and adaptive pedagogical strategies. *User Modelling and User-Adapted Interaction*, 21(1-2):137–180, 2011.

[10] S. Corrigan, T. Barkley, and Z. Pardos. Dynamic Approaches to Modeling Student Affect and its Changing Role in Learning and Performance. In *Proceedings of the 23rd International Conference on User Modeling, Adaptation, and Personalization*, pages 92–103, 2015.

[11] S. Craig, S. D'Mello, A. Witherspoon, and A. Graesser. Emote-Aloud during Learning with AutoTutor: Applying the Facial Action Coding System to Cognitive-Affective States during Learning. *Cognition and Emotion*, 22(5):777–788, 2008.

[12] S. D. Craig, A. C. Graesser, J. Sullins, and B. Gholson. Affect and learning: An exploratory look into the role of affect in learning with AutoTutor. *Journal of Educational Media*, 29(3):241–250, 2004.

[13] F. De la Torre and J. F. Cohn. Facial expression analysis. *Visual analysis of humans*, pages 377–409, 2011.

[14] M. Dennis, J. Masthoff, and C. Mellish. Adapting Performance Feedback to a Learner's Conscientiousness. In *Proceedings of the 20th International Conference on User Modeling, Adaptation, and Personalization*, pages 297–302, 2012.

[15] M. C. Desmarais and R. S. J. d. Baker. A review of recent advances in learner and skill modeling in intelligent learning environments. *User Modelling and User-Adapted Interaction*, 22(1-2):9–38, 2012.

[16] U. Dimberg and L.-O. Lundquist. Gender differences in facial reactions to facial expressions. *Biological psychology*, 30(2):151–159, 1990.

[17] S. D'Mello, B. Lehman, R. Pekrun, and A. Graesser. Confusion can be beneficial for learning. *Learning and Instruction*, 29:153–170, 2014.

[18] S. K. D'Mello. A Selective Meta-analysis on the Relative Incidence of Discrete Affective States during Learning with Technology. *Journal of Educational Psychology*, 105(4):1082–1099, 2013.

[19] S. K. D'Mello and A. C. Graesser. AutoTutor and affective AutoTutor: Learning by talking with cognitively and emotionally intelligent computers that talk back. *ACM Transactions on Interactive Intelligent Systems*, 2:1–39, 2012.

[20] P. Ekman, W. V. Friesen, and P. Ellsworth. *Emotion in the Human Face: Guidelines for Research and an Integration of Findings*. Pergamon Press, 1972.

[21] P. Ekman, W. V. Friesen, and J. C. Hager. *Facial Action Coding System: Investigator's Guide*. 2002.

[22] L. R. Goldberg. The structure of phenotypic personality traits. *American Psychologist*, 48(1):26–34, 1993.

[23] J. F. Grafsgaard, K. E. Boyer, and J. C. Lester. Predicting facial indicators of confusion with hidden Markov models. In *Proceedings of the 4th International Conference on Affective Computing and Intelligent Interaction*, pages 97–106, 2011.

[24] J. F. Grafsgaard, S. Y. Lee, B. W. Mott, K. E. Boyer, and J. C. Lester. Modeling Self-Efficacy Across Age Groups with Automatically Tracked Facial Expression. In *Proceedings of the 17th International Conference on Artificial Intelligence in Education*, pages 582–585, 2015.

[25] J. F. Grafsgaard, J. B. Wiggins, K. E. Boyer, E. N. Wiebe, and J. C. Lester. Automatically Recognizing Facial Expression: Predicting Engagement and Frustration. In *Proceedings of the 6th International Conference on Educational Data Mining*, pages 43–50, 2013.

[26] J. F. Grafsgaard, J. B. Wiggins, A. K. Vail, K. E. Boyer, and J. C. Lester. The Additive Value of Multimodal Features for Predicting Engagement, Frustration, and Learning during Tutoring. In *Proceedings of the 16th ACM International Conference on Multimodal Interaction*, pages 42–49, 2014.

[27] D. T. Green, T. J. Walsh, P. R. Cohen, C. R. Beal, and Y.-H. Chang. Gender Differences and the Value of Choice in Intelligent Tutoring Systems. In *Proceedings of the 19th International Conference on User Modeling, Adaptation, and Personalization*, pages 341–346, 2011.

[28] E. Y. Ha, J. F. Grafsgaard, C. M. Mitchell, K. E. Boyer, and J. C. Lester. Combining Verbal and Nonverbal Features to Overcome the 'Information Gap' in Task-Oriented Dialogue. In *Proceedings of the 13th Annual SIGDIAL Meeting on Discourse and Dialogue*, pages 247–256, 2012.

[29] J. A. Hall. Gender effects in decoding nonverbal cues. *Psychological bulletin*, 85(4):845, 1978.

[30] J. A. Hall and D. Matsumoto. Gender differences in judgments of multiple emotions from facial expressions. *Emotion*, 4(2):201, 2004.

[31] O. P. John and S. Srivastava. The Big Five trait taxonomy: History, measurement, and theoretical perspectives. *Handbook of Personality: Theory and Research*, 2:102–138, 1999.

[32] D. Keltner. Signs of appeasement: Evidence for the distinct displays of embarrassment, amusement, and shame. *Journal of Personality and Social Psychology*, page 441.

[33] M. LaFrance and M. A. Hecht. Option or obligation to smile: The effects of power and gender on facial expression. *The social context of nonverbal behavior: Studies in emotion and social interaction*, page 431, 1999.

[34] M. R. Lepper and M. Woolverton. The wisdom of practice: Lessons learned from the study of highly effective tutors. *Improving Academic Achievement: Impact of Psychological Factors on Education*, pages 135–158, 2002.

[35] G. Littlewort, J. Whitehill, T. Wu, I. Fasel, M. Frank, M. Javier, and M. Bartlett. The computer expression recognition toolbox (CERT). In *Proceedings of the 11th International Conference on Automatic Face & Gesture Recognition and Workshops*, pages 298–305, 2011.

[36] G. C. Littlewort, M. S. Bartlett, L. P. Salamanca, and J. Reilly. Automated measurement of children's facial expressions during problem solving tasks. In *Proceedings of the International Conference on Automatic Face & Gesture Recognition and Workshops*, pages 30–35, 2011.

[37] C. M. Mitchell, E. Y. Ha, K. E. Boyer, and J. C. Lester. Learner characteristics and dialogue: recognising effective and student-adaptive tutorial strategies. *International Journal of Learning Technology*, 8(4):382–403, 2013.

[38] A. Mitrovic. Fifteen years of constraint-based tutors: What we have achieved and where we are going. *User Modelling and User-Adapted Interaction*, 22(1-2):39–72, 2012.

[39] M. O. Z. San Pedro, R. S. J. d. Baker, S. M. Gowda, and N. T. Hefferman. Towards an Understanding of Affect and Knowledge from Student Interaction with an Intelligent Tutoring System. In *Proceedings of the 16th International Conference on Artificial Intelligence in Education*, pages 41–50, 2013.

[40] A. K. Vail, K. E. Boyer, E. N. Wiebe, and J. C. Lester. The Mars and Venus Effect: The Influence of User Gender on the Effectiveness of Adaptive Task Support. In *Proceedings of the 23rd International Conference on User Modeling, Adaptation, and Personalization*, pages 216–227, 2015.

[41] K. VanLehn. The relative effectiveness of human tutoring, intelligent tutoring systems, and other tutoring systems. *Educational Psychologist*, 46(4):197–221, 2011.

[42] K. VanLehn, A. C. Graesser, G. T. Jackson, P. W. Jordan, A. Olney, and C. P. Rosé. When Are Tutorial Dialogues More Effective Than Reading? *Cognitive Science*, 31(1):3–62, 2007.

[43] M. Wixon and I. Arroyo. When the Question is Part of the Answer: Examining the Impact of Emotion Self-reports on Student Emotion. In *Proceedings of the 22nd International Conference on User Modeling, Adaptation, and Personalization*, pages 471–477, 2014.

[44] B. P. Woolf, W. Burleson, I. Arroyo, T. Dragon, D. G. Cooper, and R. W. Picard. Affect-Aware Tutors: Recognizing and Responding to Student Affect. *International Journal of Learning Technology*, 4(3-4):129–164.

Gender Difference in the Credibility Perception of Mobile Websites: A Mixed Method Approach

Kiemute Oyibo
University of Saskatchewan
Saskatoon, Canada
kiemute.oyibo@usask.ca

Yusuf Sahabi Ali
Ahmadu Bello University
Zaria, Nigeria
sahabiali@yahoo.com

Julita Vassileva
University of Saskatchewan
Saskatoon, Canada
jiv@cs.usask.ca

ABSTRACT

To persuade people to buy a product or service online, they must be visually convinced and attracted to use the sales website. Thus, there is need to understand how different user groups perceive various designs of websites for better adaptation. A lot of research has shown that users' judgment of the credibility of a website is critical to its success. However, in the mobile domain, little has been done empirically to 1) investigate users' credibility perception of a website; and 2) how it changes as the user interface (UI) design is systematically altered. This paper bridges this gap by carrying out sentiment and statistical analyses of users' perceptions of four systematically modified mobile websites among 285 subjects from North America, Africa and Asia. The results show that mobile website design affects the perception of its credibility, with 1) females being more critical and sensitive to UI changes than males; and 2) the grid-layout website design preferred to the list-layout website design by both genders. The study contributes to knowledge in three ways. First, it provides a concise model for understanding users' UI perceptions, expectations and gender differences. Second, it presents important findings that will enable a gender-based mobile website adaptation. Third, it provides a set of empirically backed guidelines for mobile web design.

Keywords

Mobile website; user model; user interface design; visual design; navigation; layout; credibility; gender difference; adaptation.

1. INTRODUCTION

The rapid growth in information technologies, especially the Internet and smartphones, has led to unprecedented opportunities for people to connect with one another, interact and trade. So far, many people have embraced the benefits of e-commerce. Thus, in the comfort of their home, or while on the move, they can carry out online transactions through their laptops, tablets or smartphones. For example, they can order a product, book a plane ticket or hotel, etc. online without having to go to the physical store, thereby saving time and money on transportation. Even for those who make their purchases in physical stores, research has shown that 70% of them use the retailers' websites and apps on their smartphones to seek online information on the products and services of interest prior to purchasing them [20]. This makes it more important than ever before for mobile website owners, designers and advertisers to understand what exactly users expect from e-commerce websites in order to attract new customers and keep existing ones through data-driven design and adaptation [15]. Many e-commerce websites have been originally designed for use in a web browser and involve fairly complex workflows. When they are accessed on small-screen smartphones, they can create a confusing and untrustworthy experience for the user. Therefore, mobile e-commerce vendors need to provide user-friendly UIs for their customers to improve the user experience [29]. However, while there has been a number of empirical research on the influence of visual and navigational designs on web credibility, very few have been focused on the mobile domain and on the role gender plays [29]. Moreover, very few have been conducted among a mixed population, which cuts across diverse cultures, in order to arrive at more generalizable findings. For the most part, previous studies have focused on mainly Western and Asian demographics, often leaving out a continent like Africa, which happens to be one of the fastest growing mobile markets in the world today and a key player in the global mobile web [41]. To bridge this gap, we carried out a mixed-method study of four systematically modified mobile websites among a mixed sample of 285 subjects from three continents (North America, Africa and Asia). In order to foster better mobile website design and adaptation, we investigated 1) how users perceive the various mobile websites in terms of aesthetics (e.g., color and images), usability (e.g., layout and spacing) and credibility; 2) how these perceptions vary as the visual and navigational characteristics are altered; and 3) the role gender plays in the various perceptions. The findings from our analyses show that 1) mobile website design influences the perception of its credibility; 2) females are more critical and sensitive to UI changes than males; and 3) the grid-layout design is preferred by both genders over list-layout design.

The rest of this paper is organized as follows. Section 2 focuses on related work. Section 3 dwells on the study method. Sections 4 and 5 present the results and discussion respectively. Finally, Section 6 wraps up with the conclusion, contribution and future work.

2. RELATED WORK

Researchers [5], [31] have found that inherent gender differences exist between males and females in the processing of information across a wide range of cognitive tasks [38]. For example, males are known to perform better in spatial reasoning while females in verbal and linguistic activities [5], [19], [22], [30]. Females have also been found to be more visually discerning [21] and more accurate in decoding nonverbal cues [35] than males. In particular, in marketing and advertising, gender differences have been found to exist in the processing of advertising information [31], [10]; as a result, "*gender has been historically used as basis of market segmentation*" (p. 20) [38]. According to the selectivity model [25], females are *comprehensive* information processors, who respond to subtle cues by considering a product's attributes both subjectively and objectively; while males are *selective* information processors, who usually miss subtle cues because they process information heuristically. This was proven to be true by Arcand and Nantel [1], who carried out a study to investigate gender differences in search patterns and online task performance among 125 actual consumers.

UMAP '16, July 13-17, 2016, Halifax, NS, Canada
© 2016 ACM. ISBN 978-1-4503-4370-1/16/07...$15.00
DOI: http://dx.doi.org/10.1145/2930238.2930245

They found out that women spent significantly more time per page than men. Similarly, in the web domain, research [9], [16], [25], [36], [38] has shown that males and females perceive websites differently, with the latter being more critical. In a study among 76 participants, Cyr and Bonanni [9] found that gender played a major role in the assessment of information and navigation design, with males being more satisfied than females. Ferebee [15] also found that males rated websites higher on credibility than females.

In the mobile domain, very few studies, regarding the perception of websites and gender difference, have been carried out [29], using a mixed method approach and a mixed sample. Li and Ye [26] carried out a study among 200 subjects and came up with a structural equation model showing that design aesthetics indirectly impacted customer's trust. However, this study was based on a homogeneous population and did not look at the role gender plays in the perception of trust. Cyr et al. [6], in a similar study with 60 participants comprising 30 Canadians and 30 Chinese, found as well that design aesthetics indirectly influences loyalty to mobile websites, but could not find any significant influence of gender, culture or age. However, unlike our study, their sample size was small and did not include participants from Africa, which is currently one of the fastest growing markets in the world using the mobile web [41]. More recently, Lu and Rastrick [29] carried out a survey to investigate the influence of website design on the intention to adopt mobile commerce. They found that navigation design most significantly influenced users' perceived ease of use of mobile websites, and this was a more important factor for females than for males when deciding to use mobile commerce. However, their findings were based on quantitative analysis only, whereas ours adopted a mixed-method approach, focusing on the qualitative analysis, complemented and confirmed by quantitative results.

3. METHODOLOGY
In this section, we present our research design, the instruments used in measuring constructs and the demographics of participants.

3.1 Research Design
The aim of our study is to investigate users' credibility perception, how it changes as the aesthetic and usability design elements change and the role gender plays for better adaptation. So, we came up with what we called a "Mobile Web UI Transformation Framework" or, simply, "Action-Artifact (A²) Framework" to systematically modify the UI design of four hypothetical mobile webpages [32], adapted in 2014 from m.wakanow.com, mobile.united.com, mobile.utah.com and tourismwinnipeg.com. Figure 1 shows the framework in a Cartesian coordinate system [32]. The axes represent the actions (UI treatments) carried out in a clockwise direction to realize a new artifact (UI) in the next quadrant. We regard the UI pairs above and below the x-axis as low-level and high-level web designs respectively. Starting from the low-level group, we carry out a compound UI treatment (*make gray and add icon*) on A to produce B. Next, we carry out a simple UI treatment (*make unicolor*) on B to produce C. This UI transformation continues till we return to A from where we started. Finally, based on the four web UIs, we hypothesized as follows:

H1: Users' perception of credibility of mobile websites changes as the UI designs are modified.

H2: Users will be more concerned about visual design than navigational design elements in judging the mobile websites.

H3: D will be judged as the best by both genders.

H4: A will be judged as the worst by both genders.

H5: Females will be more critical in their judgment of the mobile websites than males.

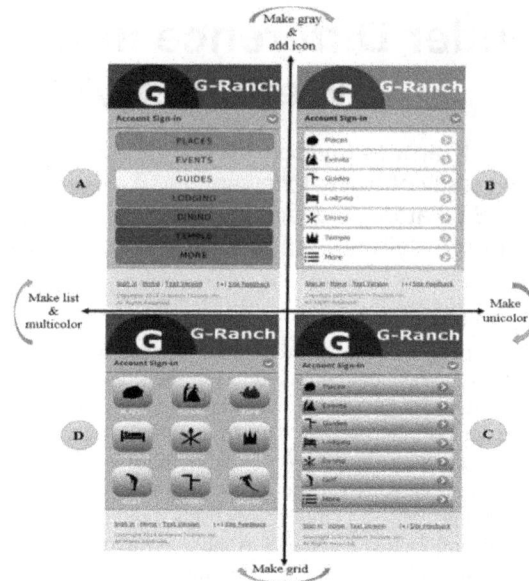

Figure 1. UI transformation framework

Our hypotheses, for the most part, were based on previous findings in the literature in the web domain, where most of the existing research has been focused. The first hypothesis (H1) was informed by the work of Robins and Holmes [34]. They found out that when the same web content was presented to users at different levels of aesthetic treatment, the one(s) with better aesthetic treatment performed better with respect to credibility assessment. The second hypothesis (H2) was informed by the work of Fogg [17], [18] and others [8], [26], [28], [27] on web credibility. They showed that, at the visceral level and for the most part, it is the perception of aesthetics, i.e., visual design, which determines users' judgment of website credibility. Thus, we believed that this would be true in the mobile domain as well despite the importance of usability, which, given the small-screen size of mobile devices, may make usability even more important. The third and fourth hypotheses (H3 and H4) stemmed from our judgement, as we viewed D and C, which belong to the high-level group, as more appealing UIs; while A and B, which belong to the low-level group, as less appealing UIs. So, between D and C, we speculated that the former (grid-based UI) will perform better than the latter (list-based UI), as the former appears to be more usable or convenient to use than the latter. We hypothesized that this better *usability* perception of D will impact the perception of the *visual design* and the *credibility* of the entire website as well due to the halo effect [39], thereby making it the best preferred. On the other hand, we surmised A will be judged as the worst due to the less professional choice and the multiplicity of colors used. Finally, the fifth hypothesis (H5) was based on gender-related findings in prior research. Using a homogeneous sample of 76 participants, Cyr and Bonanni [9] found out that significant gender differences exist in the way participants evaluated websites on the basis of design and satisfaction. Furthermore, based on a heterogeneous sample of 1156 subjects from 8 countries, Cyr et al. [7] found that men and women perceived the same websites differently based on a number of design characteristics, which included information design, navigation design, visual design, trust and satisfaction. Similarly, Flanagin and Metzger [16] found that there is a moderating effect in the way males and females evaluate website design and credibility. For example, Cyr and Bonanni [9], Flanagin and Metzger [16], and Ferebee [15] found that females rated websites less favorably than males. This was attributed to: 1) women are more critical in the judgement of things in general and information technology in particular [36], [25]; and 2) most websites are designed to meet male rather than female preferences. As cited in [3], a study of UK websites found that 94% of the sites had a masculine orientation and 74% were designed by males.

3.2 Measures

Credibility perception was measured by using a combination of quantitative method (rating and ranking) and qualitative method (comments). First, participants were asked to rate each of the webpages on a Likert scale ranging from 1 to 7 and comment on what interested or annoyed them. Second, they were requested to rank them from 1 to 4. The four webpages were not presented to them in any special order, e.g., from best to worst, or vice versa, as perceived by us the designers. Rather, they were presented out of order: C, A, B and D. We chose a single-item credibility rating scale because: 1) Bergkvist and Rossiter [2] have shown that *"there is no difference in the predictive validity of the multiple-item and single-item measures"* (p. 174); 2) the single-item has been used in a prior study [37]; and 3) we wanted to prevent participant fatigue.

3.3 Participants

The survey (online) was approved by the University of Saskatchewan Research Ethics Board. Thereafter, it was posted on the university's website and social network (Facebook) for anonymous participation. Also, invitation emails were sent to volunteer participants for a chance to participate. In order to appreciate participants for their time, they were given a chance to optionally enter for a draw to win one of our four gift cards worth $50 each. The data gathering lasted for a period of six months. A total number of 300 subjects took part in the study. However, after cleaning, we were left with 285 valid participants, which include 149 (52.3%) males and 136 (47.7%) females. Table 1 shows the participants' demographics. About 65.6% of the participants were between 18 and 24 years old, while the rest were older. Only about 66% of the participants provided comments, at least on one of the UIs (90 males and 87 females). About 45% of the participants had over ten years of internet experience, while 54% and 25.3% of them had high school and bachelor educational qualification. Further, the African, North American and Asian participants formed 54.7%, 33.3%, and 12.0% of the population sample respectively.

Table 1. Sample demographics (N=285)

Criterion	Group	Number	Percent
Gender	Male	149	52.3%
	Female	136	47.7%
Age	18-24	187	65.6%
	25-34	79	27.7%
	>44	19	6.7%
Continent	Africa	156	54.7%
	North America	95	33.3%
	Asia	34	12.0%
Country	Nigeria	147	51.6%
	Canada	92	32.3%
	China	9	3.2%
	Others	37	12.9%
Years on Internet	<10	127	44.6%
	>=10	158	55.4%
Educational Qualification	High School	154	54.0%
	Bachelor	72	25.3%
	Postgraduate	35	12.3%
	Others	24	8.4%
Commenter	Male	90	31.6%
	Female	87	30.5%

4. RESULTS

In this section, we present the results of our analysis, which include comments' word count, clustering of comment documents (files), word clouding of comment files, sentiment and statistical analyses.

4.1 Comments Word Count

We began our analysis by performing a word count on participants' comments on all four UIs, using R's *tm* package [14], in order to find out which UI resonated the most with participants and the gender differences. In total, we have eight comment documents, four for each gender. Table 2 shows the word count with stopwords removed. Overall, C and B elicited the highest and lowest number of words (709 and 451) respectively. A possible explanation for the former is that C was presented to participants first in the survey. As a result, most users, perhaps, might have commented on it the most before participant fatigue cropped in. The female group (FG) scored a higher word count (1,265) than the male group (MG, 932) across all four UIs. This suggests that, overall, the females were more stimulated to respond to the UI designs than the males, given that the ratio of male to female commenters is roughly 1 to 1 (90 to 87), as shown in Table 1. This also confirms the theory [4] that females generally tend to be more verbal or talkative than males.

4.2 Comment Files Clustering

We carried out K-Means clustering on the comments of participants in order to understand how their perceptions changed as the UI is transformed from one design to another. Figure 3 shows a principal component plot of three clusters [13]. We manually chose three clusters as against other numbers (e.g., two, four, etc.) because, heuristically, we realized they best fit the data or reflect the word content of the comment files. The first principal component represents the maximum possible variability (18%) in the eight comment files (each file contains the relevant comments for each artifact and gender), followed by the second principal component which accounts for 16% of the total variation. Cluster 1 indicates that males and females responded in a similar way to A with respect to the choice of words used. Similarly, Cluster 2 indicates males responded in a similar way to B, C and D, with more similarity existing between M_B and M_D due to their overlapping. Lastly, based on their proximity on the plot, Cluster 3 indicates that females responded in a similar way to B, C and D, with more similarity existing between F_B and F_D. We discuss the significance of the principal components in subsection 4.3.

Table 2. Comment word count with stopwords removed

Webpage	Male	Female	Global
A	211	344	555
B	201	250	451
C	324	385	709
D	196	286	482
Total	932	1,265	2,197

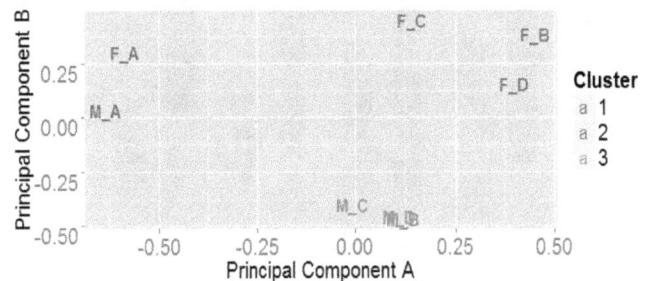

Figure 3. Principal components for comment files

4.3 Sentiment Analysis

We carried out a sentiment analysis on each of the eight comment files, using R's *tm* package [14] and QDA Miner Lite [24], in order to gain insight into: 1) what the first two principal components might represent; 2) what participants were most concerned with in each of the four UI designs. For example, *what design themes run through the comment files in each and all clusters?* QDA Miner Lite [24] was used to manually code the comments into 13 subthemes. These subthemes were further categorized into three broader themes as shown in Table 3. *Visual design*, according to [6], refers to the aesthetics of a website coupled with its emotional appeal and balance. This may be expressed through sensory design elements such as colors, shapes, font type or multimedia. *Usability*, according to our coding criteria, refers to convenience of use, ease of use, easy orientation and easy navigation of a website [40]. This can be expressed through layout, position and orientation of elements, such as buttons, texts, images, etc. *General remarks* refers to general comments relating to the site's name, professionalism and credibility. Lastly, general comments on visual design and usability as well as remarks, which do not fall under any of the sub-themes, are coded using the broader theme names, while very specific comments are coded using the subthemes names.

4.3.1 Positive vs. Negative Sentiments

Figure 4 shows a plot of the positive and negative sentiments for both genders under the 13 identified subthemes which run through all eight comment files. Overall, the male comments (Figure 4a) are characterized by more positive and less negative sentiments than the female comments (Figure 4b). For example, the files containing all the male participants' comments on artefact A (M_A) comprises 42 positive and 35 negative sentiments, denoted as (+42, -35), for brevity. In contrast, F_A comprises (+24, -72) sentiments. Similarly, M_C comprises (+72, -23) sentiments, while F_C comprises (+31, -60) sentiments. Figure 4 also provides insight into some likely characteristics that defined the clusters in Figure 3. It reveals that M_A, M_B, M_C and M_D (files with male's comments) are more positive than their respective female counterparts (F_A, F_B, F_C and F_D). This seems to account for the location of M_A, M_B, M_C and M_D below the hypothetical line, y=0, and F_A, F_B, F_C, and F_D above it. As a result, the principal component B in Figure 3 may be regarded as a measure of sentiment polarity with files (M_A, M_B, M_C M_D, F_D) below the line, y=0.25, indicating more-positive-than-negative sentiments and those above it (F_A, F_B and F_C) indicating more-negative-than-positive sentiments, as evident in Figure 4.

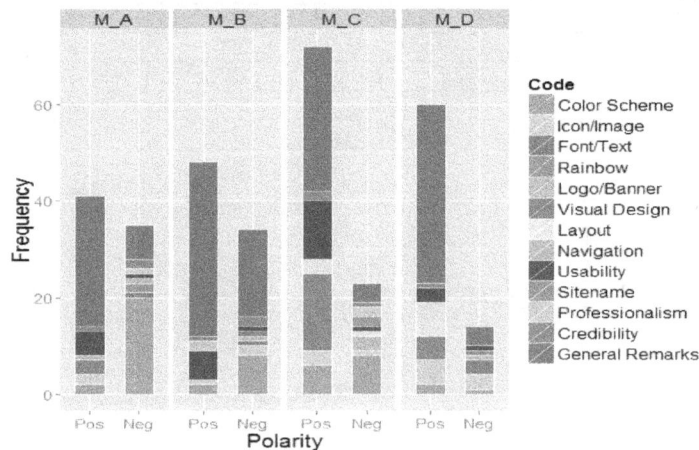

Table 3. Broad and subthemes in comment files

Broad theme	Sub-themes
Visual design	Color scheme, icon/image, font/text, rainbow theme and logo/banner
Usability	Layout and navigation
General remarks	Site name, professionalism and credibility

4.3.2 General vs. Specific Remarks

Figure 4 shows that, overall, the male group gave more general remarks in their response to the web designs than the female group. This is evident in the broader blue (general remarks) band, green (usability) band and red (visual design) band in the male than the female bar chart. For example, regarding B, the male group made 54 general remarks (+36, -18), while the female group made about 31 general remarks (+12, -19). Similarly, regarding D, the male group made 41 general remarks (+37, -4), while the female group made about 29 general remarks (+20, -9). Typical examples of general remarks include: *Everything about it appeals to me* (M_A), *very attractive* (F_A); *the design is really interesting* (M_B), *very boring but less tacky* (F_B); *the page looks blurred* (M_C); *actually the mobile page is fascinating* (F_C). One would have expected females to record more general remarks than males given the fact that the former provided more comments (see Table 2). In contrast, the female group gave more specific remarks than the male group (see subsection 4.4.2). For example, in all four UIs, females used the specific word *color* and related words (e.g. *blue*, *gray*, *black*, *white*, etc.) much more than males as indicated by the broader color scheme band in the female bar chart in Figure 4. They also noticed and made specific reference to the rainbow color scheme used in A in their comments more than the males as shown in the broader rainbow band in the female bar chart. This supports the theory in the existing literature, which states that females tend to be more visually discerning [21] and more specific in decoding nonverbal cues [35] than males.

4.4 Documents Word Clouding

We combined four of the eight comment files for each gender into one single file and carried out word clouding (minimum frequency of words = 5, scale is 5 to 1) on the resulting file using R's tm package for textual analysis [14]. We did this in order to gain insight into what specific UI design elements participants were most concerned with, choice of words used, and how they vary across gender. Figure 5 shows the word clouds for both gender. It is discussed in details in the next subsections.

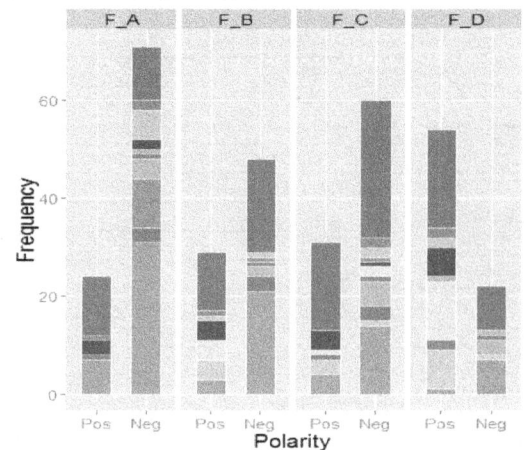

(a) Male   (b) Female

Figure 4. Gender-based sentiments for all four UIs

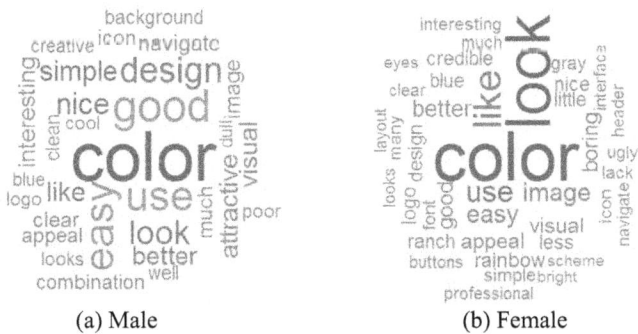

(a) Male   (b) Female

Figure 5. Word cloud for comments on all four webpages

4.4.1 Visual Design vs. Usability Concerns

The most prominent theme that runs through the comment files for both group is visual design or look and feel (as evident in the boldness of such words as *color, look, nice, appeal, visual, attractive*, etc.). This resonated more with the FG than the MG (as evident in the bolder words, such as *look* and *image* in the female word cloud and Figure 4). In particular, *color* turns out to be the overarching concern for both genders. This suggests that the color scheme chosen in the design of a mobile website is critical to its success or failure. The second most prominent theme is usability, as evident in the high occurrence of such words as *use, easy, simple, interesting, navigate*, etc. This resonated more with the MG than the FG. This is evident in the words (e.g., *easy, use* and *navigate*) occurring bolder in the male than the female word cloud.

4.4.2 Abstract/Generic vs. Concrete/Specific Words

As shown in Figure 5, males and females use different choices of words in expressing their reactions to the UI designs. Male tended to use more abstract and generic words, while females tended to use more concrete and specific words. By generic words we mean general remarks that do not refer to any specific part or element of the UI under assessment, e.g., *color, logo, icon, layout, background* etc. For example, apart from *color*, the next predominant visual design-related noun term in the male cloud is *design* (abstract and generic), while in the female cloud is *image* (concrete and specific). All in all, the graphical design-specific elements that made it into the male cloud are *color, image, icon, logo, background* and *blue*, while those that made it to the female cloud are *color, image, icon, logo, header, layout, font, buttons, rainbow, blue, gray* and *ranch* (representing "G-Ranch", i.e., the fictitious name of the websites).

4.4.3 Interface Commendation vs. Condemnation

Males tended to be more impressed with all four UIs than the females, and thus expressed more positive sentiments than the females. This is evident in such choice of words as *good, easy, attractive* and *interesting, simple, nice*, which are more frequent and prominent in the male than the female word cloud. This finding is also evident in Figure 4a where males have more positive than negative sentiments. On the other hand, the FG tended to be more critical of the UIs than the MG as evident in the negative choice of words such as *boring, ugly, lack* and *less*, which made it to the female word cloud but not to the male word cloud, having only two negative words (*poor* and *dull*). This is also evident in Figure 4 and Figure 6, which shows the overall sentiments of each gender. The overall sentiments expressed by females regarding the four interfaces, except D, is negative. This contrasts the overall sentiment expressed by males, which is positive. This qualitative result supports prior findings [15], [9], [16], [36], [25] suggesting that females are more critical of websites than males. Moreover, Figure 6 shows that the global overall sentiments for D, C and B is positive (with B almost having a zero value), while A is negative.

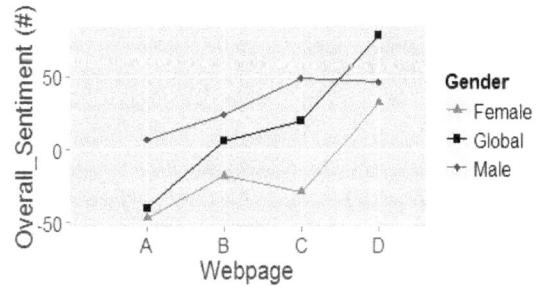

Figure 6. Overall (resultant) sentiment for all four webpages

4.5 Statistical Analysis of Credibility Scores

In addition to the qualitative analysis, we plotted the credibility rating and credibility ranking of the four UIs by participants and performed a statistical analysis on them to confirm our qualitative findings. Figure 7 shows the plot of both measures on a 0-to-100% scale for both groups. Again, just as we have seen before, males rated all four interfaces in terms of credibility higher than the females, which confirms our findings (males being less critical) in subsections 4.3 and 4.4. We also see that as we move from one interface to another, participants' perception of credibility in terms of rating and ranking changed, with D being the best and A being the worst for both genders. While males rated all four interfaces more favorably (higher) than females, females ranked D, C and B higher than males. This was only possible because the ranking was forced. As a result, females' dislike and critical condemnation of A paved the way for the other three interfaces to rank higher.

4.5.1 Verification of H5: Between-group Analysis

Given that our data did not meet the normality requirement, we carried out the non-parametric Kruskal-Wallis (one-way ANOVA) rank test [23] between the respective male and female credibility rating and credibility ranking scores of the four UIs to verify *H5: Females will be more critical in their judgment of the mobile websites than males.* Table 4 shows the result. First, with respect to the credibility rating, the test shows that there is a significant difference between the two groups. The group difference regarding A, B and C is significant at p<0.0000, while that regarding D at p<0.0001. This highlights how the two groups differ in their credibility perception, with the females being more critical than the males, as we have found before in the qualitative analysis (see Figure 4). Second, with respect to credibility ranking, only the group difference regarding A is statistically significant at p<0.001. A possible explanation for this, unlike the rating where the group difference is significant with regard to all four UIs, is that the ranking was forced and constrained between 1 and 4. Thus, there was a limited range of numbers for participants to choose from, unlike the rating having a wider range from 1 to 7. However, the highly significant group difference in credibility ranking regarding A highlights how much the MG and the FG differ in the perception of A, as seen in the qualitative result (see Figure 4). It indicates that the FG completely disapproved the color scheme used in A.

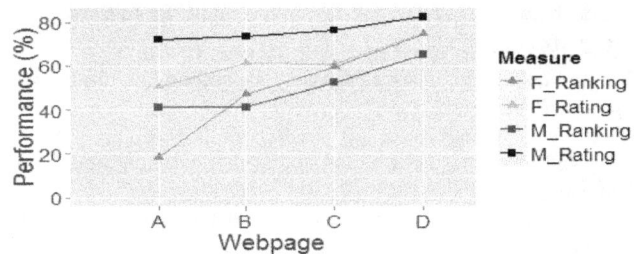

Figure 7. Credibility rating and ranking for all four webpages

Finally, based on the highly significant group difference regarding the four UIs' credibility rating at p<0.0001 (Table 4), with females scoring lower (Figure 7) and providing more negative than positive comments (Figure 4), the fifth hypothesis (H5) is validated.

4.5.2 Verification of H1: Within-group Analysis

Table 5 shows the result of the non-parametric Friedman test and Nemenyi post-hoc pairwise comparison test [33] we carried out to verify our first hypothesis (*H1: Users' perception of credibility of mobile websites changes as the UI designs are modified*). In the within-group analysis, with respect to pairwise significance, there is a correspondence between the credibility rating and credibility ranking measures for both groups. In other words, for each group, it is either both the credibility rating and ranking pairwise comparison tests for a given UI transformation are significant (p<0.05) or they are not significant (n.s). For example, for the MG, the results regarding credibility rating for UI transformations (A → D, B → D, and C → D) are significant at p<0.01, and so are the corresponding results regarding credibility ranking significant at p<0.05. Similarly, for the FG, the results regarding credibility rating for UI transformations (A → B, A → C, A → D, B → D, and C → D) are significant at p<0.01, and so are the corresponding results regarding credibility ranking at p<0.05. On the other hand, for the MG, the results regarding credibility rating for UI transformations (A → B, A → C, and B → C) are not significant, and so are those regarding credibility ranking. Similarly, for the FG, the result regarding credibility rating for transformation (B → C) is not significant, and so is the result regarding credibility ranking not significant. Therefore, since about 66% (16 out of 24) of the pairwise comparison tests are significant at p<0.05, we conclude that, for the most part, our first hypothesis (H1) is supported.

4.5.3 Verification of H3/H4: Within-group Analysis

As shown in Table 4 and Figure 7, we see that D was rated and ranked as the best by both groups. The MG rated and ranked D 82.43% and 65.34% respectively, while the FG rated and ranked D 75.18% and 74.63% respectively. Based on the within-group (pairwise) analysis result shown in Table 5 and discussed in subsection 4.5.2, between the scores of D and each of the other three UIs, there is a significant difference at p<0.05, with D being rated and ranked as the highest in all 12 cases. Therefore, the third hypothesis (*H3: D will be judged as the best by both genders*) is validated. On the other hand, as shown in Table 5, given that the pairwise comparison (A → B, A → C and A → D) with respect to credibility rating and credibility ranking for the FG is significant at p<0.0000, the fourth hypothesis (*H4: A will be judged as the worst by both genders*) is supported for the FG. However, for the MG, except for A → D, we see that the pairwise comparisons (A → B and A → C) with respect to credibility rating and credibility ranking is not significant. Therefore, H4, for the MG, is not supported. A possible explanation for this is that the participants in the MG were, overall, liberal and not too critical in rating and ranking A and B which we perceived as low-level designs. Thus, we see a situation where there is no significant difference in the respective rating and ranking between A and B, and between A and C for this group.

4.5.4 Verification of H2: Sentiment Analysis

We used qualitative measure to verify the second hypothesis (*H2: Users will be more concerned about visual than navigational design elements in judging the mobile websites*). Figure 4 shows that users were more concerned about visual design (aesthetics) than navigational design (usability) when assessing the mobile websites. As shown in the bar chart, the visual design bars (red-like band) are broader than the usability bars (green-like band) for all four UIs. Thus, from a qualitative standpoint, H2 is confirmed.

Table 4. Kruskal-Wallis rank test between credibility scores

Webpage	Credibility	Male	Female	Sig
A	Rating	72.07	50.62	p<0.0000
	Ranking	41.22	18.66	p<0.0010
B	Rating	73.76	61.44	p<0.0000
	Ranking	41.22	47.26	p=0.0690
C	Rating	76.58	60.70	p<0.0000
	Ranking	52.25	59.45	p=0.0560
D	Rating	82.43	75.18	p<0.0001
	Ranking	65.34	74.63	n.s

Table 5. Friedman/Nemenyi pairwise credibility post-hoc test

Credibility	Gr	Cmp	Score1	Score2	Sig
Rating	M	A→B	72.07	73.76	n.s
		A→C	72.07	76.58	n.s
		A→D	72.07	82.43	P<0.0000
		B→C	73.76	76.58	n.s
		B→D	73.76	82.43	p<0.0000
		C→D	76.58	82.43	p<0.0100
	F	A→B	50.62	61.44	p<0.0010
		A→C	50.62	60.70	p<0.0100
		A→D	50.62	75.18	p<0.0000
		B→C	61.44	60.70	n.s
		B→D	61.44	75.18	P<0.0000
		C→D	60.70	75.18	p<0.0000
Ranking	M	A→B	41.22	41.22	n.s
		A→C	41.22	52.25	n.s
		A→D	41.22	65.34	p<0.0000
		B→C	41.22	52.25	n.s
		B→D	41.22	65.34	p<0.0000
		C→D	52.25	65.34	p<0.0500
	F	A→B	18.66	47.26	p<0.0000
		A→C	18.66	59.45	p<0.0000
		A→D	18.66	74.63	p<0.0000
		B→C	47.26	59.45	n.s
		B→D	47.26	74.63	p<0.0000
		C→D	59.45	74.63	p<0.0500

5. DISCUSSION

To synthesize our findings, we created a UI transformation model to visualize and understand how the modification of the UI elements affected the credibility perception of the two groups (Figure 8). The model summarizes both the qualitative and quantitative findings. The corners of the rectangle, A, B, C, D, represent the four web designs, the blue arrows between each pair represent the UI transformations. The red and black colors represent the female and male groups respectively. The vertically stacked arrows indicate qualitative measures, where the upward and the downward directions indicate positive and negative overall sentiments respectively. The lengths of these arrows represent the number of overall sentiments elicited by the respective UIs (Figure 6). The pairs of values in brackets indicate the quantitative measures, where (v1, v2) represent credibility *rating* and credibility *ranking* scores respectively, and the asterisk (*) symbol between each male group score and each female group score indicates statistical significance when compared. The "+" sign between each pair of UIs indicates a significant increase in the perception of credibility (positive effect) when the UI is transformed from one design to another, while the "0" sign indicates no effect. These signs are based on the significance test results shown in Table 5.

5.1 UI Transformation Effect

Except from B to C, for the most part, we notice that as we transition from the low-level to the high-level designs, the perception and judgment of the UIs improve for both genders, with the FG recording more positives than the MG. The difference between the groups appears for transitions from A to B and A to C where there is a positive effect for FG and zero effect for MG.

5.1.1 Positive Effect UI Transformation

For the MG, we find that the UI transformations from any of the designs A, B and C to design D that resulted in a significant change (positive effect) in perception. For the FG, we find that all six UI transformations, except B → C, resulted in a positive effect in perception. The fact that there are more positive effects for the FG than the MG indicates that the FG's responses to the four UIs vary much more than the MG's, as we saw in the clustering of the comment files in Figure 3. The FG's overall sentiments began from negative (at A), remained negative (at B and C) and only became positive (at D). On the other hand, the MG's overall sentiments began from neutral or slightly positive (at A), and remained positive all through (at B, C and D). This suggests that, in practice, females would be more responsive or sensitive to UI upgrades in a mobile website than males (see Figure 6 and Figure 7). Thus, operators of websites should ensure such upgrades are for the better; otherwise, the credibility of the sites, especially among females, may decline.

5.1.2 Different Effect UI Transformation

The two groups differ regarding A → B and A → C. The UI transformation had a zero effect on the MG, but a positive effect on the FG. An explanation for this difference can be found in the sentiment analysis: females tend to be more sensitive to and critical of the use of color in general. Specifically, the rainbow color scheme of A was highly penalized by the FG. However, upon "improving" the multicolor scheme of A to the gray (B) and blue (C) color schemes, which they perceived as more professional and appealing respectively, they toned down their criticism, as evident in the better credibility rating and ranking scores and the less negative overall sentiments at B and C. However, the MG was not as critical of A at first as the FG, as seen in the credibility rating scores of 51 and 72 respectively. Thus, we see very close credibility rating scores between A and B, and between A and C, for the MG. For example, the credibility rating difference between A and B is 2 and that between A and C is 5, which are not significant ("0"). In contrast, for the FG, the credibility rating differences between A and B, and between A and C are high: that between A and B is 10 and that between A and C is 10, which are both significant ("+").

5.1.3 Zero-Effect UI Transformation for both Groups

The zero-effect transformation between B (a low-level design) and C (a high-level design) for both genders is also evident in the least change of global overall sentiment (see Figure 6 also). This could be explained based on participants' comments on the UIs. They generally tended to view the gray color theme of B as a professional theme and thus were not too critical about it (relative to C). This suggests that, in practice, if every other UI design characteristic is okay, users may be less bothered by a gray color scheme than by another color scheme, which may be perceived as unappealing and unprofessional, e.g. A. However, from the sentiment analysis, it seems that users would prefer a mobile site both professional and colorful, as they want to see some level of color, which appeals to their visual sense. Moreover, it is noteworthy how the FG assessed C qualitatively (Figure 4b), especially regarding its color scheme. One would have expected that its overall assessment would be positive given that blue is a common theme used by many popular websites (e.g., Facebook) and mobile websites (e.g., banking).

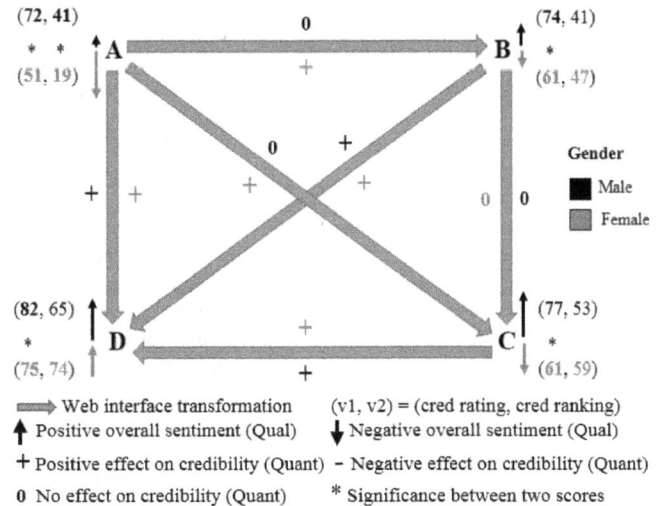

Figure 8. User model for understanding UI design perceptions

However, the FG's overall assessment of C turned out to be negative and even worse than B which employed a gray color scheme, described by some female participants as "*boring*" and "*bland*". The sentiment analysis showed that the FG was displeased with C's blue color scheme. Thus C and B ended up having the same credibility rating of 61. The reason may be due to C's unicolor scheme. Some saw this as "*boring*" and "*hard on the eyes*" Some typical comments include: 1) *The blue is horrible to look at (hard on the eyes, physically)...* 2) *The blue and blocks seems very boring, and does not make me want to use the site...* 3) *The website does not appeal to me because of the color combination.* However, on modifying C's layout from list to grid (D), the FG seemed not to be concerned about the all-blue color scheme any longer. They tended to focus on the relative "ease of use" of D, which seemed to increase its appeal to them. As a result, their overall sentiment shifted positive, with the credibility rating and ranking increasing from 61 and 59 (at C) to 75 and 74 (at D) respectively—an indication of the halo effect [11], [39]. A possible explanation for this remarkable change in perception, which also explains why D is the most preferred by both genders, is evident in participants' comments. People generally are so used to the iPhone (grid) layout for mobile apps that they expect to see it also in mobile web design. Besides, most smart phones use this layout for placing their apps on the screen, as this has become a *de facto* standard. Therefore, the participants found it more credible, professional, and aesthetic. This suggests that, in practice, due to its relative ease of use, the grid layout should be given priority by designers, especially when all the mobile web app's content (items) can fit into a single screen.

In summary, the following, based on the sentiment analysis, are noteworthy for the adaptation of mobile websites based on gender:

1. Females care more about visual design than males.
2. Females care more about the professional use of images, fonts and a multicolor theme in mobile sites than males.
3. Males care more about usability features than females.

5.2 Mobile Website Design Guidelines

Table 5 shows a set of mobile website design guidelines, informed by participants' comments. It includes key features, justifications and snapshots of participants' comments. The first key feature emphasizes the need to use a color scheme that is both appealing and professional, as improper application of colors may cause users to doubt the website's credibility. The second key feature focuses

Table 5. Empirically backed feature set of guidelines for the design of mobile websites

	User-Expected Key Feature	Justification	Comment
1.	The color scheme or theme used in the mobile website design should be appealing as well as professional.	Most participants felt the color scheme used in A was unprofessional and amateurish, while that used in B, though might be more credible, was old-fashioned and boring.	*More colors make it more fascinating, but it still looks sort of amateurish. Maybe it's the font type? (F_A). It looks nice but the grey scale is very boring (F_A).*
2.	The mobile website's name and logo should be intuitive as much as possible to give first-time users a quick insight into what products and services the mobile website offers.	Some participants felt the logo/banner of the hypothetical website was not good enough, the name did not reflect its services. A few participants suggested a green theme best suited the website given the name "G-Ranch", which reflected tourism.	*"G" ranch makes me think its not a legit, I would use something else. Company logo or some info or anything would make it look less fake (F_C). Name plays into the credibility level too. G-Ranch doesn't make me think it's a real place because it sounds too simple and made up (M_C).*
3.	Icon menu should be preferred to color-bar menu if the website content (items) is to be presented using a list layout.	Most participants preferred D, B and C (which used icon menu) to A (which used color bars). They believe this is more intuitive in the presentation of contents.	*This web page is outstanding and the pictorial illustrations are self-explanatory such that even if one cannot read English, the symbols will guide such ones. Its excellent job done (M_D).*
4.	Grid should be preferred to list layout if all items fit into a page. Otherwise, users should be provided with a layout option.	Most participants (both males and females) preferred D to C, as they felt it was more navigable and less prone to error in the course of selecting (clicking on) an item.	*The menu are well spelt out and are easy to navigate (M_D). The buttons would probably be easy to press with my stubby fingers without accidentally hitting the wrong one (F_D).*
5.	Help should be provided to assist non-expert users in navigating the site easily.	Some participants expected to see a help feature where supportive information on the usage of the site could be sought.	*There should be a "Help" button to understand the app better. An intro to the app would have increased its credibility (F_B).*
6.	Search feature should be provided users to help users find information easily.	Some participants requested a search box where they could type in and search for information they wanted.	*I don't see any place where I can type in a search for what I want (F_C). It's annoying that there is no option to search (F_C).*
7.	Language option or translation feature should be provided if possible.	A couple of participants suggested language option be provided to enable the non-default language speakers to use the site as well.	*Great layout but language option should be added for non-English speaking countries (F_B).*
8.	Extraneous allusions should be avoided in the website design, branding and presentation of information.	A couple of participants were put off by the rainbow menu used in A, as they deemed this inappropriate, unprofessional and un-connected to the site.	*Looking more credible but the bright rainbow colors are not necessary (F_A). The colorful rainbow does not look professional (F_A). Is this App for Kids? Rainbow Menu (M_A).*
9.	Users should be allowed to access site, at least its basic features, without having to sign up or sign in.	A couple of participants were bothered with the sign-in button below the site banner, as they felt reluctant to sign-in before having full access to what the site had to offered.	*It looks as if there is a sign-in option, which would worry me - do I need to waste time entering my info? (F_C).*

on the site name and logo. Users want to see a site whose name and logo, as much as possible, reflect the products and services of the site. For example, given that the hypothetical website we presented relates to tourism, some participants expected the site to have a green theme, which reflected the fictitious name "*G-Ranch*" and services, such as *golf*. Other key features, which they expected to see on the site, include *search, help, language option*, etc. Finally, thanks to the useful information on users' expectations, gathered from the sentiment analysis, we recommend that in the design of a mobile website, as a way of formative evaluation, potential users (with a gender balance) should be involved in the design process in order to gather useful qualitative information on users' needs [12].

5.3 Limitation
Our study has some limitations. First, the order in which the mobile webpages (C, A, B and D) were presented to participants might have affected the results. It would have been better if we had been able to randomize it. Second, our findings are based on users' perception of, and not actual interaction with, the four web designs.

6. CONCLUSION AND FUTURE WORK
We have presented the findings of a mixed-method study on users' perceptions of four systematically modified mobile websites and the role gender plays based on a mixed sample of 285 subjects from North America, Africa and Asia. We showed both quantitatively

and qualitatively that the design of a mobile website affects the perception of its credibility, with females being more critical, responsive and sensitive to UI changes than males, and the grid-layout preferred to the list-layout design by both genders. Our findings, by implication, reiterates the need for mobile website vendors to provide users with customizable mobile websites, which they can tailor to their thematic and layout preferences. More important, it would be better off if vendors can infer the gender and preferences of their visitors/users and personalize the essential look-and-feel features, such as theme and layout, accordingly instead of having users do it themselves. Our contributions to knowledge are in two fold. First, regarding mobile web design: 1) we confirmed the existing theory that holds that females are more critical in the judgement of websites than males; 2) we showed that as UI design characteristics change, users' perceptions change also, with females being more sensitive and responsive to those changes; 3) we showed that both genders prefer the grid to the list layout; and 4) we presented an empirically backed set of guidelines for the design of mobile websites. Second, regarding mobile web adaptation, we presented important findings that can inform a gender-based website adaptation, e.g., females liking ample colors professionally used alongside images and fonts. Finally, in future work, we intend to investigate how the perceptions of the respective UIs' aesthetics, usability and credibility influence one another.

7. REFERENCES

[1] Arcand, M. and Nantel, J. 2005. *Gender differences in processing information: Implications for online search patterns and task performance.* HEC Montréal.

[2] Bergkvist, L. and Rossiter, J.R. 2007. The Predictive Validity of Multiple-Item Versus Single-Item Measures of the Same Constructs. *Journal of Marketing Research.* 44, 2 (2007), 175–184.

[3] Boiano, S. et al. 2006. Gender Issues in Hci Design for Web Access. *Advances in Universal Web Design and Evaluation: Research, Trends and Opportunities.* S. Kurniawan and P. Zaphiris, eds. Idea Group Publishing. 116–153.

[4] Brizendine, L. 2006. *The female brain.* Morgan Road, New York.

[5] Burstein, B. et al. 1980. Sex differences in cognitive functioning: Evidence, determinants, implications. *Human Development.* 23, 5 (1980), 289–313.

[6] Cyr, D. et al. 2006. Design aesthetics leading to m-loyalty in mobile commerce. *Information and Management.* 43, 8 (2006), 950–963.

[7] Cyr, D. 2009. Gender and website design across cultures. *17th European Conference on Information Systems.* (2009), 279–291.

[8] Cyr, D. et al. 2008. Web site design, trust, satisfaction and e-loyalty: the Indian experience. *Online Information Review.* 32, 6 (2008), 773–790.

[9] Cyr, D. and Bonanni, C. 2005. Gender and website design in e-business. *International Journal of Electronic Business.* 3, 6 (2005), 565.

[10] Darley, W.K. and Smith, R.E. 1995. Gender differences in information processing strategies: An empirical test of the selectivity model in advertising response. *Journal of Advertising.* 24, 1 (1995), 41–56.

[11] Deng, L. and Poole, M.S. 2010. Affect in Web Interfaces: a Study of the Impacts of Web Page Visual Complexity and Order. *Mis Quarterly.* 34, 4 (2010), 711–730.

[12] Faulkner, X. 2000. *Usability Engineering.* Palgrave.

[13] Feinerer, I. 2008. An Introduction to Text Mining in R. *R News.* 8, (2008), 51–88.

[14] Feinerer, I. and Hornik, K. 2014. TM: Text Mining Package. R package version 0.6. (2014), 2014.

[15] Ferebee, S. 2008. The influence of gender and involvement level on the perceived credibility of web sites. *Lecture Notes in Computer Science (including subseries Lecture Notes in Artificial Intelligence and Lecture Notes in Bioinformatics).* 5033 LNCS, (2008), 279–282.

[16] Flanagin, A.J. and Metzger, M.J. 2003. The perceived credibility of personal Web page information as influenced by the sex of the source. *Computers in Human Behavior.* 19, 6 (2003), 683–701.

[17] Fogg, B.J. et al. 2003. How do users evaluate the credibility of Web sites?: a study with over 2,500 participants. *Proceedings of the 2003 conference on Designing for user experiences* (2003), 1–15.

[18] Fogg, B.J. et al. 2001. What Makes Web Sites Credible ? A Report on a Large Quantitative Study CHI 2001. *Sigchi'01* (2001), 61–68.

[19] Geary, D.C. 1996. Sexual selection and sex differences in mathematical abilities. *Behavioral and Brain Sciences.* 19, 02 (1996), 229.

[20] Google 2014. Digital Impact on In-Store Shopping: Research Debunks Common Myths. *Think with Google.* October (2014).

[21] Holbrook, M.B. 1986. Aims, Concepts, and Methods for the Representation of Individual Differences in Esthetic Responses to Design Features. *Journal of Consumer Research.* 13, 3 (1986), 337.

[22] Hyde, J.S. and Linn, M.C. 1988. Gender differences in verbal ability: A meta-analysis. *Psychological Bulletin.* 104, 1 (1988), 53–69.

[23] Kruskal, W.H. and Wallis, W.A. 1952. Use of Ranks in One-Criterion Variance Analysis. *Source Journal of the American Statistical Association.* 4710087, 260 (1952), 583–621.

[24] Lewis, R.B. and Maas, S.M. 2007. QDA Miner 2.0: Mixed-Model Qualitative Data Analysis Software. *Field Methods.* 19, (2007), 87–108.

[25] Li, N. et al. 2001. Cross-cultural comparison of women students' attitudes toward the Internet and usage: China and the United Kingdom. *CyberPsychology & Behavior.* 4, 3 (2001), 415–426.

[26] Li, Y.M. and Yeh, Y.S. 2010. Increasing trust in mobile commerce through design aesthetics. *Computers in Human Behavior.* 26, 4 (2010), 673–684.

[27] Lindgaard, G. et al. 2006. Attention web designers: You have 50 milliseconds to make a good first impression! *Behaviour & Information Technology.* 25, 2 (2006), 115–126.

[28] Liu, C.-H. et al. 2010. The Influence of HCI Design Aesthetics on Website Creditability--Using on Online Banking Website Interfaces as an Example. *Springer.* (2010), 1–20.

[29] Lu, Y. and Rastrick, K. 2014. Impacts of Website Design on the Adoption Intention of Mobile Commerce: Gender as a Moderator. *New Zealand Journal of Applied Business Research.* 12, 2 (2014), 51–69.

[30] Meyers-Levy, J. 1989. Gender Differences in Information Processing: A Selectivity Interpretation. *Cognitive and Affective Responses to Advertising.* (1989), 219–260.

[31] Meyers-Levy, J. and Maheswaran, D. 1991. Exploring Differences in Males' and Females' Processing Strategies. *Journal of Consumer Research.* 18, 1 (1991), 63–70.

[32] Oyibo, K. et al. 2016. An Empirical Analysis of the Perception of Mobile Website Interfaces and the Influence of Culture. *Worshop on Personalization in Persuasive Technology (PPT'16)* (Salzburg, Austria, 2016), 44–56.

[33] Pohlert, T. 2014. The pairwise multiple comparison of mean ranks package (PMCMR). R package. *R package.* (2014), 1–9.

[34]   Robins, D. and Holmes, J. 2008. Aesthetics and credibility in web site design. *Information Processing & Management*. 44, 1 (2008), 386–399.

[35]   Rosenthal, R. and DePaulo, B.M. 1979. Sex Differences in Accommodation in Nonverbal Communication. *Skill in Nonverbal Communication: Individual Differences*. R. Rosenthal, ed. Oelgeschlager, Gunn and Hain. 68–103.

[36]   Schumacher, P. and Morahan-Martin, J. 2001. Gender, Internet and computer attitudes and experiences. *Computers in human behavior*. 17, 1 (2001), 95–110.

[37]   Setterstrom, S. 2010. *Assessing credibility and aesthetic perception across different exposure times on a health care information website*. Iowa State University.

[38]   Simon, S.J. 2001. The impact of culture and gender on web sites: an empirical study. *SIGMIS Database*. 32, 1 (2001), 18–37.

[39]   Soper, D.S. 2014. User Interface Design and the Halo Effect : Some Preliminary Evidence. *Twentieth Americas Conference on Information Systems, Savannah* (2014), 1–11.

[40]   Sutcliffe, A. and De Angeli, A. 2005. Assessing interaction styles in web user interfaces. *Human-Computer Interaction-INTERACT 2005* (2005), 405–417.

[41]   The fastest-growing mobile phone markets barely use apps: 2015. *http://qz.com/466089/the-fastest-growing-mobile-phone-markets-barely-use-apps/*. Accessed: 2016-03-03.

Personalizing Reminders to Personality for Melanoma Self-checking

Kirsten A. Smith
University of Aberdeen
Aberdeen, UK
r01kas12@abdn.ac.uk

Matt Dennis
University of Aberdeen
Aberdeen, UK
m.dennis@abdn.ac.uk

Judith Masthoff
University of Aberdeen
Aberdeen, UK
j.masthoff@abdn.ac.uk

ABSTRACT

This paper investigates whether different types of persuasive reminder should be sent to patients with different personalities. We describe a study where we presented participants with a personality measure, then describe a scenario with a fictional patient, who has not performed a skin check for recurrent melanoma. We asked patients to imagine they are in that situation and rate validated reminders based on Cialdini's 6 principles of persuasion for their suitability. Participants then chose their favourite reminder, and an alternative reminder to send if that one failed. We found that persuasive reminders that use 'Authority' and 'Liking' are the most popular overall. We also found that personality had an effect when deciding on the type of persuasive reminder to use. In particular, we have found that those with high emotional stability are more responsive to any kind of persuasion, those with low agreeableness rated all types of reminder higher than those with high, and that conscientiousness matters when selecting an alternative reminder.

Keywords

Reminders, Personality, Persuasion, eHealth

1. INTRODUCTION

There is a growing area of research surrounding digital behaviour interventions (also known as persuasive technology) that attempt to change people's attitudes or behaviour. Personalization can play an important role in optimising the effectiveness of these interventions. For example, a meta-analysis by Noar et al. [37] suggests that tailored messages are more effective in causing health behaviour change, and another meta-analysis by Wantland et al. [45] found that tailored messages increased system use. This paper focuses on adapting reminders that prompt people to self-monitor. Whilst this paper is particularly concerned with prompting skin self-examinations, we believe that the applicability of the research is more general, as reminding people to

UMAP '16, July 13-17, 2016, Halifax, NS, Canada

© 2016 ACM. ISBN 978-1-4503-4370-1/16/07...$15.00

DOI: http://dx.doi.org/10.1145/2930238.2930254

self-monitor is an important technique used in many digital behaviour interventions. For instance, in the domain of healthy eating and physical activity interventions, Michie et al.'s meta-analysis of 122 studies [33] led to them recommend the inclusion of five behaviour change techniques, of which prompting self-monitoring behaviour was one. Despite the case having been made for personalizing digital behaviour interventions [29, 3], research in this area is still quite limited and this paper adds to the research on adapting behaviour change techniques to personality.

Our research aims to encourage people who have been treated for subcutaneous melanoma (skin cancer) to perform Total Skin Self-Examinations (TSSEs). Melanoma is one of the most common cancers in 15-34 year olds and kills over 2,000 people a year in the UK [1]. Early detection of recurrences is a critical goal of follow-up programmes for people who have been previously treated for melanoma [36], as the risk of malignant melanoma is between 8-15 times greater [2] and there is up to a 63% reduction in mortality [11, 25] when patients detect their own recurrences. Hence, experts have argued that patients need to be advised to perform TSSEs at frequent intervals [5]. However, even if patients are taught to self-check often, it is likely that their self-checking will decrease over time without an intervention to sustain their behaviour [21, 24].

Extensive evidence suggests that digital interventions can help promote health behaviour change (e.g. [16, 46, 40])and that apps (i.e. mobile or tablet applications) can be used to support a sustained health self-management strategy [47]. With this in mind, the *ASICA* (Achieving Self-directed Integrated Cancer Aftercare) skin self-examinations app was developed in 2013, as part of an intervention aiming to remove barriers between patients treated for melanoma and dermatology specialists by enabling remote screening and diagnosis of skin changes. One goal was to ensure that patients complete skin self-examinations at least once per month. In a six month pilot study, 20 patients were provided with a tablet with the skin checker app. The same reminder was sent by the team monthly to all patients. Reminders were generally effective, but not for all patients. Accordingly, we decided to investigate how reminders could be personalised. It is likely that personality plays a role in a patient's response to a reminder (along with other relevant factors such as their affective state, daily schedules, etc.), and as personality is relatively stable in adults, it seems a relevant characteristic to consider for the personalization of reminders.

For this research, the Five-Factor model of Personality [18] is used, as it is one of the most popular and reliably validated constructs in use by psychologists. This model describes five personality dimensions: Agreeableness (I), Extraversion (II), Conscientiousness (III), Emotional Stability (IV) and Openness to Experience (V).

This paper builds on previous research [14], which examined the selection of reminders based on Cialdini's 6 principles of persuasion [10]. In the previous study, participants rated 12 reminders for their suitability for a patient with either low or high conscientiousness (as expressed through a story about the patient). There were three main issues arising from that study. The first issue is that the participants' own personality may have impacted their decisions about the suitability of the reminders for the described patients, and that they may have had difficulty to understand what may work best for a patient with a radically different personality to their own. In this paper, we will measure participants' personality and let them rate reminders for a patient with the same (or very similar) personality to their own.

A second issue is that the reminders used were not stringently validated as expressing the correct Cialdini persuasive principle. In this paper, we will report on the validation of the reminder messages and use these validated messages in the main study.

A third issue is that the previous study only investigated Conscientiousness. In this paper, we will investigate the effect of all Five-Factor Model personality traits.

The paper is organized as follows: Section 2 summarises the related work; Section 3 reports on the validation of a set of 12 reminders (2 for each of Cialdini's 6 principles); and Section 4 reports a study using these reminders where participants rated these reminders for their suitability for a patient with a personality similar to their own. Participants also selected their favourite reminder, an alternative reminder to send if that one failed, and indicated the amount of time they would wait between sending the first and second reminder. Section 5 concludes the paper and discusses future work. From the results of this study, we aim to discover which reminders are most effective for certain personalities, which will allow the ASICA app to intelligently select these in the future. Additionally, as there are many e-health interventions which incorporate self-monitoring for long term conditions, it is hoped that the findings from this work will allow such interventions to adapt to the patient personality and improve adherence to self-monitoring.

2. RELATED WORK

Many behaviour changes techniques exist (for example, [34] identified 137 techniques). The use of prompts (also called triggers) is one of the most used techniques, and this paper focusses on a special kind of prompts namely reminders. Many studies across the healthcare domain have shown the effectiveness of digital reminders (e.g. [39, 15, 48, 22, 4]).

To produce effective reminders, we use Cialdini's 6 principles of persuasion [10] (shown in Table 1), as they have been used in multiple contexts and can be easily implemented as reminders [27]. For example, they have been used in reminders for clinic appointments [44] and interaction with an activity monitor app [27].

It has been argued that personalization of prompts will make them more effective. For example, [17] argued that prompts need to be adapted to the user's motivation and

Table 1: Cialdini's 6 principles of persuasion [9, 27].

Principle	Description
Liking (LIK)	"People like those who like them." If a request is made by someone we like, we are more likely to say yes.
Reciprocity (REC)	"People repay in kind." People are more likely to do something for someone they feel they owe a favour.
Consensus (CON)	"People follow the lead of similar others." People will do the same as other people who are similar to them.
Commitment and Consistency (COM)	"People align with their clear commitments." People will do something if they have committed to it. Also, they will act consistently with previous behaviour.
Authority (AUT)	"People defer to experts." If a doctor advises you to take a medication, you are likely to comply.
Scarcity (SCA)	"People want more of what they can have less of." People will take the opportunity to do something that they can't leave until later.

ability. Based on this, he distinguishes three types of prompts: *spark prompts* that motivate people who lack motivation to act, *facilitator prompts* that make behaviour easier for motivated people with low ability, and *signal prompts* that remind motivated people with high ability to act. This paper does not consider this kind of adaptation and the reminders that are studied are closest to spark prompts, even though a basic level of motivation can be assumed given the users have been treated for skin cancer. There is also some evidence that prompts may need to be personalized to user demographics. For example, Masthoff et al. [30] showed that prompts in the charity domain may need to be personalized to gender, age, religion and country affinity and Brown et al. [6] suggested that older people are more sensitive to Cialdini's *consistency* technique. Again, demographic characteristics are not considered in this paper though we recognize that user characteristics such as gender and cultural background may well influence the relative effectiveness of prompts.

Personalisation in reminders is a relatively new field. McGee et al. [32] identified the need for the personalising reminder systems, as current personalisation is often limited to only preferred time. Some research has been done on personalising reminders – e.g. adapting to the user's location and movement when providing medication reminders [28] and tailoring mammography reminders to personal risk and the patient's personal barriers to having a mammogram [31].

It has been argued that persuasive techniques or even the choice of a persuasive technique may need to be adapted to the user's personality. For example, studies by Kaptein (e.g. [26]) have investigated the effectiveness of adapting the strategy used in a persuasive prompt (for example, appeal to authority, appeal to commitment) to the user's susceptibility to Cialdini's six social persuasion principles. Dennis et al. [13] have investigated the adaptation of feedback and emotional support to personality. Orji et al. [38] have investigated the adaptation of the selection of persuasive technique to gamer types.

The link between personality and the result of reminders in the healthcare domain has also been investigated, e.g [23] found that conscientious people would likely be the most successful at achieving their health objectives, and persuasive categories with a social aspect were likely to be the most successful for conscientious people. Patients low in conscientiousness typically have lower adherence to treatments [7,

Table 2: Reminder messages selected for Study 2 based on the validation results of Study 1

Category	ID	Message	LIK	REC	CON	COM	AUT	SCA	OTH	Kappa
SCA	SCA1	This is your last opportunity for your monthly skin check. Do not miss out - please check your skin now.	0	1	0	7	4	47	1	0.781
	SCA2	You are running out of time to check your skin this month. Please check your skin now.	0	1	0	4	1	21	3	0.421
AUT	AUT1	According to experts, checking your skin regularly is an effective way of identifying recurrent skin cancer. Please check your skin now.	0	0	3	3	54	0	0	0.649
	AUT2	Expert dermatologists emphasize the benefits of regular skin checking. Please check your skin now.	0	0	1	2	56	1	0	0.618
COM	COM1	When you decided to participate, you agreed that checking your skin monthly is a good idea. Please check your skin now.	1	5	1	47	5	0	1	0.849
	COM2	You promised that you would use the Skin Checker iPad to check your skin. Please check your skin now.	1	5	2	49	3	0	0	0.715
CON	CON1	Thousands of people are actively checking their skin each month. Join them - please check your skin now.	1	1	53	4	1	0	0	0.746
	CON2	Other users have found the Skin Checker iPad very helpful. Please check your skin now.	2	1	50	3	2	0	2	0.748
LIK	LIK1	Your family would appreciate it if you performed your monthly skin check so they don't need to worry about you as much. Please check your skin now.	42	8	5	1	0	1	3	0.744
	LIK2	Lots of people care about you and would feel better if you took the time to check your skin. Please check your skin now.	44	6	4	3	2	0	1	0.68
REC	REC1	The Skin Checker iPad was provided to you to help you check your skin. Please return the favour by doing something for us - check your skin now.	0	24	1	3	0	2	0	0.584
	REC2	We spent a lot of time developing this app to help you. Please check your skin for us now.	0	24	2	1	3	0	0	0.584

8]. Therefore, it is likely that patients who are low in conscientiousness would require different types of reminders, and perhaps more frequently, than those patients who are normally highly conscientious.

3. STUDY 1: REMINDER VALIDATION

This section describes our approach to categorize and validate reminder messages. Initially we produced a wide range of reminders attempting to provide wide coverage of Cialdini's principles. We validated the categorisation of these messages in categories linked to Cialdini's principles shown in Table 1. We adopted the approach used in [13], who investigated the categorization of emotional support statements.

3.1 Study Design

3.1.1 Participants

Participants were recruited from Amazon's Mechanical Turk service [35], a crowd-sourcing tool. For this validation experiment, participants had to be based in the US and have an acceptance rate of 90% (meaning that 90% of the work they do is accepted by other requesters as good quality) and were paid $0.50. We used a Cloze Test [43] for English fluency due to the language based nature of the study. Workers who failed the test were excluded. The validation was run in two studies. 30 participants completed the first study (21 male; 16 aged 18-25, 10 aged 26-40, 12 aged 41-65) and 30 participants the second study (18 male; 7 aged 18-25, 18 aged 26-40, 5 aged 41-65).

3.1.2 Procedure

Participants were introduced to the categories and their definitions (as described in Table 1). Next, they were shown a message and asked to place it into one of the categories (still seeing the definitions). Participants could rate the reminder as 'other' if they did not think the reminder fitted any of the categories. This was repeated for each message. 24 messages were used in Study 1A and 24 in Study 1B. Participants were advised that there were no right or wrong answers and that it was their opinion that counted. The order of messages was randomized.

3.1.3 Validation Measure

We use Free-Marginal Kappa [41] as a metric for establishing how well categorized our reminder messages were. The kappa value describes agreement amongst raters, with 1 indicating unanimous agreement, 0.7 excellent and 0.4 moderate agreement. To be reliably categorized, the kappa score for the message had to be ≥ 0.4.

3.2 Results

In Study 1A, 16 out of 24 messages obtained a kappa ≥ 0.4, 11 of which obtained a kappa ≥ 0.7. However, no messages at all were validated with kappa ≥ 0.4 for the *Reciprocity* category, and only one for *Scarcity* (and none with kappa ≥ 0.7). A second run of the study was therefore performed (Study 1B) with 8 new messages (4 designed for Reciprocity and 4 for Scarcity) as well as the 16 messages which had validated in the first study (to ensure there were enough different messages to make it a proper categorization task). For messages used in both studies, an overall kappa was calculated based on both studies. The valida-

Meet John

John's Doctor has given him an iPad with an app on it which helps him to check his skin. When John has used the app to do a full skin check, a notification is sent to his doctor automatically. John has been advised to check his skin monthly.

A month has passed, and John has not checked his skin yet.

John has a **very similar personality to you.**

Reminder number 1 of 12:

"When you decided to participate, you agreed that checking your skin monthly is a good idea. Please check your skin now."

Please rate this reminder for the following qualities:

	Very unmotivating				Very motivating
Motivational	▮	▮	▮	▮	▮
	▮	▮	▮	▮	▮
	▮	▮	▮	▮	▮
	▮	▮	▮	▮	▮

Read the two stories below, which describe two people. Decide which person you are most like, and then move the slider to indicate how similar that you feel they are to you.

For example, if you move the slider all the way to one of the stories, you are exactly like the person. If you are only a bit like them, move the slider less far.

Elizabeth procrastinates and wastes her time. She finds it difficult to get down to work. She does just enough work to get by and often doesn't see things through, leaving them unfinished. She shirks her duties and messes things up. She doesn't put her mind on the task at hand and needs a push to get started. Elizabeth tends to enjoy talking with people.

Jennifer is always prepared. She gets tasks done right away, paying attention to detail. She makes plans and sticks to them and carries them out. She completes tasks successfully, doing things according to a plan. She is exacting in his work; she finishes what she starts. Jennifer is quite a nice person, tends to enjoy talking with people, and quite likes exploring new ideas.

Next

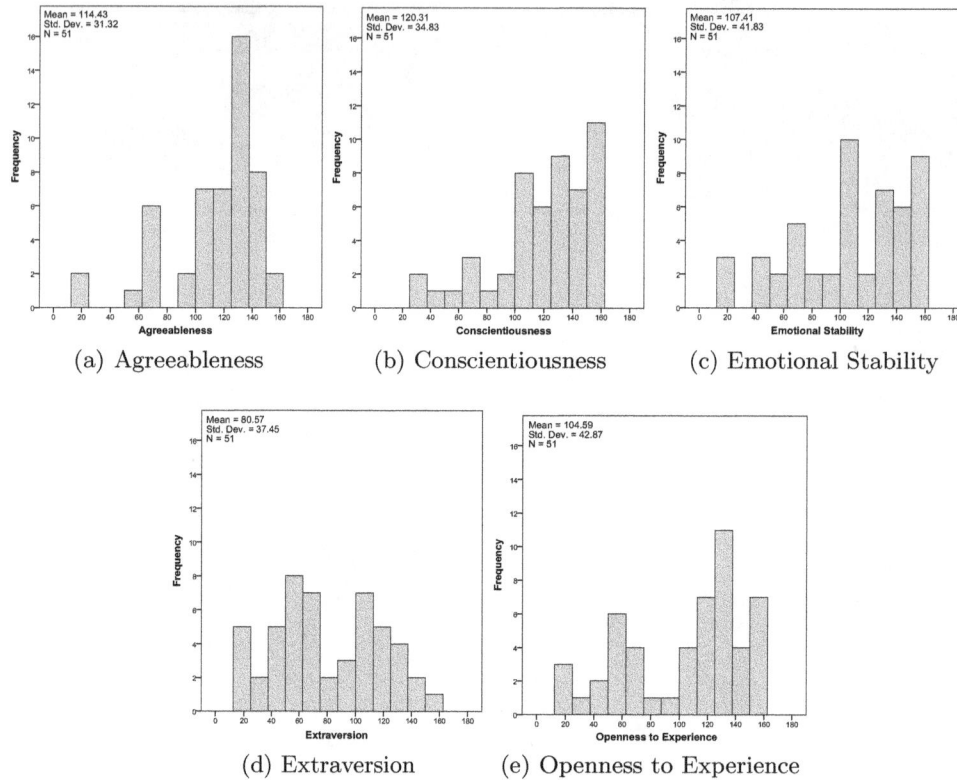

(a) Agreeableness　(b) Conscientiousness　(c) Emotional Stability

(d) Extraversion　(e) Openness to Experience

Figure 3: Personality Trait Distributions

Table 4: Homogeneous subsets for Reminder Type

Subset	Reminder Type	Mean Rating	S.E.
1	AUT	3.70	0.09
	LIK	3.37	0.10
2	LIK	3.37	0.10
	SCA	3.15	0.10
	CON	3.11	0.11
	COM	2.96	0.10
3	COM	2.96	0.10
	REC	2.54	0.12

Effects of Personality and Reminder Type on Mean Rating. A 6-way ANCOVA of Reminder Type on Mean Rating was performed with covariates of each personality trait score. This was significant ($F(5, 601) = 14.29$, $p < 0.001$) and is shown in Figure 4. Post-hoc tests revealed 3 homogeneous subsets (see Table 4). Authority and Liking were the highest rated categories and Commitment & Consistency and Reciprocity were the lowest rated. This supports *H1*. There were significant effects for the covariants Agreeableness ($F(1, 601) = 4.98$, $p = 0.03$) and Emotional Stability ($F(1, 601) = 12.24$, $p = 0.001$), providing support for *H1a*.

Effects of Personality on Mean Rating. To explore *H1a* further, partial correlations were performed for each personality trait (controlling for other traits) for each Re-

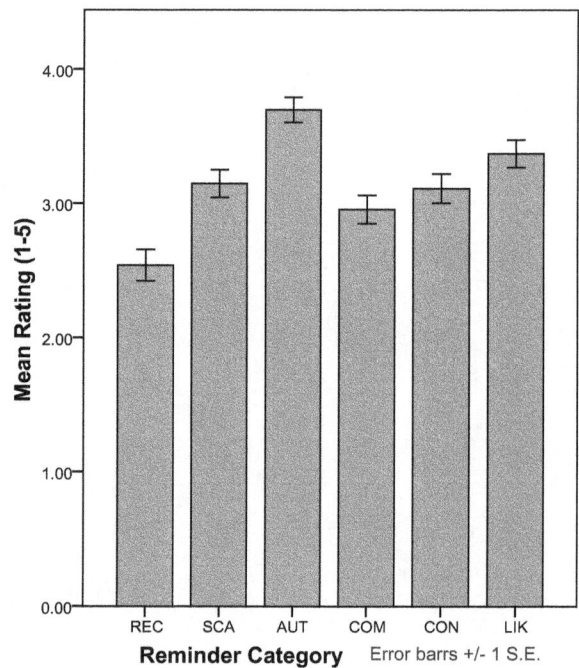

Figure 4: Mean ratings for each category

Table 5: Chi-Squared frequencies for alternative reminder type, for Conscientiousness

CONC	Reminder Type						Total
	AUT	CON	COM	LIK	REC	SCA	
Low	0*	0	4	0	0	5*	9
High	15*	0	10	11	1	5*	42
Total	15	0	14	11	1	10	51

minder, each Reminder Category and Overall. The correlations are shown in Table 3. There were significant correlations for Agreeableness for COM2 and COM, Agreeableness for REC1 and REC and Agreeableness overall. There was also an overall effect for Emotional stability. Participants with low agreeableness rated COM and REC higher than participants with high agreeableness. Participants with high Emotional Stability rated reminders higher that participants with low emotional stability. It should be noted that the correlations we found are quite small and may be of small use to adapt to without further investigation.

Effects of Personality on Best and Alternative Reminder Category. To test *H2*, a Multinominal Logistic Regression was performed of all personality trait scores on the category of the first reminder that was chosen to give to John. This showed no significant effects.

To test *H3a*, a Multinominal Logistic Regression was performed of all personality trait scores on the category of the alternative reminder that was chosen to give to John if the first reminder failed. This showed a significant effect for Conscientiousness ($\chi^2(4) = 14.45$, $p < 0.01$). To investigate the direction of this effect, we divided participants into 2 groups for conscientiousness - a 'low' group with scores less than the midpoint of the scale and a 'high' group. We then ran a χ^2 analysis of Alternative Reminder Category × Conscientiousness group. This was significant at ($\chi^2(4) = 14.14$, $p < 0.01$). The adjusted residuals show that High Conscientious participants selected AUT reminders, while low conscientious participants selected SCA reminders.

To investigate *H3*, a χ^2 analysis was run on Best Category × Alternative Category. This was significant ($\chi^2(20)=40.01$, p=0.005). Most participants selected AUT (n=19) or LIK (n=16) for the first reminder and shifted to AUT (n=15), LIK (n=11), SCA (n=10) and COM (n=14) for the second reminder. REC and CON were selected least.

Effects of Personality on Time between reminders. A correlation analysis showed no significant relation between personality trait and the time participants wanted to wait before sending the second reminder (1-30 days or 'longer'), providing no support for *H4* Most participants selected 1 or 2 days (mean 2.29±1.69; see Figure 5).

5. DISCUSSION AND CONCLUSIONS

We have found that personality should be taken into account when deciding on the type of persuasion that should be employed when sending reminders. In particular, we have found that those with high emotional stability are more responsive to any kind of persuasion. Those with low agreeableness rated all types of reminder higher than those with

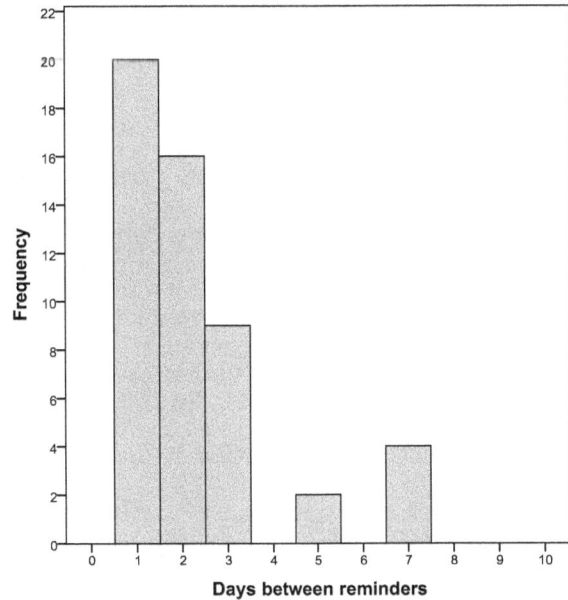

Figure 5: Days to wait between reminders

high, especially commitment/consistency and reciprocity. This is an interesting finding which requires further investigation.

We have also found that if a reminder fails to persuade, many participants picked a reminder of a different category to the first (Authority and Liking are the most popular for the first reminder, and there is a trend to using more Scarcity and Commitment for the second). There is a trend for conscientiousness– those with high conscientiousness prefer alternative reminders which use Authority, whereas those with low conscientiousness prefer Scarcity. This seems appropriate as those with low conscientiousness are more likely to procrastinate and have lower adherence to health treatments [7], so a reminder with a temporal emphasis may persuade them to act earlier. Overall, it seems that participants started with a more generic reminder for the first, then personalised the alternative one subsequently. There was no effect of personality for the time between the two reminders, with most participants waiting 1-3 days.

We have now made an important first step in the tailoring of persuasive reminders to personality. As we now have some indication of how the reminders should be selected, the next step is to consult with medical experts to establish whether they think that the adaptations are appropriate and safe. We will also consult with a patient group to identify any possible issues. These can then be incorporated into an algorithm to allow an intelligent system to utilize these adaptations. We could also make this algorithm more sophisticated by taking the patient's previous record on performing skin checks into account. For example, a neurotic patient who has always completed their skin check on time in the past may require a different reminder to a neurotic patient who is habitually late when performing their skin checks. After this process, the adaptations can be incorporated into the app, so that the effects on real patients can be tested.

In this study, we did not investigate the effect of age and gender on support type - this should be considered in future work. We also do not propose a means of determining the patient's personality so we know what to adapt to. While methods to detect personality automatically remain unreliable, we propose that a quick and easy personality test such as the Tipi test [20] or *Personality Sliders* [42] could be integrated into the set-up of the App.

Further investigations could also be performed into the generalizability of the algorithm for tailoring persuasive reminders in other domains such as physical activity, healthy-eating or other long term health conditions which require a large amount of self monitoring from patients. This would only require minor adjustments to the reminder content for the domain in question. With the rise of many health-monitoring systems and apps, this could be a valuable contribution to sustaining long-term health behaviour change.

6. ACKNOWLEDGEMENTS

This work was partially funded by the RCUK Digital Economy award to the dot.rural Digital Economy Hub, University of Aberdeen; award reference: EP/G066051/1.

7. REFERENCES

[1] Skin cancer key facts. Cancer Research UK Publications, 2014.

[2] Skin cancer risk factors. http://www.cancerresearchuk.org/cancer-info/cancerstats/types/skin/riskfactors/. Cancer Research UK, 2015.

[3] H. Akker, V. M. Jones, and H. J. Hermens. Tailoring real-time physical activity coaching systems: A literature survey and model. *User Modeling and User-Adapted Interaction*, 24(5):351–392, Dec. 2014.

[4] F. Bentley and K. Tollmar. The power of mobile notifications to increase wellbeing logging behavior. In *Proceedings of the SIGCHI Conference on Human Factors in Computing Systems*, pages 1095–1098. ACM, 2013.

[5] M. Berwick, C. B. Begg, J. A. Fine, G. C. Roush, and R. L. Barnhill. Screening for cutaneous melanoma by skin self-examination. *Natl Cancer Inst.*, 88(1):17–23, 1996.

[6] S. L. Brown, T. Asher, and R. B. Cialdini. Evidence of a positive relationship between age and preference for consistency. *Journal of Research in Personality*, 39(5):517–533, 2005.

[7] J. M. Bruce, L. M. Hancock, P. Arnett, and S. Lynch. Treatment adherence in multiple sclerosis: association with emotional status, personality, and cognition. *J. of behavioral medicine*, 33(3):219–227, 2010.

[8] A. J. Christensen and T. W. Smith. Personality and patient adherence: correlates of the 5-factor model in renal dialysis. *J. of behavioral medicine*, 18(3):305–313, 1995.

[9] R. B. Cialdini. Harnessing the science of persuasion. *Harvard Business Review*, 79(9):72–81, 2001.

[10] R. B. Cialdini. *Influence: Science and practice.* Pearson, 2001.

[11] K. M. Dalal, Q. Zhou, K. S. Panageas, M. S. Brady, D. P. Jaques, and D. G. Coit. Methods of detection of first recurrence in patients with stage i/ii primary cutaneous melanoma after sentinel lymph node biopsy. *Ann Surg Oncol*, 15(8):2206–2214, 2008.

[12] M. Dennis, J. Masthoff, and C. Mellish. The quest for validated personality trait stories. In *Proceedings of IUI 2012*, pages 273–276, New York, USA, 2012. ACM.

[13] M. Dennis, J. Masthoff, and C. Mellish. Adapting progress feedback and emotional support to learner personality. *International Journal of Artificial Intelligence in Education*, pages 1–55, 2015.

[14] M. G. Dennis, K. A. Smith, J. Masthoff, and N. Tintarev. How can skin check reminders be personalised to patient conscientiousness? *UMAP 2015 Adjunct Proceedings*, 2015.

[15] N. Dowshen, L. M. Kuhns, A. Johnson, B. J. Holoyda, and R. Garofalo. Improving adherence to antiretroviral therapy for youth living with hiv/aids: a pilot study using personalized, interactive, daily text message reminders. *J. of Medical Internet Research*, 14(2), 2012.

[16] B. S. Fjeldsoe, A. L. Marshall, and Y. D. Miller. Behavior change interventions delivered by mobile telephone short-message service. *American J. of preventive medicine*, 36(2):165–173, 2009.

[17] B. J. Fogg. A behavior model for persuasive design. In *Proceedings of the 4th international Conference on Persuasive Technology*, page 40. ACM, 2009.

[18] L. Goldberg. The structure of phenotypic personality traits. *American Psychologist*, 48:26–34, 1993.

[19] L. R. Goldberg, J. A. Johnson, H. W. Eber, R. Hogan, M. C. Ashton, C. R. Cloninger, and H. C. Gough. The international personality item pool and the future of public-domain personality measures. *J. of Reseach in Personality*, 40:84–96, 2006.

[20] S. D. Gosling, P. J. Rentfrow, and W. B. Swann Jr. A very brief measure of the big-five personality domains. *Journal of Research in personality*, 37(6):504–528, 2003.

[21] K. E. Grady. Cue enhancement and the long-term practice of breast self-examination. *Behav Med*, 7(2):191–204, 1984.

[22] I. Gurol-Urganci, T. de Jongh, V. Vodopivec-Jamsek, R. Atun, and J. Car. Mobile phone messaging reminders for attendance at healthcare appointments. *The Cochrane Library*, 2013.

[23] S. Halko and J. Kientz. Personality and persuasive technology: An exploratory study on health-promoting mobile applications. In *Persuasive Technology*, volume 6137 of *LNCS*, pages 150–161. Springer Berlin Heidelberg, 2010.

[24] S. Hall and P. Murchie. Can we use technology to encourage self-monitoring by people treated for melanoma? a qualitative exploration of the perceptions of potential recipients. *Supportive Care in Cancer*, 22(6):1663–1671, 2014.

[25] P. R. Hull, N. G. Piemontesi, and J. Lichtenwald. Compliance with self-examination surveillance in patients with melanoma and atypical moles: an anonymous questionnaire study. *Cutaneous Medicine and Surgery*, 15(2):97–102, 2010.

[26] M. Kaptein, B. De Ruyter, P. Markopoulos, and E. Aarts. Adaptive persuasive systems: a study of

tailored persuasive text messages to reduce snacking. *ACM Transactions on Interactive Intelligent Systems (TiiS)*, 2(2):10, 2012.

[27] M. Kaptein and A. van Halteren. Adaptive persuasive messaging to increase service retention: using persuasion profiles to increase the effectiveness of email reminders. *Personal and Ubiquitous Computing*, 17(6):1173–1185, 2013.

[28] P. Kaushik, S. S. Intille, and K. Larson. Observations from a case study on user adaptive reminders for medication adherence. In *Pervasive Computing Technologies for Healthcare, 2008.*, pages 250–253. IEEE, 2008.

[29] J. Masthoff, F. Grasso, and J. Ham. Preface to the special issue on personalization and behavior change. *User Modeling and User-Adapted Interaction*, 24(5):345–350, Dec. 2014.

[30] J. Masthoff, S. Langrial, and K. van Deemter. Personalizing triggers for charity actions. In *Persuasive Technology*, pages 125–136. Springer, 2013.

[31] K. D. McCaul and K. S. Wold. The effects of mailed reminders and tailored messages on mammography screening. *Journal of community health*, 27(3):181–190, 2002.

[32] M. R. McGee-Lennon, M. K. Wolters, and S. Brewster. User-centred multimodal reminders for assistive living. In *Proceedings of the SIGCHI Conference on Human Factors in Computing Systems*, pages 2105–2114. ACM, 2011.

[33] S. Michie, C. Abraham, C. Whittington, J. McAteer, and S. Gupta. Effective techniques in healthy eating and physical activity interventions: a meta-regression. *Health Psychology*, 28(6):690, 2009.

[34] S. Michie, M. Johnston, J. Francis, W. Hardeman, and M. Eccles. From theory to intervention: mapping theoretically derived behavioural determinants to behaviour change techniques. *Applied psychology*, 57(4):660–680, 2008.

[35] MT. Amazon mechanical turk. http://www.mturk.com, 2012.

[36] P. Murchie, M. Nicolson, P. Hannaford, E. Raja, A. Lee, and N. Campbell. Patient satisfaction with gp-led melanoma follow-up: a randomised controlled trial. *Brit J Cancer*, 102(10):1447–1455, 2010.

[37] S. M. Noar, C. N. Benac, and M. S. Harris. Does tailoring matter? meta-analytic review of tailored print health behavior change interventions. *Psychological bulletin*, 133(4):673, 2007.

[38] R. Orji, J. Vassileva, and R. L. Mandryk. Modeling the efficacy of persuasive strategies for different gamer types in serious games for health. *User Modeling and User-Adapted Interaction*, 24(5):453–498, 2014.

[39] S. Ornstein, D. Garr, R. Jenkins, P. Rust, and A. Arnon. Computer-generated physician and patient reminders. tools to improve population adherence to selected preventive services. *The Journal of family practice*, 32(1):82–90, 1991.

[40] G. Phillips, L. Felix, L. Galli, V. Patel, and P. Edwards. The effectiveness of m-health technologies for improving health and health services: a systematic review protocol. *BMC research notes*, 3(1):250, 2010.

[41] J. J. Randolph. Free-marginal multirater kappa: An alternative to fleiss' fixed-marginal multirater kappa. In *Joensuu University Learning and Instruction Symposium 2005*, 2005.

[42] K. A. Smith, M. Dennis, J. Masthoff, and N. Tintarev. *A Method of Bootstrapping Adapation using Personality Stories*, In Progress.

[43] W. L. Taylor. Cloze procedure: A new tool for measuring readability. *Journalism Quarterly*, 30:415–433, 1953.

[44] M. F. Walji and J. Zhang. Human-centered design of persuasive appointment reminders. In *Hawaii International Conference on System Sciences, Proceedings of the 41st Annual*, pages 236–236. IEEE, 2008.

[45] D. J. Wantland, C. J. Portillo, W. L. Holzemer, R. Slaughter, and E. M. McGhee. The effectiveness of web-based vs. non-web-based interventions: a meta-analysis of behavioral change outcomes. *Journal of medical Internet research*, 6(4):e40, 2004.

[46] T. Webb, J. Joseph, L. Yardley, and S. Michie. Using the internet to promote health behavior change: a systematic review and meta-analysis of the impact of theoretical basis, use of behavior change techniques, and mode of delivery on efficacy. *Medical Internet Research*, 12(1):e4, 2010.

[47] V. Williams, J. Price, M. Hardinge, L. Tarassenko, and A. Farmer. Using a mobile health application to support self-management in copd: a qualitative study. *Brit J Gen Pract*, 64(624):e392–e400, 2014.

[48] D. Zurovac, R. K. Sudoi, W. S. Akhwale, M. Ndiritu, D. H. Hamer, A. K. Rowe, and R. W. Snow. The effect of mobile phone text-message reminders on kenyan health workers' adherence to malaria treatment guidelines: a cluster randomised trial. *The Lancet*, 378(9793):795–803, 2011.

Harnessing Crowdsourced Recommendation Preference Data from Casual Gameplay

Barry Smyth, Rachael Rafter, Sam Banks
Insight Centre for Data Analytics
University College Dublin, Dublin, Ireland
firstname.surname@insight-centre.org

ABSTRACT

Recommender systems have become a familiar part of our online experiences, suggesting movies to watch, music to listen to, and books to read, among other things. To make relevant suggestions, recommender systems need an accurate picture of our preferences and interests and sometimes even our friends and influencers. This information can be difficult to come by and expensive to source. In this paper we describe a game-with-a-purpose designed to infer useful recommendation data as a side-effect of gameplay. The game is a simple, single-player matching game in which players attempt to match movies with their friends. It has been developed as a Facebook app and harnesses the social graph and likes of players as a source of game data. We describe the basic game mechanics and evaluate the utility of the recommendation knowledge that can be inferred from its gameplay as part of a live-user trial.

1. INTRODUCTION

Recommender systems have become a familiar part of our online experiences, suggesting products, items and services from our favourite online stores to entertainment and news sites. Today recommender systems have an influence on what we read, listen to, and watch. They often determine where we vacation and may even influence our choice of a mate.

To make good suggestions recommender systems use various types of information. Most rely on user preferences, such as item ratings [1]. Many take advantage of matrix factorisation methods to find hidden patterns within these preferences [19]. Others harness inter-user similarity to identify groups of like-minded users [7]. Some even leverage social network information to infer trust or influence relationships between users [11, 12, 27, 28]. The source of this information, and the ability to collect it at scale for many millions of users, has been the subject of much research within the recommender systems community. Many approaches have been considered, from using explicit feedback such as transaction histories to inferring interest from indirect signals such as read-times or sharing [17]. It is always interesting to consider novel ways to collect these types of data.

GWAPs (games-with-a-purpose) are casual computer games that are typically simple and fun to play. They are designed so that gameplay contributes to some secondary problem solving goal; e.g. the ESP Game invites pairs of players to guess words for a specific image [40]. Players gain points when they guess the same words and as many players compete on the same images their guesses contribute to a rich tag-based representation of the images. Similar games have been used to describe other forms of media such as audio and video [10,22,37] and more sophisticated GWAPs have been developed with other tasks in mind, from object segmentation [31] to protein folding [6].

The power of a GWAP stems from its ability to attract large numbers of players each of whom contributes some fragment of solution knowledge as part of a greater goal through their natural gameplay. GWAPs take advantage of tried and trusted game mechanics to offer players a gaming experience that is compelling and fun, often attracting large numbers of players to harness considerable collective intelligence. If GWAPs can be used for challenging tasks such as object recognition and protein folding might they also be used to help build better recommender systems?

This is the question that motivates our work. In particular, we will describe a GWAP designed to infer useful recommendation knowledge as a side-effect of gameplay. The paper builds on initial work presented in [3] which proposes a simple, single-player matching game in which players attempt to match movies with their friends. In this paper we describe how these matches can be used to infer the strength of relationships between users (an important source of knowledge for many recommender systems) as well as the likely level of interest a user will have in a particular movie (another key source of recommendation knowledge). The game has been developed as a Facebook app and harnesses the social graph and likes of players as a source of game data. In this paper we describe the basic game mechanics in detail and evaluate the utility of the recommendation knowledge that can be inferred from its gameplay as part of a live-user trial.

2. RELATED WORK

This work brings together ideas from the fields of recommender systems [1, 18, 29, 32, 34], crowdsourcing and human computation [4,14], and games-with-a-purpose [2,2,6,36,37,39]. We focus in particular on classical recommender systems (such as collaborative filtering and content-based approaches) and games-with-a-purpose to ask whether useful recommender systems data might be crowdsourced as a by-product of casual gameplay. In fact, as we shall see, the idea of crowdsourcing recommendation knowledge is gaining momentum (see, for example, [9, 20, 21, 25]) and we will discuss some specific examples of how these ideas have been adopted by some in the recommender systems community.

2.1 Recommender Systems

Generally speaking there are two common approaches when it comes to building a recommender system. Both rely on the availability of user profiles but each uses different types of information in these profiles and generates recommendations in different ways.

The most well-known recommendation approach is *collaborative filtering* which can be traced back to early work by [30]. User profiles usually take the form of user ratings over some set of items. These ratings may be provided explicitly by the user (e.g. star ratings, likes, etc.) or they may be inferred from user behaviour (e.g. purchase actions, clicks, search histories etc.). Ratings may be unary (e.g. Facebook 'likes'), binary (positive vs negative) or they may be multi-valued (e.g. Amazon's 5-point rating scale). One common collaborative filtering approach is to use these ratings directly to identify users who are similar to the target user and then select highly rated items from their profiles as suggestions for the target user; this approach is known as *user-based* collaborative filtering; see [30]. The same ratings can be used to estimate item similarities (based on ratings correlations) to suggest to the target user movies that are similar to those she has liked; so-called *item-based* collaborative filtering [33]. More recently, researchers have used matrix factorization and related ideas [19] to discover latent features within the ratings data as the basis for recommendation and prediction.

A second common recommendation approach is content-based recommendation; see [29,34]. Unlike collaborative filtering, content-based approaches rely on rich product descriptions; for example, a movie might be described in terms of its genre, actors, director, year or release etc. This data can be used to directly determine similarities between movies. Then, for a target user, recommendations can be produced by, for example, selecting and ranking items that are similar to those that the user has liked in the past.

Collaborative filtering and content-based methods have their pros and cons. The former benefits from large populations of active users, the latter from rich item descriptions. Content-based approaches can comfortably handle new items during recommendations whereas collaborative filtering approaches can only recommend new items once enough ratings have been obtained. Content-based approaches tend generate recommendations that are similar to each other and, as such, can offer limited recommendation diversity. Collaborative filtering are less susceptible to diversity issues but do tend to skew towards more popular items. However both approaches have been used to good effect and can be combined to create hybrid recommenders [5] to offer a *best-of-both-worlds* advantage.

For the purpose of this work we will focus on how a GWAP can be used to collect useful data about which users may be interested in which movies and how this data can be used to generate and rank recommendations, directly and indirectly. In due course, we will also compare these recommendations to those produced by more conventional collaborative filtering and content-based approaches.

2.2 Games-with-a-Purpose

Games-with-a-purpose are motivated by the observation that millions of people enjoy spending time playing games everyday and the tantalising prospect that it may be possible to turn some of this gameplay into solutions (or fragments of solutions) for challenging, large-scale, real-world problems. Many of these problems are classical problems such as image labeling or object recognition but others hint at the power of GWAPs to target some of life's biggest challenges, from drug discovery and protein folding to climate change.

GWAPs often trace their origins to the work of Luis von Ahn [39].

The quintessential GWAP is the ESP Game mentioned in the introduction section of this paper [41]. The ESP Game is an image labelling game; or rather the gameplay date derived from the ESP Game can be used to label images. As already mentioned, it is a two-player game in which two (random) remote players (who do not know each other and cannot communicate) are presented with the same (input) image. The goal of the game is for each player to guess a label (output) the other player will give; this style of game is referred to as an *output agreement* model. Points are awarded, and a new image is presented, when one of the players types a label that matches a label already entered by the other player. Gameplay is enjoyable and addictive, as evidenced by the large number of players and significant investment in gameplay that the ESP Game was able to attract. And as a result of this gameplay it is possible to quickly generate high quality image labels; for example, if a label is frequently entered by players for the same image then it is a strong signal that this label is valid and important for the image. The ESP Game experimented with various features to improve gameplay and encourage the submission of alternative or unusual labels for images as well as popular labels.

Another example of a well-known GWAP is TagATune; see [24]. This time two random players receive inputs (music) that are known by the game, but not the players, to be the same or different. The players provide outputs (tags) describing what the hear so that their partner may be able to assess whether they are listing to the same tune or not. And they gain points if both players correctly determine whether they are listening to the same or a different (input) tune. Thus, this style of GWAP is referred to as an *input agreement* game; see also [23].

Yet a third style of game is exemplified by Peekaboom [43], this time for locating objects in images. It is an example of the so-called *inversion-problem* model of GWAP. In Peekaboom one player ("Peek") attempts to guess the word associated with the image that is being slowly revealed by the other player ("Boom"). Boom can gradually reveal the image in 20-pixel regions and indicate to Peek whether the guesses are "hot" or "cold". If Peek guesses correctly both players receive a score. When this happens the game has generated not just an object label but information about where in the image the labeled object is located, since Boom is motivated to reveal that part of the image that goes with a particular label. The game once again proved popular and playable, attracting large numbers of players and generating significant object label data. Intriguingly, the output of the ESP Game can be used as the image labels to drive Peekaboom.

Over the last few years GWAPs have been proposed for a wide range of tasks, from improving image search [2] to protein folding [6] to large scale urban image acquisition [36]. In this paper we are especially interested in the idea that a GWAP might be a useful way to crowdsource user preferences and other forms of recommendation knowledge. This idea is not new per se, at least in the sense that GWAPs have in the past been used to elicit user preference information. Perhaps the best known example of this is the Matchin game [13] which attempts to learn image preference information by asking two randomly chosen players, "which of these two images do you think your partner prefers?" If both partners click on the same image, they both obtain points, whereas if they click on different images, neither of them receives points; it's another *output agreement* game. The game, although simple, has proven to be enjoyable, attracting tens of thousands of players and gathering millions of preference judgements. The work of [13] compares several techniques for combining these judgments between pairs of images and presents a novel algorithm for recommending unseen images to a target user based on their past judgements. In addition, and as an aside, they go on to show how merely observing user preferences on a specially chosen set of images can accurately predict a user's gender.

2.3 On Crowdsourcing and GWAPs for Recommender Systems

The work of [13] provides an early example of an intriguing link between GWAPs, human computation, crowdsourcing and recommender systems. In the meantime the recommender systems community has grown increasingly aware of, and interested in, such approaches, as evidenced by a series of annual workshops on *Crowdsourcing & Human Computation for Recommender Systems* [1].

For example, the work of [21] considers the sparsity problem in collaborative filtering, by appealing to the crowd as a source of additional information. By using reciprocal recommendations to identify not only items that are suited to users, but also users that are suited to items, they propose that it is possible to create an incentivization for users to contribute information on items. Users are motivated to contribute because the recommender system matches them with items that they find fun and interesting to comment on, review or interact with. The expected result: reduced information sparsity for an overall improvement of recommendations; see also the work of [25] for related ideas.

Felfernig et al. [9] describe how crowdsourcing ideas can be used to address some of the knowledge acquisition and engineering bottlenecks that come with some recommender systems. The authors focus on constraint-based recommenders which harness complex constraint sets that are difficult to acquire. They translate this complex task into a simpler set of micro-tasks (e.g., input an item, or validate an item against a set of characteristics) that are amenable to human computation and crowdsourcing. The crowdsourced data is then automatically converted into a richer set of constraints for the purpose of recommendation and reasoning.

On the matter of GWAPs and recommender systems one notable piece of related work describes the Curator system, a game-with-a-purpose for recommending collections of items that go together [44]. The authors present a class of GWAP for building collections where users create collections; in this case clothing or accessory collections. Players are awarded points based on the collections that match, using an output agreement model. The data from these games helps researchers to develop guidelines for collection recommender systems by, for example, noting items that are frequently collected together versus those similar items that are rarely part of the same collection.

3. THE RECOMMENDATION GAME

Our game is a simple Facebook app based around the idea of a player matching movies with their friends. Facebook was a natural platform choice, not just because of its popularity, but also because it provides access to a user's social graph (specifically the player's friends) and unary preference information (in the form Facebook likes). We will focus on movies here but of course there is no reason why a similar approach could not be used for other types of items or content such as books, music, TV shows, brands, etc. In this section we will summarise the basic architecture and game mechanics, as well as the data produced during gameplay, before detailing how this data can be used in a recommendation context.

3.1 Game Architecture

The overall system architecture is summarised in Figure 1. There are two sides to the system: the *game engine* and the *recommenda-*

tion engine. The former is responsible for managing gameplay and collecting relevant (recommendation) data as a side effect of gameplay; we will focus on this in what follows. The latter is responsible for using gameplay data to generate recommendations and we will focus on this aspect in the next section.

The system draws on two external sources of data. As mentioned previously, Facebook provides access to important user data. This includes information about a user's friends ($Friends(u)$) and their avatars, which are needed by the game engine as game targets. It also includes information about *movie likes*, that is movies that a user has explicitly liked on Facebook ($Likes(u)$). The likes of a player's friends represents one source of movies for the game.

The second source of movie data is provided by Rotten Tomatoes[2], a popular movie review site. It is used as source of movie poster graphics to represent the movies during gameplay. But it also used as an additional source of movies for gameplay (popular movies are mixed with the likes of friends during a typical game).

These sources of data, and the data generated by gameplay itself, are used to populate three data-stores of user (friends and likes), movie (posters and popular titles), and game data (matches and interests) as shown.

3.2 Basic Gameplay

Gameplay is designed to be simple but enjoyable. An example screenshot of the game in action is shown in Figure 2. During each game the player p is presented with a set of friend avatars ($f_1, ..., f_n$) at the bottom of the game arena as shown; currently $n = 5$ friends are selected randomly from $Friends(p)$. In addition a set of movies ($m_1, ..., m_k$) are chosen from the likes of these friends and including a mixture of popular movies from Rotten Tomatoes; $k = 18$ movies are currently chosen.

The objective of the game is for p to match movies with friends, on the basis that she believes a friend will like a particular movie. Player p does this by dragging and dropping a movie poster onto a friend's avatar. We refer to this as a *match* and use $match(p, m, f)$ to indicate that player p has matched movie m with friend f. The set of matches that make up a given game is denoted by $Matches(p)$ as shown in Equation 1.

$$Matches(p) = \bigcup_{\forall f \in Friends(p)} \{(p, m, f) : match(p, m, f)\}$$

$$(1)$$

To make the game more challenging, the movie posters follow different trajectories across the screen, becoming more erratic as the game progresses. The player has a limited time to make as many matches as they can. Each match is rewarded with a graphical and audible flourish (the friend's avatar explodes in a fountain of popcorn) and the player receives a variable score. We will discuss scoring shortly but first it is useful to describe the two different forms of recommendation data that can be derived from these matches.

3.3 From Matches to Recommendation Data

For a given match we either know that f likes m ($m \in Likes(f)$), which we refer to as a *known match*, or we have no such knowledge ($m \notin Likes(f)$), in which case it is an *unknown match*. In either case, we can infer useful recommendation data as follows.

In the case of a known match we learn something about p's understanding of f's (movie) interests. Intuitively, if p produces a lot of known matches for some friend f then it suggests that p knows f's interests well because their intuitions are, in some sense, con-

[1] http://crowdrecworkshop.org/

[2] see http://www.rottentomatoes.com

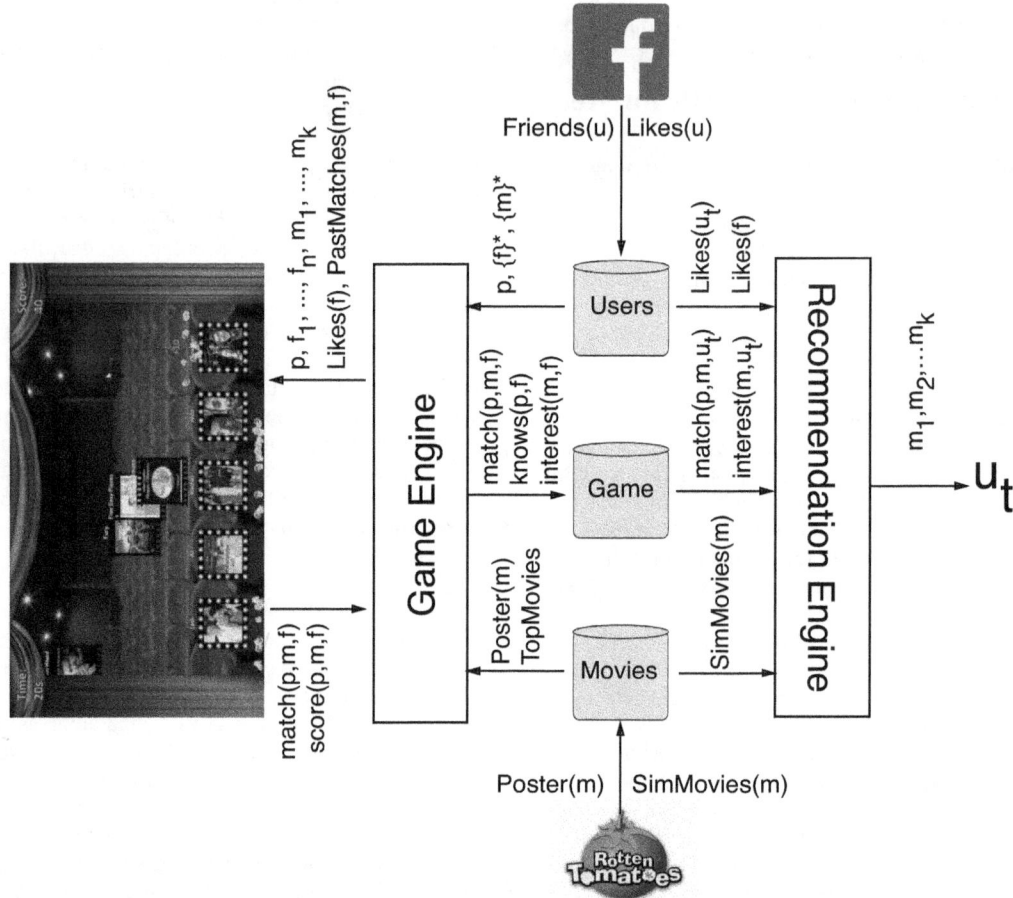

Figure 1: The Recommendation Game architecture, emphasising the game and recommendation components, information flows, and key sources of data, internal and external.

firmed by f's own Facebook likes. We can estimate $knows(p, f)$ as the proportion of known matches ($KnownMatches(p, m, f)$) that p generates for f relative to all matches p generates for f ($FriendMatches(p, m, f)$); see Equations 2 – 4.

$$FriendMatches(p, f) = \{(p, m, f^*) \in Matches(p) : f = f^*\} \quad (2)$$

$$KnownMatches(p, f) = \{(p, m, f) \in FriendMatches(p, f) : m \in Likes(f)\} \quad (3)$$

$$knows(p, f) = \frac{|KnownMatches(p, f)|}{|FriendMatches(p, f)|} \quad (4)$$

As for unknown matches, even when we have no information about f's interest in m ($m \notin Likes(f)$) this does not mean it is a poor match; remember $Likes(f)$ is not exhaustive and so there may be many movies that f likes but that are missing from her Facebook data. The fact that p assigns the match suggests that p thinks f will be interested in m. This establishes m as a potential (novel) recommendation candidate for f in the future. If other players also match m with f then this strengthens the possible relevance of m to f. Equation 5 captures this idea as an interest score

based on the number of players who have matched m with f, and how well they know f; their tie strengths with f.

$$interest(m, f) = \sum_{\forall p : match(p, m, f) \wedge m \notin Likes(f)} knows(p, f) \quad (5)$$

Thus, using these two types of matching data (known and unknown matches) we derive relationship information from known matches and we can use this information to weight the plausibility of novel recommendation candidates derived from unknown matches. Later we will describe how this information can be used in a number of different recommendation strategies, but first let us return to the scoring element of gameplay.

3.4 Scoring

Scoring is an important element of game mechanics and, in particular, how a player's score changes provides important feedback and an incentive to play. Scoring is more nuanced that might first appear. We want to encourage the player to make many matches — more matches mean more recommendation data — but we also want to reward useful matches and novel recommendation data. Intuitively we should reward p when she correctly matches m with f; that is when $m \in Likes(f)$. These matches are known to be correct in the sense that m is already known to be liked by f. But what about if m is not known to be liked by f? Such a match can still

Figure 2: The Recommendation Game in action. The game-area shows the avatars of 5 friends for the current player at the bottom of the screen. Above these we see a number of movie poster graphics, which float across the screen. If a player believes a friend will like a movie then they can drag the movie poster to the corresponding avatar to be rewarded with a graphical flourish (exploding popcorn) and a score. The scoring mechanism is designed to incentivise players to make as many matches as possible while rewarding matches based on an estimate of how useful they are likely to be as recommendation data.

be a useful source of recommendation data because it can suggest a new movie for recommendation to f.

Our scoring metric should give credit for both types of matches, known and unknown. For example, in this work we use Equation 6. In this case α can be used to adjust the relative weight given to known versus unknown matches (in this work, for simplicity, we set $\alpha = 0.5$). The score for unknown matches is inversely proportional to the number of times the same match has been generated by other players in the past ($PastMatches(m, f)$).

Equation 6 returns a score up to 10 for each match. For example, if p matches m with f, such that $m \in Likes(f)$, and 3 other players have made the same match before, then p will receive a score 6.25 ($= 10 \bullet (0.5 \bullet 1 + 0.5/4)$). If, on the other hand, $m \notin Likes(f)$ and p is the first to make such a match then p receives a score of 5 ($= 10 \bullet (0 + 0.5/1)$).

$$score(p,m,f) =$$
$$10 \bullet \left(\alpha \bullet 1[m \in Likes(f)] + \frac{1-\alpha}{1 + PastMatches(m,f)} \right) \tag{6}$$

Obviously there are many possible variations on this scoring metric that could (and should) be tested in the future. For example, in the metric above the score given to unknown matches is inversely proportional to how often the same matches have been made in the past; this was decided on the grounds that the most recent match is not producing a new potential recommendation candidate but rather validating an existing one. It could be argued that the un-

known match score should be directly proportional to the number of past matches on the grounds that more past matches suggest a higher likelihood that m will turn out to be a good candidate for f. It would be straightforward to implement this but for reasons of space we have left this as a matter for future work.

4. RECOMMENDATIONS STRATEGIES

So far we have described the type of recommendation data that can be produced as a side effect of gameplay, which includes user-user relationship information (tie strength from known matches) and novel recommendation candidates (based on unknown matches). In this section we discuss how these data can be used in an actual recommendation system. In fact we describe 3 different strategies, two using gameplay data in complementary ways, and a third that uses a purely content-based approach for the purpose of comparison. These strategies are, by design, simple and straightforward. They reflect fairly conventional approaches to recommendation rather than the current state of the art in recommender systems. Remember the aim is not to develop new recommendation techniques per se but rather to gain an understanding of the value of the gameplay data as part of such conventional recommendation techniques. If gameplay data proves to be successful in simple recommendation setups then we can be optimistic that it may prove similarly useful in more sophisticated recommendation settings. Given this, the best way to proceed is to start with the simplest possible recommendation strategies. We present each strategy in terms of how recommendation candidates are selected and then ranked for some target user u_t.

4.1 Crowdsourced Recommendations (CS)

First we adopt an approach that is based purely on crowdsourced (gameplay) data to both generate and rank candidate recommendation items. The candidates are novel movies (that is, unknown to u_t) that were matched with u_t by a player-friend during regular gameplay; see Equation 7. These candidates are movies that u_t should like according to her friends.

$$CS\_Candidates(u_t) =$$
$$\bigcup_{\forall p \in Friends(u_t)} \{m : match(p, m, u_t) \land m \notin Likes(u_t)\} \quad (7)$$

Next, these candidates are ranked by decreasing $interest(m, u_t)$, as per Equation 5. In this way movies that are frequently matched with u_t by many friends who know u_t's tastes well will be ranked higher than movies less often matched with u_t by players less familiar with u_t.

4.2 Collaborative Filtering Recommendations (CF)

Next we implement a version of classical collaborative filtering [18,32] by choosing movies from the profiles (likes) of u_t's friends as recommendation candidates; see Equation 8. The idea here is to select movies liked by friends of u_t but that are not (yet) liked by u_t under the collaborative filtering assumption that friends (similar users) are likely to like many of the same movies.

$$CF\_Candidates(u_t) =$$
$$\bigcup_{\forall f \in Friends(u_t)} Likes(f) - Likes(u_t) \quad (8)$$

Collaborative filtering typically ranks such recommendation candidates based on the similarity between u_t and the friends or neighbours from where the items originate; movies liked by a more similar user to u_t are more likely to be liked by u_t. User similarity is usually based on some form of ratings correlation in traditional collaborative filtering approaches. Here we instead use the $knows(f, u_t)$ data, which estimates how well f knows u_t, as a proxy for this user-user similarity. We score each candidate recommendation according to the sum of the $knows$ score between its source user and u_t. In other words we again rank candidates in decreasing order of $interest(m, u_t)$. Thus, the CS and the CF techniques differ primarily in the source of the candidates (gameplay vs. profiles, respectively).

4.3 Content-based Recommendations (CB)

Finally, as a convenient and complementary content-based recommendation strategy [29, 34] we use the Rotten Tomatoes API call, $movie\_similar(m)$, which returns a set of 5 movies similar to a given m, based on a variety of meta-data features. In this case we use u_t's likes as seed movies and retrieve the Rotten Tomatoes similar movies for each of these likes. Then the candidate movies for u_t are the concatenation ($\bigoplus$) of all of these Rotten Tomatoes movies returned; see Equation 9.

$$CB\_Candidates(u_t) = \bigoplus_{m \in Likes(u_t)} movie\_similar(m) \quad (9)$$

Content-based recommendations are selected from these candidates at random. Note, $CB\_Candidates(u_t)$ may contain duplicates if the same movies are returned by Rotten Tomatoes for different profile/seed movies. Hence this random selection process will tend to select movies that are more frequently represented in the candidate list. This makes sense as it effectively gives priority to those movies that are considered similar to many movies in u_t's profile thereby reflecting common themes within a user's profile.

This strategy obviously does not make use of any gameplay data. It is included as a useful benchmark for comparison against the previous strategies which both do make use of gameplay data to a greater or lesser degree.

5. EVALUATION

The primary aim of this work is to explore the potential for GWAPs to produce useful recommendation data. To this end the key objective in this section is to evaluate the potential utility of the recommendation data that is produced from our movie matching game. We describe a small pilot study involving 3 different groups of users. The users in each group play the game and then participate in a recommendation test to provide direct feedback on the relevance of a set of movie recommendations based on the above recommendation strategies.

5.1 Setup & Method

Our pilot trial involved 27 participants made up of a mixture of young (approx. 18 - 30 years old) male and females, both undergraduate and postgraduate students at our institution. The participants were made up of 3 groups of 15 (Group 1), 6 (Group 2), and 6 (Group 3). Groups 1 and 2 were sets of close mutual friends; in other words they could be expected to know each other's movie tastes well. In contrast Group 3 was made up of people who did not know each other's movie tastes well, if at all; thus Group 3 served as a useful control when it came to understanding the influence of relationship strength on the recommendation outcome.

Each group of users acted as both players and friends for the purpose of evaluation. In other words, each participant played the recommendation game, participated in the follow-up recommendation test, and their profiles also served as friends in the games of other players. For each participant we had access to their movie likes from Facebook.

The pilot study took place in two phases. Phase 1 focused on collecting recommendation data by asking users to play the game. The data collected in Phase 1 was then used in Phase 2 to generate recommendations for each of the users. We tested our 3 different recommendation strategies and users were asked to rate the resulting recommendations as satisfactory or not.

5.2 Phase 1 - Testing Gameplay

During the first part of the evaluation each user was provided with a link to the game and asked to play it a few times. During each game they were presented with a random subset of 5 friends and 18 movies. These 18 movies were made up of a mixture of movies drawn from the likes of their friends and the most popular movies on Rotten Tomatoes. This ensured a mix of movies as potential known and unknown matches.

On average participants played 11 games each and during these games they matched more than 11 movies per player per game; just over 3 of these matches were known to be correct on average. Table 1 summarises key gameplay statistics on a group by group basis and on average overall (per participant).

In terms of the generation of potential recommendation data this means that, during a typical game, the average player suggested about 8 movies as candidate recommendations; movies that were not already known to be liked by the matched friends. During

Gameplay Stats	G1	G2	G3	Mean
Members/Group	15	6	6	-
Movies/Profile	20	11	13	16.4
Games/Player	15	5	7	11
Matches/Game/Player	10.85	11.03	13.2	11.4
Known/Game/Player	2.76	3.93	3.07	3

Table 1: Gameplay statistics per group and overall per player.

these same games players correctly matched 3 movies per game with friends, which contributed the evaluation of how well a player was likely to know these friends. Thus during a typical gaming session (an average of 11 games per player) this gameplay data quickly builds to provide a detailed source of recommendation data.

5.3 Phase 2 - Evaluating Recommendations

The data collected in Phase 1 was used in Phase 2 to generate recommendations for each of the 27 participants. In each case we generated 6 ranked recommendations from each of the 3 different recommendation strategies and we asked each participant to rate all 18 recommendations as either satisfactory or unsatisfactory; that is, a simple binary rating. When producing these recommendation lists we were careful to randomise the interleaving order of recommendations from each of the strategies to ensure that there was no positional bias.

5.4 Results & Discussion

The results are presented in Figure 3 as a bar chart showing the satisfaction feedback for each of the 3 groups (Groups 1 - 3) of participants and for each of the 3 recommendation techniques (CS, CF, and CB). In each case the percentage satisfaction value is the percentage of recommendations generated by a given algorithm that enjoyed a positive satisfactory rating; so a satisfaction score of 70% for some algorithm means that 70% of the recommendations produced by that algorithm were rated as satisfactory by the participants.

We can see that the CF and CB strategies tend to produce similar satisfaction scores of between 70% - 80% across the 3 groups. However a very different result is evident for the CS strategy, which relies wholly on gameplay data. In this case we can see that the recommendations produced for Group 1 and 2 participants (those with strong social connections) enjoy much higher satisfaction scores, in both cases approximately 94%. Interestingly we see that this increased satisfaction level is not maintained by CS for Group 3. The Group 3 satisfaction scores average only 76% for CS, comparable with those for CF and CB, most likely because, unlike Groups 1 and 2, Group 3 participants are not close friends and so do not know each others movie tastes well. As a result Group 3 users should find it more difficult generate good matches for their 'friends' in the game thereby limiting the recommendation data that is produced as a result.

It is also interesting to examine the diversity of recommendations that are being made by the different approaches; diversity is often considered to be a useful measure in modern recommender systems as it speaks to the ability of the recommender to offer the user more or less choice through its suggestions [15, 35, 38]; all other things being equal, more diversity is generally viewed as desirable. As a simple measure of diversity we can look at the percentage of unique recommendations made by each of the 3 approaches and the results are presented in Figure 4.

This time the CB strategy performs best, producing recommen-

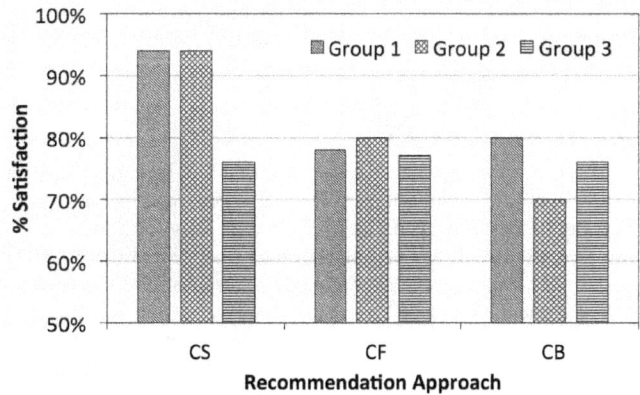

Figure 3: Recommendation satisfaction scores by group and by recommendation strategy.

dation lists with much higher diversity than both the CS and CF approaches. For example the average diversity of CB recommendations across the 3 groups is 77% (that is 77% of the recommendations are unique) compared to only 34% and 43% for CS and CF respectively. This is likely due to the limited size of user profiles in this pilot, which ultimately constrains the set of available movies for gameplay and recommendation. By comparison the CB approach calls on a much larger set of movies available through Rotten Tomatoes.

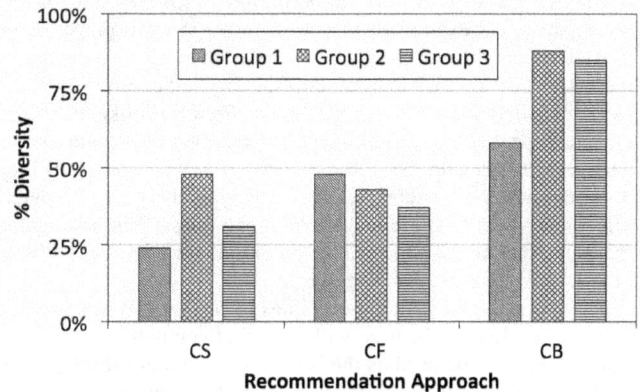

Figure 4: Recommendation diversity scores by group and by recommendation strategy.

Another part of the explanation for the low diversity scores for CS (compared with CF) is likely to be that gameplay data skews towards popular movies. Players recognise the icons/posters of popular more readily and naturally gravitate towards these during gameplay. As a result players will tend to focus on a more limited set of movies, hence the lower diversity score at recommendation time. Moreover, because these movies are popular they may also be easier to match with friends and there will be a greater likelihood that they will be liked, hence the improved satisfaction scores.

It is a matter for future work to consider this relationship between satisfaction and diversity further. It may be possible to guide gameplay towards more novel items by manipulating the size and speed of items according to the item popularity. For example, perhaps unusual movies could be presented with a larger icon and/or a slower trajectory, making them more attractive gameplay targets; scoring could also be adapted with respect to inverse item popularity to incentivize this type of behaviour.

6. DISCUSSION

The recommendation game, as described, is of course just one example of how we might use a GWAP to generate the type of data that can be useful in recommender systems. It is certainly interesting to consider alternative game styles as additional opportunities to generate useful recommendation data, perhaps for different types of recommendation tasks.

A similar type of matching game might be considered to generate the type of data that a group recommender systems might find useful; see [16]. Normally, group recommender systems assume a fixed group and the task is to identify items that will satisfy the group as a whole. An alternative formulation might be to start with an item and identify a group of users who will like the item. Indeed this format might be better adapted to group recommendation tasks such as matching movies with friends because rather than make compromises by selecting a movie for a fixed set of friends it may be better to identify a suitable set of friends for a given movie. With this in mind one could imagine a similar matching game to that presented in this paper but where friends are floating across the game arena and the task of the player is to match these friends with one of a fixed set of movies currently on release. In this way gameplay will associate groups of friends with movies. And if there is a tendency for players to associate the same (or similar) groups of friends with a movie then we can gain valuable information about the type of groups that are likely to enjoy that movie.

Another game mechanic can be borrowed from simple "snap" style games. For example, it is easy to envisage a two-player game in which each player is presented with the same friend-movie pairing. The task of each player is to quickly indicate whether the pairing is good or bad (indicating that the friend will like the movie or not, respectively). If both players agree then they both receive a score (perhaps with the fastest player receiving a bonus). If they disagree they get no score. In this way, player-agreement determines which pairings are likely to be good ones. This same game mechanic can be used to validate movie-movie pairings to obtain item-item similarity data for example.

These are just two simple examples of further GWAPs that we intend to evaluate. The trick will be to find compelling game mechanics that can be used as the basis for collecting useful recommendation data at scale. If the game is fun and addicting then it has the potential to attract large numbers of users and generate huge amounts of valuable recommendation data. Even in our small scale user study it was interesting to see that participants appeared willing to play multiple games with each game generating multiple pieces of recommendation data. For example on average each participant played an average of just over 11 games and generated about 8 new recommendation candidates. That makes for a total of 88 new recommendation candidates generated per participant. This level of recommendation data would be challenging to solicit using more traditional survey-based techniques.

7. CONCLUSIONS

The main purpose of this paper is to explore the use of a GWAP to collect recommendation data and user preferences as a side effect of casual gameplay. This is interesting because, if successful, this crowdsourcing approach has the potential to deliver preference data at scale; there are many examples of GWAPs that attract large communities of highly engaged users [42]. We have implemented

and tested a simple movie matching game and described the recommendation data that we can collect from its gameplay. These data can be used in a recommendation context and we have demonstrated its potential as part of a live-user trial.

Obviously the work in this paper is limited in many ways. The developed system is a working prototype and the small scale of our evaluation is just a first step to explore the potential role of GWAPs in recommender systems. Nevertheless we believe it serves to highlight the potential for new ways to think about recommendation data and recommender systems while contributing to a growing interest in the role of crowdsourcing in recommender systems and personalization research.

Our attention in this paper has been on the movie domain, a classical recommendation domain. Of course the approach is not limited to this specific domain, and it is likely that similar techniques can be used for other types of content such as music, TV shows, brands etc. In addition, our focus has been on deriving specific types of recommendation data, preference data and user similarity data. It will be interesting to consider whether related approaches can be used to source other forms of recommendation data such as item similarities [33], trust or reputation data [11, 26, 27], or even opinion sentiment [8] and explanations [2].

Obviously we have focused on a simple, single-player matching game and there are a great many opportunities to explore more sophisticated game mechanics. For example, our current work is exploring multi-player game designs for group recommendation tasks. Adding additional players provides an opportunity to further scale-up the generation of useful data via multi-party validation. It also introduces new game dynamics including strategic gameplay elements that have the potential to provide for a more long-lasting gaming experience.

8. ACKNOWLEDGEMENTS

This work is supported by Science Foundation Ireland under grant 07/CE/I1147.

9. REFERENCES

[1] Adomavicius, G., and Tuzhilin, A. Toward the Next Generation of Recommender Systems: A Survey of the State-of-the-Art and Possible Extensions. *IEEE Transactions on Knowledge and Data Engineering 17*, 6 (June 2005), 734–749.

[2] Ahn, L. V., Ginosar, S., Kedia, M., and Blum, M. Improving Image Search with PHETCH. *Proceedings of the 2007 IEEE International Conference on Acoustics, Speech and Signal Processing - ICASSP '07 4* (Apr. 2007).

[3] Banks, S., Rafter, R., and Smyth, B. The recommendation game: Using a game-with-a-purpose to generate recommendation data. In *Proceedings of the 9th ACM Conference on Recommender Systems, RecSys 2015, Vienna, Austria, September 16-20, 2015* (2015), 305–308.

[4] Bigham, J. P., and Parkes, D. C., Eds. *Proceedings of the Second AAAI Conference on Human Computation and Crowdsourcing, HCOMP 2014, November 2-4, 2014, Pittsburgh, Pennsylvania, USA*, AAAI (2014).

[5] Burke, R. Hybrid Recommender Systems: Survey and Experiments. *User Modeling and User-Adapted Interaction 12*, 4 (Nov. 2002), 331–370.

[6] Cooper, S., Khatib, F., Treuille, A., Barbero, J., Lee, J., Beenen, M., Leaver-Fay, A., Baker, D., Popović, Z., and Players, F. Predicting Protein Structures with a Multiplayer Online Game. *Nature 466*, 7307 (2010), 756–760.

[7] Desrosiers, C., and Karypis, G. A Comprehensive Survey of Neighborhood-based Recommendation Methods. In *Recommender Systems Handbook*, F. Ricci, L. Rokach, B. Shapira, and P. B. Kantor, Eds. 2011, 107–144.

[8] Dong, R., Schaal, M., O'Mahony, M. P., and Smyth, B. Topic extraction from online reviews for classification and recommendation. In *IJCAI 2013, Proceedings of the 23rd International Joint Conference on Artificial Intelligence, Beijing, China, August 3-9, 2013* (2013).

[9] Felfernig, A., Haas, S., Ninaus, G., Schwarz, M., Ulz, T., Stettinger, M., Isak, K., Jeran, M., and Reiterer, S. RecTurk: Constraint-based Recommendation based on Human Computation. In *Proceedings of the 3rd International Workshop on Crowdsourcing and Human Computation for Recommender Systems at ACM RecSys - CrowdRec'14* (Foster City, CA, USA, Oct. 2014), 1–6.

[10] Gligorov, R., Hildebrand, M., van Ossenbruggen, J., Schreiber, G., and Aroyo, L. On the Role of User-generated Metadata in Audio Visual Collections. In *Proceedings of the 6th International Conference on Knowledge Capture - K-CAP '11*, M. A. Musen and O. Corcho, Eds., ACM (Banff, Canada, June 2011), 145–151.

[11] Golbeck, J. Generating predictive movie recommendations from trust in social networks. In *Proceedings of the 4th International Conference on Trust Management - iTrust'06*, K. Stølen, W. H. Winsborough, F. Martinelli, and F. Massacci, Eds., vol. 3986, Springer Berlin Heidelberg (Pisa, Italy, May 2006), 93–104.

[12] Guo, G., Zhang, J., and Yorke-Smith, N. Trustsvd: Collaborative filtering with both the explicit and implicit influence of user trust and of item ratings. In *Proceedings of the Twenty-Ninth AAAI Conference on Artificial Intelligence, January 25-30, 2015, Austin, Texas, USA.* (2015), 123–129.

[13] Hacker, S., and von Ahn, L. Matchin: Eliciting User Preferences with an Online Game. In *Proceedings of the 27th International Conference on Human Factors in Computing Systems - CHI 09*, ACM Press (Boston, Massachusetts, USA, Apr. 2009), 1207.

[14] Hartman, B., and Horvitz, E., Eds. *Proceedings of the First AAAI Conference on Human Computation and Crowdsourcing, HCOMP 2013, November 7-9, 2013, Palm Springs, CA, USA*, AAAI (2013).

[15] Hurley, N. J. Personalised ranking with diversity. In *Seventh ACM Conference on Recommender Systems, RecSys '13, Hong Kong, China, October 12-16, 2013* (2013), 379–382.

[16] Jameson, A., and Smyth, B. Recommendation to groups. In *The Adaptive Web, Methods and Strategies of Web Personalization* (2007), 596–627.

[17] Kelly, D., and Teevan, J. Implicit Feedback for Inferring User Preference: A Bibliography. *ACM SIGIR Forum 37*, 2 (2003), 18 – 28.

[18] Konstan, J. A., Miller, B. N., Maltz, D., Herlocker, J. L., Gordon, L. R., and Riedl, J. Grouplens: Applying collaborative filtering to usenet news. *Commun. ACM 40*, 3 (1997), 77–87.

[19] Koren, Y., Bell, R., and Volinsky, C. Matrix Factorization Techniques for Recommender Systems. *Computer 42*, 8 (Aug. 2009), 30–37.

[20] Larson, M., Cremonesi, P., and Karatzoglou, A. Overview of ACM recsys crowdrec 2014 workshop: crowdsourcing and human computation for recommender systems. In *Eighth ACM Conference on Recommender Systems, RecSys '14, Foster City, Silicon Valley, CA, USA - October 06 - 10, 2014* (2014), 381–382.

[21] Larson, M., Said, A., Shi, Y., Cremonesi, P., Tikk, D., Baltrunas, L., Karatzoglou, A., Geurts, J., Anguera, X., and Hopfgartner, F. Activating the Crowd: Exploiting User-Item Reciprocity for Recommendation. In *Proceedings of the 2nd International Workshop on Crowdsourcing and Human Computation for Recommender Systems at ACM RecSys - CrowdRec'13* (Hong Kong, 2013).

[22] Law, E., and von Ahn, L. Input-Agreement: A New Mechanism for Collecting Data using Human Computation Games. In *Proceedings of the 27th International Conference on Human Factors in Computing Systems - CHI 09*, ACM Press (Boston, Massachusetts, USA, Apr. 2009), 1197–1206.

[23] Law, E., and von Ahn, L. Input-agreement: a new mechanism for collecting data using human computation games. In *Proceedings of the 27th International Conference on Human Factors in Computing Systems, CHI 2009, Boston, MA, USA, April 4-9, 2009* (2009), 1197–1206.

[24] Law, E. L. M., von Ahn, L., Dannenberg, R. B., and Crawford, M. Tagatune: A game for music and sound annotation. In *Proceedings of the 8th International Conference on Music Information Retrieval, ISMIR 2007, Vienna, Austria, September 23-27, 2007* (2007), 361–364.

[25] Lee, J., Jang, M., Lee, D., Hwang, W.-S., Hong, J., and Sang-Wook, K. Alleviating the Sparsity in Collaborative Filtering using Crowdsourcing. In *Proceedings of the 2nd International Workshop on Crowdsourcing and Human Computation for Recommender Systems at ACM RecSys - CrowdRec'13* (Hong Kong, Oct. 2013).

[26] McNally, K., O'Mahony, M. P., and Smyth, B. A comparative study of collaboration-based reputation models for social recommender systems. *User Model. User-Adapt. Interact. 24*, 3 (2014), 219–260.

[27] O'Donovan, J., and Smyth, B. Trust in recommender systems. In *Proceedings of the 2005 International Conference on Intelligent User Interfaces, January 10-13, 2005, San Diego, California, USA* (2005), 167–174.

[28] O'Donovan, J., and Smyth, B. Is trust robust?: an analysis of trust-based recommendation. In *Proceedings of the 2006 International Conference on Intelligent User Interfaces, January 29 - February 1, 2006, Sydney, Australia* (2006), 101–108.

[29] Pazzani, M. J., and Billsus, D. Content-based recommendation systems. In *The Adaptive Web, Methods and Strategies of Web Personalization* (2007), 325–341.

[30] Resnick, P., Iacovou, N., Suchak, M., Bergstrom, P., and Riedl, J. GroupLens: An Open Architecture For Collaborative Filtering Of Netnews. In *Proceedings of the ACM Conference on Computer-Supported Cooperative Work - CSCW 94*, ACM (Chapel Hill, North Carolina, USA, Aug. 1994), 175 – 186.

[31] Salvador, A., Carlier, A., Giro-i Nieto, X., Marques, O., and Charvillat, V. Crowdsourced Object Segmentation with a Game. In *Proceedings of the 2nd ACM International Workshop on Crowdsourcing for Multimedia - CrowdMM '13*, ACM (Barcelona, Spain, Oct. 2013), 15–20.

[32] Sarwar, B. M., Karypis, G., Konstan, J. A., and Riedl, J. Item-based collaborative filtering recommendation algorithms. In *Proceedings of the Tenth International World Wide Web Conference, WWW 10, Hong Kong, China, May 1-5, 2001* (2001), 285–295.

[33] Sarwar, B. M., Karypis, G., Konstan, J. A., and Riedl, J. Item-Based Collaborative Filtering Recommendation Algorithms. In *Proceedings of the 10th International World Wide Web Conference - WWW 10*, ACM (Hong Kong, May 2001), 285 – 295.

[34] Smyth, B. Case-based recommendation. In *The Adaptive Web, Methods and Strategies of Web Personalization* (2007), 342–376.

[35] Smyth, B., and McClave, P. Similarity vs. diversity. In *Case-Based Reasoning Research and Development, 4th International Conference on Case-Based Reasoning, ICCBR 2001, Vancouver, BC, Canada, July 30 - August 2, 2001, Proceedings* (2001), 347–361.

[36] Tuite, K., Snavely, N., Hsiao, D.-y., Tabing, N., and Popovic, Z. PhotoCity: Training Experts at Large-scale Image Acquisition through a Competitive Game. In *Proceedings of the 2011 Annual Conference on Human Factors in Computing Systems - CHI '11*, ACM Press (Vancouver, Canada, May 2011), 1383–1392.

[37] van Zwol, R., Garcia, L., Ramirez, G., Sigurbjornsson, B., and Labad, M. Video Tag Game. In *Proceedings of the 17th International World Wide Web Conference (WWW Developer Track)*, H. Jinpeng, R. Chen, H.-W. Hon, Y. Liu, W.-Y. Ma, A. Tomkins, and X. Zhang, Eds., ACM Press (Beijing, China, Apr. 2008).

[38] Vargas, S., and Castells, P. Improving sales diversity by recommending users to items. In *Eighth ACM Conference on Recommender Systems, RecSys '14, Foster City, Silicon Valley, CA, USA - October 06 - 10, 2014* (2014), 145–152.

[39] von Ahn, L. Games with a Purpose. *Computer 39*, 6 (June 2006), 92–94.

[40] von Ahn, L., and Dabbish, L. Labeling Images with a Computer Game. In *Proceedings of The ACM Conference on Human Factors in Computing Systems*, E. Dykstra-Erickson and M. Tscheligi, Eds., ACM (Vienna, Austria, Apr. 2004), 319 – 326.

[41] von Ahn, L., and Dabbish, L. ESP: labeling images with a computer game. In *Knowledge Collection from Volunteer Contributors, Papers from the 2005 AAAI Spring Symposium, Technical Report SS-05-03, Stanford, California, USA, March 21-23, 2005* (2005), 91–98.

[42] von Ahn, L., and Dabbish, L. Designing Games with a Purpose. *Communications of the ACM 51*, 8 (2008), 57.

[43] Von Ahn, L., Liu, R., and Blum, M. Peekaboom: a Game for Locating Objects in Images. In *Proceedings of the SIGCHI Conference on Human Factors in Computing Systems - CHI '06*, R. Grinter, T. Rodden, P. Aoki, E. Cutrell, R. Jeffries, and G. Olson, Eds. (Montréal, Canada, Apr. 2006), 55–64.

[44] Walsh, G., and Golbeck, J. Curator: a Game with a Purpose for Collection Recommendation. In *Proceedings of the 28th International Conference on Human Factors in Computing Systems - CHI '10*, ACM Press (Atlanta, Georgia, USA, Apr. 2010), 2079–2082.

Analyzing Aggregated Semantics-enabled User Modeling on Google+ and Twitter for Personalized Link Recommendations

Guangyuan Piao
Insight Centre for Data Analytics, NUI Galway
IDA Business Park, Galway, Ireland
guangyuan.piao@insight-centre.org

John G. Breslin
Insight Centre for Data Analytics, NUI Galway
IDA Business Park, Galway, Ireland
john.breslin@nuigalway.ie

ABSTRACT

In this paper, we study if reusing Google+ profiles can provide reliable recommendations on Twitter to resolve the *cold start* problem. Next, we investigate the impact of giving different weights for aggregating user profiles from two OSNs and present that giving a higher weight to the targeted OSN profile for aggregation allows the best performance in the context of a personalized link recommender system. Finally, we propose a user modeling strategy which combines *entity-* and *category-based* user profiles using with a discounting strategy. Results show that our proposed strategy improves the quality of user modeling significantly compared to the baseline method.

1. INTRODUCTION

With the growing popularity of Online Social Networks (OSNs) and the increased number of OSNs that users tend to use, studies of reusing or aggregating different OSN profiles for user modeling and then using it for recommendations have been widely conducted. Abel et al. [4] described *tag-based* user profiles from OSNs such as Delicious[1], StumbleUpon[2] and Flickr[3] and used the profile of other services for recommendations in the targeted OSN (e.g., reusing user profiles from Delicious for recommendations on Flickr in a cold start situation). The *targeted OSN* denotes the OSN where we recommend items to the users. Different OSNs have different characteristics. The social bookmarking and photo sharing OSNs in the study [4] have a great amount of tags in addition to their main content, and therefore *tag-based* profiles have been used. However, in a microblogging service like Twitter or other general OSNs like Google+[4], the main content usually consists of short messages, and therefore *entity-*

[1] https://www.delicious.com
[2] https://www.stumbleupon.com
[3] https://www.flickr.com
[4] https://plus.google.com

UMAP '16, July 13-17, 2016, Halifax, NS, Canada
© 2016 ACM. ISBN 978-1-4503-4370-1/16/07. . . $15.00
DOI: http://dx.doi.org/10.1145/2930238.2930278

based user profiles (i.e., user interests are represented by entities, e.g., `dbpedia`[5]`:Steve_Jobs`, `dbpedia:Apple_Inc.`) have been used [1]. On top of entity-based user profiles, researchers [3,15] proposed extending user profiles with background knowledge from Linked Data [5] (e.g., DBpedia [10]) since it provides rich semantic information about entities. We propose a mixed approach using *entity-* and *category-based* user profiles and evaluate the user modeling strategy in the context of link recommendations (category-based user profiles represent user interests using categories, e.g., `dbpedia:Category:Electronics_companies` for the entity `dbpedia:Apple_Inc.`).

The main contributions of our work are as follows: (i) an investigation of the benefits of reusing Google+ profiles for personalized link recommendations on Twitter (Section 5.1), (ii) a study of aggregation strategies with different weighting scheme for different OSN profiles (Section 5.2), and (iii) the evaluation of our mixed approach for extending user profiles using background knowledge from DBpedia (Section 5.3).

2. RELATED WORK

Mehta et al. [13] proposed cross-system personalization approaches, which aim to make recommender systems more robust against spam and cold start problems. However, they could not evaluate their methods on the Social Web data. In [4], the authors investigated aggregated *tag-based* profiles from Delicious, StumbleUpon and Flickr. They investigated how the aggregated *tag-based* user profiles impact on tag and resource recommendations, especially in cold start situations. Different user modeling strategies should be applied to different types of OSNs.. The same authors from [4] proved that the *entity-based* user profiles outperform other approaches such as *hashtag-* or *topic-based* user profiles on Twitter [1]. However, they did not evaluate aggregated *entity-based* profiles from general OSNs such as Google+ or Twitter further. In this regard, it has not been shown if the cold start problem in a more general OSN can be resolved by the aggregated entity-based profiles (as has been shown for tag-based profiles on social tagging systems).

To aggregate user profiles from different OSNs, previous studies applied the same weight to each OSN profile [4,15] but did not look at different weights for aggregating OSN profiles. A recent survey [6] also pointed out that the method of giving equal weights to different OSNs for aggregating

[5] The prefix `dbpedia` denotes http://dbpedia.org/resource/

profiles might not be enough, and a sophisticated model could be derived based on the specific needs for recommendations.

In the past years, user modeling strategies leveraging background knowledge (e.g., DBpedia) for extending user profiles have been developed [3, 9, 14, 15]. Abel et al. [3] proposed using Linked Data to extend user profiles and proved that extending user profiles with rich information from Linked Data can improve user modeling in terms of point of interest (POI) recommendations. Orlandi et al. [15] proposed *category-based* user profiles based on category information for entities from DBpedia. Besides a straightforward extension that gives equal weight to each extended category with respect to an entity [3], they also proposed a discounting strategy for those extended categories. Although *category-based* and *entity-based* user profiles showed similar performance in their user study, the authors [15] claimed that *category-based* user profiles produced almost seven times more user interests and might be helpful in the context of recommender systems. However, they did not further evaluate those user modeling strategies in the context of recommendations and left it as future work. Our work is more similar to [3, 15] in terms of the knowledge base that has been exploited.

3. CONTENT-BASED USER MODELING

In this work, we use DBpedia entities for representing the interests of users. The generic model for profiles representing users is specified in Definition 1.

Definition 1. The profile of a user $u \in U$ is a set of weighted DBpedia entities where with respect to the given user u for an entity $e \in E$ its weight $w(u, e)$ is computed by a certain function w.

$$P_u = \{(e, w(u, e)) \mid e \in E, u \in U\} \quad (1)$$

Here, E and U denote the set of entities in DBpedia and users respectively. We apply occurrence frequency as the weighting scheme $w(u, e)$, which means that the weight of an entity (interest) is determined by the number of OSN activities in which user u refers to the entity e. For instance, in a Twitter profile of user u, $w(u, \texttt{dbpedia:IPad}) = 7$ means that u published seven Twitter messages that mention the entity $\texttt{dbpedia:IPad}$. We further normalize user profiles so that the sum of all weights in a profile is equal to 1: $\sum_{e_i \in E} w(u, e_i) = 1$.

To get aforementioned user profiles, we implemented a user modeling framework that retrieves user profiles from User-Generated Content (UGC). Our framework features three main components:

Link Extractor. Given User-Generated Content (tweets and Google+ posts in this study), the component extracts all links (URLs) in the content by using a defined regex pattern. Furthermore, this component expands a URL from a shortened form (e.g., $\texttt{http://t.co/Is6l9ODiny}$), which is a common practice in OSNs.

Entity Extractor. This component extracts all DBpedia entities within UGC using the $\texttt{Aylien API}$[6]. In addition, it is used for retrieving DBpedia entities in the content of the links which were extracted by the $\texttt{Link Extractor}$.

Profile Generator. Based on the extracted entities, our framework provides a method for generating user profiles that might adhere to aggregating strategies with different weights

for different OSN profiles as well as extending strategies with background knowledge from DBpedia.

4. DATASET

Users tend to have multiple social identities in different OSNs [11]. To retrieve the ground truth data (i.e., users who are using both Google+ and Twitter), we obtained OSN accounts of users from $\texttt{about.me}$[7]. We crawled 247,630 public profile pages from $\texttt{about.me}$ during December 2014 that have at least two external links. In our dataset, the number of different OSNs (29) and the average number that each person participates in (4.48) are both larger than the numbers from a previous study [11], which are 15 and 3.92 respectively.

As $\texttt{about.me}$ dataset only contains OSN accounts of users, we need to retrieve all UGC from selected OSNs for our study. We chose Google+ and Twitter for our study due to (1) their higher degrees of openness, and (2) UGC from OSNs such as tweets has been demonstrated to be a good indicator for determining user interests in [2, 15]. As we were interested in analyzing aggregated user profiles from Google+ and Twitter, we randomly selected 480 *active* users from the $\texttt{about.me}$ dataset who had been using both OSNs. We then extracted their UGC as well as all links shared with those UGC using the aforementioned framework. Similar to other studies [8, 12], we define that a user is *active* if the user published at least 100 posts (i.e., tweets and Google+ posts). In addition, we selected users who shared at least 10 links via their tweets to construct ground truth links. After all, there were 429 *active* users in the dataset for the experiment (41 users did not have 10 links in their recent posts). The dataset is available via the supporting website of this paper [16].

5. USER MODELING FOR PERSONALIZED LINK RECOMMENDATIONS

Evaluation Methodology. Our main goal here is to analyze and compare the different user modeling strategies in the context of link recommendations. We do not aim to optimize the recommendation quality, but are interested in comparing the quality achieved by the same recommendation algorithm when inputting user profiles based on different user modeling strategies. In this regard, we adopt a lightweight content-based algorithm as the recommendation algorithm that recommends links according to their *cosine* similarity with a given user profile.

Definition 2. Recommendation Algorithm: given P_u and a set of candidate links $N = \{P_{i1}, ..., P_{in}\}$, which are represented via profiles using the same vector representation, the recommendation algorithm ranks the candidate items according to their cosine similarity to the user profile.

The ground truth of links, which we consider as *relevant* for a specific user, was given by the 10 latest links shared via the user's tweets. We used 10 links of each user from 429 users, as well as the links shared by other users but not shared by 429 users in the dataset, for constructing candidate links. As a result, the set of candidate links consists of 5,165 distinct links. The rest of tweets and Google+ posts before the recommendation time were all used for constructing user profiles. The quality of the top-N recommendations was measured via the Mean Reciprocal Rank (*MRR*) and the

---

[6]http://aylien.com

[7]https://about.me

Recall at rank N (R@N), which have been widely used in the literature [3,15]. *MRR* indicates at which rank the first item *relevant* to the user occurs on average, and R@N represents the mean probability that *relevant* items are retrieved within the top-N recommendations. We used the *bootstrapped paired t-test* for testing the significance where the significance level was set to 0.05 unless otherwise noted.

5.1 Using Google+ profiles for recommendations on Twitter in a cold start situation

RQ1: Can we reuse entity-based user profiles from Google+ to recommend links on Twitter? In [4], the authors used *tag-based* user profiles from other OSNs such as Delicious to recommend items on Flickr and showed that using other social bookmarking OSN profiles can improve recommendations in the targeted photo sharing OSN in cold start situations. In the same way, we used Google+ profiles of users for recommendations on Twitter especially in a cold start situation. To answer the research question (*RQ1*), we blinded out Twitter profiles of users and used only Google+ profiles of them to provide link recommendations on Twitter. We used the top-popular item recommender (TopPop) as a baseline, which is a common practice for a user in cold start until the user has interacted with the service enough [7].

Results. Figure 1 shows the results with respect to different evaluation methods for link recommendations by using Google+ profiles (Gonly) with the recommendation algorithm (Definition 2) and the results with TopPop recommendations on Twitter. As we can see from the figure, Gonly outperforms the baseline method TopPop significantly in terms of all evaluation methods. The value of *MRR* is 22.91%, which indicates that by using Google+ profiles, users can find a preferred link in the top 5 recommendations on Twitter on average. The results show that using Google+ profiles improves the quality of link recommendations significantly ($p < 0.01$) compared to the baseline method, and achieves comparable performance to using Twitter profiles (Tonly). In line with the results from the study [4], our results show that we can reuse Google+ profiles of users to provide personalized recommendations on Twitter in the cold start situation.

5.2 Aggregated user modeling with different weighting strategies

RQ2: Do aggregated profiles giving a higher weight to the targeted OSN perform better than those with

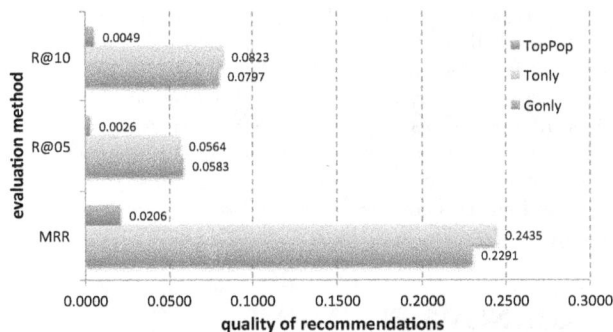

Figure 1: Performance of link recommendations on Twitter using Google+ profiles and the TopPop recommender

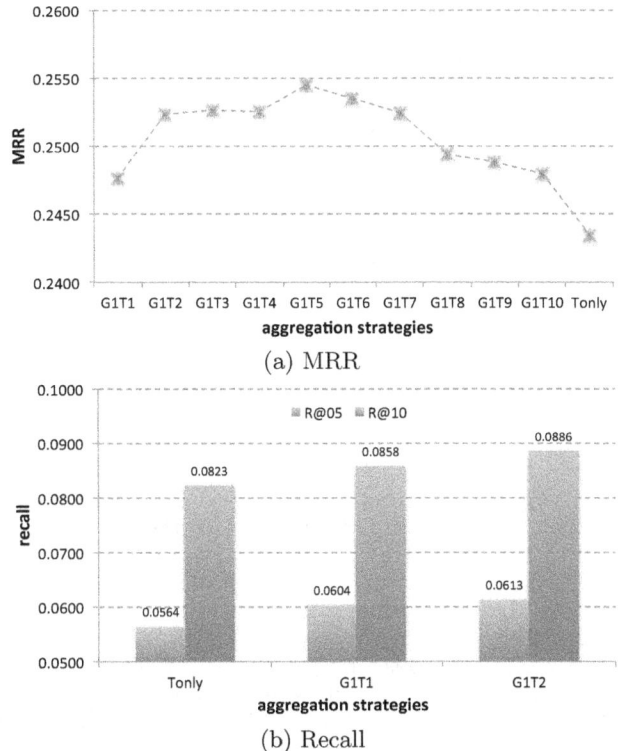

(a) MRR

(b) Recall

Figure 2: Performance of link recommendations based on different aggregating strategies for Google+ and Twitter

the same weight for each OSN? To study the impact of aggregating profiles with different weights on user modeling, we assessed different weights for Twitter profile (which is the targeted OSN here), between 1 and 10 in steps of 1 and compared to the user profile of Twitter without aggregation (Tonly) as a baseline. Where previous works improved over Tonly by giving equal weight to each OSN in the aggregated profile, our hypothesis is that we can improve this further by giving a higher weight to the targeted OSN profile.

Results. Figure 2 (a) shows the performance of recommendations based on different weighting strategies in terms of *MRR*. GmTn denotes the weights m and n for Google+ and Twitter profiles respectively. For instance, G1T1 denotes the aggregated profile with the same weight for Google+ and Twitter profiles while G1T2 denotes the aggregated profile giving weight 1 for Google+ profile and weight 2 for Twitter profile. Finally, Tonly denotes the Twitter profile without any aggregation. As we can see from the Figure 2 (a), the performance of link recommendations begins to increase by giving a higher weight to the targeted OSN and then decreases if the weight is too high. Overall, G1T5 performs best in terms of *MRR* and improves Tonly significantly while G1T1 does not. Regarding the recall of recommendations (see Figure 2 (b)), G1T2, which gives a higher weight to the targeted OSN profile, performs best as well. Similar to *MRR* result, G1T2 outperforms Tonly significantly in terms of both R@5 and R@10 while G1T1 does not. While the weight for the targeted OSN profile is different for achieving the best performance in terms of different evaluation methods, the aggregated profile with a higher weight for the targeted OSN always performs best (i.e., G1T5 and G1T2 for *MRR* and recall respectively), and improves `Tonly` significantly. This indicates that aggregated profiles with a higher weight for the targeted OSN are required to achieve the best performance in terms of link recommendations.

Therefore, we conclude that the aggregated user profile giving a higher weight to the targeted OSN performs better than that of giving equal weight to each OSN and improves `Tonly` significantly.

5.3 Extended user modeling with categories from DBpedia

In this section, we evaluate two *category-based* user profiles from [15] compared to `Tonly`. In addition, we propose combined user profiles of *entity-* and *category-based* profiles (`Tonly+T(x)`) and evaluate them in the context of link recommendations. The two *category-based* user profiles from [15] and the combined profiles are as below:

T(Cat) [15]: A straightforward way of *replacing* `Tonly` with the categories from DBpedia applying the same weights of the corresponding entities in the *entity-based* profiles.

T(CatDiscount) [15]: Instead of the straightforward extension, this method applies a discounting strategy (Equation 2) for the extended categories from DBpedia.

Tonly+T(x): This strategy combines the *entity-based* profiles (i.e., `Tonly`) as well as one of the *category-based* profiles mentioned above.

$$CategoryDiscount = \frac{1}{\alpha} \times \frac{1}{\log(SP)} \times \frac{1}{\log(SC)} \quad (2)$$

where: SP = *Set of Pages belonging to the Category, SC = Set of Sub-Categories*. SP and SC discount the category in the context of DBpedia. Thus, an extended category is discounted more heavily if it is a general one (i.e., the category has a great number of pages or sub-categories). In addition, we add the parameter α which denotes the discount of the extended *category-based* user profiles for combining the *entity-based* and *category-based* user profiles. Thus, this parameter only has an effect on the combined user modeling strategies with the discounting strategy for the extended categories, i.e., **Tonly+T(CatDiscount)**. We set $\alpha = 2$ for this experiment.

Results. Figure 3 illustrates the recommendation performance of using different user modeling strategies based on category information from DBpedia as well as the performance of using `Tonly` in terms of *MRR* and recall. As depicted in Figure 3, `Tonly+T(CatDiscount)` achieves the best performance in the context of link recommendations and significantly outperforms `Tonly` in terms of all evaluation methods. In contrast, other strategies do not perform as well as `Tonly`. For instance, *category-based* user profiles (`T(Cat)` and `T(CatDiscount)`) and the combined user profiles with the straightforward extension of categories (`Tonly+T(Cat)`) do not outperform `Tonly` but decrease the performance of link recommendations.

Different from the hypothesis from [15], *category-based* user profiles do not perform better than *entity-based* user profiles in the context of recommender systems. However, the results show that the combined user profiles of *entity-* and *category-based* profiles with the discounting strategy (`Tonly+T(CatDiscount)`), improve the *entity-based* user profiles significantly and allow the best performance in terms of link recommendations compared to other user modeling strategies.

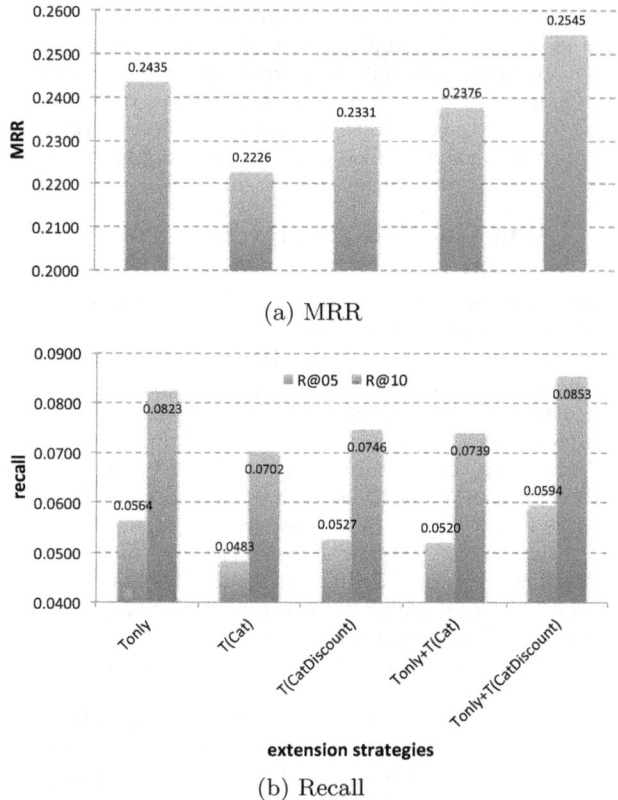

(a) MRR

(b) Recall

Figure 3: Performance of link recommendations based on extended user profiles using background knowledge from DBpedia

6. CONCLUSIONS AND FUTURE WORK

In this paper, we explored two dimensions of user modeling: (1) aggregating strategy of user profiles from different OSNs, and (2) extending strategy using background knowledge from DBpedia, and evaluated different strategies in the context of link recommendations. We investigated and proved the benefits of reusing Google+ profiles for link recommendations on Twitter in a cold start situation (refer to *RQ1*). Next, we studied different weighting strategies for aggregating Twitter and Google+ profiles. Unlike the approach from previous studies, results show that a higher weight must be given to the targeted OSN when aggregating profiles from different OSNs in order to achieve the best performance (refer to *RQ2*). Finally, we evaluated our mixed approach using entity- and category-based user profiles. Results show that our proposed user modeling strategy performs better than *category-based* user profiles as well as that with the straightforward extension strategy, and improves `Tonly` significantly. In the near future, we plan to investigate different aspects of DBpedia, such as classes and entities connected via different properties for user modeling.

7. ACKNOWLEDGMENTS

This publication has emanated from research conducted with the financial support of Science Foundation Ireland (SFI) under Grant Number SFI/12/RC/2289 (Insight Centre for Data Analytics).

8. REFERENCES

[1] F. Abel, Q. Gao, G.-J. Houben, and K. Tao. Analyzing user modeling on twitter for personalized news recommendations. In *User Modeling, Adaption and Personalization*, pages 1–12. Springer, 2011.

[2] F. Abel, Q. Gao, G.-J. Houben, and K. Tao. Semantic enrichment of twitter posts for user profile construction on the social web. In *The Semanic Web: Research and Applications*, pages 375–389. Springer, 2011.

[3] F. Abel, C. Hauff, G.-J. Houben, and K. Tao. Leveraging User Modeling on the Social Web with Linked Data. In *Web Engineering SE - 31*, pages 378–385. Springer, 2012.

[4] F. Abel, E. Herder, G.-J. Houben, N. Henze, and D. Krause. Cross-system user modeling and personalization on the social web. *User Modeling and User-Adapted Interaction*, 23(2-3):169–209, 2013.

[5] C. Bizer, T. Heath, and T. Berners-Lee. Linked Data - The Story So Far. *International Journal on Semantic Web and Information Systems*, 5(3):1–22, 2009.

[6] K. Bontcheva and D. Rout. Making sense of social media streams through semantics: A survey. *Semantic Web*, 5(5):373–403, 2014.

[7] F. Cena, S. Likavec, and F. Osborne. Property-based interest propagation in ontology-based user model. In *User Modeling, Adaptation, and Personalization*, pages 38–50. Springer, 2012.

[8] P. Jain, P. Kumaraguru, and A. Joshi. @i seek 'fb.me': identifying users across multiple online social networks. In *Proceedings of the 22nd international conference on World Wide Web companion*, pages 1259–1268, Rio de Janeiro, Brazil, 2013. International World Wide Web Conferences Steering Committee.

[9] P. Kapanipathi, P. Jain, C. Venkataramani, and A. Sheth. User Interests Identification on Twitter Using a Hierarchical Knowledge Base. In *The Semantic Web: Trends and Challenges*, pages 99–113. Springer, 2014.

[10] J. Lehmann, R. Isele, M. Jakob, A. Jentzsch, D. Kontokostas, P. N. Mendes, S. Hellmann, M. Morsey, P. van Kleef, and S. Auer. Dbpedia-a large-scale, multilingual knowledge base extracted from wikipedia. *Semantic Web Journal*, 2013.

[11] J. Liu, F. Zhang, X. Song, Y.-I. Song, C.-Y. Lin, and H.-W. Hon. What's in a name?: an unsupervised approach to link users across communities. In *Proceedings of the sixth ACM international conference on Web search and data mining*, pages 495–504. ACM, 2013.

[12] C. Lu, W. Lam, and Y. Zhang. Twitter user modeling and tweets recommendation based on wikipedia concept graph. In *Workshops at the Twenty-Sixth AAAI Conference on Artificial Intelligence*, 2012.

[13] B. Mehta. *Cross System Personalization: Enabling personalization across multiple systems*. PhD thesis, 2008.

[14] F. Narducci, C. Musto, G. Semeraro, P. Lops, and M. Gemmis. Leveraging Encyclopedic Knowledge for Transparent and Serendipitous User Profiles. pages 350–352. Springer Berlin Heidelberg, Berlin, Heidelberg, 2013.

[15] F. Orlandi, J. Breslin, and A. Passant. Aggregated, interoperable and multi-domain user profiles for the social web. In *Proceedings of the 8th International Conference on Semantic Systems*, pages 41–48. ACM, 2012.

[16] G. Piao and J. G. Breslin. Supporting website: details about datasets and additional findings, 2016.

Modelling User Collaboration in Social Networks Using Edits and Comments

Ifeoma Adaji
University of Saskatchewan
Saskatoon, Saskatchewan
Canada
Ita811@mail.usask.ca

Julita Vassileva
University of Saskatchewan
Saskatoon, Saskatchewan
Canada
jiv@cs.usask.ca

ABSTRACT

Research has shown that in Q&A social networks, collaboration between respondents results in quality answers. Since good answers are required to keep any Q&A social network active, it is important to understand the characteristics of these collaborations and the collaborators. In this paper, we investigate how Stack Overflow promotes collaboration by allowing users to edit existing questions and answers in order to improve them. Using over 40,000 answer posts, our study reveals that collaboration in answer posts is not a function of achievement earned in terms of badges, as most edits associated with "best answer" rewards were posted by users who have not earned any answer badge. Our study further shows that posts that earned the "best answer" reward have more comments than those that did not. This study though, work in progress, can aid developers in implementing collaboration strategies in social networks that work.

Keywords

User modelling, collaboration, social networks

1. INTRODUCTION

The use of collaboration has been shown to result in a greater value creation [1]. In its simplest form, collaboration is the act of working with someone or a group of people to create something. In Q&A social networks, collaboration is when users contribute to an existing post; either a question or answer post. In Q&A social networks, collaboration between authors results in better answers [2] and quality answers result in an active Q&A network [3]. Hence, the importance of studying collaboration among users who answer questions cannot be overemphasized.

In this study, we examined the characteristics of collaboration and collaborators in answers posted on Stack Overflow (SO), a successful Q&A social network. In SO, users post questions and other users attempt to answer them. The asker of a question selects the best answer provided to his or her question irrespective of how highly an answer is rated by the community.

UMAP '16, July 13-17, 2016, Halifax, NS, Canada
© 2016 ACM. ISBN 978-1-4503-4370-1/16/07...$15.00
DOI: http://dx.doi.org/10.1145/2930238.2930289

In SO, users can collaborate to improve existing questions and answers by editing them independently of who posted the questions or answers. Only those who have earned the privilege can approve such edits. Users also collaborate by commenting on existing questions and answers. Unlike question and answer posts, comments cannot be edited by other users. However, they can be voted as being useful by other users.

To determine the characteristics of collaboration and collaborators, we analyzed over 40,000 answer posts and their corresponding edits and comments. Our study showed that the collaborators are not the highest achievers in terms of badges earned as most edits associated with "best answer" reward were posted by users who have not earned any answer badge. Hence, collaboration in answer posts is not a function of achievement earned in terms of badges.

To investigate collaboration using comments, we analyzed the comments of over 20,000 answer posts. The result of our analysis showed that posts that earned the "best answer" reward have more comments than those that did not. We also discovered that the answer posts with the highest number of comments were posted by users that have earned between 1 and 5 answer badges.

This paper is still work in progress. However, the preliminary results discussed in this paper can aid developers and stake holders on strategies to adopt when incorporating collaboration in Q&A social networks.

2. RELATED WORK

2.1 Stack Overflow

Stack Overflow is a Q&A platform where users can ask and answer specific IT related questions. Through active participation and providing high quality answers, the users can gain incentives such as reputation score, badges and privileges. While all users can upvote or downvote other users' questions and answers, only the user that asked a question that can select the best answer to his/her question. Users have to earn the privilege to edit answers posted by others in a bid to improve them. Users can also comment on answers to improve them or to seek clarification. Similar to questions, comments can also be upvoted or downvoted. Upvotes and downvotes contribute to the reputation score of users.

In Stack Overflow, badges are earned by users who are especially helpful in the community[1]. Badges are awarded in several categories including question, answer, participation, tag and moderation badges. We only considered badges in the answer category because we are interested in collaboration in answer posts, since high quality answers keeps a Q&A social network active [3].

---

[1] http://stackoverflow.com/help/badges

2.2 Collaboration in social networks

Dalle et al. [4] applied game theory to the study of collaboration in social networks. Their study was based on a class of local contribution games where only neighbors of a contributor benefit from the positive effects of a contribution. This form of network is totally different from SO where respondents who post helpful answers benefit from their contribution in the form of upvotes and higher reputation scores.

In [5], McDonald focused on the use of social networks in an organization to recommend people for possible collaboration. Unlike the case of McDonald, in this study, we examined existing collaborations through *edits* and *comments* in order to identify the characteristics that make them successful.

In their study of social networks, Dalle et al. [2] studied *edits* as a means of collaboration. They concluded that collaboration between authors results in better answers. Though our research is an extension of this study, unlike Dalle et al., our focus is only on the answer posts.

Panciera et al. [6] studied collaboration in an open source project, Cyclopath. By conducting a user survey, they studied the reasons behind collaboration from the perspective of the editors and the consumers. Though we also studied the characteristics of collaborators, unlike Panciera et al., we did that by analyzing the existing data of users and not by user study. The context of their study is also different from ours; we studied a Q&A social network where incentives are earned by providing high quality questions and answers, while Panciera studied Cyclopath, a bike route finder.

In their study of interactions in Stack Overflow, Wang et al. [7] developed a topic modelling strategy that can assign a new question to existing categories of questions. Their study of collaboration did not include the use of edits and comments.

In [8], Dalip et al. proposed a *learning to rank* approach for ranking answers in Q&A collaborative networks. Using Stack Overflow as a case study, they developed an approach to rank answers based on user feedback. Though Dalip et al. used Stack overflow as a case study, their work focuses on ranking answers while ours uses edits and comments to study collaborations between users.

Yang et al. [9] studied the editing behavior of users in Stack Overflow in order to improve existing questions. They developed an approach that can automatically suggest editing actions for newly posted questions that will likely make the questions clearer to the community. The focus of their research was on improving questions in Stack Overflow using edit actions, while our focus was on the characteristics of the users that carry out edits on answer posts.

Shah Chirag and Pomerantz [10], using Yahoo! Answers, developed a model for evaluating and predicting answer quality using 13 quality criteria which were derived from questions, answers and the user. Our study differs from this as we did not predict answer quality, rather we studied the characteristics of collaborators in Stack Overflow.

To the best of our knowledge, no research has been carried out on understanding the characteristics of collaborators in answer posts in Stack Overflow using edits and comments.

3. RESEARCH METHOD & RESULTS

To study the characteristics of collaboration between respondents in SO, we collected detailed information of answers posted in response to questions that scored above the average score. We calculated the average score of questions to be 203 points[2], hence we considered answers posted to questions that earned at least 203 points. We identified 4,521 questions that met this criteria. These questions received 49,738 answers which were posted by 32,538 users. The summary of the dataset used is described in table 1.

Table 1. Summary of dataset used in this study

Number of questions	4,521
Number of answers	49,247
Number of users who posted answers	32,538
Total number of edits done on these answers	14,343
Number of users who carried out these edits	12,232

3.1 Collaboration using *edits*

To understand the use of *edits* in Stack Overflow as a method of collaboration, we identified the edits that were carried out on the 49,738 answers in the dataset. There were 14,343 edits of which 7,909 were approved. Figure 1 shows the spread of the data based on the number of edits carried out. Most posts were edited less than five times. These edits were approved because they improved the initial answer post[3].

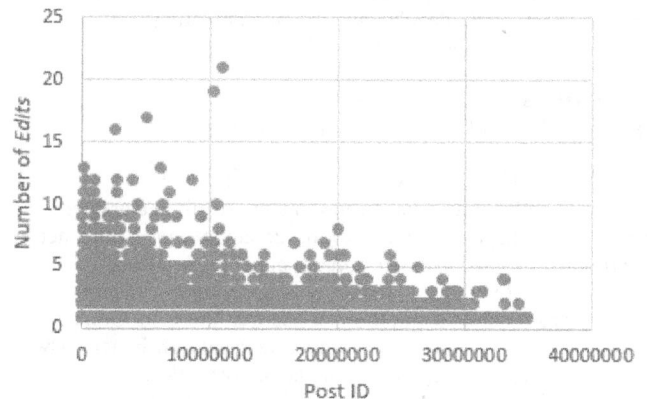

Figure 1. Number of edits in the dataset

In order to understand the characteristics of users who collaborated using these edits, we aimed to answer the following research question; are commenters high achievers in the network? In order words, is collaboration in answer posts a function of achievement in terms of badges earned? To answer these questions, we categorized users into 4 categories based on the number of answer badges the users have earned. In Stack Overflow, badges are earned by users who are especially helpful[4]. We only included users who have earned answer badges because this study is based on collaboration in answer posts. Table 2 describes the number of badges in each category and their description. The use of categories is important in order to have a narrower view of who collaborators are in the network.

---

[2] In calculating average, we only included question posts that had scored at least one point.

[3] http://stackoverflow.com/help/privileges/edit

[4] http://stackoverflow.com/help/badges

Table 2. Categories of users based on number of badges earned

Category	Description
EQ1	Users who have earned only 1 answer badge
GT1	Users who have earned between 2 and 5 answer badges inclusive
GT5	Users who have earned between 6 and 10 answer badges inclusive
GT10	Users who have earned more than 10 answer badges
NON	Users who have not earned any answer badges

Figure 2 shows the breakdown of edits carried out by users in the various categories. The users that edited most of the answer posts were users who have not earned any answer badge in the past. On the other hand, the users who have earned the most answer badges carried out the least number of edits. Hence collaboration using edits was done by non-achievers (users who have not earned any answer badge) in the network.

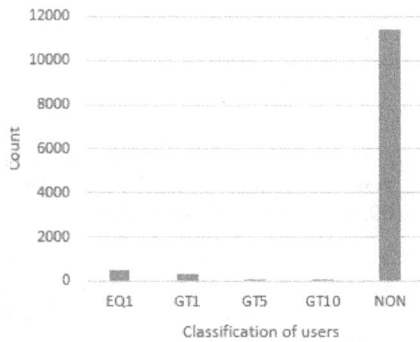

Figure 2. Number of edits in each user category

Since edits have to be approved before the suggested changes are committed, we further analyzed the approved edits. Of the 14,343 answer edits, only 7909 were approved by the community. Of these, 7,353 were posted by users who have not earned any answer badge. Hence, the users who collaborated the most were not high achievers in terms of badges earned. Only 556 edits were posted by users who have earned at least one answer badge. The breakdown of these 556 users based on the category of badges is shown in figure 3.

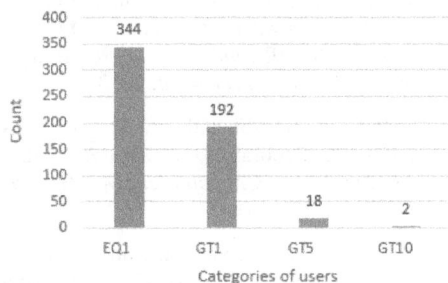

Figure 3. Categories of users who made approved answer edits

Of the approved edits posted by answer badge earners, over 60% of them were posted by users who have at least one answer badge. On the other hand, users with the most answer badges only have a few edits approved.

3.2 Collaboration using comments

The use of comments is another form of collaboration is Stack Overflow. Users can improve on existing questions and answers by posting comments related to such questions and answers. These comments could be upvoted based on how useful they are to other users.

To explore the use of comments for collaboration, we aimed to answer the following research question; does collaboration using comments lead to better answers? In other words, do posts that earn the *best answer* reward receive more comments?

To do this, we analyzed the comments of the answers identified in table 1. We considered the answers in response to questions that scored higher than the average score of 203. For this study, we only considered comments that had a vote of more than 1, hence we excluded questions that had 1 or no comment associated with it. We also excluded questions that did not have a corresponding "best answer" post. The final data set was reduced to 54,212 comments made on 20,776 answer posts in response to 4,443 questions. These were posted by 26,728 users. On the average, an answer post had 5 comments. Figure 4 describes the distribution of comments among the answer posts.

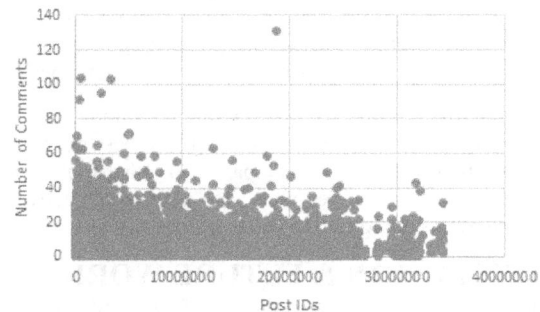

Figure 4. Number of comments for answer posts

For each question post, we identified the corresponding answer post with the highest number of comments, *MaxComment*. We also determined the answer posts with the "best answer" reward, *BestAnswer*, for each of the questions. We then compared *MaxComment* to *BestAnswer* to determine if the posts with the maximum number of comments also earned the best answer reward. 3,374 posts had *MaxComment* and also earned *BestAnswer* reward. We concluded that 75% of posts with the highest number of comments also earned the best answer reward, hence the use of comments enhances collaboration as it leads to improved answers.

To determine the level of achievement of the users who collaborate by commenting, we studied the 3,374 posts that had the highest number of comments, *MaxComment*. Figure 5 shows the participation of users based on the category of badges in table 1.

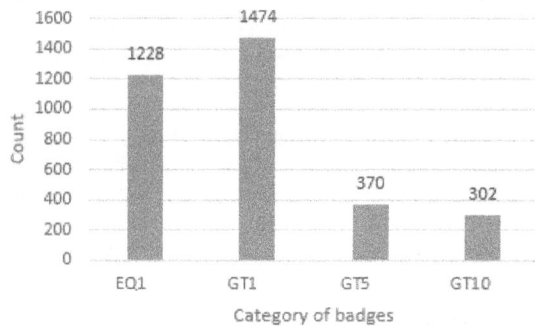

Figure 5. Categories of users with highest number of comments

The answer posts with the highest number of comments were posted by users that have earned between 1 and 5 answer badges. Answer posts of users who have earned over 10 badges had fewer comments. This result could mean that the high achievers do not engage in collaboration as much as the users with fewer comments.

3.3 Discussion

This paper aims at studying collaboration in a typical Q&A social network using *edits* and *comments*. From the results of our analysis, we can conclude the following:

Since collaboration results in better answers [2], there is a need to encourage collaboration Q&A in social networks. In Stack Overflow new persuasive strategies to encourage active collaboration through edits and comments may be required. For instance, badges or rewards that encourage editing and commenting could increase collaboration through these means.

Using comments as a form of collaboration to improve answers posted on the network, we concluded that the best answer posts usually had more comments compared to other posts. Hence networks should encourage users to participate actively in commenting as this could lead to better quality answers.

4. CONCLUSION & FUTURE WORK

In this short paper, we examined the use of *edits* and *comments* as forms of collaboration in a successful Q&A social network, Stack Overflow. Since high-quality answers to users' questions is one of the sustaining factors of a Q&A social network, it is important to understand who the collaborators are that improve existing answers.

We analyzed over 40,000 answer posts and their corresponding edits and comments. Our study showed that the collaborators are not the highest achievers in terms of badges earned, since users with more than 10 answer badges carried out only a few edits to answers that earned the "best answer" reward. This study also revealed that most edits associated with answers are posted by users who do not have answer badges. Of the users who have earned answer badges and have edited "best answer" posts, only a few of them have earned over 10 badges while about 60% of them have just one badge. Hence, collaboration in answer posts is not a function of achievement earned in terms of badges.

To investigate collaboration using *comments*, we analyzed the comments of over 20,000 answer posts. The result of our analysis showed that posts that earned best answer reward had more comments than those that did not. We also discovered that the answer posts with the highest number of comments were posted by users that have earned between 1 and 5 answer badges.

This study is still work in progress, hence further analysis has to be carried out to validate our findings. For example, there is a need to analyze the comments in order to exclude comments that do not contribute to the answers posted.

Although the study showed that the high achievers in the network who have over 10 answer badges posted answers with fewer comments, this could mean that their answers could not be improved any further based on their level of expertise. Hence we need to extend this study by analyzing the content of the posts and comments.

Finally, we propose to study collaboration in other Q&A social networks like Yahoo! Answers and Yelp to determine if the same conclusions can be drawn about these other networks.

5. REFERENCES

[1] L. Camarinha-Matos and H. Afsarmanesh, "Collaborative Networks. Value creation in a knowledge society," *International Federation for Information Processing (IFIP),* vol. 207, pp. 26-40, 2006.

[2] J.-M. Dalle, M. Devillers and M. den Besten, "Answer editing in StackOverflow," *Proceedings of 2nd Thematic Conference on Knowledge Commons: Governing Pooled Knowledge Resources,* 2014.

[3] G. Dror, D. Pelleg, O. Rokhlenko and I. Szpektor, "Churn prediction in new users of yahoo! answers,," *Proceedings of the 21st International Conference Companion on World Wide Web,* pp. 829-834, 2014.

[4] L. Dall Asta, m. marsili and P. Pin, "Collaboration in social networks," *Proc of the National Academy of Sciences of the USA,* vol. 109, no. 12, pp. 4395-4400, 2012.

[5] D. McDonald, "Recommending Collaboration with Social Networks: A Comparative Evaluation," *Proceedings of the SIGCHI Conference on Human Factors in Computing Systems,* pp. Pages 593-600, 2003.

[6] K. Panciera, M. Masli and L. Terveen., "How should I go from ___ to ___ without getting killed?": motivation and benefits in open collaboration," *Proceedings of the 7th International Symposium on Wikis and Open Collaboration (WikiSym '11). ACM,* pp. 183-192, 2011.

[7] S. Wang, D. Lo and L. Jiang, "An empirical study on developer interactions in StackOverflow," *Proceedings of the 28th Annual ACM Symposium on Applied Computing (SAC '13). ACM,* pp. 1019-1024, 2013.

[8] H. Dalip, A. Gonçalves, M. Cristo and P. Calado, "Exploiting user feedback to learn to rank answers in q&a forums: a case study with stack overflow," in *Proceedings of the 36th international ACM SIGIR conference on Research and development in information retrieval,* 2013.

[9] J. Yang, C. Hauff, A. Bozzon and G.-J. Houben, "Asking the Right Question in Collaborative Q&A systems," in *Proceedings of the 25th ACM conference on Hypertext and social media,* Chile, 2014.

[10] C. Shah and J. Pomerantz, "Evaluating and predicting answer quality in community QA," in *Proceedings of 33rd int'l ACM SIGIR conference on Research and development in information retrieval* , New Jersey, USA, 2010

Predicting Customer Satisfaction in Customer Support Conversations in Social Media Using Affective Features

Jonathan Herzig, Guy Feigenblat,
Michal Shmueli-Scheuer,
David Konopnicki
IBM Research - Haifa
Haifa 31905, Israel
{hjon,guyf,shmueli,davidko}@il.ibm.com

Anat Rafaeli
Technion-Israel Institute of Technology
Haifa 32000, Israel
anatr@ie.technion.ac.il

ABSTRACT

Providing customer support through social media channels is gaining popularity. In such a context, predicting customer satisfaction in an early stage of a service conversation is important. Such an analysis can help personalize agent assignment to maximize customer satisfaction, and prioritize conversations. In this paper, we show that affective features such as customer's and agent's personality traits and emotion expression improve prediction of customer satisfaction when added to more typical text based features. We only utilize information extracted from the first customer conversation turn and previous customer and agent social network activity. Thus, our customer satisfaction classifier outputs its prediction in an early stage of the conversation, before any interaction has taken place between the customer and an agent. Our model was trained and tested on a Twitter conversations dataset of two customer support services, and shows an improvement of 30% in F1-score for predicting dissatisfaction.

Keywords

Affective computing; classification; customer support

1. INTRODUCTION

As part of the raging societal and commercial success of social media, applications go far beyond the initial use case of person to person communication. Social media are rapidly becoming an integral part of corporate Customer Relationship Management. In this context, an interesting use case for social media is customer support, which used to assume a private conversation between a customer and a service rep (agent), and can now take place over public social media channels. A recent study shows that one in five customers in the U.S (23%) say they have used social media for cus-

tomer support in 2014, up from 17% in 2012[1]. Obviously, companies hope that such uses are associated with a positive experience. Yet, there are limited tools for assessing this.

In this work we explore the relation between *affect* evident in a conversation and satisfaction with customer support provided through social media. Our objective is to predict customer satisfaction given affective evaluations of both customers and agents. Specifically we model *affect* by considering *personality traits* and *emotions*, two aspects of individuals' intrinsic dispositions that are different in temporality: personality traits are relatively long term and permanent while emotions are relatively short term and transient. In the context of customer support, it was shown that customers tend to express negative emotions such as frustration and disappointment, as well as positive emotions such as gratitude [5]. As to *personality traits*, many studies examined the effect of specific traits of agents with respect to customer satisfaction, as well as how to interpret traits of customers. For example, customer trust and compromising traits correlate with positive satisfaction [14, 3].

With the advance of behavioral studies in social media, online services are available for assessing the *personality traits* of social media users based on their online interactions (e.g., tweets, forum posts)[2,3]. These services use text analytics to infer personality and social characteristics. As to *emotions*, analysis services based on textual messages are gaining popularity both in academic studies (cf. [16, 15]), and industry[4,5] as a method to get valuable insights about a person from their textual content.

Using these capabilities, our goal is to predict customer satisfaction from the initiation of the interaction (i.e., the first message that is posted by a customer), given the customer's and the selected agent's *personality traits* (obtained from their social media history prior to the conversation), and the *emotions* expressed by the customer in this first message. These data are utilized to predict the satisfaction of the customer from the entire conversation. Companies that provide customer support can foremost benefit from such a prediction and use it, for example in their agent assignment process (to assign an agent with personality traits

UMAP '16, July 13-17, 2016, Halifax, NS, Canada
© 2016 ACM. ISBN 978-1-4503-4370-1/16/07...$15.00
DOI: http://dx.doi.org/10.1145/2930238.2930285

---

[1] http://about.americanexpress.com/news/docs/2014x/2014-Global-Customer-Service-Barometer-US.pdf
[2] http://analyzewords.com
[3] https://watson-pi-demo.mybluemix.net/
[4] http://www.sentimetrix.com/
[5] http://apidemo.theysay.io/

that will maximize customer satisfaction), or to provide the assigned agent information about the state of the customer (e.g., the customer is angry, and not open to changes). To our knowledge, this is the first research that shows how to utilize *affect* of both parties of a conversation in order to increase the customer support satisfaction provided through social media.

2. RELATED WORK

Various works have studied customer behavior w.r.t personality traits of agents and customers. The work in [13] examined the relationship between the personality of agents and customer perceptions of service quality; it showed, for example, that openness correlated with assurance, and that conscientiousness predicted reliability. In [3] the authors analyzed which agent traits influence customer satisfaction in different settings (phone, email, on-line chats), and showed that knowledgeableness and preparedness were good indicators. In [17] the authors examined effects of personality traits on customer satisfaction patterns among mobile phone and credit card users. They report that the personality traits modesty, altruism, agreeableness and trust had strong predictive power of customer satisfaction with the two services. There are several differences between these works and ours; first, none of the previous studies considered personality traits of both agents and customers in the interaction. Second, the setting of social media enables new ways for assessments; for example, personality traits in previous work are all based on self report (e.g., IPIP questionnaire [7]), while we suggest automated extraction of traits. This means easier and greater availability and scale of our approach. Third, previous research never considered our unique research goal of optimizing service interactions by recommending a best agent to handle the interaction.

We note that companies like Mattersight[6] provide call center services that match an agent to a customer based on personality traits. Key difference with our approach is that Mattersight matches personality based on caller ID, and previous interactions with the call center. Our approach does not require previous service interactions. We utilize available social profiles and emotions in current interaction.

Works on social media have considered user personality traits [11, 4, 6], but did not focus on the unique context of customers and agents. The focus has been on general issues like engagement in social media, blog topics, discussion topics, etc.

Studies of customer support have documented emotions as part of written interactions. The work in [8], analyzed emotions in textual email communications and focused on prioritizing customer support emails based on detected emotions. Studies of online customer service (chats), such as [18] reported the impact of emotional text usage by service agents on their perception by customers.

3. METHODOLOGY

The objective of our work is to predict customer satisfaction at the end of customer service conversations delivered through social media. We treated this objective as a binary classification task, where the target classes are "satisfied" and "not-satisfied". The only part of the conversation that is used for this objective is the content of the first message

[6]http://www.mattersight.com/

posted by the customer. This means that our classifier generates its prediction as soon as a customer initiated a conversation with the customer service platform, and before a specific agent was assigned to support the customer. We use two auxiliary classifiers to extract affective features. The first auxiliary classifier generates *personality traits* scores based on previous social media posts of the customer and of a possible agent. The second classifier is an *emotion* detection classifier that detects emotions expressed in the customer's message. These settings enable us to identify and assign an agent, among all available agents, with the personality traits that would maximize the satisfaction of the customer and to prioritize conversations where customers are likely to be dissatisfied.

Below we describe the auxiliary classifiers, the features we extracted from their output and from the customer message content, and the training of our customer satisfaction classifier.

3.1 Personality Traits Classifier

To extract the *personality traits* we utilized the IBM Personality Insights service, available online publicly [7]. This service infers three models of personality, namely, *big five*, *needs* and *values*. The service was trained on social media data, including tweets and forum posts. In total, this classifier extracts percentile scores for 52 traits, as summarized in Table 1. This service requires at least $3,500$ words to have meaningful results. In our collected dataset (described below), 81% of the customers and 91% of the agents answered these requirements. To extract customer *personality traits* we used their historical public tweets as input to the personality traits classifier, and for agents we used their public customer support historical tweets. We distinguished between different agents by parsing their name which appears at the end of each agent tweet in the format of "^AGENT_NAME".

3.2 Emotion Detection Classifier

Another type of affective features we used to predict customer satisfaction is the presence of *emotions* in the content of the first customer message. The emotions are detected by an *emotion* detection classifier based on state-of-the-art features [12, 16, 2], which can detect multiple emotions in each tweet, including: *frustration, disappointment, confusion, politeness* and *anger*.

3.3 Features

We used the following features in our models.

3.3.1 Affective Features

Affective Features comprise two feature families: *personality* and *emotional*. The *personality* family of features are features extracted from *personality traits* of the customer and of the agent assigned to the customer. The extracted features, detailed in Table 2, include the raw output of the *personality traits* classifier for the customer and the agent, and features that represent the interaction of different personality traits of the two parties. These interaction features include root squared error features which capture the similarity between each customer and agent personality trait. MSE and cosine similarity features capture the similarity between a customer and an agent across all personality traits.

[7]https://www.ibm.com/smarterplanet/us/en/ibmwatson/developercloud/doc/personality-insights/index.shtml

Model	Description	Size	Trait
Big five	represents the most widely used model for generally describing how a person engages with the world	35	**Agreeableness** (Altruism, Cooperation, Modesty, Uncompromising, Sympathy, Trust), **Conscientiousness** (Achievement striving, Cautiousness, Dutifulness, Orderliness, Self-discipline, Self-efficacy), **Extraversion** (Activity level, Assertiveness, Cheerfulness, Excitement-seeking, Outgoing, Gregariousness), **Neuroticism** (Fiery, Prone to worry, Melancholy, Immoderation, Self-consciousness, Susceptible to stress), **Openness** (Adventurousness, Artistic interests, Emotionality, Imagination, Intellect, Authority-challenging)
Needs	describes which aspects of a product will resonate with a person	12	Excitement, Harmony, Curiosity, Ideal, Closeness, Self-expression, Liberty, Love, Practicality, Stability, Challenge, Structure
Values	describes motivating factors that influence a person's decision making	5	Self-transcendence, Conservation, Hedonism, Self-enhancement, Excitement

Table 1: Personality traits.

Feature Set Name	# Extracted Features	Mathematical Expression
customer personality traits	52	p_i^c
agent personality traits	52	p_i^a
root squared error	52	$\sqrt{(p_i^c - p_i^a)^2}$
mean squared error (MSE)	1	$\frac{1}{52}\sum_i (p_i^c - p_i^a)^2$
cosine similarity	1	$\frac{\sum_i p_i^c \cdot p_i^a}{\sqrt{\sum_i (p_i^c)^2} \cdot \sqrt{\sum_i (p_i^a)^2}}$

Table 2: Personality feature sets extracted from customer and agent personality traits.

We define p_i^c and p_i^a to be the percentile scores for the customer's and agent's i^{th} personality trait, respectively.

The *emotional* family of features includes the output of the *emotion* detection classifier described above, as a series of binary features (each feature describes a different emotion).

3.3.2 Textual Features

Textual features are extracted from the text of the first customer message, without considering any other information. These features include various n-grams, punctuation and social media features. Namely, *unigrams, bigrams, NRC lexicon features* (number of terms in a post associated with each affect label in NRC lexicon), and presence of *exclamation marks, question marks, usernames, links, happy emoticons,* and *sad emoticons*. These are the features we used in our baseline model detailed in the description of our experiments.

3.4 Customer Satisfaction Prediction System

We trained a binary SVM classifier with a linear kernel. The feature vector used to represent a message incorporated *affective* and *textual* features. A feature vector for a sample in the training data is generated as follows. The *emotion* detection classifier is used on the content of the initial message to output binary emotional scores, that represent whether each emotion is expressed in the content. These scores are then added as the *emotional* features to the feature vector. *Personality* features are generated by running the *personality traits* classifier for the customer and agent, and processing its output to generate the *personality* features described above. *Textual* features are also extracted from the content of the customer message and added to the feature vector. After the model is trained, a test initial message is classified by the model, after being transformed to a feature vector in the same way a train sample is transformed. The SVM classification model outputs a score s where $sign(s)$ determines the class label ("satisfied" or "not-satisfied") while $|s|$ deter-

mines the confidence of the classification (which is the distance of the sample from the separating hyper-plane). This can eventually be utilized to assign the most appropriate agent in terms of customer satisfaction confidence. Thus, for a given set of support agents, an agent is assigned such that her personality traits maximize the customer satisfaction confidence.

4. EXPERIMENTS

4.1 Dataset

We gathered data of two North America based Twitter customer service accounts that provide support in English to customers from North America. These dedicated Twitter accounts provide real-time support by monitoring tweets that customers address to it. Corporate support agents reply to these tweets through the Twitter platform. For the two companies, we extracted data from December 2014 until June 2015. For each customer that posted a tweet to the customer support accounts, we searched for the previous message, if any, to which it replied. This allowed us to trace back previous messages and reconstruct the entire conversation. We removed conversations longer than 10 turns, since 89% of the conversations include at most 10 turns, and also removed conversations that contained only 2 messages as these are too short to be meaningful (the customer never replied or provided details about the issue, and thus we can not learn about satisfaction). After applying these preprocessing steps, we had a dataset of 2,632 conversations.

4.2 Experimental Setup

As a first step to a classification model, we collected ground truth data. For this, we sampled 333 conversations from our dataset, accounting for length frequency in the data set. Each sampled conversation was initiated by a different customer, and the total number of agents in the dataset was 50. We validated that customers and agents in this dataset had enough public tweets available to extract their personality traits. We used Amazon Mechanical Turk[8] to tag the sampled conversations. Each conversation was tagged by five different MTurk's master level judges. Each judge answered the following questions given the full conversation:

- "Overall, how satisfied do you believe the customer was with the service in this communication?"

- "How likely is it that this customer will recommend this service provider to a friend or colleague?"

Each judge indicated an answer on a scale of [0...7], where 0 defines very low agreement, and 7 defines very high agreement with the statement. The average measures of intraclass

---
[8]https://www.mturk.com/

Model	Satisfied			Not-Satisfied		
	P	R	F	P	R	F
Random	0.721	0.5	0.590	0.279	0.5	0.358
M_t	0.781	0.833	0.806	0.481	0.398	0.435
Aff_{t+p}	0.803	0.833	0.818	0.524	0.473	0.497
Aff_{t+e}	0.809	**0.863**	0.835	0.571	0.473	0.518
Aff_{t+p+e}	**0.827**	0.858	**0.843**	**0.595**	**0.538**	**0.565**

Table 3: Detailed performance results for baseline and affective models.

correlation (ICC) among the judges was 0.847 and 0.845 for the first and the second questions respectively, which indicates high agreement between the judges. Cronbach's Alpha measure for the two questions was 0.942 which indicates very high internal consistency between the questions.

We generated true binary labels for the customer satisfaction classifier from the tagging of the two above mentioned questions. For each conversation, c, we calculated a summary customer satisfaction score, s_c, as the average of the responses to the two questions by each judge, and then averaged the score for all the judges. Using an average of the two ratings rather than only one question is statistically better because it accounts for errors that may have occurred in judges' ratings of one questions, and improves the reliability and validity of the score used [1]. For conversation c, we considered it to end with a positive customer satisfaction if $s_c \geq 4$. This process generated 240 conversations that ended with a positive customer satisfaction and 93 conversations that ended with a negative customer satisfaction.

We evaluated our methods by using leave-one-conversation-out cross-validation as in [10, 9]. Our baseline in all experiments, besides a random classifier, is an SVM classifier that uses only the *textual features* described above, and does not utilize *affective* features. This was used as a state-of-the-art single sentence emotion and sentiment detection approach in many cases (e.g., [12, 16, 15]). Since the classes distribution is unbalanced, we evaluated each class classification performance by using precision (P), recall (R) and F1-score (F). We used Liblinear[9] as an implementation of SVM with a linear kernel and ClearNLP[10] for *textual* features extraction.

4.3 Classification Results

Table 3 depicts the detailed classification results for both classes and a number of models we experimented with. Our baseline models are a model which assigns a label randomly (random) and a model based only on *textual* features (M_t). The novel models we experimented with added *affective* features to the baseline model: a model that uses *textual* and *personality* features (Aff_{t+p}), a model that uses *textual* and *emotional* features (Aff_{t+e}), and a model that uses *textual*, *personality* and *emotional* features (Aff_{t+p+e}). Table 3 shows that all affective models outperform baseline models, where Aff_{t+p} and Aff_{t+e} performed similarly with an average improvement of 17% in F1-score of the "not-satisfied" class, in comparison to M_t. Aff_{t+p+e}, which considered both *emotional* and *personality* affective features, yielded the best performance with an improvement of 30% in F1-score of the "not-satisfied" class, and of 5% for the "satisfied" class. Additionally, we used *McNemar's test* on the

[9]http://liblinear.bwaldvogel.de/
[10]https://github.com/clir/clearnlp

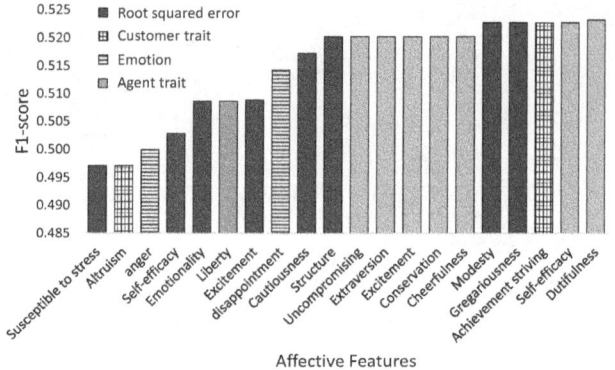

Figure 1: Model performance after excluding specific affective features. The bar's pattern associated with each feature indicates its feature set.

contingency tables derived from Aff_{t+p+e} and M_t predictions. This test showed that Aff_{t+p+e} performed statistically significantly better from M_t, under a value of 0.05. These results suggest that utilizing features based on affective components such as *personality traits* and *emotion* expression improves prediction of customer satisfaction to a reasonable level, already after the first message.

4.4 Contribution of Affective Features

We evaluated the importance of the affective features by performing the following experiment: for each affective feature, f, we generated a model which is trained using all features included in Aff_{t+p+e} except f. For each one of these models we have calculated the F1-score for the "not-satisfied" class. Figure 1 shows 20 affective features for which the lowest F1-scores were obtained, i.e., excluding these features caused performance to deteriorate the most. As Figure 1 shows, removal of each of these 20 features reduced F1 from $F1 = 0.565$ to $F1 < 0.523$. We further see that half of these high effect features describe one of the participants (traits and emotions of customers or agents), and half refer to a fit between them (root squared error). And of the 20 features, only two are emotions (anger and disappointment).

5. CONCLUSIONS AND FUTURE WORK

This paper reports on a first attempt to utilize *affect* features to improve the prediction of customer satisfaction in customer care interactions in social media. We showed how to utilize these features to gain a statistically significant improvement in predicting customer satisfaction. We discussed some practical applications such as optimizing the agent assignment for a specific customer inquiry.

We believe that this is only the tip of the iceberg, and see the following issues as future work. Extend contribution of affective features study, explore the case of virtual agents, extend beyond affect (adding contextual features, such as the topic of the dialogue), experimenting with large-scale datasets (our approach is scalable), and to predict customer satisfaction as the dialogue progresses (not just for the first customer message).

6. ACKNOWLEDGMENTS

The authors thank Michal Jacovi for constructive comments and Ishai Borovoy for assistance in data collection.

7. REFERENCES

[1] E. G. Carmines and R. A. Zeller. *Reliability and validity assessment*, volume 17. Sage publications, 1979.

[2] G. Feigenblat, D. Konopnicki, M. Shmueli-Scheuer, J. Herzig, and H. Shkedi. I understand your frustration. In *Proceedings of the 19th ACM Conference on Computer Supported Cooperative Work and Social Computing Companion*, pages 25–28. ACM, 2016.

[3] C. M. Froehle. Service personnel, technology, and their interaction in influencing customer satisfaction. *Decision Sciences*, 37(1):5–38, 2006.

[4] H. Gao, J. Mahmud, J. Chen, J. Nichols, and M. X. Zhou. Modeling user attitude toward controversial topics in online social media. In *Proceedings of the Eighth International Conference on Weblogs and Social Media, ICWSM 2014, Ann Arbor, Michigan, USA, June 1-4, 2014.*, 2014.

[5] K. Gelbrich. Anger, frustration, and helplessness after service failure: coping strategies and effective informational support. *Journal of the Academy of Marketing Science*, 38(5):567–585, 2010.

[6] A. J. Gill, S. Nowson, and J. Oberlander. What are they blogging about? personality, topic and motivation in blogs. In *Proceedings of the Third International Conference on Weblogs and Social Media, ICWSM*, 2009.

[7] L. R. Goldberg, J. A. Johnson, H. W. Eber, R. Hogan, M. C. Ashton, C. R. Cloninger, and H. G. Gough. The international personality item pool and the future of public-domain personality measures. *Journal of Research in personality*, 40(1):84–96, 2006.

[8] N. K. Gupta, M. Gilbert, and G. D. Fabbrizio. Emotion detection in email customer care. *Computational Intelligence*, 29(3):489–505, 2013.

[9] E. Ivanovic. Dialogue act tagging for instant messaging chat sessions. In *Proceedings of the ACL Student Research Workshop*, pages 79–84. Association for Computational Linguistics, 2005.

[10] S. N. Kim, L. Cavedon, and T. Baldwin. Classifying dialogue acts in one-on-one live chats. In *Proceedings of EMNLP*, pages 862–871, 2010.

[11] K. Lee, J. Mahmud, J. Chen, M. Zhou, and J. Nichols. Who will retweet this? detecting strangers from twitter to retweet information. *ACM Trans. Intell. Syst. Technol.*, 6(3):31:1–31:25, 2015.

[12] S. Mohammad. Portable features for classifying emotional text. In *Proceedings of NAACL HLT*, pages 587–591, 2012.

[13] L. Neng-Pai, C. Hung-Chang, and H. Yi-Ching. Investigating the relationship between service providers? personality and customers? perceptions of service quality across gender. *Journal of Total Quality Management*, 12(1):57–67, 2001.

[14] R. L. Oliver. *Satisfaction: A behavioral perspective on the consumer*. Routledge, 2014.

[15] A. Qadir and E. Riloff. Learning emotion indicators from tweets: Hashtags, hashtag patterns, and phrases. In *Proceedings of EMNLP*, pages 1203–1209, 2014.

[16] K. Roberts, M. A. Roach, J. Johnson, J. Guthrie, and S. M. Harabagiu. Empatweet: Annotating and detecting emotions on twitter. In *LREC*, pages 3806–3813, 2012.

[17] K. A. Siddiqui. Personality influences on customer satisfaction. *African Journal of Business Management*, 6(11):4134–4141, 2012.

[18] L. Zhang, L. B. Erickson, and H. C. Webb. Effects of emotional text on online customer service chat. In *Graduate Student Research Conference in Hospitality and Tourism*, 2011.

On the Impact of Personality in Massive Open Online Learning

Guanliang Chen*, Dan Davis†, Claudia Hauff and Geert-Jan Houben
Delft University of Technology
Delft, the Netherlands
{guanliang.chen, d.j.davis, c.hauff, g.j.p.m.houben}@tudelft.nl

ABSTRACT

Massive Open Online Courses (MOOCs) have gained considerable momentum since their inception in 2011. They are, however, plagued by two issues that threaten their future: learner engagement and learner retention. MOOCs regularly attract tens of thousands of learners, though only a very small percentage complete them successfully. In the traditional classroom setting, it has been established that personality impacts different aspects of learning. It is an open question to what extent this finding translates to MOOCs: do learners' personalities impact their learning & learning behaviour in the MOOC setting? In this paper, we explore this question and analyse the personality profiles and learning traces of hundreds of learners that have taken a *EX101x Data Analysis* MOOC on the edX platform. We find learners' personality traits to only weakly correlate with learning as captured through the data traces learners leave on edX.

Keywords

massive open online learning, personality prediction

1. INTRODUCTION

MOOCs can deliver a world-class education on virtually any academic or professional development topic to any person with access to the Internet. Millions of people around the globe have signed up to courses offered on platforms such as edX[1], Coursera[2], FutureLearn[3] and Udacity[4]. At the same time though, only a small percentage of these learners (usually between 5-10%) actually complete a MOOC suc-

cessfully [20], an issue that continues to plague massive open online learning. Keeping MOOC learners engaged with the course and platform are of major concerns to instructional designers and MOOC instructors alike.

Considerable research efforts have been dedicated to establish the effect of learner personality on learning in the classroom setting, e.g. [3, 22, 37, 26] and certain personality traits have been shown to be rather consistently correlated with learner achievement and success. Not investigated so far has been the impact of personality on learning in MOOCs — is personality predictive of success and behaviour in the current massive open online learning environments? If we were to find this to be the case, it would open avenues for personalization and adaptation of learning in MOOCs based on learners' personalities. In contrast to the classroom setting where learners form a relatively homogeneous group (in terms of age group, cultural exposure, prior knowledge, etc.), MOOC learners have very diverse backgrounds [19] — a factor we hypothesize to make the subject more complex. A second question in this context is how to *estimate* the personality of learners based on MOOC data traces. The personality of learners (or users more generally) is commonly measured through self-reported questionnaires; one of the most often employed personality models is the so-called *Big Five personality model* [11] which is commonly administered through a fifty-item self-reporting questionnaire [18]. Many learners do not take the time to fill in pre-course surveys and thus, it is also of interest to us to *estimate* learners' personality, based on their MOOC data traces alone. Such an empirical estimation of users' personality based on their digital traces has been an active area of research in the past few years, with successful predictions of personality traits based on data extracted from Facebook [17, 23, 2], Twitter [29, 16, 36, 1], Sina Weibo [15], Flickr [10] and Instagram [14]. Very diverse sets of social media traces have shown to be predictive of personality, not only behavioural (number of friends, etc.), activity and demographic features, but also image patterns and colors.

Inspired by the positive findings in these prior works, we focus on the following two **Research Questions**:

RQ1 Does personality impact learner engagement, learner behaviour and learner success in the context of MOOCs?

RQ2 Can learners' personalities be predicted based on their behaviour exhibited on a MOOC platform?

We empirically investigate our research questions on the data traces of 763 learners who participated in the *EX101x Data Analysis* MOOC running on the edX platform in 2015.

*The author's research is supported by the *Extension School* of the Delft University of Technology.

†The author's research is supported by the *Leiden-Delft-Erasmus Centre for Education and Learning.*

[1] https://www.edx.org/

[2] https://www.coursera.org/

[3] https://www.futurelearn.com/

[4] https://www.udacity.com/

UMAP '16, July 13-17, 2016, Halifax, NS, Canada
© 2016 ACM. ISBN 978-1-4503-4370-1/16/07 ...$15.00.
DOI: http://dx.doi.org/10.1145/2930238.2930240

We observe (i) significant negative correlations between a range of behavioural MOOC features and the *openness* personality trait for novice learners, and (ii) significant positive correlations between behavioural features and the *conscientious* trait for learners with a high level of prior expertise. Overall though, we find learners' MOOC data traces to be less predictive of their personality traits than data traces users leave on other social Web platforms.

Our empirical work shows that the prediction of learners' personality traits based on their interactions with the MOOC platform is possible to some extent: our predictions are statistically significant for four of the five investigated personality traits and improve as more data about our learners becomes available.

2. BACKGROUND

Two strands of work come together in our research: (1) the impact of personality on learning, and (2) the prediction of personality traits based on user activities on the social Web.

Personality and Learning.
Researchers in the field of Education Psychology have found each of the Big Five personality traits to be a reliable predictor of academic performance (as measured in the form of grade point averages) in the traditional higher-education setting [31].

Meta-analyses [28] and empirical literature reviews [27] identify *conscientiousness* as the one trait with the strongest and most consistent association with academic success.

Taking individual works into consideration, [8] found in a US-based study that *conscientiousness* is a better and more reliable predictor of future academic success (at college level) than a student's SAT score (a standardized test for college admissions in the US). Similarly, Chamorro-Premuzic & Furnham [4] found *conscientiousness* to account for more than 10% of unique variance in overall final exam marks at university level. It should be noted though, that not all empirical studies agree on this observation and some report other personality traits to be significantly correlated with academic success. Farsides & Woodfield [13], for instance, found *openness* and *agreeableness* to be the two traits most strongly correlated with academic success in a study conducted on undergraduate college students.

Other studies on education and personality do not concern themselves with academic success, but other factors such as a student's intrinsic motivation to attend college [6] and the effect of different types of feedback and emotional support [32, 12].

The above studies all employ undergraduate college students as their test subjects. However, the subjects of the present research are much more heterogeneous; given the openness of MOOCs and their accessibility, we can explore the role of personality on a new, globally diverse population of learners.

Personality Prediction based on Social Web Traces.
Predicting users' Big Five personality traits based on their activities on various social Web platforms has been a very active area of research in the past years. In Table 1 we list a number of works that inspired our own investigation. The two most often considered platforms are Facebook and Twitter; they offer a myriad of diverse user traces that can be ex-

ploited for prediction purposes such as users preferences, social and academic activities, "conversations" with individuals and groups of users and so on. Especially the textual content users produce has been shown to be particularly useful to estimate users' personality [17, 15]. Notable in Table 1 is also the diversity of the user set under investigation — ranging from a mere 71 users [1] to 180,000 users [2]. These numbers are a first pointer towards the difficulty of collecting personality ground truth data; while small user samples are gathered through questionnaires, in the two large-scale Facebook studies [23, 2] a Facebook app was developed to engage a large set of users. Studies that recruit users through crowdsourcing platforms such as Amazon Mechanical Turk, e.g. [14], may not be very reliable, due to the setup's inherent incentive for workers to quickly answer the personality questions. Finally, Table 1 can also serve as a first indicator of the expected effectiveness of our personality predictor. The features less directly related to users (e.g. the color features in their photos) yield a higher error and a lower correlation coefficient than features which are more directly related to users (the number of their friends, their use of language, etc.). Since in our scenario (personality prediction based on MOOC log traces), we also have to deal with traces which are indirectly expressing a learner's personality, we may expect our work to result in similar results as those in [10, 14].

3. MOOC DATA & PERSONALITY

Before delving into our research methodology, we briefly describe our data collection process and the specific MOOC we analyzed for this research.

3.1 MOOC

We collected personality ground truth data from learners of the *EX101x Data Analysis* MOOC — officially known as *EX101x Data Analysis: Take It to the MAX( )* — which ran from August 31, 2015 to November 9, 2015 on the edX platform.

EX101x Data Analysis teaches various introductory data analysis skills in Excel and Python. The course was set up as an xMOOC [33]: lecture videos were published throughout the ten teaching weeks. Apart from lectures, each week exercises were distributed in the form of multiple choice and numerical input questions. Each of the 146 questions was worth one point and could be attempted twice. Answers were due three weeks after the release of the respective assignment. To pass the course, $\geq$ 60% of the questions had to be answered correctly.

Overall, 23,622 users registered for the course. Less than half of the registered learners (40%) engaged with the course, watching at least one lecture video. The completion rate was 4.75% in line with similar MOOC offerings [21].

The edX platform provides a great deal of timestamped log traces, including clicks, views, quiz attempts, and forum interactions — in the *EX101x Data Analysis* MOOC a total of 9,523,840 log traces were recorded. We adapted the MOOCdb[5] toolkit to our needs and translated these low-level log traces into a data schema that is easily query-able.

3.2 Learners' Personality Traits

We included a fifty item Big Five personality questionnaire [18] in the first week of the course as an optional com-

---

[5] http://moocdb.csail.mit.edu/

	Platform	#Users	Features	Big Five Regressor
[17]	Facebook	167	network, activities, language, preferences	$r \in [0.48, 0.65]$
[23]	Facebook	58,466	likes	$r \in [0.29, 0.43]$
[2]	Facebook	180,000	likes, status updates	RMSE $\in [0.27, 0.29]$
[29]	Twitter	335	Number of followers, following and list counts	RMSE $\in [0.69, 0.85]$
[16]	Twitter	279	language, Twitter usage, network	MAE $\in [0.12, 0.18]$
[36]	Twitter	2,927	language, Twitter usage	—
[1]	Twitter	71	Number of friends, likes, groups	MAE $\in [0.12, 0.19]$
[15]	Sina Weibo	1,766	language	$r \in [0.31, 0.40]$
[10]	Flickr	300	visual patterns	$\rho \in [0.12, 0.22]$
[14]	Instagram	113	color features	RMSE $\in [0.66, 0.95]$

Table 1: Overview of a number of past works in the area of personality prediction — shown are the platform under investigation, the number of users in the evaluation set and the type of features derived from the platform. The final column lists the evaluation metrics reported in the prediction setup: each personality trait is predicted independently, the interval shows the minimum and maximum metric reported across the five traits. The evaluation metrics are either the linear correlation coefficient (r), Spearman's rank correlation coefficient (ρ), the mean absolute error (MAE) or the root mean squared error (RMSE). The latter two metrics are only meaningful when the normalization of the personality scores is known (in the reported works to scores between [1,5]).

ponent; we described our motivation for this questionnaire in an introductory text ("aligning our education with your personality"), and did not offer any compensation.

A total of $2,195$ (9.3%) registered learners began the process of filling in the personality questionnaire; $1,356$ learners eventually completed this process (5.7% of registered learners). This is a common attrition rate, due to the perceived high demand (rating fifty statements) and the lack of an immediate gain for the learners.

The fifty items are short descriptive statements such as:

```
I am the life of the party.
I am always prepared.
I get stressed out easily.
```

and are answered on a Likert scale (*disagree, slightly disagree, neutral, slightly agree* and *agree*). Based on the provided answers, for each of the five personality traits (*openness, extraversion, conscientiousness, agreeableness, neuroticism*) a score between 0 and 40 is computed which indicates to what extent the learner possesses that trait. The five traits can be summarized as follows:

- The *openness* trait is displayed by a strong intellectual curiosity and a preference for variety and novelty.

- The *extraversion* trait refers to a high degree of sociability and assertiveness.

- *Conscientiousness* is exhibited through being organized, disciplined and achievement-oriented.

- People who score high on *agreeableness* are helpful to others, cooperative and sympathetic.

- The *neuroticism* trait indicates emotional stability, the level of anxiety and impulse control.

For each learner who completed the questionnaire, we are able to compute his or her personality traits according to [18]; each learner can thus be described with a five-dimensional personality score vector.

4. APPROACH

Having gathered personality ground truth data, we now describe the features we computed for each learner based on their MOOC data traces, and the machine learning approaches employed to predict a learner's personality traits based on those features.

4.1 Features

As our work is exploratory (and to our knowledge personality prediction based on MOOC traces has not been attempted before), the features we extract are inspired by personality findings in learning outside of the MOOC setting as well as by the characteristics of the personality traits themselves.

Learners who score high on *extraversion* tend to have a strong need for gratification [5, 34, 24]. In the MOOC setting, such gratification can be fulfilled through interactions with other learners. The edX platform facilities interactions through its forums, and we thus explore features related to forum use. We also expect forum-based features to be useful to predict high levels of *agreeableness* (people who tend to help others). We hypothesize that learners who are very *conscientious* (i.e. have a high degree of self-organization and self-discipline) will be more disciplined in terms of video watching and quiz question answering than learners who score low in this trait, inspiring us to explore video & quiz related features. The *openness* trait embodies academic curiosity and we hypothesize it to correlate positively with the amount of time spent on the platform and the material.

Concretely, we extracted the following twenty features for each learner by aggregating all of the learner's activities throughout the running of the *EX101x Data Analysis* MOOC:

- *Time watching video material*: the total amount of time (in minutes) a learner spent watching video material.

- *Time solving quizzes*: the total amount of time a learner spent on the MOOC's quiz pages.

- *#Questions learners attempted to solve*: the total number of quiz questions a learner answered (independent of the answer being right or wrong).

- *#New forum questions*: the number of new forum questions created by a learner.

- *#Forum replies*: the number of replies (including replies to questions and comments to replies) created by a learner.

- *#Total forum postings*: the total number of postings a learner made to the course forum (this includes comments, questions and replies).

- *Forum browsing time*: the total amount of time a learner spent on the course forum.

- *#Forum accesses*: the number of times a learner entered the course 'Forum' page.

- *#Forum interactions*: the total number of unique learners involved in the questions a learner participated in.

- *Total time on-site*: the total amount of time (in minutes) a learner spent on the course's edX platform instantiation.

- *Average video response time*: the average number of minutes between a lecture video's release and a learner clicking the video's 'play' button for the first time.

- *Average quiz response time*: the average number of minutes between a quiz question's release and a learner making a first submission for it.

- *#Videos skipped*: the number of lecture videos a learner did not watch.

- *#Videos sped up*: the number of lecture videos a learner sped up during watching.

- *Maximum session time*: the maximum amount of time (in minutes) a learner spent in a single session on the course's edX site.

- *Average/standard deviation session time*: the average number of minutes/standard deviation in a learner's sessions on the course's edX site.

- *Average/standard deviation between-quizzes time*: the average number of minutes/standard deviation between answering subsequent quiz questions in the same quiz.

- *Final score*: the percentage of quiz questions a learner answered correctly at the end of the course.

Performing a correlation analysis between these features and the personality traits derived from the learners' personality questionnaires allows us to answer **RQ1**: the extent to which personality impacts learner behaviour, engagement and success as captured through the lense of MOOC data traces.

As many of the features described here will be impacted by a learner's prior knowledge — a learner with a high amount of prior knowledge may skip many videos, while a learner without any prior knowledge may skip close to none — we distinguish two learner groups:

- learners with *high* prior knowledge, and,

- learners with *low* prior knowledge.

We derive a learner's level of prior knowledge based on the information provided in the general pre-course survey. In the pre-course survey, learners are asked to fill in to what degree they are familiar with certain course-specific concepts such as "pivot tables" and "named range" (two spreadsheet-specific concepts). We aggregate learners' answers by weighting the difficulty of those concepts (the weighting was provided by an expert on the course's topics) and divide the learners into a low and a high prior knowledge group accordingly.

4.2 Personality Traits' Prediction

Our second goal in this work, as captured in **RQ2**, is the prediction of learners' personality traits based on their MOOC data traces. To this end, we experiment with two state-of-the-art regression models based on Gaussian Processes (GP) [30] and Random Forests (RF) [25], respectively, which have been shown to perform well in previous personality prediction works [14, 1, 15, 36].

Formally, a regression problem can be represented as $y = f(x) + \varepsilon$, where y denotes the personality trait (we predict each of the five traits independently as previous works), x denotes the features we derive for each learner, and ε denotes the intercept. To estimate the regression function $f(\cdot)$, GP considers the observed samples to have been drawn from a Gaussian distribution, while RF fits a number of classifying decision trees on various sub-samples and employs the averaging technique to improve the predictive accuracy. In our experiments, we set GP's noise parameter to 1.0; the number of trees in RF was set to 100.

Due to the limited number of learners, we resort to 10-fold cross-validation. In order to evaluate the accuracy of our personality trait predictions, we resort to Spearman's rank correlation coefficient [35] with the two variables being the learners' ground truth personality trait score (a value between 0 and 40) and the predicted trait score. Correlations are expressed as values between $[-1, 1]$ with the two boundaries indicating a perfect negative or positive alignment in ranks. Correlations close to 0 are not statistically significant and indicate that no direct relationship between the two variables exists.

5. RESULTS

In the first part of this section, we provide a basic analysis of the MOOC and the personality data we collected, and then present our findings with respect to the correlation of individual features and personality traits (Section 5.3), as well as the predictability of personality traits based on these features (Section 5.4).

5.1 EX101x Data Analysis Overview

To provide additional context of the MOOC we investigate, in Table 2 we provide its characteristics with respect to the learners that actively participated in it. We consider a registered learner to have actively participated, if the learner clicked at least once the 'Watch' button of a lecture video. Of the 23,622 registered learners, this is the case for 9,493 learners — our set of *engaged* MOOC learners. Among those, about half also submitted at least one answer to a quiz question. Overall, 12% of the engaged learners earned a certificate by answering 60% or more of the quiz questions correctly. Notably, on average, less than one hour of lecture material (of approximately 300 minutes of video lecture material) was consumed by the engaged learners. Less than 15% of engaged learners were active in the course forum; by the end of the course, a total of 4,419 posts (questions, replies and comments) had been created.

Metrics	
#Learners	9,493
Completion rate	11.82%
Avg. time watching video material (in min.)	49.61
%Learners who answered at least one question	53.90%
Avg. #questions learners answered	20.89
Avg. #questions answered correctly	16.30
Avg. accuracy of learners' answers	48.25%
#Forum posts	4,419
%Learners who posted at least once	12.18%
Avg. #posts per learner	0.47

Table 2: Basic characteristics across engaged learners of *EX101x Data Analysis*.

These statistics provide a first indicator of the issue we face in the prediction of personality based on MOOC log traces: data is sparse. While there are thousands of active learners, most learners are active only sporadically; only a small percentage of learners remain active throughout the entire MOOC. As already hinted at in Section 3, the MOOC we investigate is not an outlier with respect to engagement and learner success, it is rather representative of the average MOOC offered today on major MOOC platforms.

5.2 Learners' Personality Traits

As stated in Section 3, we received 1,356 completed personality questionnaires from our learners. We made the design decision to present learners with the personality questionnaire at the start of the MOOC, to prevent only the most persevering subset of learners to enter our learner pool, thus decreasing bias. At the same time though, this also means that we are likely to have little activity data for most of our learners that provided us with their personality scores.

Due to the length of the personality questionnaire, we suspect some learners to more or less randomly provide answers instead of truly *answering* to the personality statements. To investigate this effect, in Figure 1 we plot the amount of time (in minutes) it took our 1,356 learners to complete the questionnaire as extracted from the log traces. According to [18], completing this questionnaire should take between three and eight minutes, depending on a person's reading speed. We take a somewhat wider margin (Web users easily get distracted and might have been multi-tasking at the same time) and consider the personality data of all those learners as valid that spent at least three minutes and at most twelve minutes on the questionnaire. After this filtering step, we are left with 1,082 valid personality questionnaire responses that we continue to analyse in the remainder of this section.

In Figure 2 we plot the distribution of the five personality traits of those 1,082 learners. Our learners score lowest on *extraversion* and highest on *openness* and *agreeableness*. These results are in line with previous work exploring the personality of users that are active on social media [9]. The plot also shows the largest variety among our learners with respect to their *extraversion* and the smallest with respect to their *openness* to experience. These results are sensible and point to the validity of the responses — one of the defining characteristics of openness is intellectual curiosity, which ev-

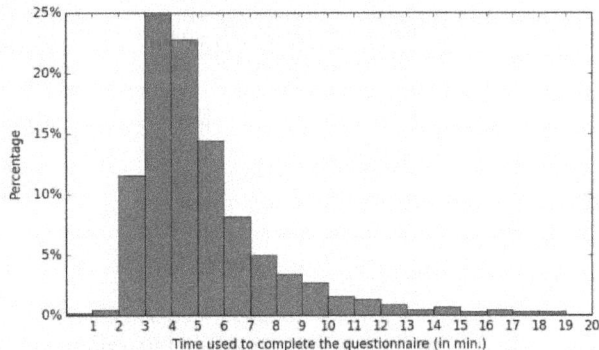

Figure 1: Overview of the fraction of learners and the time (in minutes) it took them to complete the fifty-item personality questionnaire. Only the learners that completed the whole questionnaire are included.

ery learner that starts learning through a MOOC must have to some extent. This is in contrast to the general population, where openness tends to be the trait that scores the lowest (together with extraversion), as observed for instance in [7].

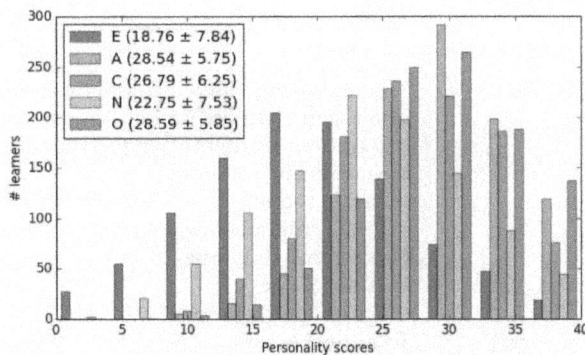

Figure 2: Histogram of the 1,082 learners' personality data. E, A, C, N, O denote Extroversion, Agreeableness, Conscientiousness, Neuroticism and Openness to experience, respectively.

We summarize the demographics of our learners with known personality traits in Table 3. The majority are male (64%) and between the ages of 20 and 40 (62%). More than 40% of our learners have completed a first university degree already.

5.3 Feature Correlation Analysis

In order to conduct a meaningful correlation analysis, we partition our 1,082 learners into two sets: those learners with high and those with low prior knowledge based on their self-reported expertise in the pre-course survey. As all questionnaires and surveys in this MOOC, the pre-course survey was voluntary and not all learners completed it. We are thus left with 763 learners who completed the personality questionnaire *and* stated their prior knowledge level.

In Tables 4 and 5 we report the Spearman's rank correlation between the features described in Section 4.1 and the learners' personality traits. As in previous works [1, 36, 15, 2], we treat each personality trait independently. Across the two sets of learners we do not observe any statistically sig-

	E	A	C	N	O
Time watching video material (in min.)	0.00	−0.04	0.15*	0.03	−0.18**
Time solving quizzes (in min.)	−0.02	0.02	0.07	0.02	−0.18**
# Questions learners attempted to solve	−0.04	−0.04	0.15*	0.03	−0.17**
# New forum questions	0.07	0.04	0.01	0.04	0.00
# Forum replies	0.12	0.12	0.00	0.01	0.03
# Total forum postings	0.11	0.10	0.03	0.03	0.02
Forum browsing time	−0.10	0.00	0.06	−0.04	−0.13
Forum accesses	−0.11	−0.04	0.06	−0.05	−0.16*
# Forum interactions	0.10	0.11	0.03	0.04	0.03
Total time on-site	−0.02	−0.03	0.12	0.01	−0.19**
Average time responded to videos	0.09	−0.04	−0.04	−0.06	−0.10
Average time responded to quizs	0.03	0.00	−0.14	−0.10	−0.15
# Videos skipped	0.02	0.07	−0.14*	−0.04	0.18**
# Videos sped up	0.00	−0.03	0.10	−0.01	−0.02
Maximum session time	−0.02	−0.05	0.10	0.00	−0.17*
Average session time	0.00	−0.03	0.05	−0.01	−0.08
Standard deviation session time	0.04	−0.01	0.11	0.02	−0.16*
Average between-quizzes time	0.03	0.10	0.00	0.02	−0.10
Standard deviation between-quizzes time	0.01	0.06	0.04	0.01	−0.14*
Final score	−0.06	−0.07	0.12	0.07	−0.15*

Table 4: Overview of the correlations (Spearman's rank) between the 360 LOW prior knowledge learners' personality traits and their MOOC-based behavioural features. The significant values (according to the Student's t distribution) are marked by: * ($p < 0.01$) and ** ($p < 0.001$).

	E	A	C	N	O
Time watching video material (in min.)	−0.08	−0.07	0.09	0.05	−0.01
Time solving quizzes (in min.)	−0.09	−0.10	0.10	0.04	−0.03
# Questions learners attempted to solve	−0.13	−0.08	0.08	0.00	−0.03
# New forum questions	−0.04	0.04	0.10	−0.03	0.03
# Forum replies	−0.02	0.03	0.15*	0.08	0.03
# Total forum postings	−0.03	0.02	0.15*	0.02	0.03
Forum browsing time	−0.11	−0.04	0.02	−0.03	−0.06
Forum accesses	−0.14*	−0.06	0.03	−0.04	−0.04
# Forum interactions	−0.02	0.02	0.15*	0.03	0.03
Total time on-site	−0.07	−0.07	0.11	0.04	−0.03
Average time responded to videos	0.05	−0.02	−0.01	0.06	0.03
Average time responded to quizs	0.03	−0.05	0.00	0.05	0.02
# Videos skipped	0.09	0.08	−0.09	−0.04	0.00
# Videos sped up	0.03	0.00	0.06	0.09	0.06
Maximum session time	−0.04	−0.04	0.11	0.04	−0.04
Average session time	0.06	−0.05	0.03	0.06	−0.04
Standard deviation session time	−0.03	−0.07	0.12	0.04	−0.04
Average between-quizzes time	0.00	−0.06	0.09	0.06	0.00
Standard deviation between-quizzes time	−0.03	−0.07	0.09	0.07	0.00
Final score	−0.12	−0.05	0.07	0.01	−0.01

Table 5: Overview of the correlations (Spearman's rank) between the 403 HIGH prior knowledge learners' personality traits and their MOOC-based behavioural features. The significant values (according to the Student's t distribution) are marked by: * ($p < 0.01$) and ** ($p < 0.001$).

nificant correlations between behavioural features and the traits of *agreeableness* and *neuroticism*. The hypothesized increased forum activities of learners with a high *agreeableness* score are not supported by our data. Only two personality traits are significantly correlated with a number of features: *openness* to experience and *conscientiousness*. Among the learners with low prior knowledge (Table 4) the amount of time spent watching video lectures and number of quiz questions learners attempted are positively correlated with *conscientiousness* to a significant degree while a significant negative correlation is found for the number of videos skipped — i.e., learners with a high-self discipline and striving for achievement are likely to be more thoroughly engaged with more learning materials than learners who are not. The same features (as well as additional related features, 10 in total) are *inversely* correlated with the *openness* to experience trait

Demographics	Distribution	
Gender	Female	304 (28.10%)
	Male	688 (63.59%)
	Unknown	90 (8.32%)
Age	< 20	117 (10.81%)
	[20, 30)	378 (34.94%)
	[30, 40)	296 (27.36%)
	≥ 40	291 (26.89%)
	Unknown	106 (9.80%)
Education level completed	Bachelor	440 (40.67%)
	Advanced degree	413 (42.75%)
	Other	133 (12.29%)
	Unknown	84 (7.76%)

Table 3: Demographics of the 1,082 learners included in our study.

to a significant degree — i.e. learners that are more intellectually curious & prefer variety are less likely to spend time focused on the learning material than learners with lower *openness* scores. As a consequence they earn a lower grade. The negative influence of this trait points to learners that are interested in a broader set of subjects (instead of steadily following a single MOOC).

In the case of learners with high levels of prior knowledge (Table 5) we observe only four significant correlations between features and personality traits: three forum features (number of replies, number of forum posts and number of forum interactions) are positively correlated with *conscientiousness*. In contrast to our expectations, learners with high levels of *extraversion* are not positively correlated with forum behaviour, in contrast, the only other significant correlation (between the amount of time spent on the forum and the *extraversion*) trait is a negative one – learners with higher levels of *extraversion* spend less time on the forum than learners with lower levels of *extraversion*.

Overall, we have to conclude that behavioural features extracted from MOOC log traces are correlated to a lesser degree with personality than lexical or behavioural features extracted from social networks such as Facebook and Twitter, possibly due to the more constraint nature of the MOOC setting.

5.4 Personality Traits' Prediction

In this section we provide an answer to **RQ2**. We are particularly interested, to what extent we are able *early on* in the course to predict a learner's personality — if we were able to predict a learner's personality traits after one or two weeks of MOOC activities the automatic adaptation and personalization based on personality would become possible. Here, we train the regression models by taking all of the learners as input with their prior knowledge level as an additional feature in the feature set[6].

In Figure 3 we plot for each of the personality traits the effectiveness our two regression approaches achieve as measured by Spearman's rank correlation coefficient. The plots also show for each week of the course the number of active learners the personality was predicted for, with 567 active

learners at the start of the course[7] (i.e., those with ground truth personality profiles) and 136 active in the last week of the course. Based on these plots, we can make a number of observations:

- significant correlations (indicating usable predictions) are achieved for four of the five personality traits — the exception is *agreeableness*, which is not surprising, considering the correlation analysis and the lack of indicative features;
- Gaussian Processes perform better in this setting than Random Forests yielding higher correlations in three of the four traits that result in significant results;
- the correlation coefficients tend to increase with increasing course weeks as more activity data about each learner is gathered, and
- *extraversion* ($\rho = 0.31$) and *neuroticism* ($\rho = 0.22$) achieve the highest prediction accuracy by the end of the course — considering that those two traits did result in a significant correlation for only one feature in our correlation analysis, we have to conclude that more complex and higher-level features are needed to capture those traits well.

6. CONCLUSIONS

In this paper we have provided a first exploration of the relationship between massive open online learning and learners' personality traits.

Our work centered around two questions, which we evaluated in the context of the *EX101x Data Analysis* MOOC and more than 1,000 learners with valid personality profiles.

We have provided initial evidence that personality can impact learners' behaviour in the MOOC setting (**RQ1**). We have explored a set of MOOC-specific behavioural features and investigated their correlation with the personality traits of the Big Five personality factor model. We found various features to be correlated with the traits of *openness* and *conscientiousness* for learners with low prior knowledge. Learners with high prior knowledge exhibited fewer significant correlations, the *conscientiousness* trait was the only trait for which we observed multiple correlated features.

With respect to **RQ2** and the prediction of personality traits we can conclude that our features provide a meaningful starting point for future work — we observed significant positive correlations with all but one personality trait. The trend that over time the correlations increase (as more log traces per user become available better predictions are made) indicates the viability of the approach as well as the need to elicit more activity log traces from MOOC learners, e.g. through the offering of additional course activities and explicit guidance towards social interactions by course instructors.

In our future work, we will expand our analysis and exploration of behavioural features extracted from MOOC log traces for personality prediction. We will investigate human-computer interaction approaches that elicit additional log traces in MOOCs to improve the early prediction of personality traits. Most importantly, we will explore to what extent the predictions of personality allow us to automatically

---

[6]The alternative of training separate models for HIGH and LOW prior knowledge learners results in similar findings.

[7]Note that this number is different from our 763 learners with prior expertise level and personality profile as not every learner was active every week.

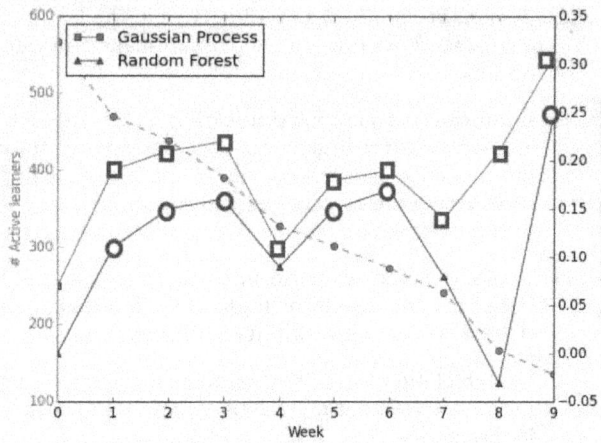

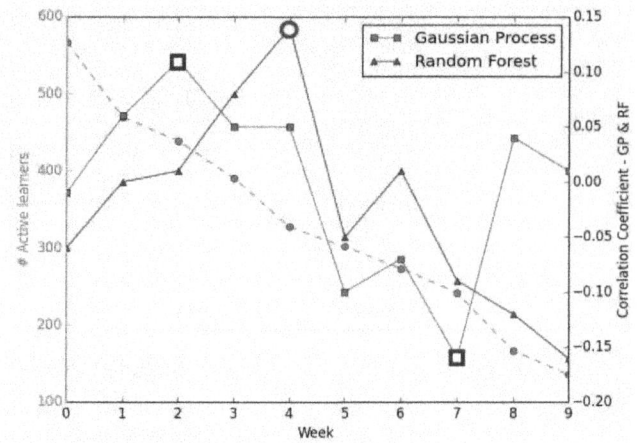

Prediction of extraversion (left) and agreeableness (right).

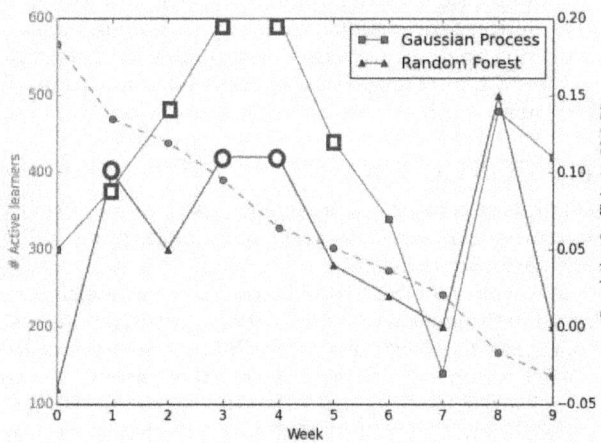

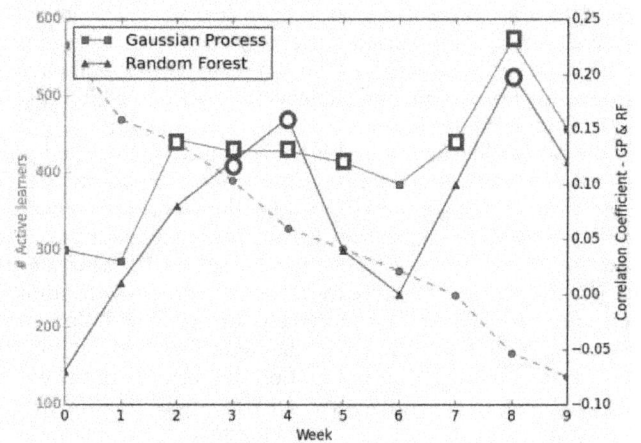

Prediction of conscientiousness (left) and neuroticism (right).

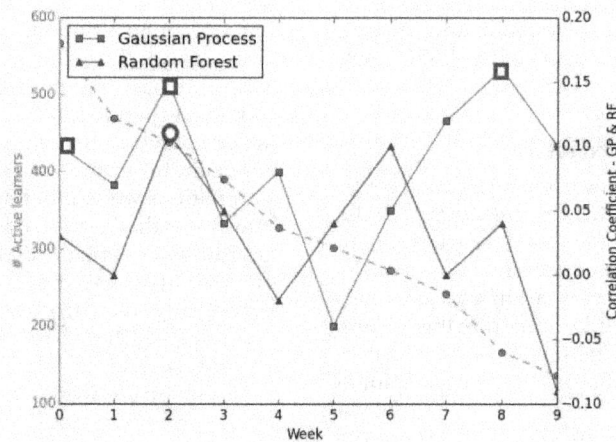

Prediction of openness.

Figure 3: Overview of personality trait predictions. Each personality trait is predicted independently. In each plot, the red (dashed) line indicates the number of learners active up to course week n. The two regression-based predictors are evaluated according to Spearman's rank correlation coefficient. The empty markers ($\square$/$\bigcirc$) denote that the corresponding results are statistically significant ($p < 0.01$).

adapt the MOOC learning material and presentation in a meaningful manner to fulfil our ultimate goals of increasing MOOC learner engagement and success.

7. REFERENCES

[1] S. Adali and J. Golbeck. Predicting personality with social behavior. In *Proceedings of the 2012 International Conference on Advances in Social Networks Analysis and Mining*, ASONAM '12, pages 302–309, 2012.

[2] Y. Bachrach, M. Kosinski, T. Graepel, P. Kohli, and D. Stillwell. Personality and patterns of facebook usage. In *Proceedings of the 4th Annual ACM Web Science Conference*, WebSci '12, pages 24–32, 2012.

[3] G. Blickle. Personality traits, learning stratigies, and performance. *European Journal of Personality*, 10(5):337–352, 1996.

[4] T. Chamorro-Premuzic and A. Furnham. Personality predicts academic performance: Evidence from two longitudinal university samples. *Journal of Research in Personality*, 37(4):319–338, 2003.

[5] S.-J. Chen and E. J. Caropreso. Influence of personality on online discussion. *Journal of Interactive Online Learning*, 3(2):1–17, 2004.

[6] M. Clark and C. A. Schroth. Examining relationships between academic motivation and personality among college students. *Learning and individual differences*, 20(1):19–24, 2010.

[7] D. A. Cobb-Clark and S. Schurer. The stability of big-five personality traits. *Economics Letters*, 115(1):11–15, 2012.

[8] M. A. Conard. Aptitude is not enough: How personality and behavior predict academic performance. *Journal of Research in Personality*, 40(3):339–346, 2006.

[9] T. Correa, A. W. Hinsley, and H. G. De Zuniga. Who interacts on the web?: The intersection of users' personality and social media use. *Computers in Human Behavior*, 26(2):247–253, 2010.

[10] M. Cristani, A. Vinciarelli, C. Segalin, and A. Perina. Unveiling the multimedia unconscious: Implicit cognitive processes and multimedia content analysis. In *Proceedings of the 21st ACM International Conference on Multimedia*, MM '13, pages 213–222, 2013.

[11] B. De Raad. *The Big Five Personality Factors: The psycholexical approach to personality*. Hogrefe & Huber Publishers, 2000.

[12] M. Dennis, J. Masthoff, and C. Mellish. Adapting progress feedback and emotional support to learner personality. *International Journal of Artificial Intelligence in Education*, pages 1–55, 2015.

[13] T. Farsides and R. Woodfield. Individual differences and undergraduate academic success: The roles of personality, intelligence, and application. *Personality and Individual differences*, 34(7):1225–1243, 2003.

[14] B. Ferwerda, M. Schedl, and M. Tkalcic. Using Instagram Picture Features to Predict Users' Personality. In Q. Tian, N. Sebe, G.-J. Qi, B. Huet, R. Hong, and X. Liu, editors, *MultiMedia Modeling*, volume 9516 of *Lecture Notes in Computer Science*, pages 850–861. 2016.

[15] R. Gao, B. Hao, S. Bai, L. Li, A. Li, and T. Zhu. Improving user profile with personality traits predicted from social media content. In *Proceedings of the 7th ACM Conference on Recommender Systems*, RecSys '13, pages 355–358, 2013.

[16] J. Golbeck, C. Robles, M. Edmondson, and K. Turner. Predicting Personality from Twitter. In *Privacy, Security, Risk and Trust (PASSAT) and 2011 IEEE Third Inernational Conference on Social Computing (SocialCom), 2011 IEEE Third International Conference on*, pages 149–156, 2011.

[17] J. Golbeck, C. Robles, and K. Turner. Predicting personality with social media. In *CHI '11 Extended Abstracts on Human Factors in Computing Systems*, CHI EA '11, pages 253–262, 2011.

[18] L. R. Goldberg. The development of markers for the big-five factor structure. *Psychological assessment*, 4(1):26–42, 1992.

[19] P. J. Guo and K. Reinecke. Demographic differences in how students navigate through MOOCs. In *Proceedings of the first ACM conference on Learning@Scale*, pages 21–30, 2014.

[20] D. Koller, A. Ng, C. Do, and Z. Chen. Retention and intention in massive open online courses. *Educause Review*, 48(3):62–63, 2013.

[21] D. Koller, A. Ng, C. Do, and Z. Chen. Retention and intention in massive open online courses: In depth. *Educause Review*, 48(3):62–63, 2013.

[22] M. Komarraju, S. J. Karau, R. R. Schmeck, and A. Avdic. The big five personality traits, learning styles, and academic achievement. *Personality and Individual Differences*, 51(4):472–477, 2011.

[23] M. Kosinski, D. Stillwell, and T. Graepel. Private traits and attributes are predictable from digital records of human behavior. *Proceedings of the National Academy of Sciences*, 110(15):5802–5805, 2013.

[24] J. Lee and Y. Lee. Personality types and learners' interaction in web-based threaded discussion. *Quarterly Review of Distance Education*, 7(1):83–94, 2006.

[25] A. Liaw and M. Wiener. Classification and regression by randomforest. *R news*, 2(3):18–22, 2002.

[26] S. T. McAbee and F. L. Oswald. The criterion-related validity of personality measures for predicting gpa: A meta-analytic validity competition. *Psychological Assessment*, 25(2):532, 2013.

[27] M. C. O'Connor and S. V. Paunonen. Big five personality predictors of post-secondary academic performance. *Personality and Individual differences*, 43(5):971–990, 2007.

[28] A. E. Poropat. A meta-analysis of the five-factor model of personality and academic performance. *Psychological bulletin*, 135(2):322–338, 2009.

[29] D. Quercia, M. Kosinski, D. Stillwell, and J. Crowcroft. Our twitter profiles, our selves: Predicting personality with twitter. In *Privacy, Security, Risk and Trust (PASSAT) and 2011 IEEE Third Inernational Conference on Social Computing (SocialCom), 2011 IEEE Third International Conference on*, pages 180–185, 2011.

[30] C. E. Rasmussen. Gaussian processes in machine learning. In *Advanced lectures on machine learning*, pages 63–71. Springer, 2004.

[31] M. Richardson, C. Abraham, and R. Bond. Psychological correlates of university students' academic performance: a systematic review and meta-analysis. *Psychological bulletin*, 138(2):353–387, 2012.

[32] J. Robison, S. McQuiggan, and J. Lester. *Intelligent Tutoring Systems: 10th International Conference, ITS 2010, Pittsburgh, PA, USA, June 14-18, 2010, Proceedings, Part I*, chapter Developing Empirically Based Student Personality Profiles for Affective Feedback Models, pages 285–295. Springer Berlin Heidelberg, Berlin, Heidelberg, 2010.

[33] O. Rodriguez. The concept of openness behind c and x-moocs (massive open online courses). *Open Praxis*, 5(1):67–73, 2013.

[34] D. Rose. Personality as it relates to learning styles in online courses. In P. Resta, editor, *Proceedings of Society for Information Technology & Teacher Education International Conference 2012*, pages 827–831. Association for the Advancement of Computing in Education (AACE), 2012.

[35] C. Spearman. The proof and measurement of association between two things. *The American journal of psychology*, 15(1):72–101, 1904.

[36] C. Sumner, A. Byers, R. Boochever, and G. Park. Predicting dark triad personality traits from twitter usage and a linguistic analysis of tweets. In *Machine Learning and Applications (ICMLA), 2012 11th International Conference on*, volume 2, pages 386–393, 2012.

[37] A. Vedel. The big five and tertiary academic performance: A systematic review and meta-analysis. *Personality and Individual Differences*, 71:66–76, 2014.

Adaptive Training Environment without Prior Knowledge: Modeling Feedback Selection as a Multi-armed Bandit Problem

Rémy Frenoy
Sorbonne University
Université de technologie de
Compiègne
CNRS UMR 7253 Heudiasyc
CS 60 319 - 60 203
Compiègne cedex
remy.frenoy@utc.fr

Yann Soullard
Sorbonne University
Université de technologie de
Compiègne
CNRS UMR 7253 Heudiasyc
CS 60 319 - 60 203
Compiègne cedex
yann.soullard@utc.fr

Indira Thouvenin
Sorbonne University
Université de technologie de
Compiègne
CNRS UMR 7253 Heudiasyc
CS 60 319 - 60 203
Compiègne cedex
indira.thouvenin@utc.fr

Olivier Gapenne
Sorbonne University
Université de technologie de
Compiègne
CNRS UMR 7338
Biomechanics and
Bioengineering
CS 60 319 - 60 203
Compiègne cedex
olivier.gapenne@utc.fr

ABSTRACT

Pedagogical Action Selection (PAS) is a major issue for intelligent tutoring and training systems. Expert knowledge provides useful insights to build strategies that relate students representation to PAS, but it can be difficult to collect. Furthermore, the influence of a specific action may vary across students, which is rarely reflected in expert knowledge. As part of an automatic gesture training system, we propose to model the co-evolution between a student and a training environment in order to provide personalized action selection. The proposed approach is based on three models representing the student, the environment, and the interactions between these two entities. The latter model sees the PAS as a multi-armed bandit problem, each arm representing a possible action. Thus, PAS personalization only relies on the interactions between the student and the learning environment, without any prior knowledge. Two experiments, one in a simulated environment and a second in a calligraphy training environment, highlight the model ability to personalize action selection, and the benefits of this ability on students skill acquisition.

UMAP '16, July 13-17, 2016, Halifax, NS, Canada

© 2016 ACM. ISBN 978-1-4503-4370-1/16/07... $15.00

DOI: http://dx.doi.org/10.1145/2930238.2930256

Keywords

Adaptive Feedback Selection; Adaptive Pedagogical Action Selection; Intelligent Tutoring System; Multi-armed Bandit

1. INTRODUCTION

The past decade has seen an enormous growth of the field of technology-enhanced learning (TEL) and more generally computer-based learning. Computer-based learning includes e-learning, mobile learning, educational games and standalone educational applications. In the recent years, the development of sensors and 3D environments has spread the influence of TEL to new possibilities, such as gesture training and augmented-reality-based training [31]. The domain will probably continue to extend in the future, TEL being more and more accepted in the everyday life [9].

One of the challenging issues in the field is the adaptation of the learning content to the student. Students have different needs and characteristics: in [22], the authors identify three stages of learning (the cognitive, associative and autonomous stages), and claim that two students in different learning phases have different needs. These differences will reflect when a particular information or stimuli will differently impact their performances, and because the stimuli which could theoretically maximize their learning is probably different. More than students current learning phases, other characteristics such as personal sensitivity or motivation can deeply impact their needs. It is thus impossible to apply a naive *one-size-fits-all* strategy, and it is essential to respond to their individual differences.

Despite the development of many representation reflecting students characteristics, learning environments are still far from having a precise and exhaustive representation of all the variables which make the difference between two individuals. Intelligent tutoring systems (ITS) have introduced student models, from which learning environments can adapt based on a set of rules provided by experts. Yet, expert knowledge can be difficult to collect (e.g. availability of experts, prohibitive cost), or to define (e.g. case of ill-defined domains).

In this paper, we propose a new way for adapting the selection of pedagogical action by modeling the relationship between the student model and the environment as a multi-armed bandit problem [29]. Adapting pedagogical action selection based on past interaction between the student and the environment is interesting since it allows to dynamically change the mapping between the student model and the selection of action. This is particularly useful within contexts where the domain knowledge is difficult to define, or when it is not precise enough to predict the influence of an action based on the student model.

Related work on student models and adaptive learning content is studied in Section 2. The multi-armed bandit problem is introduced in Section 3. Section 4 describes the theoretical basis of the model. Two experiments highlight its benefits. A first experiment on simulated data is presented in Section 5, and illustrates the model ability to converge to a stable setting. A second experiment in real conditions is presented in Section 6, and shows the benefits of the model on students skill acquisition. The benefits and limits of the model are discussed in Section 7, which concludes the paper with a description of future work.

2. RELATED WORK

To adapt to student needs and characteristics, intelligent tutoring systems have introduced *student models*. Student models are based on psychological and learning theories such as the Felder-Silverman learning style classification or the Myers-Briggs type indicator, and quickly became the base for personalization in computer-based educational applications (see [7] for a review of the last decade). Over the years, several models have been proposed and can be used on their own, or be combined with other models. The overlay model considers the student model as a subset of the domain model, which reflects the expert-level knowledge of the subject [4]. The stereotype approach, introduced by [23], allows to gather students sharing the same characteristics in a group. The constraint-based model, proposed by [21] and extensively studied since [20], sometimes combined with an overlay model [28], represents both the domain knowledge and the student model. The domain knowledge is seen as a set of constraints, and the student model is seen as the subset of these constraints that have been violated. Bayesian approaches [8] have also been extensively studied these last years, having the advantage of allowing efficient parameter learning and accurate inference [14].

From these models, ITS adapt to the student by selecting the most appropriate pedagogical action. However, action selection is based on domain knowledge, which is a clear shortcoming in several cases. This shortcoming was first pointed out in [17], where the authors propose a methodology for developing rational pedagogical action selection strategies. First, two students could have the same representation according to a student model, but still have different needs. Indeed, the students could be different in a dimension which is not considered in the student model. It is also legitimate to imagine that two perfectly matching students in term of characteristics and learning needs can have a different perception towards pedagogical actions. Second, domain knowledge is difficult to acquire, and remains uncertain (the fact that experts often disagree is a proof of the difficulty and the uncertainty of collecting domain knowledge). Domain knowledge may even be more uncertain when it comes to motor skill learning, a field which could benefit from the adaptation and personalization characteristics of ITS. Numerous studies have investigated the impact of different pedagogical actions (e.g. different feedback types and modalities) on the various phases of motor skill learning [22]. Yet, although some specific actions are known to be effective in particular situations, there is still no precise rule relating and predicting their influence given a student representation.

As stated in [12, 18, 27], a well-designed tutoring system actively undertakes two tasks: that of the diagnostician discovering the nature and extent of the student's knowledge, and that of the strategist planning a response using its findings about the learner. While the first task is extensively studied, the latter task remains a recurring issue, especially when collecting domain knowledge is difficult, or when domain knowledge is not precise enough to predict the influence of an action given a student representation. The two next sections introduce the multi-armed bandit problem, and how it can be used to dynamically adapt the selection rules based on the interactions between the student and the learning environment.

3. MULTI-ARMED BANDIT

The multi-armed bandit (MAB) problem for a gambler is to decide which arm of a K-slot machine to pull to maximize the total reward in a series of trial. Applying the multi-armed bandit problem to pedagogical action selection, each action can be seen as an arm, the goal being to maximize the benefits for the students. The reward of an action can be seen as the difference, in the student model, between student representations before and after having chosen the given action.

Numerous algorithms have been proposed to solve the MAB problem (see [5] for a review). These algorithms tackle various variations of the MAB problem, depending on the nature of the reward (stochastic or adversarial), the existence of side information associated with each arm (contextual MAB), or the possibility that the set of possible actions vary over time (sleeping MAB). A few studies [15, 29] compare MAB strategies, and point out the good performances generally obtained by simple strategies such as epsilon-greedy and SoftMax.

The epsilon-greedy strategy consists of choosing a random lever with epsilon-frequency, and otherwise choosing the lever with the highest estimated mean, the estimation being based on the rewards observed thus far. Epsilon must be in the open interval $(0, 1)$ and its choice is left to the user. The epsilon-greedy strategy is part of the semi-uniform methods where an hyper-parameter balances between exploitation of known results, and exploration of possibilities.

Contrary to the epsilon-greedy strategy, the SoftMax strategy is part of the probability matching methods. It consists of a random choice according to a Gibbs distribution. The lever i is chosen with a probability

$$p_i = \frac{e^{\frac{\hat{\mu}_i}{\tau}}}{\sum_{k=1}^{n} e^{\frac{\hat{\mu}_k}{\tau}}} \qquad (1)$$

where $\hat{\mu}_i$ is the estimated mean of the rewards brought by the lever i, and τ is a temperature parameter which balances between exploitation and exploration. The choice of τ is left to the user. When τ is high, all levers are close to be equiprobable, whereas low values of τ cause greedy selection. This trade off between exploitation and exploration (also faced in reinforcement learning) illustrates here the inclination of the model to test new actions (high values of τ) or to choose among already-tested ones (low values of τ). Considering that the optimal action may vary over time, the SoftMax strategy is preferred, as it takes into account previous interactions by remembering the successive rewards obtained by each action [24].

Modeling PAS as a MAB problem for a learning system presents two advantages. First, it adapts at the selection level (the task of the strategist), which makes it possible to consider previous interactions instead of relying on fixed heuristics to relate the student representation to the selection of an action. Second, it traces the interactions between the student and the environment, making it possible to monitor the student (as the student model already does) but also the influence of every action over the interactions. To offer these advantages, the MAB must be integrated into a meta-model combining a student model and an environment model. This meta-model is described in the next section.

4. PROPOSED APPROACH

This section describes the components of the proposed meta-model, and how they work together to model the co-evolution between the student and the learning environment. This model has two objectives: select the action which maximize the benefits for the student (exploration/exploitation trade-off) and update the environment representation to reflect its influence on the student.

4.1 Student modeling

As discussed earlier, many works proposed student models, taking into account students' characteristics and their progressions during training. The *overlay* model is one of the first approach concerning such an adaptation, considering that the student model is a subset of the domain knowledge. The first overlay models assign a Boolean value to each dimension, depending whether students master or not the given dimension. New versions of this approach improve the original model by replacing the Boolean value by a qualitative measure (good-average-poor), or a probability that a student masters the concept[1] [4]. This latter approach is particularly interesting within the context of gesture training, as it can be combined with a gesture recognition method [19].

In this paper, a dimension (i.e. a concept) is seen as a type of error which can be performed on a given type of gesture. In such a case, a student performance is represented by a vector $\vec{S} = \{s_1, s_2, \ldots, s_n\}$ where n is the number of

types of errors and s_i, for $1 < i \leq n$, is the probability that the student made the error i. These probabilities are computed using a probabilistic model which are commonly used in gesture recognition [19]. From such a student representation, $\vec{S} = \vec{0}$ refers to an expert and $\vec{S} = \{1, \ldots, 1\}$ refers to a complete novice. As in [4], the probability that a student masters the concept is represented by the vector $\{1 - s_1, \ldots, 1 - s_n\}$ describing the student capacity to accurately perform a gesture.

4.2 Environment modeling

The learning environment contains the training components (e.g. a set of feedback or learning situations[2]) which can help students during training. While the student model provides a representation of the student state in term of knowledge and characteristics, modeling the learning environment and adapting it to the student model is a non-trivial task. Indeed, on the one hand, the environment modeling should reflect a good way for selecting an appropriate action according to the student representation. On the other hand, as the impact of a given action varies among students, the training environment should change over time in order to fit well with the student individual needs.

Here, we consider that for a given student S, there is an optimal modeling of the learning environment C_S^* representing the best setting to assist the student. Let $\mathcal{A}$ be the set of actions, m be the cardinality of $\mathcal{A}$ and, as a reminder, n is the number of dimensions (i.e. concepts) in the student model. We defined each element $A^{(i)} \in \mathcal{A}$ by a vector $\{A_1^{(i)}, A_2^{(i)}, \ldots, A_n^{(i)}\}$ where each element reflects the level for which $A^{(i)}$ seems to be the most appropriate to assist a student on the concept, i.e. regarding the type of error. For a given concept j, $A^{(i)} \in \mathcal{A}$ and a student S, the optimal setting C_S^* is a $m \times n$ matrix where each component $C_S^*(i,j)$ refers to the optimal vector $A_j^{(i)}$ maximising the reward on the student performance. In Section 4.4, we propose a new way to compute, at each time t and for each $A^{(i)} \in \mathcal{A}$, an approximate setting C_t of C_S^*[3]. This provides a solution to adapt the environment modeling according to the influence of actions on the student training.

4.3 Action selection

We want to define a strategy to select an action (e.g. a type of feedback or a learning situation) according to a student performance and then provides it to the student at the next learning step.

A Softmax method allows to model learning as a co-evolution between a student/trainee and a learning environment, an idea first proposed in [25]. In this approach, the probability of choosing the action i takes into account the successive rewards previously obtained. Thus, by decomposing the mean $\hat{\mu}_i$ in Eq. 1, the probability of choosing the action i at time $t + 1$ depends, in our case, of its previous rewards obtained when the action has been selected:

---

[1] A concept can be seen as a dimension, a subset of the domain knowledge, and reaching an expert level implies mastering every one of these dimensions.

[2] In this paper, an *action* will, without distinction, refer to providing a type of feedback or a learning situation.

[3] Note that, for many applications, only a subset of $\mathcal{A}$ is available at each time t. In this case, the environment model is restrained to the available elements $A^{(i)} \in \mathcal{A}$. Also, readers can refer to sleeping multi-armed bandit methods in such a case.

$$p_{i,t+1} = \frac{e^{\frac{1}{t_i \cdot \tau} \sum_{l=0}^{t} \delta_{A_l^{(i)}} \mu_{i,l}}}{\sum_{k=1}^{n} e^{\frac{1}{t_k \cdot \tau} \sum_{l=0}^{t} \delta_{A_l^{(k)}} \mu_{k,l}}} \quad (2)$$

where $\delta_{A_t^{(i)}}$ is equal to 1 if the action $A^{(i)}$ has been selected at iteration t, otherwise 0 and with t_i the number of iterations where the action i has been selected and $\mu_{i,t}$ the reward at time t. Here, the reward $\mu_{i,t}$ is defined as the difference observed in the student model before and after having provided $A^{(i)}$. The reward is hence a vector representing the variations on a particular concept j and can be decomposed as follow:

$$\mu_{i,t+1}(j) = S_{t+1}(j) - S_t(j) \quad (3)$$

The Gibbs distribution is hence used to compute the probability of choosing the action i according to the reward on the concept j in the student model:

$$p_{i,j,t+1} \propto e^{\frac{1}{t_i \cdot \tau} \sum_{l=0}^{t} \delta_{A_l^{(i)}} (S_{l+1}(j) - S_l(j))} \quad (4)$$

where one obtains the equality in the above equation by normalizing with the following term $Z(S)$:

$$Z(S) = \sum_{k=1}^{n} e^{\frac{1}{t_k \cdot \tau} \sum_{l=0}^{t} \delta_{A_l^{(k)}} (S_{l+1}(j) - S_l(j))} \quad (5)$$

Finally, an action i is selected according to the current performance of a student and the probability of choosing the action defined in Eq. 4. For each dimension j, the student score is weighted by the probability $p_{i,j,t}$ to select the feedback i at time t. The goal is to guide the selection towards an action which has a high probability of success on the dimensions where the student performs poorly:

$$p_{i,t} = \frac{\sum_{j=1}^{n} p_{i,j,t} \cdot S_t(j)}{\sum_{k_1=1}^{m} \sum_{k_2=1}^{n} p_{k_1,k_2,t}} \quad (6)$$

The action A^* maximising the probability defined above is selected:

$$A^* = \operatorname*{argmax}_{1 \leqslant i \leqslant n} p_{i,t} \quad (7)$$

4.4 Environment update

The interaction modeling uses the previous interactions, i.e. the set of rewards obtained on the previously selected actions, to update the environment modeling so that, for a given student, the current setting of feedback C_t converges toward the optimal setting C_S^*. Hence, for a given student performance S_t, if the action $A_t^{(i)}$ has a positive reward, we hypothesize the following inequality:

$$||S_t - A_{t+1}^{(i)}|| < ||S_t - A_t^{(i)}|| \quad (8)$$

where all terms are vectors of length n (i.e. the number of concepts). Meaning that the representation of $A_t^{(i)}$ gets closer to the current situation of the student where it proved to be relevant. On the contrary, we want that a negative reward places $A_{t+1}^{(i)}$ further from S_t than was $A_t^{(i)}$. To take into account the previous interactions (positive or negative rewards), $A_t^{(i)}$ can be represented as the arithmetic mean of all

points S_t (student state when $A_t^{(i)}$ was proposed) weighted by a function of the received reward $\alpha(\mu_i)$:

$$\overrightarrow{OA_{t+1}^{(i)}} = \sum_{l=0}^{t} \delta_{A_l^{(i)}} \cdot \alpha(\mu_{i,l}) \cdot \overrightarrow{OS_l^{(i)}} \quad (9)$$

where O is the origin and, as a reminder, $\delta_{A_l^{(i)}}$ is equal to 1 if the action $A^{(i)}$ has been selected at training iteration l, otherwise 0. For a given concept j, we define each term $\alpha(\mu_{i,l})(j)$ as the probability of having the current reward $S_{l+1}(j) - S_l(j)$ at time l given the action $A^{(i)}$. Equation 9 is then rewritten as follow:

$$A_{t+1}^{(i)}(j) = \frac{1}{t_i} \sum_{l=0}^{t} \delta_{A_l^{(i)}} \cdot \frac{e^{\frac{S_{l+1}(j) - S_l(j)}{\tau}}}{\sum_{k=1}^{m} e^{\frac{S_{l+1}(k) - S_l(k)}{\tau}}} \cdot S_l^{(i)}(j) \quad (10)$$

We described in this section our meta-model containing three sub-models: the student model represents the student as a subset of the domain knowledge; the environment modeling represents every element of the set of possible actions by a vector in which every coordinate corresponds to the student's state where the action has the largest impact; finally the interaction model, modeling the selection step as a SoftMax multi-armed bandit system, select at each step the next action. It also updates the environment modeling by computing the arithmetic mean of all students states S_t where the action has been selected, weighted by the Gibbs distribution of the received rewards. The next section exhibits the results of the meta-model on a first experiment using a simulated learning process. As stated in [1, 3, 30], simulation is a widespread and widely used technique for testing educational approaches and may bring advantages.

5. EXPERIMENT IN A SIMULATED ENVIRONMENT

In the same fashion as in [10], a probabilistic model has been developed to simulate the learning process and the student performance, taking into account aspects related to the impact of feedback and learning situations on students [2, 6, 13]. First, the rules of the simulation are described. Then, the methodology of the experiment is presented and the results are discussed.

5.1 Rules of the simulation

The simulation computes the impact of an action on a student according to simple but robust heuristics. The impact of an action depending on numerous factors (student's level, characteristics, motivation), an action can have a positive or negative impact in every situation [13]. However, the closer the action is to its optimal configuration (the optimal configuration is obviously unknown by the interaction model), the better is the probability that the action will have a positive impact on the student. Each action $A^{(i)}$ in the simulation is hence defined by two vectors, one representing its current state $A_t^{(i)}$, and the other representing the optimal state where it will obtain the best reward $A^{(i)*}$. The dimension of these two vectors is equal to the dimension of the model (i.e. the number of concepts). Probability that $A^{(i)}$ obtains a positive reward on dimension j hence depends on the distance between the current student state S and the optimal state $A^{(i)*}$ on dimension j:

$$p(\mu_{i,j} > 0) = 1 - (\beta \times (\|S_j - A_j^{(i)^*}\|)) \qquad (11)$$

where β is a temperature parameter which defines how quickly the impact of an action becomes random when it moves away from its optimal state. A random draw between 0 and 1 decides whether the action will have a positive impact (if the result is inferior to $p(\mu_{i,j} > 0)$). If so, a random reward is computed within the interval $[r_{min}, r_{max}]$, r_{min} and r_{max} being parameters of the simulation representing the minimum and the maximum possible rewards. Otherwise, the reward is randomly computed in $[-r_{max}, r_{max}]$. The student representation is then updated using the computed reward r_j:

$$S_{t+1}(j) = S_t(j) + r_j \qquad (12)$$

Selection of the new action is then computed using (7). The overall algorithm for the simulation is described in Figure 1. Sources of the simulation are available upon request.

Initialize student representation
Initialize environment representation
for $t = 1, \dots, nb\ of\ steps$ **do**
  $i \leftarrow$ Select action (Eq. 7)
  for $j = 1, \dots, nb\ of\ dimensions$ **do**
    Compute $p(\mu_{i,j} > 0)$ (Eq. 11)
    random_draw = random(0,1)
    if random_draw $\leq p(\mu_{i,j} > 0)$ **then**
      reward[j] = random(r_{min}, r_{max})
    else
      reward[j] = random($-r_{max}, r_{max}$)
    end if
  end for
  Update student representation (Eq. 12)
  Update action representation (Eq. 10)
end for

Figure 1: Simulated learning algorithm

5.2 Methodology

As previously described, the interaction model updates the environment model in such a way that it converges to the optimal configuration. The optimal configuration depends on the student, but can also vary over time for a given student. These changes must be reflected in the interaction model, which should be able to update the environment model to the new optimal configuration no matter the initial one. Using a simulation is the only robust way to test the model on these aspects, as it permits to set values to the optimal configuration and hence measure the convergence. The model's behavior was tested under the three following configurations:

1. initial configuration set empirically, random optimal configuration

2. random initial configuration, optimal configuration set empirically

3. random initial configuration, random optimal configuration

For each of these configurations, the model was tested with τ varying from 0.1 to 0.9 in the Gibbs distribution.

Parameter	Value
β	2
τ	$[0.1, 0.9]$
r_{min}	0
r_{max}	0.1
nb of dimensions	2
nb of actions	4
nb of steps	50
nb of simulations	30

Table 1: Simulation parameters

Table 1 gives the values of the various parameters of the experiment. Figure 2 illustrates the results.

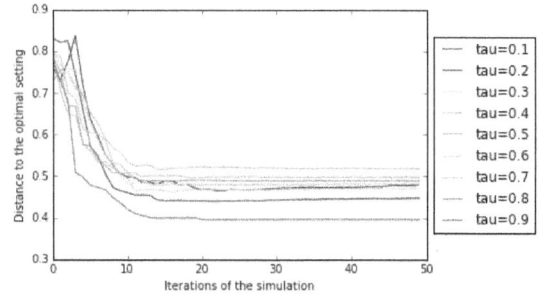

(a) Random initial configuration

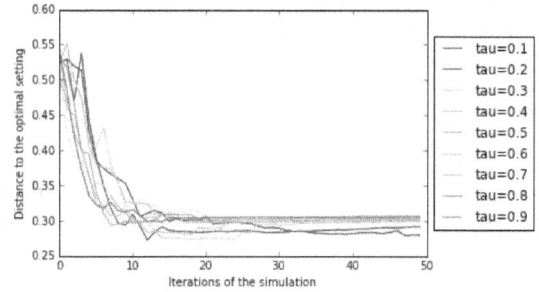

(b) Random optimal configuration

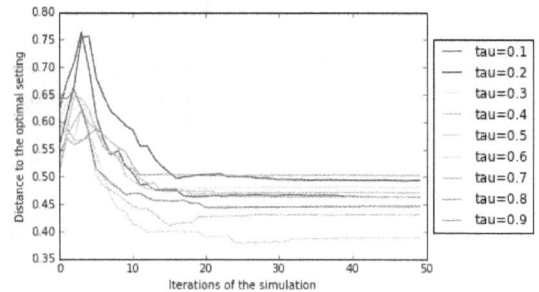

(c) Random initial and optimal configurations

Figure 2: Euclidean distance to optimal setting

5.3 Results

Whatever the experiment and the value of τ, the model converges to a configuration which is closer to the optimal configuration than the initial configuration. It appears that the initial configuration has a major impact on the asymptotic value, as the difference between experiment 2 on one side and experiments 1 and 3 on the other side suggests. As it could be expected, the model converges faster with high values of τ, as the model favors exploration over exploitation, and hence tends to test new actions more rapidly. However, except in the first experiment where a τ value of 0.9 gives the better results, low values of τ tend to make the model to a closer distance of the optimal configuration. Furthermore, considering a real learning environment, the hypothesis can be made that drastically favoring the exploration of untested actions over the exploitation of already known ones could confuse the student.

The closest an action is to its optimal configuration, the best are the chances that the best action will be chosen[4]. The number of possible actions and the number of dimensions in the student model must be taken into account when evaluating the asymptotic values. Indeed, the larger the set of possible actions, the lowest should be the accepted asymptotic value to be able to differentiate the actions. For the simulation settings, the model converges towards a stable solution after 10 (experiments 1 and 2) and 15 (experiment 3) iterations. Depending on the τ value, the distance to the optimal configuration varies from 0.4 to 0.53 in the first experiment, 0.28 to 0.32 in the second experiment and 0.38 to 0.51 in the third experiment. Taking the third experiment as a reference, as it is the experiment with the most robust settings, and keeping in mind that the experiment run on two dimensions, an asymptotic value of 0.38 implies a maximum error of 0.38 on a single dimension, or an average error of 0.19 per dimensions. With four possible actions, chances that several actions remain indistinguishable remain acceptable, especially since within the context of learning, actions should be chosen in such a way that they maximize the covering of the student model. Finally, these results are acceptable since the simulation settings highly impact the final results. In real conditions, it can indeed be expected that r_{min} and r_{max} would have higher values than their respective values of 0 and 0.1 in this simulation. To extend the results of this simulation, next section describes a second experiment in real conditions.

6. EXPERIMENT IN REAL CONDITIONS

We present a second experiment in a real learning environment. The model is integrated into an interactive software for calligraphy training. Results of the first experiment were used to configure the algorithm used in the second experiment, using a τ-value of 0.3, which outperformed other τ-values in the third simulated configuration (Figure 2c). Software runs on a Wacom table[5] and provides four types of visual guidance. Other modalities such as haptic, which is extensively studied within the context of gesture training, would be interesting features to add to the software in order to enrich the diversity of feedback. A gesture recognition module, based on a logistic regression algorithm, computes for every element of a set of errors given by an expert the probability that the student made the error. These probabilities integrates our student model as described in Section 4.1.

This experiment has two objectives. First it aims at measuring the benefits of using the proposed model on students acquisition of skills. Second, it measures the model ability to detect and withdraw actions that do not positively influence this acquisition. A previous study [11], conducted on a simpler version of the learning environment (gesture fluidity was not measured), and with feedback especially designed to correct the studied types of error, showed that adaptation based on expert knowledge without adaptation could already benefit to gesture learning.

6.1 Design and methodology

The experiment considers two main abilities: the fluency of the gesture, and the ability to draw straight strokes. The software can provide four types of feedback. These four types of feedback cannot be combined, and only one feedback is provided at a time. Each feedback was designed from a list of potentially useful types of feedback provided by calligraphy teachers. However, these types of feedback do not precisely focus on the abilities measured in this experiment. It was thus the experts job to anticipate the potential effect of these types of feedback on the considered abilities when building the rules mapping each feedback to the student model. Expert rules were defined in the same fashion as in [11]. Feedback A provides real time visual information regarding discontinuity in gesture velocity. It displays a blue line when students slow down their gesture, and a red line when students speed up their gesture. This feedback is considered by experts as useful to train gesture fluency. Feedback B displays a green dot ahead of student's pen. By constituting a target guiding students gestures, this feedback is considered by experts as useful to train the ability to draw straight lines. It can also, in certain cases, improves fluency skill as it modifies students visual focus, allowing them to untie and perform more loosely. Feedback C displays, at the beginning of a stroke, a gray display of the previous stroke. It provides useful information as it allows to compare in real time the current stroke with the previous one, but can confuse novice students who will tend to reproduce their previous errors. Finally, feedback D provides real-time visual information regarding the pen normal pressure. It colors the drawing in blue if pressure is too weak, and in red if it is too strong. Being aware of the applied pressure can be very difficult for novice students, and providing them with this type of information can have great benefits on their overall performances. However, as pressure is not considered in this experiment, this type of feedback can only give marginal benefits.

Two software configurations were implemented. For the *control group*, the selection of action was based on expert rules mapping the elements of the feedback set to the student model. For the *experimental group*, the proposed model was integrated into the software and selected the actions to perform, without any prior knowledge.

44 people participated in the experiment. Participants were people working at the university, students in computer science, design and mechanics, with no to very little expertise in calligraphy. They were randomly and evenly distributed into the two groups. The experiment consisted of four stages. First participants could perform freely on the platform in order to familiarize with the tablet and the software. Then, a first experiment without any feedback constituted the pre-test. Participants were then asked to per-

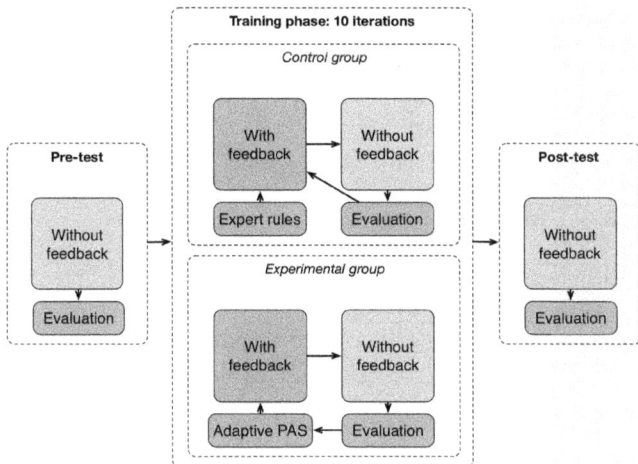

Figure 3: Design of the experiment

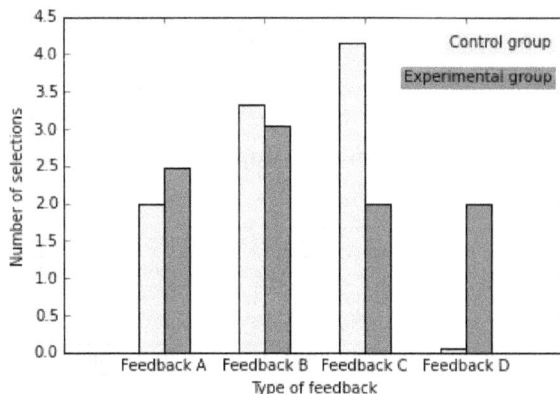

Figure 4: Average number of selection after ten iterations for the four possible actions

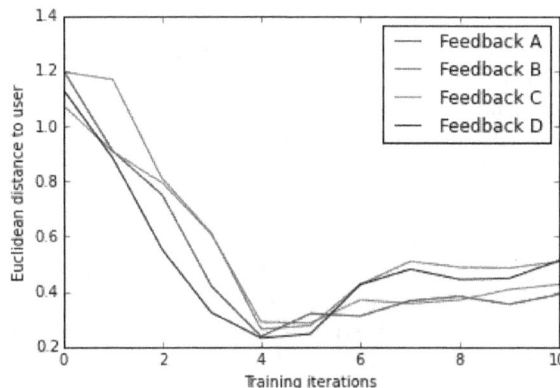

Figure 5: Average distance between feedback and student representations over training

form 10 pairs of exercises. A pair of exercise consisted of a first exercise where the software provided a feedback, and a second exercise without feedback. The reward of a specific feedback were computed during the second exercise. This way, every types of feedback were measured in the same conditions. Moreover, when provided with feedback, students often drastically change their gesture, which directly impact their performance. Evaluating students during the second exercise allows to reduce the noise produced by these changes, and have a smoother measure of the feedback influence. Finally, a last exercise without feedback constituted the post-test. Figure 3 illustrates the design of the experiment.

6.2 Results

Statistics about the two groups are presented in Tables 2 and 3. There was no significant difference between the pre-test performances of the two groups. The experimental group significantly outperformed the control group in the post-test, as confirm the t-test with a p-value under 0.05. Paired t-tests measured the improvement between pre-tests and post-tests. The experimental group improved significantly ($p = 0.03$) while there is no significance of improvement for the control group ($p = 0.53$). This difference between the two groups can be explained by the selection of feedback. Figure 4 illustrates that feedback types A and B were the most chosen in the experimental group, while the control group were mostly provided with feedback type C. Feedback type D was almost never chosen in the control group. Hence, participants in the experimental group were provided with a wider range of feedback. After a number of training iterations, the model has converged and it seems that it proposes the types of feedback which benefits the most to students. This convergence began at the fourth pair of exercise, as highlighted by Figure 5. Results among participants in the control group were very heterogeneous, with participants clearly improving while others did not, as highlighted by the large standard deviation in the post-test for this group (0.26) (Table 2). This is different from the previous study in [11], where selection based on expert rules made participants improve. This difference can be explained by the fact that in [11], feedback were especially designed for the exercise, and thus experts exactly new with which

rules each action had to be mapped to the student model. In the current experiment, experts had to make the best of a set of feedback they did not design. We can thus make the hypothesis that the expert rules in the current experiment were not as precise as they were in [11]. This is a realistic scenario, since a lack of domain knowledge, or a domain which is difficult to define, often result in approximate rules.

Finally, Figure 6 suggests that the influence of a type of feedback on a user was constant over training, as the model was not subjected to large variations and converged rather linearly to its final configuration. This conclusion may differ in a larger experiment. It is possible that the influence of a type of feedback changes after a certain number of exercises, with students feeling bored or disengaging from the task. It would thus be interesting to measure the behavior of the model on a larger experiment.

7. CONCLUSIONS

In this paper, we present a new approach for modeling the co-evolution between a student and a learning environment. It relies on a meta-model for adapting the action selection to students and updating the environment representation according to past interactions. Such a personalization of the learning environment allows to take into account hidden variables which are not necessarily reflected in the student

	Control(22)	Experimental(22)	p
Pre-test (std)	0.34(0.12)	0.30(0.13)	0.57
Post-test (std)	0.29(0.26)	0.20(0.13)	0.04
Improvement	$p = 0.53, t = -0.63$	$p = 0.03, t = -2.28$	

Table 2: Improvement between pre-test and post-test for the two groups

	Control(22)	Experimental(22)	p
After 2 training iterations (std)	0.30(0.17)	0.29(0.12)	0.73
After 4 training iterations (std)	0.28(0.19)	0.28(0.17)	0.92
After 6 training iterations (std)	0.29(0.21)	0.24(0.18)	0.38
After 8 training iterations (std)	0.30(0.22)	0.23(0.17)	0.19
After 10 training iterations (std)	0.30(0.25)	0.19(0.12)	0.07

Table 3: Comparison between the two groups through the training phase

model. It does not require expert heuristics relating action selection to a student model.

Components of the meta-model are described. A student model based on the overlay model represents the acquired knowledge as a subset of the expert-level knowledge. An environment modeling represents each possible action (providing a specific type of feedback or learning situation) by a vector which approximates the situation where the action has the biggest influence.

The action selection is modeled as a multi-armed bandit problem. A SoftMax strategy computes the probability of choosing an action depending on its influence in past interactions. The environment is updated by computing the arithmetic mean of the past student representations weighted by a Gibbs distribution of the past rewards.

The behavior of the proposed approach was tested through two experiments. The first experiment placed the model in an environment based on a probabilistic model, which simulates the learning process and the student performance. Analysis of the environment model states over the simulations showed that the model converges no matter the initial nor the objective configuration. In a second experiment, the model was integrated into a calligraphy training platform. The experiment compared two groups: a control group where action selection was based on heuristics given by an expert, and an experimental group where action selection was based on the model. The proposed approach significantly improved students skill acquisition, by favoring actions which benefited them. Action selection based on fixed heuristics cannot reflect differences between students preferences. Yet these differences exist, because although student models more and more accurately represent students learning state, they cannot perfectly reflect the complexity of human learning. Furthermore, the hypothesis can be made that two students who learn in the exact same way could still have different needs in term of pedagogical actions. The proposed approach addresses this shortcoming by adapting action selection according to past interactions.

In future works, the model should be tested on a more complex environment, considering further dimensions of the student model in order to analyze how our approach would handle scalability. Furthermore, the model should be tested on more training iterations, allowing to study the influence of a given action over time. The influence may vary over time and it is not trivial how adapt the model in such a case. One strategy could be to extend our current approach

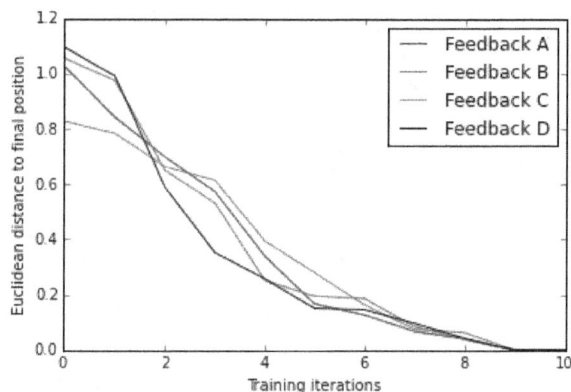

Figure 6: Average distance between feedback position and feedback final position over training

to contextual multi-armed bandit approaches [16, 26], where the reward distribution for a lever also depends on contextual information.

8. ACKNOWLEDGMENTS

This work, as part of the Descript project, is supported by the Picardy region. The authors would particularly like to thank Florian Baune for his work on the development of the platform.

9. REFERENCES

[1] S. C. Abdullah and R. E. Cooley. Using simulated students to evaluate an adaptive testing system. In *Computers in Education, 2002. Proceedings. International Conference on*, pages 614–618. IEEE, 2002.

[2] D. Boud and E. Molloy. *Feedback in higher and professional education: understanding it and doing it well.* Routledge, 2013.

[3] J. Bravo and A. Ortigosa. Validating the evaluation of adaptive systems by user profile simulation. In *Proceedings of workshop held at the fourth international conference on adaptive hypermedia and adaptive web-based systems (AH2006)*, pages 479–483, 2006.

[4] P. Brusilovsky and E. Millán. User models for adaptive hypermedia and adaptive educational systems. In *The adaptive web*, pages 3–53. Springer-Verlag, 2007.

[5] S. Bubeck and N. Cesa-Bianchi. Regret analysis of stochastic and nonstochastic multi-armed bandit problems. *arXiv preprint arXiv:1204.5721*, 2012.

[6] R. A. Calvo and R. A. Ellis. Students' conceptions of tutor and automated feedback in professional writing. *Journal of Engineering Education*, 99(4):427–438, 2010.

[7] K. Chrysafiadi and M. Virvou. Student modeling approaches: A literature review for the last decade. *Expert Systems with Applications*, 40(11):4715–4729, Sept. 2013.

[8] A. T. Corbett and J. R. Anderson. Knowledge tracing: Modeling the acquisition of procedural knowledge. *User modeling and user-adapted interaction*, 4(4):253–278, 1994.

[9] M. C. Desmarais and R. S. d Baker. A review of recent advances in learner and skill modeling in intelligent learning environments. *User Modeling and User-Adapted Interaction*, 22(1-2):9–38, 2012.

[10] F. A. Dorça, L. V. Lima, M. A. Fernandes, and C. R. Lopes. Comparing strategies for modeling students learning styles through reinforcement learning in adaptive and intelligent educational systems: An experimental analysis. *Expert Systems with Applications*, 40(6):2092–2101, May 2013.

[11] R. Frenoy, I. Thouvenin, Y. Soullard, and O. Gapenne. CalliSmart: an Adaptive Informed Environment for Intelligent Calligraphy Training. In *The Ninth International Conference on Advances in Computer-Human Interactions (ACHI 16)*, Venice, 2016.

[12] R. Glaser, A. Lesgold, and S. Lajoie. Toward a cognitive theory for the measurement of achievement. In *The influence of cognitive psychology on testing*, pages 41–85. Hillsdale: Erlbaum, 1987.

[13] J. Hattie. *Visible learning for teachers: Maximizing impact on learning*. Routledge, 2012.

[14] T. Käser, S. Klingler, A. G. Schwing, and M. Gross. Beyond knowledge tracing: Modeling skill topologies with bayesian networks. In *Intelligent Tutoring Systems*, pages 188–198. Springer, 2014.

[15] V. Kuleshov and D. Precup. Algorithms for multi-armed bandit problems. *Journal of Machine Learning*, 2010.

[16] T. Lu, D. Pál, and M. Pál. Contextual multi-armed bandits. In *International Conference on Artificial Intelligence and Statistics*, pages 485–492, 2010.

[17] M. Mayo and A. Mitrovic. Optimising ITS behaviour with Bayesian networks and decision theory. *International Journal of Artificial Intelligence in Education*, 12(2):124–153, 2001.

[18] L. N. Michaud and K. F. McCoy. Empirical derivation of a sequence of user stereotypes for language learning. *User Modeling and User-Adapted Interaction*, 14(4):317–350, 2004.

[19] S. Mitra and T. Acharya. Gesture Recognition: A Survey. *IEEE Transactions on Systems, Man and Cybernetics, Part C (Applications and Reviews)*, 37(3):311–324, May 2007.

[20] A. Mitrovic and S. Ohlsson. Constraint-based knowledge representation for individualized instruction. *Computer Science and Information Systems*, 3(1):1–22, 2006.

[21] S. Ohlsson. Constraint-based student modeling. In *Student modelling: the key to individualized knowledge-based instruction*, pages 167–189. Springer, 1994.

[22] P.M. Fitts and M.I. Posner. *Human performance*. Belmont, CA: Brooks/Cole, 1967.

[23] E. Rich. User modeling via stereotypes*. *Cognitive science*, 3(4):329–354, 1979.

[24] S. L. Scott. A modern Bayesian look at the multi-armed bandit. *Applied Stochastic Models in Business and Industry*, 26(6):639–658, Nov. 2010.

[25] E. Sklar, A. D. Blair, and J. B. Pollack. Co-evolutionary learning: Machines and humans schooling together. In *Workshop on Current Trends and Applications of Artificial Intelligence in Education: 4th World Congress on Expert Systems*. Citeseer, 1998.

[26] A. Slivkins. Contextual bandits with similarity information. *The Journal of Machine Learning Research*, 15(1):2533–2568, 2014.

[27] N. Spada and P. M. Lightbown. Instruction and the development of questions in l2 classrooms. *Studies in Second Language Acquisition*, 15(02):205–224, 1993.

[28] P. Suraweera and A. Mitrovic. An intelligent tutoring system for entity relationship modelling. *International Journal of Artificial Intelligence in Education*, 14(3, 4):375–417, 2004.

[29] J. Vermorel and M. Mohri. Multi-armed bandit algorithms and empirical evaluation. In *Machine learning: ECML 2005*, pages 437–448. Springer, 2005.

[30] M. Virvou, K. Manos, and G. Katsionis. An evaluation agent that simulates students' behaviour in intelligent tutoring systems. In *Systems, Man and Cybernetics, 2003. IEEE International Conference on*, volume 5, pages 4872–4877. IEEE, 2003.

[31] G. Westerfield, A. Mitrovic, and M. Billinghurst. Intelligent augmented reality training for assembly tasks. In *Artificial Intelligence in Education*, pages 542–551. Springer, 2013.

A Framework for Dynamic Knowledge Modeling in Textbook-Based Learning

Yun Huang
Intelligent Systems Program
University of Pittsburgh
210 S. Bouquet Street
Pittsburgh, PA, USA
yuh43@pitt.edu

Michael Yudelson
Human-Computer Interaction
Institute
Carnegie Mellon University
5000 Forbes Ave.
Pittsburgh, PA, USA
yudelson@cs.cmu.edu

Shuguang Han
School of Information
Sciences
University of Pittsburgh
135 N. Bellefield Ave.
Pittsburgh, PA, USA
shh69@pitt.edu

Daqing He
School of Information
Sciences
University of Pittsburgh
135 N. Bellefield Ave.
Pittsburgh, PA, USA
dah44@pitt.edu

Peter Brusilovsky
School of Information
Sciences
University of Pittsburgh
135 N. Bellefield Ave.
Pittsburgh, PA, USA
peterb@pitt.edu

ABSTRACT

Various e-learning systems that provide electronic textbooks are gathering data on large numbers of student reading interactions. This data can potentially be used to model student knowledge acquisition. However, reading activity is often overlooked in canonical student modeling. Prior studies modeling learning from reading either estimate student knowledge at the end of all reading activities, or use quiz performance data with expert-crafted knowledge components (KCs). In this work, we demonstrate that the dynamic modeling of student knowledge is feasible and that automatic text analysis can be applied to save expert effort. We propose a data-driven approach for dynamic student modeling in textbook-based learning. We formulate the problem of modeling learning from reading as a reading-time prediction problem, reconstruct existing popular student models (such as Knowledge Tracing) and explore two automatic text analysis approaches (bag-of-words-based and latent semantic-based) to build the KC model. We evaluate the proposed framework using a dataset collected from a Human-Computer Interaction course. Results show that our approach for reading modeling is plausible; the proposed Knowledge Tracing-based student model reliably outperforms baselines and the latent semantic-based approach can be a promising way to construct a KC model. Serving as the first step to model dynamic knowledge in textbook-based learning, our framework can be applied to a broader context of open-corpus personalized learning.

UMAP '16, July 13-17, 2016, Halifax, NS, Canada

© 2016 ACM. ISBN 978-1-4503-4370-1/16/07...$15.00

DOI: http://dx.doi.org/10.1145/2930238.2930258

Keywords

textbook-based learning, reading, learner model, Knowledge Tracing, Additive Factor Model, Performance Factor Analysis, latent topic modeling, text analysis

1. INTRODUCTION

The steadily increasing volume of online educational content makes it harder for learners to find *appropriate content* that matches their individual goals, interests, and knowledge. In the past, adaptive hypermedia (AH) techniques attempted to address this problem by providing personalized adaptive navigation support to help individual students locate, recognize, and comprehend relevant information. Evaluations of adaptive navigation support techniques have demonstrated their ability to increase learning outcomes, retention, and efficiency of student work [7, 14, 24].

Unfortunately, existing adaptive navigation support techniques can only work efficiently within a closed corpus of documents whose domain concepts and other metadata have been manually identified and indexed at the time of the system design. The open corpus educational systems of today, when the whole web could be considered the content base, present new challenges for traditional AH techniques. From these challenges, we want to address the following three: (1) how to determine the knowledge components (KCs, or skills, concepts) behind each unit of open corpus content without human engagement; (2) how to maintain dynamic student knowledge models on the level of automatically identified KCs with only reading interactions; (3) how to apply our inferred student knowledge about KCs underlying the content to make personalization decisions.

In this paper, we present our attempt to construct dynamic student knowledge models for personalized guidance in the context of online textbook-based learning environments. Such a context enables us to readily apply our approaches to a broader context of open-corpus personalized learning and to address the above-mentioned AH challenges with an open corpus. Our key idea is to automatically extract *elements of meaning* from the text and to adopt these individual elements as knowledge components for student modeling. However, current popular student models rely on in-time quiz performance data, which is often unavailable in our context. To address this, we utilize the available abundant reading interaction data and formulate the problem as a reading time prediction problem, so that existed popular student models can be applied after simple modifications. This student modeling approach allows us to implement an in-time personalized guidance approach that can distinguish between reading and skimming content pages given a student's current level of knowledge.

Specifically, for content modeling (or knowledge component modeling), we explore both bag-of-words-based approach [36] and latent semantic topic modeling approach [2]. In terms of modeling student learning, we mainly employ a widely-adopted Knowledge Tracing (KT) model [13] that models the learning process by hidden Markov models [34], and we compare it with the state-of-the-art logistic regression-based models of student learning. In the following sections, we will provide detailed descriptions of prior work, our methods and experimental results.

2. BACKGROUND

With our main research focus on tracing students' knowledge in textbook-based learning applying predictive student models, related research of our study lies in the following three areas: difficulty assessment for learning materials, predictive evaluation for students' knowledge modeling, and automatic educational content modeling.

2.1 Difficulty Assessment in Adaptive Hypermedia

Adaptive electronic textbooks frequently guide users by distinguishing between "ready to be learned" content, which bears new information without being too difficult to prevent users from understanding, and "not ready to be learned" content, which is too complicated for the current state of the user's knowledge. With fine-grained domain models that index content pages at the concept level, adaptive navigation support can be provided both easily and reliably by assessing the fraction of concepts that the user has already learned and by checking poorly known prerequisites. For example, the "traffic light" approach using a "traffic light" icon to annotate links as ready/not ready content, was introduced in the ELM-ART system [41]. Since then, this approach has been replicated in numerous educational AH systems. Later, this approach was also extended to cases that lack prerequisite links and thus doesn't allow the system to reliably judge content as "not ready." In these cases, links to content are annotated with "knowledge progression" icons presenting to what extent the user might already know the content [8, 21, 31]. Many studies confirmed the effectiveness of these approaches in the context of learning from online textbooks [3, 8, 14, 20, 31, 41].

2.2 Predictive Evaluation of Student Models

The approaches to building and evaluating student models and adaptive systems have evolved significantly over the last two decades. The classic approaches to evaluating user models and adaptive systems were mostly empirical (see [12] for a good review). A frequently used approach is A/B testing. It compares user performance and behavior in two versions

of a system: one with and one without adaptation. However, during an empirical evaluation, many factors contribute to the outcome, and the quality of the user model is just one of many. As a result, it is difficult to assess the quality of just the user modeling alone. To address this problem, several researchers advocated the use of the *layered evaluation* of adaptive systems [4, 32, 38] where each *layer* that contributes to the performance of the adaptive system (such as interface or user modeling) is evaluated separately.

In a layered evaluation context, the prediction accuracy evaluation approach emerged as a de-facto standard to isolate and assess the student modeling component of the personalized learning system. Predictive accuracy evaluation replaced live user studies with fully-automatic assessment based on real user data collected during the learning process. The idea is to split user data into two parts (training and testing). The training part of the data is used to build a student model, which is then used to predict student performance in the held-out testing part. The student model is then assessed by comparing the predicted performance to the actual performance obtained from the testing data. The classic work of Knowledge Tracing [13] presented several predictive evaluations in order to demonstrate its useful properties. Many recent studies [44, 16, 25] also compared and evaluated student models by performing a cross-validated evaluation, and they paid attention to the plausibility of the model parameters as well. The most recent internal evaluation framework [22] proposed multifaceted aspects including predictive accuracy, parameter plausibility, and consistency, and the work compared some state-of-the-art student models [17] from these multifaceted aspects.

2.3 Automatic Educational Content Modeling

Automatically modeling the content of documents has been viewed as the basis for various tasks, including user modeling [6] and text classification [37]. There are several methods that can be used for automatic content representation. The simplest approach is the bag-of-words-based approach, where the frequencies of words (terms) in both the documents and the collection are counted [26, 28, 36]. Despite its simplicity, this method has been among the most frequently used approaches for calculating the similarity among different fragments of educational content [19]. However, its limitation of not being able to capture the knowledge components inside the domain, particularly in domains related to education, is also well documented [19].

Therefore, the literature has also explored the automatic representation of educational materials considering semantics. For example, The Conceptual Open Hypermedia Services Environment (COHSE) [1] proposed a representation of online educational documents with metadata, and through integrating with an ontological reasoning service, it can form a conceptual hypermedia educational system. More recently, various latent semantic-based approaches such as topic modeling have gained attention in automatic content modeling [40]. By representing the content of documents as finite mixtures over an underlying set of latent topics, topic modeling moves beyond a bag-of-words representation, and avoids the rather expensive development cost in some earlier semantic modeling methods. In particular, Latent Dirichlet Allocation (LDA) [2] has been explored many times in content modeling [9, 35], including in supporting semantic representation in the fine-grained textbook linking [19].

3. METHODS

3.1 Problem Statement

Traditionally, student knowledge is inferred from performance data, which is collected from students' activities on questions, problems, quizzes, tests or exams. Such data carries a relatively high certainty for inferring student knowledge. However, textbook-based learning behavior investigated in this paper almost exclusively consists of students' reading activities. Problems or questions, even if in cases when they are provided as a part of reading-oriented learning, are usually found at the end of relatively large reading sections, and can only serve as a delayed assessment of student knowledge. In this situation, to maintain a highly dynamic student model that is necessary to deliver just-in-time personalization experience, we need to learn how to use students' online reading interactions to estimate changes in the students' dynamic knowledge. One benefit of using students' reading behaviors is that they are the most abundant data obtainable from the system logs in our context.

Prior literature supports our idea of linking students' reading time to their overall knowledge growth. For example, research on learning curves [29, 27] confirms that with the increases in practice opportunities, students' problem-solving time decreases, following a power law. Although reading might require less complex cognitive process than problem-solving, we argue that it is also an activity that builds up fluency through "repetition" as a learning process. In this case, "repetition" means reading the content (e.g., document, page) that contains previously covered knowledge components. In other words, students' knowledge of a knowledge component should grow as students spend time reading the related content. Meanwhile, once a student acquires the knowledge underlying a piece of learning content, they would generally spend little time on the content.

More formally, we have made two assumptions:

- If a student spends time reading a document, the student's knowledge of the knowledge components associated with the document will grow.

- If a document contains knowledge components that a student has already learned, the student is highly likely to skip or skim the document; if a document contains new knowledge components the student has not yet learned, the student is highly likely to read the document carefully. Note that like most models, our model simplifies real-world experience in order to quantify it in an efficient way. It assumes a "diligent student" who is motivated to learn and reads with few distractions. It also assumes that knowledge is the only factor that drives students' reading behaviors.

The above-mentioned student learning process is illustrated in Figure 1, where we assume that there are N knowledge components (from KC_1 to KC_n) underlying a set of reading materials (documents). For each student, the knowledge level of a knowledge component can be learned or unlearned. Through consistent content reading that contains the same knowledge component, a student can transition from the unlearned to the learned state with some probability. Also, given the knowledge levels of a set of KCs, the time that a student needs to spend reading a new document can be predicted. This formulation directly translates the problem into what traditional student modeling can address.

Instead of using performance on problems (quizzes) as observations, we can use reading time. Furthermore, to evaluate the inference of knowledge, we can examine the prediction of reading time on the held-out data. In contrast to traditional classroom studies, this method requires less time and labor, and can provide valuable insights for performing studies. In addition to evaluating predictive performance, we also examine each KC model's potential impact for real-world adaptive learning by considering its semantics, granularity, and the ability to capture transfer learning.

Note that in this hypothesized learning process, we assume binary states for both observed reading time (*Skim* or *Read*) and hidden knowledge levels (*Learned* or *Unlearned*). As mentioned before, this is a simplification for efficiency, particularly when applying classic student models which have the same binary state assumptions. Here, *Skim* corresponds to *Skim Reading* or *Scanning*, and *Read* corresponds to *Receptive Reading* or *Reflective Reading* from the typology of reading proposed in [30]. Since the logged reading time is a continuous variable, we conduct discretization on the data (see Section 4.1.2 for details). Next, we will explain how we reconstruct traditional probabilistic student models and apply automatic text analysis to model reading.

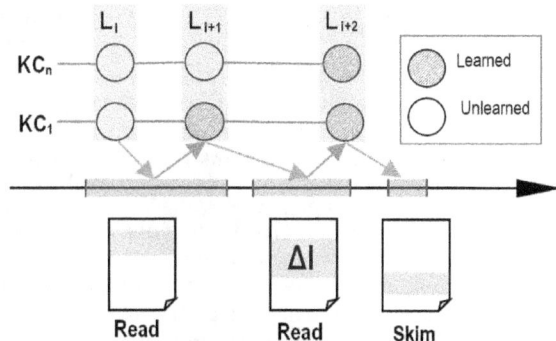

Figure 1: An illustration of knowledge modeling in textbook reading. KC_n represents the nth knowledge component (KC) and L_i denotes the students' knowledge state for each KC at i^{th} learning opportunity. ΔI indicates the content that a student reads.

3.2 Student Models for Reading

In this paper, we compare two schools of student models for reading: one uses latent variables empowering latent knowledge estimates, while the other is based on logistic regression models and serves as a high baseline.

We also compare each school of student models with a low baseline, *majority class model (Majority)*. This model makes predictions for the target variable (reading time) by using the majority class based on its distribution of the data. For example, in our final dataset, there are around 67% activities labeled as *Read*, so this model always predicts *Read* for observations.

3.2.1 Knowledge Tracing-Based Model

Knowledge Tracing (KT) [13] has been the de-facto standard for inferring student knowledge from performance data. The classic KT model relies on decomposing knowledge in a domain into individual pieces of knowledge components (KCs), and traces students' knowledge acquisition for each KC through a hidden Markov model (HMM) [34].

We use the classic KT paradigm and transform reading modeling into a traditional performance modeling problem. The variables in Knowledge Tracing for each knowledge component and their corresponding variables in our model are:

- **Observed variable:** a binary performance variable that indicates whether a question is answered correctly or not. In our reading context, this corresponds to a binary reading time variable with two possible states - *Skim* or *Read*).

- **Hidden variable:** a binary knowledge state variable with two possible states - *Learned* or *Unlearned*.

A classic KT has four parameters for each knowledge component (assuming no *forgetting* so that the probability of transferring from a Learned to an Unlearned state is zero). These four parameters and their corresponding parameters in our model are as follows:

- $\mathbf{P(L_0)}$: the probability that a student initially knows the KC, i.e., the student is in the learned state.

- $\mathbf{P(T)}$: the probability that a student transitions from an unlearned to a learned state.

- $\mathbf{P(G)}$: the probability that a student "guesses" correctly, given that the student is in the unlearned state. In our case, it is the probability of a student *skims* when being in the unlearned state.

- $\mathbf{P(S)}$: The probability that a student "slips," given that the student is in the learned state. In our case, it is the probability of a student *reads* when being in the learned state.

If we assume each reading activity as an opportunity to learn a single KC (i.e., each document only involves one KC), then each student's reading time on documents related to a KC can be ordered into a sequence, and all such sequences of a KC can serve as the input for training a KT model (an HMM) that is directly used in prediction. However, reading is a complex learning process, since it usually involves multiple KCs at the same time when a student reads a document. It is not clear how much attention each KC is allotted, based on the observation of time on the document (learning content) level. Traditional KT is constructed based on the decomposition of knowledge into units, where each unit's measurement can be directly collected. As a result, we have to develop some mechanisms in the KT framework to address the attention attribution issue in reading.

As a first attempt, we propose a simple mechanism similar to the one used in [16]. Despite its simplicity, such kind of mechanisms has achieved a relatively good level of predictive accuracy in some previous reported results on the quiz performance data [16, 42]. This mechanism can be explained via the following steps:

Parameter Learning: During the parameter learning (training) process, we assume that each KC has equal responsibility for the observed reading time, and that they are independent of each other. This means we duplicate a single observation multiple times to make sure that each underlying KC has one observation, which forms each KC's learning sequence. For example, if a student *Skims* a document that contains KCs KC_1, KC_2, KC_3, we duplicate this activity three times (labeled as *Skim*), and assign it to each of the three KCs. Then we can train an HMM for each KC as in the traditional KT.

Predicting: After the parameter fitting process, in order to perform prediction on a new document, we have to aggregate the prediction (predicted probability of *Skim*) from each underlying KC of this document. Prior literature provides several options for aggregation [16, 42, 17]: (1) multiplying each KC's predicted probability; (2) using the lowest prediction probability among all KCs (i.e., choosing the weakest); or (3) computing the average of each KC's predicted probability. We argue that the first strategy is not suitable, since a reading document typically involves a number of KCs, which easily makes the resulting probability very small. In our preliminary study we found out that the second strategy behaved the same as a majority class model, in that it ended up always predicting *Read*. Therefore, we chose the third strategy for our experiments. Equation 1 shows that the predicted probability of a student skimming a document D_i at the tth learning opportunity is the average of the predicted probabilities from each required KC k underlying this document:

$$P(D_i^t = Skim) = \frac{1}{N} \sum_{k \in D_i} \Big(P(L_k^t = Learned) \times (1 - P(S)_k) $$
$$+ P(L_k^t = Unlearned) \times P(G)_k \Big)$$
$$(1)$$

Updating: After performing prediction on a new document, the actual observation of this document can be used to update the belief of each KC's knowledge. We assume that such new evidence will have impact on all of the KCs underlying the document, so we update all the involved KCs. Equation 2 shows how we compute the posterior probability of a student in the learned state of KC k observing this student *Skimming* a document D_i at t^{th} learning opportunity based on the prior probability. Equation 3 shows how we further compute the prior probability (up-to-date estimate) of the student in the learned state of KC k at the next $(t + 1)^{th}$ learning opportunity, based on the transition probability $P(T)_k$. For updating the knowledge based on an observation of *Read*, the procedure is similar.

$$P(L_k^t = Learned)_{post} = P(L_k^t = Learned | D_i^t = Skim)$$
$$= \frac{P(L_k^t = Learned, D_i^t = Skim)}{P(D_i^t = Skim)}$$
$$= \frac{P(L_k^t = Learned)_{prior} \times (1 - P(S)_k)}{P(D_i^t = Skim)}$$
$$(2)$$

$$P(L_k^{t+1} = Learned)_{prior} = P(L_k^t = Learned)_{post}$$
$$+ P(L_k^t = Unlearned)_{post} \times P(T)_k$$
$$(3)$$

3.2.2 Logistic Regression-Based Models

There are several logistic regression-based models that are traditionally used in modeling student learning. Rasch (1PL IRT) model [39] does not model learning per se, but is used as a basis for other approaches. Rasch model assumes that the correctness of a student's response on an item (a question or a problem) depends on the student's ability and the corresponding item's difficulty. The Additive Factor Model (AFM) [11] and the Performance Factors Analysis (PFA) model [33] extend the Rasch model by actually capturing the process of learning. Instead of considering item difficulties, AFM considers knowledge components (KCs, or skills) that are linked to the corresponding item. It models student performance as a function of the student ability, the difficulty and the learning from accumulated practices of each underlying KC of the current item. Moreover, the student ability parameters can be treated as random effects [44]. Compared with AFM, traditional PFA removes student ability parameters and differentiates learning from successes and learning from failures.

Traditional AFM and PFA are constructed following the rationality (assumption) that practices should increase (the belief of) the knowledge level, as well as the chance to succeed. As explained in Section 3.1, our hypothesized learning process of reading follows a similar rationality: accessing documents about a particular KC should increase (the belief of) the knowledge level and the likelihood of skimming next documents about the same KC. Also, the discretized reading time as the dependent variable is still binary. As a result, the logistic regression models that are traditionally applied to modeling student quiz (problem) performance are directly applicable to modeling reading. We choose *Skim* as a *success* and *Read* as a *failure*. As explained in Section 3.1, this is a simplification based on assuming that students are diligent, and that they will read and only read a document when there are underlying unlearned KCs.

Equation 4 shows how we reconstruct PFA for modeling reading (similar idea can be used to reconstruct AFM). We compute the predicted probability of a student skimming a document D_i at the tth learning opportunity, based on all required KCs' corresponding counts of this student's previous *skim* activities (S_k) and *read* activities (R_k) on documents that require the same KC k:

$$P(D_i^t = Skim) = logistic(\sum_{k \in D_i} (\alpha_k + \beta_k S_k + \rho_k R_k)) \quad (4)$$

where α_k, β_k, ρ_k are coefficients interpreted as initial easiness, learning rates from previous *Skim*, or *Read* activities of each KC k.

As opposed to KT, AFM and PFA models avoid local optima when fitting the parameters, and they both have a natural mechanism to handle multiple skills per item observations by the logistic regression formulation. Prior studies have shown that PFA outperforms KT in prediction particularly in multiple skills per item cases [33, 16]. So, AFM and PFA models serve as high baselines for prediction in our study. However, AFM and PFA lack the ability to explicitly represent knowledge estimations for each individual knowledge component which can be helpful for personalization. A variety of statistical packages are available to fit mixed-effect logistic regressions (AFM) or generalized linear models (PFA).

3.3 Extracting Knowledge Components

A knowledge component (KC) is the basic knowledge unit (e.g., concept, skill) to accomplish steps in a task or a problem. In prior studies about students' knowledge modeling [13, 17], KC is often predefined and manually crafted by domain experts; however, this process can be time-consuming in an open corpus, and particularly in our context of textbook-based learning. In this paper, we explore different methods for automatically extracting KC from textbooks.

The simplest approach is to treat each single *word* (term) in a document as a KC under the bag-of-words assumption.

Although it provides fine-grained granularity and potentially captures transfer learning across a book (since words can be shared across a book), It fails to capture the semantic relationships among different words. As a result, we explore several additional approaches that aim to capture the underlying semantics among different words.

We try two approaches for estimating semantic-based knowledge components – a coarse-grained approach that estimates each *chapter* within a textbook as a KC and a fine-grained approach that mines *latent topics* as KCs using the latent Dirichlet allocation (LDA) [2] model. In addition to the granularity difference between these two approaches, they also differ in their ability to capture transfer learning: the former fails to capture transfer across chapters, since each document is mapped to one chapter only used for estimating the current chapter's knowledge level, while the latter captures transfer, since topic modeling allows different documents to share latent topics in a probabilistic way. A comparison of these approaches can be seen in Table 1 and the details are explained in Section 4.1.3.

4. EXPERIMENTS AND RESULTS

We conduct three comparison studies that demonstrate the ability of the proposed KT-based model in modeling textbook reading. We will start with description of the experiment setup in Section 4.1, then present our studies investigating different KC models under KT-based and logistic regression-based models in Section 4.2, and finally compare these two schools of student models for modeling reading.

4.1 Experiment Setup

4.1.1 System and Dataset

Our dataset was collected from two online reading platforms: *AnnotatED+* [5] and *Reading Circle* [18], which were used for a graduate course about Interactive Systems Design at the University of Pittsburgh from 2007 to 2015. The collection of online readings for the class included five textbooks on human-computer interaction. The online reading systems have many functions for engaging and helping students to learn: for example, students can leave and see comments during reading, and each student's reading progress is visualized. Every week, students were assigned reading assignments; and every other week, they were asked to take a short quiz in the class that contained questions that were highly related to the reading materials. Although it was not mandatory for students to use the reading platform, many students found it to be useful and used the system for reading the textbooks.

This dataset contains students' logged time of accessing each document of a book (we call it an activity). Each document contains one to more pages and typically corresponds to a subsection (the lowest level) of a book. In order to get more reliable information for modeling, we conducted the following filtering of the data: we removed students who read fewer than one unique document; we removed the per-page activities with too much time (> 13 minutes, which is the 95th percentile of the distribution); and we removed the documents with fewer than 10 activities in total (to reduce bias in discretization in Section 4.1.2).

The final dataset contains 10,188 activities on 325 documents from 289 students. There are around 33% activities labeled as *Skim*, and thus the majority class is *Read* (67%).

The mean (median) values of some attributes of the dataset are reported as follows: the total number of documents per student is 35 (10); the total reading time per student is 57 (13) minutes; the number of activities per document is 31 (24); and the reading time per document over all activities totaled 1.6 minutes (22 seconds).

4.1.2 Discretization of Time

We discretized time based on each document's reading time distribution (across activities), because our documents have a high variance in length (SD=314 words), which we considered as the primary factor that affects reading time, similar to [15]. In our preliminary study, we found out that the 33rd percentile of the time distribution per document constitutes a reasonable cutoff to differentiate *Skim* and *Read*. We first computed the reading speed for each activity by dividing the number of words in the corresponding document by the time spent on this document. The distribution of learning speeds across activities was highly skewed, so we obtained the median as 6 words per second, and treated it as the normal reading speed in our context. This speed is above the reported speed of an average-speed reader [23] and below the reported speed of the fastest college graduate readers [10]. We then computed the reading speed by the 33rd percentile time for each document and obtained the median as 20 words per second from the skewed distribution. We considered it as the minimum skimming speed (an activity with a reading speed above this is labeled as *Skim* and an activity with a reading speed below this is labeled as *Read*). We found out that this speed is about three times faster than the normal reading speed, which is consistent with the finding in a classic work [23] that found that speed readers and skimmers were 3 times to 2.5 times faster than normal readers. As a result, we chose this discretization method for our experiments.

Admittedly, our discretization does not consider students' individual differences, yet incorporating this aspect is non-trivial: measuring a stable reliable learning speed might require tests on students before they use the system, which may reduce students' engagement or may not be available for existing platforms, and it might require collecting enough observations and then conducting time-consuming online parameter estimations while students are using the system. It is also unclear as to whether the learning speed can be considered stable. In our current document based discretization, the system can immediately perform modeling even if a student has just entered the system, and will avoid time-consuming online parameter estimations. In the future, we plan to further improve our discretization method.

4.1.3 Knowledge Component Extraction

As mentioned in Section 3.3, we adopted three different approaches for knowledge component extraction - the pure word-based method, a coarse-grained semantic-based method (chapter-based) and a fine-grained semantic-based method (latent topic-based). Table 1 compares them.

When applying the word-based approach for knowledge component extraction, we removed stop words[1], excluded non-letter symbols (e.g., brackets and punctuations) and performed stemming. There are 8,076 words identified as KCs. For the chapter-based approach, each book chapter

[1] The stop word list is directly downloaded from Mallet (http://mallet.cs.umass.edu/).

Table 1: Knowledge component model comparison by number of KCs, whether it captures semantic relations, whether it provides enough fine-grained granularity for adaptation, and whether it captures transfer learning across chapters and books.

KC Model	#KCs	semantics	granularity	transfer
Words	8,076	no	yes	yes
Book Chapter	35	yes	no	no
Latent Topic	250	yes	yes	yes

is treated as a knowledge component directly. In total, our dataset includes 35 chapters from five textbooks. The latent topic-based approach identifies the knowledge components from the textbooks, based on latent semantic mining methods. This paper follows a previous study that works on a similar task [19]. Specifically, our LDA approach have 250 topics (this number was chosen based on our preliminary study). Since the initial document-topic probability is uniformly distributed, a probability that is higher than the cutoff 1/250 indicates the relative importance of a topic in a document. Therefore, we chose 1/250 as the cutoff probability, and represented a document using topics with an association probability bigger than 1/250.

4.1.4 Cross-Validation and Evaluation

Following the conventions of traditional KTs, we constructed KC-specific models, which means we fit parameters for each knowledge component, and evaluated our models by their ability to be generalized from trained students to test students. We conducted a 10-fold student stratified cross-validation where the data was first randomly split into 10 groups of students, and in each fold, 90% of students (from 9 groups) were used as a training set and the remaining 10% were used as the test set. Although trained models only capture KC characteristics, by the online update mechanism explained in Section 3.2.1, student models are able to maintain individual knowledge estimations for each student as their interaction evidence is accumulated.

We reported two popular prediction metrics used in evaluating student models, *root-mean-squared error (RMSE)* and *area under the receiver operating characteristic curve (AUC)*. For RMSE, a lower value is preferred; for AUC, a higher value is preferred. We computed the average RMSE or AUC across 10 folds and reported a 95% confidence interval, based on a t-distribution. In addition, we also compared the models' potential impact on real-world adaptive tutoring by considering the semantics, granularity, and the ability to capture transfer of each KC model.

4.1.5 Tools

When building the KT-based and logistic regression-based models, we used two tools that allowed us to cope with the scale of the data. The first tool, which was used for KT, is `hmm-scalable`. It is a command line utility implemented in C/C++. It targets large datasets in the order of tens of millions of records and implements a suite of solver algorithms. `Hmm-scalable` can also fit KT models with per-student parameters (individualized KT) [43]. It has been extensively tested on different datasets and is freely available[2]. We used the default values in the tool for our exper-

[2] https://github.com/IEDMS/standard-bkt

iments (p(L_0)=0.5, p(T)=0.4, p(G)=0.2, p(S)=0.2, maximum iteration=200, tolerance=0.01, solver using Gradient Descent). The other tool is LIBLINEAR, which we used for building logistic regression-based models. This tool also targets large datasets. LIBLINEAR was developed by a team at the National Taiwan University that won first prize at the 2010 Knowledge Discovery and Data Mining Cup. Although LIBLINEAR supports logistic regression, it does not support random factors. To fix that, we have developed a modified version of LIBLINEAR that implements random factors via grouped penalties. This modified version is also freely available[3].

4.2 Experimental Results

In this section, we summarize our modeling results for KT-based and logistic regression-based models under different KC extraction methods.

4.2.1 Knowledge Tracing-based Student Model with Different Knowledge Component Models

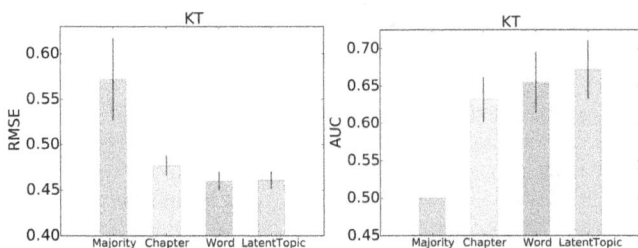

Figure 2: KT-based student model with different KC models. The reported values are averaged across 10-fold cross-validation. 95% CI is also plotted for each method.

The summary of the results of KT models with varying KC models is given in Figure 2. Here, we see that in terms of both RMSE and AUC across all KC extraction methods, our proposed KT-based models consistently outperform the majority class baseline (which predicts *Read* for all observations). Even the simple chapter model performs quite well. This shows that students' reading behaviors in our dataset can be reasonably well described under our hypothesis (assumptions) of the learning process in Section 3.1. Also, our framework of using a KT-based student model seems to be an effective approach to model learning from textbooks. Using the majority class model will suggest that students read all documents, risking the waste of a considerable amount of time that could be better used for learning new material.

Because the difference in predictive power among the three KC extraction methods is not statistically significant, it shows the robustness of our KT-based student model varying granularity and semantics of the underlying KC models. In terms of the absolute value, the KT model based on latent topics has a slight advantage over a word-based or chapter-based KC model. Despite the predictive accuracy being similar among the three models, we argue that the latent topic-based model might offer the highest benefit for personalization by examining semantics, granularity, and transfer learning (Table 1). Although the chapter-based model has clear semantic and pedagogic meaning, its knowledge modeling is too coarse-grained and it fails to capture transfer learning

[3]https://github.com/IEDMS/liblinear-mixed-models

across chapters. Although words (terms) can potentially capture transfer learning across chapters, the word-based model has weak semantic ground by treating words (terms) as knowledge components. In this context, the latent topic-based model provides a reasonable granularity level with its 250 topics operating on a sufficient semantic level, and it also maintains the ability to model transfer learning across chapters (and books). We foresee that combining latent topic modeling with textbook structure or expert knowledge can further increase the modeling capability. We plan to investigate this combination in future work.

4.2.2 Logistic Regression-based Student Models with Different Knowledge Component Models

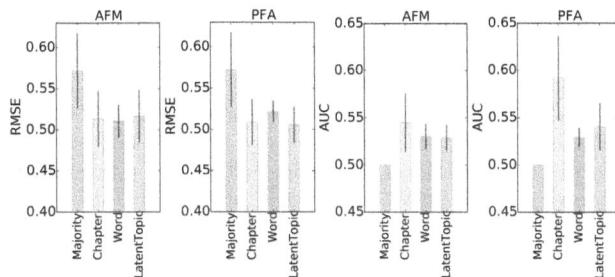

Figure 3: Logistic regression-based student models with different KC models. The reported values are averaged across 10-fold cross-validation. 95% CI is also plotted for each method.

As shown in Figure 3, we also find that logistic regression-based student models all consistently outperform the majority class baseline model. This again provides evidence to support our hypothesis (assumptions) of the learning process in reading and the effectiveness of our framework to model this learning process.

There is no clear winner in terms of the KC units used (chapters, words, or latent topics); however, the PFA model based on simple chapters does stand out in terms of AUC. This suggests the potential benefit of using a textbook structure (as an exposition of domain expert knowledge) to extract KC models. However, as mentioned in Section 3.3, 4.2.1 and Table 1, chapter-based modeling provides a too coarse-grained knowledge estimation, and even if we replace it with a more fine-grained section or subsection based representation, it still fails to capture transfer learning across units (sections/subsections). This is not the case for word-based or latent topic based models, where words or latent topics can be shared across chapters or books so that knowledge (estimations) can be transferred. Combining this with the results from the KT-based model, we further strengthen our belief that a promising future direction is to combine latent topic modeling with a textbook structure or with expert knowledge.

4.2.3 Knowledge Tracing-based Student Model Vs. Logistic Regression-based Student Models

As we can see from Figure 4, the KT-based model on average significantly outperforms logistic regression-based models for both RMSE and AUC, as well as across all knowledge component modeling units. This is different from our expectation that logistic regression-based models should have a higher predictive power, since they naturally have the ability to handle multiple skills (as features) and do not suffer

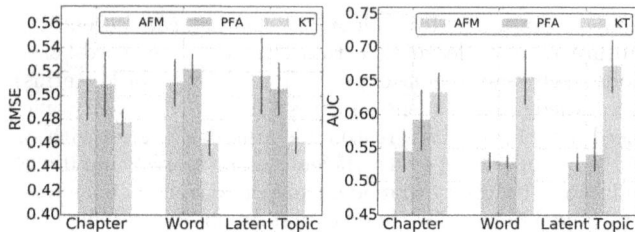

Figure 4: KT-based vs. logistic regression-based student models varying KC models. The reported values are averaged across 10-fold cross-validation. 95% CI is also plotted for each method.

from the local optimum problem. We intend to further investigate the reason for this result. Given this result, the advantage of a KT-based model over logistic regression-based models stands out: it not only has significantly higher predictive performance, but also provides additional knowledge-estimation power.

So far, among all the model variants, the best performance is achieved by the latent topic-based and KT-based model, with the average RMSE as 0.46 and AUC as 0.67 across 10 folds. While these values are not the most ideal, they are very similar to the predictive performance reported in classic student model comparisons [16].

5. DISCUSSION AND CONCLUSION

This paper proposes a novel framework for dynamic modeling of student knowledge in textbook-based learning. We summarize the main contributions and limitations as follows.

We innovatively formulated the problem of modeling knowledge in reading as a reading time prediction problem. We argue that traditional quiz performance-based student knowledge modeling is not suitable in textbook-based learning environments, but instead, that using student reading activities allows us to obtain enough data and perform in-time knowledge estimation to empower in-time personalization. Our results showed that the proposed student models significantly outperform the majority baseline with a reasonable degree of predictive power. It provides evidence that our hypothesized learning process for reading modeling is plausible and that our modeling mechanism is feasible and effective. Moreover, the quality of models could now be evaluated using prediction, which is less time- and labor-consuming than traditional classroom study-based evaluation, and provides important insights for such studies. However, we are aware that such internal data-driven evaluation is still not enough, and we plan to further examine external validity as in [13] and to conduct classroom studies in the end to examine our model's real world impact on personalization.

We built novel algorithms to model student knowledge learning from reading by reconstructing existing student models. The conventional student model, Knowledge Tracing (KT), is designed for tracing individual knowledge components (KCs) using quiz performance data. Moreover, it does not directly support situations where multiple KCs are associated with a single observed evidence. To address these limitations, we first mapped a time-prediction problem to traditional performance-prediction problems, and then we further constructed credit and blame assignment mechanisms for handling multiple KCs in the complex reading process. In our experiments, we found out that this pro-

posed KT-based model significantly outperforms not only the majority baseline model, but also state-of-the-art logistic regression-based models for student learning (which are expected to have higher predictive ability), with additional knowledge estimation power. This demonstrates that our blind assignment mechanism is simple but effective. We foresee that with improvement in the multiple KC handling mechanisms, applying the KT-based model is promising for modeling learning in reading.

Also, in order to readily apply existing classic student models, we made simplifications in terms of the hidden and observed variables (including the relation between them). We assume that students are diligent, devoted readers who will read whenever there is unlearned knowledge; that knowledge level is the only factor that affects reading time ignoring other factors (such as reading goals or strategies); and that reading time is the only observed behavior, ignoring rich behaviors such as mouse movements and specific focus on parts of a page. We also assume binary states for both knowledge levels and reading time. In particular, we follow classic student models' KC-specific perspectives without explicitly considering individual student differences. We intend to investigate such issues in the future and improve our student modeling approach.

As a next step for implementing personalized guidance based on our dynamic knowledge model, we need to distinguish content pages with suitable difficulty levels that should be read from those that are too simple or too complicated that can be skimmed or skipped, given a student's knowledge levels on KCs underlying the content. Our current model's prediction of *Read* or *Skim* needs to incorporate this aspect of suitable difficulty levels in order to be translated into effective recommendation actions.

We also explored two automatic text-analysis approaches to extract knowledge component models. By using automatically extracted KCs, we address the open corpus problem in adaptive hypermedia research. It makes the process of KC extraction less time- and labor-consuming than in traditional expert-based domain knowledge engineering. We conducted extensive studies comparing different KC extractions varying semantics, granularity, and knowledge transferring ability. We found out that using the latent topic-based KC model provides the highest predictive ability than using simple book chapters or words (for a KT-based model). Although the advantage of using latent topics over others is not significant, we argue that its level of granularity, semantic relation modeling, and transferring ability will offer significant benefits to real-world personalization. We anticipate a promising future direction of combining this approach with textbook structure or domain expert knowledge.

Overall, our work could be considered as the first step to model dynamic knowledge in textbook-based learning. We believe that our framework is promising and that its application lies beyond textbook-based learning. This framework can be applied to a broader context of open-corpus personalized learning, empowering learners with the ability to access the right reading content at the right moment, despite the huge volume of online educational content.

Acknowledgement

This research was supported by the National Science Foundation Cyber-Human Systems (CHS) Program under Grant IIS-1525186.

6. REFERENCES

[1] S. Bechhofer, C. Goble, L. Carr, W. Hall, S. Kampa, and D. De Roure. Cohse: Conceptual open hypermedia service. In *Annotation for the Semantic Web*, pages 193–210. IOS Press, 2003.

[2] D. M. Blei, A. Y. Ng, and M. I. Jordan. Latent dirichlet allocation. *Journal of Machine Learning Research*, 3:993–1022, 2003.

[3] P. Brusilovsky and J. Eklund. A study of user-model based link annotation in educational hypermedia. *Journal of Universal Computer Science*, 4(4):429–448, 1998.

[4] P. Brusilovsky, C. Karagiannidis, and D. Sampson. Layered evaluation of adaptive learning systems. *International Journal of Continuing Engineering Education and Lifelong Learning*, 14(4/5):402 – 421, 2004.

[5] P. Brusilovsky and J. Kim. Enhancing electronic books with spatial annotation and social navigation support. In *Proc. 5th Int. Conf. Universal Digital Library (ICUDL)*, 2009.

[6] P. Brusilovsky and E. Millán. User models for adaptive hypermedia and adaptive educational systems. In *The adaptive web*, pages 3–53. Springer-Verlag, 2007.

[7] P. Brusilovsky and L. Pesin. Adaptive navigation support in educational hypermedia: An evaluation of the isis-tutor. *Journal of Computing and Information Technology*, 6(1):27–38, 1998.

[8] P. Brusilovsky, S. Sosnovsky, and M. Yudelson. Addictive links: The motivational value of adaptive link annotation. *New Review of Hypermedia and Multimedia*, 15(1):97–118, 2009.

[9] K. R. Canini, L. Shi, and T. L. Griffiths. Online inference of topics with latent dirichlet allocation. In *Int. Conf. Artificial Intelligence and Statistics*, pages 65–72, 2009.

[10] R. P. Carver. *The causes of high and low reading achievement*. Routledge, 2000.

[11] H. Cen, K. R. Koedinger, and B. Junker. Comparing two irt models for conjunctive skills. In *Proc. 10th Int. Conf. Intelligent Tutoring Systems*, pages 796–798, Berlin/Heidelberg, 2008. Springer-Verlag.

[12] D. Chin. Empirical evaluations of user models and user-adapted systems. *User Modeling and User-Adapted Interaction*, 11(1-2):181–194, 2001.

[13] A. T. Corbett and J. R. Anderson. Knowledge tracing: Modelling the acquisition of procedural knowledge. *User Modeling and User-Adapted Interaction*, 4(4):253–278, 1995.

[14] A. Davidovic, J. Warren, and E. Trichina. Learning benefits of structural example-based adaptive tutoring systems. *IEEE Transactions on Education*, 46(2):241–251, 2003.

[15] R. Farzan and P. Brusilovsky. Social navigation support in e-learning: What are real footprints. In *IJCAI'05 Workshop on Intelligent Techniques for Web Personalization*, pages 49–56, 2005.

[16] Y. Gong, J. E. Beck, and N. T. Heffernan. Comparing knowledge tracing and performance factor analysis by using multiple model fitting procedures. In *Proc. 10th Int. Conf. Intelligent Tutoring Systems*, pages 35–44. Springer, 2010.

[17] J. P. González-Brenes, Y. Huang, and P. Brusilovsky. General features in knowledge tracing: Applications to multiple subskills, temporal item response theory, and expert knowledge. In *Proc. of the 7th Int. Conf. on Educational Data Mining*, pages 84–91, 2014.

[18] J. Guerra, D. Parra, and P. Brusilovsky. Encouraging online student reading with social visualization. In *The 2nd Workshop on Intelligent Support for Learning in Groups at the 16th Conference on Artificial Intelligence in Education*, pages 47–50, 2013.

[19] J. Guerra, S. Sosnovsky, and P. Brusilovsky. When one textbook is not enough: Linking multiple textbooks using probabilistic topic models. In *Scaling up Learning for Sustained Impact*, pages 125–138. Springer, 2013.

[20] N. Henze and W. Nejdl. Adaptation in open corpus hypermedia. *International Journal of Artificial Intelligence in Education*, 12(4):325–350, 2001.

[21] I.-H. Hsiao, S. Sosnovsky, and P. Brusilovsky. Guiding students to the right questions: adaptive navigation support in an e-learning system for java programming. *Journal of Computer Assisted Learning*, 26(4):270–283, 2010.

[22] Y. Huang, J. P. González-Brenes, R. Kumar, and P. Brusilovsky. A framework for multifaceted evaluation of student models. In *Proceedings of the 8th International Conference on Educational Data Mining*, pages 203–210, 2015.

[23] M. A. Just and P. A. Carpenter. *The psychology of reading and language comprehension*. Allyn & Bacon, 1987.

[24] A. Kavcic. Fuzzy user modeling for adaptation in educational hypermedia. *IEEE Transactions on Systems, Man, and Cybernetics*, 34(4):439–449, 2004.

[25] K. Koedinger, J. Stamper, E. McLaughlin, and T. Nixon. Using data-driven discovery of better student models to improve student learning. In *Proceedings of the 16th International Conference on Artificial Intelligence in Education.*, pages 412–430, 2013.

[26] H. P. Luhn. The automatic creation of literature abstracts. *IBM Journal of research and development*, 2(2):159–165, 1958.

[27] B. Martin, A. Mitrovic, K. Koedinger, and S. Mathan. Evaluating and improving adaptive educational systems with learning curves. *User Modeling and User-Adapted Interaction*, 21(3):249–283, 2011.

[28] J. T. Mayes, M. R. Kibby, and H. Watson. Strathtutor: The development and evaluation of a learning-by-browsing on the macintosh. *Computers and Education*, 12(1):221–229, 1988.

[29] A. Newell and P. S. Rosenbloom. Mechanisms of skill acquisition and the law of practice. *Cognitive skills and their acquisition*, 1:1–55, 1981.

[30] K. O'Hara. Towards a typology of reading goals. Technical Report EPC-1996-107, Rank Xerox Research Centre Cambridge Laboratory, 1996.

[31] K. A. Papanikolaou, M. Grigoriadou, H. Kornilakis, and G. D. Magoulas. Personalising the interaction in a web-based educational hypermedia system: the case of inspire. *User Modeling and User Adapted Interaction*, 13(3):213–267, 2003.

[32] A. Paramythis and S. Weibelzahl. A decomposition model for the layered evaluation of interactive adaptive systems. In L. Ardissono, P. Brna, and A. Mitrovic, editors, *10th International User Modeling Conference*, volume 3538 of *Lecture Notes in Artificial Intelligence*, pages 438–442. Springer Verlag, 2005.

[33] P. I. Pavlik Jr., H. Cen, and K. R. Koedinger. Performance factors analysis – a new alternative to knowledge tracing. In *Proceedings of the 14th International Conference on Artificial Intelligence in Education*, pages 531–538. IOS Press, 2009.

[34] L. Rabiner and B. Juang. An introduction to Hidden Markov Models. *ASSP Magazine, IEEE*, 3(1):4–16, 1986.

[35] M. Rosen-Zvi, T. Griffiths, M. Steyvers, and P. Smyth. The author-topic model for authors and documents. In *Proceedings of the 20th conference on Uncertainty in artificial intelligence*, pages 487–494. AUAI Press, 2004.

[36] G. Salton and C. Buckley. Term-weighting approaches in automatic text retrieval. *Information processing & management*, 24(5):513–523, 1988.

[37] F. Sebastiani. Machine learning in automated text categorization. *ACM computing surveys (CSUR)*, 34(1):1–47, 2002.

[38] S. Sosnovsky and P. Brusilovsky. Evaluation of topic-based adaptation and student modeling in quizguide. *User Modeling and User-Adapted Interaction*, 25(4):371–424, 2015.

[39] W. J. van der Linden and R. K. Hambleton. *Handbook of Modern Item Response Theory*. Springer Verlag, New York, NY, 1997.

[40] H. M. Wallach. Topic modeling: beyond bag-of-words. In *Proceedings of the 23rd international conference on Machine learning*, pages 977–984. ACM, 2006.

[41] G. Weber and P. Brusilovsky. Elm-art: An adaptive versatile system for web-based instruction. *International Journal of Artificial Intelligence in Education*, 12(4):351–384, 2001.

[42] Y. Xu and J. Mostow. Comparison of methods to trace multiple subskills: Is LR-DBN best? In *Proceedings of the 5th International Conference on Educational Data Mining*, pages 41–48, Chania, Greece, 2012.

[43] M. Yudelson, K. Koedinger, and G. Gordon. Individualized bayesian knowledge tracing models. In *Proceedings of 16th International Conference on Artificial Intelligence in Education (AIED 2013).*, pages 171–180, Berlin/Heidelberg, 2013. Springer-Verlag.

[44] M. Yudelson, P. Pavlik, and K. Koedinger. User modeling – a notoriously black art. In *Proceedings of the 19th International Conference on User Modeling Adaptation and Personalization (UMAP 2011)*, pages 317–328, 2011.

Modeling and Predicting User Actions in Recommender Systems

Tural Gurbanov
Free University of Bozen-Bolzano
Bozen-Bolzano, Italy
tgurbanov@unibz.it

Francesco Ricci
Free University of Bozen-Bolzano
Bozen-Bolzano, Italy
fricci@unibz.it

Meinhard Ploner
ProSiebenSat.1 Media SE
Unterföhring, Germany
meinhard.ploner@prosiebensat1digital.de

ABSTRACT

Many collaborative filtering recommender systems collect and use users' explicitly entered preferences in the form of ratings for items. However, in many real world scenarios, this form of feedback can be difficult to obtain or unavailable (e.g., news portals). In this case recommendations must be built by leveraging more abundant implicit feedback data, which only indirectly signal users' preferences or opinions. A record in such datasets is a result of an *action* performed by a user on an item (e.g., the item was clicked or viewed). State-of-the-art implicit feedback recommender systems predict whether the user will act on a target item and interpret this prediction as a discovered preference for the item. These models are trained by observations of user actions of one single type. For instance, they predict that a user will watch a video using a dataset of observed video watch actions. In this paper we conjecture that multiple types of user actions may be jointly exploited to predict one target type of actions. We present a general prediction model (MMF - Multiple action types Matrix Factorization) that implements this conjecture and we illustrate some practical examples. The empirical evaluation of MMF, which was conducted on a large real world dataset, shows that using multiple actions is beneficial and it can outperform a state-of-the-art implicit feedback model that uses only the target action data.

Keywords

Collaborative filtering; implicit feedback; matrix factorization; user actions

1. INTRODUCTION

Collaborative filtering (CF) is a popular recommendation technique where user ratings/likes are analyzed to predict missing ratings/likes. Many CF systems collect and use users' explicitly entered preferences: ratings for items. However, in many real world scenarios ratings can be difficult to obtain or unavailable (e.g., news portals). Hence, recommenders have been also built by leveraging more abundant implicit feedback data, such as the log of item/page views or item purchases [9], which only indirectly signal users' preferences or opinions [10].

We say that an item is labeled (positively) by a user if the user performed an "action" on the item (e.g., the item was viewed or purchased). We note that it might be erroneous to conclude that since the user acted on an item, then the user liked it (implicit feedback). Besides, analysing user actions, it is even harder to reliably identify which items a user does not like. In fact, usually there is no explicitly negative feedback/action, and the items not acted by the user cannot be directly assigned to the "negative" label. Furthermore, data is usually extremely sparse and unbalanced [15]: only a small part of the items is labeled with actions.

Two general approaches to treat implicit feedback data in CF have been proposed: weighting [3, 12] and sampling [12]. The first one treats all the unlabeled items as negatively labeled examples and the (label) prediction model is based on weighted low-rank approximation [8]. The second uses a sampling strategy to draw some unlabeled items and treats them as negative examples. The source data is thus split into several parts where each part has the same positive examples and different negative and unlabeled examples. The final prediction model is built by employing all these data parts. Both approaches use a non-negative matrix of weights, which are called confidence weights, that indicate the confidence in the negativeness or positiveness of the assigned label. We stress that these systems can only predict whether an item is labeled positively, i.e., a user will act on it. When these systems recommend the positively predicted items it is implicitly assumed that the user likes the items on which she has acted.

In this paper we consider, simultaneously, multiple types of user actions, e.g., user clicks, user views, and user bookmarks. We introduce a method that reinforces the confidence weights, either for the positive or negative labels of an action (e.g., view), by leveraging observations of another type of action (e.g., click). The proposed method takes advantage of the existence of a range of action types to improve the confidence in certain observations for a given target action. For example, if a user opened the description of a

UMAP '16, July 13-17, 2016, Halifax, NS, Canada

© 2016 ACM. ISBN 978-1-4503-4370-1/16/07. . . $15.00

DOI: http://dx.doi.org/10.1145/2930238.2930284

movie, read it, watched a movie trailer but did not watch the movie, then the method increases the confidence that the user will not watch this movie. This information, as we will show in this short article, may help to develop a more accurate prediction model of the video views.

We note that this research initiated when we observed the existence of a correlation between the presence of an action of type A on an item with the absence of an action of another type B. We conjectured that this type of correlations may be generalized and leveraged to overcome the data sparsity problem and to better predict users' actions.

We conducted an experimental evaluation of the proposed method using a dataset provided by the mass media company P7S1[1]. We designed a novel, multiple actions, prediction model (MMF), that extends Hu's et al. [3] weighted CF model for implicit feedback (IMF). MMF incorporates multiple action types in order to better predict a target user action. The experiment results show that the proposed model outperforms IMF.

The rest of the paper is organized as follows. We introduce state-of-the-art user actions prediction techniques in Section 2. We then describe our general model and provide concrete examples of it in Section 3. Section 4 describes the data and Section 5 contains the results of our experiments. Finally, in Section 6 we conclude the paper and indicate some future work.

2. STATE OF THE ART

We start this section by introducing a state-of-the-art model (IMF) for predicting user actions that follows the approach proposed in [3]. Later we will generalize this model by considering observations for a range of action types.

The input data for the action prediction model is a $|U| \times |I|$ non-negative matrix, whose entries a_{ui} count the number of observed actions of user u on item i, e.g., the number of clicks on an item. If no action is observed then a_{ui} is zero.

The model predicts whether the user will act on a target item, hence an indicator function p, is introduced:

$$p_{ui} = \begin{cases} 1 & a_{ui} > 0 \\ 0 & a_{ui} = 0 \end{cases}$$

The model generates predictions $\hat{p}_{ui}$ for the items i where $p_{ui} = 0$. In fact, the absence of observed actions of the user u on item i does not mean that the user will not act on the item in the future. Hu et al. [3] interprets this prediction $\hat{p}_{ui}$ as a (predicted) preference for the item. For instance, in case the action is a click, a predicted click is interpreted as a predicted preference. We will not follow this interpretation and we will simply assume that the model predicts user actions.

IMF introduces also a confidence function:

$$c_{ui} = c(a_{ui})$$

which indicates the confidence in the value assigned to p_{ui} on the base of the observation a_{ui}. In fact, if $a_{ui} > 0$, hence $p_{ui} = 1$, the model should strongly rely on this information, as it is based on real observations of user u actions on the item i. Conversely, we should not force the model to rely on information that u never acted on i ($a_{ui} = 0$): the user may act on the item in the future, that is what we want to predict.

[1]http://www.prosiebensat1.com/

Furthermore, it might be the case that the user was never exposed to the item and therefore did not act on it. Hence, the confidence that $p_{ui} = 0$, for items where $a_{ui} = 0$ (i.e., when we miss observations) must be much smaller than the confidence that $p_{ui} = 1$ for items where $a_{ui} > 0$. Otherwise, if we strongly believe that $p_{ui} = 0$ when $a_{ui} = 0$, then there will be no point in building a prediction model $\hat{p}_{ui}$ for the items where $a_{ui} = 0$.

In IMF the target action prediction $\hat{p}_{ui}$ is computed using matrix factorization (MF). Each user u and item i is associated with an f-dimensional factors vector $x_u \in \mathbb{R}^f$ and $y_i \in \mathbb{R}^f$ respectively. The predicted value is computed by the inner product of these two vectors: $\hat{p}_{ui} = x_u^T y_i$. The factor vectors are computed by minimizing the following cost function:

$$\min_{x*, y*} \sum_{u,i} c_{ui}(p_{ui} - x_u^T y_i)^2 + \lambda(\sum_u \|x_u\|^2 + \sum_i \|y_i\|^2) \quad (1)$$

The constant λ weights the regularizer term to avoid model's overfitting [13]. The value of λ is data-dependent and determined by cross-validation.

In addition to IMF, other approaches have incorporated user- or item-related information to the confidence values to improve the prediction system results [5, 14, 2]. There are also models that predict a user's immediate next action by observing sequential patterns of actions [7, 16]. Moreover, existing models can be employed as components in more complex boosting [6] or hybrid [1, 11] techniques.

3. GENERAL MODEL AND EXAMPLES

In this paper we conjecture that the prediction accuracy of a model can be improved by leveraging the observation of a range of action types, i.e., not only the actions that are to be predicted. For instance, the information whether a user bookmarked a page may be useful to predict if the user will read a page.

We now describe our general action prediction model called MMF (Multiple action types Matrix Factorization). Suppose we have a dataset of $d + 1$ types of users' actions. The variable a_{ui}^j counts or measures the observations of an action of type j performed by a user u on an item i. We assume that there is a target action $j = 0$ (predicted), and non-target actions are instead those for $j \in \{1, \ldots, d\}$ (predictive).

The indication function of the target action p_{ui}^0 and the confidence c_{ui}^0 of the target action are now functions of all the observations for all the action types:

$$p_{ui}^0 = p(a_{ui}^0, a_{ui}^1, \ldots, a_{ui}^d) \qquad c_{ui}^0 = c(a_{ui}^0, a_{ui}^1, \ldots, a_{ui}^d)$$

As in IMF, in order to build the prediction model for the target action by using MF techniques one should minimize the cost-function in Equation 1. The difference, with respect to IMF, is due to the usage of different confidence and indicator matrices: c_{ui}^0 and p_{ui}^0. Moreover, the optimization process must consider all the possible u, i pairs, and the huge number of terms prevents us from applying the most direct optimization techniques, such as stochastic gradient descent. Thus, an alternating least squares (ALS) optimization procedure was employed.

Below we illustrate two applications of MMF related to P7S1's video streaming service 7TV[2] that provides access

[2]http://www.7tv.de/

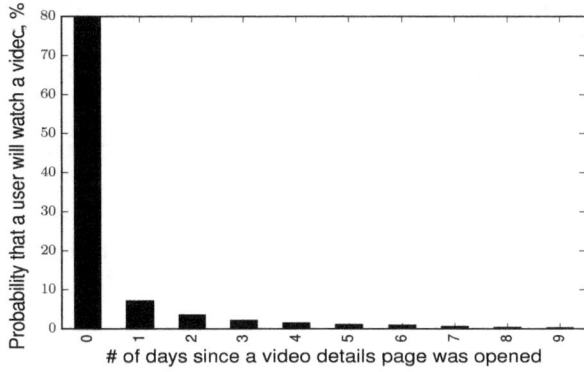

Figure 1: The distribution of probability that a user will start to watch a video after Δ days since the video details page was opened

to videos and TV-shows (a set of videos). We consider three types of actions: a user opened a video details page, a user stopped to watch a video and a user marked a TV-show as "watch later".

3.1 Predicting video views with open details actions

In the first example MMF predicts that a user will watch a video by also leveraging the observations of two additional action types: the user opened the video details page and the user stopped to watch a video.

Let $v_{ui} \in [0, 1]$ denote the percentage of video i viewed by user u. The service obtains this data when a user stops to watch a video. A positive example of the user target action (a user started to watch a video) is observed when $v_{ui} > 0$. So, in case only this target action type is used, the indicator function p can be defined as:

$$p_{ui} = \begin{cases} 1 & v_{ui} > 0 \\ 0 & v_{ui} = 0 \end{cases}$$

In general, as v_{ui} grows, we have stronger confidence that $p_{ui} = 1$. At the same time, for items where we missed observations the confidence that $p_{ui} = 0$ should be much smaller. A feasible choice for c_{ui} would be:

$$c_{ui} = 1 + \alpha v_{ui}$$

The parameter $\alpha \geq 0$ is a meta parameter that must be optimized. The value of α is data-dependent and determined by cross-validation. Increasing α places (proportionally) more weight on the non-zero observations while decreasing α places more weight on non-observed items.

Analyzing the data we noted that if a user opened a video details page but did not watch the video then there is a high probability that the user will not watch the video in the future. The probability is proportional to the time passed since the video details page was opened (Fig. 1).

This observation can be used to increase the confidence in the negative examples ($p_{ui} = 0$) of the target action. The more days are passed since the video details page was opened (the video still has not been watched), the higher must be the confidence that p_{ui} will stay equal to 0.

Let us denote with o_{ui} the variable indicating that a user has visited ($o_{ui} = 1$) or not ($o_{ui} = 0$) a video details page. Moreover, let Δ_{ui} be the number of days since the visit action, $o_{ui} = 1$, was observed, and $b^{-\Delta_{ui}}$ is the function that approximates the probability distribution displayed in Fig. 1. Then the confidence value is assumed to be as follow:

$$c_{ui} = \begin{cases} 1 + \alpha v_{ui} & v_{ui} > 0 \\ 1 + \beta(1 - b^{-\Delta_{ui}}) & v_{ui} = 0 \text{ and } o_{ui} = 1 \\ 1 & v_{ui} = 0 \text{ and } o_{ui} = 0 \end{cases}$$

Here α, β and b are data-dependent meta parameters that should be tuned. By cross-validation we found that $\alpha = 80$, $\beta = 8$ and $b = 10$ produce good results in our experiments. The parameter b should be greater than 1.

3.2 Predicting TV-show views with watch later actions

In the second example MMF predicts that a user will watch a TV-show. Even in this scenario we use observations of two action types: a user watches a video, and a user marks a TV-show as "watch later". We denote with $s_{ui} \in [0, 1]$ the percentage of a TV-show i viewed by a user u. The positive examples of the user target action (a user started to watch a TV-show) are observed when $s_{ui} > 0$.

In contrast to the previous example, the "watch later" action type can be here used to reinforce the confidence in positive examples of the target action. In fact, in 86% of cases a user watched a TV-show after she marked it as "watch later". Let $l_{ui} \in \{0, 1\}$ indicate the absence/presence of item i in the set of TV-shows that u would like to watch later. According to our data analysis, if a user adds an item to the "watch later" set, then there is a high probability that a user will watch such an item. Hence, the indicator function p can be defined as:

$$p_{ui} = \begin{cases} 1 & s_{ui} > 0 \text{ or } l_{ui} = 1 \\ 0 & s_{ui} = 0 \text{ and } l_{ui} = 0 \end{cases}$$

At the same time, we conjecture that the confidence that a user will watch a TV-show should be increased when a user marks it as "watch later". So, the confidence value can be defined as:

$$c_{ui} = \begin{cases} 1 + \alpha s_{ui} + \gamma l_{ui} & s_{ui} > 0 \text{ or } l_{ui} > 0 \\ 1 & s_{ui} = 0 \text{ and } l_{ui} = 0 \end{cases}$$

As in the previous example, α and γ are meta parameters that must be determined by cross-validation. In our experiments, setting $\alpha = 40$ and $\gamma = 5$ was found to produce optimal results.

4. DATASETS

The data[3] provided by mass media company P7S1 contains information about the interaction of users with the on-line video streaming service 7TV for one month. A user interacts with the service through a set of devices. For this reason we consider a device as a user, i.e., users are anonymised. Table 1 shows some statistics about the devices (users), videos and TV-shows (items), observations of different action types.

A "Video details opened action" record indicates that a user opened a video details page. A "Video view stopped

[3]http://www.inf.unibz.it/~gurbanov/vod_data.html

Table 1: Statistics of the used datasets

Collection name	Size
Devices	128k
Videos	23k
TV-shows	347
Video view stopped action	0.8M
Video details opened action	1.6M
Watch later action	1.1k

Table 2: "Video view stopped action" record

User	Video	Watched percent	Timestamp
4E6E8D...	380934	0.84	1438387203

Table 3: Comparison of IMF and MMF (f=20)

	Metric	IMF	MMF	Improvement
Video views prediction	MPR	12.9	12.6	2.3%
	R@20	17.1	17.3	1.1%
TV-show views prediction	MPR	27.3	24.4	10.6%
	R@20	38.8	44.8	15.5%

action" record contains the maximal percentage of a video viewed by a user. A "Watch later action" record refers to a TV-show that a user marked to watch it later. All action records contain the time when the action was performed. For the "Video view stopped action" type the *timestamp* field stores the last time a user watched the video (Table 2).

"Videos", "TV-shows" and "Devices" in Table 1 count only items that are found in the actions collections. The sparsity of the indicator and confidence values matrices are approximately 99.9%.

5. EVALUATION

In our experimental evaluation we have compared MMF with IMF. We used the actions from the first three weeks as training sets, while the more recent actions was used for validation and testing purposes. We indicate with T the test set of target actions, and the observation of an action in T is denoted with a_{ui}^t. In our datasets users often perform a target action multiple times. Because it is more interesting for a user to be recommended with items that she has not acted recently, or that she is not aware of [3], we removed from the test set T all the actions a_{ui}^t belonging to the target type that were already presented in the training set.

The models generate for each user a list of items sorted in descending order by their predicted value $\hat{p}_{ui}$. Since the test set contains only positive observations of the target action, precision based metrics are not appropriate to measure the quality of the compared models, hence, we used a recall measure: Mean Percentage Ranking (MPR) [4, 3]. MPR evaluates a user's satisfaction with an ordered list of items.

$$MPR(T) = \frac{\sum_{u,i \in T} a_{ui}^t rank_{ui}}{\sum_{u,i \in T} a_{ui}^t}$$

We denote by $rank_{ui}$ the percentile ranking of the item i within the ordered list of all the items predicted to receive the target action by user u. $rank_{ui} = 0\%$ indicates that i is predicted on top of the items that will be acted by u, while $rank_{ui} = 100\%$ indicates that i is predicted at the bottom of the ranked items for u. Lower values of MPR are better, as they indicate that users actually acted ($a_{ui}^t > 0$) on the clips that are ranked on top. Notice that a random ranking will have MPR equal to 50%. Thus, $MPR < 50\%$ indicates an algorithm better than random.

We also calculated Recall at 20 (R@20). We denote with S_u^{20} the top 20 items in the ranked list of the predicted items that will be acted by a user u, and with A_u^T the items on which the user u actually acted and present in T. If U_T

denotes the users in T then R@20 is defined as follow:

$$R@20(T) = \frac{1}{|U_T|} \sum_{u \in U_T} \frac{|S_u^{20} \cap A_u^T|}{|A_u^T|}$$

We evaluated the two example applications presented above for different number of latent factors $f \in \{10, 20, 30, 40\}$. We anticipate that for all these choices MMF outperforms IMF. Hence, we present the results only for the optimal number of latent factors, $f = 20$, which was found by cross validation on the training data.

In the first example the models predict that a user will watch a video, while in the second one the models predict that a user will watch a TV-show. IMF is trained by using only the target action data, while MMF uses also the "watch later" action type. As can be seen in Table 3, MMF outperforms IMF in terms of MPR and R@20.

We must observe that in the second example the "watch later" actions let us add positive examples of the indicator function, thereby increasing prediction recall. Conversely, in the first example by considering the "open video details" actions we can only tune the confidence of negative examples of the indicator function. That explains why the improvement brought by MMF is larger in the second case.

6. CONCLUSIONS

In this work we conjectured that multiple types of user actions, e.g., user clicks, user views, and user bookmarks, can be jointly exploited to predict one target type of actions. Hence, we have presented a general model (MMF) that predicts a target user action by leveraging information about actions of multiple types and we illustrated two practical applications of this model. The empirical evaluation of MMF, which was conducted on a large real world dataset, showed that using multiple actions is beneficial and can outperform a state-of-the-art implicit feedback model that uses only the target action data. This conclusion was not obvious since not all available action types may be relevant for the prediction of a target action. Moreover, the presence of latent relations between action types might have a negative impact on the prediction results.

The incorporation of multiple action types into the prediction requires the definition of specific indicator and confidence functions and the optimization of multiple meta parameters. Currently these functions have been identified heuristically, after an exploratory analysis of the data. As future work, we want to set up data mining solutions that can automatically discover the hidden relationships between actions of different types and compute the indicator and confidence functions. The ultimate goal of our research is the application of the proposed model as a component of a movie recommender system, hence we will also derive a preference model from the learned actions prediction model.

7. REFERENCES

[1] K. Choi, D. Yoo, G. Kim, and Y. Suh. A hybrid online-product recommendation system: Combining implicit rating-based collaborative filtering and sequential pattern analysis. *Electron. Commer. Rec. Appl.*, 11(4):309–317, July 2012.

[2] Y. Fang and L. Si. Matrix co-factorization for recommendation with rich side information and implicit feedback. In *Proceedings of the 2Nd International Workshop on Information Heterogeneity and Fusion in Recommender Systems*, HetRec '11, pages 65–69, New York, NY, USA, 2011. ACM.

[3] Y. Hu, Y. Koren, and C. Volinsky. Collaborative filtering for implicit feedback datasets. In *Proceedings of the 2008 Eighth IEEE International Conference on Data Mining*, ICDM '08, pages 263–272, Washington, DC, USA, 2008. IEEE Computer Society.

[4] C. C. Johnson. Logistic matrix factorization for implicit feedback data. *Advances in Neural Information Processing Systems*, 27, 2014.

[5] Y. Li, J. Hu, C. Zhai, and Y. Chen. Improving one-class collaborative filtering by incorporating rich user information. In *Proceedings of the 19th ACM International Conference on Information and Knowledge Management*, CIKM '10, pages 959–968, New York, NY, USA, 2010. ACM.

[6] Y. Liu, P. Zhao, A. Sun, and C. Miao. A boosting algorithm for item recommendation with implicit feedback. In *Proceedings of the 24th International Conference on Artificial Intelligence*, IJCAI'15, pages 1792–1798. AAAI Press, 2015.

[7] B. Mobasher, H. Dai, T. Luo, and M. Nakagawa. Using sequential and non-sequential patterns in predictive web usage mining tasks. In *Data Mining, 2002. ICDM 2003. Proceedings. 2002 IEEE International Conference on*, pages 669–672, 2002.

[8] N. S. Nati and T. Jaakkola. Weighted low-rank approximations. In *In 20th International Conference on Machine Learning*, pages 720–727. AAAI Press, 2003.

[9] E. R. Núñez Valdéz, J. M. Cueva Lovelle, O. Sanjuán Martínez, V. García-Díaz, P. Ordoñez de Pablos, and C. E. Montenegro Marin. Implicit feedback techniques on recommender systems applied to electronic books. *Comput. Hum. Behav.*, 28(4):1186–1193, July 2012.

[10] D. Oard and J. Kim. Implicit feedback for recommender systems. In *in Proceedings of the AAAI Workshop on Recommender Systems*, pages 81–83, 1998.

[11] V. C. Ostuni, T. Di Noia, E. Di Sciascio, and R. Mirizzi. Top-n recommendations from implicit feedback leveraging linked open data. In *Proceedings of the 7th ACM Conference on Recommender Systems*, RecSys '13, pages 85–92, New York, NY, USA, 2013. ACM.

[12] R. Pan, Y. Zhou, B. Cao, N. N. Liu, R. Lukose, M. Scholz, and Q. Yang. One-class collaborative filtering. In *Proceedings of the 2008 Eighth IEEE International Conference on Data Mining*, ICDM '08, pages 502–511, Washington, DC, USA, 2008. IEEE Computer Society.

[13] A. Paterek. Improving regularized singular value decomposition for collaborative filtering. *Proceedings of KDD Cup and Workshop*, pages 39–42, 2007.

[14] L. Peska and P. Vojtás. Evaluating the importance of various implicit factors in e-commerce. In X. Amatriain, P. Castells, A. P. de Vries, C. Posse, and H. Steck, editors, *Proceedings of the Workshop on Recommendation Utility Evaluation: Beyond RMSE, RUE 2012, Dublin, Ireland, September 9, 2012*, volume 910 of *CEUR Workshop Proceedings*, pages 51–55. CEUR-WS.org, 2012.

[15] F. Ricci, L. Rokach, and B. Shapira. *Recommender Systems Handbook*. Springer US, New York, NY, USA, 2nd edition, 2015.

[16] D. Rosaci. Cilios: Connectionist inductive learning and inter-ontology similarities for recommending information agents. *Information Systems*, 32(6):793 – 825, 2007.

Incorporating Student Response Time and Tutor Instructional Interventions into Student Modeling

Chen Lin, Shitian Shen, Min Chi
Department of Computer Science
North Carolina State University
{clin12, sshen, mchi}@ncsu.edu

ABSTRACT

Bayesian Knowledge Tracing (BKT) is one of the most widely adopted student-modeling methods. It uses *performance* (*incorrect, correct*) to infer student knowledge state (*unlearned, learned*). However, performance can be noisy and thus we explored another type of observations – student response time. Furthermore, we proposed Intervention Bayesian Knowledge Tracing (Intervention-BKT) which can incorporate multiple types of instructional interventions into the conventional BKT model. Our results show that for next-step performance predictions, Intervention-BKT is more effective than BKT; whereas to predict students' post-test scores, including student response time would yield better result than using performance alone.

Keywords

Hidden Markov Model; Input Output Hidden Markov Model; Student Modeling; Response Time

1. INTRODUCTION

Bayesian Knowledge Tracing (BKT) [5] is a widely used student-modeling approach for Intelligent Tutoring Systems (ITSs). In this paper, we extended the conventional BKT model by leveraging student response time and tutor instructional interventions. The conventional BKT model infers students' hidden knowledge states mainly from their performance (i.e., *correct, incorrect*). Nevertheless, student performance can be noisy because many ITSs allow students to refer to external resources for information. The ability to solicit help from external resources obscures the fact of whether a student has truly learned or not. On the other hand, ever since the mid-1950s, response time has been used as a preferred dependent variable in cognitive psychology [13]. It has mainly been used to assess student learning because response time can indicate how active and accessible student knowledge is. For example, it is shown that response time reveals student proficiency [11] and there was a significant negative correlation between student average response

UMAP '16, July 13–17, 2016, Halifax, Nova Scotia, Canada.

© 2016 Copyright held by the owner/author(s). Publication rights licensed to ACM.
ISBN 978-1-4503-4370-1/16/07...$15.00

DOI: http://dx.doi.org/10.1145/2930238.2930291

time and student final exam score taken at the end of the semester [7]. To build effective student modeling, in this paper we explored three types of observations: the conventional *performance*, the proposed *student response time*, and the *combined* which uses both.

To further improve our model, we incorporate multiple types of instructional interventions into the conventional BKT framework. Instructional interventions indicate actions initiated by the system to guide student learning activity. We proposed a new approach called Intervention-Bayesian Knowledge Tracing (Intervention-BKT). To determine whether introducing response time and instructional intervention lead to better student models, we constructed nine model variations {BKT, BKT (without tell), Intervention-BKT} × {*performance, time, combined*}. These nine model variations were tested on two important prediction tasks: 1) to predict students' next step performance and 2) to predict their post-test scores.

2. RELATED WORK

In recent years a variety of BKT extensions have been proposed. For example, Pardos and Heffernan [10] added problem nodes to capture item difficulty. Their model achieved performance gain on the ASSISTments dataset, but not on the Cognitive Tutor dataset. In addition, Pardos and Heffernan proposed Prior Per Student model [9], which adds a multinomial node representing student's incoming competence. They showed their model performed better than the BKT. Yudelson et al [15] later revisited the same problem and showed parametrizing student speed of learning is even more effective. Finally, Baker and Corbett [6] proposed to contextually estimate whether each student guesses or slips [1]. Their model showed greater accuracy and reliability compared to the conventional BKT model.

While much research leverages performance to assess student knowledge, relatively little research was done using student response time. Beck et.al. modeled student disengagement using student response time [8] and their models were based on the item response theory (IRT). Additionally, Shih B. et al. [12] built a response-time based indicator that can detect good bottom-out hint behaviors (i.e., exploit hints as worked examples). Finally, Wang and Heffernan [14] combined the BKT model together with student response time to predict student performance and their results showed that the proposed model was slightly better than using the BKT alone. Note that they did not incorporate response time into the BKT model while we directly incorporated response time within the Bayesian framework and explored three types of observation: *performance*, *time* and *combined* to model student knowledge.

Finally, prior research on student modeling showed that it is still an open question whether incorporating various instructional interventions into the BKT would indeed lead to better performance. For example, Beck et al. proposed the HELP model [2] to measure the impact of the tutors' help. Their results showed that HELP model did not yield a more accurate prediction compared to the BKT.

3. METHOD

Fundamentally, the BKT model is a two-state Hidden Markov Model (HMM). It is [4] characterized by five parameters *Prior Knowledge*, *Learning rate*, *Forget Rate*, *Guess* and *Slip*. The BKT [5] model continually updates its parameters based upon the observation of student's performance history. Note that, the conventional BKT does not take the different types of instructional interventions into account.

Intervention-BKT is a special case of Input Output Hidden Markov Model (IOHMM) [4], which is extended from HMM. Therefore, fundamentally the Intervention-BKT model is an extension to the BKT model. The Bayesian network topology of the Intervention-BKT is displayed in Figure 1. Compared with BKT, Intervention-BKT adds a sequence of unshaded input nodes I. The input nodes I represent instructional interventions. Each input node I carries a pair of extra edges with arrows pointing to the corresponding knowledge state S and student observation nodes O. The arrows between input nodes I and student observation nodes O represent how instructional interventions affect a student's performance. The arrows between input nodes I and knowledge state nodes S represent how instructional interventions affect a student's hidden knowledge state. Thus, the Intervention-BKT employs $1 + 4 \times K$ parameters (compared with 5 parameters of BKT). The Prior Knowledge share the same definition as the conventional BKT: Prior Knowledge= $P(S_0=\text{learned})$. For each of the K types of interventions $A_j, j \in [1, K]$, the Intervention-BKT defines four conditional parameters, the *Learning rate*, *Forget Rate*, *Guess* and *Slip* parameters for A_j :

Learning Rate$_{A_j}$ = P(learned|unlearned, $I_t = A_j$)
Forget$_{A_j}$ = P(unlearned|learned, $I_t = A_j$)
Guess$_{A_j}$ = P(correct|unlearned, $I_t = A_j$)
Slip$_{A_j}$ = P(incorrect|learned, $I_t = A_j$)

In this paper, we mainly focus on modeling two types of instructional intervention (K=2) *elicit* and *tell*. A possible sequence of instructional interventions is suggested above input node in Figure 1. Note that the Intervention-BKT model is trained from a sequence of instructional interventions and a sequence of corresponding performance extracted from the log files directly.

The second goal of our paper is to explore the benefits of using student response time to infer student hidden knowledge, instead of using students' performance alone. Response time measures how long a student has spent on a given attempt. It is denoted by one of two symbols: *quick* and *slow*. The symbols were assigned by comparing the student's response time on that given step with the median response time of all students on the same step. If the time

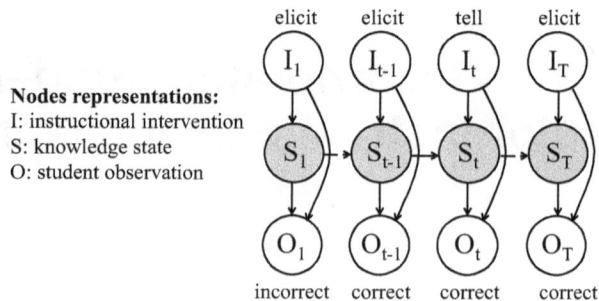

Figure 1: The Bayesian network topology of the Intervention-BKT model

is greater than the median, we classify it as *slow*, otherwise, *quick*. Note that, when tutor *tells*, we automatically assigned the symbol *quick* based on the assumption that all students spent the same amount of time reading the content.

In short, we constructed both the BKT and the Interventional-BKT with three types of observations: 1) *performance*: the correctness of entry on a step; 2) *time*: the speed of the student's response on a step and 3) *combined*: a combination of *performance* and *time*.

4. TRAINING CORPUS

Cordillera is a Natural Language ITS teaching college level introductory physics. All participants in our training corpus experienced identical procedure: 1) completed a survey; 2) read a textbook; 3) took a pretest; 4) solved seven training problems, and finally 5) took a post-test.

In the learning literature, it is commonly considered that relevant knowledge in domains such as math and science is structured as a set of independent but co-occurring Knowledge Components (KCs). A *Knowledge Component (KC)* is the atomic unit of knowledge. It is: "a generalization of everyday terms like concept, principle, fact, or skill, and cognitive science terms like schema, production rule, misconception, or facet" . It is assumed that the student's knowledge state at one KC has no impact on the student's understanding of any other KCs. This is an idealization, but it has served ITS developers well for many decades, and is a fundamental assumption made by many student models [5].

Cordillera consists of a subset of the physics work-energy domain, which is characterized by five primary KCs: Kinetic Energy(KE), Gravitational Potential Energy(GPE), Spring Potential Energy (SPE), Total Mechanical Energy (TME) and Conservation of Total Mechanical Energy (CTME). Given the KCs' independence assumptions, our student model was constructed and evaluated for each of the five primary KCs individually. However, in Cordillera, some steps have mixed KC, thus we also trained on sequences of observations irregardless of the KCs involved (denoted by OVERALL).

Cordillera provides two types of instructional interventions *elicit* and *tell*. *Elicit* usually takes the form of a question, e.g., which principle will help you calculate the rock's instantaneous magnitude of velocity at T1? *Tell* usually takes the form of a written statement, i.e., to calculate the rock's instantaneous magnitude of velocity at T1, we will apply the definition of kinetic energy again.

In our datasets, the instructional intervention *elicit* or *tell* were guided by different pedagogical rules. We used

Table 1: Accuracy in Next Step Performance Prediction

KC	Data		BKT			BKT (without tell)			Intervention-BKT		
			Perf 1	Time 2	Comb 3	Perf 4	Time 5	Comb 6	Perf 7	Time 8	Comb 9
K	Eff	1	0.814*	0.636	0.814*	0.787	0.484	0.805	0.814*	0.535	0.751
	Acr	2	0.740	0.652	0.740	0.734	0.496	0.740	0.749*	0.630	0.746
	Ine	3	0.717	0.682	0.717	0.716	0.512	0.708	0.728*	0.670	0.728*
G	Eff	4	0.766	0.557	0.766	0.772*	0.530	0.757	0.763	0.602	0.763
	Acr	5	0.704*	0.643	0.704*	0.704*	0.532	0.704*	0.696	0.608	0.692
	Ine	6	0.685*	0.668	0.685*	0.685*	0.530	0.685*	0.683	0.611	0.679
S	Eff	7	0.825*	0.779	0.825*	0.825*	0.318	0.825*	0.825*	0.782	0.820
	Acr	8	0.713	0.713	0.713	0.713	0.440	0.713	0.720*	0.713	0.720*
	Ine	9	0.680	0.680	0.680	0.649	0.474	0.660	0.700*	0.680	0.700*
T	Eff	10	0.778*	0.599	0.778*	0.762	0.466	0.778*	0.777	0.538	0.675
	Acr	11	0.689	0.593	0.689	0.693	0.480	0.689	0.701*	0.598	0.694
	Ine	12	0.660	0.601	0.660	0.667	0.486	0.660	0.675*	0.628	0.675*
C	Eff	13	0.771	0.771	0.771	0.771	0.628	0.771	0.734	0.775*	0.725
	Acr	14	0.657	0.657	0.657	0.650	0.593	0.650	0.665*	0.629	0.650
	Ine	15	0.635	0.635	0.635	0.555	0.584	0.628	0.650*	0.604	0.626
O	Eff	16	0.790	0.659	0.785	0.782	0.507	0.787	0.794*	0.542	0.786
	Acr	17	0.708	0.650	0.708	0.699	0.511	0.708	0.722*	0.598	0.712
	Ine	18	0.683	0.663	0.683	0.678	0.521	0.683	0.698*	0.604	0.694

Note: the highest accuracy are marked by * and best models are shaded

three types of training datasets *Effective, Ineffective* and *Across*. According to prior literature [3], *Effective* was generated from training corpus implementing effective pedagogical rules; while the *Ineffective* datasets was generated from training corpus implementing ineffective rules contributing less to student learning. *Across* contained both datasets. Since students learn differently in each training corpus, we trained a separate model for each of them.

The overall dataset comprises 38028 data points from 158 students. Among them, 5810 data points from 29 students belong to the *Effective* dataset and 32218 data points from 129 students belong to the *Ineffective* dataset. There were no significant training time difference among these three datasets. On average, it took students roughly 4-9 hours to complete the training. The average number of Cordillera-student interactions was more than 280. A data point in our training datasets is either the first attempt by a student in response to a system *elicit*, or a system *tell* during the student's training on Cordillera.

5. EXPERIMENT

In our experiment, nine models {BKT, BKT (without tell), Intervention-BKT} × {performance, time, combined} were evaluated across three corpus {*Effective, Across, Ineffective*} on six primary KCs {KE, GPE, SPE, TME, CTME, OVERALL}. Thus, we constructed nine models for the eighteen datasets. Note that BKT (without tell) only considers the student observation corresponding to a tutor elicits, while BKT considers the correctness in a log file irregardless of whether it is generated by tutor *elicits* or tutor *tells*.

We focused on two prediction tasks. The first task is to predict students' next step performance in training, referred to as "next step performance predictions". The second task is to predict their post-test scores, referred to as "post-test scores predictions". For the first task, the model estimates $P(S_t = learned)$ at each learning opportunity, then uses the previous state probability to predict the next observation $P(O_t = correct)$ by using the formula below. The formula for conventional BKT is shown in Equation (1) and (2).

$$P(S_t = learned) \qquad (1)$$
$$= P(S_{t-1} = learned)*(1 - Forget) + P(S_{t-1} = unlearned)* Learning\ Rate$$

$$P(O_t = correct) \qquad (2)$$
$$= P(S_t = learned)*(1 - Slip) + P(S_t = unlearned)*Guess$$

For Intervention-BKT, it uses a similar equations but with *Learning Rate, Forget Rate, Guess* and *Slip* parameters conditioned on the intervention type at time t, that is I_t.

Note that for different types of observations, *Slip* and *Guess* were calculated differently. When we used *performance*, *Slip* and *Guess* have already been learned and their values can be looked up in the emission probability table. When we used *time*, the model could not estimate *Slip* and *Guess*, as it only learns the probability that, given the students' learning states, whether their observation of response time is *quick* or *slow*. Therefore, we set both *Slip* and *Guess* to be 0.2 based on expert guess. When we used *combined*, we calculated *Slip* and *Guess* by looking up the values of the entries in emission tables. And calculate the *Guess* and *Slip* using the formula as shown below for BKT. Similarly, for Intervention-BKT, *Guess* and *Slip* are conditioned on the corresponding instructional interventions.

$$Slip = P(incorrect, slow|learned) \qquad (3)$$
$$+ P(incorrect, quick|learned)$$

$$Guess = P(correct, slow|unlearned) \qquad (4)$$
$$+ P(correct, quick|unlearned)$$

For the second task, both BKT and Intervention-BKT

Table 2: RMSE in Post-test Score Prediction

KC	Data		BKT			BKT (without tell)			Intervention-BKT		
			Perf 1	Time 2	Comb 3	Perf 4	Time 5	Comb 6	Perf 7	Time 8	Comb 9
K	Eff	1	0.295	0.236	0.288	0.279	0.298	0.214*	0.271	0.260	0.235
	Acr	2	0.357	0.235	0.359	0.263	0.242	0.241	0.249	0.190*	0.244
	Ine	3	0.378	0.234	0.380	0.261	0.222	0.245	0.246	0.183*	0.242
G	Eff	4	0.229	0.165	0.226	0.160*	0.285	0.167	0.175	0.248	0.176
	Acr	5	0.306	0.263	0.306	0.212*	0.306	0.218	0.233	0.267	0.229
	Ine	6	0.330	0.276	0.330	0.261	0.222	0.245	0.246	0.183*	0.242
S	Eff	7	0.368	0.254	0.367	0.283	0.290	0.288	0.317	0.215*	0.316
	Acr	8	0.420	0.319	0.418	0.278	0.296	0.279	0.289	0.264*	0.286
	Ine	9	0.434	0.335	0.432	0.278*	0.300	0.279	0.286	0.279	0.284
T	Eff	10	0.287	0.254	0.277	0.233	0.281	0.194*	0.218	0.232	0.196
	Acr	11	0.347	0.233	0.343	0.236	0.282	0.204	0.229	0.198*	0.220
	Ine	12	0.363	0.236	0.355	0.231	0.277	0.211	0.229	0.194*	0.222
C	Eff	13	0.307	0.216*	0.296	0.246	0.263	0.244	0.256	0.258	0.254
	Acr	14	0.326	0.278	0.323	0.244*	0.319	0.246	0.254	0.295	0.252
	Ine	15	0.336	0.293	0.334	0.244*	0.330	0.250	0.257	0.303	0.256
O	Eff	16	0.332	0.180*	0.331	0.284	0.256	0.234	0.268	0.220	0.249
	Acr	17	0.367	0.249	0.367	0.256	0.270	0.240*	0.277	0.244	0.262
	Ine	18	0.381	0.269	0.382	0.252	0.274	0.242*	0.279	0.253	0.266

Note: the lowest RMSE are marked by * and best models are shaded

traced a student's knowledge until the last step on Cordillera. Then the probability that a student gives a correct response in post-test can be calculated based on the probability that the student is in the learned state on the final step. We assume that no learning occurs during the post-test and thus the students' knowledge state would not change.

6. RESULTS

Accuracy and Leave One Out Cross Validation Root Mean Square Error (LOOCV RMSE) were used to evaluate the outcomes of these two prediction tasks respectively. Accuracy evaluates how well our models correctly identify an *incorrect* or a *correct* student responses: the higher the value, the better. LOOCV RMSE measures the difference between our predicted post-test scores and the actual post-test scores: the lower the value, the better.

Table 1 shows the model's **accuracy** in predicting students' next step performance during training. Columns represent 9 different models. Rows represent 18 different datsets: 6 primary KCs (denoted by K, G, S, T, C and O) on 3 types of training corpus (denoted by Eff, Acr and Ine). The highest accuracy among the 9 models for each dataset is marked *. Then the best model is selected among the ones producing the highest accuracy and when there is a tie, the best model is the one *involving the least number of parameters*. The cells contain the best model are shaded.

Table 1 shows that 12 out of the 18 shaded cells are produced by Intervention-BKT. 5 of them are BKT (without tell) and only 1 of them is BKT. Thus, the Intervention-BKT seemingly leads to better prediction than BKT-based models. Moreover, among the three types of observations, performance is the best choice for next step performance prediction since 16 out of 18 best models used performance.

Table 2 presents the **LOOCV RMSE** for Post-test Scores Predictions. For this task, the lowest LOOCV RMSE are all marked * and the best models are shaded. From the shaded cells we can see there is no clear winner between BKT (without tell) and Interventional-BKT as they generate 9 and 7 best models respectively. The conventional BKT produces the worst result. 13 out of 18 best models use *time* or *combined* observations while only 5 are produced by using *performance*. It seems including students' response time makes better predictions than using *performance* only.

7. DISCUSSION

In this paper, we made two major contributions: 1) we leveraged student response time to infer students' knowledge, and 2) we proposed Intervention-BKT that can incorporate different types of instructional interventions into student models and learn different parameters for each type of interventions. We trained nine different model variations and tested them on two types of predictions: 1) students' next step performance prediction and 2) students' post-test scores predictions.

For future work, we will explore other *Guess* and *Slip* parameter when using *time* instead of using 0.2 based on expert guess. Secondly, we will explore other ways to classify students' response time: for example, classifying them into {*too fast, reasonable, too slow*} instead of {*quick, slow*}. Third, we will evaluate the effectiveness of our models to other datasets in other domains to determine whether our proposed model is indeed robust. Finally, we will apply our model in systems that involve other types of tutor instructional interventions, such as *skip* (*elicit* a question without asking students for explanation) and *justify* (ask students to explain after they give an answer).

Acknowledgments

This research was supported by the NSF Grant 1432156 "Educational Data Mining for Individualized Instruction in STEM Learning Environments".

8. REFERENCES

[1] J. Beck. Difficulties in inferring student knowledge from observations (and why you should care). In *Educational Data Mining: Supplementary Proceedings of the 13th International Conference of Artificial Intelligence in Education*, pages 21–30, 2007.

[2] J. E. Beck, K.-m. Chang, J. Mostow, and A. Corbett. Does help help? introducing the bayesian evaluation and assessment methodology. In *ITS*, pages 383–394. Springer, 2008.

[3] M. Chi, K. VanLehn, and D. Litman. Do micro-level tutorial decisions matter: Applying reinforcement learning to induce pedagogical tutorial tactics. In *Intelligent Tutoring Systems*, pages 224–234. Springer, 2010.

[4] S. Chiappa and S. Bengio. Hmm and iohmm modeling of eeg rhythms for asynchronous bci systems. Technical report, IDIAP, 2003.

[5] A. T. Corbett and J. R. Anderson. Knowledge tracing: Modeling the acquisition of procedural knowledge. *UMAP*, 4(4):253–278, 1994.

[6] R. S. d Baker, A. T. Corbett, and V. Aleven. More accurate student modeling through contextual estimation of slip and guess probabilities in bayesian knowledge tracing. In *Intelligent Tutoring Systems*, pages 406–415. Springer, 2008.

[7] W. J. González-Espada and D. W. Bullock. Innovative applications of classroom response systems: Investigating students' item response times in relation to final course grade, gender, general point average, and high school act scores. *Electronic Journal for the Integration of Technology in Education*, 6:97–108.

[8] E. Joseph. Engagement tracing: using response times to model student disengagement. *Artificial intelligence in education: Supporting learning through intelligent and socially informed technology*, 125:88, 2005.

[9] Z. A. Pardos and N. T. Heffernan. Modeling individualization in a bayesian networks implementation of knowledge tracing. In *UMAP*, pages 255–266. Springer, 2010.

[10] Z. A. Pardos and N. T. Heffernan. Kt-idem: Introducing item difficulty to the knowledge tracing model. In *User Modeling, Adaption and Personalization*, pages 243–254. Springer, 2011.

[11] D. L. Schnipke and D. J. Scrams. Exploring issues of examinee behavior: Insights gained from response-time analyses. *Computer-based testing: Building the foundation for future assessments*, pages 237–266, 2002.

[12] B. Shih, K. R. Koedinger, and R. Scheines. A response time model for bottom-out hints as worked examples. *Handbook of educational data mining*, pages 201–212, 2011.

[13] R. D. L. V. S. Thomas et al. *Response Times: Their Role in Inferring Elementary Mental Organization: Their Role in Inferring Elementary Mental Organization*. Oxford University Press, USA, 1986.

[14] Y. Wang and N. T. Heffernan. Leveraging first response time into the knowledge tracing model. *International Educational Data Mining Society*, 2012.

[15] M. V. Yudelson, K. R. Koedinger, and G. J. Gordon. Individualized bayesian knowledge tracing models. In *Artificial intelligence in education*, pages 171–180. Springer, 2013.

An Eye-Tracking Study: Implication to Implicit Critiquing Feedback Elicitation in Recommender Systems

Li Chen and Feng Wang
Department of Computer Science
Hong Kong Baptist University, China
{lichen,fwang}@comp.hkbu.edu.hk

ABSTRACT

The *critiquing-based recommender system* (CBRS) stimulates users to critique the recommended item in terms of its attribute values. It has been shown that such *critiquing feedback* can effectively improve users' decision quality, especially in complex decision environments such as e-commerce, tourism, and finance. However, because its explicit elicitation process unavoidably demands extra user efforts, the application in real situations is limited. In this paper, we report an eye-tracking experiment with the objective of studying the relationship between users' eye gazes as laid on recommended items and their critiquing feedback. The results indicate the feasibility of inferring users' feedback based on their eye movements. It hence points out a promising roadmap to developing unobtrusive eye-based feedback elicitation for recommender systems.

CCS Concepts

•**Human-centered computing → Empirical studies in interaction design;** *User models; User studies;* •**Information systems** → *Recommender systems;*

Keywords

Recommender systems; feedback elicitation; critiquing; eye tracking; user study

1. INTRODUCTION

During the past decade, recommender systems have popularly been applied in various online scenarios to aid users in confronting overwhelming information and making effective decisions. It has been shown that the existing techniques such as collaborative filtering and content-based approaches are capable of estimating users' preferences based on their historical data like ratings [20]. However, in practical situations, especially in complex decision environments (e.g., e-commerce, tourism, and finance domains), where users have

UMAP '16, July 13-17, 2016, Halifax, NS, Canada

© 2016 ACM. ISBN 978-1-4503-4370-1/16/07...$15.00

DOI: http://dx.doi.org/10.1145/2930238.2930286

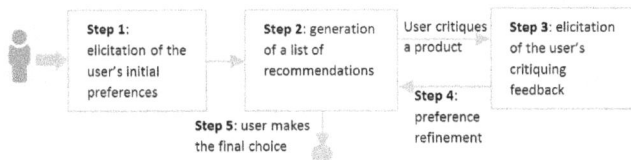

Figure 1: Workflow of a representative critiquing-based recommender system called Example Critiquing [4].

left few transaction records, it is difficult to adopt these techniques to predict user preferences and generate recommendation. In order to resolve this problem, the *critiquing-based recommenders system (CBRS)* has emerged, which distinguishes itself in feedback elicitation [1, 16, 4, 7]. Concretely, it involves users in a conversational dialog with the system so as to elicit their feedback and construct their preference model on site. Figure 1 shows the workflow of a representative CBRS called Example Critiquing [4]. It first presents some example products to a user according to her/his initially specified preferences. It then stimulates the user to select a near-satisfactory product and critique it in terms of its attribute values (such as "*I would like to see some laptops with different manufactures and higher processor speed*"). The system will refine its understanding of the user's preferences based on her/his critique and generate a new set of recommendations in the next interaction cycle. For a user to reach his/her target choice, a number of critiquing cycles are usually required. Prior work states that a typical user has many constraints and preferences, but s/he can only become aware of these latent preferences when some solutions are proposed [3]. Obtaining their critiques to recommendation has hence been regarded as an effective mechanism to disclose their latent preferences and help them to improve decision quality [7].

However, the applicability of existing CBRSs is limited as they mostly require users to *explicitly* specify their critiques in each recommendation cycle. As shown in previous studies, some users are subject to avoid making critiques due to the extra efforts it causes [5, 12]. The challenging question that CBRS faces is: *Is it possible to elicit users' critiquing feedback through implicit and unobtrusive way?*

In this paper, we are interested in investigating the relationship between users' eye-gaze behavior when they view recommendations and their critiquing feedback. The results could thus be suggestive for developing eye-based feedback elicitation in CBRS. Indeed, the eye and its movements, being "a window to the mind", are tightly coupled with human cognitive processes [15]. Given that advanced eye-tracking instrument makes it feasible to identify how a user's attention is directed in relation to an interface, we may treat the eye measures as implicit feedback to sense the user's interest and intention. With this objective, we have performed an eye-tracking experiment that in depth examines users' eye-gaze behavior at both *product level* and *attribute level*.

2. RELATED WORK

The development of eye tracking technology has enabled academic and commercial sectors to apply it in various interaction designs [14, 10, 17]. In recommender systems, it has mainly be adopted for two purposes. One is to evaluate the usability of a recommendation interface. For instance, one user experiment measured the effect of interface layout on users' visual searching pattern [6]. It shows that users tend to fixate more on the top area if recommended items are displayed in a list layout, but will be directed to view more items if they are arranged in a category structure. Another experiment investigated whether users would gaze at recommendation during their entire product searching process [2]. Its results clarify the important role of recommendation in users' purchase decision.

As the second purpose, some researchers have exploited eye-gaze metrics to elicit users' implicit *relevance feedback* on recommendation, i.e., "positive" or "negative" (or called "like" or "dislike"). For instance, in [11], the documents that users consume higher number of fixations and longer average fixation time are regarded with "positive" feedback. They then use clustering and content based techniques to retrieve similar documents and recommend them to the user. Some studies aim at developing algorithms, e.g., interactive genetic algorithm [8], evolutionary programming [13], and attention prediction method [23], to incorporate the eye-based *relevant feedback* into the process of inferring users' preferences for images, documents, videos, or e-commerce products.

However, little work has exerted to elicit users' specific feedback to product attributes through eye tracking. The eye-based application in CBRS is even rare. As mentioned before, CBRS aims to obtain users' *critiquing feedback*, which contains not only the user's preference for a product to critique, but also her/his multi-type critiquing criteria for the product's attributes. Its elicitation procedure is hence more challenging than that for relevance feedback.

3. EXPERIMENT SETUP

3.1 Materials and Participants

We choose Example Critiquing as the experiment system to obtain users' explicit critiques. Its laptop catalog was extracted from a commercial e-commerce website. During each recommendation cycle, 25 laptops that best match the user's current preferences are returned. Each laptop is described by three blocks of information in the recommendation interface: title (e.g., "Apple 15 MacBook Pro Notebook"), image, and ten major attributes' values (i.e., manufacturer, price, operating system, battery life, display size, hard drive capacity, installed memory, processor class, processor speed, and weight). Within the set of recommendations, if the user cannot locate her/his target choice, s/he can select one product that is near-satisfactory and provide critiquing

feedback on it. Specifically, for each attribute of the selected product, the user can make one of the following three critiques: "**Keep**" - keeping the attribute's existing value (default choice); "**Improve**" - improving the attribute's value, e.g., "cheaper", "bigger size"; "**Compromise**" - accepting a compromised value. Essentially, the critique that involves both "improve" and "compromise" is a kind of tradeoff decision, i.e., accepting an outcome that is undesirable in some respects but advantageous in others [19].

The experiment is in form of a controlled lab study. A Tobii 1750 eye-tracker that is integrated with a 17" TFT screen is used to record each subject's eye movements when s/he views recommended products. Its resolution setting is 1290x1024 pixels, and can sample the position of a user's eyes by every 20ms. The monitor frame has near infra-red light-emitting diodes, which allow for natural eye tracking without placing many restrictions on the user.

We recruited 18 participants (2 females) to join the study (according to [9], this scale is acceptable for an eye tracking study), who were interested in buying a laptop at the time of experiment. They are from nine different countries (e.g., China, Switzerland, Italy, Spain, India, USA, etc.), and most of them were students pursuing Master or PhD degree in the university.

3.2 Experiment Procedure and Measurement

The user task was to "*find a product you would purchase if given the opportunity by using the Example Critiquing system.*" An administrator was present in each experiment. She debriefed the experiment's objective to the participant and asked her/him to fill in a demographic questionnaire at the beginning. Then, the participant was prompted to get familiar with the Example Critiquing system's interfaces during a warm-up period. Afterwards, the eye-tracker calibration was performed, and the participant started to use the system to accomplish the given task. In the mean time, her/his eye-gaze behavior and mouse clicking actions were automatically recorded by the eye-tracker.

The process of deriving useful information from eye-gaze recordings is usually to analyze users' fixations. Each fixation is a spatially stable gaze point, during which most information acquisition and processing occur. We set its minimum duration as 200ms according to [21]. We performed two levels of fixation analysis: *product level* and *attribute level*. At product level, any fixations that fall inside the boundary of a product that contains its title, image and major attributes' values are treated equally. At attribute level, fixations laid on different attributes (e.g, price and operating system) are analyzed individually.

Regarding fixation metrics, we adopted three commonly used measures [18, 9, 22]: **Fixation Count (FC)** - the number of times the user fixates on a product or an attribute; **Total Fixation Duration (TFD)** - the sum of the duration of all fixations the user has laid on a product or an attribute; **Average Fixation Duration (AFD)** - the average duration of a fixation on a product or an attribute. These three metrics generally represent users' relative engagement with the interface object [18, 22]. More fixations on an object suggest that it is more noticeable and important. A longer duration may indicate that the fixated object is more engaging in some way.

From users' clicking actions, we retrieved their actual **critiquing feedback** in each recommendation cycle, which includes the *critiqued product* (i.e., the product selected for critiquing) and the user's *critiquing criteria* (i.e., "keep", "improve", or "compromise") for the product's attributes.

4. RESULTS ANALYSIS

4.1 Critiquing Application

The results show that each user provided at least one critiquing feedback before s/he made the final choice. The total number of critiques made by all 18 users is 38 (mean = 2.11, st.d. = 1.45, min = 1, max = 6). Moreover, the number of *improvement-based critiques* (that "improve" some attribute values) is largely higher than that of *similarity-based critiques* (that "keep" all attribute values of the critiqued product) (36 vs. 2). Among those improvement-based critiques, 88.9% (32 out of 36) involve multiple attributes to "improve" (average 2.69 attributes) and/or "compromise" (average 1.94 attributes) (that are called *compound critiques* in [16]). Through computing conditional probability (Equation (1)), we find $P("improve"|"compromise") = 1$, whereas $P("compromise"|"improve") = 0.72$, which indicates that the appearance of "compromise" in a compound critique is always contingent on that of "improve", but not vice versa. It hence suggests that users are inclined to *improve* certain attribute values of a product in their critiques, which will (but not always) be at the cost of *compromising* some of other attributes' values for the purpose of tradeoff.

$$P(h|e) = \frac{N(h \wedge e)}{N(e)} \quad (1)$$

where $N()$ denotes the number of observations within all compound critiques.

4.2 Product-Level Fixation Analysis

Figure 2 shows the example of a user's gaze plot on recommended products, where each fixation is illustrated with a blue circle and its radius represents the duration of the fixation. Because the eye-tracker we used cannot automatically map a fixation onto the specific product or attribute that is displayed on the recommendation interface, we did the mapping manually. Concretely, two researchers first independently examined each fixation point for corresponding it to the actual information shown on the interface. If it fell into a product-level area, they associated it with that product's ID; if it was placed on an attribute's value, they associated it with both product ID and that attribute's name (e.g., price). They then met together to resolve any divergences. In this way, we identified 2,493 fixation points at product level (see next section for the attribute-level fixation analysis results).

More specifically, within the set of 25 products recommended to the user in each cycle, we find on average 9.87 products (st.d. = 5.73) were viewed. We use FC-p, TFD-p, and AFD-p to respectively denote the measures of fixation count, total fixation duration, and average fixation duration at product level. It shows for every viewed product the mean values of FC-p, TFD-p, and AFD-p are respectively 6.57 (st.d. = 5.59), 2,308.87msec (st.d. = 2,011.55), and 345.43msec (st.d. = 50.95).

We then compute *Hit-Ratio@N* (shorted as *H@N*) (Equation (2)) and *Mean Reciprocal Rank (MRR)* (Equation (3)): 1) *Hit-Ratio@N* measures whether the user's critiqued

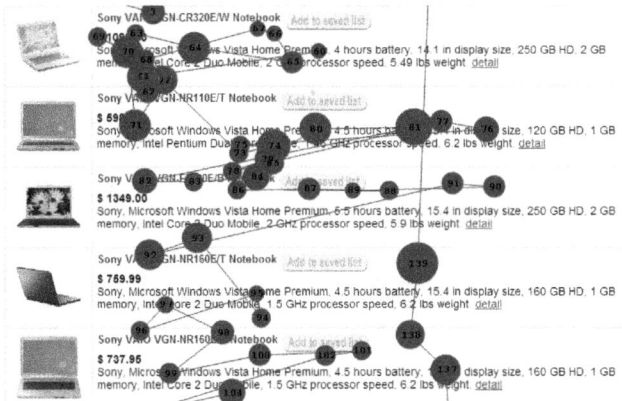

Figure 2: A user's eye-gaze plot on recommended products.

product appears in the top-N viewed products as ranked in descending order of FC-p, TFD-p, or AFD-p values, and 2) *MRR* denotes the critiqued product's position in this ordering.

$$H@N = \frac{\sum_{c \in C} 1_{rank(p_c) \leq N}}{|C|} \quad (2)$$

$$MRR = \frac{\sum_{c \in C} \frac{1}{rank(p_c)}}{|C|} \quad (3)$$

where $|C|$ is the total number of critiquing cycles by all users, and $rank(p_c)$ gives the ranking position of the critiqued product p_c within the top-N viewed products (in cycle c) as ranked by FC-p, TFD-p, or AFD-p.

From Table 1, we can see that Rank-by-FC-p and Rank-by-TFD-p are of higher accuracy than Rank-by-AFD-p and RAM (RAM refers to random ranking of viewed products), in terms of locating the critiqued product. For example, when $N = 1$, the hit ratios of Rank-by-FC-p and Rank-by-TFD-p are around 0.5, showing that within about half of all critiquing cycles, the product with the highest fixation count or total fixation duration was the one that the user selected to critique. When N is increased to 5, the hit ratios of Rank-by-FC-p and Rank-by-TFD-p both achieve 0.868. As for Rank-by-AFD-p, its hit ratio is relatively low (maximum 0.605 at $N = 5$). MRR results again imply that Rank-by-FC-p and Rank-by-TFD-p are more predictive than Rank-by-AFD-p and RAM (0.635 and 0.628, vs. 0.378 and 0.36). Moreover, as the differences between Rank-by-FC-p and Rank-by-TFD-p are not obvious across all measures, we can infer they might be equivalent in terms of inferring users' critiquing intention at product level.

The above observations thus imply that if a user takes more times in viewing a product (with corresponding higher FC-p and TFD-p), the chance s/he selects it for critiquing will be higher than that of selecting others. In comparison, the average fixation duration (AFD-p), which mainly reflects a fixation's average dwell time, is less powerful to predict the critiqued product.

4.3 Attribute-Level Fixation Analysis

For the next step of analysis, we look into fixation data at attribute-level for identifying their relationship with users'

Table 1: Relationship between product-level fixations and critiqued products

	H@1	*H@2*	*H@3*	*H@4*	*H@5*	*MRR*
Rank by FC-p	0.474	**0.605**	**0.789**	0.842	**0.868**	0.628
Rank by TFD-p	**0.5**	**0.605**	0.711	**0.868**	**0.868**	**0.635**
Rank by AFD-p	0.184	0.368	0.447	0.526	0.605	0.378
RAM	0.316	0.342	0.342	0.553	0.5	0.36

Table 2: Relationship between attribute-level fixations and critiquing criteria (*note*: C for "Compromise", and the superscript indicates significant difference, i.e., $p < 0.05$)

	Average FC-a	*Average TFD-a (msec)*	*Average AFD-a (msec)*
"Keep" attr.	3.165^C	$1,088.92^C$	289.23^C
"Improve" attr.	2.64^C	$1,038.19^C$	340.35^C
"Compromise" attr.	1.42	448.42	143.96
ANOVA test	$F = 3.42, \mathbf{p = 0.036}$	$F = 4.045, \mathbf{p = 0.02}$	$F = 21.34, \mathbf{p < 0.001}$

critiquing criteria for product attributes. There are in total 1,227 fixation points associated with the 10 major attributes (e.g., manufacturer, price, operating system, battery life). On average, the number of distinct attributes viewed by a user within each set of recommendations is 7.13 (st.d. = 2.64), with mean FC per attribute (FC-a) 3.83 (st.d. = 3.15), mean TFD per attribute (TFD-a) 1,360.6msec (st.d. = 1,199.9), and mean AFD per attribute (AFD-a) 338.4msec (st.d. = 54.1).

In addition, it shows the differences among attributes that were respectively critiqued with "keep", "improve", and "compromise" are significant in terms of FC-a, TFD-a, and AFD-a by means of ANOVA test (see Table 2). Pairwise comparisons via paired samples T-test further reveal that the fixation values of "keep" and "improve" attributes are significantly higher than those of "compromise" attributes. Specifically, the mean fixation count (FC-a) of "keep" attributes is 3.165 and that of "improve" attributes is 2.64, against 1.42 of "compromise" attributes ("keep" vs. "compromise": $t = 2.36$, $p = 0.02$; "improve" vs. "compromise": $t = 3.01$, $p < 0.01$). Similar trends are observed for total fixation duration (TFD-a) and average fixation duration (AFD-a). As for the difference between "keep" and "improve" attributes, it is just moderately significant regarding AFD-a (289.23msec vs. 340.35msec, $t = 1.75$, $p = 0.088$).

The results hence suggest that if a user's eyes fixate more on one attribute, s/he may tend to "keep" or "improve" it during critiquing, whereas for the attribute with fewer attentions, s/he may "compromise" it.

4.4 Discussion

The practical implication of this study is that: suppose we know a user's eye-gaze behavior on a recommendation interface, we can infer what product s/he is inclined to critique, and furthermore what attributes of the product s/he will be likely to "keep", "improve", or "compromise". The system could then suggest some critiques for the user to choose, instead of requiring the user to specify critique by her/himself. Moreover, the system could automatically refine the user's preference model for augmenting product recommendation simultaneously. For instance, the critiqued product's attribute values will become default acceptable value thresh-

olds, and the weight of "kept" or "improved" attribute will be increased, while the weight of "compromised" attribute will be decreased. We may then adjust the utility computed for each candidate product to enhance products' ranking. By this way, we can not only reduce users' critiquing efforts, but also help them to locate the target choice earlier.

5. CONCLUSIONS AND FUTURE WORK

In conclusion, this work indicates the feasibility of inferring users' critiquing feedback from their eye movements on recommendations. There are two major findings: 1) The fixation count and total fixation duration at product level (i.e., FC-p and TFD-p) are helpful for estimating users' interest in a product for critiquing, since the one with higher FC-p or TFD-p was more frequently selected as critiqued product. 2) The differences among critiqued attributes in terms of their fixation values are significant, especially between "kept"/"improved" and "compromised" attributes. It suggests that attributes with higher FC-a/TFD-a/AFD-a are more likely to be "kept" or "improved", whereas those with lower values will be "compromised".

The findings inspire us to conduct more studies in the future. We will attempt to identify which fixation metric, among FC-a, TFD-a, and AFD-a, would be more precise to infer users' critiquing criteria for attributes. We will also manage to recover users' decision process of comparing different attribute values of recommended products, by investigating their fixations on attributes' actual values and scanpath. Particularly, scanpath analysis can help detect users' *pairwise* value comparison behavior, as each scanpath shows a complete saccade-fixate-saccade sequence [22]. Eventually, we will develop an eye-based feedback elicitation and preference prediction model for critiquing-based recommender systems (CBRS), and perform more user studies to verify its practical performance.

6. ACKNOWLEDGMENTS

We thank participants who took part in the experiment. We also thank Hong Kong RGC and China NSFC for sponsoring the described research work (under projects RGC/HKBU12200415 and NSFC/61272365).

7. REFERENCES

[1] R. D. Burke, K. J. Hammond, and B. Young. The FindMo approach to assisted browsing. *IEEE Expert: Intelligent Systems and Their Applications*, 12(4):32–40, July 1997.

[2] S. Castagnos, N. Jones, and P. Pu. Eye-tracking product recommenders' usage. In *Proceedings of the 4th ACM Conference on Recommender Systems*, RecSys '10, pages 29–36. ACM, 2010.

[3] L. Chen. *User Decision Improvement and Trust Building in Product Recommender Systems*. PhD thesis, Ecole Polytechnique Federale De Lausanne (EPFL), Lausanne, Switzerland, August 2008.

[4] L. Chen and P. Pu. Evaluating critiquing-based recommender agents. In *Proceedings of the 21st National Conference on Artificial Intelligence - Volume 1*, AAAI'06, pages 157–162. AAAI Press, 2006.

[5] L. Chen and P. Pu. Interaction design guidelines on critiquing-based recommender systems. *User Modeling and User-Adapted Interaction*, 19(3):167–206, Aug. 2009.

[6] L. Chen and P. Pu. Eye-tracking study of user behavior in recommender interfaces. In *Proceedings of the 18th International Conference on User Modeling, Adaptation and Personalization*, UMAP '10, pages 375–380. Springer-Verlag, 2010.

[7] L. Chen and P. Pu. Critiquing-based recommenders: survey and emerging trends. *User Modeling and User-Adapted Interaction*, 22(1-2):125–150, 2012.

[8] S. Cheng, X. Liu, P. Yan, J. Zhou, and S. Sun. Adaptive user interface of product recommendation based on eye-tracking. In *Proceedings of the 2010 Workshop on Eye Gaze in Intelligent Human Machine Interaction*, EGIHMI '10, pages 94–101. ACM, 2010.

[9] C. Ehmke and S. Wilson. Identifying web usability problems from eye-tracking data. In *Proceedings of the 21st British HCI Group Annual Conference on People and Computers: HCI...But Not As We Know It - Volume 1*, BCS-HCI '07, pages 119–128. British Computer Society, 2007.

[10] C. Eickhoff, S. Dungs, and V. Tran. An eye-tracking study of query reformulation. In *Proceedings of the 38th International ACM SIGIR Conference on Research and Development in Information Retrieval*, SIGIR '15, pages 13–22. ACM, 2015.

[11] D. Giordano, I. Kavasidis, C. Pino, and C. Spampinato. Content based recommender system by using eye gaze data. In *Proceedings of the Symposium on Eye Tracking Research and Applications*, ETRA '12, pages 369–372. ACM, 2012.

[12] G. Haübl and V. Trifts. Consumer decision making in online shopping environments: The effects of interactive decision aids. *Marketing Science*, 19(1):4–21, Jan. 2000.

[13] J. Jung, Y. Matsuba, R. Mallipeddi, H. Funaya, K. Ikeda, and M. Lee. Evolutionary programming based recommendation system for online shopping. In *Signal and Information Processing Association Annual Summit and Conference (APSIPA), 2013 Asia-Pacific*, pages 1–4, Oct 2013.

[14] S. Kardan and C. Conati. Comparing and combining eye gaze and interface actions for determining user learning with an interactive simulation. In *Proceedings of the 21st International Conference on User Modeling, Adaptation and Personalization*, UMAP '13, pages 215–227, 2010.

[15] S. Liversedge, I. Gilchrist, and S. Everling. *The Oxford Handbook of Eye Movements*. Oxford University Press, 2011.

[16] K. McCarthy, J. Reilly, L. McGinty, and B. Smyth. Experiments in dynamic critiquing. In *Proceedings of the 10th International Conference on Intelligent User Interfaces*, IUI '05, pages 175–182. ACM, 2005.

[17] Y. I. Nakano and R. Ishii. Estimating user's engagement from eye-gaze behaviors in human-agent conversations. In *Proceedings of the 15th International Conference on Intelligent User Interfaces*, IUI '10, pages 139–148. ACM, 2010.

[18] A. Poole and L. J. Ball. Eye tracking in human-computer interaction and usability research: Current status and future prospects. In *Prospectsąś, Chapter in C. Ghaoui (Ed.): Encyclopedia of Human-Computer Interaction*. Pennsylvania: Idea Group, Inc, 2005.

[19] P. Pu and L. Chen. Integrating tradeoff support in product search tools for e-commerce sites. In *Proceedings of the 6th ACM Conference on Electronic Commerce*, EC '05, pages 269–278. ACM, 2005.

[20] F. Ricci, L. Rokach, B. Shapira, and P. B. Kantor. *Recommender Systems Handbook*. Springer-Verlag New York, Inc., New York, NY, USA, 1st edition, 2010.

[21] D. D. Salvucci and J. H. Goldberg. Identifying fixations and saccades in eye-tracking protocols. In *Proceedings of the Symposium on Eye Tracking Research & Applications*, ETRA '00, pages 71–78. ACM, 2000.

[22] T. Tullis and W. Albert. *Measuring the User Experience: Collecting, Analyzing, and Presenting Usability Metrics*. Morgan Kaufmann Publishers Inc., San Francisco, CA, USA, 2008.

[23] S. Xu, H. Jiang, and F. C. Lau. Personalized online document, image and video recommendation via commodity eye-tracking. In *Proceedings of the 2008 ACM Conference on Recommender Systems*, RecSys '08, pages 83–90. ACM, 2008.

Tag-Enhanced Collaborative Filtering for Increasing Transparency and Interactive Control

Tim Donkers	Benedikt Loepp	Jürgen Ziegler
University of Duisburg-Essen	University of Duisburg-Essen	University of Duisburg-Essen
Duisburg, Germany	Duisburg, Germany	Duisburg, Germany
tim.donkers@uni-due.de	benedikt.loepp@uni-due.de	juergen.ziegler@uni-due.de

ABSTRACT

To increase transparency and interactive control in Recommender Systems, we extended the Matrix Factorization technique widely used in Collaborative Filtering by learning an integrated model of user-generated tags and latent factors derived from user ratings. Our approach enables users to manipulate their preference profile expressed implicitly in the (intransparent) factor space through explicitly presented tags. Furthermore, it seems helpful in cold-start situations since user preferences can be elicited via meaningful tags instead of ratings. We evaluate this approach and present a user study that to our knowledge is the most extensive empirical study of tag-enhanced recommending to date. Among other findings, we obtained promising results in terms of recommendation quality and perceived transparency, as well as regarding user experience, which we analyzed by Structural Equation Modeling.

Keywords

Recommender Systems; Interactive Recommending; Matrix Factorization; Tags; Human Factors; User Experience

1. INTRODUCTION

Letting users influence the recommendation process and making it more comprehensible is increasingly considered an important goal in *Recommender Systems* (RS) research [17, 27, 15]. Interactive RS have been proposed that use, for instance, user-provided tags for eliciting preferences [30]. This has the advantage of relying on concepts that are meaningful to users without requiring explicit item descriptions, thus being promising for improving user control and comprehension [28]. However, tag-based RS in general (e.g. [28, 30]), and, specifically attempts to increase interactivity (e.g. [4, 2]), have mostly been developed independently of established *Collaborative Filtering* (CF) methods, and can therefore not benefit from existing long-term user profiles based on rating data or implicit feedback. Moreover, the availability of precise and efficient model-based CF algorithms such as the widely used *Matrix Factorization* (MF) [18] is usually not exploited. What is lacking, thus, are combinations of the accuracy-related benefits of model-based RS with the easy-to-understand semantics of tags.

We recently proposed an interactive recommending approach that integrates latent factors automatically derived by MF with tags users provided for the items [5]. In contrast to other approaches that enhance latent factor models with further data [13, 9, 22, 29, 8], we utilize the additional information to also allow users to interactively express their preferences and control the recommendation process

UMAP '16, July 13 - 17, 2016, Halifax, NS, Canada
Copyright is held by the owner/author(s). Publication rights licensed to ACM.
ISBN 978-1-4503-4370-1/16/07...\$15.00
DOI: http://dx.doi.org/10.1145/2930238.2930287

through selecting and weighting tags, thus indirectly determining their profile in the factor space. Besides, the tags serve as a means to elicit preferences in cold-start situations without requiring the user to rate items. Following offline experiments [5], we now present a user study with a prototype system to further evaluate our approach. To our knowledge, it is the most extensive empirical study of a tag-enhanced RS to date. Among several promising findings, e.g. regarding choice difficulty and interaction process, it shows that integrating tags into MF also increases perceived recommendation quality, which previously has only been observed offline. To analyze the user experience we used *Structural Equation Modeling* (SEM) [23]. Still rarely used in RS research [15], this method gave us interesting insights into user behavior when tag-based interaction is offered in a RS, and emphasizes the value of the increased level of transparency introduced by our approach.

2. RELATED WORK AND BACKGROUND

Interactive recommenders (e.g. [30, 4, 2, 20]) are especially useful in cold-start situations when no historical data is available for new users or when a user does not want an existing profile to be applied. This common issue has been addressed in CF in several ways, but attempts to increase interactivity are overall typically independent of CF: Various approaches have been proposed, but they usually rely on their own concepts to recommend items instead of building on the benefits of established model-based CF techniques. Thus, even when available, previously given ratings or past browsing behavior cannot be considered. Overall, the availability of precise and efficient algorithms such as MF is typically not exploited by interactive RS. Latent factor models, in particular MF, have in turn been improved primarily with respect to objective accuracy metrics [17, 15], for instance, by complementing ratings with further data. The additional information used may be rather generic, such as implicit feedback or temporal effects [18], but also more specific, predefined metadata are taken into account [9]. Other approaches integrate the models with contextual information [13] or topics inferred from semantically analyzed product reviews [22]. In contrast, only a few rely on user-provided information such as tags [29, 8]. There are indeed recommending approaches that primarily use tags [28, 12, 25], but apart from e.g. *MovieTuner* [30], these tag-based RS are not particularly aimed at giving users more control. Developed independently of model-based CF techniques, they also cannot benefit from the algorithms' maturity and the availability of explicit or implicit user rating feedback.

The range of methods for integrating further data into CF is very broad. When using common SVD-like MF [18], constraints or regularization terms may be added when training the model [18, 22, 29, 8]. However, the latent factors then exhibit no interpretable association with the additional information as this is calculated into the factor values. Thus, the relationship between data and factors, and consequently items, cannot be accessed by users. In contrast, in [9], a content-related association with the factors is explicitly established: By proposing a regression-constrained formulation, they are considered as functions of content attributes. In our previous work [5], we initially followed this approach by integrating item-specific tag relevance information, but then also derived user-tag relevance scores as well as tag-factor relations. With $\mathbf{P} \in \mathbb{R}^{|U| \times |F|}$ and $\mathbf{Q} \in \mathbb{R}^{|I| \times |F|}$ being the user/item-factor matrices, this leads to:

$$\mathbf{R} \approx \mathbf{PQ}^{\mathrm{T}} = {}^{\mathrm{u}}\mathbf{A} \Lambda {}^{\mathrm{i}}\mathbf{A}^{\mathrm{T}}$$

where ${}^{\mathrm{u}}\mathbf{A} \in \mathbb{R}^{|U| \times |T|}$ describes how strongly each user relates to each tag, ${}^{\mathrm{i}}\mathbf{A} \in \mathbb{R}^{|I| \times |T|}$ is the equivalent on item side, and $\Lambda \in \mathbb{R}^{|T| \times |T|}$ contains the latent factor information. This method proposed in [5] thus gives us the opportunity to access the previously abstract user/item-factor vectors in a much more comprehensible way: Based on the model learned, user profiles now comprise information related to both tags and latent factors. As the tag concept is easily understood, this allows us to let users actively adjust their user profile. Therefore, we define a weight vector $w_u \in [0,1]^{|T|}$ to hold the user feedback regarding the tags (where 0 means no and 1 maximal interest), which is added to a_u for calculating recommendations:

$$\tilde{r}_{ui} = (a_u + w_u) \Lambda a_i^{\mathrm{T}}$$

Beyond that, latent factor models have only rarely been exploited for purposes other than improving algorithmic performance. Exceptions comprise visualizations [10, 24] or choice-based preference elicitation methods [21, 11]. Still, the derived factors are overall hard to explain and it is particularly difficult from a system-perspective to relate them to an intelligible meaning [18]. Thus, users lack a deeper understanding of the recommendations and can typically not be provided with interactive control. While such aspects related to user experience are increasingly considered important for RS research, only few evaluations go beyond measuring accuracy in offline experiments [17, 27, 15]. Tag-enhanced RS have not been extensively analyzed by user studies, and especially integrating additional data into latent factor models has not yet been examined in terms of its actual influence on users. To evaluate user experience, the model proposed in [15] may serve as an important means that explains how subjective system aspects (e.g. perceived quality or effort) mediate the influence of objective system aspects (e.g. differences in recommender algorithms). Although considered particularly useful, advanced methods such as SEM are however only rarely used in RS research [15]. Exceptions have investigated, for instance, effects of objective system aspects on user perception of results [6], influence of choice-based preference elicitation compared to conventional ratings [11], or how the number of recommended items affects choice difficulty and satisfaction [1].

3. EMPIRICAL USER STUDY

To demonstrate and to evaluate our tag-enhanced recommending approach proposed in [5], we developed a web-based movie RS and conducted a user study. We used the Stochastic Gradient Descent MF algorithm from the Apache Mahout library as a baseline, and extended this algorithm (in same configuration) according to our method considering a limited number of 25 most popular tags as additional training data. We also implemented online-updating of factor vectors. As datasource for items and associated ratings and tags, we created an intersection of the well-known MovieLens 10M dataset and the MovieLens Tag Genome dataset. Reducing these datasets to those movies included in both left us with 8 429 movies, 9 964 745 ratings and 9 507 912 tag relevance scores.

For comparing our approach with conventional CF, we implemented two versions of the system: one used the standard MF algorithm, the other our tag-enhanced method. In the standard MF version, the top-10 recommended movies were displayed together with their movie posters and some metadata. Users could only rate the items recommended and explicitly search further titles in order to rate them as well. Upon rating an item, the result set was updated

immediately. In the version based on our approach, users could additionally select tags and change their weight. For a screenshot and a more detailed description, please refer to [5].

3.1 Goals

We were especially interested in evaluating user experience as well as subjective perception of recommendation quality, transparency, and in particular, the preference elicitation in our system and its interactive features. We hypothesized that including tags would lead to better recommendations in terms of perceived quality, and would also increase transparency of the results, especially in cold-start situations. We also assumed that users would prefer tag-based interaction while the perceived effort would be acceptable despite the increased level of interactivity offered by our approach.

3.2 Method

Participants: We recruited 46 participants (33 female) with an average age of 22.89 (*SD*=6.88), most of them students (85 %). The study was designed as an experiment under controlled conditions.

Questionnaire/Log data: Participants had to fill in a questionnaire that was primarily based on the pragmatic evaluation procedure for RS described in [16], containing items regarding, among others, recommendation quality and usage effort. This framework based on [15] is reduced to stable operationalizations of the subjective constructs and, after repeated validation, appears to measure user experience in RS reasonably well with a limited number of questionnaire items [16]. In addition, we used items from [26] to assess recommendation transparency and interface adequacy, as well as self-generated items to ask which system version participants prefer. Further, we applied the *System Usability Scale* (SUS [3]) and *User Experience Questionnaire* (UEQ [19]), and gathered data about demographics, participants' interest in movies and their familiarity with this domain. Apart from UEQ (7-point bipolar scale), all items were assessed on a positive 5-point Likert-scale (1–5). We also logged users' interaction behavior and measured task times.

Procedure: First, participants were asked to complete two preliminary tasks in counter-balanced order that served to elicit an initial set of preferences. In one task, participants were asked to rate 10 out of the 30 most popular movies. Items were shown in random order and could be skipped when unknown. In the other task, participants should select 3 tags they liked out of the 20 most popular ones (also shown in random order), which are then used to initialize a meaningful user-tag vector a_u. Next, based on the two system versions implementing standard MF and our tag-enhanced approach, respectively, we assigned the participants in counter-balanced order to three different conditions in a within-subject design:

1. *Standard MF:* Standard MF with initial recommendations based on the 10 user ratings. The only interaction possible was to rate more items.
2. *TMF-Rating:* Our tag-enhanced MF with initial recommendations based on the 10 user ratings. Users could interactively select and weight tags, and also rate more items.
3. *TMF-Tag:* Our tag-enhanced MF with initial recommendations based on the 3 selected tags. User interaction was similar to the previous condition.

In each condition, participants were initially shown the top-6 recommendations obtained with the respective algorithm. First, they were asked to choose one movie from the six recommended ones they would actually like to watch. Second, they rated their satisfaction with each recommendation on a 5-point Likert-scale (1–5). Third, they filled in the questionnaire described above. Next, participants were asked to interact with the current system version to further refine recommendations and to receive a result set that better matched their personal interests. After participants finished interaction at their own discretion, they were again presented with the (now adjusted) top-6 recommendations. Again, they had to select one movie out of them, rate how satisfying each recommendation was, and fill in a questionnaire (which was now complemented with questions regarding the interaction process). For each condition, the respective variables were thus assessed at two different points in time, before and after the corresponding interaction phase.

3.3 Results

Participants reported that they liked movies a lot (M=4.22, SD=0.63) while having average knowledge about movies in general (M=3.07, SD=0.80) as well as about newer movies (M=2.93, SD=0.98). We conducted two-way repeated measures ANOVAs to compare the effect of condition and point in time on the dependent variables. For the three conditions, marginal mean values and standard errors are presented in Table 1.

Table 1. Results for the different conditions.

	MF		TMF-Rating		TMF-Tag	
	M	SE	M	SE	M	SE
Perc. Rec. Quality	3.16	0.11	3.31	0.13	3.65	0.10
Mean Item Rating	3.11	0.10	3.29	0.11	3.55	0.10
Choice Satisfaction	4.00	0.10	4.10	0.13	4.35	0.09
Choice Difficulty	34.50	3.10	27.80	2.62	28.37	2.32
Transparency	3.20	0.15	3.41	0.15	3.73	0.13

Perceived Recommendation Quality: Concerning subjective quality, there was a statistically significant effect with α=0.05 for condition, $F(2,90)$=7.40, p<.001. Post hoc comparisons using Bonferroni correction indicate that the mean score for TMF-Tag was significantly higher than for both, TMF-Rating, p=.028, and standard MF, p<.001. However, there was no significant difference regarding perceived quality of recommendations before and after the interaction phase, $F(1,45)$=0.02, p=.904.

Mean Item Rating: We found similar differences between the conditions with regard to the individual satisfaction participants stated for each recommended item, $F(2,90)$=11.19, p=.001. Again, TMF-Tag received significantly higher ratings than TMF-Rating, p=.025, and standard MF, p<.001.

Choice Satisfaction: Regarding satisfaction with the movie participants finally selected from the set of recommendations, we also found statistical evidence for differences between the conditions, $F(2,90)$=4.72, p=.011. Post hoc Bonferroni tests indicate that the mean score for TMF-Tag was significantly higher than for standard MF, p=.009. No differences were found between TMF-Rating and other conditions. Furthermore, the mean values before and after the interaction tasks are statistically discriminable, $F(1,45)$=5.07, p=.029. Before interaction (M=4.28, SE=0.10) users were more confident with their selected movies than afterwards (M=4.02, SE=0.11). Since the interaction term of condition and point in time was not significant, we deduce that this applies to all conditions.

Choice Difficulty: With respect to objective difficulty to decide, operationalized as the total time participants spent for choosing one movie they would actually like to watch from the shown recommendations, the within-subjects main effect yielded significant differences for condition, $F(2,90)$=6.42, p=0.02. Post hoc comparisons denote that users took more time to decide in the standard MF condition compared to TMF-Rating, p=.012, and TMF-Tag, p=.027. Additionally, users tended to decide more quickly after they interacted with the system, $F(1,45)$=29.23, p<.001.

Transparency: We also found a significant effect of condition on transparency, $F(2,90)$=6.22, p=.003. Results from standard MF

were perceived less transparent than from TMF-Tag, p=.003. No differences were found between TMF-Rating and other conditions.

Effort and Usability: The version allowing for interaction via tags was assessed significantly ($t(45)$=4.15, p<.001) better (M=3.76, SD=1.02) than the other (M=2.83, SD=1.00). Without tags, participants spent 165.54 sec (SD=114.64) for the entire interaction task, in the two conditions with tags, they needed on average 209.68 sec (SD=103.26). Although interaction phases were thus significantly longer ($t(45)$=-2.43, p=.019), perceived interaction effort was not higher: a one-way ANOVA yielded no significant effect for condition, $F(2,90)$=1.40, p=.253. Also, the usability was rated as "good" with a SUS-score of 78 and values between 0.95 and 1.96 on the different scales of the UEQ. In particular, the subscale for transparency yielded an excellent score (M=1.96) and efficiency was rated above average (M=1.16), which corresponds to the very promising assessment of interface adequacy (M=4.13, SD=0.48).

Structural Equation Modeling: Using SEM we further analyzed the questionnaire data to investigate the effects of varying recommender algorithm (*Standard MF* vs. *Tag-enhanced MF*) and method for eliciting initial preferences (*Ratings* vs. *Tags*) on user experience and interaction behavior. We were especially interested in differences between the three conditions in cold-start where the system must deal with a high level of uncertainty when presenting the first recommendations. We also considered personal characteristics to deduce assumptions about how different dispositions may influence those relations. Following [15], we define algorithms and preference elicitation methods as *Objective System Aspects* (OSA) that cannot be influenced by the user. *Perceived Rec. Quality* and *Transparency* are seen as *Subjective System Aspects* (SSA), which represent the user's perception of OSA. SSA are conceived as mediating variables between OSA and user experience [15]. User experience may be substantially influenced by using different algorithms and preference elicitation methods (see, e.g. [14, 4, 6, 15, 7]). We assume that user experience is affected by changes with respect to *Perceived Rec. Quality* and *Transparency* when a novel means for eliciting initial preferences is used, i.e. selecting tags according to our approach. We included *Choice Satisfaction* as an indicator of the user's *Experience* (EXP). The user's *Interaction Behavior* (INT) is also influenced by SSA. We therefore complement the more general *Perceived Rec. Quality* by capturing the specific feedback regarding each recommended item, i.e. the *Mean Item Rating*. Finally, we in line with the underlying framework assume that certain *Personal Characteristics* (PC) such as *Domain Knowledge* and *Trust in Technology* have an impact on attitude and behavior concerning the varied system aspects.

We set up the theoretical model shown in Figure 1 that yielded a good fit with the data ($\chi^2(12)$=13.669, p=.322, CFI=.995, TLI=.989, $RMSEA$=.032). It explains a large amount of variance regarding our dependent variables *Choice Satisfaction* (R^2=.401), *Mean Item Rating* (R^2=.693) and *Perceived Rec. Quality* (R^2=.523), and also a reasonable proportion with respect to *Transparency* (R^2=.234). Direct effects of the two different algorithms used in the three conditions were not significant for any dependent variable or the mediator. Thus, the algorithms (*Standard MF* vs. *Tag-enhanced MF*) were eventually not considered in our model. In contrast, the variation of the preference elicitation method (*Ratings* vs. *Tags*) seems to account for a significant explanation of *Transparency*. While *Domain Knowledge* as one of the personal characteristics shows a meaningful influence only on *Transparency*, *Trust in Technology* also influences *Choice Satisfaction* and *Mean Item Rating*. Further analysis shows that *Transparency* seems to be a substantial causal factor for *Perceived Rec. Quality*, which is an overall subjective assessment that in turn acts as a complete mediator for the effects on our dependent variables, i.e. the more specific *Choice Satisfaction* and *Mean Item Rating*. In particular, this route appears to completely mediate the otherwise significant predictive power of the different methods to elicit initial preferences (*Ratings* vs. *Tags*).

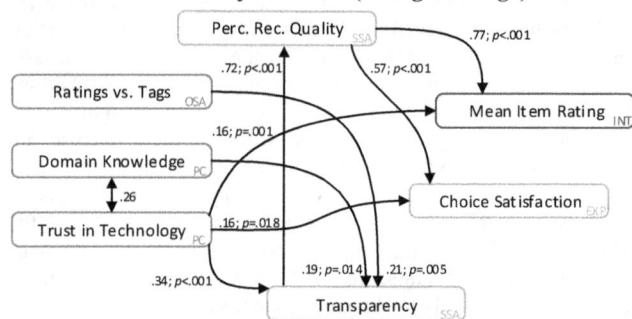

Figure 1. Path model for comparing the influence of preference elicitation via ratings or tags. On the edges, standardized regression weights and p-values are displayed.

3.4 Discussion

In general, including additional content information into MF seems to be beneficial in terms of objective recommendation quality. We observed this for our approach [5], thereby validating results of offline experiments performed by several others, e.g. [13, 9, 29, 22, 8]. However, by conducting a user study we could for the first time confirm that this finding also applies to the users' subjective perception. TMF-Tag received significantly higher scores with respect to perceived recommendation quality, satisfaction with the chosen movie, and transparency. Significant differences between conditions before the interaction phases (with tag-enhanced MF being superior) further suggest that the few interaction steps performed at the beginning to elicit preferences by selecting a small number of tags are already sufficient to improve user experience, in particular perceived quality and transparency. Regarding choice difficulty, condition and point in time both account for significant effects. The latter was to be expected as users may already have decided for an item during interaction, and therefore needed less time to settle on a recommended movie. However, it is particularly interesting that with standard MF, participants needed significantly longer to select a movie than in the tag-enhanced conditions. They further perceived recommendations to be significantly more transparent with TMF-Tag—also before the interaction, without knowing that the results were just based on the initially selected tags. Our tag-based preference elicitation approach thus seems to help users also implicitly when judging recommendations.

Because of these findings, we further examined the role of transparency in context of generating satisfying recommendations, particularly in cold-start situations, by using SEM. As indicated by our model, selecting tags instead of rating items to elicit initial preferences significantly improves transparency. We therefore deduce that tags import semantics into the result set which are more natural to understand by users than deriving a meaning from recommendations based on numerical ratings. Thus, our tag-enhanced recommending approach seems to lead to more comprehensible results. In general, increasing transparency seems to positively influence user satisfaction with recommendations. The high standardized regression weight of .72 supports that transparency is a substantial predictor. Consequently, the significant influence of preference elicitation method on transparency emphasizes that our approach is a promising means to alleviate the cold-start problem.

The fact that only varying the algorithm yielded no significant differences in recommendation quality is generally in line with recent research stating that different or objectively more accurate recommenders do not necessarily produce better results from a subjective perspective [17, 27, 6]. Instead, the entire result set should express some kind of inner consistency, which in case of our proposed method is reached through relating latent factors learned by MF with user-provided tags. While even increasing objective accuracy [5], our approach to use tags for eliciting preferences thus makes recommendations more transparent and thereby in fact also improves perceived recommendation quality. The recommendations then seem to refer to each other implied by the easy-to-understand semantics of tags. Conversely, although it may achieve high accuracy scores, a list of items detached from such a meaningful superordinate context might not be as satisfactory for the user.

Highly significant regression weights suggest that recommendation quality is the main predictor for choice satisfaction and users' individual rating feedback for recommended items. However, also domain knowledge, for instance, may increase users' satisfaction with the results as it helps to better comprehend why certain items were recommended. By increasing transparency, our approach thus seems to be especially useful for users with little domain knowledge. The influence of trust in technology on the dependent variables is in contrast not fully mediated via transparency. This is another indicator for the importance of aspects that go beyond recommendations themselves: Concerning the satisfaction with chosen item as well as mean item rating, it suggests that some personal characteristics might alter the way perceived recommendation quality is translated into numerical ratings. As a result, datasets comprising user feedback in form of ratings may suffer from non-systematic deviations, i.e. users whose trust in technology is low would provide lower ratings in a more technically-oriented system. This, in turn, is another argument for using more natural ways than ratings to interact with CF recommenders.

Finally, regarding interaction, participants assessed our system's usability very positively. They preferred the tag-enhanced version, which might be a reason why they spent more time using it. Although the richer possibilities for interaction may also contribute to this finding, perceived interaction effort did not differ. Overall, our interactive recommending approach based on tags thus seems to be of value for providing users with more control over the recommendation process and for improving its transparency.

4. CONCLUSIONS AND OUTLOOK

Our user study confirmed that additional content information can be used in conjunction with MF not only to increase accuracy, but at the same time also improves perceived recommendation quality and transparency. Furthermore, users were more satisfied with the chosen movie while it was easier to settle for an item. Interestingly, besides the fact that users liked the interaction via tags generally more than just rating items, tag-enhanced MF yields particularly promising results when preferences were elicited initially by tags. Thus, our approach seems useful to interactively adapt results when a rating-based profile is already available as well as to set up a new profile in cold-start situations since a small number of selected tags leads to a user profile at least as good as when rating a larger number of items up front. Using SEM, we further analyzed these findings, focusing on the role of this new method to elicit initial preferences and its positive influence on the aforementioned aspects. In future work, we plan to exploit tags as well as other content-related or contextual data more extensively, for instance, to explain user profiles and to establish even richer interaction possibilities in MF recommenders. Finally, we are interested in comparing our system with other tag-based RS and in adapting it to different domains.

5. REFERENCES

[1] Bollen, D., Knijnenburg, B. P., Willemsen, M. C., and Graus, M. P. 2010. Understanding choice overload in recommender systems. In *Proc. RecSys '10*. ACM, 63–70.

[2] Bostandjiev, S., O'Donovan, J., and Höllerer, T. 2012. Taste-Weights: A visual interactive hybrid recommender system. In *Proc. RecSys '12*. ACM, 35–42.

[3] Brooke. J. 1996. SUS – A quick and dirty usability scale. In *Usability Evaluation in Industry*, Taylor & Francis, 189–194.

[4] Chen, L. and Pu, P. 2012. Critiquing-based recommenders: Survey and emerging trends. *User Mod. User-Adap. 22*, 1-2, 125–150.

[5] Donkers, T., Loepp, B., and Ziegler, J. 2015. Merging latent factors and tags to increase interactive control of recommendations. In *Poster Proc. RecSys '15*.

[6] Ekstrand, M. D., Harper, F. M., Willemsen, M. C., and Konstan, J. A. 2014. User perception of differences in recommender algorithms. In *Proc. RecSys '14*. ACM, 161–168.

[7] Ekstrand, M. D., Kluver, D., Harper, F. M., and Konstan, J. A. 2015. Letting users choose recommender algorithms: An experimental study. In *Proc. RecSys '15*. ACM, 11–18.

[8] Fernández-Tobías, I. and Cantador, I. 2014. Exploiting social tags in matrix factorization models for cross-domain collaborative filtering. In *Proc. CBRecSys '14*, 34–41.

[9] Forbes, P. and Zhu, M. 2011. Content-boosted matrix factorization for recommender systems: Experiments with recipe recommendation. In *Proc. RecSys '11*. ACM, 261–264.

[10] Gansner, E., Hu, Y., Kobourov, S., and Volinsky, C. 2009. Putting recommendations on the map: Visualizing clusters and relations. In *Proc. RecSys '09*. ACM, 345–348.

[11] Graus, M. P. and Willemsen, M. C. 2015. Improving the user experience during cold start through choice-based preference elicitation. In *Proc. RecSys '15*. ACM, 273–276.

[12] Guan, Z., Wang, C., Bu, J., Chen, C., Yang, K., Cai, D., and He, X. 2010. Document recommendation in social tagging services. In *Proc. WWW '10*. ACM, 391–400.

[13] Karatzoglou, A., Amatriain, X., Baltrunas, L., and Oliver, N. 2010. Multiverse recommendation: N-dimensional tensor factorization for context-aware collaborative filtering. In *Proc. RecSys '10*. ACM, 79–86.

[14] Knijnenburg, B. P. and Willemsen, M. C. 2010. The effect of preference elicitation methods on the user experience of a recommender system. In *Ext. Abstr. CHI '10*. ACM, 3457–3462.

[15] Knijnenburg, B. P. and Willemsen, M. C. 2015. Evaluating recommender systems with user experiments. In *Recommender Systems Handbook*. Springer US, 309–352.

[16] Knijnenburg, B. P., Willemsen, M. C., and Kobsa, A. 2011. A pragmatic procedure to support the user-centric evaluation of recommender systems. In *Proc. RecSys '11*. ACM, 321–324.

[17] Konstan, J. A. and Riedl, J. 2012. Recommender systems: From algorithms to user experience. *User Mod. User-Adap. 22*, 1-2, 101–123.

[18] Koren, Y., Bell, R. M., and Volinsky, C. 2009. Matrix factorization techniques for recommender systems. *IEEE Computer 42*, 8, 30–37.

[19] Laugwitz, B., Held, T., and Schrepp, M. 2008. Construction and evaluation of a user experience questionnaire. In *Proc. USAB '08*. Springer, 63–76.

[20] Loepp, B., Herrmanny, K., and Ziegler, J. 2015. Blended recommending: Integrating interactive information filtering and algorithmic recommender techniques. In *Proc. CHI '15*. ACM, 975–984.

[21] Loepp, B., Hussein, T., and Ziegler, J. 2014. Choice-based preference elicitation for collaborative filtering recommender systems. In *Proc. CHI '14*. ACM, 3085–3094.

[22] McAuley, J. and Leskovec, J. 2013. Hidden factors and hidden topics: Understanding rating dimensions with review text. In *Proc. RecSys '13*. ACM, 165–172.

[23] Muthén, B. 1984. A general structural equation model with dichotomous, ordered categorical, and continuous latent variable indicators. *Psychometrika 49*, 1, 115–132.

[24] Németh, B., Takács, G., Pilászy, I., and Tikk, D. 2013. Visualization of movie features in collaborative filtering. In *Proc. SoMeT '13*, 229–233.

[25] Nguyen, T. T. and Riedl, J. 2013. Predicting users' preference from tag relevance. In *Proc. UMAP '13*. Springer, 274–280.

[26] Pu, P., Chen, L., and Hu, R. 2011. A user-centric evaluation framework for recommender systems. In *Proc. RecSys '11*. ACM, 157–164.

[27] Pu, P., Chen, L., and Hu, R. 2012. Evaluating recommender systems from the user's perspective: Survey of the state of the art. *User Mod. User-Adap. 22*, 4-5, 317–355.

[28] Sen, S., Vig, J., and Riedl, J. 2009. Tagommenders: Connecting users to items through tags. In *Proc. WWW '09*. ACM, 671–680.

[29] Shi, Y., Larson, M., and Hanjalic, A. 2013. Mining contextual movie similarity with matrix factorization for context-aware recommendation. *ACM Trans. Intell. Syst. Technol. 4*, 1, 16:1–16:19.

[30] Vig, J., Sen, S., and Riedl, J. 2011. Navigating the tag genome. In *Proc. IUI '11*. ACM, 93–102.

Eliciting Users' Attitudes toward Smart Devices

Kai Zhan
Faculty of Information Technology
Monash University
Clayton, Victoria 3800, Australia
Kai.Zhan@monash.edu

Ingrid Zukerman
Faculty of Information Technology
Monash University
Clayton, Victoria 3800, Australia
Ingrid.Zukerman@monash.edu

Masud Moshtaghi
Melbourne School of Engineering
The University of Melbourne
Melbourne, Victoria 3010, Australia
masud.moshtaghi@unimelb.edu.au

Gwyneth Rees
Centre for Eye Research Australia
The University of Melbourne
Melbourne, Victoria 3010, Australia
grees@unimelb.edu.au

ABSTRACT

This paper presents a study to determine users' attitudes toward smart devices. We conducted a web survey to elicit users' ratings for devices and combinations of tasks and devices; the results of this survey led to the development of a *Recommender System (RS)* for smart devices for particular tasks. We investigated user- and item-based Collaborative Filters, and compared their performance with that of global and demographic RS baselines. We then developed a technique based on Principal Components Analysis to select a subset of the original survey questions that supports the prediction of users' ratings for device-task combinations. Our results show that the accuracy of an RS that asks only a small subset of the survey questions is similar to that of an RS that predicts users' answers to one survey question on the basis of their answers to all the other questions.

Keywords

Attitude modeling; information elicitation; rating prediction.

1. INTRODUCTION

Intelligent systems, which have become ubiquitous in recent times, range from wearable accessories, such as smart watches and fitbits, and personal companions, like Aibo and Nao, to interactive virtual agents or environments on a screen, and the Internet of Things (IoT). In modern society, many people interact with smart devices on a daily basis. However, people's attitudes toward devices may vary in general or depending on the context of device usage.

The goal of this research is to understand users' attitudes toward smart devices, in order to support the recommenda-

UMAP '16, July 13 - 17, 2016, Halifax, NS, Canada

© 2016 Copyright held by the owner/author(s). Publication rights licensed to ACM.
ISBN 978-1-4503-4370-1/16/07. . . $15.00

DOI: http://dx.doi.org/10.1145/2930238.2930241

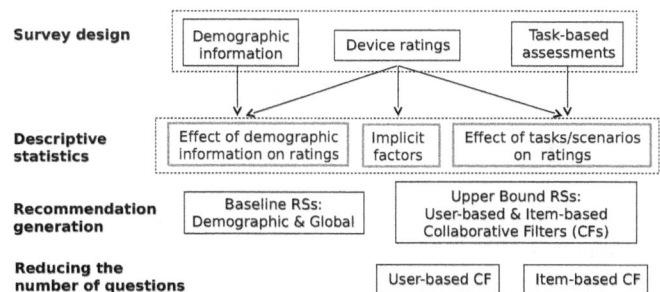

Figure 1: Main research topics

tion of (existing and future) devices to users, and influence the design of devices, thereby increasing their acceptability,[1] and hence, their adoption.

As a first step in this project, we conducted a web survey, where people provided demographic information, rated individual devices, and rated devices in the context of specific tasks (top panel in Figure 1). The results of our survey show that demographic information does not adequately explain users' ratings of devices, while the task influences device ratings; our analysis also revealed implicit factors that affect device ratings (second panel in Figure 1).

These results led to the development of *Recommender Systems (RSs)* as a means of understanding users' attitudes toward devices (third panel in Figure 1). However, there are significant differences between common RS applications and ours: (1) our participants often rated items on the basis of the information we provided, rather than from personal experience; and (2) our dataset is not sparse [4], due to the fact that the participants answered all the 178 questions in our survey. Clearly, such a large number of questions is not suitable for a recommendation setting, which brings us to an additional contribution of our research: an approach to minimize the number of questions required for making adequate recommendations (bottom panel of Figure 1).

This paper is organized as follows. An overview of related

---

[1]We distinguish between *acceptability*, which is prospective, and *acceptance*, which takes place after being exposed to a device [28].

Table 1: List of factors: manually defined and derived from data

Device factors	Description	Factor weighting
MANUALLY DEFINED		
Mains powered	Powered at the wall socket (robotic arm, virtual agent), battery-powered otherwise (robot, smart clothing)	4.182
Mobile	Moves by itself (humanoid robot, mobile robot)	3.611
Portable	Light and small enough to be carried (robotic pet, control interface)	0.823
Vital-sign monitor	Measures human vital signs (health-monitoring device, smart shirt)	-0.538
Humanoid	Has a face, and could have body and legs (humanoid robot, humanoid virtual agent)	0.236
Physical	Has a physical presence (robot), virtual otherwise (agent on a screen)	0.159
Wearable	Smart watch, glasses, shoes, shirt, gloves	
DERIVED FROM DATA		
Accessory-like	Can be worn or carried like an accessory (smart watch, glasses, control interface)	3.458
Clothing-like	Integrated into clothing (smart shoes, shirt, gloves)	3.129
Realistic	Looks like a real person (realistic humanoid robot, virtual human)	-0.622
Bionic	Mimics a natural life form (robotic pet, humanoid robot), functional otherwise (mobile robot)	-0.498
Cute/Cartoon	Animated, cartoon-like or cute device (emoticon, cartoon character, robotic pet)	-0.498

work appears in Section 2. Section 3 describes our survey, and presents its results. Our RSs and their evaluation appear in Section 4, and the paper concludes in Section 5.

2. RELATED RESEARCH

In this section, we describe related work on three main types of smart devices: robotic agents, screen-based assistants and accessory/wearable devices.

- *Robotic agents*, or personal service robots, have been employed in diverse areas, such as elderly support, health-care and entertainment [9, 14, 31]. The growing market for service robots has prompted studies on the interaction between robots' and users' attributes, and the influence of these attributes on users' perceptions. Examples are [2,5], which investigate the influence of people's cultural background and prior experiences with a particular robot, like Aibo or Nao, on their attitude toward robots. Other studies focus on the general acceptance of robots [7], and on their acceptance in various settings, e.g., domestic environments [21], health-care [3] and education [22].

- *Screen-based assistants* may have a functional design or take the form of virtual agents. Among the former are devices for environmental monitoring and control [24]; smart walkers [20], which provide navigation assistance to older adults across public areas; and the smart kitchen environment *Kochbot* [1], which helps people with cooking tasks through spoken interactions. Virtual agents, which may be represented as people or characters, have been shown to enable an emotional relationship between people and assistive technologies [19, 29, 30]. Recently, virtual agents have been used in job interviews [6] and skill training [18], with associated studies to evaluate users' acceptance of virtual agents for teaching or training purposes [10, 17].

- *Accessories / wearable devices*, such as smart phones, watches, glasses and clothes, have increased in popularity due to advances in ubiquitous computing. Spagnolli *et al.* [26] measure users' acceptance of a range of wearable devices through a questionnaire that includes multiple dimensions of the Technology Acceptance Model [27] that are particularly relevant to wearable devices, such as perceived usefulness, effort expectancy, psychological attachment and facilitating conditions.

Despite the increased interest in smart devices, the factors that influence users' attitudes toward these devices remain unclear. Further, the influence of the context or task on the acceptability of a device has not been considered to date. These issues are addressed in this paper, together with the construction of an RS-based model of users' attitudes.

3. USER STUDY

In this section, we describe our survey, and present its main results. Prior to conducting the survey, we selected representative devices as follows. We defined the hypothetical factors listed at the top of Table 1 on the basis of an initial set of devices, and selected a subset of 17 devices that together covered these factors. Table 2 displays these devices, separated into three main categories (robotic, screen-based and wearable). Note that we have included some technologies that are not typically considered smart devices, e.g., robotic arm or driverless car. However, in principle, these technologies can perform many of the tasks performed by smart devices.

Upon completion of the survey, we performed *Principal Component Analysis* (*PCA*) on the participants' answers, which yielded additional factors, and refined the wearable factor (bottom of Table 1; the weightings in the third column were obtained by means of linear regression, Section 3.2.2).

3.1 Survey Design

Our survey[2] had three main segments: demographic information, device ratings, and task-based device ratings.

- *Demographic information* (10 questions): this segment collected information about participants' gender, age, country of residence, work situation, occupation, educational background and experience with technology.

---

[2] Available at https://goo.gl/tKxt3s.

Table 2: List of devices in our survey

Robotic	Screen-based	Wearable
Robotic pet Realistic humanoid robot	Control interface Virtual human	Smart glasses Smart watch
Humanoid robot Mobile robot	Emoticon Cartoon character	Smart shirt Smart gloves
Robotic arm Self-driving vehicle	Health monitoring device	Smart shoes
Cleaning robot		

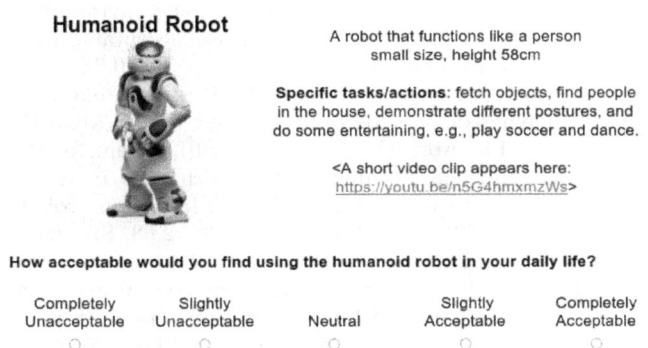

Humanoid Robot

A robot that functions like a person
small size, height 58cm

Specific tasks/actions: fetch objects, find people in the house, demonstrate different postures, and do some entertaining, e.g., play soccer and dance.

<A short video clip appears here: https://youtu.be/n5G4hmxmzWs>

How acceptable would you find using the humanoid robot in your daily life?

Completely Unacceptable	Slightly Unacceptable	Neutral	Slightly Acceptable	Completely Acceptable
○	○	○	○	○

Figure 2: Survey component for the Nao robot

- *Device ratings* (17 questions): this segment showed an image for each of the 17 devices, provided information about the size and functionality of each device, and gave a link to a short video that demonstrates the operation of the device. The participants rated on a 1-5 Likert scale how acceptable they find using each device in daily life, where 1 means "Completely Unacceptable", and 5 means "Completely Acceptable". Figure 2 illustrates this component with respect to a humanoid robot.

- *Task-based device ratings* (151 questions): this segment provided a list of tasks that the devices could potentially perform, which reflect users' daily activities and requirements at home and at work. Although some of the devices in Table 2 may be designed for specific tasks (e.g., the cleaning robot), in many cases, there is no technical impediment to such devices performing additional tasks (e.g., finding objects in the home). Hence, we excluded from this segment only device-task combinations where the physical limitations of devices prevented them from performing a task (e.g., smart clothing was excluded from the devices that could perform physical actions). In addition, we reduced the number of devices in the task-based questions by combining the virtual human, emoticon and cartoon into one virtual agent; the smart glasses and watch into accessories; and the smart shirt, gloves and shoes into smart clothing. This yielded a maximum of 12 devices for each task; Table 3 lists the tasks and the number of devices considered for each task. Similarly to the second segment, participants rated the acceptability of the devices for each task on a 1-5 Likert scale. Figure 3 illustrates this component for the task of performing physical actions at home and at work at the user's command, for which seven devices are suitable.

Table 3: List of tasks in our survey

#	Task	# of devices
1	Inform you about an emergency in a place	12
2	Inform you about an emergency of a person	12
3	Adjust your home environment at your command	11
4	Adjust your work environment at your command	11
5	Automatically adjust your home environment	11
6	Automatically adjust your work environment	11
7	Locate misplaced objects at home	11
8	Locate misplaced objects at work	11
9	Perform physical actions at your command at home	7
10	Perform physical actions at your command at work	7
11	Autonomously perform physical actions at home	7
12	Autonomously perform physical actions at work	7
13	Provide you with general information	11
14	Give you reminders about your daily life	11
15	Entertain you and your family	11

Figure 3: Survey component for physical actions at home and at work

3.2 Survey Results

Participants for this survey were recruited through professional mailing lists, a Monash University volunteer web-site, social media and health-care centers. We collected responses from 161 participants, of which the majority (93.6%) live in Australia. We excluded responses from participants who gave the same answer for all the questions, did not answer some questions, or finished the survey unreasonably quickly (e.g., within 10 minutes — our survey was designed to be completed in about 30 minutes). This left 93 valid responses: 33 of the respondents were male and 60 female; 42 participants were under 30 years of age, 31 between 30 and 50 years, and 20 over 50 years; 54 users worked full-time, 27 worked part-time and 12 were unemployed; 17 users had a secondary education, 25 a Bachelor degree, 38 a Master and 13 a PhD; and 61 participants self-rated as having a medium technological expertise, and 32 as having a high expertise.

3.2.1 Users, Devices and Tasks

This section presents salient insights yielded by our survey (statistically significant with $p\text{-}value \leq 0.05$, obtained with t-test for paired samples, and with one-way ANOVA for more than two samples, validated with Tukey's range test).

Users and Devices.

Participants found familiar devices, such as the cleaning robot (M=4.83, SD=0.54), health-monitoring device (M=4.74, SD=0.62) and control interface (M=4.56, SD=0.96), more acceptable than less common devices.

Male participants (M=4.08, SD=0.50) were more likely to accept smart devices than female participants (M=3.68, SD=0.63), with statistically significant differences taking place for the robotic pet, realistic humanoid robot, mobile platform, robotic arm, cleaning robot and smart glasses, shirt and gloves. In addition, users with higher technological expertise gave higher ratings to devices (M=4.09, SD=0.52) than users with lower expertise (M=3.69, SD=0.61). Although in general, age did not influence device ratings, this was not the case for the robotic pet, which was disliked by participants over 50 years of age.

In general, users rated realistic humanoid devices, viz the realistic humanoid robot (M=2.94, SD=1.30) and the realistic virtual agent (M=3.14, SD=1.23), lower than other devices. The smart gloves (M=3.17, SD=1.29) also had low ratings, probably because of their cumbersomeness, rather than realism issues. However, note the high standard deviations, which indicate that other factors, such as specific user attributes or tasks, may affect device ratings.

Users and Tasks.

Similarly to *Users and Devices*, there was a statistically significant difference between the views of male participants (M=3.60, SD=0.41) and those of female participants (M=3.05, SD=0.58) about tasks being performed by devices. The most generally acceptable tasks pertained to informing users about emergency conditions of a place (M=3.95, SD=0.33) or a person (M=3.93, SD=0.47).

Overall, having devices perform activities automatically (e.g., Tasks 5, 6, 11 and 12) was less acceptable than performing activities at a user's command (e.g., Tasks 3, 4, 9 and 10). For example, adjusting the home environment automatically (M=2.42, SD=0.4) was less acceptable than adjusting it at a user's command (M=3.44, SD=0.6).

In addition, there was no statistically significant difference between having devices perform tasks at home (M=3.17, SD=0.63) and at work (M=3.04, SD=0.56), except for the robotic pet and the cleaning robot, which were more acceptable at home (pet: M=3.06, SD=0.84; cleaning robot: M=3.57, SD=0.72) than at work (pet: M=2.68, SD=0.60; cleaning robot: M=3.28, SD=0.61).

Finally, participants with a high technological expertise favoured autonomously performing physical actions at home (M=3.35, SD=1.25) and at work (M=3.30, SD=1.30) compared to participants with lower expertise (home: M=2.53, SD=1.12; work: M=2.42, SD=1.20).

Devices and Tasks.

Looking at the ratings participants gave to devices for the different tasks, the smart clothing (M=4.03, SD=0.35) and the control interface (M=3.98, SD=0.56) were deemed more acceptable than other devices over all tasks. In contrast, the realistic humanoid robot (M=2.97, SD=0.53), the robotic arm (M=2.84, SD=0.58) and the driverless vehicle (M=2.78, SD=0.59) were deemed less acceptable than other devices. We posit that this is because users associate these devices

(a) Correlations between device-task—device for each task

(b) Correlations between device-task—device for each device

(c) Mean device ratings and device-task—device correlations

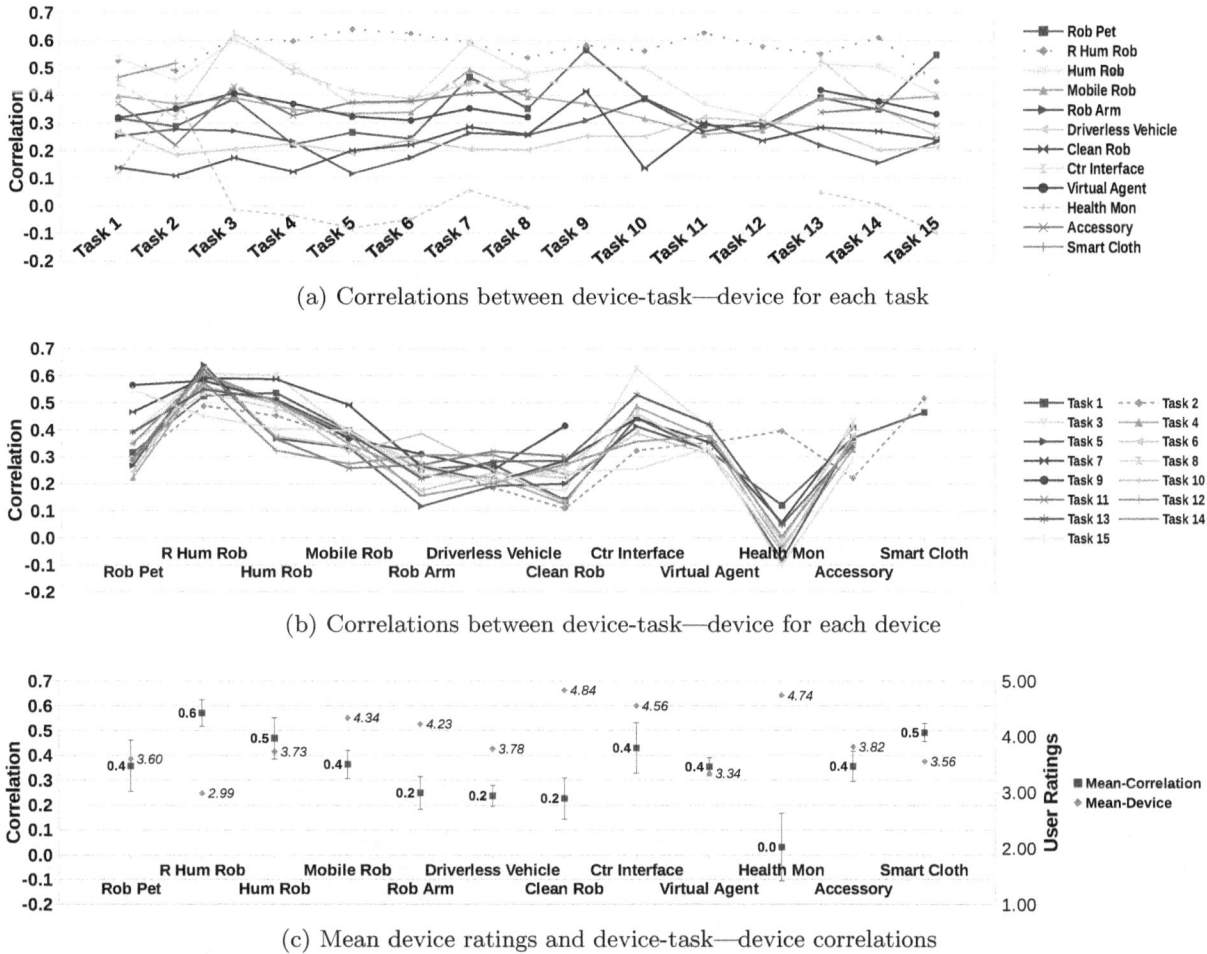

Figure 4: Correlations between devices and device-task combinations

with specific tasks. This idea is corroborated by the observation that participants found it more acceptable for devices to perform their designated tasks than other tasks, e.g., it was more acceptable for the cleaning robot to perform physical actions at home (M=4.61, SD=0.79) than other tasks (M=3.08, SD=0.49), and for the health-monitoring device to inform about an emergency condition of a person (M=4.69, SD=0.8) than to perform other tasks (M=2.82, SD=0.53).

Interestingly, the participants' ratings of devices in isolation were higher (M=3.96, SD=0.58) than their ratings when the devices were associated with specific tasks (M=3.25, SD=0.50). This indicates that when the participants' thinking was focused on the usage context, the devices were assessed more carefully, compared to the "first impressions" assessment performed in the second segment of the survey. This observation prompted us to further analyze the relationship between devices and tasks. To this effect, we computed Pearson's correlation coefficient between the ratings of the 12 devices in isolation and their ratings when associated with the 15 tasks in Table 3.

Figure 4(a) displays these correlations for tasks and devices, where the x-axis represents the tasks (Table 3), and each line depicts a device (Table 2). The realistic humanoid robot has the highest correlation between its usage for each task and its rating in isolation, with a low average device rating (M=2.99, SD=1.3) and device-task rating (M=3.05,

SD=0.5). This means that the realistic humanoid robot is not very acceptable, regardless of the tasks it performs. Next are the humanoid robot, control interface and smart clothing (two tasks only). In contrast, the task-based and device-only correlation for the health-monitoring device is quite low, with a high device-only rating (M=4.74, SD=0.62), but lower ratings for most tasks (M=3.16, SD=0.77), except Task 2, which is informing about an emergency of a person. This means that participants are positively inclined toward the health-monitoring device, but are unlikely to accept it for tasks that are unrelated to its perceived purpose.

Figure 4(b) represents the same data from a different point of view, where the x-axis represents the devices (Table 2), and each line depicts a task (Table 3). Here we can see that most task ratings follow a similar trend across devices. The plot also highlights the relatively high correlations between the ratings of the realistic humanoid robot, humanoid robot, control interface and smart clothing in isolation with their ratings across all tasks; and reiterates the results shown in Figure 4(a) for the health-monitoring device.

Figure 4(c) depicts average device ratings (orange diamonds), and average correlation between device ratings in isolation and device ratings over all tasks (blue squares, with error bars). These correlations corroborate our intuition that general device ratings alone are insufficient for selecting devices for specific tasks.

Table 4: Factors ≥ 0.4 for the main PCA components

Component/Device	Accessory	Bionic	Cartoon	Physical	Clothing	Realistic
Robotic pet		0.6292				
Humanoid robot		0.5519				
Realistic hum. rob.						0.5820
Virtual human						0.7643
Mobile robot				0.5482		
Robotic arm				0.4873		
Self-driving vehicle				0.5305		
Emoticon			0.6497			
Cartoon character			0.7307			
Control interface	0.4072					
Smart glasses	0.5161					
Smart watch	0.4469					
Smart shirt					0.4572	
Smart gloves					0.6845	
Smart shoes					0.4022	
% of Variance:	35.76	19.06	9.01	8.13	4.58	4.46

3.2.2 Implicit Device Factors

Implicit factors represent latent information that will hopefully improve our understanding of users' attitudes toward devices, and enhance the factors in Table 1. To obtain implicit factors, we performed PCA with Varimax rotation [15] on the rating matrix of devices obtained from the second segment of our survey (Section 3.1). PCA yields component vectors of dimension N, where N is the number of devices, such that each element in a vector contains a score for a device. We retained only components with eigenvalue greater than 1 [16], which produced six PCs that account for 81% of the total variance. For each component, we employed a minimum threshold of 0.4 to accept a device as defining the component [8], which resulted in the removal of the health-monitoring device and the cleaning robot from all the components. Table 4 displays the PCs and the devices that exceeded the threshold, which provided the basis for naming the components. These components constitute the five factors at the bottom of Table 1 (physicality already appears at the top of Table 1).

It is worth noting that the scores from the PCA do not provide information about whether a factor has a positive or a negative effect on device acceptability; they just indicate the strength and direction of the influence of a factor on a PC, which may not directly reflect people's attitudes. For example, as seen in Table 4, Realism (as in the realistic humanoid robot and the virtual human) has a strong positive influence on the sixth PC. However, this does not tell us whether our participants liked or disliked this factor.

To obtain this information, we performed a linear regression where we fitted factors to device ratings. We first combined the factors inferred from the PCA (bottom of Table 1) with the manually devised factors (top of Table 1), splitting the wearable feature into clothing-like and accessory-like factors. The data for the regression was a binary matrix obtained by manually assigning a binary code to each device for each factor, e.g., a robotic pet is physical and is not humanoid, so we assigned 1 to the factor Physical and 0 to Humanoid. The weightings shown in the third column of Table 1 represent the impact of the factors in question on users' ratings of devices. For example, being Mains Powered has a high positive effect, while Realism has a small nega-

tive effect, which, at first glance, seems to contradict the high PCA score of the Realism component in Table 4. This seeming discrepancy may be explained by the fact that the importance of the components obtained by PCA stems from their ability to represent high variations in the data. However, importance in terms of variation does not necessarily lead to a high coefficient in linear regression. In addition, combining components inferred from PCA with manually designed components may result in some factors losing importance when others are presented.

4. RECOMMENDER SYSTEMS

The results in Section 3.2 indicate that device acceptability depends on the task at hand. To model users' attitudes toward a device-task combination, we employed an RS approach, where we built user- and item-based *Collaborative Filters* (*CFs*) [11,13,23,25] that predict the rating of a target user for a particular device-task combination.

In order to obtain an upper bound on performance, we used leave-one-out cross validation. Specifically, our models were built from the ratings given by all participants except the target user for all device-task combinations, and the ratings given by the target user for all device-task combinations except the one we are predicting (i.e., the models were obtained from a corpus of $93 \times 151 - 1 = 14042$ responses). This procedure was repeated for all the device-task combinations rated by the target user, and for all the participants. Clearly, it is not reasonable to ask a user to answer 150 questions in order to obtain a rating for the 151st device-task combination (we might as well ask about that combination). However, this approach yields an upper bound on performance due to its use of the maximum number of data points to predict one rating.[3]

To determine the performance range for an RS that predicts the ratings of devices for tasks, we investigated two baseline RSs, viz global RS and demographic RS.

- The global RS simply returns the average of all participants' ratings for a device-task combination.

- The demographic RS uses the ratings of the nearest neighbours of a user, in terms of the demographic features obtained from the first segment of our survey, to predict unseen ratings. The neighbourhood comprises 10 users nearest to the target user based on the Euclidean distance of their demographic information.

Table 5 displays the *Mean Absolute Error* (*MAE*) and *Root Mean Square Error* (*RMSE*) of the baseline RSs (global and demographic) and the upper-bound RSs (user- and item-based CFs). The top half of the table displays the RSs' performance for all ratings, and the bottom half for ratings above 3, which are the ratings of interest when one is making a recommendation.

Our results show that, surprisingly, the demographic RS performed similarly to the global RS. In addition, as expected, both the user- and item-based CFs outperformed the baseline RSs (statistically significant with p-value$\ll 0.01$, calculated with t-test for paired samples). The MAE and

---

[3]We employed the standard implementation of user- and item-based CF, rather than implementations that have improvements such as shrinkage to the mean [12] (significance weighting [11] is not relevant, as all device-task combinations have been rated).

Table 5: Performance of baseline RSs and CFs

RSs	MAE	RMSE
All Ratings		
Global	1.2744	1.4801
Demographic	1.2714	1.5050
User-based CF	0.8434	1.0547
Item-based CF	0.7498	0.9844
Ratings > 3		
Global	1.2588	1.4343
Demographic	1.2102	1.4250
User-based CF	0.8266	1.0365
Item-based CF	0.7055	0.9436

RMSE obtained by the item-based CF were lower than those obtained by the user-based CF (but the differences in predicted ratings were not statistically significant). Regardless of the good performance of the CFs, as indicated above, it is not realistic to expect users to answer 150 questions. In the next section, we describe our approach for reducing the number of questions.

4.1 Reducing the Number of Questions

In this section, we demonstrate that the ratings obtained from all the questions in our survey (except one) are not necessary to infer a user's rating of a particular device-task combination. We offer a *key question* (*KeyQ*) method that identifies a significantly smaller subset of important questions, which extract the most representative information about device-task combinations. The idea is that new users need to provide answers only to these key questions in order to enable a KeyQ-based CF to infer these users' answers to the remaining questions (we still require an initial set of complete survey results for training).

4.1.1 Identifying key questions

To identify key questions, we first performed *Weighted Principal Components Analysis* (*WPCA*) with Varimax rotation on the rating matrix of device-task combinations obtained from the third segment of our survey (Section 3.1). WPCA generated 36 components with eigenvalue greater than 1 (we also tried PCA, but it produced more components than WPCA); these components differ from the components obtained by PCA for devices (Section 3.2.2). Algorithm 1 was then applied to identify key questions on the basis of the top 10 components, which have an eigenvalue greater than 5, and explain 75.4% of the total variance.

In Step 2, the algorithm computes a 151×151 correlation matrix $\mathbf{M}$ of the 151 questions about the acceptability of device-task combinations (at a 95% confidence interval). The algorithm goes over each PC (10 in our case), and identifies key question $KeyQ_i$ as the question with the highest WPCA score among the 151 questions in PC_k (Step 6). In Steps 7-8, the algorithm appends $KeyQ_i$ to $\mathbf{KeyQ}$, and removes $KeyQ_i$ from $\mathbf{M}$; followed by the removal of the question that is most correlated to $KeyQ_i$, provided the correlation coefficient equals or exceeds 0.5 (Steps 9-13). The identification-removal steps are performed for each PC. Thus, after 10 iterations, the algorithm returns 10 key questions, and will have removed a maximum of 10 questions. This process is repeated until all the questions in $\mathbf{M}$ have been removed. At this point $\mathbf{KeyQ}$ contains a list of key questions (61 in our case) ranked in descending order of im-

---

Algorithm 1 Identifying key questions

```
1: procedure
2:     Compute correlation matrix M between all questions
3:     Set i = 1, KeyQ = ∅
4:     while M ≠ 0 do
5:         for k = 1 to NumberOfPCs do
6:             KeyQ_i ← arg max_{j=1}^{151}(abs(PC_{jk}))
7:             KeyQ ← append(KeyQ, KeyQ_i)
8:             M(KeyQ_i, *) = 0
9:             maxcf = max M(*, KeyQ_i)
10:            Q_maxcf = arg max M(*, KeyQ_i)
11:            if maxcf ≥ 0.5 then
12:                M(Q_maxcf, *) = 0
13:            end if
14:            Set i = i + 1
15:        end for
16:    end while
17:    Return KeyQ
18: end procedure
```

Table 6: Top 10 questions chosen by our algorithm

#	Device	Task
1	Cleaning robot	Give you reminders about your daily life
2	Driverless vehicle	Perform physical actions at your command at home
3	Wearable device	Give you reminders about your daily life
4	Robotic pet	Entertain you and your family
5	Cleaning robot	Inform you about an emergency condition of a person
6	Virtual agent	Adjust your home environment at your command
7	Mobile robot	Perform physical actions at your command at work
8	Realistic hum. robot	Locate misplaced objects at home
9	Robotic pet	Adjust your work environment at your command
10	Driverless vehicle	Autonomously perform physical actions at work

portance (i.e., one question for the highest-scoring factor of each PC_1-PC_{10}, one question for the highest-scoring factor of each PC_1-PC_{10} after one iteration, etc). Table 6 shows the top-10 questions chosen by our algorithm, where the questions have the following format: "How acceptable would you find for a *device* to *task*?", e.g., "How acceptable would you find for a *cleaning robot* to *give you reminders about your daily life*?" (Question 1). The tasks in some of these questions, e.g., a driverless vehicle performing physical actions at work, differ significantly from the tasks for which the devices were designed. However, these device-task combinations are highly predictive with respect to users' answers to a range of questions.

4.1.2 KeyQ user- and item-based CFs

The KeyQ user- and item-based CFs compute the ratings of $151-N$ device-task combinations after asking N key questions, which are selected from $\mathbf{KeyQ}$ in descending order of importance. For the KeyQ user-based CF, the similarity scores between a new user and users in the training set are calculated from the ratings given by all users to N device-task combinations; the new user's ratings for the re-

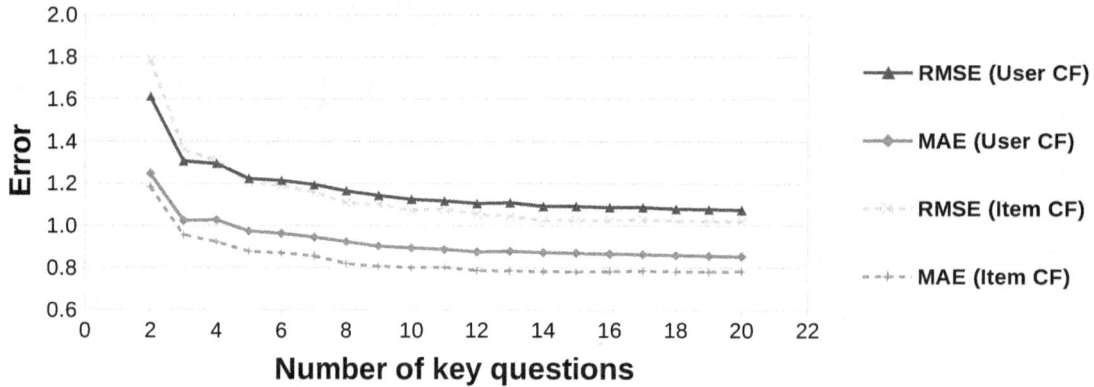

Figure 5: RS performance as a function of number of questions

Table 7: Results for key questions

# of Qs	User-based CF		Item-based CF	
	MAE	RMSE	MAE	RMSE
All Ratings				
10	0.8940	1.1228	0.8008	1.0710
20	0.8524	1.0737	0.7825	1.0186
30	0.8447	1.0641	0.7773	1.0054
40	0.8287	1.0410	0.7601	0.9809
50	0.8199	1.0299	0.7512	0.9703
Ratings > 3				
10	0.8650	1.0989	0.7425	1.0122
20	0.8296	1.0502	0.7419	0.9751
30	0.8367	1.0568	0.7575	0.9886
40	0.7995	1.0127	0.7156	0.9312
50	0.7953	1.0056	0.7129	0.9269

maining $151 - N$ device-task combinations are imputed on the basis of the ratings given by the other users, moderated by the similarity scores. For the KeyQ item-based CF, the similarity scores between all the device-task combinations are pre-computed on the basis of the ratings in the training set; after a new user has rated N device-task combinations, his/her ratings for the remaining $151 - N$ combinations are imputed on the basis of their similarity with the N rated combinations.

4.1.3 Performance Evaluation

Table 7 displays the MAE and RMSE obtained by the KeyQ user- and item-based CFs for different numbers of key questions. As seen in Tables 5 and 7, the KeyQ CFs significantly outperform both baselines after asking as few as 10 questions (statistically significant with $p\text{-}value \ll 0.01$). In addition, as expected, their performance generally improves as the number of questions increases (the only exception is between 20 and 30 questions for ratings greater than 3, where performance deteriorates slightly for both KeyQ CFs). As for the upper-bound case, the MAE and RMSE obtained by the KeyQ item-based CF are lower than those obtained by the KeyQ user-based CF (but the difference is not statistically significant).

Our results show that KeyQ user- and item-based CFs reach a similar level of performance to that of the corresponding upper-bound CFs. Specifically, the KeyQ user-based CF performs similarly to the upper-bound user-based

CF after asking 30 questions, yielding a slightly lower MAE and RMSE for 40 or more questions. The KeyQ item-based CF performs similarly to the upper-bound item-based CF after 40 questions. Although this is of theoretical interest, in a practical setting, one would not ask more than 20 questions, for which the KeyQ item-based CF has a creditable performance. As expected, the results for ratings above 3 follow this trend, but with better values for MAE and RMSE, which corroborate the practicality of our approach.

Figure 5 displays the performance metrics for our KeyQ CFs as a function of the number of questions. As seen in Figure 5, the errors decrease dramatically from 2 to 3 questions, with a relative flattening after 10 questions. This indicates that even asking a few questions can be of value.

5. CONCLUSIONS AND FUTURE WORK

In this paper, we described a survey that elicits people's views about smart devices in isolation and in the context of task performance. We have demonstrated how acceptability varies among different devices, and identified implicit factors that influence peoples' attitudes toward these devices. In addition, our results show how the task at hand influences the acceptability of individual devices.

We also applied an RS approach to model users' attitudes toward device-task combinations, and proposed a method for identifying key questions, which can significantly reduce the amount of effort and time required to model peoples' attitudes toward a range of device-task combinations. Our results show that user- and item-based CFs built with a relatively low number of well-chosen questions can obtain an acceptable level of accuracy, similar to that obtained by CFs built with a much higher number of questions. This finding paves the way for new avenues of investigation about the generation of minimal, coherent sets of questions for RSs.

In the future, we propose to use our results to help users select devices for specific tasks, thereby improving device adoption. We also aim to conduct a study that investigates factors that influence device acceptance after usage.

Acknowledgments.

This material is based upon work supported by the Air Force Office of Scientific Research, Asian Office of Aerospace Research and Development (AOARD), under award number FA2386-14-1-0010. The authors thank Duy Han Phan for his initial assistance on this project.

6. REFERENCES

[1] J. Alexandersson, U. Schäfer, M. Rekrut, F. Arnold, and S. Reifers. Kochbot in the intelligent kitchen speech-enabled assistance and cooking control in a smart home. In *AAL-Kongress 2015*, 2015.

[2] C. Bartneck, T. Suzuki, T. Kanda, and T. Nomura. The influence of people's culture and prior experiences with aibo on their attitude towards robots. *AI & Society*, 21(1):217–230, 2006.

[3] E. Broadbent, I. H. Kuo, Y. I. Lee, J. Rabindran, N. Kerse, R. Stafford, and B. A. MacDonald. Attitudes and reactions to a healthcare robot. *Telemedicine and e-Health*, 16(5):608–613, 2010.

[4] R. Burke. Hybrid recommender systems: Survey and experiments. *User Modeling and User-Adapted Interaction*, 12(4):331–370, 2002.

[5] D. Conti, A. Cattani, S. Di Nuovo, and A. Di Nuovo. A cross-cultural study of acceptance and use of robotics by future psychology practitioners. In *RO-MAN 2015 – Proceedings of the 24th IEEE International Symposium on Robot and Human Interactive Communication*, pages 555–560, 2015.

[6] D. DeVault, R. Artstein, G. Benn, T. Dey, E. Fast, A. Gainer, K. Georgila, J. Gratch, A. Hartholt, M. Lhommet, et al. SimSensei Kiosk: A virtual human interviewer for healthcare decision support. In *AAMAS 2014 – Proceedings of the 2014 International Conference on Autonomous Agents and Multi-agent Systems*, pages 1061–1068, 2014.

[7] Eurobarometer. Public attitudes towards robots. Technical Report 382, European Commission, Directorate-General for Information Society and Media, 2012.

[8] E. Ferguson and T. Cox. Exploratory factor analysis: A users' guide. *International Journal of Selection and Assessment*, 1(2):84–94, 1993.

[9] D. Fischinger, P. Einramhof, K. Papoutsakis, W. Wohlkinger, P. Mayer, P. Panek, S. Hofmann, T. Koertner, A. Weiss, A. Argyros, and M. Vincze. Hobbit, a care robot supporting independent living at home: First prototype and lessons learned. *Robotics and Autonomous Systems*, 75, Part A:60 – 78, 2016.

[10] N. Gesundheit, P. Brutlag, P. Youngblood, W. T. Gunning, N. Zary, and U. Fors. The use of virtual patients to assess the clinical skills and reasoning of medical students: initial insights on student acceptance. *Medical Teacher*, 31(8):739–742, 2009.

[11] J. L. Herlocker, J. A. Konstan, A. Borchers, and J. Riedl. An algorithmic framework for performing collaborative filtering. In *SIGIR-99 – Proceedings of the 22nd Annual International ACM SIGIR Conference on Research and Development in Information Retrieval*, pages 230–237, 1999.

[12] W. James and C. M. Stein. Estimation with quadratic loss. In *Proceedings of the Fourth Berkeley Symposium on Mathematical Statistics and Probability, vol. 1*, pages 361–379, 1961.

[13] D. Jannach, M. Zanker, A. Felfernig, and G. Friedrich. *Recommender Systems: An Introduction*. Cambridge University Press, 2010.

[14] C. Jayawardena, I. H. Kuo, U. Unger, A. Igic, R. Wong, C. I. Watson, R. Stafford, E. Broadbent, P. Tiwari, J. Warren, et al. Deployment of a service robot to help older people. In *IROS 2010 – Proceedings of the IEEE/RSJ International Conference on Intelligent Robots and Systems*, pages 5990–5995, 2010.

[15] H. F. Kaiser. The Varimax criterion for analytic rotation in factor analysis. *Psychometrika*, 23(3):187–200, 1958.

[16] H. F. Kaiser. The application of electronic computers to factor analysis. *Educational and psychological measurement*, 20(1):141–151, 1960.

[17] M. W. Link, P. P. Armsby, R. C. Hubal, and C. I. Guinn. Accessibility and acceptance of responsive virtual human technology as a survey interviewer training tool. *Computers in Human Behavior*, 22(3):412 – 426, 2006.

[18] R. Lyons, T. R. Johnson, M. K. Khalil, and J. C. Cendán. The impact of social context on learning and cognitive demands for interactive virtual human simulations. *PeerJ*, 2:e372, 2014.

[19] M. M. Morandell, A. Hochgatterer, S. Fagel, and S. Wassertheurer. Avatars in assistive homes for the elderly. In *Proceedings of the 4th Symposium of the Workgroup on Human-Computer Interaction and Usability Engineering of the Austrian Computer Society*, pages 391–402, 2008.

[20] L. Palopoli, A. Argyros, J. Birchbauer, A. Colombo, D. Fontanelli, A. Legay, A. Garulli, A. Giannitrapani, D. Macii, F. Moro, P. Nazemzadeh, P. Padeleris, R. Passerone, G. Poier, D. Prattichizzo, T. Rizano, L. Rizzon, S. Scheggi, and S. Sedwards. Navigation assistance and guidance of older adults across complex public spaces: the DALI approach. *Intelligent Service Robotics*, 8(2):77–92, 2015.

[21] N. Reich and F. Eyssel. Attitudes towards service robots in domestic environments: The role of personality characteristics, individual interests, and demographic variables. *Paladyn, Journal of Behavioral Robotics*, 4(2):123–130, 2013.

[22] N. Reich-Stiebert and F. Eyssel. Learning with educational companion robots? Toward attitudes on education robots, predictors of attitudes, and application potentials for education robots. *International Journal of Social Robotics*, 7(5):875–888, 2015.

[23] P. Resnick and H. R. Varian. Recommender systems. *Communications of the ACM*, 40(3):56–58, 1997.

[24] A. Saha, M. Kuzlu, M. Pipattanasomporn, S. Rahman, O. Elma, U. S. Selamogullari, M. Uzunoglu, and B. Yagcitekin. A robust building energy management algorithm validated in a smart house environment. *Intelligent Industrial Systems*, 1(2):163–174, 2015.

[25] U. Shardanand and P. Maes. Social information filtering: Algorithms for automating "word of mouth". In *CHI-95 – Proceedings of the SIGCHI Conference on Human Factors in Computing Systems*, pages 210–217, 1995.

[26] A. Spagnolli, E. Guardigli, V. Orso, A. Varotto, and L. Gamberini. Measuring user acceptance of wearable symbiotic devices: Validation study across application scenarios. In *Symbiotic 2014: Proceedings of the Third*

International Workshop on Symbiotic Interaction, pages 87–98, 2014.

[27] V. Venkatesh, M. G. Morris, G. B. Davis, and F. D. Davis. User acceptance of information technology: Toward a unified view. *MIS quarterly*, pages 425–478, 2003.

[28] F. M. Verberne, J. Ham, and C. J. Midden. Trust in smart systems: Sharing driving goals and giving information to increase trustworthiness and acceptability of smart systems in cars. *Human Factors*, 54(5):799–810, 2012.

[29] P. Wu and C. Miller. Results from a field study: The need for an emotional relationship between the elderly and their assistive technologies. *Foundations of Augmented Cognition*, 11:889–898, 2005.

[30] R. Yaghoubzadeh, M. Kramer, K. Pitsch, and S. Kopp. Virtual agents as daily assistants for elderly or cognitively impaired people. In *IVA 2013 – Proceedings of the 13th International Conference on Intelligent Virtual Agents*, pages 79–91, 2013.

[31] S. Yoshida, T. Shirokura, Y. Sugiura, D. Sakamoto, T. Ono, M. Inami, and T. Igarashi. RoboJockey: Designing an entertainment experience with robots. *IEEE Computer Graphics and Applications*, 36(1):62–69, 2016.

Interactive Modeling of Concept Drift and Errors in Relevance Feedback

Antti Kangasrääsiö° Yi Chen° Dorota Głowacka* Samuel Kaski°
°Helsinki Institute for Information Technology HIIT, Department of Computer Science, Aalto University
* Helsinki Institute for Information Technology HIIT, Department of Computer Science,
University of Helsinki
first.last@hiit.fi

ABSTRACT

In exploratory search tasks, users usually start with considerable uncertainty about their search goals, and so the search intent of the user may be volatile as the user is constantly learning and reformulating her search hypothesis during the search. This may lead to a noticeable concept drift in the relevance feedback given by the user. We formulate a Bayesian regression model for predicting the accuracy of each individual user feedback and thus find outliers in the feedback data set. To accompany this model, we introduce a timeline interface that visualizes the feedback history to the user and gives her suggestions on which past feedback is likely in need of adjustment. This interface also allows the user to adjust the feedback accuracy inferences made by the model. Simulation experiments demonstrate that the performance of the new user model outperforms a simpler baseline and that the performance approaches that of an oracle, given a small amount of additional user interaction. A user study shows that the proposed modeling technique, combined with the timeline interface, made it easier for the users to notice and correct mistakes in their feedback, resulted in better and more diverse recommendations, allowed users to easier find items they liked, and was more understandable.

CCS Concepts

•**Information systems** → *Personalization; Query reformulation; Search interfaces; Probabilistic retrieval models; Recommender systems;* •**Human-centered computing** → Interface design prototyping;

Keywords

Concept drift; Exploratory search; Interactive user modeling; Probabilistic user models; User interfaces

UMAP '16, July 13-17, 2016, Halifax, NS, Canada
© 2016 ACM. ISBN 978-1-4503-4370-1/16/07. . . $15.00
DOI: http://dx.doi.org/10.1145/2930238.2930243

1. INTRODUCTION

Search can be broadly divided into two categories: (1) exploratory search, where the goals are ill-defined and may change as search progresses, and (2) lookup search, where the user has a specific target in mind [21, 28]. A lookup search begins with the users expressing their information need as precisely as possible to reach the correct area of the information space. By contrast, user behavior in exploratory search is highly dynamic. Users begin exploration with no clear search goals in mind and issue search queries that are imprecise at first. They browse through the search results and iteratively reformulate their queries using new keywords they discover [21]. As they gradually learn from the results, they reformulate their search goals as well as the the criteria for judging the relevance of result items.

For example, an exploratory search session could progress as follows. A user wants to find a nice warm place for spending a holiday. She may start her search with a very general query, such as "warm holiday resorts". At this point, all of the results related to warm holiday resorts would be relevant. After browsing some of the results, the user learns of different types of resorts and realises that she is particularly interested in seaside resorts, and that there are nice seaside resorts in colder regions as well. As her goal drifts, results related to inland resorts are no longer relevant, whereas results related to seaside resorts in colder regions become relevant. She may then adjust her search query to make it reflect her current search interests, such as by adding the keyword "seaside" and removing the keyword "warm".

In addition to being uncertain of the search goal, users are often also uncertain about how to formulate and refine their search queries in exploratory tasks [8]. A recently developed search system called *SciNet* [13, 14, 15] aims to assist the user in exploratory search tasks by allowing her to interactively refine her search query. The user starts the search with a general keyword query and gradually refines the system's user model through interactive relevance feedback to keywords suggested by the system. However, the user model in this system assumes that: (1) all the user feedback is equally accurate, (2) the user makes no mistakes in giving the feedback, and (3) no learning or changes in the user's search interests occurs as the search progresses. In short, the system does not take the possibility of concept drift [12, 27] into account.

To illustrate concept drift in practice, let us return to the previous example. Imagine that the user initially searched for "warm holiday resorts", but then decided to add the keywords "seaside" and "arctic", as she remembered that ice fishing was something she had always wanted to try out. However, now the search query contains both keywords "warm" and "arctic". This presents a challenge for the search engine, as there may not be any results that fulfill both requirements. In this case, it would be sensible if the search engine could recognize the conflict in the user feedback, and ask the user for clarification. For example, the search engine might suggest that the user removes the keyword "warm" from her query, as the keyword "arctic" is more recent. In absence of this clarification, it might be sensible for the search engine to decide whether "warm seaside holiday resorts" or "arctic seaside holiday resorts" is more likely to be what the user wanted to find, and return results based on the most likely model of the user's interests.

In this paper, we improve over the existing SciNet system by formulating a user model that is able to deal with concept drift. The proposed user model is a Bayesian regression model that is able to estimate both the current search intent of the user and the accuracy of the relevance feedback provided by the user. The model also allows the user to make corrections to the accuracy inferences made by the model.

To accompany this model, we introduce a timeline interface that shows the user her recent feedback history. Relevance feedback with low estimated accuracy is highlighted in the timeline. The interface allows the user to refine previously given feedback to update the model. The interface also allows the user to specify which past feedback is certainly accurate.

We demonstrate that the proposed model is able to improve retrieval performance in a simulation experiment. In the user study, participants report that this system makes it easier for them to notice mistakes in their feedback and make corrections to the user model. In addition, it also resulted in better and more diverse recommendations, allowed users to find items they liked easier and was more understandable to use.

The paper is organised as follows. In the next section we present a brief overview of related literature. Next, we describe the proposed user model and the new interface that allows the user to adjust the user model. Finally, we present results from a simulation study and a user study.

2. RELATED WORK

In most interactive systems, the user has a concept in mind that the system is trying to learn while the user interacts with the system, for example, a particular genre of music or specific types of documents. Many of such systems rely on machine learning techniques to help the system to identify the concept that the user has in mind. However, as human interests are often quite complex, it is common that the predictions will have errors, especially if the data are noisy or there are only very little of them. Therefore, in recent years there has been a growing interest in developing new applications that would allow the user to correct the model of her needs that a machine learning system has built [10, 16, 18, 24]. This type of a system explains the reasons for its predictions to the user, who in turn explains corrections back to the system. This both helps the system to make a better model of the user's interests and helps the user to build a mental model to predict how the system will behave. Researchers have explored using this cycle of quick interactions to train instance-based classifiers [11], elicit labels for the most important instances [7], and to improve reinforcement learning for automated agents [17]. However, none of the above applications deal with the idea of involving the user in the interactive search loop in the concept drift setting.

Open user models are another important branch of research in the area of user modeling [1, 4]. A user model is an internal representation of the user's knowledge or interests that an adaptive information retrieval system (IR) can use to recommend new items to a given user. In most IR systems, the user model is hidden from the user. However, adaptive IR systems with open user models allow the user to view the system's representation of her interests or

search goals and edit it. Open user modeling has been very popular in the e-learning community [6, 9] and has also been applied in other domains, such as news recommendation [2] or Wikipedia page recommendation [19]. Recent studies show that interactive open user models can improve user performance and user satisfaction [4, 13, 15]. However, these systems assume that the user interests are fixed and do not change over a search session. Our modeling technique combined with the proposed interactive user model visualisation takes into account the gradual concept drift that frequently occurs in exploratory search.

3. THE USER MODEL

We assume that we have a large collection of items that we could recommend to the user. Each item i has a feature vector $\boldsymbol{x}_i$ and our main goal is to estimate the relevance y_i of each item, based on observations made about the user's search interests. In general, these observations are based on relevance feedback provided by the user: the user indicates that the relevance of item i is y_i.

We make the simplifying assumption that the function that predicts the relevance of an item based on its features is approximately linear. We assume that the errors made by the model are normally distributed so the general accuracy of this model is described by the variance σ^2. To accommodate observations that have different accuracies, we assume that each observation has an accuracy factor w_i that scales the global model variance. This gives us the following observation model:

$$y_i \sim Normal(\boldsymbol{x}_i\boldsymbol{\phi}, \sigma^2/w_i), \tag{1}$$

where $\boldsymbol{\phi}$ are the linear model coefficients.

To make the model fully Bayesian, we assume prior distributions for the parameters:

$$\phi_j \sim Normal(\mu_\phi, \lambda_\phi), \tag{2}$$

$$\sigma^2 \sim InverseGamma(\alpha_{\sigma^2}, \beta_{\sigma^2}), \tag{3}$$

$$w_i \sim Gamma(\alpha_w, \beta_w), \tag{4}$$

$$w_i^{fix} \sim Delta(1.0), \tag{5}$$

where ϕ_j is the jth component of the vector $\boldsymbol{\phi}$. Generally, we assume that the accuracies of the observations are unknown and drawn from a Gamma distribution. However, we also allow the user to inform the system about the accuracy of her feedback: if the user has explicitly marked certain feedback as accurate, we use w_i^{fix} instead of w_i, making the accuracy for that feedback equal to 1. We also assume that the most recent feedback is always similarly accurate. In this paper we will refer to this model as the *ARD model*, as the determination of observation weights can be seen as Automatic Relevance Determination [20].

To estimate the posterior of the parameters $(\boldsymbol{\phi}, \sigma^2, \boldsymbol{w})$ given the observations $\{(y_i, \boldsymbol{x}_i)\}$ and hyperparameters $(\mu_\phi, \lambda_\phi, \alpha_{\sigma^2}, \beta_{\sigma^2}, \alpha_w, \beta_w)$, we use mean-field variational inference [3]. Initial values of the variables are drawn from the prior. The estimates of the relevance values are calculated by using the mean of the posterior distribution of $\boldsymbol{\phi}$.[1]

Variational inference on a linear Gaussian model with individual accuracies for observations was first introduced in [26]. A similar

---

[1]For keywords that the user had given explicit feedback to, we adjusted the relevance value to be the mean of the given feedback and estimated relevance. The reason for this was that in a pilot study the users sometimes complained that the keywords did not go where the user dragged them. This "control problem" was also discussed in [15] and our current approach is a simplified way to address it.

model has been used successfully for outlier detection in robotics [25]. Our model differs from it by allowing the user to correct the inferences, and also by estimating σ^2 with variational inference instead of using a point estimate. Taking full distributions into account is important because only a very small amount of user feedback is available for fitting the model.

In the user experiments, we made a model for the relevance of the various keywords that appear in the recommended documents. The feature vectors of the keywords were constructed dynamically based on the TF-IDF scores of the keywords in the top 400 documents. The feature vectors were normalized to unit length (L2 norm). User relevance feedback was in the range $[0, 1]$, where larger values indicate higher relevance. The documents were ranked based on the estimated relevance of the most relevant keywords (more details can be found in [13]).

4. USER INTERFACE

A timeline user interface, shown in Figure 1, was designed to allow the user to interact with the model. The primary purpose of the new interface was to notify the user when past feedback was estimated to be inaccurate and to allow her to make suitable corrections, either to her feedback or to the inferences made by the model. The motivation for the visual design was to give the user a simple overview of the feedback she has given in the current search session. In longer sessions, it is likely that the user will not remember the details of the feedback she has given earlier.

The timeline interface is integrated to a search interface that is similar to the one presented in [15]. The full interface is shown in Figure 2. The search results (a list of 10 most relevant documents recommended to the user) are displayed on the right side of the screen. On the left side, the user intent model is presented as a radar visualisation. The user can adjust the model by moving keywords to new locations on the radar (i.e. provide relevance feedback to the keywords). The timeline interface is situated under the radar.

The search starts with the user typing in an initial query in the search bar. This initial query is then transformed into a corresponding set of relevance feedback, which is added to the timeline and used to fit the initial user model.[2] The top 10 relevant keywords then appear in the center of the radar visualisation, and the list of recommended documents is presented on the right hand side of the screen.

While the user is performing the search, the timeline displays the keywords used so far in chronological order. The most recent feedback given by the user appears at the top of the timeline. Each feedback on the timeline has a green bar on the right hand side of the timeline to indicate the relevance of its keyword. The longer the bar, the higher the relevance the user has given to the keyword.

Feedback with low estimated accuracy is made salient to the user by yellow backgrounds.[3] Highlighting is expected to help the user to find feedback in need of revision more efficiently. The user can adjust the relevance value of a feedback by clicking on the corresponding position on the bar. She can also indicate that a feedback

---

[2]These "pseudo feedbacks" were generated by finding the most common keywords that appear in the documents that were retrieved based on the initial query alone. Keywords that were at least half as common as the most common keyword were selected. The feedback values were in proportion to the frequency of appearance, so that the most common keyword received feedback 1. This relevance feedback was used to initialize the user model.

[3]Feedback is highlighted with increasing intensities when the estimated accuracy w_i is below the threshold values 0.65 (light yellow), 0.55 (medium yellow) or 0.45 (dark yellow). These values were tuned by hand.

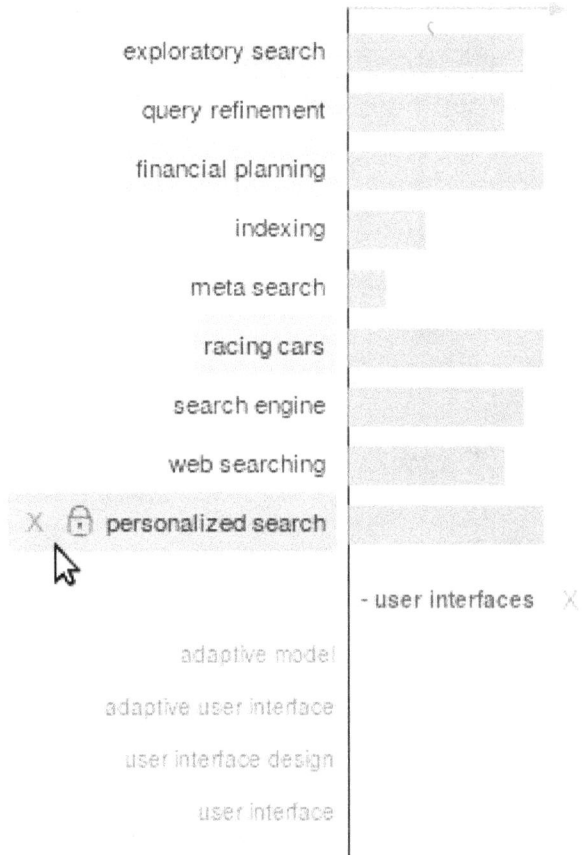

Figure 1: The timeline interface visualizes past feedback (recent feedback on top) and provides the user with ways to interact with it. The interface for deleting and marking feedback as accurate is hidden unless the user hovers the mouse on top of the keyword (blue background with mouse). Feedback most likely in need of revision is highlighted with yellow background. Highlighted feedback has an explanatory tooltip: "Is this feedback still accurate?". The user can click the lock icon to indicate that she is sure that it is accurate. The user can also adjust the relevance of a given keyword using the green bar. The feedback can be removed by clicking the X icon. The user can give feedback to keywords used in previous sessions by clicking on the area right of the keyword (blue keywords at the bottom). Hovering the mouse above the area shows a blue bar visualizing the feedback value (not shown in this image).

is accurate by clicking the lock icon, or delete a feedback by clicking the X-icon (removes the effect of the feedback from the model). The option to react to both true and false highlights (respectively by adjusting keyword relevance and marking feedback as accurate) was motivated by the results of the simulation experiment.

Keywords from previous search sessions are added as expandable lists at the bottom of the timeline. These lists can be removed by clicking the X-icon. The motivation for this feature was to provide the user with a convenient way to re-use keywords she interacted with in previous sessions.

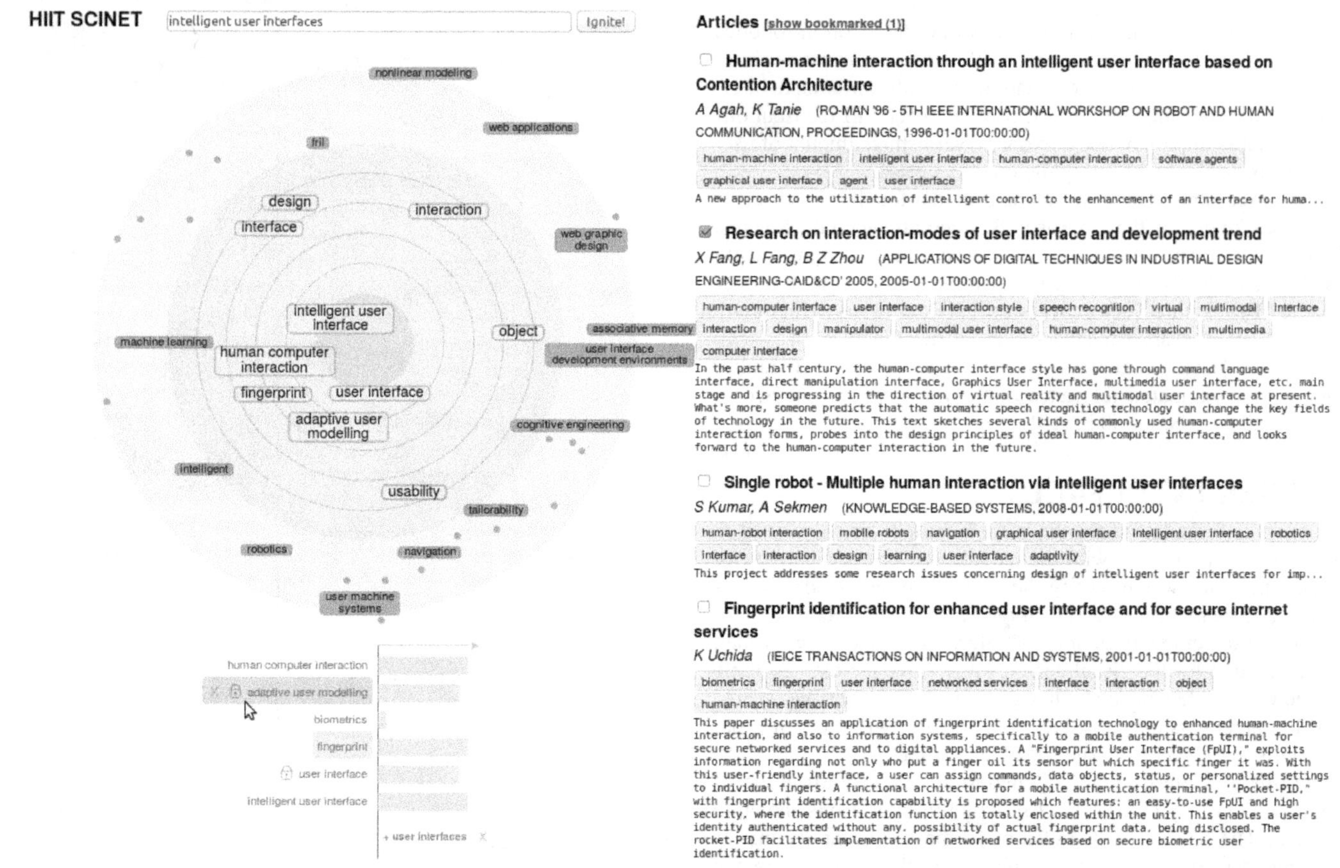

Figure 2: The system's search interface. At the top of the screen there is a keyword search bar. Below it, a visualization of the current user model is shown using a radar metaphor: relevant keywords are closer to the center and less relevant ones are further away from the center. At the very edge of the radar there are keyword suggestions. At the bottom of the screen is the proposed timeline interface, showing the feedback the user has given so far in the current search session, as well as lists of keywords used in past sessions. On the right hand side of the radar visualisation there is a list of the most relevant documents. The abstract of each document can be expanded by clicking on it. The user can also bookmark articles to be able to access them at a later time by opening the bookmark list (blue link at the top).

5. SIMULATION EXPERIMENT

To study the performance of the user model, we conducted an experiment with a simulated user. As a dataset we used the 20 Newsgroups dataset [23] containing 2000 newsgroup messages, 100 from each of 20 newsgroups. L2-normalized TF-IDF feature vectors of length 539 were generated for the posts. Terms with document frequency over 0.2 or under 0.04 were thresholded to remove too rare and too common terms.

In each repeated experiment the simulated user selected at random one of the 20 newsgroups as the search target. The user then initialized the query by indicating two positive examples from this group at random. The user model replied with a list of 50 most relevant documents and, depending on the scenario, one highlighted past feedback the user should re-evaluate. The user then replied by giving noisy feedback to one item in the list of 50 and, depending on the scenario, by possibly revising the highlighted feedback. This cycle was repeated 100 times. After each step, the F1-score of the list of 50 items was stored (representing the quality of found items).

The user's noisy feedback was generated as follows. From the list of items, 70% of the time the user selected a positive example and gave it relevance feedback with value 1. The user selected a negative example 10% of the time, and gave it relevance feedback 0. 20% of the time the user selected a random item from the list and gave it relevance feedback 1 with 87.5% probability or 0 with 12.5% probability. The proportions of negative and positive feedback reflect our past experience with user behavior with similar systems. The proportion of noise was chosen to be small,[4] but sufficient to demonstrate the effect of the new user model.

The experiment was repeated in four different scenarios. In Scenario A, no items were highlighted to the user, and thus the user made no revisions to given feedback. In Scenario B, the user revised the highlighted feedback if it did not have the correct relevance value (i.e. revised true positive highlights) and indicated that the feedback was accurate if it already had the correct relevance value (i.e. indicated false positive highlights). In Scenario C, the user only revised true positive highlights, and in Scenario D the user only indicated false positive highlights.

We compared the performance of the ARD model to a baseline and an oracle. The baseline was a Linear Gaussian model that was otherwise similar to the ARD model, except that all feedback was

---

[4]Assuming half of the items in the list were relevant, the average proportion of false positive feedback was 1.25% and false negative feedback was 8.75%

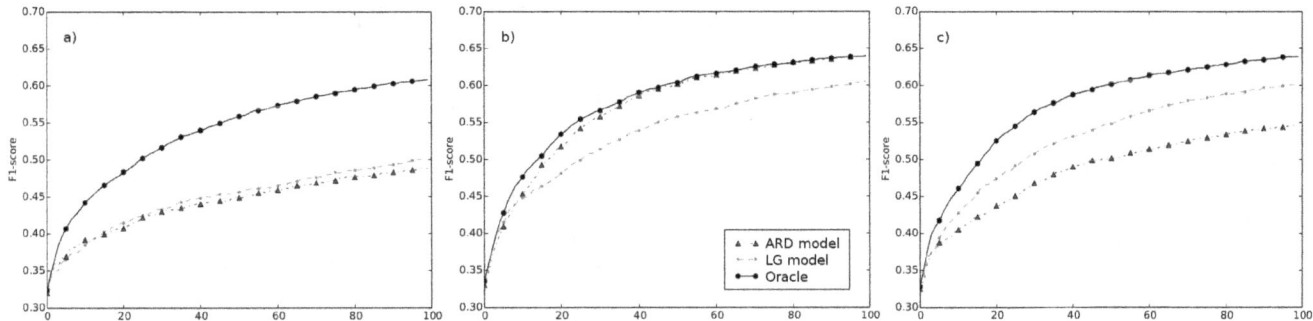

Figure 3: Simulated F1-scores during 100 feedback iterations (iteration number in x-axis), averaged over 200 search sessions, in three of the four different scenarios. a) No items highlighted to the user. b) One item highlighted to the user at each step, user revises true positives and indicates false positives. c) One item highlighted to the user at each step, user revises true positives but does not indicate false positives. The results from the scenario where the user indicates false positives but does not revise true positives were similar to a) and were left out to save space.

assumed to be equally accurate (i.e. $w_i = 1$). We will call this the *LG model*. The *Oracle* knew which feedback was correct[5] and only used correct observations in fitting the model, otherwise being similar to the LG model.

The ARD model chose the feedback to be highlighted by selecting the feedback having the lowest w_i value. Draws were resolved randomly. The LG model sampled the highlighted feedback uniformly and the Oracle highlighted randomly chosen incorrect feedbacks.

The prior parameters of all the algorithms were hand tuned over a small number of iterations to avoid over-fitting. The used parameters were $\mu_\phi = 0.0, \lambda_\phi = 0.1, \alpha_{\sigma^2} = 2.5, \beta_{\sigma^2} = 0.5, \alpha_w = 0.7$ and $\beta_w = 1.0$. All the models were fit using variational approximation. The convergence criterion was set to be an absolute change of less than 0.1 in the unnormalized KL-divergence. The initial state was drawn from the prior.

The retrieval performance is shown in Figure 3. We observe that the ARD model performed similarly to the LG model if no corrections were made to the historical feedback (Scenario A). If the user reacted to both true and false highlights (Scenario B), the performance of the ARD model approached that of the Oracle. The LG model did not improve as much in this case, as the method for selecting the highlighted items was random. If the user made corrections to only the true positive highlighted items, the ARD model improved the retrieval performance from Scenario A, but the performance was not as good as in Scenario B. Surprisingly, the LG model performed better than the ARD model in this scenario. The reason for this was that if the ARD model made a mistake in identifying an outlier, this was not corrected by the user in this scenario, and thus the model always highlighted this particular item instead of trying some other items. In comparison, the LG model would eventually find the correct items to highlight through random sampling. If the user made corrections to only the false positive highlighted items (Scenario D), the improvements were small.

We also measured the average runtimes of the models per step in wall clock time. Averaged over all scenarios, after 10 steps ARD had an average runtime of 0.6 s, whereas LG had 0.4 s. After 100 steps the average runtimes were 1.4 s for ARD and 0.8 s for LG. Simulations were made in a computing cluster equipped with 2.6 GHz processors.

Overall, we observed that the ARD model provided improve-

ments over the simple baseline without increasing the runtime considerably. We also observed that the user should be able to react to both true and false highlights for the best performance when using the ARD model.

In this experiment the user model directly estimated the relevance of the newsgroup posts, instead of the keywords appearing in the posts. This was done to simplify the situation. However, the general results should apply to the more complex case as well, where we first estimate the relevance of keywords, and then order the documents based on the most relevant keywords.

6. USER STUDY

We ran a user study to understand how the new user model and interface affect (1) the ability of the user to notice mistakes in her feedback and make corrections to the user model, (2) quality of the recommendations, measured both objectively (evaluated by an external expert) and subjectively (reported by the users), (3) user interaction with the system, such as interaction strategies and amount of interaction events.

6.1 Methodology

We compared the proposed interface and user model to a baseline with a simpler user model and interface. In the baseline, the timeline visualization was hidden from the user and the LG model was used for predicting the relevance of keywords. Thus the differences in user behavior are attributable to either the new user model or the new interface.

Eighteen participants (three female), aged 20 – 30, took part in the user study. All of the participants were university students. Each participant was compensated with a movie ticket worth approximately 10 EUR.

Each participant performed two tasks – one with each interface. The order of tasks and interfaces was balanced as was the pairing of interfaces with tasks. Before performing the two tasks, the participants were shown a video tutorial on how to use the two interfaces. This was followed by a 30 minute practice session to allow the users to familiarize themselves with the systems at their own pace. In the practice session the participants were instructed to perform a free search related to their own study interests. The timeline interface was used in the practice session as it covers all the features present in both interfaces.

In the main tasks, the user was instructed to write a short draft of an essay on a given topic. The task descriptions followed the template: "Many types of X exist in the field of Y. Try to find up to

---

[5]Whether a feedback was correct or not was recorded when it was generated. This information was only available to the Oracle.

189

five types of X used in Y. Give some concrete examples of different X. Write your answer as an essay draft and bookmark at least 10 relevant articles that you could use as a reference in writing the article." The two topics were "algorithms used in robotics" and "examples of information retrieval systems". Before performing each task, participants rated their familiarity with the topic on a 5-point Likert scale. All users reported familiarity between 1 and 4 (average 1.9 for task 1, 2.1 for task 2). The duration of each task was 20 minutes with a short break between the tasks.

After each task, the participants completed the SUS [5] questionnaire with 10 questions (Table 1) and a modified version of the ResQue questionnaire [22] with 19 questions (Table 2). The ResQue questions were the same as the ones used in [15] with four additional questions (No. 10, 11, 13 and 15 in Table 2). The aim of the additional questions was to learn how useful the participants found the system in situations when the user had made an error or when concept drift was happening. The motivation to use the SUS questionnaire was to find out if there was any big differences in the general usability of these two systems. The modified ResQue questionnaire was used both to evaluate the overall quality of the search engines, and to answer the more detailed research questions regarding the performance in concept drift situations.

During the experiments we logged the keywords seen and manipulated by the users at each iteration, the documents presented to the users, as well as the documents bookmarked by the users. After both tasks were completed, we conducted a semi-structured interview with the participants.

The parameters of the user model were hand tuned over a small number of iterations to avoid over-fitting. The used parameters were: $\mu_\phi = 0.0, \lambda_\phi = 0.1, \alpha_{\sigma^2} = 2.0, \beta_{\sigma^2} = 0.1, \alpha_w = 1.0$ and $\beta_w = 1.0$. The algorithm was limited to 10 iterations of the variational fitting to guarantee fast on-line performance. Based on initial tests the algorithm often converged before the limit.

6.2 User Study Results

Below, we report on the analysis of the user study results. Two participants were excluded from the analysis as they were not able to complete one of the tasks successfully.[6]

6.2.1 Questionnaire Results

The SUS scores (Table 1) were similar for both interfaces. The average total score was 68 for the baseline and 72 for the new interface ($p = 0.7$).[7] This indicates that the usability of the system did not suffer from the added functionality.

The new interface got better ResQue scores (Table 2). The average total score was 50 for the baseline and 55 for the new interface ($p = 0.04$). User ratings indicate that the new user model generates better and more diverse results (ResQue 1, 3, 16). It was easier for the users to find items they liked using the new system (ResQue 2, 14, 15). It was easier for users to notice mistakes in previous feedbacks and make corrections to the model using the timeline interface (ResQue 9, 10, 11, 13). The users were able to understand the search engine behavior better with the new interface (ResQue 4, 5, 6, 12, 18; SUS 6).

6.2.2 Log Data Analysis

We logged the actions of the users during the experiment. The users performed on average 5.6 keyword queries per task with the

---

[6]Users were excluded from analysis if two independent experts rated their task performance as 1 out of 5 in at least one task.

[7]The reported p-values were calculated with the paired two-sided Wilcoxon signed-rank test and rounded up. Each p-value was calculated independently and was reported as such for completeness.

N	B	p	Question
3.8	**3.8**	0.9	1: I think that I would like to use this system frequently
2.6	**2.3**	1.0	2: I found the system unnecessarily complex
3.9	**3.9**	1.0	3: I thought the system was easy to use
2.0	**2.0**	1.0	4: I think that I would need the support of a technical person to be able to use this system
3.6	**3.6**	0.8	5: I found the various functions in this system were well integrated
2.2	2.9	0.2	6: I thought there was too much inconsistency in this system
4.3	**4.4**	0.4	7: I would imagine that most people would learn to use this system very quickly
2.1	**2.0**	0.9	8: I found the system very cumbersome to use
3.9	**4.0**	0.6	9: I felt very confident using the system
1.8	1.9	0.8	10: I needed to learn a lot of things before I could get going with this system

Table 1: SUS score question averages for the new interface (N) and the baseline (B) system with p-values. Questions were scored on a 5-point Likert scale from 1 (disagree) to 5 (agree). The better value in each row is in boldface; higher is better for odd numbered questions and lower is better for even numbered questions.

baseline and 3.8 with the new interface ($p = 0.2$). The number of keyword-related interactions (giving feedback to a keyword, removing or marking feedback as accurate) was larger with the new interface. Users did on average 5.5 keyword interactions per task with the baseline and 10.8 with the new interface ($p = 0.001$). The interactions with the new interface consisted of on average 6.8 keyword feedback on the radar ($p = 0.09$ compared to baseline), 1.2 keyword feedback on the timeline, 1.9 keyword deletions from the timeline, 0.9 feedback marked as accurate and 0.1 feedback given to archived keywords from past search sessions. These results indicate that users interacted more frequently with the new system. This was not entirely due to the fact that they had more interaction options, as on average users also performed more interactions with the radar when using the new interface. Users also seemed to write fewer keyword queries, likely resulting from the increased interaction options.

Various proxies for users' engagement and quality of the retrieved results were also monitored. Users expanded to view on average 15 articles' abstracts with the baseline and 17 with the new interface ($p = 0.5$). The average number of viewed unique articles per task was similar for both interfaces: 61 for the baseline and 63 for the new interface ($p = 0.4$). The average numbers of viewed unique keywords per task were 43 central and 197 peripheral for the baseline, and 41 central and 233 peripheral for the new interface (local: $p = 0.8$, peripheral: $p = 0.1$). It appears that the new system provided more diverse keyword suggestions to the user.

6.2.3 Expert Evaluations

Task performance was assessed in a blind manner by two independent experts based on the written answers and bookmarked articles. The ratings were done on 5-point Likert scale from 1 (bad) to 5 (good). The average task performance was 3.6 with the baseline and 3.5 with the new interface ($p = 0.6$). This indicates that there was no significant difference in the task performance between the two systems. Inter-rater reliability[8] was 0.6 for both tasks.

We asked an expert to evaluate the keywords shown to the users

---

[8]Inter-rater reliability was calculated with Spearman's rho and rounded down.

N	B	p	Question
4.1	3.9	0.3	1: The items recommended to me matched what I was searching for
4.6	4.1	0.02	2: The recommender system helped me discover new items
4.0	3.5	0.05	3: The items recommended to me are diverse
3.8	3.4	0.08	4: The layout of the recommender interface is adequate
3.6	3.2	0.2	5: The recommender explains why the items are recommended to me
3.8	3.4	0.2	6: The information provided for the recommended items is sufficient
3.6	3.4	1.0	7: I found it easy to tell the system what I want / don't want to find
4.1	**4.3**	0.5	8: I became familiar with the recommender system very quickly
4.2	3.8	0.2	9: I found it easy to modify my search query in the recommender
3.6	3.1	0.06	10: I found it easy to notice if some of my query modifications were not correct any more
3.9	3.6	0.3	11: I found it easy to find suitable ways to modify my query
3.9	3.5	0.05	12: I understood why the items were recommended to me
3.5	2.9	0.09	13: I found it easy to notice if I had made a mistake in modifying my query
3.9	3.6	0.05	14: Using the recommender to find what I like is easy
3.5	3.2	0.3	15: I found it easy to re-find items I had been recommended before
4.3	4.0	0.2	16: The recommender gave me good suggestions
4.0	3.8	0.5	17: Overall, I am satisfied with the recommender
4.3	4.0	0.3	18: The recommender can be trusted
4.1	3.9	0.5	19: I would use this recommender again, given the opportunity

Table 2: ResQue score question averages for improved (I) and baseline (B) system with p-values. Questions were scored on a 5-point Likert scale from 1 (disagree) to 5 (agree). The better value in each is in boldface; higher is better.

in the center of the radar. The keywords were divided into three categories: *general*, containing keywords generally relevant to the topic; *specific*, containing keywords specifically relevant to the topic; and *irrelevant*, containing keywords not relevant to the topic. The proportions of general, specific and irrelevant keywords shown on average to the user were 41%, 47%, 11% with the baseline and 48%, 47%, 5% with the new interface ($p = 0.6, 1.0, 0.2$). This indicates that the keywords shown to the user were slightly more relevant with the new system compared to the baseline.

We also asked an expert to evaluate the articles shown to the users. The articles were divided into three categories: *obvious*, containing common articles related to the topic; *novel*, containing articles that are less common but relevant to the topic; and *irrelevant*, containing articles that are not relevant to the topic. The proportions of obvious, novel and irrelevant articles shown on average to the user were 7%, 80%, 13% with the baseline and 6%, 81%, 13% with the new interface ($p = 0.3, 0.8, 1.0$). This indicates that the quality of the articles shown to the user were approximately the same between the systems.

6.2.4 User Interview Analysis

After the main tasks, we conducted a semi-structured interview with each user. Almost all of the users reported that they preferred the new interface to the baseline. The most often mentioned bene-

fits of the new interface were: (1) Helped users to track and compare relevance of keywords they had interacted with, (2) Gave the user subjectively more control over the system, as the users felt that the relevance bars in the timeline make it easier and more accurate to set and modify the relevance of keywords, and (3) Enabled users to re-use keywords from past search sessions.

The delete function was used mostly as we expected. For example, users reported to have removed feedbacks which were no longer valid when switching to another sub-topic, or when they wanted to remove the effect of a particular feedback. According to the interviews, many users did not appreciate the function of "marking feedback as accurate", and several users reported having not used this function at all. However, a few users used it in a creative way, for example, "locking" the feedback to the core keywords related to the topic while trying to explore different sub-topics. The highlighting of feedback was reported to attract attention, and some users tried to respond to each of them, although some users felt that sometimes too many keywords were highlighted. The users also made the following suggestions as features they would like to add to the system: (1) Ability to perform multiple queries simultaneously instead of being restricted to one active session at a time, (2) Ability to give feedback to multiple keywords at once rather than just one at a time, (3) Availability to go back to a specific previous state, and (4) Ability to see more search results for the same query if needed.

7. DISCUSSION AND CONCLUSIONS

We introduced a new user model that is able to take into account concept drift and user errors in relevance feedback in exploratory search tasks, as well as a timeline interface that allows the user to interact with the model.

In a simulation experiment we showed that the new user model is able to improve the search results over a baseline when the user responds to the highlights made by the model. However, we also noticed that for best performance, the user needs to be able to make corrections to both her own feedback and model predictions.

We also conducted a user study, where we investigated the combined effect of the new model and interface in exploratory search tasks, using multiple measures related to user performance, satisfaction and actions with the system. In general, it was easier for users to notice mistakes in previous feedbacks and make corrections to the model using the new system. The new system also made better and more diverse recommendations, allowed users to easier find items they liked easier, and was more understandable.

Ability of users to notice and correct mistakes

It seems that the new model was able to make sensible suggestions regarding what user feedback was in need of adjustment, and that the interface made this information salient enough for the user to notice it. However, there is still space for improvement, as some users reported that too many keywords were highlighted at times.

Quality of recommendations

The quality of the recommendations with the new system was rated more highly by the users. However, we were not able to directly confirm this with the expert evaluations. Although the keyword suggestions given by the new system were more diverse and the most relevant model keywords were slightly better, the task performance and the quality of the articles found by the users was approximately the same between the systems. As the quality of results in exploratory search can be a very subjective matter, we trusted the user evaluations more in this case. One explanation for the results we got is that we did not evaluate the quality of the results per each individual query, but only with respect to the general relatedness to the topic of the given search task. It may be that users were occasionally exploring areas not directly related to the topic given by us, and thus the subjective result quality could well be higher than the results rated by the expert.

User interaction

Users interacted more frequently with the new interface, and this was not only because of the new interaction options related to the presence of the timeline – users also gave more feedback using the radar interface in the new system. Additionally, users issued fewer keyword queries with the new interface, indicating that the new interface options made it easier for them to modify the query in other ways. In post-experiment interviews, users reported that the new interface helped them to easily track and compare the feedback they had given, enabled them to re-use keywords from past sessions, and that the new interface gave them subjectively more control over the system. The usage of the added functionality was mostly as expected, although users also found novel ways to use the functions that we had not thought of before the experiment.

Overall, the users seemed to prefer the new system over the baseline and the results suggest that further research in this field is warranted. Further research questions include: (1) Are there better models for estimating which user feedback is still relevant in modeling the current interests of the user? (2) Are there better ways to ask the user for clarification to her feedback? (3) What is the relationship between the task performance and the quality of the user model in realistic scenarios? How good a user model is "good enough" for the user to perform adequately?

To the best of our knowledge, this is the first search system that both models the accuracy of individual user feedback in a search setting and allows the user to directly interact with this model.

8. ACKNOWLEDGMENTS

This work has been partly supported by the Academy of Finland (Finnish Centre of Excellence in Computational Inference Research COIN) and TEKES (Re:Know). The research leading to this results has received funding from the European Union Seventh Framework Programme (FP7/2007-2013) under grant agreement no 611570. We acknowledge the computational resources provided by the Aalto Science-IT project.

9. REFERENCES

[1] J. Ahn and P. Brusilovsky. Adaptive visualization of search results: Bringing user models to visual analytics. *Information Visualization*, 8(3):167–179, 2009.

[2] J. Ahn, P. Brusilovsky, J. Grady, D. He, and S. Y. Syn. Open user profiles for adaptive news systems: Help or harm? In *Proc. of the 16th International Conference on World Wide Web*, WWW '07, pages 11–20. ACM, 2007.

[3] H. Attias. Inferring parameters and structure of latent variable models by variational Bayes. In *Proc. of the Fifteenth Conference on Uncertainty in Artificial Intelligence*, UAI'99, pages 21–30. Morgan Kaufmann Publishers Inc., 1999.

[4] F. Bakalov, M.-J. Meurs, B. König-Ries, B. Sateli, R. Witte, G. Butler, and A. Tsang. An approach to controlling user models and personalization effects in recommender systems. In *Proc. of the 2013 International Conference on Intelligent User Interfaces*, IUI '13, pages 49–56. ACM, 2013.

[5] J. Brooke. SUS–A quick and dirty usability scale. *Usability Evaluation in Industry*, 189:194, 1996.

[6] S. Bull. Supporting learning with open learner models. In *Proc. of 4th Hellenic Conference on Information and Communication Technologies in Education*, pages 47–61, 2004. Keynote.

[7] M. Cakmak, C. Chao, and A. L. Thomaz. Designing interactions for robot active learners. *Autonomous Mental Development, IEEE Transactions on*, 2(2):108–118, 2010.

[8] S. Chowdhury, F. Gibb, and M. Landoni. Uncertainty in information seeking and retrieval: A study in an academic environment. *Information Processing & Management*, 47(2):157–175, 2011.

[9] V. Dimitrova, J. Self, and P. Brna. Applying interactive open learner models to learning technical terminology. In *Proc. of User Modeling*, pages 148–157. Springer, 2001.

[10] J. A. Fails and D. R. Olsen Jr. Interactive machine learning. In *Proc. of the 8th international conference on Intelligent user interfaces*, pages 39–45. ACM, 2003.

[11] J. Fogarty, D. Tan, A. Kapoor, and S. Winder. CueFlik: Interactive concept learning in image search. In *Proc. of the SIGCHI Conference on Human Factors in Computing Systems*, pages 29–38. ACM, 2008.

[12] J. Gama, I. Žliobaitė, A. Bifet, M. Pechenizkiy, and A. Bouchachia. A survey on concept drift adaptation. *ACM Computing Surveys*, 46(4):1–37, 2014.

[13] D. Glowacka, T. Ruotsalo, K. Konuyshkova, K. Athukorala, S. Kaski, and G. Jacucci. Directing exploratory search: Reinforcement learning from user interactions with keywords. In *Proc. of the 2013 International Conference on Intelligent User Interfaces*, IUI '13, pages 117–128. ACM, 2013.

[14] A. Kangasrääsiö, Y. Chen, D. Glowacka, and S. Kaski. Dealing with concept drift in exploratory search: An interactive Bayesian approach. In *Companion Publication of the 21st International Conference on Intelligent User Interfaces*, IUI '16 Companion, pages 62–66. ACM, 2016.

[15] A. Kangasrääsiö, D. Glowacka, and S. Kaski. Improving controllability and predictability of interactive recommendation interfaces for exploratory search. In *Proc. of the 20th International Conference on Intelligent User Interfaces*, IUI '15, pages 247–251. ACM, 2015.

[16] A. Kapoor, B. Lee, D. Tan, and E. Horvitz. Interactive optimization for steering machine classification. In *Proc. of the SIGCHI Conference on Human Factors in Computing Systems*, pages 1343–1352. ACM, 2010.

[17] W. B. Knox and P. Stone. Reinforcement learning from human reward: Discounting in episodic tasks. In *RO-MAN, 2012 IEEE*, pages 878–885. IEEE, 2012.

[18] T. Kulesza, M. Burnett, W.-K. Wong, and S. Stumpf. Principles of explanatory debugging to personalize interactive machine learning. In *Proc. of the 20th International Conference on Intelligent User Interfaces*, pages 126–137. ACM, 2015.

[19] S. Lehmann, U. Schwanecke, and R. Dörner. Interactive visualization for opportunistic exploration of large document collections. *Information Systems*, 35(2):260–269, 2010.

[20] D. J. C. MacKay. Bayesian nonlinear modeling for the prediction competition. *ASHRAE transactions*, 100(2):1053–1062, 1994.

[21] G. Marchionini. Exploratory search: From finding to

understanding. *Communications of the ACM*, 49(4):41–46, 2006.

[22] P. Pu, L. Chen, and R. Hu. A user-centric evaluation framework for recommender systems. In *Proc. of the fifth ACM conference on Recommender systems*, pages 157–164. ACM, 2011.

[23] J. Rennie and K. Lang. The 20 Newsgroups dataset, January 2008. http://qwone.com/~jason/20Newsgroups/.

[24] S. Stumpf, V. Rajaram, L. Li, W.-K. Wong, M. Burnett, T. Dietterich, E. Sullivan, and J. Herlocker. Interacting meaningfully with machine learning systems: Three experiments. *International Journal of Human-Computer Studies*, 67(8):639–662, 2009.

[25] J. Ting, A. D'Souza, and S. Schaal. Automatic outlier detection: A Bayesian approach. In *Robotics and*

Automation, IEEE International Conference on, pages 2489–2494. IEEE, 2007.

[26] M. Tipping and N. Lawrence. A variational approach to robust Bayesian interpolation. In *Neural Networks for Signal Processing, IEEE 13th Workshop on*, NNSP '03, pages 229–238. IEEE, 2003.

[27] A. Tsymbal. The problem of concept drift: Definitions and related work. Technical Report TCD-CS-2004-15, Computer Science Department, Trinity College Dublin, 2004.

[28] R. W. White, B. Kules, S. M. Drucker, and M. C. Schraefel. Supporting exploratory search. *Communications of the ACM*, 49(4):36–39, 2006.

Relating Newcomer Personality to
Survival and Activity in Recommender Systems

Raghav Pavan Karumur
GroupLens Research
University of Minnesota, Twin Cities
Minneapolis, MN USA
+1 – (612) 626 2057
raghav@cs.umn.edu

Joseph A. Konstan
GroupLens Research
University of Minnesota, Twin Cities
Minneapolis, MN USA
+1 – (612) 625 1831
konstan@umn.edu

ABSTRACT

In this work, we explore the degree to which personality information can be used to model newcomer retention, investment, intensity of engagement, and distribution of activity in a recommender community. Prior work shows that Big-Five Personality traits can explain variation in user behavior in other contexts. Building on this, we carry out and report on an analysis of 1008 MovieLens users with identified personality profiles. We find that Introverts and low Agreeableness users are more likely to survive into the second and subsequent sessions compared to their respective counterparts; Introverts and low Conscientiousness users are a significantly more active population compared to their respective counterparts; High Openness and High Neuroticism users contribute (tag) significantly more compared to their counterparts, but their counterparts consume (browse and bookmark) more; and low Agreeableness users are more likely to rate whereas high Agreeableness users are more likely to tag. These results show how modeling newcomer behavior from user personality can be useful for recommender systems designers as they customize the system to guide people towards tasks that need to be done or tasks the users will find rewarding and also decide which users to invest retention efforts in.

CCS Concepts

• **Human-centered computing→Human computer interaction (HCI)→HCI design and evaluation methods→Usermodels.**
• **Information systems→Information retrieval→Retrieval tasks and goals→Recommender Systems**.

Keywords

newcomer retention; newcomer engagement; new users; personality; Big-Five Personality Traits; recommender systems;

1. INTRODUCTION
1.1 User Activity in Recommender Systems

From non-personalized feedback about items to personalized recommendations, recommender systems have become ubiquitous over the last decade and half. Within these systems, participation

UMAP'16, July 13–17, 2016, Halifax, NS, Canada
© 2016 ACM. ISBN 978-1-4503-4370-1/16/07...$15.00
DOI: http://dx.doi.org/10.1145/2930238.2930246

can take many forms. Users can browse through items (could be places, businesses, products, songs, movies, etc.), consume them (visit, buy, listen, watch etc.) or contribute items (add products, movies, videos or songs to the catalog). They can write reviews, rate or tag items, or provide other forms of feedback such videos (of products they use and how they find them), or pictures, or just view some of these forms of feedback. Through these explicit and implicit actions, users provide their preferences. Recommender systems learn these preferences and make suggestions.

Under-contribution [9, 12], lack of diversity in contribution [29, 52, 55], and early user dropouts [18, 29, 39, 57] are challenges that are historically plaguing many online communities, and recommender systems are no exception. Indeed, these challenges have a much greater impact on the performance of recommender systems, particularly during the cold-start phase [1, 44], for they also hinder their ability to gather sufficient (and diverse) information about users as well as items and make appropriate recommendations. In this work, we are interested in the properties of users that might help us understand their specific preferences for activity.

Our goal is to identify attributes that recommender systems operators could use to evaluate these properties and determine the users who are likely to contribute and ways they are likely to contribute to select and guide them to activities/experiences they are more likely to find fulfilling. We hope that this improves overall user satisfaction, activity, and retention, simultaneously increasing the annotations about the products.

1.2 Personality

Personality is known to explain variation in user preferences and behaviors across a variety of online [7, 15, 34, 47, 56] and offline contexts [8, 31, 32], and prior research suggests that it is a stable attribute across the human lifespan [14, 41]. Personality is commonly represented using the Five Factor Model [16, 26, 35, 51]. Therefore, we are interested in knowing how personality can model newcomer usage of a recommender.

1.3 Research Questions

In this paper, we measure usage using three classes of metrics: metrics about retention, metrics about early time investment and metrics about distribution and level of activity. Specifically, we ask the following questions:

RQ1. How is personality related to newcomer retention?

RQ2. How is personality related to newcomer investment?

RQ3. How is personality related to newcomer intensity of engagement?

We extract various high-level measures characterizing survival, engagement intensity, and level of activity of newcomers in MovieLens, a movie recommender system (movielens.org). We show how these measures correlate with users' personality, as measured by a standard Big Five-Factor Model questionnaire.

1.4 Findings and Contributions

In this paper, we find that personality information can be used to model newcomer retention, investment, intensity of engagement and distribution of activity in a community movie recommender system. In particular, we find trend evidence for the following:

- Introverts and low Agreeableness user users are more likely to survive into second and subsequent sessions compared to their respective counterparts.

- Introverts and low Conscientiousness users are a significantly more active population compared to their respective counterparts.

- High Agreeableness users are more likely to tag whereas low Agreeableness users are more likely to rate.

- High Openness users and high Neuroticism users contribute significantly more tags compared with their counterparts, but their counterparts browse and bookmark more.

2. BACKGROUND AND RELATED WORK

2.1 Newcomer Motivations, Activity and Retention

Newcomer retention and activity have been studied in a variety of online communities such as Wikis [39], Q&A sites [17, 57], Online Role Playing Games [30], social networks [10, 20] and recommender systems [21, 29]. Some of the prior work identified factors such as desires to volunteer online, help others, be social, gain reputation, develop in one's career, improve one's skills, have fun/intellectual stimulation, or having prior experience in the area motivate contribution (and lead to greater retention) in these communities. [21, 28, 37, 54]. Others also showed improved participation and engagement by use of personalized early interventions in the context of social networks [20]. However, in order to make accurate recommendations on multiple categories which is the usual case in a typical recommender system, it seems essential to capture the fundamental nature of each individual. Prior research has shown that personality can account for individual differences in attitudes, motivations, experiences, and emotions [35]. We therefore explore personality to model both retention and user activity in the system.

2.2 Personality and The Big Five Model

Research on personality traits in social psychology and computer-mediated communication since the 1990s has shown that personality can predict user preferences and behaviors in all kinds of contexts, ranging from media [32], to activities such as reading books and attending concerts [32], to appreciation for arts such as music and paintings [41, 58], to job success [8] and marital satisfaction [31], and to the amount of internet and social media usage [7, 15, 34, 43, 46]. A lot of studies focused on understanding how internet usage varied among people with different personality type and we summarize them below under each personality type.

The Big Five Model on Personality, also known as the Five Factor Model is a well-researched and widely accepted model of personality traits and is commonly used in studies examining

personality and human behavior [16, 26, 35, 51]. This model has been found to be reliable after testing across multiple languages and cultures [45]. The Five Dimensions of this Model, often abbreviated using the acronym OCEAN are:

Openness (to experience): High Openness people tend to be characterized by higher creativity, imagination and ability to ideate. They possess greater intellectual curiosity and appreciation for novelty or variety in experiences and diversity in interests. Low Openness users are more down-to-earth and conservative.

Prior work found positive correlations for Openness and use of internet for entertainment [53] and games [48, 53]. This may be due to their proclivity for new experiences and variety and curiosity. It was also found in [46] that high Openness users stayed online longer. Others found that Openness to experience was positively related to the use of social networking sites and features such as instant messaging [15]. High Openness is associated with an interest in more complex and exciting recreational activities [32].

Conscientiousness: High Conscientiousness people tend to be highly disciplined, organized, consistent, cautious, and dutiful in their behavior, whereas those with low Conscientiousness tend to be more impulsive, creative, easy-going, and flexible.

Several works report that high Conscientiousness is negatively correlated with general internet use and time spent online on entertainment, leisure and social networking sites [11, 33, 42]. On the other hand, high Conscientiousness is positively correlated with time spent on academic/work related sites [33]. Some researchers [7, 34] reason that conscientious people tend to have less interest in activities related to entertainment such as playing games or listening to music as they involve less planned use of time and are more spontaneous activities, which is opposed to their nature of being cautious and self-disciplined, possessing impulse control and having planned behavior [23]. Also, in [24], low Conscientiousness people were found to rate more items, whereas high Conscientiousness people were found to rate only the required number of items, and such cautious behavior is again characteristic of high Conscientiousness users. Others found that Conscientiousness was negatively related to ability to undertake difficult or unconventional activities [32].

Extroversion: Extroverts tend to be more sociable, out-going, energetic and desire the company of others and stimulation in external environments. Introverts are more reserved, self-absorbed, low-key, and seek environments in which stimulation is much lower.

Some researchers claim that Extroverts tend to prefer face-to-face interactions while Introverts tend to prefer use of online channels for self-expression [3]. Amiel et al found high Extroversion to be negatively associated with comfort in online communication [4]. Anolli et al. found a negative relationship between Extroversion and use of online chat [5]. Whereas in [13], Extroversion was negatively associated with addiction to gaming, Teng [48] found that Extroverts were significantly more into gaming compared to Introverts. Others have found positive associations between high Extroversion and the use of internet for communication and emails [50, 56] as well as more direct face-to-face friendships [50]. Yet others have also found Extroversion to be positively correlated with social network usage [43, 15]. Some found that Extroverts do a lot of liking, commenting and expressing their appreciation or sympathy for others, befriending a lot of people [7]. Others suggest that Extroverts may use the internet for more networking and Introverts may use it to escape their offline personas [38].

Agreeableness: High Agreeableness persons tend to be more cooperative, submissive, flexible, adaptable, tolerant, and empathize with others, whereas low Agreeableness persons are more competitive, challenging and tend to exercise their authority over others.

Some works did not find any relationship for Agreeableness with performance and internet use [8, 34]. Others found high Agreeableness to be negatively related to the time spent online [33], and activities such as playing online games [13, 40]. While Agreeableness was negatively associated with ability to undertake unconventional and difficult activities [32], high Agreeableness users were found to be associated with higher number of tags in [7]. It was found in [24] that high Agreeableness users tend to give ratings that are more positive.

Neuroticism: Users high in Neuroticism tend to be more sensitive, insecure, pessimistic, self-conscious, and are more susceptible to anger, frustration, anxiety, hopelessness and negative emotions. They are more likely to experience stress and depression. People with low Neuroticism, on the other hand, tend to be calmer and more emotionally stable.

Because High Neuroticism users are susceptible to a lot of negative emotions, use of the internet could provide venues to alleviate such emotions, get rid of insecurity/loneliness and find a sense of belonging. A lot of studies found high levels of Neuroticism of users to be associated with higher use and a greater amount of time spent on the internet, in particular on social networks [2, 4, 6, 11, 15, 34, 38, 42, 56]. Some researchers also found activities of leisure such as playing music or watching movies to be attractive for users with high Neuroticism [47, 56]. At the same time, other researchers found that High Neuroticism users are less likely to use the internet to seek information [2, 53]. One reason for this may be their insecurity and inability to trust any source of information. Another might be due to their nature of lacking hope and being susceptible to frustration.

Some of prior work has connected personality to rating behaviors [19, 25] in recommender systems, but we are aware of no work that specifically highlighted relationship between personality and newcomer survival, time investment, level and distribution of early user activity in a system. In this work, we are specifically interested in using personality to model newcomer retention and level of activity since newcomer survival and activity are intricately connected to community success [9, 12, 18, 29, 39, 57].

3. RESEARCH METRICS

RQ1. *How is personality related to newcomer retention?* We measure retention using the following metrics:

- Number of sessions at the end of first month, and at the end of the first four months.

- Odds of returning for a 2nd, 5th or 10th session[1].

- Time to first return.

- Average return time (time between sessions) during the first four months

---

[1] We choose these sessions to be consistent with prior work [29].

RQ2. *How is personality related to newcomer investment (time committed to early sessions)?* To answer this question, we measure:

- Length of first session[2].

- Average session length for first four months of activity.

RQ3. *How is personality related to newcomer intensity of engagement?* We define level of activity to be number of ratings, number of tags applied, number of items the person adds to their wish list, proportion of tags to ratings, number of page views and so forth. We now measure:

- Level of activity for first-session.

- Average level of activity per session for the first 4 months.

- Aggregate (total amount of) activity for the first four months.

We look at a variety of metrics to address the three research questions. We recognize that the underlying constructs and metrics have overlap. For example, we categorize metrics such as frequency of logging in as retention, but they can also be measures of intensity of engagement. Our goal is to understand user behavior characterized by these metrics. So we have chosen a single organization for our investigation, and report the resulting data to allow others to draw further conclusions.

In the next section, we discuss the structure and properties of the MovieLens platform. We frame the hypotheses for user behavior in a system like MovieLens based on existing knowledge of personality types. We then present our findings, summarize them and draw implications from them before we conclude the paper with limitations and future directions.

4. PLATFORM, STUDY DESIGN AND METHODOLOGY
4.1 MovieLens

MovieLens (movielens.org) is a standalone movie recommendation engine which provides an opportunity for its users to express preferences through rating, tagging and wishlisting movies, while allowing them to view movie details at different levels (summary of plot, trailers, posters, etc). With more than 200,000 registered users worldwide, and an average of 50 new user registrations every day, MovieLens is a suitable platform for studying user engagement, participation, retention and commitment in recommender systems.

MovieLens is primarily used for obtaining movie recommendations based on individual taste preferences. Rating is much more common than tagging, both because ratings build user personalization profiles and because the site design permits ratings at every movie display (with a simple click) while tagging requires visiting a detail page and typing. Clicking on a movie brings up a "movie details page" with plot and cast information, the tagging interface, and various other ways to interact with the movie. Users can add movies to a wishlist anywhere they can rate them, but wishlists are a not a widely-used feature. Very rarely, some users suggest movies to be added to MovieLens through an interface for suggesting movies. MovieLens runs several recommendation algorithms, which it calls "The Peasant", "The

---

[2] First session in MovieLens is considerably different from other sessions as most users provide a majority of ratings during this session.

Bard", "The Warrior", and "The Wizard" and provides different kinds of recommendations depending on what the user selects as their primary recommender. Occasionally, users change their recommenders too. Our data also suggests that occasionally, users view the posters and watch the trailers on the movie details page. Since rating, tagging and wishlisting movies are the three primary activities on MovieLens, and findings on these activities are generalizable to other recommender systems, we mostly focus our analyses on these three activities. However, we do report results on the number of movie detail pages a user visits and the total number of activities the user performs (which may include all the above activities) as well, for completeness.

4.2 Dataset

In order to collect personality information for improving recommendations, Tien Nguyen of GroupLens Research administered a questionnaire based on [22] to MovieLens users during the summer of 2015. Users were asked to respond to questions assessing their personality on a Likert Scale with responses ranging from 1 (Strongly Disagree) to 7 (Strongly Agree). Based on these answers, a score for each of the five personality dimensions was computed for each user on the scale 1-7. We use the results of this survey to study retention, early time investment and activity level of new users.

Table 1. Counts of users in low and high personality types

Personality	#low users	#high users
Openness	62	430
Conscientiousness	33	228
Extroversion	222	87
Agreeableness	34	113
Neuroticism	59	213

We pick 1008 of these users, who registered between 01 July 2015 and 01 October 2015 and extract their activity log for four months along with their personality scores on the scale 1-7 for this study. MovieLens makes it optional for users to enter any profile information and so only a very small fraction of users have some information about their gender and age. We are therefore unable to report summary statistics about age groups, gender, and location of these users.

Finding effect sizes that are small is a known challenge in personality related research methods. In order to circumvent this problem, increase the sensitivity of statistical analyses used, and ensure comparability of results some researchers [43, 46] divide the personality dimensions into thirds in terms of percentiles and compare the users scoring in the higher third with the users scoring in the lower third. We realized that these approaches might have the possibility of users with similar scores (such as a score of 5 on Openness) coming in two different thirds (in this example, the middle third as well as the upper third). So, we partition the users such that those scoring less than or equal to 2 on each dimension are the low personality type, and those scoring greater than or equal to 6 are the high personality type and those with no strong preferences (scoring between 2 and 6) are the medium personality type. Most results reported in the next section are based on a comparison between the users in the low and high personality types. However, since we had too few low Openness users based on this approach to draw statistically significant conclusions, in order to explore the effect of Openness trait in a useful way, we set the threshold for low Openness at 3.5. Since 4 on the Likert scale corresponds to 'Neither Agree Nor Disagree', 3.5 for Openness has the same directional effect as 2. However,

since our goal is to also optimize the sensitivity of our analyses, we retained the lower threshold of 2 for the remaining four personality types. We report the counts of users with low and high personality types in Table 1.

4.3 Hypotheses

Based on the existing knowledge about personality and user behavior, we frame the following hypotheses for newcomer behavior in the context of MovieLens[3]:

4.3.1 Hypotheses for Openness:

Because Openness is characterized by a tendency to seek variety, and a system like MovieLens offers a diverse collection of movies for users to keep returning, we expect high Openness users to last longer. Because Openness is positively associated with use of internet for entertainment and games [48, 53] and MovieLens does not offer movies to watch, we expect high Openness users to invest shorter durations of time in their visits, maybe just enough to find movies for watching. Because creative activities excite high Openness users [32] and tagging exercises one's creativity we expect high Openness users to tag more. Because high Openness users have greater curiosity and a desire for entertainment, we expect them to have already watched a lot of movies and therefore add less movies to their wish lists compared to low Openness users. Because curiosity is characteristic of Openness users, we expect them to visit more movie detail pages.

O1: Openness is positively correlated with likelihood of retention.

O2: Openness is negatively correlated with time investment per session.

O3: Openness is positively correlated with tagging movies.

O4: Openness is negatively correlated with wishlisting movies.

O5: Openness is positively correlated with visiting movie detail pages.

4.3.2 Hypotheses for Conscientiousness:

Because Conscientiousness is characterized by self-discipline and planned behavior, we expect high conscientious users to be more judicious with the amount of time they spend on a site aimed at entertainment. So, we expect lower activity and lower number of movie detail views from high Conscientiousness users who are less spontaneous and easy-going. Prior work [24] found evidence for negative correlation between Conscientiousness and rating items, and Conscientiousness and ability to undertake difficult activities. So we have the following hypotheses in relation to Conscientiousness:

C1: Conscientiousness is negatively correlated with likelihood of retention.

C2: Conscientiousness is negatively correlated with time investment per session.

C3: Conscientiousness is negatively correlated with rating movies.

C4: Conscientiousness is negatively correlated with tagging movies.

---

[3] We do not state all possible combinations of hypotheses for each personality type because nothing we know of their nature suggests an expected behavior for certain actions for some personality types.

C5: Conscientiousness is negatively correlated with wishlisting movies.

C6: Conscientiousness is negatively correlated with visiting movie detail pages.

C7: Conscientiousness is negatively correlated with aggregate activity per session.

4.3.3 Hypotheses for Extroversion:

Prior work suggests that extroverts primarily enjoy environments which stimulate them and so would show positive associations in online environments that are social, and help them network or compete with others, but otherwise have negative correlations with online activity in standalone systems like MovieLens. So we make the following hypotheses:

E1: Extroversion is negatively correlated with likelihood of retention.

E2: Extroversion is negatively correlated with time investment per session.

E3: Extroversion is negatively correlated with rating movies.

E4: Extroversion is negatively correlated with tagging movies.

E5: Extroversion is negatively correlated with wishlisting movies.

E6: Extroversion is negatively correlated with visiting movie detail pages.

E7: Extroversion is negatively correlated with aggregate activity per session.

4.3.4 Hypotheses for Agreeableness:

Because high Agreeableness is associated with a tendency to trust others [27], we expect more consumption behavior from high Agreeableness users. Because low Agreeableness persons tend to exercise their authority over others, we expect them to actively critique and thus contribute to activities such as rating and tagging movies. Since MovieLens is primarily a rating system, we expect low Agreeableness users to stay longer and offer their critiques. So, we have the following hypotheses in relation to Agreeableness:

A1: Agreeableness is negatively correlated with likelihood of retention.

A2: Agreeableness is negatively correlated with time investment per session.

A3: Agreeableness is negatively correlated with rating movies.

A4: Agreeableness is negatively correlated with tagging movies.

4.3.5 Hypotheses for Neuroticism:

Neuroticism is associated with insecurity and loneliness and a tendency to seek a sense of belonging. So prior work found Neuroticism to be positively related to time spent on social networks and sites with leisure activities such as playing games or watching movies. Since MovieLens is only a movie recommender, we don't necessarily expect any relation to time spent online. Since high Neuroticism users are insecure, there may be a tendency to exercise their opinion on a group of people. So we expect positive correlation with activities such as rating and tagging which annotate the system's items. Since high Neuroticism users often change their mood, it may be hard to understand their wishlisting behavior and we hypothesize that low Neuroticism users or emotionally stable users have higher activity on tasks such as wishlisting movies. High Neuroticism users are known to be not good at information-seeking, a behavior that may be likely due to their inability to trust any source of information [2, 53]. We therefore expect negative correlation to browsing pages about movie details:

N1: Neuroticism is positively correlated with rating movies.

N2: Neuroticism is positively correlated with tagging movies.

N3: Neuroticism is negatively correlated with wishlisting movies.

N4: Neuroticism is negatively correlated with visiting movie detail pages.

4.4 Method

To validate the hypotheses, we compute several metrics at several points in time. Due to space constraints, we report only a few of them that typified our results in this paper.

We use the term 'session' to mean a normal login period that begins with the user signing in and ends with the user logging out or with the expiration of the cookie. However, since most users multitask (use multiple tabs and switch between them), they make it harder to record their true session length as there is no explicit logout action in the MovieLens data log. So we computed session lengths explicitly as the differences between their first recorded activity and their last recorded activity per unique session ID.

The samples in the low and high groups, although independent are not necessarily normally distributed. So, we use the Wilcoxon-Mann-Whitney-test to determine whether the users in the low and the high personality type groups differ significantly in terms of their behavior in relation to the metrics listed in the research questions section. In the cases where one of the groups has a lot of zeros for the metric under consideration (this is mostly the case with the number of tags or the number of movies the user adds to their wishlist), we step away from comparing low and high personality groups and use the personality scores on the original 1-7 scale. We employ the Poisson, Negative Binomial, Zero-inflated Poisson, or Zero-inflated Negative Binomial models, as appropriate, subsequently testing the assumptions for each, to draw conclusions about effect sizes. Our interpretations will therefore follow two different patterns, one directly making a comparison between high and low personality type and the other talking about the change in the metric score associated with an increase/decrease in the particular personality score. We report results that are significant (at 0.05 level) and marginally significant (at 0.1 level) in the Results section.

5. RESULTS

First we combine the findings for the three research questions and report the results grouped by each personality type.

Table 2. Summary Statistics for some of the metrics

Metric	Min	1st Q	Median	3rd Q	Max
Metrics related to newcomer retention (RQ1)					
Number of Sessions during first month	1	2	5	11	120
Number of Sessions during first four months	1	3	7	19	451
Return time for second session (in seconds)	0	8863	54960	253500	10190000
Average return time between sessions (in seconds)	0	151200	334000	780700	10190000
Metrics related to newcomer investment (RQ2)					
First session length (in seconds)	19	860	1945	3907	35860
Average session length (in seconds)	45.25	587.8	963.9	1456	7218
Metrics related to newcomer intensity of engagement (RQ3)					
Number of ratings in first session	0	28	62	134	1372
Total number of movie detail page views in first session	1	18	41	87	1753
Total number of activities during first session	1	59	119	250	3143
Total number of ratings for the first four months	0	61	143	305	6364
Total number of activities for the first four months	1	158	352	731	9833
Total number of movie detail views for the first four months	1	65	162	360	4689
Average number of ratings per session during the first four months	0	8	16	35	516
Average number of movie detail page views per session	1	11	18	31	266
Average number of activities per session	1	22	39	74	679

In Table 2, we report the five summary statistics for some of the measures we use in the results section. In this table, the minimum values for first return time and average return time are zero. Return times have been computed by subtracting the beginning time of a session from the ending time of the previous session. However, a very small proportion of users logged in simultaneously from another device while using MovieLens from one device and for these cases, our approach yields negative return times. In order to resolve this issue, we consider these users to return in "no time" and assign zeros. Also, 44 users did not return after the first session. We exclude these users for the results reported on first and average return times. The user who had the longest inter-session time had only 2 sessions resulting in the same maximum value of 10190000 sec for average return time between sessions and return time for second session.

Openness We find a trend of high Openness users having a 21% higher odds of returning for the fifth session compared to low Openness users ($p < 0.1$[4]). We also find a trend of high Openness users having sessions that are 7.2 minutes shorter than low Openness users during the first session ($p < 0.1$). A unit increase in Openness score on the scale ranging from 1 to 7 is associated with a 21% increase in the expected number of tags from them during the first session ($p < 0.05$) and a 28.3% increase in the expected number of tags from them per session on an average for all the sessions during the first four months ($p < 0.05$) supporting our hypothesis O3. We also find that a unit increase in Openness score on the scale ranging from 1 to 7 is associated with a 156% increase in the odds of producing both nonzero ratings as well as tags on the aggregate during the four month period ($p < 0.05$) and

a 177% increase in the odds of producing both nonzero ratings as well as tags per session on an average during the first four months ($p < 0.05$). We find a trend of high Openness users adding an average of 58.4% of total number of movies added by low Openness users to their wish lists during the first session ($p < 0.1$).

Conscientiousness We find that low Conscientiousness users return by a median of 39.2 hours earlier for the next session on an average for all session return times during the first four months ($p < 0.05$) and also a trend of returning 5.4 hours earlier for the second session ($p < 0.1$) compared to high Conscientiousness users supporting our hypothesis C1 that low Conscientiousness users show more likelihood of retention compared to their counterparts. We find that low Conscientiousness users last longer per session by a median of 8.6 minutes on an average for all sessions during the first four months compared to high Conscientiousness users ($p < 0.05$) confirming our hypothesis C2 on time investment per session. Low Conscientiousness users rate a median of 42 more movies during the first session ($p < 0.05$), 7 more movies on an average per session for all sessions ($p < 0.05$) and 63 more movies on the aggregate for the first four months ($p < 0.05$) compared to high Conscientiousness users. These findings support our hypothesis C3 on rating movies. We do not find statistically significant difference between number of tags produced by users in the high and low Conscientiousness groups. A unit increase in Conscientiousness is associated with a 13% decrease in the number of movies wishlisted on an average per session for all sessions ($p < 0.05$) supporting our hypothesis C5. We find a trend of low Conscientiousness users viewing a median of 15 additional movie detail pages during the first session ($p < 0.1$) and a statistically significant median of 8 additional movie detail pages per session on an average for all sessions during the first four months ($p < 0.05$) compared to their counterparts. This supports our hypothesis C6 on visiting movie detail pages. We find that low Conscientiousness users perform a

---

[4] We note analyses with $0.05 < p < 0.1$ to provide trend information that may be useful to guide future work, but not as statistically significant results.

Table 3. Summary of findings (selected results listed for each hypothesis)

Hyp	Results	Data	Summary
RQ1. *How is personality related to newcomer retention?*			
O1	Not Supported	High Openness users have 21% higher odds of returning ($p < 0.1$)	Marginally significant for fifth session*
C1	Supported	Low Conscientiousness users return 39.2 hours earlier ($p < 0.05$)	Significant per session on average
E1	Supported	Introverts have 33% higher odds of returning ($p < 0.05$)	Significant for fifth and tenth sessions
A1	Supported	Low Agreeableness users return earlier for a second session ($p < 0.05$)	Significant for second session
RQ2. *How is personality related to newcomer investment (time committed to early sessions)?*			
O2	Not Supported	Sessions for High Openness users are 7.2 minutes shorter ($p < 0.1$)	Marginally significant for first session*
C2	Supported	Low Conscientiousness users last 8.6 minutes longer ($p < 0.05$)	Significant per session on average
E2	Supported	Introverts last 3.6 minutes longer ($p < 0.05$)	Significant per session on average
A2	Not Supported		Not Significant
RQ3. *How is personality related to newcomer intensity of engagement and distribution of activity?*			
O3	Supported	21-28% more tags per unit increase in Openness score ($p < 0.05$)	Significant for first session, first four months
O4	Not Supported	Low Openness users wishlist 1.6 times more movies ($p < 0.1$)	Marginally significant for first session*
O5	Not Supported		Not Significant
C3	Supported	+42 in first session, +7 per session on average, +63 in all ($p < 0.05$)	Significant for all mentioned periods
C4	Not Supported		Not Significant
C5	Supported	13% less tags/session per unit increase in Conscientiousness ($p < 0.05$)	Significant per session on average
C6	Supported	+15 in first session, +8 per session on average ($p < 0.05$)	Significant for all mentioned periods
C7	Supported	+65 in first session, +18 per session on average ($p < 0.05$), +121 in all	Significant for mentioned periods
E3	Supported	+26 in first session, +52 in all ($p < 0.05$)	Significant for first session, first four months
E4	Supported	29% less tags/session per unit increase in Extroversion ($p < 0.05$)	Significant per session on average
E5	Not Supported	+1 additional movie ($p < 0.1$)	Marginally significant for first four months*
E6	Supported	+30 in first session, +6 per session on average, +81 in all ($p < 0.05$)	Significant for all mentioned periods
E7	Supported	+67 in first session, +10 per session on average, +156 in all ($p < 0.05$)	Significant for all mentioned periods
A3	Not Supported	+25 during first session, +45 in all ($p < 0.1$)	Marginally significant results found*
A4	Not Supported	24% more tags/session per unit increase in Agreeableness ($p < 0.05$)	Significant per session on average
N1	Not Supported	62% higher odds of nonzero ratings/session per unit increase ($p < 0.1$)	Marginally significant per session on average*
N2	Supported	16% more tags per unit increase in Neuroticism ($p < 0.05$)	Significant for first session, first four months
N3	Supported	26% decrease in wishlists per unit increase in Neuroticism ($p < 0.05$)	Significant per session on average
N4	Not Supported		Not Significant

* We saw marginally significant effects ($p < 0.1$) at this amount and we report them as trend evidence; these might deserve further investigation.

median of 65 more activities during the first session ($p < 0.05$), 18 more activities on an average per session for all sessions ($p < 0.05$) and a trend of 121 more activities on the aggregate for the first four months ($p < 0.1$) compared to high Conscientiousness users. These findings support our hypothesis C7 on overall activeness of low Conscientiousness users.

Extroversion Introverts visit more frequently by a median of 1 additional session during the first month ($p < 0.05$). We also find a trend of introverts visiting more frequently by a median of 1 additional session on the aggregate four month period ($p < 0.1$) compared to extroverts. Introverts have 34.5% higher odds of returning for the fifth session ($p < 0.05$) and 33.5% higher odds of returning for the tenth session ($p < 0.05$) compared to extroverts. We find a trend of Introverts returning a median of 3.2 hours earlier than extroverts for a second session ($p < 0.1$). All these confirm our hypothesis E1 that Introverts are more likely to retain in the community compared to extroverts. Introverts last for a median of 215 seconds more on an average per session for all sessions during the first four months compared to extroverts, supporting our hypothesis E2 on investment. Introverts rate a median of 26 more movies during the first session ($p < 0.05$) and

52 more movies on the aggregate for the first four months ($p < 0.05$) compared to extroverts, supporting our hypothesis E3 on relationship between Extroversion and rating movies. A unit increase in Extroversion on the score ranging from 1 to 7 is associated with a 40% decrease in the expected number of tags during the first session ($p < 0.05$) and a 29% decrease in the expected number of tags per session on an average for all the sessions during the 4 month period ($p < 0.05$). These findings support E4. We find a trend of Extroverts wishlisting an average of about 55.4% of the total number of movies wishlisted by Introverts during the first session ($p < 0.1$) and Introverts wishlisting a median of 1 additional movie on the aggregate during the entire four month period compared to extroverts ($p < 0.1$). Introverts view a median of 30 additional movie detail pages during the first session ($p < 0.05$), 6 additional movie detail pages on an average per session for all sessions ($p < 0.05$) and 81 additional movie detail pages on the aggregate for the first four months ($p < 0.05$) compared to extroverts supporting our hypothesis E6. Introverts perform a median of 67 additional activities ($p < 0.05$) during the first session, 10 additional activities per session on an average for all sessions during the first four months ($p < 0.05$) and 156 additional activities on the

aggregate for the first four months ($p < 0.05$) compared to extroverts, supporting our hypothesis E7.

Agreeableness Low Agreeableness users show a trend of visiting more frequently (by a median of 3 sessions more) during the first month ($p < 0.1$) and having a 35% higher odds of returning for the fifth session ($p < 0.1$) compared with high Agreeableness users. We find that low Agreeableness users return for the second session 4.7 hours earlier than high Agreeableness users ($p < 0.05$). We find a trend of low Agreeableness users rating a median of 25 more movies during the first session ($p < 0.1$) and a median of 45 additional movies on the aggregate during the first four months ($p < 0.1$) compared to high Agreeableness users. A unit increase in Agreeableness is found to be associated with a 24.3% increase in the expected number of tags per session on average for all sessions during the first four months ($p < 0.05$). Here we find a direction opposite to the assertion we made for hypothesis A4. One reason for this might be that these users are mostly producing tags similar to what others have produced before just by adding existing tags, which is characteristic of Agreeableness users (to agree with others). This may also be a reason why we do not find any statistically significant relationship between Agreeableness and early time investment. Both high and low Agreeableness users might be investing in different activities (rating and tagging). Bachrach et al (2012) find Agreeableness to be a hard trait to predict using Facebook profile features and report very low R^2 for their model (0.01) [7]. Others [8, 34] do not find any relationship between Agreeableness and internet use. So, it is not surprising that many of our results are only significant at 0.1 instead of 0.05.

Neuroticism We find a trend of a unit increase in Neuroticism being associated with a 61.5% increase in the odds of having both nonzero ratings and tags per session on an average during the first four months ($p < 0.1$). A unit increase in Neuroticism on scale with scores ranging from 1 to 7 is associated with a 16.5% increase in the expected number of tags during the first session ($p < 0.05$). This finding supports our assertion in hypothesis N2 on the relationship between Neuroticism and tagging activity. A unit increase in Neuroticism is found to be associated with an average decrease of 26.4% in the number of movies wishlisted per session for all sessions during the first four months ($p < 0.05$). Low Neuroticism users wishlist a median of 2 additional movies on the aggregate for the first four months compared to high Neuroticism users ($p \sim 0.05$). These findings support our hypothesis N3. We do not find any statistically significant results to support our assertion on visiting movie detail pages. This may again be due to opposite behaviors on rating and tagging, and wishlisting.

We summarize and report selected findings grouped by the research questions in Table 3.

6. DISCUSSION
The above results suggest that different personality types use the system differently. Specifically, we find that users with certain personality types (low Extroversion, low Agreeableness) have a higher likelihood of returning to the community compared to their counterparts; users with certain other personality types (low Extroversion and low Conscientiousness) are more active in a system like MovieLens compared with their counterparts; users with some other personality types show different activity preferences (low Agreeableness users are more likely to rate and high Agreeableness users are more likely to tag); and low and high personality types can show a preference towards consumption vs contribution (ex: high Openness users and high Neuroticism users contribute more compared to their

counterparts). All in all, our results show that the challenges of newcomer churn and activity levels can be approached by making use of their personality information.

6.1 Implications
Our findings show that there is value in using a stable trait such as personality in deciding how to adapt a recommender system and customize interaction for specific personality types, which features to present to them or how to nudge them towards various existing features, who to recruit at cold-start (e.g., personality types that contribute more annotations), who to recruit for specific tasks (e.g., rating vs tagging), whether to invest particular efforts in them, or how to retain them.

7. LIMITATIONS AND FUTURE WORK
In this paper, we investigate the relationship between newcomer retention and activity, and their personality. We expand the theory on personality traits and online behavior by contributing our hypotheses and findings of user activity in one recommender system, MovieLens.

7.1 Limitations
MovieLens has the common features of a standalone recommender system with primarily anonymous features. It is not representative of all recommender systems. In particular, it is not a social system. There are limitations in the kind of data that we have and the kind of activities people can do on MovieLens.

7.2 Future Work
One future direction would be to exploit this idea in a wider variety of systems (e.g., that are not standalone, or those which are not anonymous) with different types of social affordances. High Conscientiousness users might use Amazon differently. Extroverts might use social systems differently. We leave all such investigations to future work.

There is also future work to be done in customizing the interface to match personality where it is known. Tkalcic and Chen [49] explore other ways in which personality can be used to improve performance of recommender systems such as determining whether or not to present novel, diverse items, improving performance of collaborative filtering algorithms, improving group recommendations and so forth. We focus here on issues of newcomer retention and feature usage which were not explored earlier using personality, but we wish to explore some of these in future.

We had few low Openness users in our dataset. So, in order to explore the effects of Openness trait in a useful way, we set a different lower threshold for Openness. Future work should explore whether finding few low Openness users is endemic to recommender systems or just an artifact of MovieLens. Also, in this work we analyzed personality traits in isolation from each other based on their theoretical independence. Future work, however, should explore ways in which the combination of traits found in each individual can be used to look at relationships with user retention, investment, intensity of engagement, and distribution of activity in various domains.

8. ACKNOWLEDGMENTS
This work was supported by the National Science Foundation under the grant IIS-13-19382. We thank Tien T. Nguyen of GroupLens Research for providing us this dataset and the MovieLens users who took the personality survey. We also thank the anonymous reviewers for their valuable comments.

9. REFERENCES

[1] Adomavicius, G. and Tuzhilin, A. 2005. Toward the next generation of recommender systems: A survey of the state-of-the-art and possible extensions. *Knowledge and Data Engineering, IEEE Transactions on*, 17, 6 (June 2005) 734-749. DOI= 10.1109/TKDE.2005.99.

[2] Amichai-Hamburger, Y. and Ben-Artzi, E. 2000. The relationship between extraversion and neuroticism and the different uses of the Internet. *Computers in human behavior*, 16, 4, (July 2000), 441-449.

[3] Amichai-Hamburger, Y., Wainapel, G. and Fox, S. 2002. "On the Internet no one knows I'm an introvert": Extroversion, neuroticism, and Internet interaction. *Cyber Psychology & Behavior*, 5, 2 (April 2002), 125-128.

[4] Amiel, T. and Sargent, S.L. 2004. Individual differences in Internet usage motives. *Computers in Human Behavior*, 20, 6 (Oct 2004), 711-726.

[5] Anolli, L., Villani, D. and Riva, G. 2005. Personality of people using chat: An on-line research. *Cyber Psychology & Behavior*, 8, 1 (Feb 2005), 89-95.

[6] Armstrong, L., Phillips, J.G. and Saling, L.L. 2000. Potential determinants of heavier Internet usage. *International Journal of Human-Computer Studies*, 53, 4 (Oct 2000), 537-550.

[7] Bachrach, Y., Kosinski, M., Graepel, T., Kohli, P. and Stillwell, D. 2012. Personality and patterns of Facebook usage. In *Proceedings of the 4th Annual ACM Web Science Conference* (Evanston, Illinois, June 22-24, 2012).WebSci '12. ACM, New York, NY, 24-32. DOI= http://dx.doi.org/10.1145/2380718.2380722.

[8] Barrick, M.R. and Mount, M.K. 1991. The big five personality dimensions and job performance: a meta-analysis. *Personnel psychology*, 44, 1 (March 1991), 1-26.

[9] Beenen, G., Ling, K., Wang, X., Chang, K., Frankowski, D., Resnick, P., and Kraut, R. E. 2004. Using social psychology to motivate contributions to online communities. In *Proceedings of the 2004 ACM conference on Computer supported cooperative work* (Chicago, Illinois, Nov 06-10, 2004). CSCW '04. ACM, New York, NY, 212-221. DOI= http://dx.doi.org/10.1145/1031607.1031642.

[10] Burke, M., Marlow, C. and Lento, T. 2009. Feed me: motivating newcomer contribution in social network sites. In Proceedings of the SIGCHI Conference on Human Factors in Computing Systems (Boston, MA, April 04-09, 2009).CHI '09. ACM, New York, NY, 945-954. DOI= http://dx.doi.org/10.1145/1518701.1518847.

[11] Butt, S. and Phillips, J.G. 2008. Personality and self-reported mobile phone use. *Computers in Human Behavior*, 24, 2 (March 2008), 346-360.

[12] Butler, B.S. 2001. Membership Size, Communication Activity, and Sustainability: A Resource-Based Model of Online Social Structures. *Information Systems Research*, 12, 4 (Dec 2001), 346-362.

[13] Charlton, J.P. and Danforth. D.W. Validating the distinction between computer addiction and engagement: Online game-playing and personality *Behavior & Information Technology*, 29, 6 (Oct 2009), 601-613.

[14] Cobb-Clark, D. A. and Schurer, S. 2012. The stability of big-five personality traits. *Economics Letters* 115, 1 (April 2012), 11-15. doi:10.1016/j.econlet.2011.11.015.

[15] Correa, T., Hinsley, A.W., and Gil de Zúñiga, H. 2010. Who interacts on the Web?: The intersection of users' personality and social media use. *Comput. Hum. Behav.* 26, 2 (March 2010), 247-253. DOI= http://dx.doi.org/10.1016/j.chb.2009.09.003.

[16] Costa Jr, P.T. and McCrae, R.R. 1992. Neo personality inventory–revised (neo-pi-r) and neo five-factor inventory (neo-ffi) professional manual. *Odessa, FL: Psychological Assessment Resources*.

[17] Dror, G., Pelleg, D., Rokhlenko, O., and Szpektor, I. 2012. Churn prediction in new users of Yahoo! answers. In *Proceedings of the 21st international conference companion on World Wide Web* (Lyon, France, April 16-20, 2012). WWW '12. ACM, New York, NY, 829-834. DOI= http://doi.acm.org/10.1145/2187980.2188207.

[18] Ducheneaut. N. 2005. Socialization in an Open Source Software Community: A Socio-Technical Analysis. *Comput. Supported Coop. Work*, 14, 4 (Sep 2005), 323-368.

[19] Elahi, M., Braunhofer, M., Ricci, F., & Tkalcic, M. 2013. Personality-based active learning for collaborative filtering recommender systems. In *AI* IA 2013: Advances in Artificial Intelligence*, Springer International Publishing. 360-371.

[20] Freyne, J., Jacovi, M., Guy, I., and Geyer, W. 2009. Increasing engagement through early recommender intervention. In *Proc RecSys '09*. ACM, New York, NY, 85-92. DOI= http://dx.doi.org/10.1145/1639714.1639730

[21] Fuglestad, P. T., Dwyer, P. C., Moses, J. F., Kim, J. S., Mannino, C. A., Terveen, L., and Snyder, M. 2012. What Makes Users Rate (Share, Tag, Edit...)? Predicting Patterns of Participation in Online Communities. In *Proceedings of the ACM 2012 conference on Computer Supported Cooperative Work* (Seattle, Washington, Feb 11-15, 2012). CSCW '12. ACM, New York, NY, 969-978. DOI= http://dx.doi.org/10.1145/2145204.2145349.

[22] Gosling, S. D., Rentfrow, P.J., and Swann, W.B. 2003. A very brief measure of the Big-Five personality domains. *Journal of Research in Personality* 37, 6 (Dec 2003), 504–528.

[23] Hogan, J. and Ones, D.S. 1997. Conscientiousness and Integrity at Work. *Handbook of Personality Psychology* (1997), 849–870.

[24] Hu, R. and Pu, P. 2013. Exploring Relations between Personality and User Rating Behaviors. In *UMAP Workshops*.

[25] Hughes, D.J., Rowe, M., Batey, M. and Lee, A. 2012. A tale of two sites: Twitter vs. Facebook and the personality predictors of social media usage. *Computers in Human Behavior*, 28, 2 (March 2012), 561-569.

[26] John, O.P. The Big Five factor taxonomy: Dimensions of personality in the natural language and in questionnaires. *Handbook of personality: Theory and research*, 14 (1990) 66–100.

[27] Judge, T.A. and Ilies, R. 2002. Relationship of personality to performance motivation: a meta-analytic review. *Journal of applied psychology*, 87, 4 (Aug 2002), 797-807.

[28] Kairam S.R, Wang, D.J., and Leskovec, J. 2012. The life and death of online groups: predicting group growth and longevity. In *Proceedings of the fifth ACM International Conference on Web Search and Data Mining* (Seattle, Washington, Feb 8-12, 2012).WSDM '12. ACM, New York, NY, 673-682. DOI= http://doi.acm.org/10.1145/2124295.2124374.

[29] Karumur R.P., Nguyen T.T, and Konstan J.A. 2016. Early Activity Diversity: Assessing Newcomer Retention from First-Session Activity. In *Proceedings of the 19th ACM Conference on Computer-Supported Cooperative Work & Social Computing* (San Francisco, California, Feb 27 – Mar 02, 2016).CSCW '16. ACM, New York, NY, 595-608. DOI= http://dx.doi.org/10.1145/2818048.2820009.

[30] Kawale, J., Pal, A. and Srivastava, J. 2009. Churn prediction in MMORPGs: A social influence based approach. In *12th International Conference on Computational Science and Engineering* (Vancouver, BC, Aug 29-31, 2009) CSE'09. IEEE, NJ, 423-428. DOI= http://dx.doi.org/10.1109/CSE.2009.80.

[31] Kelly, E.L. and Conley, J.J. 1987. Personality and compatibility: a prospective analysis of marital stability and marital satisfaction. *Journal of personality and social psychology*, 52, 1 (Jan 1987), 27-40.

[32] Kraaykamp, G. and Van Eijck, K., 2005. Personality, media preferences, and cultural participation. *Personality and individual differences*, 38, 7 (May 2005), 1675-1688.

[33] Landers, R.N. and Lounsbury, J.W. 2006. An investigation of Big Five and narrow personality traits in relation to Internet usage. *Computers in Human Behavior,* 22, 2 (March 2006), 283–293.

[34] Mark, G. and Ganzach, Y. 2014. Personality and Internet usage: A large-scale representative study of young adults. *Computers in Human Behavior,* 36 (July 2014), 274–281.

[35] McCrea, R. and John, O. An introduction to the five-factor model and its applications. *Journal of personality*, 60, 2 (June 1992), 175–215.

[36] McCrea, R.R. and Costa Jr, P.T. A five-factor theory of personality. L.A. Pervin, O.P. John (Eds.), *Handbook of personality: Theory and research*, Guilford, NY (1999), 139–153.

[37] Nov, O. 2007. What motivates Wikipedians? *Communications of the ACM*, 50, 11 (Nov 2007), 60-64. DOI= http://doi.acm.org/10.1145/1297797.1297798.

[38] Orchard, L.J. and Fullwood, C. 2010. Current perspectives on personality and Internet use. *Social Science Computer Review*, 28, 2 (May 2010), 155–169.

[39] Panciera, K., Halfaker, A. and Terveen, L., 2009, May. Wikipedians are born, not made: a study of power editors on Wikipedia. In *Proceedings of the ACM 2009 international conference on supporting group work* (Sanibel Island, Florida, May 10-13, 2009), GROUP '09, ACM, New York, NY, 51-60. DOI= http://dx.doi.org/10.1145/1531674.1531682.

[40] Phillips, J., Butt, S., and Blaszczynski, A. 2007. Personality and Self-Reported Use of Mobile Phones for Games. *Cyber Psychology & Behavior*, 9, 6 (Jan 2007), 753–758.

[41] Rentfrow, P.J., and Gosling, S.D. 2003. The do re mi's of everyday life: the structure and personality correlates of music preferences. *J Pers Soc Psychol*. 84, 6, (Jun 2003), 1236-1256.

[42] Ryan, T. and Xenos, S. 2011. Who uses Facebook? An investigation into the relationship between the Big Five, shyness, narcissism, loneliness, and Facebook usage. *Computers in Human Behavior,* 27, 5 (Sep 2011), 1658–1664.

[43] Ross, C., Orr, E. S., Sisic, M., Arseneault, J. M., Simmering, M. G., and Orr, R. R. 2009. Personality and motivations associated with Facebook use. *Computers in Human Behavior,* 25, 2 (March 2009), 578-586.

[44] Schein A.I., Popescul, A., Ungar, L.H., and Pennock, D. M. 2002. Methods and metrics for cold-start recommendations. *Proceedings of the 25th annual international ACM SIGIR conference on Research and development in information retrieval* (Tampere, Finland, Aug 11-15, 2002), SIGIR '02, ACM, New York, NY, 253-260. DOI= http://dx.doi.org/10.1145/564376.564421.

[45] Schmitt D., J. Allik, R. McCrae, and V. Benet-Martinez. 2007. The geographic distribution of Big Five personality traits: Patterns and profiles of human self-description across 56 nations. *Journal of Cross-Cultural Psychology*, 38, 2, (March 2007), 173-212.

[46] Schrammel, J., Köffel, C. and Tscheligi, M. 2009. Personality traits, usage patterns and information disclosure in online communities. In *Proceedings of the 23rd British HCI Group annual conference on people and computers: Celebrating people and technology* (Cambridge, UK, Sep 01-05, 2009). BCS-HCI '09. British Computer Society, Swinton, UK, 169-174.

[47] Swickert, R.J., Hittner, J.B., Harris, J.L. and Herring, J.A. 2002. Relationships among Internet use, personality, and social support. *Computers in human behavior*, 18, 4, (July 2002), 437–451.

[48] Teng, C. 2008. Personality Differences between Online Game Players and Nonplayers in a Student Sample. *CyberPsychology & Behavior,* 11, 2, (April 2008), 232–234.

[49] Tkalcic, M. and Chen L. 2015. Personality and Recommender Systems. In *Recommender Systems Handbook*, Springer US. 715–739.

[50] Tosun, L. P., and Lajunen, T. 2010. Does Internet use reflect your personality? Relationship between Eysenck's personality dimensions and Internet use. *Computers in Human Behavior*, 26, 2, (March 2010), 162–167.

[51] Tupes, E.C., and Christal, R.E. 1992. Recurrent personality factors based on trait ratings. *Journal of Personality*, 60, 2, (April 2006), 225–251.

[52] Turner T.C., Smith, M. A., Fisher, D., and Welser, H. T. 2005. Picturing Usenet: Mapping computer mediated collective action. In *Computer-Mediated Communication*. 10, 4, (June 2006), 00-00.

[53] Tuten T.L., and Bosnjak M. 2001. Understanding Differences In Web Usage: The Role Of Need For Cognition And The Five Factor Model Of Personality. *Social Behavior and Personality: an international journal soc behav pers,* 29, 4 (January 2001), 391–398.

[54] Wasko M.M, and Faraj, S. 2000. "It is what one does": why people participate and help others in electronic communities

of practice. *Journal of Strategic Information Systems* 9, 2-3 (Sep 2000), 155-173.

[55] Welser, H.T., Gleave, E., Fisher, D., and Smith, M. 2007. Visualizing the signatures of social roles in online discussion groups. *Journal of social structure*, 8, 2, (July 2007), 1-32.

[56] Wolfradt, U., and Doll, J. 2001. Motives of adolescents to use the Internet as a function of personality traits, personal and social factors. *Journal of Educational Computing Research*, 24, 1, (Jan 2001), 13-27.

[57] Yang, J., Wei, X., Ackerman, M.S. and Adamic, L.A. 2010. Activity Lifespan: An Analysis of User Survival Patterns in Online Knowledge Sharing Communities In Proceedings of the Fourth International AAAI Conference on Web and Social Media (Washington, DC, May 23-26, 2010). ICWSM '10. AAAI, Palo Alto, CA, 186-193.

[58] Zuckerman, M., Ulrich, R.S., and McLaughlin, J. 1993. Sensation seeking and reactions to nature paintings. *Personality and Individual Differences,* 15, 5, (Nov 1993), 563-576.

Plate and Prejudice: Gender Differences in Online Cooking

Markus Rokicki, Eelco Herder
L3S Research Center
Hannover, Germany
{rokicki,herder}@L3S.de

Tomasz Kuśmierczyk
NTNU
Trondheim, Norway
tomaszku@idi.ntnu.no

Christoph Trattner[*]
Know-Center
Graz, Austria
ctrattner@know-center.at

ABSTRACT

Historically, there have always been differences in how men and women cook or eat. The reasons for this gender divide have mostly gone in Western culture, but still there is qualitative and anecdotal evidence that men prefer heftier food, that women take care of everyday cooking, and that men cook to impress. In this paper, we show that these differences can also quantitatively be observed in a large dataset of almost 200 thousand members of an online recipe community. Further, we show that, using a set of 88 features, the gender of the cooks can be predicted with fairly good accuracy of 75%, with preference for particular dishes, the use of spices and the use of kitchen utensils being the strongest predictors. Finally, we show the positive impact of our results on online food recipe recommender systems that take gender information into account.

Keywords

online food; cooking; gender differences; classification; food recommender systems

1. INTRODUCTION

There are numerous suggestions in the literature that men and women behave differently and have different preferences on when, how, and why they cook. As discussed in the related work, professional cooking has traditionally been the domain of men and domestic cooking was considered a woman's duty [3]. Several studies and anecdotal evidence indicate that similar differences can still be observed: men tend to cook more for special occasions and their recipes are more ambitious and elaborate; women concentrate more on everyday recipes and pay more attention to health and balanced meals [5]. If such differences also exist in online recipe communities, it might be beneficial to take gender into account for usage analysis or personalization purposes.

In this paper, we look for quantitative evidence on differences between men and women in the domain of cooking, making use of recipes and interaction data from a large German online recipe

[*]Work was carried out during the tenure of an ERCIM "Alain Bensoussan" fellowship at NTNU, Norway.

UMAP '16, July 13-17, 2016, Halifax, NS, Canada

© 2016 ACM. ISBN 978-1-4503-4370-1/16/07. . . $15.00

DOI: http://dx.doi.org/10.1145/2930238.2930248

community. We will discuss to what extent popular stereotypes hold and how this translates into recipe uploading and commenting behavior. Our intention is not to speculate about the origin of such differences - there is plenty of sociological and popular literature on that topic - but to show that they do exist and that they are - quantitatively - significant. In addition, we collected a large number of features on the popularity, textual description, composition, and complexity of recipes and used these features to create models that are able to predict a user's gender in a quite reliable manner.

We believe that confounding factors, such as gender, impact the way popular recommendation methods - like collaborative filtering - work and that these factors generate biases that need to be taken into account [19, 2, 4]. Recommending food is believed to be more complex than recommending books or movies, for several reasons. Among others, food preferences are not only guided by taste, but also by dietary needs, seasonality, availability of ingredients, and societal conventions and expectations. As discussed in the related work, there are many indications that there are (strong) differences in societal expectations, dietary choices and cooking preferences between men and women. However, to the best of our knowledge, these differences have not yet been sufficiently quantified.

Contributions. We investigate gender differences with respect to cooking in three different ways. First, we statistically analyze gender differences, by illustrating and confirming or refuting *six prejudices* that are commonly mentioned: Men are better cooks (*H1*), men cook to impress (*H2*), women cook sweet dishes and men meat dishes (*H3*), women use spices more subtly (*H4*), men use more gadgets (*H5*), and men are more innovative (*H6*). Second, we investigate which of these differences are most discriminative by means of a *gender classification* experiment. Finally, we investigate how *food recommendation* can be improved by taking gender into account. Using these three different approaches, we aim to provide more insight on the nature as well as the impact of gender differences in the field of cooking and food preferences.

Outline. The structure of this paper is as follows: Section 2 highlights relevant related work in the field. Section 3 introduces our data set and Section 4 features the results of our empirical data analysis. Section 5 and Section 6 present results of our classification and recommendation experiments while Section 7 finally concludes the paper with a summary of our findings and future directions of our work.

2. RELATED WORK

Genderification of Cooking and Eating. In Western culture, there has always been a separation between genders when it comes to cooking [3]: everyday, private domestic cooking was the domain of women, whereas professional cooking and haute cuisine were strictly the domain of men. In earlier days, it was unacceptable to have a female chef in a professional kitchen. This separation is not as strict anymore, but many differences are believed to still hold - not only in the form of prejudices or stereotypes, but also in actual differences in food preference.

According to sociologist Eva Barlösius [3], actual differences in eating preferences between men and women are relatively small and hard to quantify in small-scale studies. In contrast, food itself is often classified as 'male' or 'female'. For example, if a restaurant order comprises roast, baked potatoes and a beer for one person, and salad with grilled chicken and a white wine for the other person, it seems obvious to virtually all that the first person is a man and the second person a woman[1].

Still, it is undeniable that males talk and write differently about food than females - see for example [20]. In a non-representative but still telling study[2], panelists concluded that gender 'certainly affects how chefs cook', but they could not articulate how and why exactly. Common prejudices were that women chefs use spices more subtly and that male chefs tend to cook to impress.

Cavazza et al. [5] carried out a study that confirmed that women preferred 'feminine food' to more 'male food'. In short, smaller and more elegantly presented meals were considered more feminine than larger, rough meals; meat was more associated with masculine meals. It has been speculated that these differences in preference might be partially related to preferences in self-presentation - in other words, how to conform (or not to conform) to expectations from society and peers. However, Dibb-Smith and Brindal [7] did not find any significant differences in food choice in different user contexts with different table companions.

Our study complements these works, providing large-scale empirical evidence on gender differences in cooking behavior.

Analysis of Patterns in Cooking and Eating Preferences. An in-depth analysis on how users choose and adapt recipes is given by Teng et al. [25]. Making use of complement and substitution networks, they show which ingredients users add, remove, pair or substitute. This allows them to predict which variation of a recipe will receive the best ratings.

Kusmierczyk et al. and Trattner et al. analyzed data from the German community platform Kochbar.de and found clear seasonal and weekly trends in online food recipe production, both in terms of nutritional value (fat, proteins, carbohydrates, and calories) [15, 26] and in terms of ingredient combinations and experimentation [14]. Similar patterns were observed by Wagner et al. [28] when investigating viewing logs. West et al. [29] found slightly different patterns for the American population. They also found correlations between search preferences and real-world health related issues. Similar observations were made recently by Said & Bellogin [23], De Coudhury et al. [6] and Abbar et al. [1] in the context of Allrecipes.com, Instagram and Twitter.

Rokicki et al. [22] investigated differences in nutritional values between user recipes created by different user groups. They found that recipes from females are, on average, richer in carbohydrates. Further, the amount of carbohydrates decreases with age - as recommended by most nutrition advice centers. Finally, there is the study of Wagner & Aiello [27], who studied gender differences in eating preferences in the context of the online platform Flickr. However, these works do not provide an in-depth analysis on gender differences expressed in recipe publishing behavior.

---

[1]Example by Barlösius in http://www.zeit.de/2016/06/ernaehrung-kultur-soziologie

[2]http://www.serious eats.com/2009/06/do-men-cook-differently-than-women-gender-in-the-kitchen-grant-achatz-dana-cowin.html

recipes	405,868	users	199,749
ratings	7,794,868	publishing users	18,212
recipes with at least 10 ratings	240,518	users with at least 10 recipes	4976
ingredients	1485	ratings users	19,444
categories	246		

Table 1: Overview of the dataset.

Online Food Recommendation. In a seminal paper, Pazzani [19] compared the performance of different basic recommender algorithms for creating recommendations from a pool of 58 restaurants to 44 users. Despite the – by current standards – small dataset, they showed that collaborative filtering, content-based methods, and recommendations directly based on demographics – all had their strengths and weaknesses.

Harvey et al. [11] carried out a long-term study to analyze factors that influence people's food choices. Users indicated that reasons for liking or disliking a recipe include particular ingredients or combinations and the preparation time. Reasons for positive ratings include the type of dish and the novelty of the recipe. In addition, there are health-conscious users who also take nutritional information into account – which is only implicitly given in terms of the ingredients used and the quantities. A mobile health-aware food recommender system was recently introduced by Ge et al. [10].

Preferences for particular kinds of dishes and ingredients – as determined by nationality, season, previous experience and other factors – can be captured to a certain extent by collaborative filtering methods, based on food preferences of a neighborhood of similar people. Svensson et al. [24] designed a social navigation system for recipes and found that users liked and acted on aggregated user trails. Users claimed that they were more influenced by user comments than by the reputation of the author or specific ingredients. In a feasibility study on recipe recommendation, Freyne and Berkovsky found that both content-based (e.g., ingredients) and collaborative approaches (taste, context) should be taken into account [8]. In combination, these works motivate and provide a basis for our food recommendation experiments.

3. DATASET

For the purpose of our study, we rely on a large-scale crawl from Kochbar.de[3], a German online food community website to which users can upload and rate cooking recipes, obtained in [14]. The dataset encompasses more than 400 thousand recipes published between 2008 and 2014 (see Table 1). Ingredients are lists of arbitrary strings given as free-form text by users. We resolve word variants, misspellings, etc. in the same way as described in [14]. Almost 200 thousand users provided more than 400 thousand recipes, 2.7 million comments, and 7.7 million ratings. The ratings are on a Likert scale, but – surprisingly – they are overwhelmingly positive (99.1% gave a rating of 5). Hence, ratings were treated as binary feedback in our work, i.e. when there was a rating we counted it as positive. Gender and age information was given by 95 thousand and 57 thousand users, respectively. More than 18 thousand users have also actively contributed recipes to the platform; among them almost 5 thousand have published 10 recipes or more (888 male, 3807 female users).

Data Enrichment. In addition to the information inherent in the data, our analysis of common assumptions in connection to specific types of ingredients (meat and spices), types of dishes (sweet or hearty), and the use of gadgets relies on additional information described in the following paragraphs.

---

[3]https://www.kochbar.de

To identify red meat ingredients, we manually constructed a list of red meat types and matched them with food items from the USDA nutrition database[4], finding a total of 31 read meat ingredients. We identified spices in our dataset by matching them to a list of spices and herbs obtained from wikipedia[5], yielding 52 spices. By matching these ingredients to USDA food items, we expanded the list to a total of 80 spices.

Likewise, we identified cooking utensils that are mentioned in ingredient lists and preparation instructions. To this end, we performed exact string matching to a list of 350 cooking utensils and 22 categories extracted from the German Wikipedia.[6]

Our approach for identifying sweet dishes was inspired by the ingredient network analysis done by Teng et al. [25]. First, we computed a co-occurrence network of ingredients. Manual inspection of the graph using Gephi[7] revealed patterns similar to those found in their analysis: two dominant clusters around ingredients that are associated with sweet and hearty dishes. To obtain a high precision labeling of sweet dishes (with possibly imperfect coverage), we identified a small set of central ingredients in the sweet cluster and a larger list of ingredients in the hearty cluster. This way, 57 thousand recipes containing sweet ingredients, but none of the hearty ones, were marked as sweet dishes.

4. EMPIRICAL DATA ANALYSIS

In this section, we report the results of our empirical data analysis in accordance to six prejudices and respective hypotheses, as stated in or suggested by the literature discussed in the related work.

4.1 Methodology

In our data analysis we compared relevant measurable indicators, such as the number of ingredients, number of downloads or preparation time, of which the means or medians can be compared using statistical tests. Whenever we compare users, we only considered those users who have published at least ten recipes - this ensures a sufficient amount of information on publishing behavior. When comparing recipes published by authors of different genders, we considered only recipes that received at least ten ratings, thus reducing noise in the data. In the statistical tests, the population size may vary due to missing values - mainly user profile data that a user has not provided. In the following paragraphs, we introduce measures we rely on in our analysis to capture comment sentiment, ingredient diversity, and innovativeness.

Comment Sentiment. Sentiment of comments was computed using the German version of SentiStrength[8], judging expressed sentiments in terms of a positive sentiment score and a negative sentiment score. Based on this, two measures can be derived to capture *attitude* – the predominant sentiment – and *sentimentality* – the magnitude of sentiments [13].

Ingredient Diversity. Following Hill's work on diversity measures for species diversity in ecology [12], we use two measures to capture different qualities of diversity. First, for each user we measure diversity in terms of the number of different ingredients used (d_0). Second, we employ a measure that weighs rare occurrences less, based on Shannon Entropy ($d_1 = \exp(-\sum p_i \ln p_i)$).

[4]http://ndb.nal.usda.gov

[5]https://en.wikipedia.org/wiki/List_of_culinary_herbs_and_spices

[6]https://de.wikipedia.org/wiki/Liste_von_Küchengeräten

[7]https://gephi.org/

[8]http://sentistrength.wlv.ac.uk

level	% recipes	% Men	% Women
easy	94.4	19.0	81.0
moderate	5.3	28.6	71.4
difficult	.3	35.3	64.7

Table 2: Ratio of recipes published by male and female users for easy, moderate and difficult recipes.

Innovation. We compute innovativeness of users in a similar way to [14]. Innovation of recipe r captures to what extend it differs from the most similar of previous recipes r':

$$IF(r) = 1 - \max_{r' \prec r} sim(r, r'),$$

where $\prec$ is temporal precedence and $sim \in [0, 1]$ measures similarity between two recipes - in our case the *Jaccard Similarity* over ingredients is employed. In order to study user-level innovation, we compare the mean innovation over recipes of users, computed over all recipes in the dataset.

4.2 H1. Men Are Better Cooks

'Better' is a very broad term and encompasses both objective and subjective measures of goodness, including self-judgement. It is known from the literature that 'professional cooking' historically is the domain of men; everyday, domestic cooking has traditionally been a woman's job. This leads to the expectation that when men cook, this will usually be for special occasions - and consequently be more festive, less everyday. As a result, one would expect that recipes from men are more time-consuming, more complicated, and more appreciated.

As a first step, we investigate the ratio between male and female users among – self-reported – difficulty levels, as shown in Table 2. Most published recipes are labeled as 'easy'. Apparently, Kochbar.de users have a preference for everyday recipes that do not require that much effort. Interestingly, the percentage of male authors is significantly higher for moderate and difficult recipes – $\chi^2(2, N = 268856) = 918.7, p < .001$.

If men are indeed better cooks, we would expect that their recipes are more popular. In order to verify this assumption we compared several popularity indicators. Recipes from men indeed seem to attract more comments than recipes from females ($M = 4.12$ versus $M = 3.30$; $W = 10268000, p < .001, r = .12$) as well as more views ($M = 825$ versus $M = 771, W = 11270000, p < .001, r = .04$). As expected, the average rating was similar between both genders (4.95 stars), due to the overwhelming amount of five-star ratings.

Interestingly, the sentiment of comments on recipes of both male and female authors shows a different picture. Female recipe authors receive more positive comments in terms of attitude ($M = .257$) compared to male recipe authors ($M = .238$) – $W = 1053998$, $p < .001, r = .11$. In addition, we also compare average sentimentality. Surprisingly, male recipe authors receive more sentimental comments ($M = .405$) than female recipe authors ($M = .390$) - $W = 1261516, p < .001, r = .07$. This indicates that male recipes elicit more controversial feedback.

In summary, the indicators show that men tend to publish more difficult recipes (or at least label them as more difficult). Recipes from male authors attract more views and more comments, but the sentiment of these comments is more diverse and on average less positive than comments on recipes from females. This effect may be explained by our second hypothesis: men cook for impressing, which may not always lead to better results.

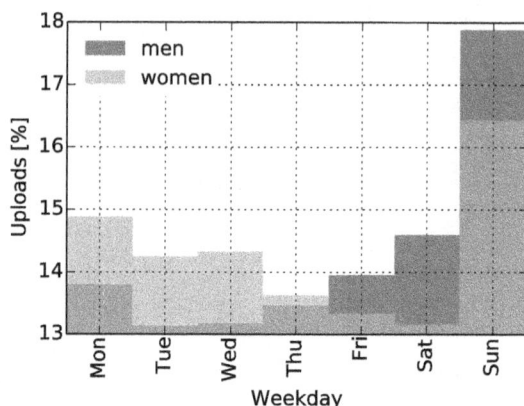

Figure 1: Comparison of women and men (with at least 10 uploads) in terms of activeness over the week. Both genders follow weekly rhythms – men are relatively more active on weekends, whereas women upload more between Mondays and Wednesdays.

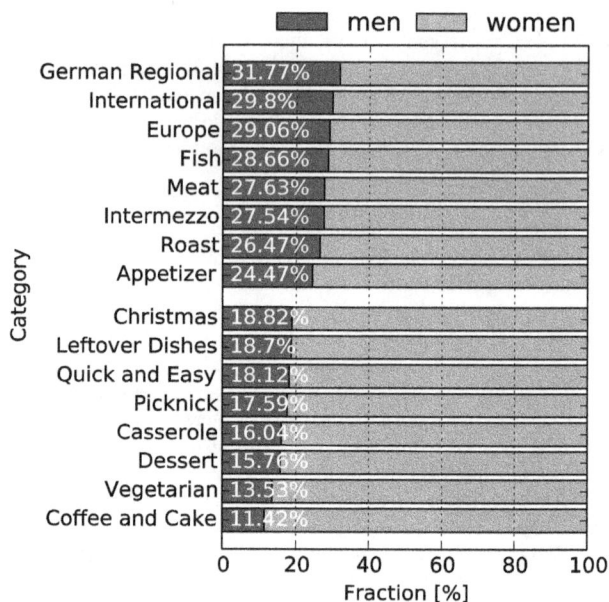

Figure 2: Popular categories with the highest and lowest percentages of recipes provided by men.

4.3 H2. Men Cook to Impress

Even though simple meals are often the best, elaborate meals are arguably the more impressive ones. Therefore, we compare the number and variety of ingredients used, the preparation time and the length of the recipe descriptions. We also investigate on which days of week both genders cook (=upload recipes in Kochbar.de).

The average number of ingredients that men use per recipe ($M = 10.22$) is slightly but significantly higher than for recipes by females ($M = 9.66$; $W = 9659100$, $p < .001$, $r = .17$). However, with respect to *diversity* of the used ingredients – as measured by the number of different ingredients used in a random sample of recipes (d_0, see Section 4.1) – we observe only moderate differences between men ($M = 57.3$) and women ($M = 54.7$; $W = 1905100$, $p < .001$, $r = .13$). The median preparation time is significantly higher (37.14 minutes versus 30.51 minutes; $W = 7840200$, $p < .001$, $r = .33$), confirming our previous observation on higher self-reported difficulty levels in male recipes.

Differences can also be found in how preparation instructions are written. Men use more words in preparation instructions ($M = 101.9$ versus $M = 86.8$; $W = 2044384$, $p < .001$, $r = .21$) and their instructions contain significantly more sentences ($M = 9.3$ versus $M = 8.8$; $W = 1801611$, $p < .001$, $r = .07$). These are indications that men indeed cook slightly more complex, time-consuming meals than women - rather than everyday meals attributed to women.

As men tend to cook more elaborate meals, they probably also cook more often for special occasions or during the weekend. Therefore, we expect different temporal behavior for males than for females, who tend more to provide everyday recipes. We compared user activity in terms of recipe uploads over the course of the week in Figure 1. The observed differences show that users indeed follow temporal patterns - the χ^2 test for uniformity strongly rejects the hypothesis that differences between days of the week are caused by chance with $\chi^2(6, N = 31805) = 368.83$, $p < .001$ for men and $\chi^2(6, N = 122104) = 649.33$, $p < .001$ for women. What is more, significant differences in patterns can be observed between genders, $\chi^2(6, N = 153909) = 66825.92$, $p < .001$. Men show relatively more active behavior during the weekends, whereas women upload more between Monday and Wednesday, supporting our initial hypothesis that motivations for preparing food of men and women differ.

4.4 H3. Women Prefer to Cook Sweet Dishes, Men Prefer to Cook Meat Dishes

A common prejudice is that men tend to eat – and probably cook – heftier dishes, preferably with meat and fish [20]. There is indeed a significant difference in the distribution of male and female recipes over the 244 categories in Kochbar.de ($\chi^2(2, N = 2256419) = 22698$, $p < .001$). Figure 2 illustrates these differences by showing the most popular categories (containing more than 10,000 recipes) with the highest and the lowest percentages of recipes provided by men. Males indeed appear to prefer meat-related categories (meat, roast), whereas dessert, coffee and cake are categories that attract mainly women.

To more closely examine this aspect, we analyzed the use of red meat in particular. In order to avoid a bias towards sweet recipes for women, we only considered recipes in the main dish category. Male authors use red meat in 40.8% of their main dish recipes – significantly more than female authors (34.4%; $\chi^2(2, N = 64026) = 141.5$, $p < .001$). Taking a closer look at the stereotypical male ingredient bacon, we would expect even more pronounced differences. This is not the case, though: men use bacon in 10.6% of their main dish recipes, women in 9.3% of their main dishes, $\chi^2(2, N = 64026) = 26.0$, $p < .001$.

We now turn to female preference for sweet dishes. We compare the fraction of sweet dishes using the labeling introduced in Section 4.1. Among recipes published by female cooks, 16.5% were identified as sweet dishes, significantly more than the fraction of 7.8% for male cooks, $\chi^2(2, N = 226835) = 2068.7$, $p < .001$. Our findings thus confirm both aspects of this hypothesis: men tend to cook meat dishes, women have a preference for sweet dishes.

4.5 H4. Women Use Spices More Subtly

Are there differences in how men and women employ spices? We investigate this by comparing the average number of spices used per recipe, the diversity of spices used by recipe authors of different genders, and which spices are used more by females and which are

Gender	N	d_0 Mean	d_0 Sd	d_1 Mean	d_1 Sd
Men	321	11.97	3.87	8.88	3.03
Women	1171	10.45	3.51	7.78	2.65

Table 3: Descriptive statistics for spice diversity results in main dish recipes.

used more by males. Our analysis is based on recipes from the main dish category from authors who published at least 10 main dishes.

Females use a lower number of different spices per main dish ($M = 2.30$) compared to males ($M = 2.61$), $W = 139129.5, p < .001, r = .26$. In this light, female use of spices in main dishes appears to be more reserved, but not necessarily more subtle.

Do men, apart from using more spices, also use a greater variety of spices? We investigate this using the diversity measures introduced in Section 4.1. To avoid biases due to differences in the number of published recipes, our computations are based on a random sample of 10 recipes per author. Table 3 shows descriptive statistics of the results on spice diversity for the main dishes. Men indeed use a significantly higher number of different spices (d_0) in their main dish recipes than women, $W = 232101, p < .001, r = .23$. In addition, male authors also achieve significantly higher d_1 diversity values, $W = 229959, p < .001, r = .22$.

A greater number and a higher diversity of spices are indications that men use spices in a less subtle manner. However, the choice of spices is of influence as well. Therefore, we further investigated spices that were used in at least 500 main dishes by ordering them according to the fraction of recipes that were published by male cooks. The results are shown in Figure 3. Spices that attract the highest fraction of males include heavy spices that are often used in hefty dishes and stews, such as caraway, bay leaf, rosemary and cloves. Spices with the lowest fraction of recipes from males, the 'female spices' appear to be more everyday (pepper, nutmeg, paprika) and commonly used in salads, soups and other light dishes (mustard, dill, basil). Interestingly, the use of the general word 'spice' as a placeholder seems to be be mainly used by women - which might indicate that women consider spices as something to support the taste of a meal, whereas men use spices more to influence the taste. This observation is in line with the previously observed male preference for more complex, impressive dishes for special occasions.

4.6 H5. Men Use More Gadgets for Cooking

In the introduction of a typical cookbook targeted at men [20] it is stated that '*you should know how to execute kitchen tasks with confidence, aplomb, and – I dare say – showmanship*. Typical male kitchen tasks involve the use of sharp knives and other impressive devices – or gadgets.

As a proxy for the use of gadgets, we compare gadget mention rates in recipes with at least 10 ratings. Male authors mention any kitchen utensil in 86.7% of recipes, in comparison to 83.5% for recipes published by female authors, $\chi^2(2, N = 226865) = 263.3, p < .001$. As these differences may be caused by the type of dishes cooked, we also looked at more constrained subsets. Within the main dish category, kitchen utensils are mentioned more often overall, with a small, but still significant, difference between male and female recipes (90.4% versus 89.7%; $\chi^2(2, N = 64033) = 6.3, p < .05$). Also, in the 'female' category desserts, kitchen utensils are mentioned slightly but significantly more often than in male recipes (89.1% versus 86.3%, $\chi^2(2, N = 23831) = 19.5$,

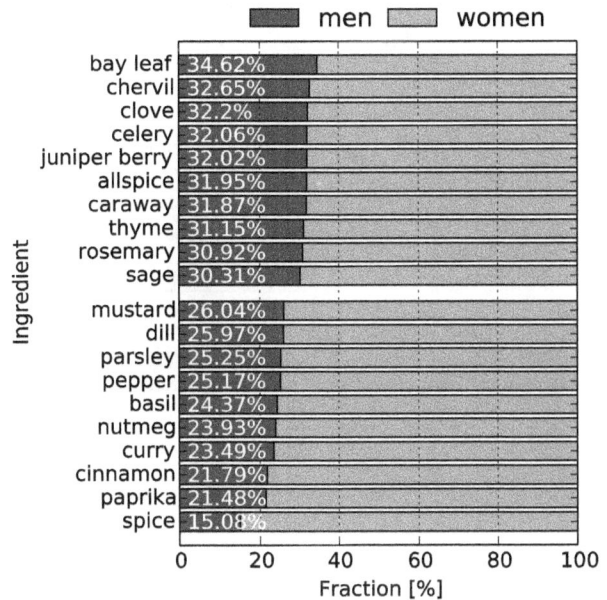

Figure 3: Popular spices used in at least 500 main dish recipes, with the highest percentage of male recipes (at the top) and the highest percentage of female recipes (at the bottom).

$p < .001$. Equally pronounced is the difference between men and women for the dishes containing red meat (89.8% versus 87.6%), $\chi^2(2, N = 48831) = 43.1, p < .001$).

We also investigated which gadgets are predominantly used by men and by women. An analysis based on all recipes mainly revealed a bias towards utensils for baking by females (e.g. forms and trays, or measuring devices) and utensils associated with hearty meals by men (e.g. knives), which is in line with our observations regarding H3, but not overly surprising. We therefore restricted our further analysis again to main dish recipes. Table 4 shows the mentioning rates of different gadgets. Utensils mentioned more often in male recipes include knives, utensils for separating, pots, pans and kettles. Although differences between these categories are significant, effect sizes are small. Still small but slightly more pronounced is the difference for forms and trays, which tend to be mentioned more often in female recipes. Surprisingly, we do not find gender differences in mentioning 'electrical devices' (3.62% versus 3.58%; $\chi^2(1, N = 93997) = .04, p = .8$).

These differences in gadget use can at least partially be explained preferences for different types of dishes. For instance, women mention casserole dishes more often, evidence for a preference of 'souffles' and other similar dishes – 13.94% versus 9.34%; $\chi^2(1, N = 93997) = 95.1, p < .001$. Male cooks, on the other hand, are more likely to employ hatchets (7.59% versus 5.13%; $\chi^2(1, N = 93997) = 188.7, p < .001$) and roasters (5.76% versus 3.42%; $\chi^2(1, N = 93997) = 240.0, p < .001$) – tools associated with the preparation of roast and other meat dishes. This confirms our observations on male preference for meat dishes.

4.7 H6. Men Are More Innovative

Given the tendencies of men to create more elaborate, time-consuming recipes that attract more polarized comments, it is likely to assume that male recipes are more innovative than recipes from women (for better or for worse). To verify this, we compared the

Category	Male Recipes ($N = 21{,}896$)	Female Recipes ($N = 72{,}101$)	χ^2
Knives	7.77%	5.21%	201.4*
Separating	10.90%	8.47%	120.4*
Pots, pans, kettles	64.42%	59.92%	143.1*
Hand tools	12.86%	12.01%	11.2*
Warming devices	36.33%	34.85%	16.1*
Containers, bowls	47.51%	46.93%	2.3
Mixing	7.28%	7.98%	11.2*
Forms, trays	9.98%	14.99%	352.6*

Table 4: Mention rates for gadget categories that occur in at least 5000 main dish recipes, ordered such that categories mentioned relatively more often in male or female recipes are at the top and bottom, respectively. Results marked with * are significant at $p < .001$.

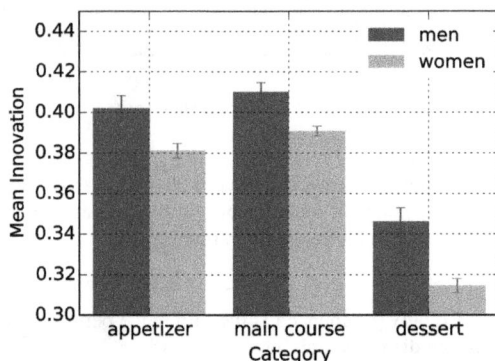

Figure 4: Comparison of innovation in recipes uploaded by women and men (with at least 10 uploads) for three meal categories present in Kochbar.de.

two genders in Kochbar.de in terms of their *innovation factor* (see Section 4.1). To remove the effect of high innovation rates for recipes from the early period (due to the absence of previous content), we evaluated only uploads starting with January 2010. Indeed, we observed a strong, statistically significant difference between genders ($D = .19$, $p < .001$), with men on average being more innovative ($M = .38$) than women ($M = .35$), with a large effect size ($W = 8.99$, $p < .001$, $r = .994$).

Figure 4 illustrates differences in innovation of men and women for three different food categories. The figure shows on the one hand that innovation varies between categories – for example, it seems to be more difficult to innovate in 'desserts' than in appetizers and main dishes. In addition, the innovation gap between genders differs between categories ($W = 3.46$, $p < .001$, $r = .995$ for appetizers, $W = 4.45$, $p < .001$, $r = .996$ for main courses, and $W = 4.18$, $p < .001$, $r = .995$ for desserts). Desserts appear to have the biggest innovation gap between genders.

5. GENDER CLASSIFICATION

In the previous section, we have shown that there are pronounced differences between men and women in terms of cooking preferences. To find out which of these differences are most discriminative, we carried out a gender classification experiment for identifying male and female cooks based on their cooking preferences.

5.1 Methodology

Feature Engineering. We selected 88 features that are related to the hypotheses that we investigated in the previous section. Below we briefly summarize these features, with the feature sets corresponding to the hypotheses.

- **Men are better cooks** (*H1*). We derived 11 features that capture the distribution of published recipes across difficulty levels, number of views, ratings, and comments, as well as sentiment and sentimentality in comments on recipes of the user.
- **Men cook to impress** (*H2*). This hypothesis is covered by 16 additional features, including preparation time, ingredients per recipe, ingredient diversity, average word length, average number of words, characters, and sentences in instructions. Further features capture the temporal behavior in terms of the distribution of uploads across days of the week and regularity of publishing behavior [9].
- **Women cook sweet dishes and men meat dishes** (*H3*). These differences in preferences and cooking practice are captured by 19 features, including the fractions of recipes containing red meat, bacon, and recipes labeled as sweet dishes, as well as the distribution across the categories preferred by male and female cooks (listed in Figure 2).
- **Women use spices more subtly** (*H4*). We derived 3 features based on the use of spices, quantifying the diversity of spices used in a sample of recipes and the average number of spices used per dish.
- **Men use more gadgets** (*H5*). We modeled the use of gadgets with 18 features that capture the frequency of mentioning any gadget, as well as gadgets in the 17 most frequently mentioned categories.
- **Men are more innovative** (*H6*). 19 Features capture innovation, measuring overall innovation, as well as innovation in main dishes and recipe categories preferred by male and female cooks.

Dataset Preparation. Our classification experiments were evaluated on a balanced dataset: we under-sampled women, so their number was equal to the men. Further, to ensure sufficient evidence, we focused our analysis on active users who published at least 10 recipes. Overall, the preprocessing resulted in 888 users in the class 'men' and 888 users in the class 'women'.

Feature Selection. Discriminative power of features was compared with the help of Information Gain (IG) and decrease in Random Forest (RF) accuracy [17]. Information Gain weights features according to their correlation with class attribute (gender) based on entropy. The mean decrease in accuracy of Random Forests measures the classification performance in comparison to using permuted or randomly chosen feature values.

Classification. The classification experiment was conducted with the help of the Weka[10] machine learning suite. We employed the popular classifiers Random Forests (RF), Logistic Regression (LR), and AdaBoost (AB) with standard parameter settings. The evaluation protocol we employed was 10-fold cross-validation.

---

[9] The three features capturing difficulty levels are also redundantly included in this category.

[10] http://www.cs.waikato.ac.nz/ml/weka/

feature name	IG	rank	RF	rank	H
sweet recipes	.058	1	9.325	4	H3
'forms' gadgets	.045	2	16.122	1	H5
spices per recipe	.043	3	11.019	3	H4
'pots & pans' gadgets	.039	4	3.358	18	H5
red meat recipes	.034	5	7.335	6	H3
'coffee & cake' recipes	.027	6	13.567	2	H3
bacon recipes	.025	7	2.260	30	H3
distinct spices count	.023	8	1.376	49	H4
preparation time	.021	9	4.181	12	H2
international category	.018	10	1.521	43	H3
spices diversity	.018	11	1.468	47	H4
'knives' gadgets	.016	12	2.112	35	H5
innovation in 'coffee & cake'	.016	13	8.146	5	H6
regional category	.016	14	−1.086	85	H3
'pounding' gadgets	.016	15	.696	61	H5
average words in instructions	.015	16	2.743	23	H2
average char count in instructions	.015	17	2.695	25	H2
Europe category	.015	18	.517	66	H3
innovation	.014	19	5.985	7	H6
dessert category	.012	20	.609	64	H3

Table 5: Top-20 features (out of 88) with gender as a target feature, according to Information Gain (IG) and mean decrease in accuracy of Random Forests (RF). Most of the best features stem from hypotheses H3 (preferences for sweet/meat dishes) and H5 (use of gadgets).

5.2 Results

Feature Selection. The 20 best features along with the evaluation measures (obtained with the FSelector package in R[11]) are presented in Table 5. We note that both measures (IG and RF) correlate to a high extent for the top-ranked features.

Figure 5 shows all 88 features, ranked according InfoGain - this measure is classifier-independent and we already noted that results between the two feature selection methods do not vary to a great extent. We observe a large diversity in feature quality and also differences in the quality of features from the six hypotheses that we investigated. A few top features are related to H3 (men prefer meat whereas women sweet dishes), with the highest InfoGain for 'sweet recipes' (the fraction of recipes marked as 'sweet'). Two more of the best features are related to H5 (men use more gadgets): the use of cooking forms (#2) and pots (#4). The feature 'spices per recipe' (H4) ranks at #3. Finally, one feature related to H2 (men cook to impress) is also in the top-10 features: preparation time.

Among the middle-quality features with InfoGain between .001 and .02 we find several other features related to H3, H4, and H5, which delivered the best-performing features. The middle field also contains some features regarding innovation (H6) and cooking for impressing (H2), but popularity and difficulty features related to H1 (men are better cooks) performed quite poorly.

Finally, there is a long tail of a very weak features (with almost zero InfoGain) from almost all hypotheses. This includes almost all features related to hypothesis H1 (men are better cooks than women), which - and this may be of relief to some women - confirms the weakness of such a claim.

---

[11]https://cran.r-project.org/web/packages/FSelector/FSelector.pdf

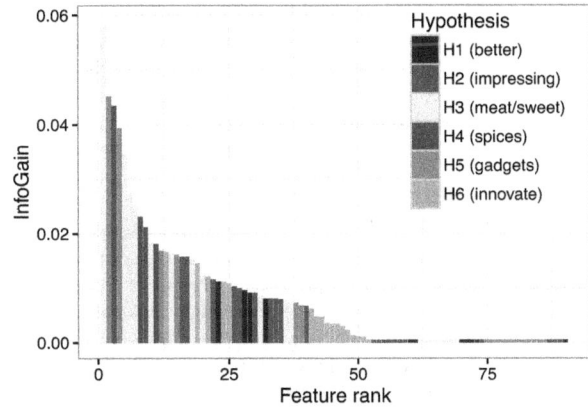

Figure 5: Ranking of the quality of features according to Information Gain. The feature classes are color-coded. The most useful features are related to hypotheses H3, H5 and H4.

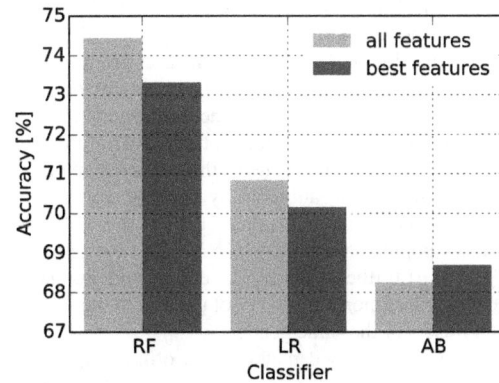

Figure 6: Classification accuracy for Random Forests (RF), Logistic Regression (LR), and AdaBoost (AB), using a complete set of features and the top 20 features (according to Information Gain).

Classification Accuracy. Figure 6 compares the results of our classification experiment in two settings: with all features and with only the top 20 best (according to InfoGain). When both classes (genders) are balanced, a random classifier would achieve exactly 50% of accuracy. As shown, all three classifiers improve significantly over this baseline: the best classifier, RandomForests, reaches an accuracy level of almost 75% when all features are considered. Similar results are observed with the Logistic Regression classifier, which reaches almost 71% accuracy. The worst among the three considered classifiers is AdaBoost reaching almost 69% of accuracy when only the 20 best features are used.

Although the differences between methods are meaningful, all of them perform satisfactorily, which demonstrates that our selection of features effectively captures differences between men and women. The most discriminative features are related to preferences regarding meat or sweet dishes (H3), spices (H4) and kitchen gadgets (H5).

6. GENDER-AWARE RECOMMENDATION

In the previous sections, we found that there are various effects between the user's gender and several preferences and tendencies concerning recipes and cooking. Particularly features concerning preferences for meat or sweet dishes as well as the use of spices and gadgets were strong enough to classify users as either male or female. In this section, we will show the impact of 'gender filtering' on the success of recipe recommendation. We adapt two common recommendation strategies by restricting them to users of the same gender, and to recipes from authors of the same gender.

6.1 Methodology

We first selected users who have rated at least 20 items and items (recipes) that have been rated at least 50 times. This procedure was performed to ensure that enough data is present in the user profile to learn from and to remove the bias of unpopular items in our dataset (see e.g., [18]). After that, we employed the MyMediaLite[12] recommender framework to run two different recommender strategies that are often employed in real-world systems [9]. The first recommender strategy we chose is known as the *MostPopular* approach, which recommends the most popular items (in terms of obtained ratings) to the user. The second strategy we chose was user-based *collaborative filtering* with k-Nearest Neighborhood (*KNN*) search. To show the effect of gender on the two baseline methods MostPopular (*MP*) and Collaborative Filtering (*CF*), we adapted the methods in the following forms.

The first restriction of *MP* concerns the user group of which the most popular items were drawn: $MP(g)$ recommends the items that are most popular among users of the same gender. As a second restriction, we filter the items based on the gender of the recipe author: $MP(g|g)$ recommends the items that are most popular among users of the same gender, authored by users of the same gender. We restrict *CF* in a similar manner: $CF(g)$ recommends items that are most popular among the *KNN* of users with the same gender. $CF(g|g)$ further restricts the recommendation strategy to items most popular among the *KNN* of users with the same gender, authored by users of the same gender.

To evaluate the proposed methods, an offline experiment was conducted using MyMediaLite's 5-fold cross validation evaluation protocol and Mean Average Precision (*MAP*) – over the whole item list – as accuracy metric. The parameter k for the user-based *CF* method was set to 80, which delivered the best results within the three presented methods (cross-validated on holdout data).

6.2 Results

As highlighted in Figure 7, all gender-aware methods improve over the baselines MP ($MAP = .011$) and CF ($MAP = .059$). While the results for $MP(g)$ ($MAP = .015$) and $CF(g)$ ($MAP = .062$) are not so pronounced, more significant differences can be observed when additionally filtering the items (recipes) based on the gender of the author, with $MAP = .026$ for the most popular approach $MP(g|g)$ and $MAP = .086$ for collaborative filtering $CF(g|g)$.

While the proposed methods are rather basic, the obtained results are insightful, demonstrating the impact of gender on food preferences and showing the benefits of 'gender filtering' in the context of online food recommender systems. Better results might be obtainable by employing better recommender methods, such as Factorization Machines [21], which we see as possible extensions of this work and out of the scope of this paper.

7. CONCLUSIONS

In this paper, we investigated to which extent differences between men and women in terms of online cooking behavior do exist. Even though there are many beliefs hinting at significant gender differences in the context of food preparation, no profound, quantitative

---

[12]http://www.mymedialite.net/

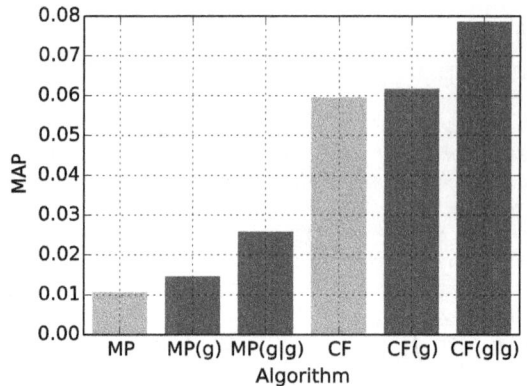

Figure 7: Mean Average Precision (*MAP*) for the context-blind recommender MostPopular (*MP*) and User-based Collaborative Filtering (*CF*) compared to the context-aware methods $MP(g)$, $MP(g|g)$, $CF(g)$ and $CF(g|g)$. As shown, *MAP* is improving over the baseline methods (highlighted in orange) when user gender (g) and additionally item gender ($g|g$) are considered.

study has been yet conducted to confirm these prejudices. To contribute to knowledge in this area, we conducted a large-scale empirical study in which we mined and analyzed online traces of almost 200 thousand users and their recipes in the German online cooking platform Kochbar.de, one of the largest communities on the Web.

Our results show that there are indeed significant differences between men and women in terms of cooking, arguably even larger than anticipated. For instance, we statistically confirmed that men tend to prepare dishes with more ingredients and a longer preparation time. Women are less inclined to prepare meat dishes and they use spices more subtly than man do. Recipes from males receive more attention and feedback, but females receive more positive and less polarized feedback.

To further investigate the magnitude and importance of the identified gender differences, we conduced a classification experiment using 88 features – derived from our empirical analysis – to predict the user's gender. Our results show that the most discriminative differences concern preferences for meat or sweet dishes, as well as the use of spices and kitchen gadgets. Finally, a simple recommender system experiment shows the usefulness of employing gender as context in the online food recipe recommendation task. Particularly restricting recommendations to recipes from authors of the same gender had a significant impact.

In summary, in this paper we quantified and analyzed differences between genders in the domain of cooking and showed the benefits of taking gender, a feature that is commonly available in user profiles, explicitly into account in the recommendation process.

Future Work. One natural extension of this work would be to apply our framework to other online food community platforms to examine cultural differences [16]. Further, one could enhance our classifier framework with a more diverse set of features, like rating behavior or nutrition values. In addition, it would be interesting to study other user characteristics, such as age or geographic origin.

8. ACKNOWLEDGMENTS

The authors would like to thank Eva Barlösius for fruitful discussions during the study phase. The work was partially funded by the German BMBF project GlycoRec (16SV7172). The Know-Center GmbH is funded within the Austrian COMET Program, managed by the Austrian Research Promotion Agency (FFG).

9. REFERENCES

[1] S. Abbar, Y. Mejova, and I. Weber. You tweet what you eat: Studying food consumption through twitter. In *Proc. of CHI'15*, 2015.

[2] G. Adomavicius and A. Tuzhilin. Context-aware recommender systems. In *Recommender systems handbook*, pages 217–253. Springer, 2011.

[3] E. Barlösius. *Soziologie des Essens*. Juventa Verlag, 1999.

[4] J. Beel, S. Langer, A. Nürnberger, and M. Genzmehr. The impact of demographics (age and gender) and other user-characteristics on evaluating recommender systems. In *Research and Advanced Technology for Digital Libraries*, pages 396–400. Springer, 2013.

[5] N. Cavazza, M. Guidetti, and F. Butera. Ingredients of gender-based stereotypes about food. indirect influence of food type, portion size and presentation on gendered intentions to eat. *Appetite*, 91:266–272, 2015.

[6] M. De Choudhury and S. S. Sharma. Characterizing dietary choices, nutrition, and language in food deserts via social media. In *Proc. of CSCW '16*, 2016.

[7] A. Dibb-Smith and E. Brindal. Table for two: The effects of familiarity, sex and gender on food choice in imaginary dining scenarios. *Appetite*, 95:492–499, 2015.

[8] J. Freyne and S. Berkovsky. Recommending food: Reasoning on recipes and ingredients. In *Proc. of UMAP'10*, pages 381–386, 2010.

[9] Z. Gantner, S. Rendle, C. Freudenthaler, and L. Schmidt-Thieme. Mymedialite: A free recommender system library. In *Proc. of RecSys'11*, pages 305–308, 2011.

[10] M. Ge, F. Ricci, and D. Massimo. Health-aware food recommender system. In *Proc. of RecSys '15*, pages 333–334, 2015.

[11] M. Harvey, B. Ludwig, and D. Elsweiler. Learning user tastes: a first step to generating healthy meal plans? In *Proc. of LIFESTYLE'12*, page 18, 2012.

[12] M. O. Hill. Diversity and evenness: a unifying notation and its consequences. *Ecology*, 54(2):427–432, 1973.

[13] O. Kucuktunc, B. B. Cambazoglu, I. Weber, and H. Ferhatosmanoglu. A large-scale sentiment analysis for yahoo! answers. In *Proc. of WSDM'12*, pages 633–642. ACM, 2012.

[14] T. Kusmierczyk, C. Trattner, and K. Nørvåg. Temporal patterns in online food innovation. In *Proc. of WWW'15 Companion*, 2015.

[15] T. Kusmierczyk, C. Trattner, and K. Nørvåg. Temporality in online food recipe consumption and production. In *Proc. of WWW'15*, 2015.

[16] P. Laufer, C. Wagner, F. Flöck, and M. Strohmaier. Mining cross-cultural relations from wikipedia-a study of 31 european food cultures. *arXiv preprint arXiv:1411.4484*, 2014.

[17] G. Louppe, L. Wehenkel, A. Sutera, and P. Geurts. Understanding variable importances in forests of randomized trees. In *Advances in Neural Information Processing Systems 26*, pages 431–439. Curran Associates, Inc., 2013.

[18] D. Parra-Santander and P. Brusilovsky. Improving collaborative filtering in social tagging systems for the recommendation of scientific articles. In *Proc. of WI'10*, pages 136–142, 2010.

[19] M. J. Pazzani. A framework for collaborative, content-based and demographic filtering. *Artificial Intelligence Review*, 13(5-6):393–408, 1999.

[20] S. Raichlen. *Man Made Meals*. Workman Publishing Company, 2014.

[21] S. Rendle. Factorization machines with libfm. *ACM Transactions on Intelligent Systems and Technology (TIST)*, 3(3):57, 2012.

[22] M. Rokicki, E. Herder, and E. Demidova. What's on my plate: Towards recommending recipe variations for diabetes patients. *Proc. of UMAP'15 LBRS*, 2015.

[23] A. Said and A. Bellogín. You are what you eat! tracking health through recipe interactions. In *Proc. of RSWeb'14*, 2014.

[24] M. Svensson, K. Höök, and R. Cöster. Designing and evaluating kalas: A social navigation system for food recipes. *ACM TOCHI*, 12(3):374–400, 2005.

[25] C. Teng, Y. Lin, and L. A. Adamic. Recipe recommendation using ingredient networks. *CoRR*, abs/1111.3919, 2011.

[26] C. Trattner, T. Kusmierczyk, and K. Nørvåg. FOODWEB - studying food consumption and production patterns on the web. *ERCIM News*, 2016(104), 2016.

[27] C. Wagner and L. M. Aiello. Men eat on mars, women on venus? an empirical study of food-images. In *Proc. of WebSci'15 Posters*, 2015.

[28] C. Wagner, P. Singer, and M. Strohmaier. The nature and evolution of online food preferences. *EPJ Data Science*, 3(1):1–22, 2014.

[29] R. West, R. W. White, and E. Horvitz. From cookies to cooks: Insights on dietary patterns via analysis of web usage logs. In *Proc. of WWW'13*, pages 1399–1410, 2013.

Effect of Different Implicit Social Networks on Recommending Research Papers

Shaikhah Alotaibi
University of Saskatchewan
181 Thorvaldson Building
110 Science Place
Saskatoon, SK, Canada
Shaikhah.otaibi@usask.ca

Julita Vassileva
University of Saskatchewan
178 Thorvaldson Building
110 Science Place
Saskatoon, SK, Canada
jiv@cs.usask.ca

ABSTRACT

Combining social network information with collaborative filtering recommendation algorithms has successfully reduced some of the drawbacks of collaborative filtering and increased the accuracy of recommendations. However, all approaches in the domain of research paper recommendation have used explicit social relations that users have initiated which has the problem of low recommendation coverage. We argued that the available data in social bookmarking Web sites such as CiteULike or Mendeley could be exploited to connect similar users using implicit social connections based on their bookmarking behavior. In this paper, we proposed three different implicit social networks—readership, co-readership, and tag-based—and we compared the recommendation accuracy of several recommendation algorithms using data from the proposed social networks as input to the recommendation algorithms. Then, we tested which implicit social network provides the best recommendation accuracy. We found that, for the most part, the social recommender is the best algorithm and that the readership network with reciprocal social relations provides the best information source for recommendations but with low coverage. However, the co-readership network provide good recommendation accuracy and better user coverage of recommendation.

Keywords

Social networks; hybrid recommendation; paper recommendation; social bookmarking Web sites; collaborative filtering.

1. INTRODUCTION

Scholarly papers both help to update researchers on new research in their areas of interest and serve as a directory of other researchers with similar interests with whom researchers can collaborate. However, as publishers, online journals, and conferences proliferate, the number of new published papers has become overwhelming. For this reason, many recommender systems (RSs) have been proposed to help readers in these tasks by suggesting a list of potential papers to users. The two main algorithms used by RSs are content-based filtering (CBF) and collaborative filtering (CF). CBF is based on information retrieval techniques that compare a paper's features (e.g., title, abstract, keywords, publication year) with the researchers' features (e.g., interests or previous search queries) to find matches [2]. In contrast,

UMAP '16, July 13-17, 2016, Halifax, NS, Canada
© 2016 ACM. ISBN 978-1-4503-4370-1/16/07…$15.00
DOI: http://dx.doi.org/10.1145/2930238.2930293

CF (e.g., [13]) uses the similarity of paper ratings to find users similar to the target user and recommend papers that these users have liked. Hybrid recommending approaches (e.g., [18]) use a combination of the CBF and CF approaches to alleviate the drawbacks of both approaches. With the advent of social networks in applications such as social bookmarking systems (e.g., CiteULike, Mendeley), which researchers often use to manage their digital paper repositories and bookmark libraries, users can be connected through different social relations. A social bookmarking service provides many clues for interest similarities between users based on their behavior in the system and their publication authorship. Surprisingly, however, none of the popular social bookmarking tools have used the wealth of social data they store to build a social RS. There are some studies that incorporate social information into CF techniques to increase the recommendation accuracy. Although such social recommenders perform well, the social information about users that they require is not readily available for all users. Thus, these social recommenders have lower user coverage [8]. User coverage is the ratio of users who receive nonempty recommended sets to the total number of users [3]. Previous studies also showed that there is a tradeoff between the recommendation accuracy and the coverage of the recommendation [5]. We aim to analyze different data resources available in social bookmarking systems for research papers, that can help identify similar users and to test which resource and which recommender approach give the best balance between accuracy and coverage. Therefore, we propose three implicit social networks that exploit data from the users' publication list (if there is one) and bookmarked papers. Users need not enter additional social data in the system (e.g. about friendships, following relationships etc.).

We have organized the rest of the paper as follows. Section 2 briefly discusses related work. Section 3 describes the three proposed implicit social networks. Section 4 describes our experiment design and the dataset used, and section 5 explains the experiments and analysis of the results. Finally, section 6 discusses our conclusions and future work.

2. RELATED WORK

Social recommendation can be defined to be any recommender system that includes social relations as an extra input [17]. Thus, social recommenders are hybrid recommender systems that combine social relationships (e.g. membership, friendship, following relations) with another recommendation method, most commonly CF. Rather than using only the user–item matrix as the traditional CF, a social recommendation mechanism uses two matrices: a user–item matrix, which represents the items that are rated by the user, and a user–user matrix, which represents the social relations between users. Many studies demonstrate that using social information in the recommendation process reduces the effect of the data sparsity and cold start problems [12] and enhances prediction accuracy [10].

There are many approaches combining CF recommender with a social network based on *explicit* social relations between users (e.g. [12, 14]). Explicit relationships are those that are initiated by users, for example, following on Twitter or CiteULike, being friends on Facebook, or in general connection that is made with the awareness or agreement of both users. For example, Massa and Avesani [12] propose a trust graph–based RS that uses trust values given by users in addition to similarity measures to reduce the data sparseness that affects new users.

Existing research has explored also the use of implicit networks in social recommender systems. Implicit social networks are constructed by inferring relationships between users that may not exist in the real world, and the users may be unaware of them. For example, the users that belong to the same neighbourhood in a CF could be considered as part of an implicit network constructed by relating users who gave similar ratings to the same items. These implicit relationships have been often called "trust" [1, 4, 14].

However, very few studies incorporate social relations in the domain of research paper recommendations. For example, PubRec is an RS that suggests to the target user, for a particular paper of interest, the most related papers from the libraries of other users to whom that user is socially connected [15]. PReSA [16] takes advantage of the available data on social bookmarking Web sites (e.g., CiteULike), such as bookmarked papers, metadata, and users' connections, to recommend papers from the users' connections' libraries that are similar and popular among the users' social connections. Both PubRec and PReSA consider the explicit relationships among users in the recommendation process. Lee and Brusilovsky studied three explicit social networks—watching networks [6], group membership [7], and collaboration networks [8]—to find the extent of interest similarities between users involved in those networks and compare the recommendations watching networks produced to the recommendations traditional CF produced [6]. Their results showed that the watching network cannot compete with CF, that the similarities between users' libraries in group membership networks are insignificant [7], and that the similarity between two users connected using co-authorship networks is comparable to user connections using explicit networks, which require agreement between the parties [8]. All of the above studies in recommending research papers depend on the existence of users' social connections to make recommendations; however this social data is not usually available for all users. Thus, the number of users who can get recommendations is reduced (low coverage).

3. PROPOSED IMPLICIT SOCIAL NETWORKS

Using data collected from CiteULike, we built three implicit social networks (ISNs) based on users' bookmarking behavior. CiteULike is a social bookmarking Web site for bookmarking research papers that has been in active use since November 2004; the site currently has 8,217,384 bookmarked papers.

3.1 Network 1: Readership Implicit Social Network

The readership ISN connects users to the authors of the papers that they have bookmarked. We assume that if users bookmark specific papers, interest overlap exists between the bookmarkers and the authors of the papers; this overlap increases with the increase in the number of papers users bookmark from the same author. The relation could be unidirectional or reciprocal. The relation is unidirectional if only one of the users in this relation has bookmarked the other user's publications. The relation is reciprocal if both users have bookmarked

each other's publications. Figure 1 shows the relations in this network, which are depicted as black arrows. For example, the relation between user 3 and user 5 is reciprocal, while the relation between user 3 and user 1 is unidirectional; user 3 is the paper's bookmarker and user 1 is the paper's author. The numbers on the arrows represent the strength of the relations. For example, the strength of the relation between user 3 and user 1 is five, which means that user 3's library contains five bookmarked papers authored by user 1.

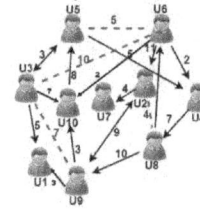

Figure 1. Sample of relations in implicit networks

3.2 Network 2: Co-readership Implicit Social Network

The co-readership ISN connects users who bookmark (and presumably read) papers written by the same authors. If user 1 and user 2 have both bookmarked papers written by user 3, then user 1 and user 2 are connected using the co-readership ISN. This network structure is useful for users who do not yet have publications and therefore cannot have relations in network 1. The assumption is that users who bookmark the same paper(s) also have similar interests. The strength of the relationship is measured by the number of authors whose libraries overlap. Figure 1 shows an example of the relationships in this network in blue. For example, user 5 and user 6 are connected because they both bookmarked papers written by the same authors; the number of overlapping author names here is five. We show only a part of the graph, and it includes only one of those five authors (user 4).

3.3 Network 3: Tag-based Implicit Social Network

The tag-based ISN connects users if they use the same tags to annotate their bookmarked papers. However, we do not check whether users use the same tags to annotate the same papers. We consider the tag similarity between the entire tag cloud associated with each user. We assume that the more similar tags the users have, the higher the interest similarity. While the previous two networks are based on the papers' metadata, this network is based on user-generated data. To build this network, the tags used to annotate the papers are aggregated for each user. The data is preprocessed to make the tags comparable. We follow the method described in [9] to preprocess the tags. All tags are preprocessed by converting them to lowercase, removing the stop words, and then using the porter stemmer tool to remove any additional letters added to the root word to eliminate the effect of the word variation (e.g., the word "social" could have different variations, such as "socialize", "socialization" or "socializing"). The relations in this network also have strengths. The strength of the relation between two users is measured by the number of tags they share. The assumption is that the more tags two users share, the stronger the relationship is between them.

4. EXPERIMENT DESIGN AND DATASET

We have conducted different offline experiments to evaluate the recommendation accuracy. We compared three different recommenders that either use pure social relations in the recommendation or incorporate the social relations in collaborative filtering (CF). In addition, we compared the recommenders using each ISN with the corresponding CF used as a baseline approach. We then compared the best recommender for each ISN to test whether any of proposed ISN's recommendations outperform those of the others.

4.1 Recommendation Approaches

To determine the effectiveness of different ISNs as good sources for recommendations, we compared the following various existing social recommendation approaches. These recommendation approaches were applied previously to datasets that have explicit social relations and numeric ratings of items (i.e. rating of items using Likert scale). We applied the same approaches to dataset that has implicit social relations and unary ratings of items (i.e. existence of the paper in the user's library).

4.1.1 Social Recommender

The social recommender was proposed by [3]. It simply replaces the anonymous nearest neighbors in the user-based CF with the target user's social friends in the social network. To apply the social recommender to one of the proposed ISNs, we found the social friends of each user and used the data from those friends in the same way that we used anonymous peers in CF by picking the top N peers and using their bookmarked papers to find candidate papers to recommend to the user. However, in social recommender we replaced the similarity between users that is used in the predication of the target user's rating for unseen items with the weighted strength between users in ISNs.

4.1.2 Combined Recommender

The combined recommender integrates neighbors from conventional user-based CF and the target user's social friends to construct a new nearest neighborhood set for the target user [3]. We then used the data from users in the new combined neighbors in the recommendation following the same way as social recommender.

4.1.3 Amplified Recommender

The amplified recommender amplifies the social friends' preferences in CF nearest neighbors [10]. First, the nearest neighborhood peers were identified by CF top-N technique. Then, if the user's social friends were also in the top-N neighbors, we used an amplifying approach to give the preferences from those social friends more weight in the recommendation process. The amplifying function that we used is the one used in [10], which is given by (1):

$$\text{Min} (S_{ij} \times (1+((N_{ij}/N_{all,j})),1) \qquad (1)$$

where j is the target user, i is one of the user's social friends, S_{ij} is the similarity between user (j) and user (i) which is calculated by CF approach using the papers that are co-bookmarked by both users, N_{ij} is the number of interaction between the target user (j) and the user's social friend (i), and $N_{all,j}$ is the total number of interactions between the target user (j) and all of the user's social friends. Because the similarity value cannot be greater than 1, we chose a minimum value between 1 and the amplified value. The interactions between the target user and one of the user's social friends were based on the type of ISN on which we were trying to apply the approach. For example, if we use the co-readership ISN, the number of interactions equals the number of authors that both users have in common (i.e., the number of authors one or more of whose papers both users bookmark).

4.2 Dataset

We collected the data for this study from the CiteULike.org social bookmarking Web site, which allows social features such as connecting users, watching users (like following on Twitter), and sharing references. Users of CiteULike can import scientific reference data from other resources such as PubMed and can assign tags to the bookmarked references for future easy access. Using the snowball method, we crawled the CiteULike Web site, starting with 500 randomly chosen, recently active users whose publications and bookmark data we collected. Then, we branched to collect the users' data for the users who had bookmarked their publications or who had bookmarked the same papers as the initial users. The total number of users in this dataset is 13,189 with average number of 1.52 publications, 98.79 bookmarks and 3.81 tags per user. The total number of publications, bookmarks, and tags are 19,774, 1,323,065, and 3,086,565 respectively.

5. Experiments and Analysis of Results

In order to evaluate the relevancy of recommended items using the aforementioned ISNs as recommendation resources, information-retrieval-based evaluation methods are usually used such as precision, recall, and F-measure. We conducted two offline experiments using N-fold cross-validation. It is a random selection technique that selects one fraction of the user's bookmarks of size (1/N) as a testing set and uses the remaining (N-1)/N fractions of the user's bookmarks to train the algorithm's model. This process is repeated N times, each time with different test and training sets. We then judged the prediction's accuracy by calculating the precision and the recall. Our experiments used fivefold cross validation and three different ranks for precision and recall (top two, top five, and top ten).

The first experiment examined which recommendation algorithm produces the best prediction accuracy for each ISN, while the second experiment compared the prediction accuracy of the recommendation for different ISNs. For each ISN, we compared the performance of the three recommendation algorithms—social recommender, combined recommender, and amplified recommender—using precision and recall prediction accuracy measures at three different ranks (N=2, 5, and 10). We compared the accuracy differences of the algorithms at 95 percent significance level using a one-way ANOVA, which tests the null hypothesis that no statistical difference exists between the mean values of precision and the recall of the three recommendation approaches, followed by the Tukey post hoc test to rank the algorithms based on the mean differences at all ranks.

5.1 Results of Different Recommenders for Each ISN

5.1.1 Readership ISN (Reciprocal Relations)

The results of comparing the prediction accuracy of the three recommenders showed statistically significant differences between the means of the precision values (see Figure 2). However, the recall values were insignificant. By applying one-way ANOVA at $p < 0.05$, we found F = 5.61 for P@2, F = 3.724 for P@5, and F = 9.77 for P@10. We then applied the Tukey post hoc test to rank the algorithms based on the mean differences of the precision values. We found that the social recommender outperformed the combined recommender, but the difference between the social and the amplified recommenders was insignificant. This means that the amplified recommender benefited from the data from the social friends that make the differences between the social and the amplified recommenders invisible, in contrast with the combined recommender, which deals with the data from anonymous peers and social peers similarly.

5.1.1 Readership ISN (Unidirectional Relations)

Using social relations that relate two users if one user bookmarks a paper written by the other caused the social recommender to perform worst. As Figure 2 shows, the social recommender had the lowest precision and recall values in all ranks. One-way ANOVA showed statistically significant differences in both precision and recall values at p < 0.05 (F = 25.12 for P@2, F = 27.71 for P@5, F = 29.50 for P@10, F = 14.23 for R@2, F = 14.10 for R@5, and F = 7.35 for R@10). The Tukey post hoc tests showed that the combined recommender had the highest precision and recall values, followed by the amplified recommender and the social recommender, whose values for all precision and recall are the lowest. Fusing data from CF in combined and amplified recommenders enhanced the recommendation in both recommenders similarly, which means that the social data had no effect in this case.

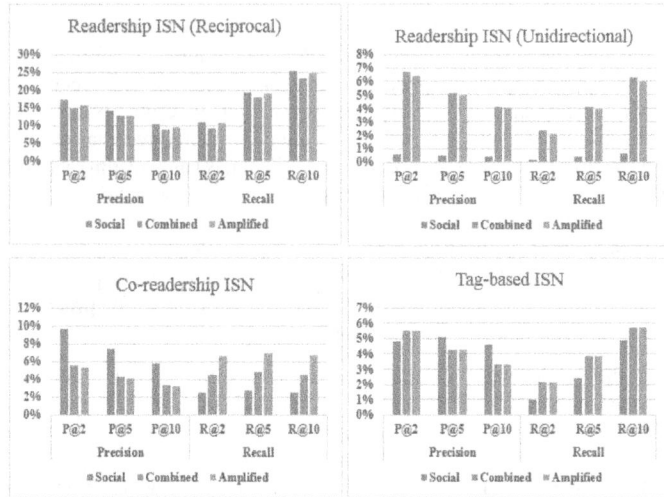

Figure 2: Prediction accuracy measures for different recommendation approaches in each ISN

5.1.2 Co-readership ISN

Figure 2 shows that the social recommender outperformed the other two recommenders in precision but not in recall values. To test the significance of the differences, application of one-way ANOVA showed statistical significant differences between the precision values at p < 0.05 (F = 14.84 for P@2, F = 15.1 for P@5, and F = 20.13 for P@10). However, the recall values were insignificant, which means that all the recommenders have similar recall. By applying the T wetea5wetea5qwqwukey post hoc tests to the precision values for different ranks, we found that the social recommender had the best prediction accuracy, followed by the combined recommender and, finally, the amplified recommender. These results were valid for P@5 and P@10. However, although the precision for the combined and amplified recommenders is similar when recommending two papers, the social recommender has the highest precision value.

5.1.3 Tag-based ISN

As Figure 2 shows, the combined and the amplified recommenders displayed almost the same performance for all ranks, which was higher than that of the social recommender with regard to most of the precision and recall values. However, the only significant differences occurred for precision when the top 10 papers were recommended and the recall value as R@2. One-way ANOVA showed significant difference of P@10 (F = 7.46, p < 0.05), and the Tukey post hoc test showed that the social recommender outperformed both the combined and the amplified recommenders. One-way ANOVA also showed a significant difference of R@2 (F = 8.47, p < 0.05), and the Tukey post hoc test showed that the combined and amplified recommenders outperformed the social recommender. However, no statistical difference existed between their mean differences. The insignificant

results probably occurred because users do not have sufficient number of tags – the average number of tags per user is only 3.81.

5.2 Comparing Results with Collaborative Filtering

In the previous subsection, we compared three recommenders: the social recommender, which uses only the data from social peers, and the combined and amplified recommenders, which incorporate social data into CF. Therefore, we compared the three previous approaches with pure collaborative filtering as a baseline; Table 1 shows the results. We used a T-test to compare each recommender with CF (significant results are in boldface). The social recommender performs better than CF in the co-readership ISN and in the readership ISN when the social relations are reciprocal, while CF outperformed the social recommender in readership ISN when the social relations were unidirectional. The results were consistent for all ranks (N= 2, 5, 10). In the tag-based ISN, the social recommender prediction accuracy was higher than CF only when ten papers were recommended. The combined recommender also performed better than CF in some cases (co-readership and unidirectional readership ISNs). In most of the cases for insignificant differences, the prediction accuracy for the three recommenders examined was higher than the CF. That is to say, the recommendation using ISNs as data sources performed better or at least the same as CF.

Table 1. Comparison between Collaborative Filtering (CF), Social Recommender (SR), Combined Recommender (CR) and Amplified Recommender (AR)

	RS	Mean value (T-test value and significance level (p-value))		
		P@2	P@5	P@10
Readership ISN (reciprocal)	SR	17.37%(t=4.017, p<0.05)	12.83%(t=4.42,p<0.05)	9.53%(t=3.28,p<0.05)
	CR	14.78%(t=1.23,p=0.25)	12.62%(t=1.27,p=0.24)	8.87%(t=0.367,p=0.84)
	AR	15.74%(t=2.52,p<0.05)	12.83%(t=1.74,p=0.12)	9.53%(t=2.063,p=0.73)
	CF	13.66%	11.81%	8.79%
Readership ISN (unidirectional)	SR	0.56%(t=-49.64,p<0.05)	0.46%%(t=-55.2,p<0.05)	0.39%%(t=-79.6,p<0.05)
	CR	6.72%%(t=2.49,p<0.05)	5.13%(t=1.19,p=0.26)	4.10%(t=1.79,p=0.11)
	AR	6.39%(t=0.17,p=0.871)	5.00%(t=-0.47,p=0.64)	4.04%(t=0.28,p=.078)
	CF	6.39%	5.04%	4.02%
Co-readership ISN	SR	9.72%(t=3.96,p<0.05)	7.42%%(t=-8.39,p<0.05)	5.82%%(t=10.26,p<0.05)
	CR	5.56%(t=2.57,p<0.05)	4.25%(t=4.19,p<0.05)	3.30%(t=3.93,p<0.05)
	AR	5.33%(t=-0.15,p=0.89)	4.09%(t=0.65,p=0.53)	3.21%(t=0.89,p=0.40)
	CF	5.33%	4.06%	3.17%
Tag-based ISN	SR	4.81%(t=-0.98,p=0.36)	5.09%(t=1.76,p=0.116)	4.60%(t=2.73,p<0.05)
	CR	5.47%(t=-1.83,p=0.10)	4.28%(t=-0.26,p=0.79)	3.33%(t=0.44,p=0.96)
	AR	5.49%(t=-1.52,p=0.16)	4.25%(t=-0.98,p=0.35)	3.32%(t=-0.36,p=0.73)
	CF	5.57%	4.28%	3.33

We gathered information about the performance from the comparisons in Figure 2 and from Table 1. We conclude that the best recommender for each ISN is

- Readership ISN (reciprocal): social recommender
- Readership ISN (unidirectional): combined recommender
- Co-readership ISN: social recommender
- Tag-based ISN: social recommender

5.3 Which ISN is the Best Recommendation Source?

We compared the accuracy values of the best performing recommender for each ISN to test, which ISN is the best as a source of recommendation. One-way ANOVA showed significant differences of precision and recall values at p < 0.05 (F = 81.19 for P@2, F = 123.66 for P@5, F = 139.88 for P@10, F = 164.80 for R@2, F = 190.91 for R@5, and F = 251.76 for R@10). Then, the Tukey post hoc test showed that the readership ISN (reciprocal) has the highest precision performance, followed by the co-readership ISN. Then, the readership

ISN (unidirectional), and the tag-based ISN with similar performances. For the recall, the only significant result was that the readership ISN (reciprocal) had the highest recall value.

5.4 User Coverage

While measuring the prediction accuracy of recommendation to filter several recommendation approaches is important, it is not the only way to evaluate the performance of a certain recommendation approach. Non-performance measures, such as serendipity, diversity, novelty, or coverage, can also evaluate recommendation approaches [11]. One measure that compares the capability different recommending approaches to produce recommendations for a larger set of users is the coverage measure, which is the ratio of users who receive nonempty recommended sets to the total number of users. The more coverage provided, the better the recommending algorithm.

Because we used social networks to find research papers from the target user's social friends, the user coverage for each recommendation approach using any of the ISNs is the number of users who have social relations using that ISN. We found that the co-readership ISN had the highest user coverage (87.25 percent), then tag-based (85.55 percent), readership ISN (with unidirectional relations) (37.22 percent), and readership ISN (with reciprocal relations) (1.59 percent). A tradeoff exists between the prediction accuracy and the user coverage: the more accurate the prediction, the smaller the user coverage. Therefore, finding relevant papers using our proposed ISNs is generally beneficial and specifically increases recommendation coverage. We found that in the CiteULike dataset that we used in this study, only 18 percent of users have explicitly social friends (i.e., invited), and the average number of social relations per user is only 0.31.

6. Conclusions and Future Work

We proposed three different ISNs based on user bookmarking behavior. We tested three recommendation approaches for each ISN. We then tested them in comparison with CF. We found that in most cases the social recommender produces the best prediction accuracy. We also found that the readership ISN with reciprocal social relations is the best recommendation information resource, followed by the co-readership ISN. However, the co-readership ISN has more user coverage.

In the future, we want to test the proposed implicit social networks with other datasets and/or with different applications to enable us to generalize our findings. We also want to test the recommendations produced by fusing data from explicit and implicit social networks or fusing data from different ISNs. We hypothesize that fusing data from both explicit and implicit social networks can increase the user coverage for the explicit social networks while at the same time increasing the prediction accuracy for the ISNs whose accuracy rates are lower. We also want to test the recommendations produced by ISNs with real users.

Acknowledgement: This work has been supported by a PhD fellowship of the Institute of Public Administration, Riyadh, Saudi Arabia and by the NSERC Discovery Grant program.

7. References

[1] Avesani, P., Massa, P., and Tiella, R. A Trust-Enhanced Recommender System Application: Moleskiing. In *Proceedings of the 2005 ACM Symposium on Applied Computing*, (New York, USA, 2004), ACM Press, 1589–1593.

[2] Basu, C., Hirsh, H., Cohen, W.W., and Nevill-Manning, C. Technical Paper Recommendation: A Study in Combining Multiple Information Sources. *J Artif Int Res* 14 (2001), 231–252.

[3] Bellogín, A., Cantador, I., and Castells, P. A Study of Heterogeneity in Recommendations for a Social Music Service. In *Proceedings of the First International Workshop on Information Heterogeneity and Fusion in Recommender Systems*, (New York, NY, USA, 2010), ACM, 1–8.

[4] Golbeck, J. FilmTrust: Movie Recommendations from Semantic Web-Based Social Networks. In *ISWC2005 Posters & Demonstrations*, 2005, PID–72.

[5] Herlocker, J. L., Konstan, J. A. , Terveen, L. G. and Riedl, T. Evaluating collaborative filtering recommender systems, In *ACM Trans. Inf. Syst.*, 22 (2004), 5–53.

[6] Lee, D.H., and Brusilovsky, P. Improving Recommendations Using Watching Networks in a Social Tagging System. In *Proceedings of the 2011 iConference*, (New York, NY, USA, 2011)), ACM, 33–39.

[7] Lee, D.H., and Brusilovsky, P. Interest Similarity of Group Members: The Case Study of CiteULike. In the *WebSci10: Extending the Frontiers of Society On-Line,* Raleigh, NC: USA, 2010).

[8] Lee, D. 2013. *Personalized Recommendations Based On Users' Information-Centered Social Networks*. Doctoral Dissertation. University of Pittsburgh.

[9] Liu, B. Informational Retrieval and Web Search. In *Web Data Mining: Exploring Hyperlinks, Contents and Usage Data*, (New York, NY, 2007), Springer , 183–236.

[10] Liu, F., and Lee, H.J. Use of Social Network Information to Enhance Collaborative Filtering Performance. *Expert Syst. Appl.* 37 (2010), 4772–4778.

[11] Ma, H., Yang, H., Lyu, M.R., and King, I. (2008). SoRec: Social Recommendation Using Probabilistic Matrix Factorization. In *Proceedings of the Seventeenth ACM Conference on Information and Knowledge Management*, (New York, NY, USA, 2008), ACM, 931–940.

[12] Massa, P., and Avesani, P. Trust-Aware Recommender Systems. In *Proceedings of the 2007 ACM Conference on Recommender Systems*, (New York, NY, USA, 2007), ACM, 17–24.

[13] McNee, S.M., Albert, I., Cosley, D., Gopalkrishnan, P., Lam, S.K., Rashid, A.M., Konstan, J.A., and Riedl, J. On the Recommending of Citations for Research Papers. In *Proceedings of the 2002 ACM Conference on Computer Supported Cooperative Work*, (New York, NY, USA, 2002), ACM, 116–125.

[14] O'Donovan, J., and Smyth, B. Trust in Recommender Systems. In *Proceedings of the Tenth International Conference on Intelligent User Interfaces*, (New York, NY, USA, 2005), ACM, 167–174.

[15] Pera, M.S., and Ng, Y.-K. A Personalized Recommendation System on Scholarly Publications. In *Proceedings of the Twentieth ACM International Conference on Information and Knowledge Management*, (New York, NY, USA, 2011), ACM, 2133–2136.

[16] Pera, M.S., and Ng, Y.-K. Exploiting the Wisdom of Social Connections to Make Personalized Recommendations on Scholarly Articles. *J. Intell. Inf. Syst.* 42 (2014), 371–391.

[17] Tang, J., Hu, X., and Liu, H. Social Recommendation: *A Review. Soc. Netw. Anal. Min.* 3 (2013), 1113–1133.

[18] Torres, R., McNee, S.M., Abel, M., Konstan, J.A., and Riedl, J. Enhancing Digital Libraries with TechLens+. In *Proceedings of the Fourth ACM/IEEE-CS Joint Conference on Digital Libraries*, (New York, NY, USA, 2004), ACM, 228–236

Trust and Reliance Based on System Accuracy

Kun Yu*   Shlomo Berkovsky   Dan Conway
Ronnie Taib   Jianlong Zhou   Fang Chen
Data61, CSIRO
13 Garden Street, Eveleigh, NSW 2015, Australia
{firstname.lastname}@data61.csiro.au

ABSTRACT

Trust plays an important role in various user-facing systems and applications. It is particularly important in the context of decision support systems, where the system's output serves as one of the inputs for the users' decision making processes. In this work, we study the dynamics of explicit and implicit user trust in a simulated automated quality monitoring system, as a function of the system accuracy. We establish that users correctly perceive the accuracy of the system and adjust their trust accordingly.

Keywords

User-system trust; system accuracy; trust formation; reliance

1. INTRODUCTION

User-system trust is an important construct in human-computer interaction as well as in many practical user-facing systems. It is particularly important for systems where users are required to make decisions based, at least partially, on machine recommendations. For instance, consider a medical decision support system or an e-commerce recommender system. In both, a user decides on the course of actions – be it medical treatment for a patient or product to purchase – in uncertain conditions and based (in part) on the system's suggestions. Due to the possible negative implications of incorrect decisions, the lack of user trust may deter the user from following these suggestions and be detrimental to the acceptance of system recommendations.

Hence, trust in automation, and in particular decision support information technologies, has been the focus of many studies over the last decades [1], [2]. It has mainly been studied in the context of task automation and industrial machinery. In one of the seminal works in this field, Muir et al [3] found a positive correlation between the level of user trust and the degree to which the user delegated control to the system. Furthermore, McGuirl and Sarter [4] found similar responses specifically within an automated decision support system. Note that both works measured the impact of establishing and maintaining trust based on user reliance on system suggestions, indirectly deriving the uptake of the system.

Although much work has been devoted to the impact of system performance [5] and transparency [6] on user trust, less attention has been paid to the temporal variations of trust. In this work, we set out to investigate the fine-grained dynamics of trust in an experiment that simulates an Automated Quality Monitoring (AQM) system that alerts users to of the existence of faulty items,

UMAP '16, July 13-17, 2016, Halifax, NS, Canada
© 2016 ACM. ISBN 978-1-4503-4370-1/16/07...$15.00
DOI: http://dx.doi.org/10.1145/2930238.2930290

in a fictional factory production line scenario. In the experiment, 22 participants interacted with four AQM systems, each exhibiting a different level of accuracy. After each trial (30 per AQM system), the users reported their perceived level of trust in the system, which we refer to as *explicit trust*. In addition, we also measured *implicit trust* through reliance, quantified by the portion of times the user has followed the AQM's suggestions so far.

Two hypotheses guided our work:

- H1: Trust would stabilise over time to a level correlated with the system's accuracy;
- H2: Users would exhibit thresholds of acceptable accuracy for the system, under which reliance would drop.

This work experimentally validates these hypotheses and draws practical conclusions that can help system designers maintain user trust in systems. In the following sections, we first present related work on user-system trust, followed by a detailed description of the experimental protocol. We then present and discuss the results, and finally conclude with a discussion on practical steps that might be taken to sustain user trust.

2. RELATED WORK

Human-machine trust has generated an extensive body of literature since it was originally investigated within the context of industrial automation systems in the nineties. Although multiple definitions, frameworks and decompositions of trust exist, there is convergent evidence about its central characteristics. We adopt the definition proposed by Lee and See [7] where '*trust can be defined as the attitude that an agent will help achieve an individual's goals in a situation characterised by uncertainty and vulnerability.*' This succinctly encapsulates the primary sources of variance (the user, the system, the context) and identifies a key aspect of this relationship – that of vulnerability. Similar definitions exist by Rousseau et al. [8], Mayer et al. [9] and Hoff and Bashit [2]. Trust is a hypothesised variable that has been shown to be a key mitigating factor in system use/disuse (i.e., reliance) [1]. It can be inferred from both self-reported and behavioural measures [10], and importantly, is dynamic, with acquisition and extinction curves, subject to the user's perception of system performance.

Trust has also been proposed to be a multi-dimensional construct with a number of models existing in the current literature, each with slightly different proposed component subscales. We have adopted the model of [2], which was based on an empirical research overview of existing literature. This model proposes that three conceptual types of factors influence user-system trust. *Dispositional* trust reflects the user's natural tendency to trust machines and encompasses cultural, demographic, and personality factors. *Situational* trust refers to more specific factors, such as the task to be performed, the complexity and type of system, user's workload, perceived risks and benefits, and even mood. Lastly, *learned* trust encapsulates the experiential aspects of the construct, which are directly related to the system itself. This variable is further decomposed into two components. One is *initial learned* trust, which consists of any knowledge of the system acquired before interaction, such as reputation or brand awareness. This initial state of learnt trust is then also affected by *dynamic learned trust*, which develops as the user interacts with the system and begins to develop experiential knowledge of its performance characteristics such as reliability, predictability, and usefulness. The relationships and interplay between these factors influencing trust are complicated and subject to much discussion. In our work we focussed on how trust changes through human-machine interaction and, therefore, seek to manipulate experimental variables thought to influence dynamic learned trust whilst keeping situational and dispositional variables static.

3. METHODOLOGY

3.1 Context

We operationalised a binary decision making task in our experiment for two reasons. Firstly, any complex decision process can be arguably decomposed into a series of binary decisions. The decision-trust relationship, thus, can be easily generalised into complicated decision-making problems. Secondly, the simplified decision making protocol we implemented, similar in effect to the 'micro-worlds' discussed by Lee and See [7], makes it convenient to map trust to decisions without other parameters' interference.

The scenario of the experiment was a typical industrial quality control task. This simulated task consisted of checking the quality of drinking glasses on a production line, with the assistance of a decision support system called an *Automatic Quality Monitor* (AQM). However, the AQM was not always correct, i.e., it would occasionally exhibit false positives (suggesting failing a good glass) and misses (suggesting passing a faulty glass).

3.2 Trials

Each trial required the participant to make a decision about whether to pass or fail a glass, with no other information about the glass other than the AQM's suggestion. Trials were presented sequentially, providing a time-based history of interaction with a given AQM. In each trial, the participant could trust the AQM or override it and make his/her own decision.

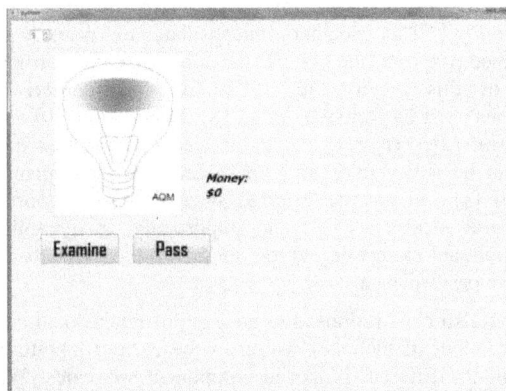

Figure 1: The trial starts with an AQM suggestion.

Each trial starts with the AQM providing a suggestion for a new glass as shown in Figure 1, by illuminating a red warning light-bulb if it predicts the glass to be faulty. Otherwise the warning light remains off. It should be noted that the status of the AQM light and the possible quality of the glass are both binary features to help generalise results, as mentioned above. The participant must then decide whether to pass the glass by clicking the *Pass* button, or conversely to fail the glass by clicking the *Examine*

button. The actual glass is then displayed, so the participant receives direct feedback on their decision, as shown in Figure 2.

Furthermore, we gamified the experiment in an attempt to increase motivation and attention: each time the participant made a correct decision, i.e., examined a faulty glass or passed a good glass, they earned a fictional $100 reward. However, each incorrect decision cost them a fictional $100 fine. The total earnings were updated and displayed after each decision. Note that the rewards and the fines were used for gamification purposes only, and no actual remuneration was offered to the participants.

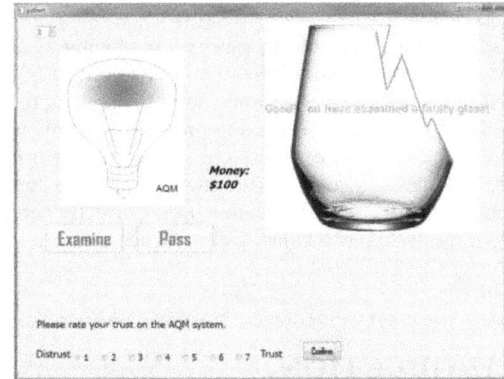

Figure 2: Upon the participant's decision, the actual glass condition is shown and score is updated.

3.3 AQM Accuracy and Blocks

The experiment session was separated into four blocks, and participants were instructed that a different AQM was used for each block. The accuracy of each of the four AQMs presented was manipulated by varying the average rate of false positives and false negatives exhibited by each system. These errors were presented in a randomised order within the 30 trials presented for each participants and each AQM.

We used four different AQM accuracies, i.e. 100%, 90%, 80% and 70% respectively. In order to capture a trust baseline for each participant, each experiment session always started with the 100% accuracy AQM, followed by the other three AQMs used in a random order. Each AQM was used for 30 task trials. The AQM made errors randomly over the trials, but in a way that the mean accuracy for respective AQM was as defined. For instance, the 80% AQM would make, on average, 6 errors over the 30 trials (on average, 3 false positives and 3 false negatives).

3.4 Participants and Data Collection

Twenty-two participants took part in the 45 minute experiment. The participants were university students and IT professionals. No specific background or requirements were required to complete the task. Recruitment and participation were conducted in accordance to an approved ethics plan for this study. No reward or compensation was offered for taking part in the experiment.

For each trial, we collected:

- The participant's binary decision (pass or examine);
- The AQM suggestion (light on or light off);
- The actual glass condition (good or faulty);
- The subjective trust rating, collected after the actual state of the glass had been revealed. This rating was collected using a 7-point Likert scale ranging from 1=distrust to 7=trust. In the instructions issued at the outset of the experiment we explained that a rating of 4 meant neutral, or no disposition in either direction.

One of the participants had consistently rated the trust at extreme levels (either 1 or 7) of the 7-point scale across the four AQMs, hence, their data was excluded from the analysis. Considering individual differences, the trust data was normalised to the [0,1] range on individual basis, for all the trials conducted on the four AQMs. The binary decisions of the participants were further quantified in terms of a reliance score, i.e., ratio between the number of decisions consistent with the AQM suggestions and the total decisions for a set number of consecutive trials.

4. RESULTS

In this section we present and discuss the results of our examinations on trust in the light of our hypotheses.

4.1 Trust Correlation to System Accuracy

We start with the investigation of acquisition and extinction of trust, as observed over the course of user interactions with the AQMs. The level of trust is measured subjectively after each trial, as described earlier. Since the AQM errors were randomised over the 30 trials for each AQM, and given the small number of participants, trust variations for each trial exhibit a number of local fluctuations. We address this by applying a simple low-pass filter; specifically, a 5-trial sliding window, reducing our data to 25 points per AQM. That is, the level of trust after trial N was computed as the average trust across the last 5 trials. Figure 3 shows the aggregated normalised trust scores for all 21 participants.

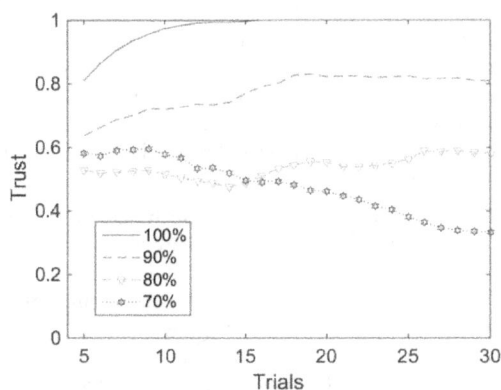

Figure 3: Mean trust for all participants, all AQMs.

Initially, trust in the 90%, 80%, and 70% AQMs seems comparable, as would be expected, since participants know that each new AQM is different from the others they may have encountered, and the order is randomised. However, the initial trust in the 100% AQM appears to be above the other AQMs, as it was the first AQM that users interacted with.

An analysis of variance showed that the effect of the AQM accuracy on the first trust point (trust mean over the first five trials) was significant for all participants, $F(3, 80)=6.463$, $p<0.001$. Post hoc Tuckey tests show there is a significant difference between the 100% AQM and both the 80% and 70% AQMs. We hypothesise that this may be linked to the sliding window we used to capture trust, as the participants started to form a preliminary trust judgment of each AQM by the time of the first trust point (recall that the first point is actually after 5 trials).

As a side note, the test of homogeneity (Levene's) for the first reliance point was significant, hence violating ANOVA's assumption of equal variances. However, the sample sizes being equal, this statistic should be robust. Hence, we accept the results.

Looking at the temporal fluctuations of the trust values, we observe that these stabilise with important differences observed between the AQMs. As expected, trust in the 100% AQM stabilises at 1 after 13 trials only. Also the 90% AQM converges to reasonably high levels of trust from trial 19. The 80% AQM is initially stable but exhibits a slight increase in trust starting from trial 15, while the trust in the 70% AQM steadily declines after less than 10 trials and eventually drops as low as 0.33.

An analysis of variance showed that the effect of the AQM accuracy on the last trust point (trust mean over the last five trials) was significant for all the participants, $F(3, 80)=27.03$, $p<0.001$. Post hoc Tuckey tests show there is a significant difference between the 100% AQM and both the 80% and 70% AQMs, as well as between the 90% AQM and the 70% AQM, and, again, between the 80% AQM and the 70% AQM.

It should be noted that the final order of the trust ratings corresponds to that of the AQM accuracies. That is, the 100% AQM stabilises at the highest trust level, followed by the 90% AQM, 80% AQM, and 70% AQM, in this order. This finding supports our hypothesis H1 that *trust would stabilise over time to a level correlated with the systems' accuracy*.

In addition, since only a small set of discrete accuracies were examined, it can be interesting to analyse our results from a rank-ordering problem perspective. Indeed, this would provide an indication of whether the reported trust ranking aligns to the discrete accuracy levels of the AQMs. A Friedman's test shows significant differences between the trust levels (Friedman's $\chi2$ (20, 3) = 45.31, p < 0.001), with mean ranks of 3.8, 2.9, 2.0 and 1.3 for the 100%, 90%, 80% and 70% AQMs, respectively. These statistics suggest that trust ratings correlate with increased levels of AQM accuracy, when considered as discrete values (here, 10% increments), again, supporting our hypothesis H1.

4.2 Acceptable Accuracy and Reliance

The dynamics of reliance are regarded as an objective measure of trust. Recall that reliance was measured implicitly during each trial as described earlier. Again, we applied in this case a simple low-pass filter, but this time we used a 10-trial sliding window, reducing our data to 20 points per AQM. The reason for this larger window is mainly because reliance is a binary feature (at every trial the participant either did or did not follow the AQM's suggestion). Hence, local variations tend to add weight to the reading for a small window size. Figure 4 shows the aggregated reliance for all the 21 participants and all four AQMs.

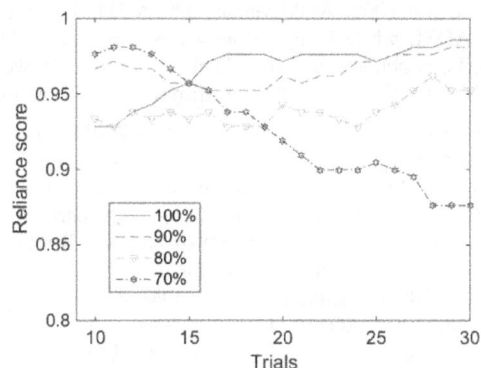

Figure 4: Mean reliance for all participants, all AQMs.

We observe that despite the twice larger sliding window, the reliance curves are less stable than the trust curves. We believe that the reason for this observation is two-fold. Firstly, the effect of a binary feature on smoothing is strong and could require a wider sliding window, but this would mean losing temporal accuracy in our analysis of reliance dynamics. Secondly, we posit that while participants exhibit relatively uniform trust trends, they have different strategies to deal with it and this comes through the objectively measured reliance values.

All curves, except for the 70% AQM, demonstrate slight (and often unstable) increases and their final levels are in the range of 0.95-0.98. The 100% and 90% AQMs seem to converge strongly, while the 70% AQM exhibits a steady decline in reliance. The 80% AQM seems close to the 100% AQM baseline. This could indicate that the acceptable level of accuracy for a system is around the 80% mark, since the reliance of the 80% AQM is slightly lower.

An analysis of variance showed that the effect of the AQM accuracy on the first reliance point was not significant for all participants, $F(3, 80)=01.597, p=0.197$ n.s. That is, the apparent reliance pairs observed are not significant in view of the variance, further demonstrated by Figure 5. This means that the participants interacted with all four AQMs with a comparable level of dispositional trust, as indicated by the implicit reliance measure.

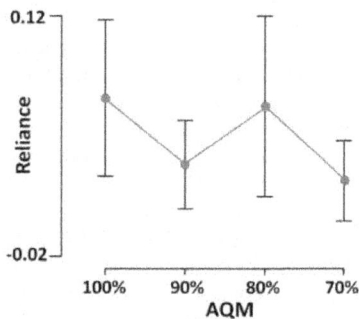

Figure 5: First reliance point variance for all participants.

Focusing on the last reliance observed after 30 trials, an analysis of variance showed that the effect of the AQM accuracy on the last reliance point was significant for all participants, $F(3, 80)=4.182, p=0.008$. The test of homogeneity (Levene's) was significant, but, again, the sample sizes are equal.

Due to the binary notion of reliance, we can test our hypothesis of acceptable level of accuracy by comparing all the AQMs to the 100% AQM baseline, in order to determine where the threshold for accuracy may lay. To do so, we applied a simple contrast in the ANOVA for the last reliance point, and obtained significance only for the pair 100% AQM versus 70% AQM. This means that the 80% AQM, while being visually apart from the 100% and 90% AQMs, is actually not significantly different. However, the 70% AQM is significantly different from the other three AQMs.

These results support our hypothesis H2 that *users have thresholds of acceptable accuracy for a system, under which the reliance drops*. Since there is no significant difference between the AQMs in terms of the initial reliance levels, participants start interacting with the AQMs free of pre-disposition. But later on we observed a different behaviour only for the 70% AQM, whereby the reliance of the participants on that AQM declined significantly compared to other AQMs. This indicates that a threshold of acceptable accuracy in the AQMs, as observed from our participants, lies somewhere between the 70% and 80% levels.

Having said that, the high values and narrow range of reliance values should be highlighted. Over the course of the whole experiment, reliance curves of all the four AQMs remain fairly compact and above the 0.9 mark. This behaviour is not surprising,

however, and can be explained by the relatively high accuracies exhibited by all the AQMs. Even the poorest AQM operating at the 70% accuracy can correctly monitor the quality of a glass in 7 cases out of 10, which is well above chance. We hypothesise that the participants rightfully perceived this benefit of the AQM over pure random choice. Hence, they followed the AQM's suggestions, leading to very high levels of reliance.

5. DISCUSSION AND CONCLUSION

In this work, we investigated the fine-gained dynamics of user-system trust, an important construct of human interaction with a decision support system. We specifically focused on an automated quality monitor (AQM) simulation, which provided indication of faulty glasses being produced. In our study, each user interacted with four AQMs and out of these interactions we populated the explicit trust and implicit reliance scores.

We analysed the temporal dynamics of both trust and reliance, as well as their dependence on the accuracy exhibited by the AQM. It was found that the reported trust levels aggregated across the entire cohort of users, stabilised over time and, in general, corresponded to the accuracy of the AQMs. Somewhat surprisingly, we discovered that the implicit reliance levels were very high and comparable across the four AQMs. We attribute this finding to the relatively high accuracy levels of the AQMs in our experiment.

Hence, the obtained experimental results support the hypotheses raised at the beginning of the paper. Firstly, we observe that the learned user-system trust stabilised over time and generally correlated with the level of accuracy exhibited by the system. Secondly, our findings indicate that at reasonably high levels of system accuracy, user reliance is high, whereas once the system accuracy falls below an acceptance threshold, the reliance is likely to deteriorate as well.

It should be noted that our findings are based on a reasonably limited cohort of participants, all having reasonably short interactions with the system. In the future, we would like to increase the number of interactions so that we may reduce the frequency of users reporting their explicit trust. For example, we could collect the explicit trust level every second interaction, allowing us to double the length of interactions without over-burdening the users. This would allow us to collect more solid empirical evidence and better support our hypotheses.

Finally, more work is needed to address the fine-grained dynamics of trust acquisition and extinction. In our work, we assumed a stable level of accuracy of every system. This, however, may vary over the course of user interaction. Hence, it is important to validate the evolution of user trust as a function of the user's initial trust disposition, observed system performance, and temporal aspects of this performance (e.g., initial failures vs. failures when the trust was already formed). Furthermore, it is possible to depict different user's trust evolving path according to their decision making patterns, and hence users can be categorized in the light of their respective trust profiles. We highlight the importance of these research questions, but leave this work for the future with expanded collection of user trust and interaction data.

ACKNOWLEDGMENTS

NICTA is funded by the Australian Government through the Department of Communications and the Australian Research Council through the ICT Centre of Excellence Program. This work was also partially supported by the Asian Office of Aerospace Research & Development (AOARD) under grant No. FA2386-14-1-0022 AOARD 134131.

REFERENCES

[1] J. D. Lee and N. Moray, "Trust, self-confidence, and operators' adaptation to automation," *Int. J. Hum.-Comput. Stud.*, vol. 40, no. 1, pp. 153–184, Jan. 1994.

[2] K. A. Hoff and M. Bashir, "Trust in Automation Integrating Empirical Evidence on Factors That Influence Trust," *Hum. Factors J. Hum. Factors Ergon. Soc.*, vol. 57, no. 3, pp. 407–434, May 2015.

[3] B. M. Muir, "Trust in automation: Part I. Theoretical issues in the study of trust and human intervention in automated systems," *Ergonomics*, vol. 37, no. 11, pp. 1905–1922, Nov. 1994.

[4] J. M. McGuirl and N. B. Sarter, "Supporting Trust Calibration and the Effective Use of Decision Aids by Presenting Dynamic System Confidence Information," *Hum. Factors J. Hum. Factors Ergon. Soc.*, vol. 48, no. 4, pp. 656–665, Dec. 2006.

[5] W. Wang and I. Benbasat, "Attributions of Trust in Decision Support Technologies: A Study of Recommendation Agents for E-Commerce," *J. Manag. Inf. Syst.*, vol. 24, no. 4, pp. 249–273, Apr. 2008.

[6] J. Zhou, "Transparent Machine Learning—Revealing Internal States of Machine Learning," in *Proceedings of IUI2013 Workshop on Interactive Machine Learning*, Santa Monica, CA, 2013.

[7] J. D. Lee and K. A. See, "Trust in Automation: Designing for Appropriate Reliance," *Hum. Factors J. Hum. Factors Ergon. Soc.*, vol. 46, no. 1, pp. 50–80, Mar. 2004.

[8] D. M. Rousseau, S. B. Sitkin, R. S. Burt, and C. Camerer, "Not So Different After All: A Cross-Discipline View Of Trust," *Acad. Manage. Rev.*, vol. 23, no. 3, pp. 393–404, Jul. 1998.

[9] R. C. Mayer, J. H. Davis, and F. D. Schoorman, "An Integrative Model Of Organizational Trust," *Acad. Manage. Rev.*, vol. 20, no. 3, pp. 709–734, Jul. 1995.

[10] J.-Y. Jian, A. M. Bisantz, and C. G. Drury, "Foundations for an Empirically Determined Scale of Trust in Automated Systems," *Int. J. Cogn. Ergon.*, vol. 4, no. 1, pp. 53–71, Mar. 2000.

[11] J. Rotter, "An new scale for the measurement of interpersonal trust," *J. Pers.*, vol. 35, no. 4, pp. 651–665, 1967.

[12] C. L. Scott, "Interpersonal Trust: A Comparison of Attitudinal and Situational Factors," *Hum. Relat.*, vol. 33, no. 11, pp. 805–812, Nov. 1980.

[13] I. L. Singh, R. Molloy, and R. Parasuraman, "Automation-Induced 'Complacency': Development of the Complacency-Potential Rating Scale," *Int. J. Aviat. Psychol.*, vol. 3, no. 2, pp. 111–122, Apr. 1993.

[14] P. Madhavan and D. A. Wiegmann, "Similarities and differences between human–human and human–automation trust: an integrative review," *Theor. Issues Ergon. Sci.*, vol. 8, no. 4, pp. 277–301, Jul. 2007.

[15] P. C. Earley, "Computer-generated performance feedback in the magazine-subscription industry," *Organ. Behav. Hum. Decis. Process.*, vol. 41, no. 1, pp. 50–64, Feb. 1988.

[16] B. J. Dietvorst, J. P. Simmons, and C. Massey, "Algorithm aversion: People erroneously avoid algorithms after seeing them err," *J. Exp. Psychol. Gen.*, vol. 144, no. 1, pp. 114–126, 2015.

[17] M. T. Dzindolet, L. G. Pierce, H. P. Beck, and L. A. Dawe, "The Perceived Utility of Human and Automated Aids in a Visual Detection Task," *Hum. Factors J. Hum. Factors Ergon. Soc.*, vol. 44, no. 1, pp. 79–94, Mar. 2002.

[18] S. Berkovsky, J. Freyne, and H. Oinas-Kukkonen, Eds., "Influencing Individually: Fusing Personalization and Persuasion," *ACM Trans Interact Intell Syst*, vol. 2, no. 2, pp. 9:1–9:8, Jun. 2012.

[19] S. Merritt and D. Ilgen, "Not all trust is created equal: Dispositional and history-based trust in human-automation interactions," *Hum. Factors*, vol. 50, no. 2, pp. 194–210, 2008.

Semantics-aware Graph-based Recommender Systems Exploiting Linked Open Data

Cataldo Musto
Dept. of Computer Science
University of Bari Aldo Moro
Via E. Orabona, 4 - Bari, Italy
cataldo.musto@uniba.it

Pasquale Lops
Dept. of Computer Science
University of Bari Aldo Moro
Via E. Orabona, 4 - Bari, Italy
pasquale.lops@uniba.it

Pierpaolo Basile
Dept. of Computer Science
University of Bari Aldo Moro
Via E. Orabona, 4 - Bari, Italy
pierpaolo.basile@uniba.it

Marco de Gemmis
Dept. of Computer Science
University of Bari Aldo Moro
Via E. Orabona, 4 - Bari, Italy
marco.degemmis@uniba.it

Giovanni Semeraro
Dept. of Computer Science
University of Bari Aldo Moro
Via E. Orabona, 4 - Bari, Italy
giovanni.semeraro@uniba.it

ABSTRACT

The ever increasing interest in semantic technologies and the availability of several open knowledge sources have fueled recent progress in the field of recommender systems. In this paper we feed recommender systems with features coming from the Linked Open Data (LOD) cloud – a huge amount of machine-readable knowledge encoded as RDF statements – with the aim of improving recommender systems effectiveness. In order to exploit the natural graph-based structure of RDF data, we study the impact of the knowledge coming from the LOD cloud on the overall performance of a graph-based recommendation algorithm. In more detail, we investigate whether the integration of LOD-based features improves the effectiveness of the algorithm and to what extent the choice of different feature selection techniques influences its performance in terms of *accuracy* and *diversity*. The experimental evaluation on two state of the art datasets shows a clear correlation between the feature selection technique and the ability of the algorithm to maximize a specific evaluation metric. Moreover, the graph-based algorithm leveraging LOD-based features is able to overcome several state of the art baselines, such as collaborative filtering and matrix factorization, thus confirming the effectiveness of the proposed approach.

Keywords

Graph-based Recommender Systems; Linked Open Data; Graphs; PageRank; Feature Selection; Diversity

1. INTRODUCTION

The Linked Open Data (LOD) cloud is a huge set of interconnected RDF statements forming a global graph and cov-

UMAP '16, July 13-17, 2016, Halifax, NS, Canada

© 2016 ACM. ISBN 978-1-4503-4370-1/16/07. . . $15.00

DOI: http://dx.doi.org/10.1145/2930238.2930249

ering many topical domains, such as geographical locations, people, companies, books, scientific publications, films, music, TV and radio programs, genes, proteins, drugs, online communities, statistical data, and so on. At the time of writing more than 3,400 datasets are available with more than 85 billions of RDF statements[1].

Figure 1 shows a fragment of the Linked Open Data cloud, where the typical *entry point* to all this plethora of data is DBpedia [2], the RDF mapping of Wikipedia which is commonly considered as the *nucleus* of the emerging *Web of Data*.

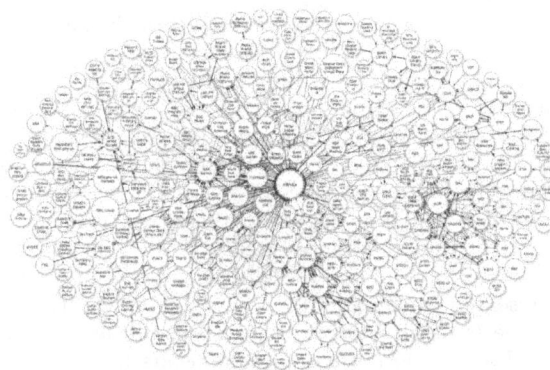

Figure 1: Fragment of the Linked Open Data cloud.

Thanks to the widespread availability of this free machine-readable knowledge, a big effort is now spent to investigate whether and how data gathered from the LOD cloud can be exploited to improve intelligent and adaptive applications, such as Recommender Systems.

Features extracted from the LOD cloud can be easily used to enrich the representation of the *items* to be recommended with novel interesting (and non-trivial) features. For example, as shown in Figure 2, in a *movie recommendation* scenario, the information encoded in DBpedia allows from one hand to describe each movie with classical information such as *director*, and *music composer*, and on the other hand to also discover some unexpected connections, for example that

[1]http://stats.lod2.eu/

229

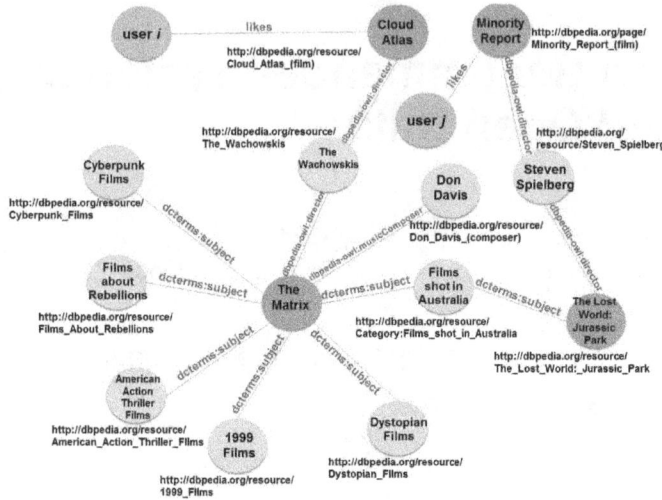

Figure 2: A (tiny) portion of the connections between users, items and entities encoded in Linked Open Data cloud. Purple nodes represent users, blue nodes represent items, yellow nodes represent entities.

both *The Matrix* and *The Lost World: Jurassic Park* movies have been shot in Australia (this is encoded through the property `dcterms:subject`, which connects both movies). It immediately follows that recommender systems can benefit of this information, since such novel features can be introduced to better represent the items as well as the connections between them.

As a first attempt, we study the impact of the knowledge coming from the LOD cloud on the effectiveness of a graph-based recommendation algorithm. Indeed, we exploit the natural graph-based structure of RDF data, which allows to use a *uniform* formalism to represent both *collaborative* and *LOD-based* (content) features. In the former case, users and items are represented as nodes of the graph, while preferences are represented as edges. In the latter case, entities from the LOD cloud are represented as nodes while the connections between them (expressed through RDF properties) are represented as edges. Given such a representation, we adopt PageRank with Priors [10], also known as Personalized PageRank, as graph-based recommendation algorithm. This choice is due to the fact that our previous investigations in the area [3] showed that Personalized PageRank obtained competitive performance even when compared well-performing *ensemble* of different algorithms.

Due to the huge number of available LOD-based features, in this work we also compare several techniques to automatically select the best subset of LOD-based features, i.e. the best subset of edges modeled in the resulting representation, with the aim to investigate to what extent the choice of the feature selection technique can influence the overall behavior of the algorithm and can lead to a higher *accuracy* or a higher *diversity* of the recommendations.

The experimental evaluation carried out on two state of the art datasets related to movies and books shows a clear correlation between the feature selection algorithm and the ability of the recommender system to provide more accurate or diverse recommendations.

Moreover, our graph-based algorithm fed with LOD-based

features is able to overcome several state of the art baselines, further confirming the insight that LOD-based features can be effectively exploited in recommender systems research.

The contributions of the paper is threefold:

1. We propose a methodology to automatically feed a graph-based recommendation algorithm with features coming from the LOD cloud;

2. We provide some guidelines to drive the choice of the feature selection technique, according to the need to optimize different objectives, such as accuracy or diversity;

3. We validate our methodology by evaluating its effectiveness with respect to two state of the art datasets.

The rest of the paper is organized as follows: Section 2 analyzes the related literature. The description of the graph-based recommender system and the overview of several feature selection techniques are provided in Section 3. The details of the experimental evaluation on two state of the art datasets are described in Section 4, while conclusions and future work are presented in Section 5.

2. RELATED WORK

This work investigates two different research lines: graph-based recommender systems and LOD-based recommender systems.

Graph-based Recommender Systems: A very early work in the area of graph-based recommender systems is due to Aggarwal et al. In [1], they present Horting, an approach which models users along with their similarity as nodes in a graph. Given this representation, predictions are calculated by walking the graph to nearby nodes and combining the opinions of the nearby users.

Next, due to the large popularity of PageRank [19], several papers introduced approaches inspired by Random Walk in the area of recommender systems as well. The main difference between the approaches lies in the topology of the graph-based representation: for example, FolkRank has been proposed by Hotho et al. [11] for tag recommendation in social bookmarking systems. The model proposed an adaptation of PageRank relying on a graph-based representation of resources along with the tags the community used to annotate them. In [4], Bogers proposed ContextWalk, a movie recommender system relying on PageRank, which also models tags, genres and actors. Another attempt is due to Gori [9], who defined the graph on the ground of co-viewing users behavior.

One of the distinguishing aspects of our work is that none of the current literature investigated the integration of LOD-based data sources in graph-based recommender systems. The only recent similar attempt has been presented in [18], in which the authors extract the paths connecting users to items by merging the information coming from user preferences with those extracted from the LOD cloud. Given this hybrid data model, the relevance of an item is calculated by counting the number of paths connecting a user and an item: the more the paths, the more the relevance. Differently from this work, we encoded LOD-based features in a graph-based representation and we exploited the personalized PageRank as recommendation technique.

LOD-based Recommender Systems: An updated and detailed review of the literature on recommendation approaches leveraging Linked Open Data is presented in [5]. In that survey, those approaches are classified as *top-down semantic approaches*, i.e. relying on the integration of external knowledge sources.

Research in the area of LOD-based recommender systems takes its root in the field of ontology-based recommender systems, introduced by Middleton et al. [14]. More recent attempts towards the exploitation of Linked Open Data to build recommender systems are due to Passant [20], who proposed a music recommender system based on semantic similarity calculations based on `DBpedia` properties. Even if several work showed that the adoption of more expressive representation languages, as those based on extensions of First-Order Predicate Logic (FOPL), and more complex similarity measures may improve the effectiveness of these systems [8], this research line has been poorly investigated in literature. Indeed, also Musto et al. in [16] propose a framework for similarity calculation based on the LOD cloud, but they did not investigate more complex similarity measures. Specifically, in that work user preferences in music extracted from Facebook are used as input to find other relevant artists and to build a personalized music playlist. A relevant paper has been also presented by Di Noia et al. [7], who performed a preliminary comparison of different manually-selected LOD properties in a movie recommender system. Recently, the use of LOD-based data sources has been the core of the ESWC 2014 Recommender Systems Challenge [17]: in that setting, the best-performing approach [3] was based on ensembles of several widespread algorithms, such as Random Forests, Logistic Regression and PageRank, running on diverse sets of features gathered from the LOD cloud.

It is worth to note that none of the above described work tackles the issue of selecting the best subset of LOD-based features. To this end, in this paper we perform an extensive study aiming to understand to what extent each of the features extracted from the LOD cloud contributes to the overall accuracy and diversity of a graph-based recommender system. This paper continues and extends the preliminary work presented in [15].

3. GRAPH-BASED RECOMMENDATIONS

3.1 Basics

The main idea behind our graph-based recommender system is to represent *users* and *items* as *nodes* in a graph.

Formally, given a set of users $U = \{u_1 \ldots u_n\}$ and a set of items $I = \{i_1 \ldots i_m\}$, a *bipartite* graph $G = \langle V, E \rangle$ is instantiated. Given that for each user and for each item a node is created, $|V| = |U| + |I|$. Next, an (undirected) edge connecting a user u with an item i is created for each positive feedback expressed by that user, so $E = \{(u, i) | likes(u, i) = true\}$.

Given this basic formulation, built on the ground of simple *collaborative* data points (we just modeled user-item pairs as in collaborative filtering, i.e. purple and blue nodes in Figure 2), each item $i \in I$ can be provided with a relevance score, computed using a variant of the PageRank, called *PageRank with priors* [10], or *personalized PageRank*. Differently from PageRank, which assigns an evenly distributed prior probability to each node ($\frac{1}{N}$, where N is the number of nodes), the *personalized PageRank* adopts a *non-uniform*

personalization vector assigning different weights to different nodes to get a bias towards some nodes (specifically, the preferences of a specific user). In our algorithm the prior probability to the nodes is distributed by defining a simple heuristics, set after a rough tuning: 80% of the total weight is evenly distributed among items liked by the user (0% assigned to items disliked by the user), while 20% is evenly distributed among the remaining nodes.

Given this setting, the personalized PageRank is executed for each user (this is mandatory, since the prior probabilities change according to user preferences), and nodes are ranked according to their PageRank score which is in turn calculated on the ground of the connectivity in the graph. The output of the algorithm is a list of nodes ranked according to PageRank scores, labeled as L. Given L, recommendations are built by extracting only *non-voted* nodes $i_1 \ldots i_n \in I$.

3.2 Enriching the Graph with LOD-based Features

The graph built on the ground of the collaborative data points could be enriched by introducing *additional* nodes and edges, extracted from the LOD cloud (yellow nodes in Figure 2). Formally, we define an extended graph $G_{LOD} = \langle V_{LOD_{ALL}}, E_{LOD_{ALL}} \rangle$, where $V_{LOD_{ALL}} = V \cup V_{LOD}$ and $E_{LOD_{ALL}} = E \cup E_{LOD}$. E_{LOD} represents the new connections resulting from the properties encoded in the LOD cloud (e.g. *subject*, *genre*, ...), while V_{LOD} represents the new set of nodes which are connected to the items $i_1 \ldots i_m \in I$ through the properties of the LOD cloud. G_{LOD} becomes a *tripartite* graph, containing users, items and LOD-based properties describing the items.

As an example, if we consider the movie *The Matrix*, the property `http://dbpedia.org/property/director` encoding the information about the director of the movie is available in the LOD cloud. Consequently, an extra node *The Wachowski Brothers* is added in V_{LOD} and an extra edge, labeled with the name of the property, is instantiated in E_{LOD} to connect the movie with its director. Similarly, if we consider the property `http://dbpedia.org/property/starring`, new nodes and new edges are defined, in order to model the relationship between *The Matrix* and the main actors, as *Keanu Reeves*, for example. In turn, given that *Keanu Reeves* acted in several movies, many new edges could be added to the graph and many new paths now connect different movies: these paths would not have been available if only *collaborative data points* were instantiated.

To sum up, we enriched the data model by introducing a new node for each entity connected to the main node describing the items in the catalogue. In this first setting we did not filter the properties available in the LOD, since all the available ones are addded. Clearly, due to the resulting enriched representation, the overall graph and the PageRank scores of the nodes change accordingly to the new graph topology. Hence the recommendations, which are based on the PageRank scores, change as well. The first goal of our experimental session is to investigate whether graph-based recommender systems can benefit of the introduction of novel LOD-based features.

3.3 Selecting LOD-based Features

Thanks to the data points available in the LOD cloud, many new information are encoded in the graph. However, as the number of additional nodes and edges grows, the computational complexity of the personalized PageRank algorithm grows as well. Hence, it necessary to identify the most useful properties, among those gathered from the LOD cloud, able to improve the effectiveness of the recommendation strategy.

A very *simple* approach is the manual selection of the most relevant LOD-based features, according to simple heuristics or to the domain knowledge (e.g. properties as `director`, `starring`, `composer` may be considered as relevant for the *movie* domain, whereas properties as `runtime` or `country` may be not). This basic approach has several drawbacks: it requires a manual effort, it is strictly domain-dependent, and it is not possible to arbitrarily state that a certain property is useful and another one is not, without an extensive experimental evaluation. Hence, we propose a methodology based on the use of *features selection techniques* to automatically select the most *useful* LOD-based features.

Our idea is to take as input E_{LOD}, the overall set of LOD-based properties, and to produce as output $E_{LOD-FS_T} \subseteq E_{LOD}$, the set of properties a specific feature selection technique T returned as relevant. Clearly, the exploitation of a feature selection technique T also produces a set $V_{LOD-FS_T} \subseteq V_{LOD}$, containing all the LOD-based nodes connected to the properties in E_{LOD-FS_T}. Each feature selection technique causes a change in the topology of the graph, hence the personalized PageRank needs to be executed again for each user. In this setting, given a FS technique T, PageRank will be executed on the graph $G_{LOD-T} = \langle V_{LOD-T}, E_{LOD-T} \rangle$, where $V_{LOD-T} = V \cup V_{LOD-FS_T}$ and $E_{LOD-T} = E \cup E_{LOD-FS_T}$. In the experimental session the effectiveness of all these topologies will be evaluated, by comparing also different techniques for LOD-based feature selection.

3.4 Overview of Feature Selection Techniques

In the following we provide a high-level description of each features selection technique exploited in this work. All the techniques have been exploited in a *top-K selection* setting, i.e. given a set of features $F = \{f_1 \ldots f_r\}$, a FS technique T produces a ranked list of features $F_T = \{f_1 \ldots f_k\}, k \leq r$. Most of the techniques rank each feature f_i and return the first K features[2] to feed the graph-based recommendation algorithm. However, other techniques as the PCA *generate* a new set of k features to feed the algorithm. A brief description of the FS techniques adopted in this work follows:

Principal Component Analysis (PCA): PCA [13] aims at identifying the subset of features (called *Principal Components*, PC) which are relevant, mutually uncorrelated and able to maintain most of the information conveyed by the whole set of features. Operationally, PC are extracted in three steps: 1) an item-property matrix X encoding the distribution of the properties along the items is built; 2) the matrix Σ, calculated as the covariance matrix of X, is obtained and its eigenvectors are calculated; 3) the K eigenvectors of matrix Σ with the highest eigenvalues are labeled as PC and are returned as output of the processing.

Chi-Squared Test (CHI): CHI is a statistical test largely adopted to evaluate the dependency between a feature and a *class attribute*. We considered each item as a different *class* and we calculated to what extent a specific feature is relevant for that class. As described in [23], the

overall score of each feature is the average value returned by Chi-Squared tests run throughout the available items (classes). The K features obtaining the higher CHI scores are the output of the FS process.

Information Gain (IG): IG measures the decrease of entropy when a feature is *given* versus when it is *absent*. Formally, given a feature f_i, IG is calculated as follows:

$$IG(f_i) = E(I) - \sum_{v \in dom(f_i)} \frac{|I_v|}{|I|} * E(I_v) \qquad (1)$$

where $E(I)$ is the overall entropy on the data, I_v is the number of items in which feature f_i assumes a value equal to v, and $E(I_v)$ is the entropy of the data calculated only on data where feature f_i has value v. Intuitively, IG of a specific feature is high when the overall sum is high, so a specific feature has a high IG if $E(I_v)$ is low. By exploiting this FS technique, features are ranked according to their IG and the top-K are returned as output.

Information Gain Ratio (GR): the goal of GR is to extend the classical IG to penalize the attributes that assume a broad range of different values throughout the data. This is done by introducing a normalization term calculated as follows:

$$Norm(I, f) = - \sum_{v \in dom(f)} \frac{|I_v|}{|I|} * log \frac{|I_v|}{|I|} \qquad (2)$$

Next, GR is calculated as the ratio between $IG(f)$ and $Norm(I, f)$. As for IG, the K features with the highest GR scores are returned as output.

Minimum Redundancy Maximum Relevance (mRMR): mRMR [21] aims to identify the subset of features which are highly relevant but enough *diverse* from each other. To this end, two functions based on Mutual Information are defined. Given a subset of features, the first one tries to minimize the average mutual information calculated between all the possible couples of features, while the second one tries to maximize their correlation with the target class. In our setting, we extracted our K features by adopting a Greedy strategy to build a set of features which was gradually larger.

PageRank (PR): PR itself can be used as FS technique. In this setting, differently from the process described in Section 3.1, for each property gathered from the LOD cloud and for each item to be recommended *a new node* is created. Next, an edge between an *item* node i_j and a *property* node p_k is instantiated whenever an item i_j is described by the property p_k. Finally, classical PageRank is run and the relevance score associated to each property node is calculated. Properties are ranked according to their PR score and the first K are returned. Given that the relevance score of each node is calculated on the ground of its connectivity in the graph, the insight behind this technique is that the more a *property node* in the graph is connected with other nodes, the more is the likelihood that it will be labeled as *relevant*.

Support Vector Machines (SVM): even if SVM [12] has been largely used as classification framework, it can be adopted for FS as well. Indeed, given the previously described set of features F, for each item i a classification hypothesis $H = \theta_0 f_0 + \theta_1 f_1 + \ldots + \theta_r f_r$ is learned by SVM in a *one-vs-all* fashion (that is to say, the item itself along

---

[2]Hereafter, the concepts of *features* and *properties* are considered as synonyms, since each property gathered from the LOD is a feature of our graph-based model.

with its features is labeled as *positive* example, while all the other items are labeled as *negative*). The variables $\theta_0 \dots \theta_r$ are the parameters of the hyphothesis learned by SVM, and their values (typically called *magnitude*) describe the importance of the corresponding feature in the model. When SVM is used as FS technique, features are ranked according to the average magnitude learned over the classes $i_1 \dots i_m$, and the first K are returned as output of the process.

4. EXPERIMENTAL EVALUATION

The main goal of the experimental evaluation is to validate the hypothesis that graph-based recommender systems benefit of the introduction of LOD-based features (experiment 1). We also assess the impact of the previously presented feature selection techniques on the recommendations accuracy (experiment 2), and on the trade-off between accuracy and diversity (experiment 3). Finally, we perform a comparison with the performance of several state of the art techniques (experiment 4).

4.1 Description of the datasets

The evaluation is performed on two state of the art datasets:

1. MovieLens[3], a widespread dataset for movie recommendations;

2. DBbook[4], a dataset for book recommendations which comes from the previously mentioned Linked-Open Data-enabled Recommender Systems challenge.

Some statistics about the datasets are provided in Table 1, which shows their different nature.

	MovieLens	DBbook
Users	943	6,181
Items	1,682	6,733
Ratings	100,000	72,372
Sparsity	93.69%	99.83%
Positive Ratings	55.17%	45.85%
Avg. ratings/user $\pm \sigma$	84.83±83.80	11.70±5.85
Median/mode per user	50/20	11/5
Avg. ratings/item $\pm \sigma$	48.48±65.03	10.74±27.14
Median/mode per item	22/1	4/1

Table 1: Description of the datasets.

Both the datasets are very sparse (the *mode* of ratings per item is equal to 1), even though MovieLens is denser than DBbook (93.69% vs. 99.83% sparsity). Each Movielens user voted 84.83 items on average (against the 11.70 votes given by DBbook users). DBbook has in turn the peculiarity of being unbalanced towards negative ratings (only 45% of positive preferences). Furthermore, MovieLens items were voted more than DBbook ones (48.48 vs 10.74 votes per item, on average).

4.2 Experimental protocol

Experiments were performed by adopting a a 5-fold cross validation as regards MovieLens, while a single training/test split for DBbook[5]. In both cases we used the splits which are

[3]http://grouplens.org/datasets/movielens/
[4]http://www.di.uniba.it/%7Eswap/datasets/dbbooks_data.zip
[5]http://challenges.2014.eswc-conferences.org/index.php/RecSys

commonly used in literature. We face a Top-N recommendation task: given that MovieLens preferences are expressed on a 5-point Likert scale, we deem as *positive* ratings only those equal to 4 and 5. On the other side, DBbook is already available as *binarized*, thus no further processing was needed. As recommendation algorithm we used the personalized PageRank (damping factor equal to 0.85, as in [19]), set as explained in Section 3.1. We compared the effectiveness of our graph-based recommender by considering three different graph topologies:

- G, which models the basics *collaborative* information about user ratings;

- G_{LOD}, which enrichs G by introducing LOD-based features gathered from DBpedia;

- G_{LOD-T}, which lighten the load of the personalized PageRank by relying on the features selected by a FS technique T.

In order to enrich the graph G with LOD-based features, each item in the dataset was mapped to a DBpedia entry. As regards MovieLens, 1,600 movies were successfully mapped (95.12% of the items) while 6,600 items (98.02%) from DBbook dataset were associated to a DBpedia node. The mapping was performed by querying a DBpedia SQL Endpoint by using the *title* of the movie or the *name* of the book. The items for which a DBpedia entry was not found were only represented by using *collaborative* data points. MovieLens entries were described through 60 different DBpedia properties, while DBbook ones using 70 properties.

We adopted all the feature selection techniques described in Section 3.4 to produce a ranked feature list, from which we have selected the top-K LOD-based features ($K = 10, 30, 50$). As baseline, we also consider a feature selection technique which selects the 10 *most popular properties* from the LOD cloud. The performance of each graph topology was evaluated in terms of:

- *accuracy* of the recommendation list, using the F1-measure, using different list sizes;

- *diversity* of the recommendation list, using the Intra-List Diversity (ILD) [24], computed as follows:

$$ILD(R) = 1 - \frac{\sum_{j,k=1(j \neq k)}^{N} sim(I_j, I_k)}{|R|} \quad (3)$$

where R is the recommendation list, I_j and I_k are a pair of items in R, and $sim(I_j, I_k)$ is the cosine similarity measure between I_j and I_k.

Moreover, we also calculated the overall running time[6] of each experiment with a specific graph topology. Statistical significance was assessed by exploiting Wilcoxon and Friedman tests, chosen after running the Shapiro-Wilk test[7], which revealed the non-normal distribution of the data. Finally, the source code of our graph-based recommendation framework has been published on GitHub[8].

[6]Experiments were run on an Intel-i7-3770 CPU3.40 GhZ, with 32GB RAM.
[7]http://en.wikipedia.org/wiki/Shapiro-Wilk_test
[8]https://github.com/cataldomusto/lod-recsys/

	MovieLens		DBbook	
	G	G_{LOD}	G	G_{LOD}
F1@5	0.5406	**0.5424**	0.5502	**0.5504**
F1@10	0.6068	**0.6083**	0.6431	0.6421
F1@15	0.5956	**0.5963**	0.5926	0.5926
F1@20	0.5678	**0.5686**	0.4906	0.4906
Run (minut.)	72	880	100	2,433
Nodes	2,625	53,794	12,914	211,611
Edges	100,000	178,020	72,372	534,841

Table 2: Experiment 1: Accuracy of the graph-based recommender fed with LOD-based properties (configurations overcoming the baseline are emphasized in bold).

4.3 Discussion of the Results

4.3.1 Experiment 1

In the first experiment, whose results are summarized in Table 2, we validate the hypothesis that graph-based recommender systems benefit of the introduction of properties gathered from DBPEDIA. As regards MovieLens, a statistically significant improvement ($p << 0.0001$, assessed through a Wilcoxon test) was obtained. On the other side, the nature of DBbook data (much sparser and negatively balanced) made the recommendation task more challenging since we got a statistically significant improvement only for F1@5. It is worth to underline that DBbook results for F1@15 and F1@20 are the same, regardless the specific graph topology. This was expected since, the average number of ratings in the test set for each user is less than 15. From now on, only F1@5 and F1@10 will be presented for such dataset.

As expected, the expansion of the graph with LOD-based features caused an exponential growth of the run time of the algorithm, due to the enrichment of the graph with many new nodes and edges (see Table 2). The growth is particularly significant for both the datasets: as regards MovieLens about 51,000 new nodes and 78,000 new edges were added to the graph, while for DBbook almost 200,000 new nodes and more than 460,000 new edges are introduced.

4.3.2 Experiment 2

In this experiment we evaluate the impact of the feature selection techniques on the recommendation accuracy. Results are presented in Table 3.

As regards MovieLens, most of the feature selection techniques (5 out of 7) obtained their best results with 50 features ($K = 50$). Given that the overall number of LOD-based properties was equal to 60, it is possible to state that most of the properties encoded in the extended graph G_{LOD} can be deemed as relevant. Indeed, the baseline which selects the 10 most popular properties from the LOD cloud (Pop-10) is always outperformed by the recommender taking into account the whole set of LOD features (G_{LOD}). Results showed that the only techniques obtaining better results with a smaller number of features are PageRank and mRMR, while all the other techniques benefit of the introduction of more data points. PageRank behavior was somehow expected, since properties with a low PageRank score are those poorly connected in the graph, thus it is not surprising that their exploitation did not provide any benefit to the effectiveness of the recommendation strategy. Overall,

the best performing configuration was PCA, which was the only technique always overcoming the baseline with $K = 50$. A Friedman test also showed that PCA statistically overcomes the other techniques.

On the other side, by analyzing results for DBbook dataset, different outcomes emerge. Results show that the application of FS techniques is much more useful for sparser datasets as DBbook. Indeed, in most of the comparisons (35 out of 42) feature selection produces a significant increase over the G_{LOD} baseline (for MovieLens FS techniques helped to overcome the baseline only 18 out of 84 times). This means that FS techniques are likely to be useful, especially when the expansion of the graph with data gathered from the LOD cloud produces an exponential growth of nodes and edges (+200,000 nodes and +460,000 edges, as previously shown).

Another interesting insight emerging from the analysis of Table 3 is that the best-performing configurations on DBbook exploit just 10 features ($K = 10$). This happened in 10 out of 14 comparisons, thus it is likely that only a few DBpedia properties encode the knowledge useful for this recommendation scenario, while the others are just noise. This also caused a different behavior of the single FS techniques, since in this case Information Gain and Gain Ratio – its normalized counterpart – were the best-performing ones. This is probably due to the fact that entropy-based techniques are more effective when most of the information is hold by just a few properties. It is not by chance that the gap between IG and GR and the other techniques is larger with $K = 10$, while it progressively decreases when $K = 30$ and $K = 50$, since such techniques are more effective in picking a smaller set of highly informative properties. On the other side, when the useful knowledge is encoded in a larger set of properties, as for MovieLens, techniques as PageRank and PCA (which has also good performance on DBbook) were the best. The good performance of the Pop-10 baseline confirms the usefulness of just 10 features to obtain accurate results, even though it is not enough to consider the most popular ones to obtain the best results.

Beyond the significant increase in terms of F1, it is worth to note that the use of FS techniques leads to a tremendous saving of computational resources to run the personalized PageRank on the graph G_{LOD-T} (with T equal to PCA for MovieLens and to IG for DBbook). As shown in Table 4, the adoption of FS caused a huge decrease of the run time of the algorithm equal to 44.9% for DBbook (from 2,433 to 1,341 minutes) and to 34% for MovieLens (from 880 to 581 minutes). This is due to the smaller number of nodes and edges in the graphs (-58.1% nodes and -73.4% edges were removed for DBbook, while -8.6% nodes and -4.8% edges were removed for MovieLens).

It is also worth to note that, thanks to the huge amount of noisy nodes and edges, now G_{LOD-IG} with K=10 also overcomes the simple graph G for F1@10 on DBbook data (differently from experiment 1). This further validates the effectiveness of techniques for automatic feature selection, which resulted to be tremendously useful to improve the effectiveness of LOD-boosted graph-based recommendation methodologies.

4.3.3 Experiment 3

In this experiment we investigate whether the adoption of a specific FS technique can *endogenously* induce a higher

MovieLens	#ft	PR	PCA	SVM	CHI	IG	GR	mRMR
F1@5	10	0.5418	0.5406	0.5382	0.5414	0.5397	0.5372	0.5397
G_{LOD} = 0.5424	30	**0.5429(*)**	0.5413	0.5413	0.5419	0.5396	0.5398	**0.5429(*)**
Pop-10=0.5413	50	0.5412	**0.5431(*)(↑)**	0.5421(*)	0.5420(*)	0.5412(*)	0.5406(*)	0.5421
F1@10	10	0.6069	0.6045	0.6043	0.6056	0.6039	0.6033	0.6039
G_{LOD} = 0.6083	30	**0.6084(*)**	0.6081	0.6074	0.6070	0.6055	0.6059	0.6072(*)
Pop-10=0.6070	50	0.6070	**0.6088(*)(↑)**	0.6081(*)	0.6079(*)	0.6072(*)	0.6078(*)	0.6077
F1@15	10	**0.5964**	0.5948	0.5943	0.5955	0.5950	0.5938	0.5950
G_{LOD} = 0.5963	30	**0.5967(*)**	**0.5967**	**0.5964**	**0.5967**	0.5955	0.5960	0.5961
Pop-10=0.5962	50	0.5955	**0.5970(*)(↑)**	**0.5966(*)**	**0.5972(*)**	0.5962(*)	**0.5968(*)**	0.5962(*)
F1@20	10	0.5684(*)	0.5667	0.5666	0.5672	0.5668	0.5666	0.5668
G_{LOD} = 0.5686	30	0.5684	**0.5688**	0.5679	0.5679	0.5675	0.5675	0.5679
Pop-10=0.5678	50	0.5682	**0.5689(*)(↑)**	0.5683(*)	0.5686(*)	0.5685(*)	**0.5687(*)**	0.5685(*)
DBbook	**#ft**	**PR**	**PCA**	**SVM**	**CHI**	**IG**	**GR**	**mRMR**
F1@5	10	**0.5515**	**0.5513(*)**	0.5507	0.5512	**0.5540(*)(↑)**	**0.5524(*)**	0.5493
G_{LOD} = 0.5504	30	**0.5518(*)**	**0.5510**	**0.5519**	**0.5517(*)**	**0.5519(*)**	**0.5523**	**0.5519(*)**
Pop-10=0.5518	50	**0.5517**	0.5512	**0.5512(*)**	0.5505	**0.5511**	0.5503	**0.5511**
F1@10	10	**0.6431(*)**	**0.6433(*)**	**0.6434(*)**	**0.6423(*)**	**0.6445(*)(↑)**	**0.6435(*)**	**0.6435(*)**
G_{LOD} = 0.6421	30	**0.6422**	**0.6432**	**0.6430**	0.6420	**0.6427**	**0.6431**	**0.6427**
Pop-10=0.6441	50	0.6418	**0.6428**	**0.6426**	0.6419	0.6419	**0.6425**	0.6419

Table 3: Experiment 2: Impact of the feature selection techniques on the recommendation accuracy. Pop-10 represents the baseline which selects the 10 most popular properties. Configurations overcoming the baseline G_{LOD} are emphasized in bold. For each technique: the number of features which led to the highest F1 is indicated with (*); the overall highest F1 score for each method is indicated with (*)(↑). The column of the feature selection technique which performed the best on a specific dataset is coloured in grey.

	MovieLens		DBbook	
	G_{LOD}	$G_{LOD-PCA}$	G_{LOD}	G_{LOD-IG}
F1@5	0.5424	**0.5431**	0.5504	**0.5540**
F1@10	0.6083	**0.6088**	0.6421	**0.6445**
F1@15	0.5963	**0.5970**	0.5926	0.5926
F1@20	0.5686	**0.5689**	0.4906	0.4906
Run(minut.)	880	581	2,433	1,341
K	60	50	70	10
Nodes	53,794	49,158	211,611	88,669
Edges	178,020	169,405	534,841	142,334

Table 4: Experiment 2: Run time and size of the graph of the best-performing feature selection technique.

diversity of the recommendation list, and to what extent this leads to a loss of accuracy in terms of F1. Results are depicted in Figure 3a and 3b, which show the accuracy-diversity tradeoff.

For the sake of brevity, only the results for F1@10 are provided. In both charts we used four different symbols to identify the different behaviors of each technique: the baseline G_{LOD} is identified by a black square; we used a *circle* for the techniques not improving neither F1 nor diversity; a *triangle* is used to identify the techniques providing an F1 improvement, while a *diamond* is used when an increase in diversity was noted; finally, a *colored square* was used for the ideal situation, i.e. when both F1 and diversity got an improvement after the application of FS.

By analyzing the results, it emerged that CHI was the less useful technique, since it did not provide any significant benefit to neither F1 (on MovieLens data was even noted a decrease) nor diversity. Next, PageRank showed a sim-

ilar behavior on both datasets, since it provided a (small) improvement on F1 and it did not significantly change the diversity of the recommendations. Generally speaking, it emerged that the application of FS on MovieLens led to both an improvement in F1 (two techniques are positioned to the right of the baseline) and diversity (tre techniques out of seven improve it). On the other side, the application of FS on DBbook produced a big improvement on both F1 (all the techniques improve it) and diversity (five out of seven

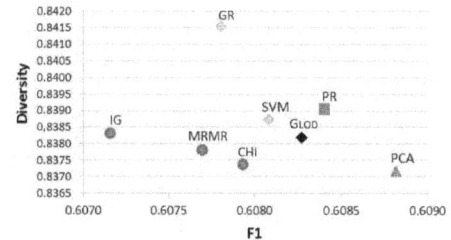

(a) MovieLens dataset

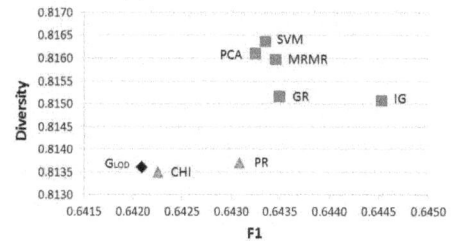

(b) DBbook dataset

Figure 3: Trade-off between accuracy (F1) and diversity

produced a significant increase). In both cases, the techniques obtaining the highest diversity were GR and SVM, for `MovieLens` and `DBbook`, respectively. Moreover, also the behavior of PCA was noteworthy, since it led to the highest F1 on the `MovieLens` (with a small decrease in terms of diversity) and to a very good compromise between F1 and diversity on `DBbook`.

To sum up, these results show that the choice of a particular FS technique has a significant impact on the overall behavior of the recommendation algorithm. Some techniques have the ability of inducing a higher diversity (or F1) at the expense of a little of F1 (or diversity, respectively), whereas others can provide a good compromise between both metrics. Clearly, more investigation is needed to deeply analyze the behavior of each technique, especially for those as IG and mRMR which performed differently on both datasets, but these results already give some general guidelines which can drive the choice of the FS technique which best fits the requirements of a specific recommendation scenario.

4.3.4 Experiment 4

In the last experiment we compared the effectiveness of our graph-based recommendation algorithm with respect to current state of the art techniques. We compared the performance of the graph-based recommender enriched with the LOD-features selected using the feature selection method inducing the highest accuracy. We exploited MyMediaLite Recommender System library[9] to evaluate how well other widespread baselines perform on `MovieLens` and `DBbook` data. As baselines, User-to-User Collaborative Filtering (U2U-KNN), Item-to-Item Collaborative Filtering (I2I-KNN), a simple popularity-based approach, a random baseline and the Bayesian Personalized Ranking Matrix Factorization (BPRMF) presented in [22] were used. As regards U2U-KNN and I2I-KNN, neighborhood size was set to 80, while BPRMF was run by setting the number of latent factors equal to 100. In all these settings we used the optimal values for such parameters. Results are depicted in Figures 4a and 4b.

Our graph-based recommender significantly outperforms all the baselines for all the metrics taken into account. It is worth to note that our approach obtained a higher F1 also when compared to a well-performing matrix factorization algorithm as BPRMF. Results further confirmed how challenging the recommendation task on `DBbook` is, since in this very sparse and negatively unbalanced dataset the second best-performing configuration was the simple popularity-based baseline. However, also in this setting our graph-based recommender system boosted with LOD-based features obtained the best results and definitely confirmed the effectiveness of our approach.

5. CONCLUSIONS AND FUTURE WORK

In this work we proposed a graph-based recommendation methodology based on the personalized PageRank algorithm, and we evaluated different techniques to automatically feed such a graph-based representation with features extracted from the LOD cloud. We investigated the impact of LOD-based features on the recommendation algorithm and the results of the experimental evaluation showed that graph-based recommenders can benefit of the infusion of novel knowledge coming from the LOD cloud. Moreover,

---

[9]http://www.mymedialite.net/

the adoption of feature selection techniques further improved the results obtained by our graph-based recommender, especially in scenarios with high data sparsity. Further investigations showed a clear correlation between the adoption of a specific FS technique with the overall results of the recommender, since some techniques *endogenously* showed the ability of increasing also the diversity of the recommendations generated by the algorithm. We also showed that our methodology was able to overcome several state of the art baselines on two state of the art datasets. A publicly available implementation of the framework as well as of the splits used for the evaluation guarantee the reproducibility of the experimental results.

As future work, we will perform the evaluation on other different datasets, besides those related to movies and books, in order to generalize the results to to different recommendation scenarios. Moreover, we will deeply study the impact of LOD-based features on other types of LOD-based recommender systems, besides the graph-based ones. As a matter of fact, we will perform the same evaluation using recommendation approaches based on text classification techniques, as Random Forests, Support Vector Machines; or techniques based on Vector Space models. Finally, we will investigate to what extent the data sparsity level influences the overall performance of the recommendation framework and will continue the analysis of the quality of recommendations by taking into account several evaluation metrics, such as *novelty* and *serendipity* [6].

Acknowledgments. This work fulfills the research objectives of the project MAIVISTO - Massive Adaptive Internet Video Streaming Using the Cloud, Bando START UP, PAC "Piano Azione e Coesione", Avviso D.D. 436 del 13 Marzo 2013, Linea 1 - Big Data (2014-2016) and is supported by the IBM Faculty Award "Deep Learning to boost Cognitive Question Answering".

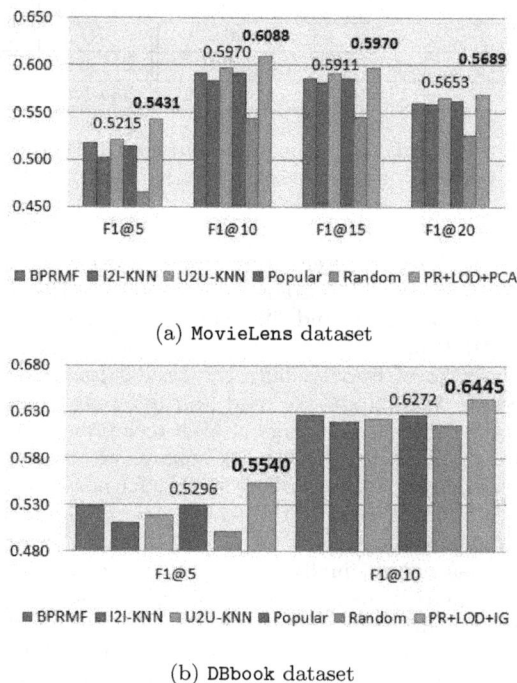

(a) `MovieLens` dataset

(b) `DBbook` dataset

Figure 4: Comparison to state of the art baselines.

6. REFERENCES

[1] C. Aggarwal, J. Wolf, K.L. Wu, and P. Yu. Horting hatches an egg: A new graph-theoretic approach to collaborative filtering. In *Proceedings of the 5th ACM SIGKDD Conference*, pages 201–212. ACM, 1999.

[2] S. Auer, C. Bizer, G. Kobilarov, J. Lehmann, R. Cyganiak, and Z. Ives. *DBpedia: A nucleus for a web of open data*. Springer, 2007.

[3] P. Basile, C. Musto, M. de Gemmis, P. Lops, F. Narducci, and G. Semeraro. Aggregation strategies for linked open data-enabled recommender systems. In *European Semantic Web Conference*, 2014.

[4] T. Bogers. Movie recommendation using random walks over the contextual graph. In *Proc. of the 2nd Intl. Workshop on Context-Aware Recommender Systems*, 2010.

[5] M. de Gemmis, P. Lops, C. Musto, F. Narducci, and G. Semeraro. Semantics-aware Content-based Recommender Systems. In Francesco Ricci, Lior Rokach, and Bracha Shapira, editors, *Recommender Systems Handbook, 2nd Edition*, pages 119–159. Springer, 2015.

[6] M. de Gemmis, P. Lops, G. Semeraro, and C. Musto. An Investigation on the Serendipity Problem in Recommender Systems. *Information Processing and Management*, 51:695–717, 2015.

[7] T. Di Noia, R. Mirizzi, V. C. Ostuni, and D. Romito. Exploiting the web of data in model-based recommender systems. In *Proceedings of the ACM RecSys Conference*, pages 253–256. ACM, 2012.

[8] Floriana Esposito, Donato Malerba, and Giovanni Semeraro. Flexible matching for noisy structural descriptions. In *IJCAI*, pages 658–664, 1991.

[9] M. Gori, A. Pucci, and V. Roma. Itemrank: A random-walk based scoring algorithm for recommender engines. In *IJCAI*, volume 7, pages 2766–2771, 2007.

[10] T. H. Haveliwala. Topic-Sensitive PageRank: A Context-Sensitive Ranking Algorithm for Web Search. *IEEE Trans. Knowl. Data Eng.*, 15(4):784–796, 2003.

[11] A. Hotho, R. Jäschke, C. Schmitz, G. Stumme, and K.-D. Althoff. Folkrank: A ranking algorithm for folksonomies. In *LWA*, volume 1, pages 111–114, 2006.

[12] T. Joachims. *Text categorization with Support Vector Machines: Learning with many relevant features*. Springer, 1998.

[13] I. Jolliffe. *Principal Component Analysis*. Wiley Online Library, 2002.

[14] S. E. Middleton, D. De Roure, and N. R. Shadbolt. Ontology-based recommender systems. In *Handbook on ontologies*, pages 477–498. Springer, 2004.

[15] C. Musto, P. Basile, M. de Gemmis, P. Lops, G. Semeraro, and S. Rutigliano. Automatic Selection of Linked Open Data Features in Graph-based Recommender Systems. In Toine Bogers and Marijn Koolen, editors, *Proceedings of the 2nd Workshop on New Trends on Content-Based Recommender Systems co-located with 9th ACM Conference on Recommender Systems (RecSys 2015), Vienna, Austria, September 16-20, 2015*, volume 1448 of *CEUR Workshop Proceedings*, pages 10–13. CEUR-WS.org, 2015.

[16] C. Musto, G. Semeraro, P. Lops, M. de Gemmis, and F. Narducci. Leveaaging social media sources to generate personalized music playlists. In *E-Commerce and Web Technologies - 13th International Conference, EC-Web 2012*, volume 123 of *Lecture Notes in Business Information Processing*, pages 112–123. Springer, 2012.

[17] T. Di Noia, I. Cantador, and V. C. Ostuni. Linked open data-enabled recommender systems: ESWC 2014 challenge on book recommendation. In V. Presutti, M. Stankovic, E. Cambria, I. Cantador, A. Di Iorio, T. Di Noia, C. Lange, D. Reforgiato Recupero, and A. Tordai, editors, *Semantic Web Evaluation Challenge - SemWebEval 2014 at ESWC 2014, Anissaras, Crete, Greece, May 25-29, 2014, Revised Selected Papers*, volume 475 of *Communications in Computer and Information Science*, pages 129–143. Springer, 2014.

[18] V. C. Ostuni, T. Di Noia, E. Di Sciascio, and R. Mirizzi. Top-n recommendations from implicit feedback leveraging linked open data. In *Proceedings of the ACM Conference on Recommender Systems*, pages 85–92. ACM, 2013.

[19] L. Page, R. Brin, S.and Motwani, and T. Winograd. The pageRank citation ranking: bringing order to the web. 1999.

[20] A. Passant. dbrec - Music Recommendations Using DBpedia. In *International Semantic Web Conference, Revised Papers*, volume 6497 of *LNCS*, pages 209–224. Springer, 2010.

[21] H. Peng, F. Long, and C. Ding. Feature selection based on mutual information criteria of max-dependency, max-relevance, and min-redundancy. *Pattern Analysis and Machine Intelligence, IEEE Transactions on*, 27(8):1226–1238, 2005.

[22] S. Rendle, C. Freudenthaler, Z. Gantner, and L. Schmidt-Thieme. Bpr: Bayesian personalized ranking from implicit feedback. In *Proceedings of the Twenty-Fifth Conference on Uncertainty in Artificial Intelligence*, pages 452–461. AUAI Press, 2009.

[23] Y. Yang and J. O. Pedersen. A comparative study on feature selection in text categorization. In *ICML*, volume 97, pages 412–420, 1997.

[24] C-N. Ziegler, S. M. McNee, J. A Konstan, and G. Lausen. Improving recommendation lists through topic diversification. In *Proceedings of the 14th International Conference on World Wide Web*, pages 22–32. ACM, 2005.

Lifestyle Recommendations for Hypertension through Rasch-based Feasibility Modeling

Mustafa Radha
Personal Health, Philips
Research
High Tech Campus 34
5656 AE
Eindhoven, The Netherlands
mustafa.radha@philips.com

Martijn C. Willemsen
Human-Technology
Interaction, Eindhoven
University of Technology
P.O. Box 513
IPO 1.20, 5600 MB
Eindhoven, The Netherlands
m.c.willemsen@tue.nl

Mark Boerhof
Human-Technology
Interaction, Eindhoven
University of Technology
P.O. Box 513
IPO 1.20, 5600 MB
Eindhoven, The Netherlands
m.boerhof@student.tue.nl

Wijnand A. IJsselsteijn
Human-Technology
Interaction, Eindhoven
University of Technology
P.O. Box 513
IPO 1.20, 5600 MB
Eindhoven, The Netherlands
w.a.ijsselsteijn@tue.nl

ABSTRACT

In this work we investigate the use of behavior feasibility to adapt and personalize lifestyle-targeting recommender systems for the prevention and treatment of hypertension. Based on survey data (N=300) we modeled the feasibiliy of 63 behaviors through a Rasch model, describing the engagement in a behavior as a function of the behavior's difficulty and the person's ability. We formulate two feasibility-tailored recommendation strategies that utilize the Rasch model. The *engagement maximization strategy* aims at maximizing the probability of engagement by proposing very feasible behaviors while the *motivation maximization strategy* aims to challenge users by matching the difficulty of the advice with the ability of the user, thereby maximizing motivation. In an online study (N=150) we assessed user preference for either strategies (embodied as virtual coaches) in comparison with a random control strategy. Our results show that coaches selecting feasible health advice resonate better with the patient than control. In general persons significantly preferred the engagement maximization strategy over random advice on most factors, while persons with a medium level of ability significantly preferred the motivation maximization strategy on multiple factors.

UMAP '16, July 13–17, 2016, Halifax, Nova Scotia, Canada.

© 2016 Copyright held by the owner/author(s). Publication rights licensed to ACM.
ISBN 978-1-4503-4370-1/16/07...$15.00

DOI: http://dx.doi.org/10.1145/2930238.2930251

Keywords

Feasibility; User Modeling; Recommender Systems; Patient-Centered Design; Behavior change theory; Lifestyle interventions; Rasch model

1. INTRODUCTION AND CONTEXT

Hypertension, or high blood pressure, is a key risk factor for cardiovascular diseases [29]. Effective hypertension management is therefore a major concern for public health. Besides blood pressure medication, non- pharmacological lifestyle interventions have been proven successful in hypertension management [10]. Appropriate lifestyle modifications may not only lower or control blood pressure in hypertensive patients but also effectively delay or prevent hypertension in non-hypertensives [17]. The European Societies of Hypertension and Cardiology endorse a wide variety of lifestyle interventions for the reduction of blood pressure: salt restriction, moderation of alcohol consumption, a diet rich in vegetables, fruits and low-fat dairy products, weight reduction, regular exercise and smoking cessation [17].

1.1 Recommender systems

Despite the obvious health benefits, adherence to lifestyle recommendations in the hypertensive population is generally low [28]. Changing behavior requires effort from the user and support from the environment. The American Heart Association stated the potential of mobile health applications to provide the information and support that is necessary to counsel and motivate individuals attempting to improve their lifestyle [5]. The first of these digital coaching services are recommender systems which rely on the pervasiveness of mobile media to support the patient at times where the care provider is unable to do so. These systems are outperforming traditional means of lifestyle recommendation for heart failure patients [8]. The content of these systems has focused on advice with a high expected health benefit by tailoring the recommendations based on the health needs of the user (e.g. weight loss recommendations for obese patients).

1.2 Feasibility

Besides the health benefit other factors also contribute to adherence. The classical Health-Belief Model [18, 19] coins (amongst other factors) the barriers for the patient to follow the recommendation as an additional predictor of adherence. This notion reoccurs as a prominent determinant of behavior in many other psychosocial theories where it is called the behavior difficulty, cost or *feasibility* [3]. In this paper we will call this factor *feasibility*, though the other terms will also be used interchangeably.

Recent work [21] has incorporated a notion of feasibility. For each monitored behavior, feasibility was measured as the frequency with which the user performs it. The authors relate the resulting feasibility parameters to self-efficacy (a person's belief in their own ability [1]). Subsequently, the feasibility and the benefit of the behavior were weighed against each other to find recommendations that are both feasible and beneficial. The resulting recommender system outperformed random control by most measures, including adherence to the recommendation [22]. This approach makes excellent use of the user's data, yet also has its limitations. The method measures seperate self-efficacy parameters for each behavior, while usually self-efficacy is seen as a trait of the person that can influence a large amount of behaviors simultaneously, leading their feasibility to be correlated within an individual.

Modeling the feasibility in health behaviors as a combination of the behavior's inherent difficulty level and the individual's personal level of self-efficacy allows knowledge about a behavior's difficulty to be generalized to different individuals. This has two benefits: first of all, knowing the relative difficulty of behaviors amongst each other can be used as a priori information to start an intervention with behaviors that are more feasible; the other benefit is that after observing the engagement of the user in a small subset of the behaviors, knowledge about how difficult those behaviors are can predict the self-efficacy level of the user, which then can in turn be used to predict how likely it would be for the user to engage in the remainder of the behaviors that were not observed (given the corresponding difficulty levels). This interaction between a pre-determined level of behavior difficulty with a personal level of self-efficacy can be used to remedy some common problems in recommender systems, such as dealing with the cold-start problem (i.e. system needs too much data from the user before it can generate personalized content) or being able to reason about behavior that is hard to monitor or observe with the technology at hand.

1.3 The Rasch model as a feasibility model

We have selected the Rasch model [4] as a simple, one-dimensional user model for the modeling of the feasibility of behaviors in the form of a generic ability level with the benefits outlined above. The Rasch model is based on item-response theory (IRT), which deals with modeling a latent trait (i.e. a person's ability) given the difficulty of a set of tasks that relate to that latent trait (i.e. behavior difficulty). The classical use of the Rasch model is in psychometrics (e.g. mathematical capability testing) but it has recently been applied successfully on lifestyle behaviors such as dietary habits [12], salt intake restriction [20], mindfulness habits [24] and even across multiple dimensions of health behavior [6] as a measure of *health performance*. The success of the Rasch model in describing engagement and difficulty of behaviors as well as the performance of individuals in these behaviors across a multitude of health-related categories motivates the use of the Rasch model as a user model of feasibility, capturing both the notion of a behavior-specific difficulty and a person-specific ability level.

Statistically, the Rasch model assumes a *unidimensional latent variable* (i.e. a user's ability of, attitude towards or self-efficacy in living a healthy lifestyle) given observations of the patient's engagement in manifest behaviors (of which the difficulty is assumed to have a transitive ordering). This information is captured on a single scale (the Rasch scale) which corresponds to a continuous latent trait (i.e. self-efficacy or ability). Behaviors are then modeled as probabilistic functions on this latent trait. Such a function is referred to as the item-characteristic curve (ICC), a function that describes the probability of engagement of a user in the behavior given their ability score on the Rasch scale. An ICC for a behavior n with difficulty β_n returns $P(X_{ni} = 1)$ (i.e. the probability of a person i engaging in n) given that person's ability δ_i:

$$P(X_{ni} = 1) = \frac{e^{\beta_n - \delta_i}}{1 + e^{\beta_n - \delta_i}} \qquad (1)$$

This means that as the user's ability level δ_i increases, the probability of them engaging in some behavior also increases logistically. Vice versa, as the difficulty of a behavior increases, the probability of some user engaging in it decreases. The β of a behavior is proportional to the number of people in a population who perform it, while the δ of an individual is proportional to the number of the behaviors he or she performs. Figure 1 illustrates the concepts of behavior difficulty, patient ability and the item-characteristic curves visually with examples of 3 behaviors related to hypertension management. The x-axis represents the latent trait (i.e. the ability of the user to live a healthy lifestyle). Each ICC represents the probability of engagement in a certain behavior given the ability. They show that some behaviors are easier than others (e.g. behavior 1 always higher probability than behavior 2), reflecting the idea of a transitive ordering of the behaviors in terms of their difficulty. In the remainder of this paper the the difficulty of a behavior will refer to the mean of its ICC (i.e. 50% probability point). The actual likelihood of engagement also depends on the ability. For example, person X with an ability of 1.9 has a 50% likelihood to ask for low sodium (behavior 2), is more likely to compare calories (behavior 1, 75%) but less likely to use an activity tracker (behavior 3, 25%). Person Y, that has a higher ability (2.9) is more likely to do all these behaviors.

1.4 Feasibility-based recommendation strategies

In this work we use the Rasch model (fitted to a target user populations' behavioral patterns) to obtain two mea-

Figure 1: Item-characteristic curves (ICC) from the Rasch model that represent the probability of engagement for three different recommendations (related to weight loss, salt restriction and exercise) as a function of the patient's ability.

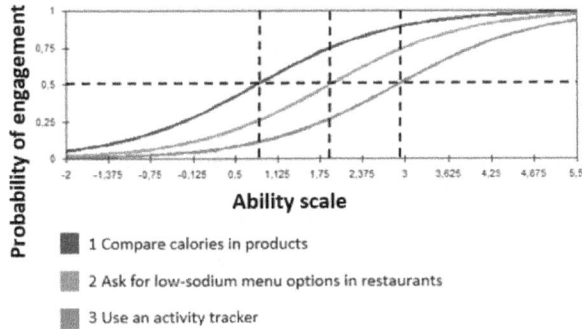

1 Compare calories in products
2 Ask for low-sodium menu options in restaurants
3 Use an activity tracker

sures. The first is the difficulty of a behavior (which defines its ICC). This metric is independent of the user but does provide prior knowledge about the difficulty ordering of lifestyle interventions. The second parameter is the ability of the user (which can be estimated from the engagement patterns of the user in a subset of the behaviors). This metric can be used to estimate the probability of engagement (see equation 1) in each of the behaviors for that specific user. Based on these measures two distinct advice generation strategies were motivated from a perspective of behavioral change theory. The *engagement maximization strategy* uses only the behavior difficulty measure while the *motivation maximization strategy* also uses the user's ability. The following sections describe these strategies.

1.4.1 Engagement maximization strategy (EMS)

For any patient with an arbitrary ability level, the Rasch model predicts a higher probability of engagement in behaviors that are relatively easy when compared to more difficult behaviors. According to the Campbell paradigm [13], such a high probability of engagement implies that the benefit of performing these behaviors is outweighed by their costs. Thus, maximizing the probability of engagement is equivalent to minimizing the cost-to-benefit rate of the behavior. The health-belief model also poses a positive contribution of the behaviors' cost-to-benefit rate towards the individuals' engagement in the behavior. The engagement maximization strategy (EMS) will therefore always recommend the most feasible behaviors from the Rasch scale (from the subset of behaviors that the patient is not already engaged in). This notion is supported by research on decision-support systems for the energy savings domain where it was shown that people ranked more feasible measures as more preferable [26].

1.4.2 Motivation maximization strategy (MMS)

While advising the most feasible behaviors can already be a strong enhancement for recommender systems, it could also be argued that for persons with a higher ability level such advice would not be appropriate for a number of reasons. First of all, the mismatch between ability and the limited challenge of easy recommendations could lead to suboptimal motivation [9]. In addition, persons who perform most easy behaviors might have other reasons for not engaging in the small set of remaining easy behaviors (e.g., physical disability to do certain exercises or allergies that prevent consumption of certain foods). These persons will not desire advice about these behaviors. Finally, theories on cognitive development suggest that the experience of mastering a difficult task could be rewarding by itself and contribute to self-efficacy [2]. These arguments suggest that the patient's ability level (as derived from the Rasch model) should be taken into account for personalization. Therefore the motivation maximization strategy (MMS) will select behaviors for which difficulty is close to the patient's ability on the Rasch scale.

2. RESEARCH OBJECTIVES

The goal of this study is to understand how feasibility as derived from the Rasch model can be used to improve recommender systems for lifestyle-based blood pressure management. The first research question is whether a good (i.e. reliable, universal and unidimensional) Rasch model can be fitted on a multi-domain set of recommended lifestyle interventions for the reduction of blood pressure. The second research question concerns how this model can be employed as a user model to enhance recommendation systems and which of the strategies discussed (EMS or MMS) is the most effective. We will first present the development and evaluation of the Rasch model in section 3 and then present an evaluation of the recommendation strategies in section 4.

3. MODEL DEVELOPMENT

This section describes the development and evaluation of the Rasch model. The feasibility of a diverse set of behaviors related to blood pressure reduction was modeled (detailed in section 3.1) based on the reported engagement of 300 individuals in those behaviors (online survey, population characteristics detailed in section 3.2). The fitting and statistical evaluation of the model is described in section 3.3.

3.1 modeled behaviors

International guidelines on blood pressure management were surveyed and 63 recommended lifestyle behaviors were identified. The behaviors are related to exercise [15], salt restriction [20], weight loss [7] and the dietary approaches to stop hypertension (DASH) [23].

3.1.1 Diet and weight loss

The daily or weekly intake was queried for a subset of DASH items to check adherence to serving recommendations [14, 23]. A second set of dietary behaviors aimed at weight loss was also queried to gain insight into more specific behaviors, such as limiting the consumption of sugary beverages or red meats. Engagement in these behaviors was measured on a 4-point frequency-scale (Rarely/ Never, Sometimes, Often, Always).

3.1.2 Physical activity

Engagement in exercise recommendations was measured by querying a participants' daily or weekly amount of physical activity. More specific behaviors [6] were queried using a dichotomous (yes/no) or a 4 point interval scale (Rarely/ Never, Sometimes, Often, Always). For example, dichotomous for 'I hold a membership for sport facilities' and a 4 point frequency scale for 'I stand during phone calls'.

Table 1: Demographic characteristics of the population on which the the Rasch model was trained

Health status

Normotensive	50.0%
(Pre-)hypertensive	50.0%
Multiple chronic diseases	32.9%
Physical disabilities	22.7 %

Demographics

Female	51.4%
Age 40-49	50.3%
Age 50-59	49.7%

Education

High school or less	22%
Secondary vocational education	48.6%
Bachelor's degree or above	29%

Lifestyle advice from care professional

Received diet advice	17.1%
Received sodium advice	13.9%
Received exercise advice	11.2%
Received any advice	30.8%

Figure 2: Spread of behavior difficulty and person ability on the Rasch scale

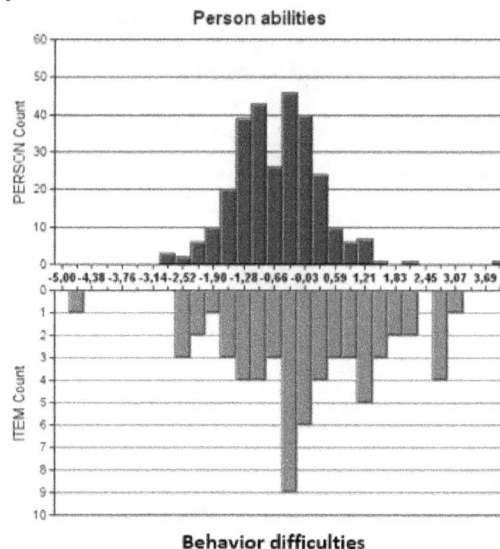

3.1.3 Sodium restriction

Questions related to sodium-intake were extracted from [20] who assessed engagement in sodium-intake behaviors in Canada. The list of behaviors was based on expert opinions and national (Canadian) studies and surveys on sodium. All items were measured on a 4 point frequency scale (Rarely/Never, Sometimes, Often, Always).

3.2 Population characteristics

The population included 300 Dutch participants between 40 and 60 years olds as this age segment is considered at relatively high risk of developing hypertension. The population was stratified to include about as many (pre-)hypertensive as normotensive subjects to allow the use of the model for both treatment of hypertensive patients as well as prevention for healthy individuals (see [17] for definitions of the stages of hypertension). All population characteristics are outlined in table 1.

3.3 Model fitting and analysis

The Rasch model was fitted on the survey data. The resulting model consisted of 63 ICCs (of which 3 are shown in figure 1). The distribution of all the behavior difficulties and person abilities along the latent variable are shown in figure 2, where it is visible that both the population and behaviors are well-spread along the latent trait, though on average behaviors were slightly difficult (relative to the populations' abilities). The transitive difficulties of behaviors (from easiest to most difficult) is illustrated in figure 3.

The evaluation of a Rasch model is based on established criteria [4]. The main properties of the Rasch model (which quantify how well the model fits the data) are the *Rasch reliability, uni-dimensionality* and *universality*. *Rasch reliability* is the ability of the model to distinguish between the difficulty of behaviors and the ability of different persons. Low reliability implies that there is no clear difference between the behaviors and persons in terms of engagement patterns. *Uni-dimensionality* is the existence of only a single latent trait (i.e. feasibility) to account for the engagement in the behaviors. The existence of multiple latent traits implies that the feasibility of behaviors and the ability of persons cannot be expressed on a single one-dimensional scale, making the Rasch model an inappropriate modeling technique. *Universality* of the model means that the estimated behavior difficulties in the model are representative of and apply for the entire population under study. If this is not the case, the model will fail in describing certain segments of the population and subsequently also fail in predicting the feasibility of behaviors. In the next sections we evaluate the model on these criteria. All tests were performed using the Winsteps software [16].

3.3.1 Rasch reliability

The behavior and person reliabilities of the constructed model are respectively 0.99 and .84. A reliability higher than .80 is generally considered sufficient [4, 16]. The outfit statistic [16] was used to inspect whether individual persons were showing unexpected engagement patterns. It is sensitive to unexpected engagement in highly unfeasible behaviors and vice-versa. Only 6% of the population had outfit statistics considered as bad (< 0.5 or > 1.5). The individual behaviors were diagnosed with both the outfit statistic (analogous to the outfit statistic for persons) and the infit statistic, which mainly measures whether persons who have an ability close to the behaviors' difficulty have expected engagement statistics. All behaviors had acceptable infit and outfit statistics.

3.3.2 Uni-dimensionality

Behaviors from different subcategories (exercise, diet and sodium-intake) are well-spread in terms of behavior difficulty (figure 3). The average behavior difficulties of exercise (M

Figure 3: The Rasch scale. The estimated behavior difficulty (i.e. feasibility) is shown. Behaviors are grouped by their type.

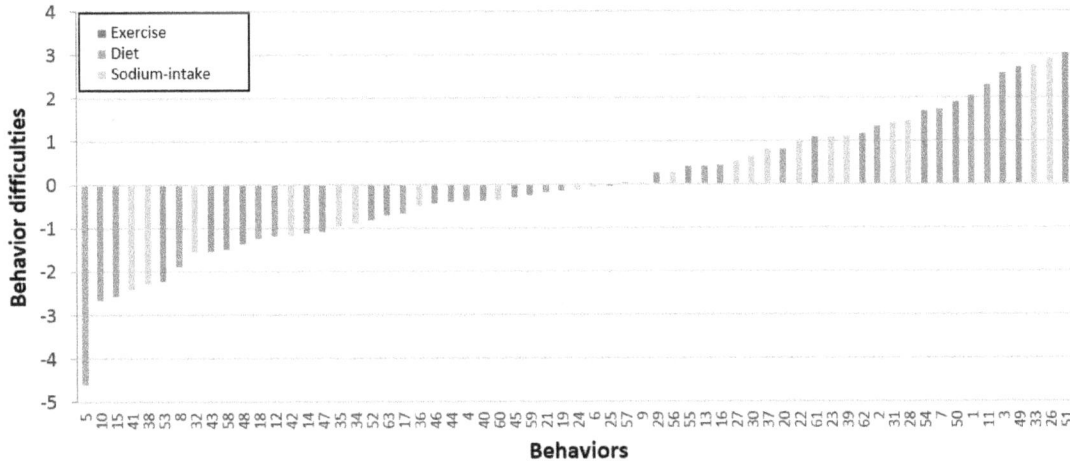

= .06, SD = 1.41), diet (M = -.23, SD = 1.70 and sodium-intake (M = .17, SD = 1.43) were also comparable. A third (33.8%) of the total variance in the data is explained by the Rasch model. Only 4.1 % of the unexplained variance was explained by the first contrast (i.e. first principal component in the residuals) showing that a one-dimensional solution is adequate.

3.3.3 Universality

Behavior difficulties should not be significantly different between subgroups of participants in order to measure a single latent trait. Differential Test Functioning (DTF) calculates the difficulty of behaviors over subgroups of the population after stratification based on ability level. Computing the correlation coefficient of the resulting behavior difficulties between the subgroups is a measure of universality of the model amongst those subgroups. DTF was performed between the lower and upper median split of the population based on the person ability, which is also known as Ben Wright's challenge [4]. A Pearson's correlation of $r = 0.927$ was measured. This DTF analysis is visualized in figure 4. The 90% confidence bounds reveal that some of the salt restriction behaviors (yellow) are significantly easier for the entire high ability population, yet the number of such outlier behaviors is limited. In addition, demographic subgroups were also contrasted with DTF analysis in the same manner: males against females ($r = 0.941$), high education against other education levels ($r = 0.941$), those who did receive doctor's advice to change lifestyle versus those who didn't $r = 0.918$ and between hypertensives and non-hypertensives ($r = 0.952$). These high correlations strongly suggest a universal model of feasibility to be sufficient.

3.3.4 Discussion

The performed tests all give evidence of a well-fitting model of feasibility. The model can distinguish between the difficulty of different behaviors and the ability of different users with high reliability. The feasibility of the behaviors is reasonably unidimensional, though it is clear that there are also other factors that determine engagement in a behavior that are not captured (in line with psychosocial the-

Figure 4: Ben Wright's challenge to test the universality of behavior difficulties amongst different ability segments of the population

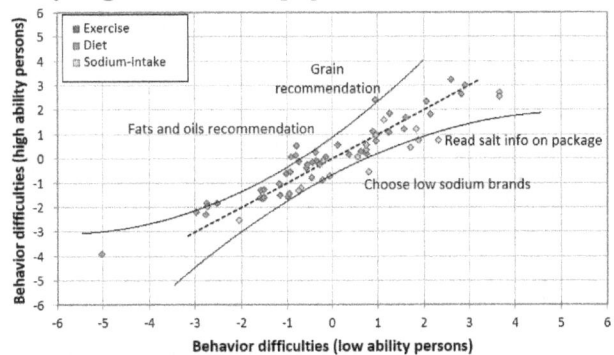

ories). Finally, the difficulty of behaviors seems to change only slightly from one sub-population to another, making the same model applicable to both hypertensive and healthy persons as well as to different demographic subgroups.

4. USER EVALUATION OF THE RECOMMENDATIONS

This section describes the evaluation of feasibility-enabled recommendation strategies in a user study. First, a description of how the strategies introduced in section 1.4 were implemented is given. Then the study design, data acquisition and results are presented.

4.1 Recommendation strategies

The following strategies will be considered in the evaluation (also see section 1.4):

1. The *engagement maximization strategy* (EMS) selects the behaviors with lowest difficulty. EMS takes into account the behavior difficulty measure from the Rasch model without personalization to the specific user.

2. The *motivation maximization strategy* (MMS) selects

Table 2: Comparative questions used in the user evaluation of virtual coaches with their original factors in the left column. In the right column the loading of the questions on the three found factors in factor analysis is presented. Italic questions are asked negatively (and reversed during analysis). High loading (>0.60) is in bold.

Original factor	Question	F1	F2	F3
Intention	If you would have to perform ALL of the recommendations from Coach X or Coach Y for the upcoming three months, which coach would you prefer?	**0,80**	0,28	0,31
Intention	If you would have to perform ONE of the recommendations from Coach X or Coach Y for the upcoming three months, which coach would you prefer?	**0,72**	0,25	0,32
Personalization	Which coach takes into account your skills?	**0,61**	0,20	**0,66**
Personalization	Which coach takes into account your circumstances?	0,53	0,28	**0,73**
Personalization	Which coach understands you well?	0,58	0,26	**0,69**
Rec. quality	Which coach presents the most relevant recommendations?	0,52	**0,67**	0,15
Rec. quality	*Which coach presents more bad recommendations?*	0,03	-0,11	0,16
Rec. quality	Which coach presents the most exciting recommendations?	**0,65**	0,43	0,32
Engagement	Which coach would you find more engaging?	**0,81**	0,26	0,30
Engagement	Which coach would help you to push your limits?	0,56	0,42	0,18
Engagement	Which coach would drive you to achieve your health goals?	**0,79**	0,35	0,28
Health Benefit	Which coach allows you to make more health gains if you implement all recommendations?	0,29	**0,86**	0,06
Health Benefit	Which coach can lower you blood pressure the most?	0,24	**0,91**	0,03
Health Benefit	Which coach enables you to reach your health goals more effectively?	0,39	**0,83**	0,07

the items for which the behavior difficulty is close to the person ability. This strategy takes into account both the behavior difficulty and the person ability measures from the Rasch model.

As we sought to compare the use of these strategies to current practices, we introduced a third control strategy which does not take into account any measure of feasibility.

3. The *random control strategy* (RCS) randomly selects behaviors, not taking into account any Rasch measure.

From the set of modeled behaviors, only the ones that the user does not engage in were selectable for recommendation by the recommendation strategies. This approach prevented the evaluation of the participants to be biased by their ability level. Especially for people with higher abilities, recommending from all behaviors would make the EMS strategy to be more likely to provide easy recommendations a user might already engage in, compared to RCS and MMS. This fact could potentially mediate the user's perception, resulting in a bias towards EMS. This is not a necessary restriction in practical deployment of these strategies (reinforcing existing healthy behaviors is not negative), but merely a necessity to ensure that the measured user's perception only related to the way the feasibility model is used.

As a consequence of limiting the selectable list of recommendations to ones that the user does not already perform, the MMS strategy might have a higher probability of selecting behaviors that are on average more difficult than the user's ability level. To remedy this, behaviors were discretized into bins of easy, medium and hard behaviors while user's ability was discretized into low, medium and high ability. The boundaries were the 33rd and 66th percentiles of the population ability from the first data collection, ensuring that by random sampling in a statistically equivalent population an equal number of participants would fall into each

of the categories. The MMS strategy can therefore pick a random set of recommendations from the bin of behaviors that corresponds to the patient's ability bin. This discretization is also not a restriction on any practical deployment of the MMS strategy, but a necessary condition to ensure that the MMS strategy behaves more in line with its theoretical specification.

4.2 Study design

The study aim was to compare advice generated by either strategies against a randomized control strategy by people considered as target users of the system. In addition, we sought to compare the user's perception of both strategies. To enable these evaluations, a *comparitive design* was employed in which users were presented with pairs of strategies for comparison [11]. Strategies were presented as recommendations by virtual coaches.

The first part of the study was a questionnaire querying the participants' engagement in the complete set of recommended lifestyle behaviors. The response was used to (1) determine the subset of behaviors that the user does not engage in and (2) determine the patient's ability level based on the Rasch model. The three virtual coaches were instantiated. According to the recommendation strategy of the coach, each selected one recommendation about exercise, one about calorie restriction and a third about salt restriction. This way preference to a coach could not be biased towards specific types of presented recommendations.

In the second part, participants compared all three possible coaching combinations against each other (EMS-RCS, MMS-RCS and EMS-MMS) that were presented side-by-side on the web-page (one comparison per screen). The order of each pair and the presentation order of the three screens was randomized as to avoid familiarity bias. Each pair of coaches A and B were compared with 14 questions related to Intention, Achievability, Recommendation Quality, Moti-

Figure 5: Score distribution of the comparisons on each of the factors, given per ability level. Each histogram denotes preference to the strategies (middle bar means no preference). Filled stars and open stars respectively indicate significant effects ($p < 0.05$) and trends ($p < 0.10$) (see 4.4 for description of statistical tests).

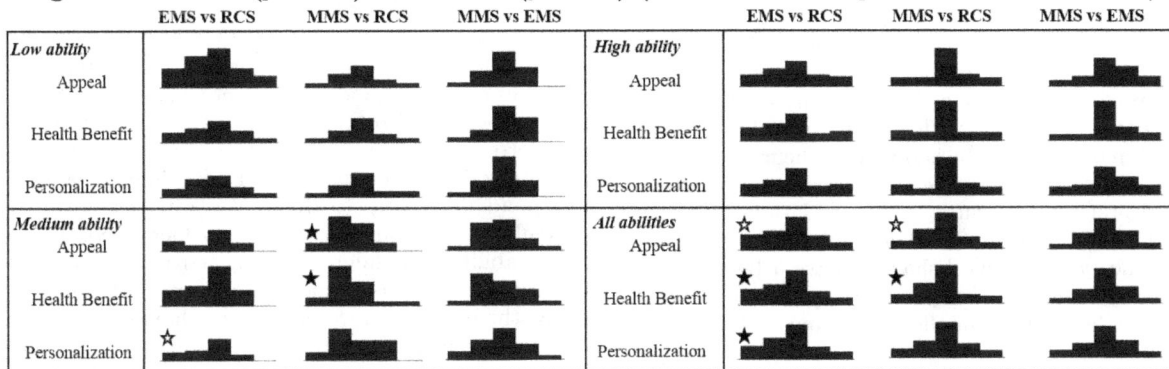

vation and Health Benefit (see table 2), on a 5 point-scale from -2 to +2 (tagged as: Strong preference coach A; mild preference coach A; No preference; Mild preference coach B; strong preference coach B). Finally participants also had to make a binary preference choice for either coach A or B.

4.3 Participants

A new sample of (pre-)hypertensive participants was recruited through a professional on-line panel service. All demographic statistics were comparable to those of the sample used for model construction (table 1). When a strategy failed to find valid recommendations, the comparisons that involved the strategy were excluded from further analysis. If two of the strategies selected an identical set of recommendations, the comparison between them was excluded. The number of comparisons that remained after the exclusions is summarized in table 3.

4.4 Results

An exploratory factor analysis (ie. principal component analysis) on the 14 evaluative questions resulted in three main factors: F1, F2 and F3. The factors explained respectively 23.6%, 22.7% and 18.0% of the variance in the responses. The loading of each of the evaluative questions on these factors (ie. the extent to which a question varies on a factor) is presented in table 2. Based on the intuitive interpretation of the analyzed questions, we summarize the factors as the general appeal (F1), perceived health benefit (F2) and personalization (F3) of the recommendations. The scores on these factors per response were calculated. Significance tests of preference were performed using the 1-sample sign test on the factors. This test was chosen as it is non-parametric and does not assume symmetry around the mean. A left-tailed test was used in the EMS vs RCS and MMS vs RCS tests to test against the null hypothesis that EMS and MMS are not preferred over control. A two-sided test was used for the EMS vs MMS comparison to test against the null hypothesis that there is no preference to either strategy. Figure 5 shows the score distribution per comparison for all of the factors. The scores are given not only for the total group of partipants, but also broken down per ability level, where we distinguished between low, medium and high ability using the same cut-offs as used for

Table 3: Number of comparisons analyzed. The columns denote the type of comparison. The rows denote the ability level segment of the participant.

	Comparison		
Ability	MMS vs RCS	MMS vs EMS	EMS vs RCS
Low	37	19	31
Medium	21	20	23
High	37	37	39
Total	83	76	93

behavior difficulties (see table 3 for number of samples per ability segment). Only significant effects ($p < 0.05$) and trends ($p < 0.10$) will be considered for reporting. In figure 5, the significance level of the tests is indicated with open (trend) and closed (significant effect) stars.

The general population (i.e. population with all ability levels included) preferred EMS over RCS in terms of health benefit ($p = 0.02$), personalization ($p = 0.03$) and appeal ($p = 0.06$). MMS was preferred over RCS in terms of health benefit ($p = 0.04$) and appeal ($p = 0.09$). The comparison of EMS vs MMS could not reject the null hypothesis that these strategies are evaluated equally for any of the factors. Medium-ability users attributed a higher appeal ($p = 0.01$) and health benefit ($p = 0.007$) to MMS over RCS and found the EMS advice more personalized ($p = 0.07$) than RCS. The null hypothesis could not be rejected for any of the factor comparisons in low ability and high ability individuals.

In the final preference question participants had to select one of either coaches as their generally preferred coach. We tested whether the selection patterns were significantly non-random by a one-sided binomial test (the null hypothesis is that the odds of participants selecting either preference is equal). For the general population, EMS was selected more than MMS (56%, $p = 0.07$) and also more than RCS (57%, $p = 0.04$). The preference of EMS over MMS was also significant in the low ability subgroup ($p = 0.05$). The preference of EMS over RCS was significant in the medium ability subgroup ($p = 0.04$).

245

4.5 Discussion

4.5.1 EMS versus RCS

The general trend (over all ability levels) is that EMS is preferred over RCS. This preference is visible in the Appeal, Health Benefit and Personalization factors as well as the general preference question. The hypothesis underlying EMS, namely that behaviors with a higher probability of engagement are more likely to be adopted by the user, appears to hold in this test and is in line with previous work where attitude and preference towards recommendations inversely correlated with the difficulty of advice [26]. It also supports the notion that very feasible behaviors have a better cost-benefit rate and therefore are appealing [6]. When grouped per ability very few significant effects remained, which could be due to the limited sample size within each ability group.

4.5.2 MMS versus RCS

While the general population (including all ability levels) did not find MMS more appealing than RCS, they did attribute a higher health benefit and appeal to it. These effects are not visible for low and medium ability individuals, but are strong for individuals of medium ability. Persons with medium levels of ability might have a higher self-efficacy than persons with a low ability and thus are more willing to accept challenging recommendations. It can also be that behaviors with a medium level of difficulty (which are recommended to this population segment by MMS) have a better perceived health benefit while being relatively feasible. The counter-intuitive result that high ability users (who according to above argumentation would have an outstanding self-efficacy) did not prefer the MMS strategy could then be because the difficult behaviors have a very high cost that outweighs their perceived benefit. From figure 2 it is apparent that there are many behaviors with a difficulty that clearly exceeds the high ability population's level. For example, one of the most difficult behaviors in our set (performing muscle exercises while brushing teeth) has a relatively low health benefit due to the short duration of teeth brushing. Another reason could be that the cause of blood pressure elevation in this segment of the population cannot be remedied by lifestyle interventions (or is caused by lifestyle aspects not covered in our model such as smoking [27] or chronic stress [25]), which would explain why this high ability segment still suffers from hypertension while complying to a large number of lifestyle behaviors. These reasons could explain why high ability users are not attracted to engaging in difficult behaviors, leading to many neutral preferences in the MMS versus RCS tests.

4.5.3 MMS versus EMS

None of the factor scores were significantly leaning to either strategy across all ability levels. On the preference question, 56% of participants favored EMS over MMS. This is most likely due to the varying perceptions of the MMS strategy over different ability groups. For low ability individuals, MMS and EMS will recommend very similar advice (both at the lower end of the Rasch scale) and thus no large differences may be expected. The medium ability individuals have a marked preference for MMS over RCS (see section above) which is unique to this ability segment. High ability individuals might not prefer MMS due to the above-mentioned reasons.

5. CONCLUSIONS

In conclusion, our results show that the use of feasibility models (using the Rasch model as an underlying one-dimensional user model) to select feasible health advice in a patient-centered recommender system leads to significantly preferred advice when contrasted with a random control strategy. To understand better why different ability groups respond differently to different strategies, future research should aim at understanding what factors contribute to the user ability that might explain attitude towards the feasibility level of a recommendation (e.g. self-efficacy [1]) and how the benefit of recommended behaviors scales with their difficulty. Identifying objective health benefit is a difficult task as hypertension can be treated with a large variety of lifestyle interventions, yet not all might be as effective for each patient (and perceived health benefit is even further confounded by other factors). A similar approach as [8] (introduced in section 1) could be a starting point.

The large variations in the coach preference of users related to their ability level implies that there is no "one-size-fits-all" strategy. We show that medium ability individuals respond differently to MMS than other groups. The ability parameter is therefore an important property of the user that should be used for personalization, though how this exactly should be done needs further exploration. A starting point could be to recommend medium ability individuals with medium difficulty behavior, while recommending the other groups only the most feasible behaviors. The ability level can be easily estimated from a person's engagement in a subset of behaviors, either through objective monitoring or through a short questionnaire [26].

The proposed recommendation strategies also deserve to be evaluated in trials to assess not only preference but also effectiveness once actually implemented by a user. Such trials can help to establish that the preference towards feasible behaviors, as shown in this study, corresponds to the actual adherence towards the intervention.

The current conclusions motivate the implementation of the Rasch model in recommender systems for lifestyle-based management of chronic disease. It is a simple and elegant model based on a considerable body of psychological literature that provides a wealth of information about the feasibility of behavior in a very structured way for use in recommendation generation. It is trivial to adapt to different behavioral recommendation domains, while also overcoming some problems of existing feasibility models [21] such as the "cold start" problem or the limitation that a behavior needs to be monitored before its feasibility can be assessed.

6. REFERENCES

[1] A. Bandura. Self-efficacy: toward a unifying theory of behavioral change. *Psychological review*, 84(2):191, 1977.

[2] A. Bandura. Perceived self-efficacy in cognitive development and functioning. *Educational psychologist*, 28(2):117–148, 1993.

[3] A. Bandura. Health promotion by social cognitive means. *Health education & behavior*, 31(2):143–164, 2004.

[4] T. Bond and C. M. Fox. *Applying the Rasch model: Fundamental measurement in the human sciences.* Routledge, 2015.

[5] L. E. Burke, J. Ma, K. M. Azar, G. G. Bennett, E. D. Peterson, Y. Zheng, W. Riley, J. Stephens, S. H. Shah, B. Suffoletto, et al. Current science on consumer use of mobile health for cardiovascular disease prevention a scientific statement from the american heart association. *Circulation*, 132(12):1157–1213, 2015.

[6] K. Byrka and F. G. Kaiser. Health performance of individuals within the campbell paradigm. *International journal of psychology*, 48(5):986–999, 2013.

[7] A. V. Chobanian, G. L. Bakris, H. R. Black, W. C. Cushman, L. A. Green, J. L. Izzo, D. W. Jones, B. J. Materson, S. Oparil, J. T. Wright, et al. Seventh report of the joint national committee on prevention, detection, evaluation, and treatment of high blood pressure. *Hypertension*, 42(6):1206–1252, 2003.

[8] C. K. Chow, J. Redfern, G. S. Hillis, J. Thakkar, K. Santo, M. L. Hackett, S. Jan, N. Graves, L. de Keizer, T. Barry, et al. Effect of lifestyle-focused text messaging on risk factor modification in patients with coronary heart disease: a randomized clinical trial. *Jama*, 314(12):1255–1263, 2015.

[9] M. Csikszentmihalyi. Flow. the psychology of optimal experience. 1990.

[10] H. O. Dickinson, J. M. Mason, D. J. Nicolson, F. Campbell, F. R. Beyer, J. V. Cook, B. Williams, and G. A. Ford. Lifestyle interventions to reduce raised blood pressure: a systematic review of randomized controlled trials. *Journal of hypertension*, 24(2):215–233, 2006.

[11] M. D. Ekstrand, F. M. Harper, M. C. Willemsen, and J. a. Konstan. User perception of differences in recommender algorithms. *Proceedings of the 8th ACM Conference on Recommender systems - RecSys '14*, pages 161–168, 2014.

[12] S. Henson, J. Blandon, and J. Cranfield. Difficulty of healthy eating: A rasch model approach. *Social Science & Medicine*, 70(10):1574–1580, 2010.

[13] F. G. Kaiser, K. Byrka, and T. Hartig. Reviving campbell's paradigm for attitude research. *Personality and Social Psychology Review*, 14(4):351–367, 2010.

[14] N. M. Kaplan. *Kaplan's clinical hypertension.* Lippincott Williams & Wilkins, 2010.

[15] A. H. Lichtenstein, L. J. Appel, M. Brands, M. Carnethon, S. Daniels, H. A. Franch, B. Franklin, P. Kris-Etherton, W. S. Harris, B. Howard, et al. Diet and lifestyle recommendations revision 2006 a scientific statement from the american heart association nutrition committee. *Circulation*, 114(1):82–96, 2006.

[16] J. M. Linacre. A user's guide to winsteps ministep rasch-model computer programs. *Chicago IL: Winsteps. com*, 2006.

[17] G. Mancia, R. Fagard, K. Narkiewicz, J. Redon, A. Zanchetti, M. Böhm, T. Christiaens, R. Cifkova, G. De Backer, A. Dominiczak, et al. 2013 esh/esc lines for the management of arterial hypertension: the task force for the management of arterial hypertension of the european society of hypertension (esh) and of the european society of cardiology (esc). *Blood pressure*, 22(4):193–278, 2013.

[18] D. F. Marks and B. Evans. *Health psychology. Theory, research and practice.* Sage, 2005.

[19] D. Meichenbaum and D. C. Turk. *Facilitating treatment adherence: A practitioner's guidebook.* Plenum Press, 1987.

[20] J. E. Mendoza, G. A. Schram, J. Arcand, S. Henson, and M. L'Abbe. Assessment of consumers' level of engagement in following recommendations for lowering sodium intake. *Appetite*, 73:51–57, 2014.

[21] M. Rabbi, M. H. Aung, M. Zhang, and T. Choudhury. MyBehavior: automatic personalized health feedback from user behaviors and preferences using smartphones. *Ubicomp '15, September 7-11, 2015, Osaka, Japan*, pages 707–718, 2015.

[22] M. Rabbi, A. Pfammatter, M. Zhang, B. Spring, and T. Choudhury. Automated personalized feedback for physical activity and dietary behavior change with mobile phones: a randomized controlled trial on adults. *JMIR mHealth and uHealth*, 3(2):e42, 2015.

[23] F. M. Sacks, L. P. Svetkey, W. M. Vollmer, L. J. Appel, G. A. Bray, D. Harsha, E. Obarzanek, P. R. Conlin, E. R. Miller, D. G. Simons-Morton, et al. Effects on blood pressure of reduced dietary sodium and the dietary approaches to stop hypertension (dash) diet. *New England journal of medicine*, 344(1):3–10, 2001.

[24] S. Sauer, H. Walach, M. Offenbächer, S. Lynch, and N. Kohls. Measuring mindfulness: a rasch analysis of the freiburg mindfulness inventory. *Religions*, 2(4):693–706, 2011.

[25] F. Sparrenberger, F. Cichelero, A. Ascoli, F. Fonseca, G. Weiss, O. Berwanger, S. Fuchs, L. Moreira, and F. Fuchs. Does psychosocial stress cause hypertension? a systematic review of observational studies. *Journal of human hypertension*, 23(1):12–19, 2009.

[26] A. Starke, M. Willemsen, and C. Snijders. Tailoring energy-saving advice using a unidimensional rasch scale of conservation measures. *Proceedings of the 2nd International Workshop on Decision Making and Recommender Systems*, pages 5–8, 2015.

[27] M. H. Talukder, W. M. Johnson, S. Varadharaj, J. Lian, P. N. Kearns, M. A. El-Mahdy, X. Liu, and J. L. Zweier. Chronic cigarette smoking causes hypertension, increased oxidative stress, impaired no bioavailability, endothelial dysfunction, and cardiac remodeling in mice. *American Journal of Physiology-Heart and Circulatory Physiology*, 300(1):H388–H396, 2011.

[28] S. Uzun, B. Kara, M. Yokusoglu, F. Arslan, M. B. Yilmaz, and H. Karaeren. The assessment of adherence of hypertensive individuals to treatment and lifestyle change recommendations. *The Antolian Journal of Cardiology*, 9(2):102–9, 2009.

[29] A. WHO. Global brief on hypertension. *World Health Organization*, 2013.

User-Oriented Context Suggestion

Yong Zheng
Center for Web Intelligence
DePaul University
Chicago, Illinois, USA
yzheng8@cs.depaul.edu

Bamshad Mobasher
Center for Web Intelligence
DePaul University
Chicago, Illinois, USA
mobasher@cs.depaul.edu

Robin Burke
Center for Web Intelligence
DePaul University
Chicago, Illinois, USA
rburke@cs.depaul.edu

ABSTRACT

Recommender systems have been used in many domains to assist users' decision making by providing item recommendations and thereby reducing information overload. Context-aware recommender systems go further, incorporating the variability of users' preferences across contexts, and suggesting items that are appropriate in different contexts. In this paper, we present a novel recommendation task, "Context Suggestion", whereby the system recommends contexts in which items may be selected. We introduce the motivations behind the notion of context suggestion and discuss several potential solutions. In particular, we focus specifically on *user-oriented context suggestion* which involves recommending appropriate contexts based on a user's profile. We propose extensions of well-known context-aware recommendation algorithms such as tensor factorization and deviation-based contextual modeling and adapt them as methods to recommend contexts instead of items. In our empirical evaluation, we compare the proposed solutions to several baseline algorithms using four real-world data sets.

Categories and Subject Descriptors

H.3.3 [**Information Search and Retrieval**]: Information filtering

Keywords

Recommendation; Context; Context Suggestion, Context-aware Recommendation

1. INTRODUCTION AND MOTIVATION

Recommender systems (RS) are effective at alleviating information overload by tailoring recommendations to users' personal preferences. Context-aware recommender systems

UMAP '16, July 13-17, 2016, Halifax, NS, Canada

Copyright 2016 ACM 978-1-4503-4370-1/16/07. . . $15.00

http://dx.doi.org/10.1145/2930238.2930252

(CARS) have the additional goal of adapting those recommendations to specific contexts in which users will select or use recommended items. CARS take contextual factors into account in modeling user profiles and in generating recommendations. In CARS, context is generally defined as "any information that can be used to characterize the situation of entities" [10]. We believe the context information usually refers to the dynamic attributes which may change when the same activity (e.g., watching a movie, listening to a music, etc) is performed repeatedly [24], such as the scenarios of the activities (such as time, location, companion) and dynamic factors from users (such as emotional states).

In rating-based application domains, such as those involving movie or book ratings, the standard formulation of the recommendation problem begins with a two dimensional matrix of ratings, organized by user and item: *Users × Items → Ratings*. The key insight of context-aware recommender systems is that users' preferences for items may be also a function of the context in which those items are encountered. Incorporating contexts requires that we estimate user preferences using a multidimensional rating function – *R*: *Users × Items × Contexts → Ratings* [1].

Both traditional RS and CARS are designed to provide item recommendations. However, incorporating the notion of context into the recommendation process, enables such systems to also recommend contexts, themselves, to users. There are many situations where recommending an appropriate context may be important and beneficial to users. For example, users may need context suggestions in a movie domain, including *When*, *Where* and with *Whom* to watch a specific movie. In a music streaming application, the best context in which a particular song should be played (such as the type of activity or time of the day) may be useful information in selecting the song. Similarly, in the travel domain, the desire to visit a particular destination may vary depending on the season.

The goal of *Context Suggestion* is to recommend a list of appropriate contexts to users in order to optimize their experience when consuming the items (e.g., watching a movie, listening to music, enjoying a trip). There are at least three ways that context suggestion can be useful:

- *Recommending the right context at the appropriate time may lead to a better user experience.* User experience refers to a person's emotions and attitudes about using a particular product, system or service. It is not always sufficient to suggest a set of items to a user based on his or her preferences. The right item should be delivered to the right person at the right *time* and in the right *place*. As shown by Figure 1, users may have different experiences if they are going to watch the movie "*Life of PI*" with different *companions* in different *locations*. Knowing the context in which this movie can be enjoyed the most may affect the user's decision in selecting it during a particular interaction.

Figure 1: Different User Experience in Movie domain

- *Context suggestion can derive the context acquisition process used in context-aware systems.* Context information can be collected explicitly (such as through user surveys) or implicitly (such as through Web or mobile activity and usage logs). These approaches have well-known disadvantages: user surveys require additional human efforts, and usage logs only present limited context information, such as time and location. Alternatively, through context suggestion, a predefined list of contexts can be ranked and recommended to users, and the user's taste in different contexts can be inferred from their interactions with the suggested contexts. For example, in Google Music (see Figure 2), the system is able to suggest a list of pre-defined contexts (e.g., workout, study, hanging out) to the user. Note that there is a mutually reinforcing relationship between the notions of *context acquisition* and *context suggestion*. There are many predefined context categories in Google Music, but only a limited number of them can be presented to a user. A "context recommender" is needed to rank the list of contexts based on a variety of factors, including possibly, the user's past behavior and interests. On the other hand, the acquired context information from users can in turn be used for model learning in the future. Besides, the context suggestion in this example also shares something in common with the topic of *activity recommendation* [8]. We interpret the activities to be recommended as users' intents which fall into the notion of contexts in our case. In addition, not only the activities, but also the attributes of the activity, such as time, location and companion can be suggested, which reveals another difference between context suggestion and activity recommendation.
- *Context suggestions can also be viewed as the process for enabling context-aware recommendation.* As the example of Google Music suggests, the user's choice on the contexts can be viewed as an explicit query to the system effectively providing a constraint on the choice of items that can be recommended. Therefore, music recommendation in the selected context can be formulated as a context-aware recommendation task. This approach allows systems to integrate

Figure 2: Context Suggestion in Google Music

context suggestion and context-aware recommendation in order to further assist user's decision making.

In this paper, we focus specifically on *user-oriented context suggestion* which involves recommending appropriate contexts based on a user's profile. We propose extensions of well-known context-aware recommendation algorithms such as tensor factorization and deviation-based contextual modeling and adapt them as methods to recommend contexts instead of items.

We introduce the related work in Section 2 and the specific problem setting in Section 3. Our evaluation methodologies are presented in Section 4, followed by the experimental results in Section 5, comparing the proposed solutions to several baseline algorithms using four real-world data sets.

2. RELATED WORK

A Context-aware recommender system (CARS) [1] aims to adapt to users' preference models to different contextual situations. The context information may include time, location, companion, emotions, occasion, and so forth. In recent years, context-aware recommendation has proved effective in many applications, and several context-aware recommendation algorithms have been developed, including algorithms based on collaborative filtering [26], context-aware matrix factorization [6] and tensor factorization [12].

By contrast, context suggestion recommends the appropriate contexts to users in order to improve their experience with a given set of items. The idea of recommending context was first mentioned in the tutorial [2] on context-aware recommender systems by Adomavicius and Tuzhilin in 2008, where context recommendation was presented as a potentially new recommendation opportunity. Since then, there have been few research efforts exploring the notion of context suggestion.

Table 1: Uses of Context Suggestion

	Inputs	Outputs
Context Suggestion	user	a list of contexts
	item	a list of contexts
	user, item	a list of contexts
Context Suggestion As Explanations	user	items + contexts
	item	users + contexts
Bundle Suggestion	user, item	contexts + items
	user, item	contexts + users

In earlier work, we have discussed different uses of context suggestion [23] which are summarized in Table 1. We briefly describe these uses below.

- **context suggestion**, for the purpose of recommending an appropriate context, always has a list of contexts as output, but the inputs could be a single user, a single item, or a user-item pair resulting in different recommendation tasks. For example, we may suggest an appropriate time (day, season, etc.) for a user to go on a vacation. Or, we may suggest the best season for tourists to visit Alaska, in which case the item (i.e., Alaska) is the input. If in addition, the suggestions are customized to the user based on his or her interests, then both user and item are considered inputs. The first attempt to solve this problem was made by Baltrunas, et al. [5], where the goal was to predict the best contexts for users listening to a specific music track. They proposed different K-nearest neighbor classifiers to predict the contexts. In our previous work, we comprehensively explored the use of multi-label classification techniques as the basis for personalized context suggestions [28].

- **Context suggestion as explanations** provides a finer-grained way to recommend a combination of appropriate contexts together with a list of users or items. For example, the system may recommend the user to listen to a list of *songs* during a *workout*. The suggested contexts can be viewed as the explanations for why the system recommends this item to the user.

- Context suggestions could be used to recommend both contexts and items in the form of a **bundle suggestion**. For example, when a user is browsing items on an e-commerce Web site, the system may suggest an appropriate occasion (e.g., Mother's Day, birthdays, etc.) for users to gift a specific item. Similarly, the system can simultaneously provide other recommended items which are appropriate as gifts for the same specific occasions.

These applications can be derived from two basic recommendation tasks. One task is *UI-Oriented Context Suggestion* which recommends contexts given a user-item pair and it has been explored by our previous work [28]. For example, what is the suggested *time* and *location* if a user is going to watch *"Life of PI"*. Another recommendation task is *User-Oriented Context Suggestion* in which the suggested context for each user is used as a way to constrain the space of recommended items. This latter task is similar to what's used in Google Music (see Figure 2), Pandora, and Youtube. Currently, Google Music and Pandora only use time as a constraint to rank contexts. For example, "Wake up" is only recommended to users in early mornings, "Focus" is suggested to the users during the working period (such as 9AM to 5PM), and "Relaxing at home" is recommended after work (such as 6 PM to 11 PM). In this paper, we present and analyze finer-grained methodologies for user-oriented context suggestion going beyond simple solutions using only one factor as constraint. Another possible task could be *Item-Oriented Context Suggestion*, but we

specifically explore *User-Oriented Context Suggestion* in this paper, since user personalization is expected to be more significant in this task.

3. PROBLEM SETTING

For user-oriented context suggestion, we use the same problem setting as commonly used for the context-aware item recommendation tasks. Accordingly, we use similar data sets used in training in context-aware recommendation models. A sample of a context-aware movie ratings data set is shown in the table below.

Table 2: Sample of Context-aware Movie Data Set

User	Item	Rating	Time	Location
U1	T1	3	Weekend	Home
U1	T2	4	Weekend	Cinema
U1	T1	5	Weekday	Cinema
U2	T2	3	Weekday	Cinema
U2	T3	4	Weekday	Home
U2	T4	5	Weekend	Home

We use *contextual dimension* to denote a contextual variable, such as "Time" or "Location". The term *contextual condition* refers to a specific value in a dimension, e.g. "Weekday" and "Weekend" are two conditions for "Time". In the table above, there are six rating profiles given by two users on four movies within different contextual situations. In user-oriented context suggestion, the system recommends a list of appropriate contextual conditions to each user, similar to the Google Music example earlier.

Without user's explicit preferences on context conditions, it is difficult to evaluate the quality and accuracy of our suggested contexts. There are two alternative solutions: one is to use the usage frequency to indicate how a user likes or dislikes a context condition. In Table 2, user *U1* may prefer to watch a movie on the *weekend* and in the *cinema* rather than at *home* or on the *weekday*, since, *U1* has two rating profiles at *weekend* and in *cinema*, respectively. Note that we ignore the combinations of contexts and directly recommend individual context conditions in the task of user-oriented context suggestion. However, most context-aware data sets are collected from user surveys, and subjects may be asked to rate items in pre-defined contextual situations, resulting in potentially unreliable data for evaluation.

Table 3: User-Context Rating Data Matrix

	Weekend	Weekday	Home	Cinema
U1	3.5	5	3	4.5
U2	5	3.5	4.5	3

Another solution is to use the user's average item rating in each context to represent user's preferences on contexts. In other words, the multidimensional context-aware data matrix shown in Table 2 can be converted to a 2-dimensional user-context rating matrix (UC rating matrix) as shown in Table 3, where the value in each cell is obtained by the average rating given by each user on multiple items in each specific context condition, and the item information is eliminated from the rating matrix. Note that using users' average rating in each context may also result in unreliable evaluations, if the number of ratings by a user on a context condition is limited. We plan to collect a real-world data with users' explicit preferences on context in our future work. Given the fact that we do not have such a data with users' explicit preferences on contexts, we use the 2-dimensional UC rating matrix as the ground truth in our experimental evaluations.

4. EXPERIMENTAL APPROACHES

We split a context-aware data set (e.g., data matrix shown in Table 2) into training and testing data sets with multidimensional context information. We then convert these data sets into 2-dimensional training and testing matrices (e.g., UC rating matrix shown by Table 3). Next, we propose to build different recommenders to suggest contexts first using the original multidimensional training set, and then using the derived 2-dimensional testing set for evaluation purpose. Namely, the rating data in the 2-dimensional test set is used as the ground truth for evaluation purposes.

In the remaining part of this section, we present several baseline algorithms for context suggestion and then introduce two novel approaches based on traditional context-aware recommendation models.

4.1 Baselines

As noted previously, we use user's average rating in context conditions to represent the ground truth. Therefore, the most straightforward methodology is to reuse this strategy to build recommenders for context suggestion. Note that these baseline approaches will only use the derived 2-dimensional training set (based on the original multidimensional training set) to build models and perform the evaluations based on the derived 2-dimensional testing set. More specifically, we build three approaches as baselines for our evaluations:

4.1.1 Context Average

The predicted score for a user u on context condition c can be obtained by the average rating given in c from the 2-dimensional training data set (i.e., UC rating matrix). This is a non-personalized method which produces the same ranking of contexts to each user based on how popular the contexts are as inferred from the UC rating matrix. Of course, this approach may not be very effective if the number of rating profiles in a particular context condition is limited.

4.1.2 User-Context Average

A finer-grained approach is to create a user-personalized recommender based on user's average item ratings in each context. In other words, the rating given by a user u on context condition c in the 2-dimensional training data set can be directly used as the predicted score for u on context c in the testing data set. If u did not rate items in c in the training set, we are able to downgrade the prediction in other ways: we use the average rating in c, and adopt the average rating by u as an alternative way if c is a cold-start condition. This approach suffers from data sparsity too – the prediction may introduce biases if the number of rating profiles given by u in context c is limited.

4.1.3 Recommenders Based on UC Rating Matrix

To alleviate the data sparsity problem in the two approaches above, we can apply a traditional recommender to the 2-dimensional training set (i.e., UC rating matrix). In this paper, we use the biased matrix factorization introduced by Koren et al. [13], using the prediction function in Equation 1.

$$\hat{r}_{uc} = \mu + b_u + b_c + p_u^T q_c \qquad (1)$$

$\hat{r}_{uc}$ is our predicted score for user u's preference on c. It is broken down into four components: global average rating μ, user bias b_u, context bias b_c, and user-context interaction $p_u^T q_c$ which presents the dot product of a user vector p_u and a context vector q_c. The algorithm assigns N latent factors for each user and context vector. p_u can describe how u likes these factors, while q_c denotes how c obtains these factors.

Note that the three approaches introduced above are built upon the 2-dimensional training set which is represented by a UC rating matrix. Next, we present our approaches to the context suggestion problem.

4.2 By Contextual Rating Deviations

In addition to building a recommender based on the 2-dimen-sional UC rating matrix, we can reuse the outputs of context-aware recommendation algorithms built on the multidimensional context-aware data sets. More specifically, we introduce the contextual rating deviations (CRDs) which can be obtained by deviation-based contextual modeling approaches in context-aware recommendation. CRDs represent how a user's rating is different in each context condition. The idea of context rating deviation has been incorporated into matrix factorization [6] and sparse linear method [29] as the underlying approach to building context-aware recommendation algorithms.

In context-aware matrix factorization (CAMF) for example, the predictions for two variants CAMF_C and CAMF_CU can be described by Equation 2 and 3 respectively.

$$\hat{r}_{uic_1c_2...c_N} = \mu + b_u + b_i + \sum_{j=1}^{N} CRD(c_j) + p_u^T q_i \qquad (2)$$

$$\hat{r}_{uic_1c_2...c_N} = \mu + \sum_{j=1}^{N} CRD(c_j, u) + b_i + p_u^T q_i \qquad (3)$$

Assume there are N context dimensions, and c_j ($j = 1, 2, ..., N$) represents the context conditions in the j_{th} context dimension. In CAMF_C, the prediction score for u on item i in context $c_1c_2...c_N$, $\hat{r}_{uic_1c_2...c_N}$, is composed of five components: global average rating, user bias, item bias, user-item interaction and the aggregated context rating deviations $CRD(c_j)$.

The intuition behind extending this approach to the problem of context suggestion is that we can apply the CAMF_C model to the multidimensional training set and obtain the deviation values of $CRD(c_j)$ for various context conditions. The different CRD values can tell us how users prefer each context condition generally. For example, if CRD in "weekend" is 1 and CRD in "weekday" is 0.3, this deviation might indicate that users prefer to watch movies on weekends rather than during the weekday. Therefore, the ranked list of context conditions based on those CRD values can be viewed as the list of contexts suggested to users. Note, the outputs by CAMF_C provide a non-personalized context suggestion.

By contrast, CAMF_CU is able to learn a CRD value for each user in each context condition which is denoted by $CRD(c_j, u)$ in Equation 3. Thus, we can generate a user-personalized context suggestion based on the CRD values for each user in each context condition. The drawback in this model is that we cannot obtain the $CRD(c_j, u)$ if u did not rate items in context c_j. In this case, we learn a CAMF_C model first, and use $CRD(c_j)$ as a substitution.

The CRD values can also be obtained by the deviation-based contextual sparse linear method (CSLIM) [29, 30]: CSLIM_C and CSLIM_CU. In a summary, we reuse the outputs in context-aware recommendation algorithms to rank the context conditions for user-oriented context suggestion. In this way, the quality of context suggestion may rely on the performance of selected deviation-based contextual modeling approaches, i.e., how good the CRDs are that have been learned in using the specific modeling approach.

4.3 By UI-Oriented Context Suggestion

Recall that the task in UI-oriented context suggestion is to recommend a list of contexts given a user-item pair.

Table 5: Predictions By UI-Oriented Context Suggestion

User	Item	Weekend	Weekday	Home	Cinema
U1	T1	3	5	3	4
U2	T2	5	3	4	3
U1	T3	3	4	4	4
U2	T4	4	4	3	3

In UI-oriented context suggestion, we are able to learn a predictive model based on the multidimensional training set and make predictions based on each user-item pair in the multidimensional testing set. An example of such predictions is depicted in Table 5 where the numerical values denote the predicted score for each context condition given by a user on a specific item.

Table 6: User-Context Predictions

	Weekend	Weekday	Home	Cinema
U1	3	4.5	3.5	4
U2	4.5	3.5	3.5	3

We are able to aggregate the outputs in Table 5 to obtain the user's average ratings on each context condition as shown in Table 6. Recall that we generate the outputs in Table 5 based on the user-item pairs in the testing set for evaluation purposes. In other words, we first use a solution in UI-oriented context suggestion to provide context predictions for each pair of users and items in the testing set, and then aggregate a list of context suggestions for each user.

The aggregation is simply a process of averaging a user's predicted score on each context conditions over all the items he or she rated in the testing set. This approach could be quite useful in practice in a variety of situations. For example, we may promote a list of items to a user, and then use this approach to generate a list of suggested contexts for that user.

In earlier work, we evaluated different multilabel classification (MLC) [20] techniques as the solution for UI-oriented context suggestion [28], and found that Label Powerset (LP) method [21] is the best performing MLC approach for this task. LP considers each unique set of context conditions as one of the classes of a new single-label classification task, and tries to learn the best unique set of contexts as the prediction by learning from features. Simply, we use user and item ids, as well as a binary value as features, where the binary value is used to indicate relevance, and it can be obtained by setting a rating threshold in the data. However, it works effectively at the price of computational costs if there are many rating profiles or several context conditions.

In this paper, we explore pairwise interaction tensor factorization (PITF) as a new solution for UI-oriented context suggestion. PITF [19] was originally developed as a solution for personalized tag recommendation. Here, we view the UI-oriented context suggestion as a task of tag recommendation, where each context condition is considered as an individual tag to be recommended. We create three dimensions in the PITF: user, item and context. All the context conditions are put into a single dimension so that PITF can be applied directly to provide context suggestions for each user-item pair. Then, we are able to aggregate all the predictions to generate a list of context suggestions for each user, as shown in Table 6. The quality of context suggestion generated in this way may rely on the performance of solutions for UI-oriented context suggestion.

5. EVALUATIONS AND RESULTS

In this section, we present our data sets, evaluation protocols, experimental results and our findings.

5.1 Data Sets

As noted before, we try to reuse the data sets in the context-aware recommendation task. Note that the number of data sets is very limited in this domain, and most of these data sets were collected from surveys, which results in small and sparse data sets. We choose data sets in four domains: restaurant, music, movie and mobile applications, as shown in Table 4.

- Restaurant data [18] is a data set collected from survey. Subjects gave ratings to the popular restaurants in Tijuana, Mexico by considering two contextual variables: time and location.

- Music data [4] was collected from InCarMusic which is an Android mobile application offering music recommendations to the passengers of a car. Users are requested to enter ratings for some items using a web application. There are 8 contextual factors and 34 contextual conditions in total.

Table 4: Descriptions of Multidimensional Context-aware Data Sets

	Restaurant	Music	LDOS-CoMoDa	Frappe
# of users	50	42	112	957
# of items	40	139	1232	4082
# of ratings	2,309	3,938	2294	87,580
rating scale	1-5	1-5	1-5	Raw frequency
rating sparsity	9.62E-02	7.49E-06	8.12E-07	3.11E-04
# of context dimensions	2	8	6	3
# of context conditions	7	34	32	12
context dimensions	Time, Location	DrivingStyle, Landscape, Mood, NaturalPhenomena, RoadType, Sleepiness, TrafficConditions, Weather	time, location, dayOfWeek, mood, dominantEmo, endEmo	Time of the day, Day of the week, Location

- LDOS-CoMoDa data [14] is a publicly available context-aware movie data collected from surveys. There are originally 12 context dimensions which captured users' various situations, and we use a subset of contexts which are proved to be influential ones in this data [17], including time, location, day of the week, and three emotional variables.

- Frappe data [3] comes from the mobile usage in the app named as Frappe which is a context-aware app discovery tool that will recommend the right apps for the right moment. We used 3 context dimensions for experimental evaluations, including time of the day, day of the week and location. This data captures the usage frequencies of an app by each user within 2 months. We employ a log transformation on the raw frequency numbers. And this data is the only large data set for public research in context-aware recommendation.

The rating sparsity in Table 4 is obtained by Equation 4. D_i denotes the size of each dimension, such as the number of users, the number of items, or the number of conditions in a specific context dimension. The music and LDOS-CoMoDa rating data are highly sparse since there are more context conditions than the other two data sets.

$$Sparsity = \frac{\text{Number of total ratings}}{\prod_i D_i} \qquad (4)$$

5.2 Evaluation Protocols

We apply a 5-fold cross validation strategy on these four data sets, i.e., each fold of data is viewed as a testing set, and the other four folds are used as training set. As mentioned in Section 3, for each fold evaluation, we have four groups of data: multidimensional training and testing sets, and the derived 2-dimensional training and testing sets (i.e., UC rating matrices).

We use three baseline approaches described in Section 4.1: Context Average, User-context Average and biased matrix factorization which are denoted by ContextAvg, UCAvg and BiasedMF respectively in Figure 3. In addition, we also evaluate the solutions based on deviation-based contextual modeling introduced in Section 4.2. More specifically, we evaluate four approaches: CAMF_C and CSLIM_C which provides a non-personalized context suggestion based on contextual rating deviations in each context condition, CAMF_CU and CSLIM_CU which suggest personalized

contexts based on contextual rating deviations by each user on a specific context condition. Furthermore, we also add the solution based on PITF (see Section 4.3) as another comparison. Note that we only use the relevant or positive profiles in PITF. More specifically, in the 2-dimensional UC rating matrix, we only retain the rating profiles when its rating is no less than a threshold when we perform the PITF algorithm. We set this threshold as 3 for the three rating-based data sets, and the mean of logged frequency value (i.e., 0.981) in the Frappe data. Furthermore, we add multilabel classification as another baseline to be compared with PITF approach. We use label powerset (LP) as the MLC algorithm and choose Random Forest [15] as the classification algorithm. We use the same rating threshold adopted in PITF to segment the rating profiles to relevant and irrelevant ones.

For CAMF and CSLIM algorithms, we use an open-source context-aware recommendation library, CARSKit [31] [1], to obtain the contextual rating deviations. For PITF, we use the toolkit [2] provided by the authors [19].

In addition, we present data statistics (see Table 7) based on the 2-dimensional training sets (i.e., UC rating matrix) in order to get insights about how reliable our baseline approaches may work on these data. The rating density is the number of total ratings divided by the number of users and the number of context conditions. The rating density by context is the average number of ratings given in each condition divided by the number of total ratings. We can see that the rating density in restaurant data is 93.4% which tells that most users have given ratings to each context condition in this data. Therefore, the predictions by UCAvg on this data may be more reliable than the ones in other data sets. Accordingly, the rating density by context in music and LDOS-CoMoDa data is only around 3.0% which may indicate the predictions by ContextAvg in these data is not as reliable as others.

We evaluate the proposed approaches based on top-N recommendation. Five and ten are the most popular choices for the value of N. We use 5 since the number of context conditions is limited in the data sets. The choice of N may also depend on the specific applications. For example, a smaller number, e.g., 2 or 4, may be appropriate to be adopted in mobile applications, since the display space on mobile screen is limited. We choose two series of evaluation

---

[1]CARSKit, https://github.com/irecsys/CARSKit
[2]PITF, http://www.libfm.org/tagrec.html

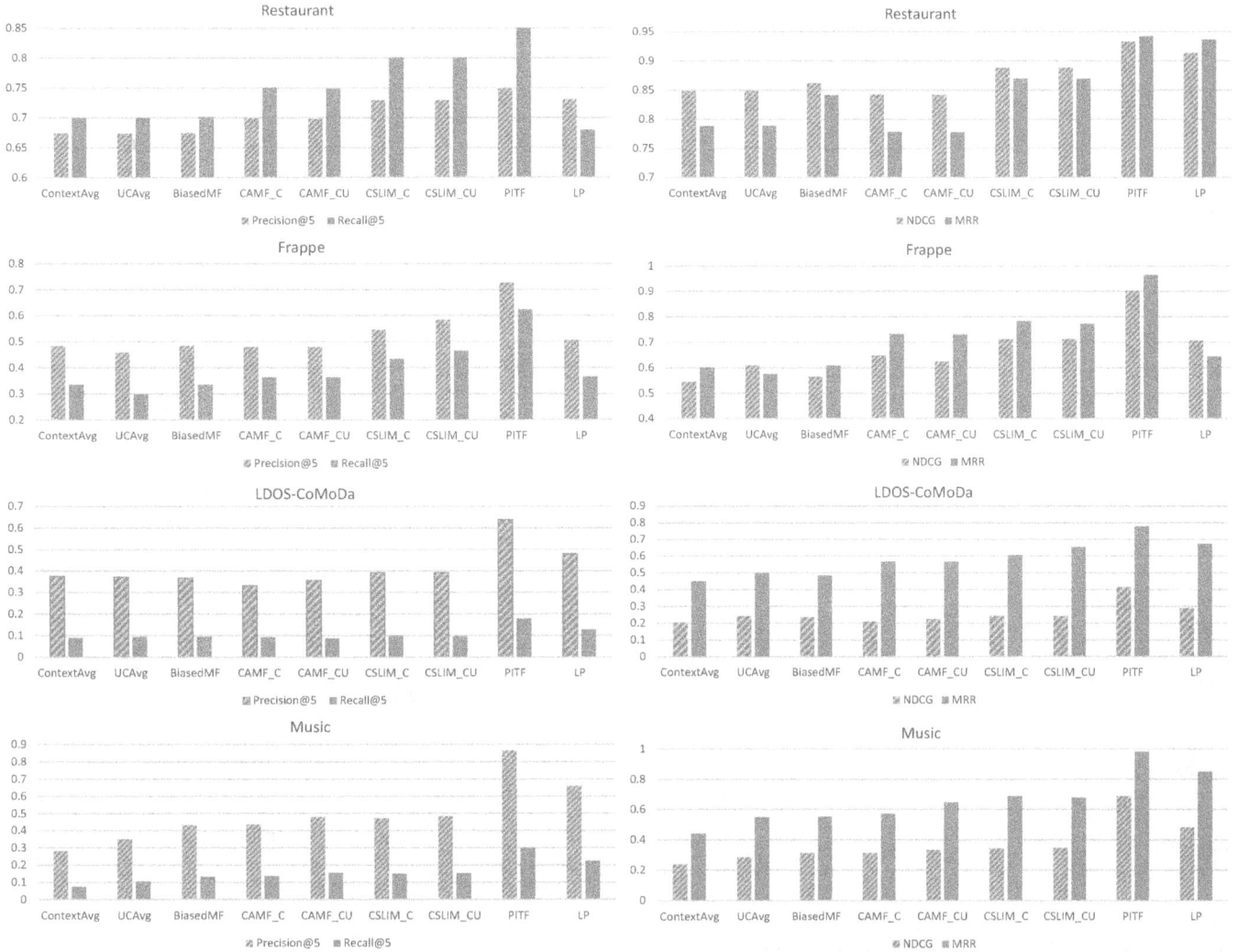

Figure 3: User-Oriented Context Suggestion: Experimental Evaluations

Table 7: Data Description of UC Rating Matrix

	Restaurant	Music	LDOS-CoMoDa	Frappe
# of users	50	42	112	957
# of conditions	7	34	32	12
# of ratings	327	1015	1484	6681
rating density	93.4%	71.1%	41.4%	58.1%
rating density by context	14.3%	2.9%	3.0%	8.3%

metrics: relevance metrics, including precision and recall for top-5 context suggestion, and ranking metrics, including Normalized Discounted Cumulative Gain (NDCG) [11] and Mean Reciprocal Rank (MRR) [22]. More specifically, precision is calculated as the ratio of relevant items selected to the number of items recommended, and recall presents the probability that a relevant item will be selected.

NDCG is a measure from information retrieval, where positions are discounted logarithmically. Assuming each user u has a "gain" g_{ui} from being recommended an item i, the average Discounted Cumulative Gain (DCG) for a list of J items is defined as shown in Equation 5.

$$DCG = \frac{1}{N} \sum_{u=1}^{N} \sum_{j=1}^{J} \frac{g_{ui_j}}{max(1, log_b j))} \qquad (5)$$

NDCG is the normalized version of DCG given by Equation 6, where DCG^* is the maximum possible DCG.

$$NDCG = \frac{DCG}{DCG^*} \qquad (6)$$

The MRR is the average of the Reciprocal Rank (RR) across all the recommendation lists for individual users. RR measures how early in the list (i.e. how highly ranked) is the first relevant recommended item. MRR can be calculated base on Equation 7, where L denotes the relevant items in the testing set for each user, and $Rank_i$ indicates the position of the i_{th} relevant item in the recommendation list.

$$MRR = \frac{1}{|L|} \sum_{i=1}^{|L|} \frac{1}{Rank_i} \qquad (7)$$

5.3 Experimental Results

The experimental results can be described by Figure 3. The figures on the left side present precision and recall results for top-5 context suggestion, and the figures on the right side present results based on NDCG and MRR.

Among the three baseline approaches, BiasedMF generally works better than ContextAvg and UCAvg in precision, recall and MRR. Its advantage is more significant on the Music data than the ones in other data sets. ContextAvg, as a non-personalized solution, only works sightly better than UCAvg in the Frappe data in terms of precision, recall and MRR. Note that the rating density by context is only 2.9%, 3.0% and 8.3% (see Table 7) in the Music, LDOS-CoMoDa and Frappe data respectively, which may introduce biases in these baseline approaches, especially the ContextAvg and UCAvg. Generally, UCAvg is able to outperform the ContextAvg based on the results shown in the figure, which indicates that personalization is required in the user-oriented context suggestion task.

Among the deviation-based contextual modeling approaches, we can see that CSLIM algorithms are able to obtain more accurate results in contextual rating deviations than the CAMF algorithms. That, in turn, results in better context suggestions in terms of both relevant and ranking metrics. This is not surprising since our previous work [29] has demonstrated that CSLIM outperforms CAMF in the task of context-aware recommendation. We also observe that user-personalized approaches work better than the non-personalized ones, even if the advantage is not that significant in some data sets. But we do find some evidences, for example, CSLIM_CU performs better than CSLIM_C in Frappe data in terms of precision and recall. CSLIM_CU works better than CSLIM_C in LDOS-CoMoDa data in terms of MRR, and CAMF_CU works better than CAMF_C in the music data in both relevance and ranking metrics. This finding confirms that user-personalization is required in the task of context suggestion.

In addition, we also reuse the outputs in the UI-oriented context suggestion task to aggregate a list of suggested contexts to each user. LP is the one using label powerset as the multilabel classification solution in this case, and PITF is the one we proposed in this paper which views context suggestion task being analogy to tag recommendations. We can see that LP generally outperforms the baseline approaches, especially the simple approach based on matrix factorization, which shows consistent results with our previous work [25]. The LP approach also works better than deviation-based approaches in the music and LDOS-CoMoDa data in terms of precision and ranking metrics. It also shows better ranking results in the restaurant data. PITF is shown to be the best performing algorithm among all the examined approaches in both relevance and ranking

metrics. And PITF runs much more effectively than LP, especially when it comes to larger data set, such as the Frappe data. It is reasonable to see these results, since PITF is shown to work better than the LP approach in the UI-oriented context suggestion task. One possible explanation to interpret why PITF and LP algorithms work better than deviation-based approaches is that they predict a score for each context condition towards a pair of user and item, and then aggregate the score across all the user-item pairs, which is exactly how we generate the ground truth in Section 3.

As a summary, deviation-based approaches are able to outperform the baselines, and CSLIM is a better way to learn contextual rating deviations than CAMF. It is not surprising since SLIM [16] is an algorithm specifically designed for top-N recommendation and it was demonstrated to outperform the several state-of-the-art algorithms in traditional recommender systems. Note SLIM is not a learning-to-rank algorithm which directly optimizes ranking metrics. Meanwhile, reusing the outputs by UI-oriented context suggestion is viewed as the most effective approach. LP is able to work better than the deviation-based approach in terms of ranking metrics in some data sets. PITF is proved to be the best performing solution among all these examined algorithms in both relevance and ranking metrics. Its advantage is significant in terms of improvement compared with other approaches, and it is viewed as an effective and efficient solution finally.

6. CONCLUSIONS AND FUTURE WORK

In this paper, we have explored several solutions for user-oriented context suggestion which aims to recommend a list of appropriate contexts to a given user. Based on our experimental evaluations, we find that the Pairwise Interactive Tensor Factorization adapted to context suggestion is the best solution for learning to rank contextual conditions. We also explored approaches based on contextual rating deviations and found that the extension of the Contextual Sparse Linear Method (CSLIM) is able to generate more accurate contextual rating deviations than the approaches based on Context-Aware Matrix Factorization.

As introduced previously, Google Music currently uses time as constraint to filter or rank the context conditions. This strategy can also be further applied as a post-processing on the context suggestions by our approaches. The approaches explored in this work are general enough to be applied in any scenario, and they can be combined with other constraints beyond the temporal factors used in Google Music.

Context suggestion is still a novel and promising research direction. The main challenge in current stage are the ground truth and evaluations. In our future work, we plan to collect preferences on contexts by user surveys or studies. Furthermore, we will explore the extensions of other context-aware recommendation algorithms as the the basis for context suggestion. For example, the context-aware splitting approaches [7, 27] could be reused to explore context suggestion. Similarity of contexts [9, 32, 33] can also be adopted as one resource to rank the recommendations. In addition, we will explore learning-to-rank algorithms to rank contexts by optimizing the ranking metrics directly.

7. REFERENCES

[1] G. Adomavicius, B. Mobasher, F. Ricci, and A. Tuzhilin. Context-aware recommender systems. *AI Magazine*, 32(3):67–80, 2011.

[2] G. Adomavicius and A. Tuzhilin. Tutorial on Context-aware Recommender Systems, the 2nd ACM Conference on Recommender Systems. http://ids.csom.umn.edu/faculty/gedas/talks/RecSys2008-tutorial.pdf.

[3] L. Baltrunas, K. Church, A. Karatzoglou, and N. Oliver. Frappe: Understanding the usage and perception of mobile app recommendations in-the-wild. *CoRR*, abs/1505.03014, 2015.

[4] L. Baltrunas, M. Kaminskas, B. Ludwig, O. Moling, F. Ricci, A. Aydin, K.-H. Lüke, and R. Schwaiger. Incarmusic: Context-aware music recommendations in a car. In *E-Commerce and Web Technologies*, pages 89–100. Springer, 2011.

[5] L. Baltrunas, M. Kaminskas, F. Ricci, R. Lior, B. Shapira, and K.-H. Luke. Best usage context predictions for music tracks. In *The 2nd Workshop on Context-aware Recommender Systems*, 2010.

[6] L. Baltrunas, B. Ludwig, and F. Ricci. Matrix factorization techniques for context aware recommendation. In *Proceedings of the fifth ACM conference on Recommender systems*, pages 301–304. ACM, 2011.

[7] L. Baltrunas and F. Ricci. Experimental evaluation of context-dependent collaborative filtering using item splitting. *User Modeling and User-Adapted Interaction*, 24(1-2):7–34, 2014.

[8] V. Bellotti, B. Begole, E. H. Chi, N. Ducheneaut, J. Fang, E. Isaacs, T. King, M. W. Newman, K. Partridge, B. Price, et al. Activity-based serendipitous recommendations with the magitti mobile leisure guide. In *Proceedings of the SIGCHI Conference on Human Factors in Computing Systems*, pages 1157–1166. ACM, 2008.

[9] V. Codina, F. Ricci, and L. Ceccaroni. Exploiting the semantic similarity of contextual situations for pre-filtering recommendation. In *User Modeling, Adaptation, and Personalization*, pages 165–177. Springer, 2013.

[10] A. K. Dey. Understanding and using context. *Personal and ubiquitous computing*, 5(1):4–7, 2001.

[11] K. Järvelin and J. Kekäläinen. Cumulated gain-based evaluation of ir techniques. *ACM Transactions on Information Systems (TOIS)*, 20(4):422–446, 2002.

[12] A. Karatzoglou, X. Amatriain, L. Baltrunas, and N. Oliver. Multiverse recommendation: n-dimensional tensor factorization for context-aware collaborative filtering. In *Proceedings of the fourth ACM conference on Recommender systems*, pages 79–86. ACM, 2010.

[13] Y. Koren, R. Bell, and C. Volinsky. Matrix factorization techniques for recommender systems. *IEEE Computer*, 42(8):30–37, 2009.

[14] A. Košir, A. Odic, M. Kunaver, M. Tkalcic, and J. F. Tasic. Database for contextual personalization. *ELEKTROTEHNISKI VESTNIK*, 78(5):270–274, 2011.

[15] A. Liaw and M. Wiener. Classification and regression by randomforest. *R news*, 2(3):18–22, 2002.

[16] X. Ning and G. Karypis. SLIM: Sparse linear methods for top-n recommender systems. In *IEEE 11th International Conference on Data Mining*, pages 497–506. IEEE, 2011.

[17] A. Odic, M. Tkalcic, J. F. Tasic, and A. Košir. Relevant context in a movie recommender system: UsersŠ opinion vs. statistical detection. *ACM RecSys Workshop on Context-aware Recommender Systems*, 2012.

[18] X. Ramirez-Garcia and M. Garca-Valdez. Post-filtering for a restaurant context-aware recommender system. In *Recent Advances on Hybrid Approaches for Designing Intelligent Systems*, volume 547 of *Studies in Computational Intelligence*, pages 695–707. Springer International Publishing, 2014.

[19] S. Rendle and L. Schmidt-Thieme. Pairwise interaction tensor factorization for personalized tag recommendation. In *Proceedings of the third ACM international conference on Web search and data mining*, pages 81–90. ACM, 2010.

[20] G. Tsoumakas, I. Katakis, and I. Vlahavas. Mining multi-label data. In *Data mining and knowledge discovery handbook*, pages 667–685. Springer, 2010.

[21] G. Tsoumakas and I. Vlahavas. Random k-labelsets: An ensemble method for multilabel classification. In *Machine learning: ECML 2007*, pages 406–417. Springer, 2007.

[22] E. M. Voorhees et al. The trec-8 question answering track report. In *Trec*, volume 99, pages 77–82, 1999.

[23] Y. Zheng. Context suggestion: Solutions and challenges. In *Proceedings of the 15th IEEE International Conference on Data Mining Workshops*, pages 1602–1603. IEEE, 2015.

[24] Y. Zheng. A revisit to the identification of contexts in recommender systems. In *Proceedings of the 20th ACM Conference on Intelligent User Interfaces Companion*, pages 133–136. ACM, 2015.

[25] Y. Zheng. Context-driven mobile apps management and recommendation. In *Proceedings of the 31st Annual ACM Symposium on Applied Computing*, pages 633–634. ACM, 2016.

[26] Y. Zheng, R. Burke, and B. Mobasher. Recommendation with differential context weighting. In *User Modeling, Adaptation, and Personalization*, pages 152–164. 2013.

[27] Y. Zheng, R. Burke, and B. Mobasher. Splitting approaches for context-aware recommendation: An empirical study. In *Proceedings of the 29th Annual ACM Symposium on Applied Computing*, pages 274–279. ACM, 2014.

[28] Y. Zheng, B. Mobasher, and R. Burke. Context recommendation using multi-label classification. In *Proceedings of the 13th IEEE/WIC/ACM International Conference on Web Intelligence*, pages 288–295. IEEE/WIC/ACM, 2014.

[29] Y. Zheng, B. Mobasher, and R. Burke. CSLIM: Contextual SLIM recommendation algorithms. In

Proceedings of the 8th ACM Conference on Recommender Systems, pages 301–304. ACM, 2014.

[30] Y. Zheng, B. Mobasher, and R. Burke. Deviation-based contextual SLIM recommenders. In *Proceedings of the 23rd ACM Conference on Information and Knowledge Management*, pages 271–280. ACM, 2014.

[31] Y. Zheng, B. Mobasher, and R. Burke. CARSKit: A java-based context-aware recommendation engine. In *Proceedings of the 15th IEEE International Conference on Data Mining Workshops*, pages 1668–1671. IEEE, 2015.

[32] Y. Zheng, B. Mobasher, and R. Burke. Integrating context similarity with sparse linear recommendation model. In *User Modeling, Adaptation, and Personalization*, volume 9146 of *Lecture Notes in Computer Science*, pages 370–376. Springer Berlin Heidelberg, 2015.

[33] Y. Zheng, B. Mobasher, and R. Burke. Similarity-based context-aware recommendation. In *Web Information Systems Engineering*, volume 9418 of *Lecture Notes in Computer Science*, pages 431–447. Springer Berlin Heidelberg, 2015.

Modeling Individual Users' Responsiveness to Maximize Recommendation Impact

Masahiro Sato
Fuji Xerox Co., Ltd.
6-1 Minatomirai, Nishi-ku, Yokohama, Kanagawa, Japan
+81-45-755-9159
sato.masahiro@fujixerox.co.jp

Hidetaka Izumo
Fuji Xerox Co., Ltd.
6-1 Minatomirai, Nishi-ku, Yokohama, Kanagawa, Japan
+81-45-755-8237
izumo.hidetaka@fujixerox.co.jp

Takashi Sonoda
Fuji Xerox Co., Ltd.
6-1 Minatomirai, Nishi-ku, Yokohama, Kanagawa, Japan
+81-45-755-8551
takashi.sonoda@fujixerox.co.jp

ABSTRACT

Recommender systems provide personalized information based on a user's preferences. Differences in preferences among users are estimated from past records such as click logs or purchase logs. Recommender systems typically assume that users will respond to recommendations, provided that their favorite items are correctly selected. However, the responsiveness to recommendations depends on the type of users; while some users might be easily persuaded to take action, others might be more hesitant. In this paper, we propose a purchase prediction model that incorporates the differences in the responsiveness. We derived the individual users' responsiveness from a combination of purchase logs and recommendation logs. Improvement in the accuracy of purchase prediction was verified using a grocery shopping dataset. Another relatively unexplored yet important objective of recommender algorithms is to maximize recommendation impact, which is defined as the increase in purchase probability through recommendations. The impact of recommendations by our model exceeded that of a conventional model that ignores individual users' responsiveness. These results demonstrate the importance of modeling the responsiveness of individual users. In cases where recommendation logs are insufficient, the responsiveness needs to be estimated from other sources. Consequently, we investigated the correlation of the responsiveness with user attributes and item attributes. The estimates of the responsiveness from the correlated attributes outperformed the mean estimates. Furthermore, the recommendation impact of the model estimated from the correlated attributes was almost comparable to that of the model estimated from recommendation logs. These findings can help overcome the cold-start problem of inadequate recommendation logs. Our study presents a new direction in the field of personalization based on the responsiveness to recommendations.

Keywords

Purchase Prediction; Profit Maximization; Grocery Shopping; Matrix Factorization; Personality; Cold-Start Problem.

UMAP'16, July 13-17, 2016, Halifax, NS, Canada
© 2016 ACM. ISBN 978-1-4503-4370-1/16/07...$15.00
DOI: http://dx.doi.org/10.1145/2930238.2930259

1. INTRODUCTION

Recommender systems are prevalent in many fields. Electronic commerce websites display items that users might like to buy, and social networking services find people whom users might know and want to connect with. Recommendation research has attracted the interest of both academics and practitioners.

Much effort has been dedicated to algorithms that estimate individual users' preferences. Preferences can be extracted from past records of explicit feedbacks such as five-point ratings and implicit feedbacks such as click logs and purchase logs. Traditionally, recommendation research has focused on the personal differences in item preferences. On the other hand, it has been indifferent to other personal differences.

Recently, however, new kinds of personal differences have drawn the attention of researchers. For example, the propensity to diversity depends on personality [23, 24]. Novelty-seeking behavior differs among users [12, 25]. Some users accept higher risks for higher returns from recommendations, while others avoid such risks [26]. Moreover, the change rate in preferences over time is unique to each user [19].

In addition to these personal differences, the responsiveness to recommendations, which is defined as the effect of recommendations to increase a user's rating of an item, might also depend on the user. However, responsiveness has been treated as independent of the users [3, 10, 22] and the individual differences have never been investigated, to the best of our knowledge. The responsiveness to recommendations is directly connected to the success of recommendation and requires further investigation in order to design better recommender systems.

Along with the dependence of the responsiveness on users, individual items might trigger different responses in users. This possibility is implied by in-situ experiments in real stores [14, 17]. Researchers have demonstrated that while certain items in some categories sell easily through recommendations, other items in other categories do not.

In this paper, we propose a recommender system that incorporates individual differences in responsiveness. We formulate the purchase probability as a sigmoid function of the sum of a rating and recommendation response. Recommendation responsiveness is decomposed into common responsiveness, user-specific responsiveness, and item-specific responsiveness. The responsiveness is inferred from a combination of purchase logs and recommendation logs, so as to maximize the likelihood of the model.

We evaluated the effectiveness of our model in terms of purchase prediction and impact maximization, using a grocery shopping dataset. The accuracy of the predictions made by our model was compared to the accuracy of a conventional model that assumes constant responsiveness. The recommendation impact, which we define as the increase in purchase probability as a result of recommendations, was also compared between the proposed model and the conventional model.

In order to clarify the characteristics of responsiveness and estimate responsiveness despite inadequate recommendation logs, we investigated the correlation between responsiveness and the other attributes of users and items. For the analysis, we used demographic information about users and features extracted from purchase records. The correlated features were then applied to predict user- and item-specific responsiveness. Furthermore, we evaluated the recommendation impacts of an individualized responsiveness model, estimated exclusively from the correlated features, without using recommendation logs.

The outline for this paper is as follows. In the next section, we review related work. In Section 3, we introduce our model, along with a conventional model and the dataset we used for our evaluation. Section 4 presents performance comparisons between our model and the conventional model in terms of prediction accuracy and recommendation impact. Section 5 describes the correlation of recommendation responsiveness to other attributes and the estimate of responsiveness from correlated attributes. Finally, we summarize and conclude this paper in Section 6.

2. RELATED WORK
There are two branches of research that relate closely to this work; meta-personalization beyond item preference, and purchase prediction of recommended items.

2.1 Meta-Personalization
Accurately predicting item preferences does not in itself lead to user satisfaction [16]. Consequently, there is a discrepancy between online performance and offline performance [5]. New perspectives have thus been introduced to recommender systems. For instance, diversity and novelty are vogue topics in recommendation research [4].

As research into diversity and novelty progresses, it is becoming apparent that the desired degree of diversity and novelty differs among users. The propensity to diversity has been measured in terms of the entropy in item selection, and the diversity of recommendations for each user can be adjusted accordingly [6]. Indeed, the preference for diversity is correlated to personality [24], and in particular to "openness to experience" [23]. Recommender systems that adapt to the novelty-seeking traits of users have also been proposed [12, 25].

Such meta-personalization is not limited to diversity and novelty. Individual differences in risk tolerance have been introduced to recommender systems in order to adjust the allowable degree of the variance in rating estimates for each user [26]. Dynamics of preference, or fickleness, also differ among users, and this has been taken into account for recommendations [19].

We believe that our work in modeling individual users' responsiveness will shed new light on the field of meta-personalization.

2.2 Recommended Purchase Prediction
A conventional task of recommender systems with implicit feedback is to predict which items users will click or buy [9, 11,

18]. However, such predictions do not always consider the effect of recommendations.

Recommendation naturally increases the probability that an item will be clicked or purchased. Recently, the effect of recommendations on purchase predictions has been modeled in several ways. Shani et al. [22] assumed that the increase in purchase probability from recommendations is proportional to the purchase probability without recommendations. Jianga et al. [10] imposed the constraint that consumers buy an item only if the valuation is more than the price of the item. They assumed that recommendation increases the valuation of the item and that the increase is constant. Bodapati [3] decomposed purchase probability into awareness probability and satisfaction probability, and assumed that recommendations guaranteed awareness of the item.

Whereas the responsiveness to recommendations was considered to be independent of the user in the previous work, we introduce user-dependent responsiveness, in an effort to advance purchase prediction a step further.

3. INDIVIDUALIZED RESPONSIVENESS
In this section, we first describe a base model for purchase prediction. We next explain the dataset we used in Subsection 3.2. Subsection 3.3 shows our preliminary experiment, which indicates individual differences in recommendation responsiveness. Finally, we introduce user- and item-specific responsiveness in Subsection 3.4.

3.1 Base Model for Purchase Prediction
The probability of binary implicit feedback, such as clicks or purchases, can be formalized in a sigmoid function of a rating of user u on item i (r_{ui}) [11]:

$$p = \sigma(r_{ui}) = \frac{1}{1 + \exp(-r_{ui})}. \quad (1)$$

The sigmoid function converts an unbounded real value to a range between zero and one. This is a popular choice for converting a rating to a probability.

We used matrix factorization, which is known to perform well in rating prediction [13]. Matrix factorization decomposes a rating to the latent factors of the user and the item. Adding bias terms is a common technique, because ratings are not zero-centered. Hence rating r_{ui} is expressed as:

$$r_{ui} = b_c + b_u + b_i + \theta_u^T \varphi_i, \quad (2)$$

where b_c is a bias common to all the users and items, b_u is a user-specific bias, and b_i is an item-specific bias. Further, θ_u and φ_i denote the latent factors of the user and the item, respectively. Equation (2) is expressed equivalently in matrix form as follows:

$$\mathbf{R} = \mathbf{B} + \Theta^T \Phi,$$
$$\{\mathbf{R}\}_{ui} = r_{ui}, \{\mathbf{B}\}_{ui} = b_c + b_u + b_i, \{\Theta\}_{u*} = \theta_u, \{\Phi\}_{i*} = \varphi_i. \quad (3)$$

Recommending an item should increase the probability of purchasing the item. Adding recommendation responsiveness γ to rating r_{ui}, Equation (1) becomes

$$p = \frac{1}{1 + \exp(-(b_c + b_u + b_i + \theta_u^T \varphi_i + \delta_{rec}\gamma))}, \quad (4)$$

where δ_{rec} is an indicator function of the recommendation. Here, $\delta_{rec} = 1$ when item i is recommended to user u; otherwise, $\delta_{rec} = 0$. Furthermore, γ can be constant or dependent on the user and the item, as discussed below in Subsection 3.4.

In our models, the parameters $\wp$ to be learned are:

$$\wp = \{b_c, b_u, b_i, \theta_u, \varphi_i, \gamma \mid u \in U, i \in I\}. \quad (5)$$

From purchase records and recommendation records, each term is determined such that it minimizes the negative log likelihood (NLL):

$$
\begin{aligned}
\text{NLL} &= -\ln(\prod_{purchase} \sigma(r_{ui} + \delta_{rec}\gamma) \\
&\times \prod_{non\text{-}purchase} (1 - \sigma(r_{ui} + \delta_{rec}\gamma)) \\
&= \sum_{purchase} \ln(1 + \exp(-(r_{ui} + \delta_{rec}\gamma))) \\
&+ \sum_{non\text{-}purchase} \ln(1 + \exp(+(r_{ui} + \delta_{rec}\gamma))).
\end{aligned} \quad (6)
$$

We define each term in the summation of purchase records and the summation of non-purchase records as $l_{ui}^{purchase}$ and $l_{ui}^{non\text{-}purchase}$, respectively.

$$l_{ui}^{purchase} \equiv \ln(1 + \exp(-(r_{ui} + \delta_{rec}\gamma))), \quad (7)$$

$$l_{ui}^{non\text{-}purchase} \equiv \ln(1 + \exp(+(r_{ui} + \delta_{rec}\gamma))). \quad (8)$$

We used a stochastic gradient descent (SGD) method for iterative learning. For each iteration, an SGD randomly picks a user-item pair and updates the parameters in the opposite direction of the gradient. The gradients of $l_{ui}^{purchase}$ and $l_{ui}^{non\text{-}purchase}$ are:

$$\frac{\partial}{\partial \wp} l_{ui}^{purchase} = -\left(\frac{1}{1 + \exp(r_{ui} + \delta_{rec}\gamma)} \right) \frac{\partial}{\partial \wp}(r_{ui} + \delta_{rec}\gamma), \quad (9)$$

$$\frac{\partial}{\partial \wp} l_{ui}^{non\text{-}purchase} = \left(\frac{1}{1 + \exp(-(r_{ui} + \delta_{rec}\gamma))} \right) \frac{\partial}{\partial \wp}(r_{ui} + \delta_{rec}\gamma). \quad (10)$$

Parameters are updated as:

$$\wp \leftarrow \wp + \zeta_\wp \left(-\frac{\partial}{\partial \wp} l_{ui}^{purchase} - \lambda_\wp \wp \right), \quad (11)$$

$$\wp \leftarrow \wp + \zeta_\wp \left(-\frac{\partial}{\partial \wp} l_{ui}^{non\text{-}purchase} - \lambda_\wp \wp \right), \quad (12)$$

where $\zeta_\wp$ is the learning rate and is the $\lambda_\wp$ regularization coefficient of the parameter. Learning the parameters of the model with the SGD always converged in our experiments.

3.2 Dataset
We used proprietary data from a grocery shop. The dataset included purchase logs and recommendation logs. We could not find any publically available open data with recommendation logs, which are crucial for our experiments. Hence, we used only this dataset. The grocery shop mainly deals in foods like vegetables, meat, fish, and various processed foodstuffs. The club members of the shop received the catalogs of available items each week and made purchases by mail order. For each week, several "recommended items of the week" were selected by the shop owner. The

recommended items were selected from diverse categories of foods in the shop. Flyers with one of the items printed were bundled with the catalog and posted for the club members over ten weeks. The members targeted for recommendation were chosen randomly each week. Members received at most one flyer per week and a flyer recommended only one item. Table 1 summarizes the dataset.

From the purchase records, we created non-purchase records, which are user-item pairs comprising users who use the shop on a certain week and the items that they do not purchase despite their availability in that week's catalog. The shop changes the merchandize assortment weekly. We generated 155,236,964 non-purchase records. Both purchase records and non-purchase records are necessary in order to evaluate the purchase probability of items.

We merged purchase records, non-purchase records, and recommendation records each week. We assumed that the influence of recommendation continued for a week, because the flyers showcased "recommended items of the week" and the merchandize assortment changed each week. Table 2 shows examples of the merged dataset. Recommended items differ depending on the week and the user. For example, Item 1 might be available on Week 1 but not on Week 2. Moreover, the same user can repeatedly buy the same item; in this example, User 1 buys Item 2 on both Week 1 and Week 2.

Table 1. Summary of the dataset.

Type	#records	#users	#items	#weeks
Purchase	3,743,300	6,937	4,150	39
Recommend	30,174	6,897	36	10

Table 2. Sampling examples of the merged dataset.

User ID	Item ID	Week ID	Purchase?	Recommend?
1	1	1	True	True
1	2	1	True	False
2	1	1	True	False
2	2	1	False	True
1	2	2	True	True
1	3	2	False	False

3.3 Preliminary Experiment
We first learned the components of the rating, $b_c, b_u, b_i, \theta_u, \varphi_i$, from data without recommendations (Recommend? = False), so as to minimize the NLL. We reserved 10 % of the data for validation and tuned hyper-parameters such as the learning rate and regularization coefficient with the validation data. We adjusted the matrix dimensions from 10 to 1000, and the improvement of the NLL saturated at 300 dimensions. Hence, we set the matrix dimensions to 300.

We next investigated the relationship between the predicted purchase probability without recommendations and the observed purchase probability with recommendations. For all user-item pairs in the recommendation logs (Recommend? = True), we

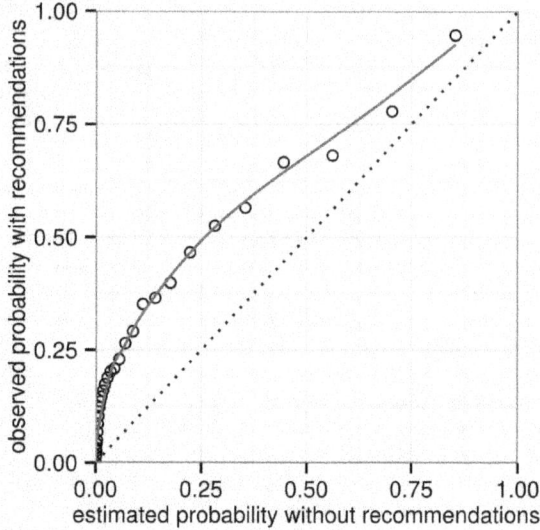

Figure 1. Purchase probabilities with and without recommendations.

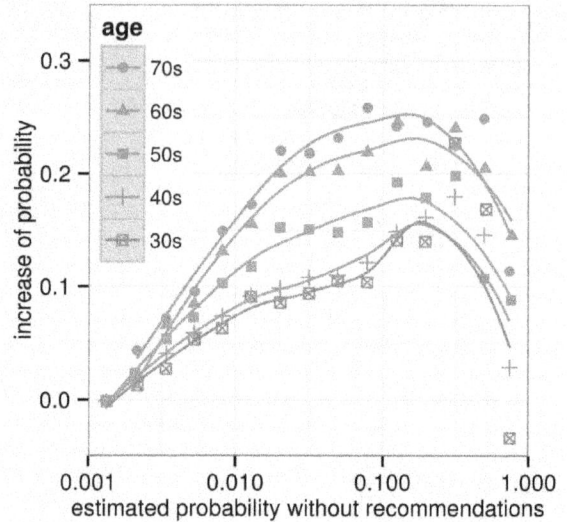

Figure 2. Increase in purchase probability from recommendations for various ages. The x-axis is a log scale.

calculated the purchase probability without including the recommendation responsiveness γ. Then, we clustered user-item pairs according to the similarity of the probability. We averaged the estimated probability for each cluster. Finally, we calculated the observed purchase probability with recommendations for each cluster, which is defined as:

$$\frac{the\ number\ of\ purchases\ in\ a\ cluster}{the\ size\ of\ the\ cluster}. \quad (13)$$

Figure 1 shows the results. The x-axis and the y-axis represent the estimated purchase probability without recommendations and the observed probability with recommendations, respectively. If recommendations do not influence purchase probability, both the probabilities should be the same, i.e., y = x, as represented by the dotted line in Figure 1. The solid line represents the moving average. Here, the solid line is above the dotted line, meaning that recommendations boost the purchase probability. While the probability without recommendations is merely an estimate, we confirmed that the prediction is fairly accurate (the average NLL, defined later in Equation (15), was 0.032 for data without recommendations). In addition, we can assume that the prediction error is unbiased, and averaging within the clusters should decrease the error.

We compared the increase in purchase probability among users of different ages. While personality information regarding the users was unavailable to us, it is known that some personality traits are correlated with age. For example, age has positive correlations with agreeableness and conscientiousness, and negative correlations with neuroticism, extraversion, and openness [15]. Conscientious people might notice recommendations more often than others, and agreeable people might accept recommendations relatively easily. Hence, we expected that the effect of recommendations might depend on age. We split the cluster of user-item pairs according to age, by grouping users in their 30s, 40s, 50s, 60s, and 70s. Figure 2 illustrates the difference in the probability increase. Indeed, the increase becomes more significant with advancing age. This result implies that the responsiveness to

recommendations depends on the type of user. This supplies the motivation for personalizing responsiveness.

3.4 Individualized Responsiveness

From the observations in Subsection 3.3, we hypothesized that the responsiveness to recommendations differs for each user and each item. Whether a user accepts a recommendation might depend on his or her personality, e.g., the user's agreeableness. In addition, some items might induce impulse shopping, whereas others might entail more deliberation.

We split recommendation responsiveness γ into a common term γ_c, a user-specific term γ_u, and an item-specific term γ_i:

$$\gamma = \gamma_c + \gamma_u + \gamma_i. \quad (14)$$

These terms can be obtained through SGD using the purchase logs and the non-purchase logs with recommendations (Recommend? = True in Table 2). We expect that this formulation will explain the observed differences in Subsection 3.3.

4. COMPARATIVE EVALUATION

In this section, we evaluate the effect of individualizing recommendation responsiveness. We measured the accuracy of the purchase predictions and the impact of the recommendations. The effectiveness of the model was examined by comparing it with a conventional model, in which responsiveness is constant for all users and items.

4.1 Accuracy Comparison

We compared the accuracy of purchase prediction in terms of NLL and precision. We calculated the NLL for each user-item pair in the testing data and took the average of them.

$$l_{ui}^{ave} = \frac{\sum_{purchase} l_{ui}^{purchase} + \sum_{non\text{-}purchase} l_{ui}^{non\text{-}purchase}}{(the\ number\ of\ the\ test\ data)}. \quad (15)$$

The precision was calculated for user-item pairs from the top n % in purchase probability:

$$\text{Precision} = \frac{\textit{the number of purchase within top } n\%}{\textit{the number of } u-i \textit{ pairs within top } n\%}. \quad (16)$$

In the dataset, 27.1% of all the recommendations were purchased; the baseline for the precision obtained by random recommendation was thus 0.271. We set n = 27.1%, because precision and recall are the same at this threshold, and this facilitates the comparison.

We compared four models: constant responsiveness ($\gamma = \gamma_c$, CR), user-specific responsiveness ($\gamma = \gamma_c + \gamma_u$, USR), item-specific responsiveness ($\gamma = \gamma_c + \gamma_i$, ISR), and user- and item-specific responsiveness ($\gamma = \gamma_c + \gamma_u + \gamma_i$, UISR). After pre-training of the components of the rating, $b_c, b_u, b_i, \theta_u, \varphi_i$, from the data without recommendations (Recommend? = False), γ for each model was trained using data with recommendations (Recommend? = True).

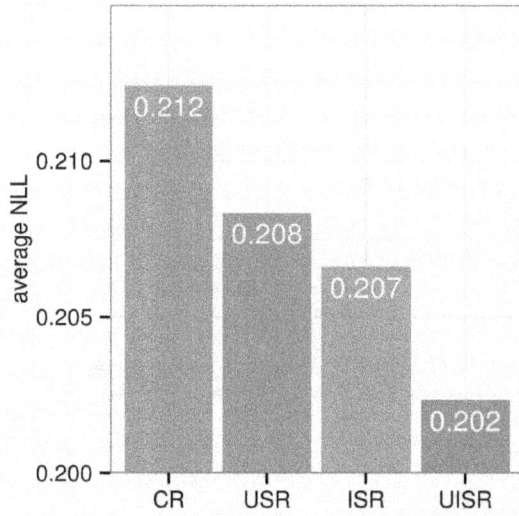

Figure 3. Comparison of the average NLL.

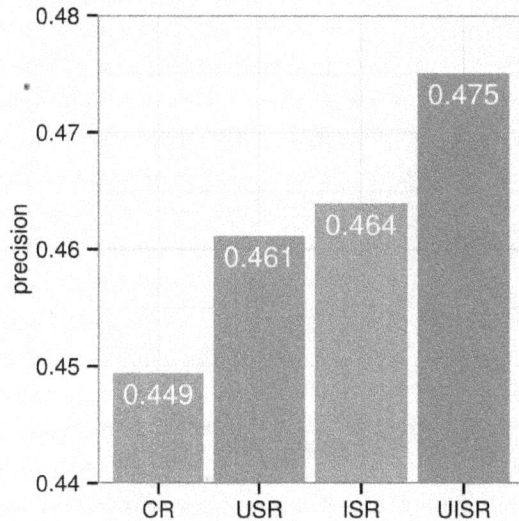

Figure 4. Comparison of precision.

We performed ten-fold cross validation on each model, and calculated the average of the results obtained.

Figure 3 shows a comparison of the mean NLL (l_{ui}^{ave}), and Figure 4 shows a comparison of the precision. UISR clearly outperformed CR with both metrics. Both user- and item-specific terms improved the accuracy and combining them further improved it.

We also confirmed the significance of the results. The paired Wilcoxon signed rank test was performed for CR vs. USR/ISR and USR/ISR vs. UISR in terms of both NLL and precision. All of the differences were significant with p-value = 0.014 for CR vs. USR in precision and p-value < 0.007 for the other comparisons. These results demonstrate the effectiveness of modeling user- and item-specific responsiveness for accurate purchase predictions.

4.2 Impact Maximization

We next evaluated the recommendation impact, which is defined as the increase in purchase probability through recommendations. We believe this is an important evaluation metric, despite the fact that it is uncommon in the field of recommendation research.

Traditional recommender systems are designed to predict whether a user will purchase an item, regardless of whether it is recommended. They then recommend the item with the highest purchase probability. These systems adopt the tacit assumption that there is a positive correlation between the increase in purchase probability from recommendations and the purchase probability without recommendations:

$$(p(\delta_{\text{rec}} = 1) - p(\delta_{\text{rec}} = 0)) \propto p(\delta_{\text{rec}} = 0). \quad (17)$$

However, this assumption is not necessarily true. Consider an extreme example where an item is recommended to a user who has already decided to buy the item in spirit; the purchase probability without a recommendation is almost 100% in this case, and there is no space for a recommendation to further increase this probability. This corresponds to $x \simeq 1$ in Figure 1. On the other hand, recommending an item that a user has no intention of buying will not affect the purchase probability either. This corresponds to $x \simeq 0$ in Figure 1. As can be seen in Figures 1 and 2, the increase in purchase probability from recommendations is a convex function of the purchase probability without recommendations. We argue that the convexity is universal in any recommendation domains based on the above observations, whereas peak positions might be domain-dependent. Recommending items that are most likely to be purchased without a recommendation is not an optimum strategy.

Recommender systems can be designed for various objectives [20]; End-users might want to maximize utility surplus, which is defined as item utility minus price [8], and maximizing profit is a major concern for retailers [2]. Maximizing recommendation impact can be seen as another form of maximizing the utility surplus or the profit. However, our definition of recommendation impact aims to evaluate the net influence of recommendations.

In order to calculate the recommendation impact, the purchase probability is needed both with and without recommendations. Although we cannot know their exact values, our model is capable of estimating them. Their difference yields the impact of each recommendation. Summing this impact is equivalent to the expected value of the increase in sales volume through recommendations. Hence, maximizing impact leads directly to profit maximization when commercial goods are recommended for purchase.

We compared the recommendation impacts obtained with two strategies: 1) the strategy used by traditional systems that recommend items that have the highest purchase probability without recommendations (HP); and 2) recommending items that will result in the largest increase in probability through recommendations (LI). For the latter strategy, we tested four models introduced in Subsection 4.2: the CR, USR, ISR, and UISR models (LI-CR, LI-USR, LI-ISR, and LI-UISR, respectively). We acquired recommendation logs for 6897 users and 36 items, and there are 248,292 possible user-item pairs. We selected the best m pairs (the highest probability for Strategy 1 and the largest increase for Strategy 2) from the possible combination, and calculated the average impact. We set $m = 3017$, which is the average number of recommendations per week in our dataset. We used the UISR model to estimate the impacts, because it is the most accurate.

The results are presented in Figure 5. LI-CR outperformed HP, proving that maximizing the increase in probability is a superior strategy. Furthermore, LI-UISR had more of an impact than LI-CR. Both LI-USR and LI-ISR surpassed LI-CR, meaning that both user- and item-specific responsiveness contribute for improvement. This result demonstrates the importance of individualized responsiveness for maximizing recommendation impact.

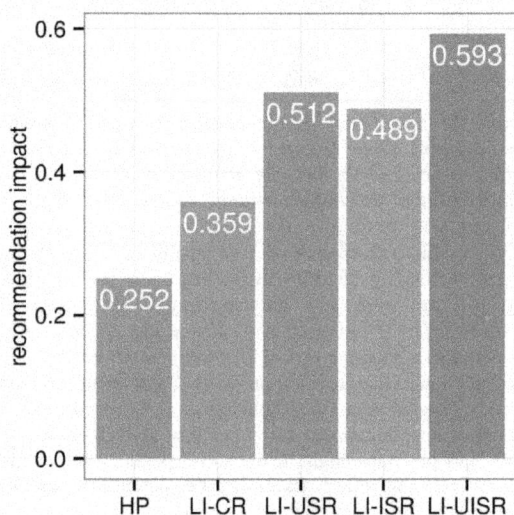

Figure 5. Comparison of recommendation impacts.

5. RESPONSIVENESS ESTIMATION

In order to clarify the characteristics of responsiveness and enable estimations of it despite insufficient recommendation logs, we investigated the correlation between responsiveness and other user and item attributes. This investigation is described in Subsection 5.1. We also evaluated the prediction accuracy of responsiveness from the correlated attributes, the results for which are described in Subsection 5.2.

5.1 Correlation Analysis

Understanding the correlation between recommendation responsiveness and user and item attributes can lead to reveal the origin of personal differences in recommendation responsiveness.

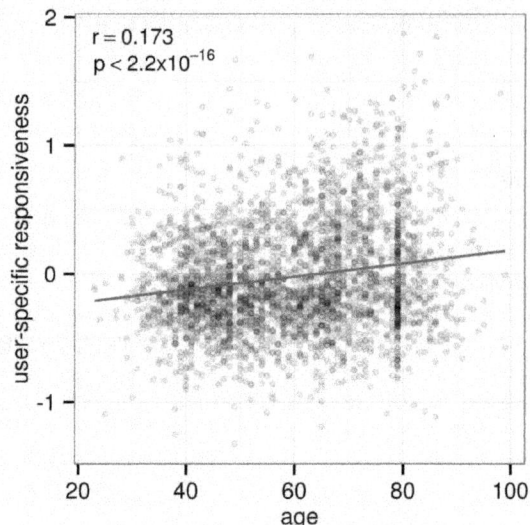

Figure 6. Correlation between user-specific responsiveness (γ_u) and age (η_{age}).

We analyzed the demographic information of users and features derived from purchase records.

The demographic features available comprised age and family size. Among these features, only age was correlated significantly with user-specific recommendation responsiveness, as shown in Figure 6. The line shows a linear regression. A positive correlation was found, meaning that elderly people are more easily persuaded to buy an item. It is known that age is positively correlated with agreeableness and conscientiousness [15], and this result might originate from the positive correlations of user-specific responsiveness to agreeableness and conscientiousness.

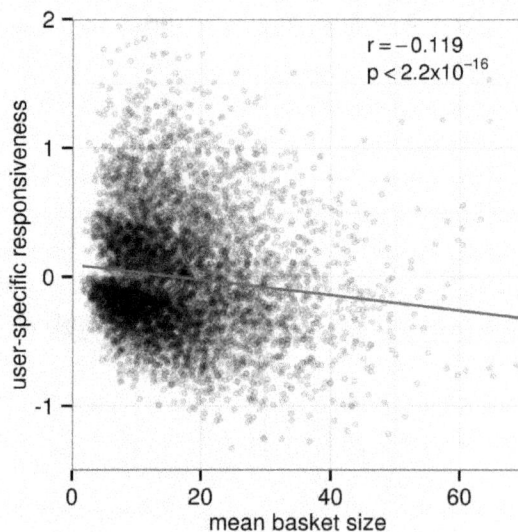

Figure 7. Correlation between user-specific responsiveness (γ_u) and the mean basket size (η_{bas}).

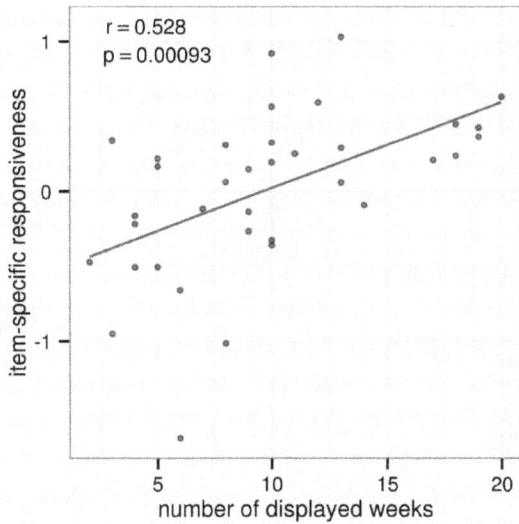

Figure 8. Correlation between item-specific responsiveness (γ_i) and the number of weeks items were displayed (η_{fam}).

Some users buy many items at once, while others buy a few at a time. We define the mean basket size of each user as the average number of items purchased at one time. The mean basket size was negatively correlated with recommendation responsiveness, as shown in Figure 7. This result suggests that bulk buyers tend to be indifferent to recommendations.

Regarding item-specific responsiveness, we examined the relationship between the number of weeks an item was displayed (η_{fam}) and the number of purchases per week (η_{pop}). We found that item-specific responsiveness increases the more time an item is displayed (see Figure 8) and decreases with the number of weekly purchases (see Figure 9). The number of weeks an item is

displayed is related to its familiarity to the user, and the number of weekly purchases tracks the popularity of the item. Hence these results suggest that familiar yet unpopular items are good candidates for recommendations.

5.2 Estimating Individual Responsiveness

Predicting user- and item-specific recommendation responsiveness is important when the recommendation logs are insufficient. Retail shops often keep purchase logs, but they rarely keep recommendation logs. Even when recommendation logs are properly recorded, we do not know the responsiveness when we first making recommendations to a user or when recommending a particular item for the first time.

The situation above resembles a situation, in which purchase logs of new users or new items are insufficient for extracting preferences. This problem is known as a cold-start problem in recommender systems [1, 21]. In our case, purchase logs are abundant, but recommendation logs are inadequate. This is a new form of the cold-start problem with our model.

In order to overcome the cold-start problem, we estimate the responsiveness from other sources. We built a linear regression model to predict individual responsiveness. Owing to the correlation analysis conducted in Subsection 5.1, effective predictors are already known. Thus, user-specific responsiveness can be predicted merely from the age and the mean basket size:

$$\gamma_u = a_1 \cdot \eta_{\text{age}} + a_2 \cdot \eta_{\text{bas}} + a_3, \qquad (18)$$

and item-specific responsiveness can be predicted from the familiarity and the popularity:

$$\gamma_i = b_1 \cdot \eta_{\text{fam}} + b_2 \cdot \eta_{\text{pop}} + b_3. \qquad (19)$$

The coefficients obtained were, $a_1 = 0.0052$, $a_2 = -0.0080$, $b_1 = 0.0047$, and $b_2 = -0.00055$. We confirmed that all of the coefficients are statistically significant ($p < 0.01$).

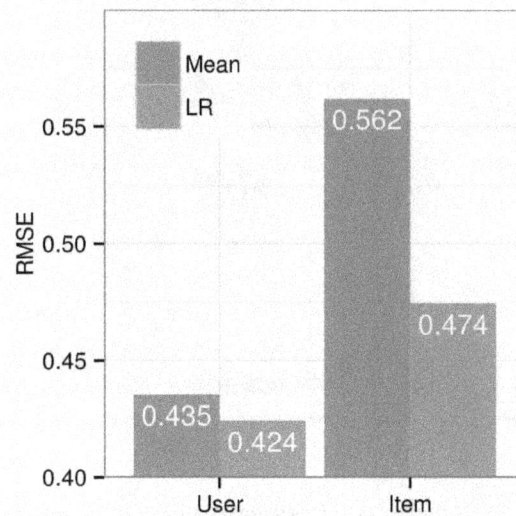

Figure 9. Correlation between item-specific responsiveness (γ_i) and the number of purchases per week (η_{pop}).

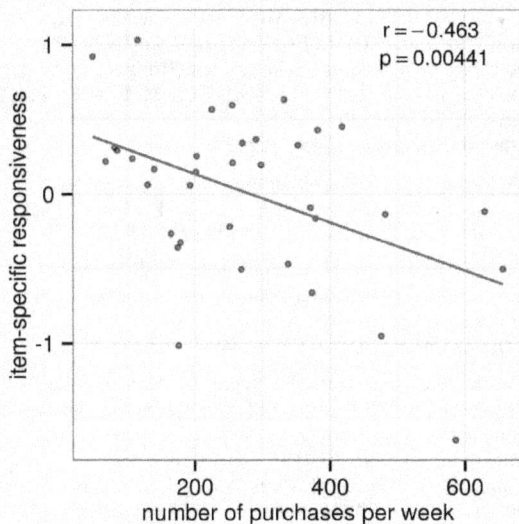

Figure 10. Predictive performance of user- and item-specific responsiveness: comparing mean estimates with linear regression estimates.

265

We evaluated the predictive performance with twelve-fold cross validation. We chose twelve-fold instead of ten-fold cross validation, because there are 36 items with item-specific responsiveness and 36 is divisible by 12. Figure 10 shows the root mean square errors (RMSEs) from predicting user-specific responsiveness ("User" in the figure) and item-specific responsiveness ("Item" in the figure). The accuracy of the linear regression model (LR) was compared to the accuracy of the mean estimate (Mean). The linear regression outperformed the mean estimate when predicting both user- and item-specific responsiveness. Indeed, item-specific responsiveness improved relatively more than user-specific responsiveness. However, both results were statistically significant (the p-value from the paired Wilcoxon signed rank tests was 2.6×10^{-6} for user-specific responsiveness and 0.047 for item-specific responsiveness). The individual responsiveness can be estimated at some level merely from the demographic information and purchase logs.

Finally, we evaluated the recommendation impact obtained from the estimated responsiveness. We used the user- and item-specific responsiveness estimated from Equations (18) and (19) for the UISR model (UISR-E), and recommended an item with the largest increase in purchase probability for each user (Strategy 2 in Subsection 4.2, LI). Figure 11 shows the comparison of the impact among LI-CR, LI-UISR, and LI-UISR-E. Note that the results for the LI-CR and LI-UISR models are the same as the results in Figure 5. They are again provided in order to facilitate the comparison. LI-UISR-E exceeded LI-CR with the statistical significance ($p < 2.2 \times 10^{-16}$ by the Wilcoxon signed rank test). LI-UISR was superior to LI-UISR-E, and learning responsiveness directly from recommendation logs is desirable, where available. However, LI-UISR-E closely aligned with LI-UISR. This result shows the potential applicability of our model, despite inadequate recommendation logs.

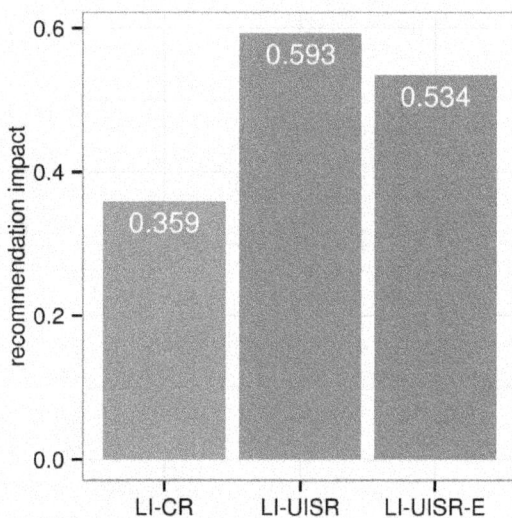

Figure 11. Comparison of recommendation impacts among the constant responsiveness model (LI-CR), the user- and item-specific responsiveness model estimated from recommendation logs (LI-UISR), and the model estimated from the correlated attributes (LI-UISR-E).

6. CONCLUSION

In this paper, we proposed a purchase prediction model that incorporates individual differences in recommendation responsiveness. Our model improved the accuracy of purchase prediction and the impact of recommendations. These results confirmed the importance of modeling individualized responsiveness. We found a correlation between user-specific responsiveness and both age and the mean basket size. We also found a correlation between item-specific responsiveness and both familiarity and popularity. The estimated responsiveness from the correlated attributes outperformed the mean estimates. We further confirmed that the recommendation impact of the user- and item-specific responsiveness model estimated from the correlated attributes exceeds the impact of the constant-responsiveness model. These findings demonstrate the applicability of our model, even when there are insufficient recommendation logs. This work offers a new research direction in personalizing recommender systems based on recommendation responsiveness.

In future work, we shall compare our impact-maximization approach with other approaches, such as diversity- and novelty-seeking approaches. This comparison would be helpful for uncovering the best recommendation tactics. Whereas we applied a sigmoid function to convert ratings into purchase probabilities, other methods are available, such as Poisson distribution [7]. We plan to evaluate these methods. This research was based on the analysis of purchases and recommendations in grocery shopping. Therefore, investigating the effectiveness of individualized responsiveness in other domains remains for future work. Finally, recommendation responsiveness might relate closely to personality, and investigating this relationship can lead to a better understanding of why users are affected by recommendations.

7. REFERENCES

[1] Adomavicius, G. and Tuzhilin, A. 2005. Toward the next generation of recommender systems: a survey of the state-of-the-art and possible extensions. *IEEE T. Knowl. Data En.* 17, 6 (June 2005), 734-749. DOI= http://dx.doi.org/10.1109/TKDE.2005.99.

[2] Azaria, A., Hassidim, A., Kraus, S., Eshkol, A., Weintraub, O., and Netanely, I. 2013. Movie recommender system for profit maximization. In *Proceedings of the 7th ACM conference on Recommender systems* (Hong Kong, China, October 12 – 16, 2013). RecSys '13. ACM, New York, NY, USA, 121-128. DOI= http://dx.doi.org/10.1145/2507157.2507162.

[3] Bodapati, A. V. 2008. Recommendation systems with purchase data. *J. Marketing Res.* 45(1) (February 2008), 77-93. DOI= http://dx.doi.org/10.1509/jmkr.45.1.77.

[4] Castells, P., Hurley, N. J., and Vargas, S. 2015. Novelty and diversity in recommender systems. In *Recommender Systems Handbook.* Springer US, 881-918. DOI= http://dx.doi.org/10.1007/978-1-4899-7637-6_26.

[5] Cremonesi, P., Garzotto, F., Negro, S., Papadopoulos, A. V., and Turrin, R. 2011. Looking for "good" recommendations: a comparative evaluation of recommender systems. In *Proceedings of the13th IFIP TC13 Conference on Human-Computer Interaction* (Lisbon, Portugal, September 05 – 09, 2011). INTERACT '11. Springer Berlin Heidelberg. 152-168. DOI= http://dx.doi.org/10.1007/978-3-642-23765-2_11.

[6] Di Noia, T., Ostuni, V. C., Rosati, J., Tomeo, P., and Di Sciascio, E. 2014. An analysis of users' propensity toward

diversity in recommendations. In *Proceedings of the 8th ACM Conference on Recommender Systems* (Silicon Valley, California, USA, October 06 - 10, 2014). RecSys '14. ACM, New York, NY, USA, 285-288. DOI= http://dx.doi.org/10.1145/2645710.2645774.

[7] Gopalan, P., Hofman, J. M., and Blei, D. M. Scalable recommendation with hierarchical Poisson factorization. 2015. In *Proceedings of the 31st Conference on Uncertainty in Artificial Intelligence* (Amsterdam, Netherlands, July 12 – 16, 2015). UAI '15. AUAI Press.

[8] Gu, W., Dong, S., and Zeng, Z. 2014. Increasing recommended effectiveness with Markov chains and purchase intervals. *Neural Comput. Appl.* 25(5) (October 2014), 1153-1162. DOI= http://dx.doi.org/10.1007/s00521-014-1599-8.

[9] Hu, Y., Koren, Y., and Volinsky, C. 2008. Collaborative filtering for implicit feedback datasets. In *Proceedings of the 8th IEEE International Conference on Data Mining* (Pisa, Italy, December 15 - 19, 2008). ICDM '08. IEEE Computer Society, Washington, DC, USA, 263-272. DOI= http://dx.doi.org/10.1109/ICDM.2008.22.

[10] Jiang, Y., Shang, J., Liu, Y., and May, J. 2015. Redesigning promotion strategy for e-commerce competitiveness through pricing and recommendation. *Int. J. Prod. Econ.* 167 (September 2015), 257-270.

[11] Johnson, C. C. 2014. Logistic matrix factorization for implicit feedback data. In *Proceedings of NIPS 2014 Workshop on Distributed Machine Learning and Matrix Computations*.

[12] Kapoor, K., Kumar, V., Terveen, L., Konstan, J. A., and Schrater, P. 2015. "I like to explore sometimes": adapting to dynamic user novelty preferences. In *Proceedings of the 9th ACM Conference on Recommender Systems* (Vienna, Austria, September 16 – 20, 2015). RecSys '15. ACM, New York, NY, USA, 19-26. DOI= http://dx.doi.org/10.1145/2792838.2800172.

[13] Koren, Y., Bell, R., and Volinsky, C. 2009. Matrix factorization techniques for recommender systems. *Computer* 42, 8 (August 2009), 30-37. DOI= http://dx.doi.org/10.1109/MC.2009.263.

[14] Lawrence, R. D., Almasi, G. S., Kotlyar, V., Viveros, M., and Duri, S. S. 2001. Personalization of supermarket product recommendations. *Data Min. Knowl. Discov.* 5, 1-2 (January 2001), 11-32. DOI= http://dx.doi.org/10.1023/A:1009835726774.

[15] McCrae, R. R., Costa, P. T., de Lima, M. P., Simões, A., Ostendorf, F., Angleitner, A., Marušić, I., Bratko, D., Caprara, G. V., Barbaranelli, C., Chae, J. H., and Piedmont, R. L. 1999. Age differences in personality across the adult life span: parallels in five cultures. *Dev. Psychol.* 35(2) (March 1999) 466-477. DOI= http://dx.doi.org/10.1037/0012-1649.35.2.466.

[16] McNee, S. M., Riedl, J., and Konstan, J. A. 2006. Being accurate is not enough: how accuracy metrics have hurt recommender systems. In *CHI '06 Extended Abstracts on Human Factors in Computing Systems* (Montreal, Quebec, Canada, April 24 – 27, 2006). CHI EA '06. ACM, New York, NY, USA, 1097-1101. DOI= http://dx.doi.org/10.1145/1125451.1125659.

[17] M Dias, M. B., Locher, D., Li, M., El-Deredy, W., and Lisboa, P. J. 2008. The value of personalised recommender systems to e-business: a case study. In *Proceedings of the 2nd ACM Conference on Recommender Systems* (Lausanne, Switzerland, October 23 - 25). RecSys '08. ACM, New York, NY, USA, 291-294. DOI= http://dx.doi.org/10.1145/1454008.1454054.

[18] Pan, R., Zhou, Y., Cao, B., Liu, N. N., Lukose, R., Scholz, M., and Yang, Q. 2008. One-class collaborative filtering. In *Proceedings of the 8th IEEE International Conference on Data Mining* (Pisa, Italy, December 15 - 19, 2008). ICDM '08. IEEE Computer Society, Washington, DC, USA, 502-511. DOI= http://dx.doi.org/10.1109/ICDM.2008.16.

[19] Rafailidis, D. and Nanopoulos, A. 2014. Modeling the dynamics of user preferences in coupled tensor factorization. In *Proceedings of the 8th ACM Conference on Recommender Systems* (Silicon Valley, California, USA, October 06 - 10, 2014). RecSys '14. ACM, New York, NY, USA, 321-324. DOI= http://dx.doi.org/10.1145/2645710.2645758.

[20] Said, A., Tikk, D., Shi, Y., Larson, M., Stumpf, K., and Cremonesi, P. 2012. Recommender systems evaluation: a 3D benchmark. In *Proceedings of RecSys 2012 Workshop on Recommendation Utility Evaluation: Beyond RMSE.* 21-23.

[21] Schein, A. I., Popescul, A., Ungar, L. H., and Pennock, D. M. 2002. Methods and metrics for cold-start recommendations. In *Proceedings of the 25th Annual International ACM SIGIR Conference on Research and Development in Information Retrieval* (Tampere, Finland, August 11 - 15, 2002). SIGIR '02. ACM, New York, NY, USA, 253-260. DOI= http://dx.doi.org/10.1145/564376.564421.

[22] Shani, G., Heckerman, D, and Brafman, R. I. 2005. An MDP-based recommender system. *J. Mach. Learn. Res.* 6 (December 2005), 1265-1295.

[23] Tintarev, N., Dennis, M., and Masthoff, J. 2013. Adapting recommendation diversity to openness to experience: a study of human behaviour. In *Proceedings of the 21th Conference on User Modeling, Adaptation, and Personalization* (Rome, Italy, June 10 - 14, 2013). UMAP '13. Springer Berlin Heidelberg, 190-202. DOI= http://dx.doi.org/ 10.1007/978-3-642-38844-6_16.

[24] Wu, W., Chen, L., and He, L. 2013. Using personality to adjust diversity in recommender systems. In *Proceedings of the 24th ACM Conference on Hypertext and Social Media* (Paris, France, May 1 – 3, 2013). HT '13. ACM, New York, NY, USA, 225-229. DOI= http://dx.doi.org/10.1145/2481492.2481521.

[25] Zhang, F., Zheng, K., Yuan, N. J., Xie, X., Chen, E., and Zhou, X. 2015. A novelty-seeking based dining recommender system. In *Proceedings of the 24th International Conference on World Wide Web* (Florence, Italy, May 18 – 22, 2015). WWW '15. ACM, New York, NY, USA, 1362-1372. DOI= http://dx.doi.org/10.1145/2736277.2741095.

[26] Zhang, W., Wang, J., Chen, B., and Zhao, X. 2013. To personalize or not: a risk management perspective. In *Proceedings of the 7th ACM Conference on Recommender Systems* (Hong Kong, China, October 12 – 16, 2013). RecSys '13. ACM, New York, NY, USA, 229-236. DOI= http://dx.doi.org/10.1145/2507157.2507167.

Recommendations with Optimal Combination of Feature-Based and Item-Based Preferences

Mona Nasery
Politecnico di Milano
Milano, Italy
mona.nasery@polimi.it

Matthias Braunhofer
Free University of
Bozen-Bolzano
Bolzano, Italy
mbraunhofer@unibz.it

Francesco Ricci
Free University of
Bozen-Bolzano
Bolzano, Italy
fricci@unibz.it

ABSTRACT

Many recommender systems rely on item ratings to predict users' preferences and generate recommendations. However, users often express preferences by referring to features of the items, e.g., "I like Tarantino's movies". But, it has been shown that user models based on feature preferences may lead to wrong recommendations. In this paper we cope with this issue and we introduce a novel prediction model that generate better item recommendations, especially in cold-start situations, by exploiting both item-based and feature-based preferences. We also show that it is possible to optimize the combination of the two types of preferences when actively requesting them to users.

Keywords

Preference Model; Recommender Systems; Active Learning; Cold-Start

1. INTRODUCTION

Many recommender systems (RSs) compute recommendations exploiting ratings or likes for items, hence user evaluations for items, not for their specific properties. But with the increased availability of on-line information, a number of researches have tried to leverage information about features of items (e.g., in the movie domain, movie genres, cast, etc.) in order to better estimate users' true interests. Despite the large differences between the proposed approaches, which are discussed in the next section, all of them are item-centric, and only ratings or likes over items do describe the user preferences.

However, it is common for users to search for items by features and to express their preferences for items by commenting their properties/attributes. For instance, a user may argue that she likes a movie because of the actors, and may not be interested in, or like, other features of the considered item. Aiming at understanding the relationships between user preferences expressed over items and on their features, in a previous work [12] we collected a dataset of explicitly formulated preferences, in terms of likes of users for both movie features and movies. We discovered that these two types of preferences often do not align and user models based on these two types of information may lead to different recommendations.

So, if these two types of preferences are conflicting can we still effectively leverage both of them? And, more precisely, can the preferences expressed over item features still be useful to predict which items the user will like? In this paper, we address this issue which is detailed in the following two questions:

- Can preferences over features and over items be beneficially combined in order to generate better recommendations?

- If the system has the option to collect selectively any of them, what is the optimal combination of these two types of preferences?

We tackle the first question by proposing a novel matrix factorization method, which is called FPMF (Feature Preferences MF) that incorporates user feature preferences to predict user likes and we compare it with: a) plain matrix factorization, b) most popular recommendations, which are both based only on item "likes", and c) content based filtering, which is based only on feature "likes". In order to address the second question, we consider a feature like or an item like as one single piece of information that could be asked to a user. Hence, we identify the right assortment of preference types when one, two, three, etc. preferences (likes) are available or can be asked to the user. We evaluated the performance of the proposed model with respect to various metrics (accuracy, novelty and coverage). Our results show that the combined model, based on both item likes and feature preferences, is effective and outperforms the compared models, especially in the new-user situation.

2. RELATED WORK

Many recent research works have tried to build recommender systems by exploiting additional information about users or items, i.e., in addition to the user preferences collected in a rating matrix. In [5] the authors proposed a feature-based recommender for situations when there are not enough ratings to measure the similarity between users or items. Their idea is that users who bought items with specific features also buy items with the same/similar features. Ning and Karypis [14] developed four algorithms that

UMAP '16, July 13-17, 2016, Halifax, NS, Canada
© 2016 ACM. ISBN 978-1-4503-4370-1/16/07...$15.00
DOI: http://dx.doi.org/10.1145/2930238.2930282

incorporate item features for top-N recommender systems and showed that their methods achieve a performance improvement (Hit Rate and Average Reciprocal Hit-Rank) by exploiting side information. Item features information have been also leveraged in latent factor models [8]. Notwithstanding the fact that these approaches do use information about item features to improve the recommender, they differ from our approach as they do not consider signals of user preferences for features, as we do.

Other research works have used user-defined features (e.g., tags) to generate better recommendations. Sen et al. in [17] proposed "Tagommenders", tag-based recommendation algorithms that predict users' ratings for movies based on their inferred tag preferences. Lops et al. in [11] addresses the cold start problem by introducing a tag-based recommender system that combines collaborative filtering with content-based technique. In [3] tags together with ratings data were used in a cross-domain scenario to address the cold start problem. We note that, although tags seems to convey preferences over features, the two are different concepts and tagging an item does not necessarily signal the preference of the user for the attribute denoted by the tag.

On another direction, some researchers have tried to actively elicit user preferences over items [16], or contextual conditions that influence the user preferences [1]. One drawback of eliciting preferences on items is that the user might not know the items that are asked to rate. In this article we show that item and feature preferences can be combined in an optimal mix, thus enabling a new kind of active learning approach so that if the user is not able to reply to the system request to rate an item, she can easily tell the system what features of the proposed item she likes.

3. FEATURE PREFERENCE MF

In order to incorporate known feature preferences of the users in a matrix factorization prediction model, we follow a strategy similar to that used in [2, 9, 4]. Hence, we interpret user u's likes for features as user's attributes and we map them to a set of Boolean attributes $A(u)$ of u. For instance, a user u who likes *action*, and *horror* genre movies as well as movies with actor *sylvester_stallone*, will be considered as possessing the Boolean attributes $A(u) = \{ genre_{action}, genre_{horror}, actor_{sylvester\_stallone} \}$.

Having done that, the resulting set of Boolean attributes $A(u)$ can be taken into account when computing item like predictions by introducing a new additional latent factor vector y_a for each attribute $a \in A(u)$. Accordingly, given a user $u \in U$ and an item $i \in I$, u's like for item i, x_{ui}, is estimated using the following model, which is called Feature Preferences Matrix Factorization (FPMF):

$$\hat{x}_{ui} = (p_u + \sum_{a \in A(u)} y_a)^\top q_i \qquad (1)$$

where p_u, y_a and q_i are f-dimensional latent factor vectors corresponding to user u, attribute a and item i respectively. This model is ideal for cold-start situations as it is capable of computing like (or rating) predictions even if no prior likes for the user are available. In this case the latent factor vector p_u is ignored and predictions are calculated solely on the basis of feature preferences.

In this paper, we deal with a positive-only user feedback dataset (likes), which is a very common situation. To effi-

ciently handle this kind of feedback, we adopt the Alternating Least Squares (ALS) optimization technique proposed by Hu et al. [6] and compute the model parameters by minimizing the following cost function:

$$\min_{p*,q*,y*} \sum_{u,i} c_{ui}(x_{ui} - \hat{x}_{ui})^2 + \lambda(\sum_u ||p_u||^2 + \sum_i ||q_i||^2 + \sum_a ||y_a||^2) \qquad (2)$$

Here, $x_{ui} = 1$ if user u liked item i, and $x_{ui} = 0$ otherwise. $\hat{x}_{ui}$ is the prediction according to the model in Equation 1. The confidence parameter c_{ui} controls how much the model penalizes mistakes in the prediction of x_{ui}, and is set to $c_{ui} = 1 + \alpha x_{ui}$ as proposed in [6]. The constant α models the increase in confidence for observed feedback. Finally, the regularization parameter λ is used to avoid overfitting the training data.

The model parameters p_u, q_i, y_a are found by minimizing the cost function over all user-item training pairs. To this aim, we extend the ALS-based method with an extra step to compute the additional y_a parameters. ALS is based on the observation that when all parameters except one are fixed, Equation 2 becomes a standard least-squares problem that can be readily computed. The first step is computing the user factors, i.e., we fix the item and user attribute factors, and solve the problem analytically for each p_u, by setting the gradient to zero:

$$p_u = (Q^\top C^u Q + \lambda I)^{-1} Q^\top C^u (x(u) - Q \sum_{a \in A(u)} y_a) \qquad (3)$$

where Q is a $|I| \times f$ matrix containing all item factors, C^u is a diagonal $|I| \times |I|$ matrix where $C_{ii}^u = c_{ui}$, and $x(u)$ is a column vector containing all the preferences by u (i.e., the x_{ui} values). Then, we fix the user and user attribute factors, to solve each q_i in a similar fashion:

$$q_i = (Z^\top C^i Z + \lambda I)^{-1} Z^\top C^i x(i) \qquad (4)$$

where Z is a $|U| \times f$ matrix containing the vectors $z_u = p_u + \sum_{a \in A(u)} y_a$, C^i is a diagonal $|U| \times |U|$ matrix where $C_{uu}^i = c_{ui}$, and x_i is a column vector containing all the preferences for i. Finally, we fix the user and item factors, and optimize for each y_a:

$$y_a = (Q^\top \sum_{u \in U(a)} C^u Q + \lambda I)^{-1} \sum_{u \in U(a)} Q^\top C^u (x(u) - Q z_{u \backslash a}) \qquad (5)$$

where $U(a) = \{ u \in U \mid a \in A(u) \}$ is the set of users with attribute a, and $z_{u \backslash a} = p_u + \sum_{b \in A(u), b \neq a} y_b$ is defined as before but excluding user attribute a. It is important to note that differently from the user and item factors, the user attribute factors depend on the state of all the other attribute factors through the $z_{u \backslash a}$ and thus can not be computed in a parallel fashion.

4. EXPERIMENTAL EVALUATION

4.1 Dataset

We tested our research hypothesis and the FPMF prediction model on a dataset that contains both item and feature likes. The PoliMovie dataset was collected through an online

Table 1: Statistics of PoliMovie dataset

Items / Features	Distinct # of items / features liked	Total # of likes
Movies	1962	4208
Genres	421	2439
Actors	492	1333
Directors	358	890
Movie periods	8	684
Production countries	45	409

survey application which was integrated into a crowdsourcing service called "Microworkers", where 420 users provided their preferences on movies and on various features of them [12]. The preferences in this dataset are positive feedback, i.e., we only have likes on movies and features – not dislikes. Table 1 presents some statistics about the likes we acquired in the PoliMovie survey.

In a previous work, we built two types of user profiles: one based on the user's likes for movies and another based on the user's likes for movie features. We compared them, i.e, the features present in the movies liked by a user versus the features she explicitly liked. The closeness of the two profiles was measured by Jaccard similarity. Our results showed that the two profiles often do not match well [12].

4.2 Evaluation Procedure

In order to address whether preferences over features and over items can be beneficially combined to generate better recommendations, we have measured the performance of our FPMF method on user profiles containing an increasing amount of item preferences (i.e., likes). Then, in a second experiment we tried to identify the best combination of feature and item likes given a fixed amount of available (or askable) preferences of both types.

To achieve this, we conducted a user-based 5-fold cross validation, similar to that proposed in [4, 7]. In particular, we first shuffled the set of users in the whole dataset and split it into five (roughly) equally sized subsets. Then, in each cross-validation iteration, we used all the item and feature likes coming from four merged user subsets as training set to build the prediction model. For each user u in the fifth subset, i.e., the test users, we randomly split her item likes into two subsets: (i) a training set, which is initially empty and then incrementally filled with u's item likes to simulate different numbers of item level preferences, and (ii) a testing set, which is used to compute the performance metrics, namely *Mean Average Precision (MAP)* [10], *Average Popularity* [18] and *Spread* [7], which measure ranking accuracy, novelty and coverage of the recommendations respectively. We also measured *Half-Life Utility (HLU)* [15] and *Mean Percentage Ranking (MPR)* [6], but the results were similar to MAP so we do not report them in Section 5.

Then, in order to reply to the second question we built several models, each one using a fixed number of preferences per user, and we varied the combination of the number of item and feature likes. In this way we were able to measure the effect of different combinations of preference types for a given total number of known preferences.

4.3 Baseline Methods for Evaluation

We have compared the performance of FPMF with the following baseline methods:

- *IMF* computes like predictions using the MF model for implicit feedback datasets proposed by Hu et al. [6] and does not use feature likes. It is known that this method struggles to give accurate predictions in cold-start situations, when little or no information about the users' preferred items is available.

- *CBF* is a pure content-based method that completely ignores item likes and recommends items based on how well their features match the user's features that she likes, based on Jaccard similarity. This method can compute item likes predictions also for users with no item likes history at all.

- *Most Popular* is a non-personalized method which always recommends the most popular items, i.e., those items that received the highest number of likes.

We note that the parameter settings for FPMF and IMF were obtained using the Nelder-Mead optimization method [13], and were as follows: for FPMF, α, f and λ were set to 7.35, 40 and 2.95, whereas for IMF, α, f and λ were set to 15.21, 39 and 13.51.

5. EVALUATION RESULTS

5.1 Evaluation of FPMF Model

Here FPMF uses all the available feature preferences, and the goal is to investigate whether it is beneficial to exploit them along with item preferences. By observing the results in Figure 1 one can note that by exploiting all available feature preferences (i.e., director, cast, country, year and genre preferences) FPMF is able to better rank the recommended items compared to the other models. The improvement of MAP@10 with respect to IMF is larger in the severe cold-start situations: when zero or only a few (i.e., up to 4) users' item likes are available. In particular, when zero item preferences are available, it can be seen that FPMF achieved a MAP@10 of 0.029, which is statistically significantly higher than the MAP@10 of 0.020 and 0.002 achieved by CBF (Wilcoxon signed-rank test, $p = 0.03$) and IMF (Wilcoxon signed-rank test, $p = 0.03$), respectively. Most Popular has the same MAP@10 as FPMF when profile size is zero, but similarly to CBF, which is usable only when no users' item preferences are at disposal, they can not compete with both IMF and FPMF as more and more item preferences become available. It is worth stressing that CBF is based on exactly the same preferences that FPMF exploits to improve IMF, but while in FPMF they are useful to improve the performance achieved by IMF, in CBF they do not seem to bring much information. Apparently this is preference data that cannot be used alone.

In addition to the relevance of the recommended items, we also analyzed the coverage and the popularity of the recommendations produced by the different methods. In Figures 2 and 3 we show the average popularity and the spread of the items recommended by the different methods. We can observe that FPMF and IMF recommend items with similar popularity, except for new users with no or only one item preference. In that case, IMF provides recommendations for items that are less popular – possibly too unpopular – to users, compared to FPMF. The same applies to the CBF method, which recommends the same unpopular items regardless of the number of available item preferences.

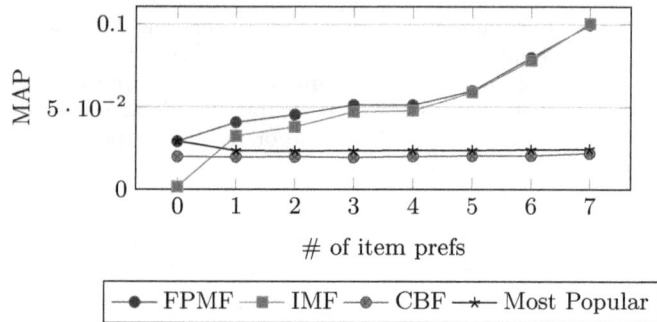

Figure 1: MAP@10 results for different amounts of item preferences/likes

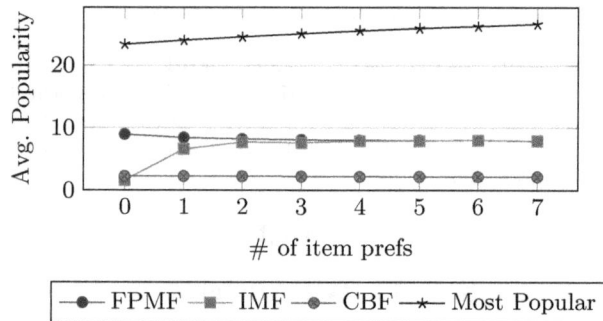

Figure 2: Average Popularity results for different amounts of item preferences/likes

In terms of coverage, the spread of the item distribution is similar among the different methods, except for IMF which recommends the same items over and over to users with zero item preferences.

5.2 Optimal Combination of Item-Based and Feature-Based Preferences

Moving to the second part of our analysis, we considered a feature or item preference as one single piece of information to be asked to the user, and we were interested in finding the best combination of feature-based and item-based preferences. To achieve this, we employed a brute-force feature selection strategy to select the true best combination of information of size k from the given set of N available pieces of information – with k varying from 1 to N. Specifically, for

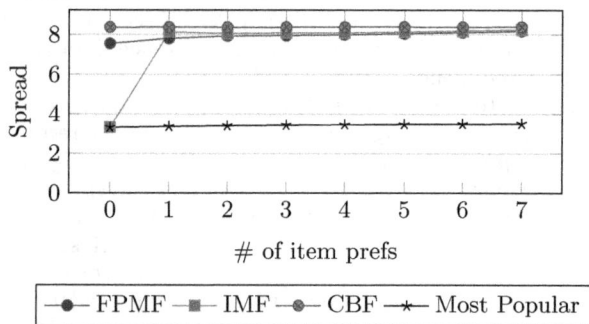

Figure 3: Spread results for different amounts of item preferences/likes

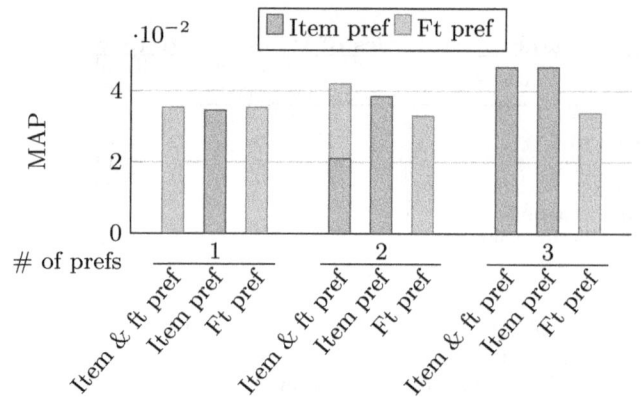

Figure 4: MAP@10 results for different types and amounts of preferences/likes

a given k, we trained FPMF on all possible k-combinations of feature-based and item-based preferences and computed the evaluation metrics on the test set in order to identify the best combination of information.

The results of this analysis are illustrated in Figure 4. It is shown the MAP@10 obtained by FPMF when trained on the best combination of preference information – either feature-based or item-based likes (i.e., "Item & ft pref") – compared to the case when only either item-based likes (i.e., "Item pref") or feature-based likes (i.e., "Ft pref") are used. We note that in the figure the number of preferences (likes) that we considered goes only up to 3 in order to focus on the situations where only a small number of preferences is acquired from the user. In fact, we found that when more than 3 likes can be elicited, the best performance is achieved by considering only item-based preferences.

In conclusion, in the cold start case, in order to achieve the best performance, which type of preferences should be asked to the user must be chosen with care; eliciting only feature preferences can clearly lead to lower MAP@10. Acquiring feature preferences can be useful only when a small number of likes can be requested to the users.

6. CONCLUSIONS AND FUTURE WORK

In this paper, we have presented a model based on both item-based and feature-based preferences (likes) of users, which extends plain MF by incorporating users expressed features preferences to generate better predictions, i.e., better predicting what items the users like. We evaluated the performance of our model in an offline experiment by considering three different metrics: MAP, Average Popularity and Spread. Our main finding is that our model led to more relevant recommendations especially in the severe cold start situation and that can be optimally used in situations where both item-based and feature-based preferences may be available or requested to the user.

As future work, we would like to perform additional experiments on more datasets where both types of preferences are available. Furthermore, we plan to perform an online experiment by conducting a live user study where we could better study the interactions between these two types of preferences and examine the usefulness (performance) of our combined recommendation model.

7. REFERENCES

[1] M. Braunhofer and F. Ricci. Contextual information elicitation in travel recommender systems. In *Information and Communication Technologies in Tourism 2016*, pages 579–592. Springer, 2016.

[2] M. Elahi, M. Braunhofer, F. Ricci, and M. Tkalcic. Personality-based active learning for collaborative filtering recommender systems. In *AI* IA 2013: Advances in Artificial Intelligence*, pages 360–371. Springer, 2013.

[3] M. Enrich, M. Braunhofer, and F. Ricci. Cold-start management with cross-domain collaborative filtering and tags. In *E-Commerce and Web Technologies*, pages 101–112. Springer, 2013.

[4] I. Fernández-Tobías, M. Braunhofer, M. Elahi, F. Ricci, and I. Cantador. Alleviating the new user problem in collaborative filtering by exploiting personality information. *User Modeling and User-Adapted Interaction*, pages 1–35, 2015.

[5] E.-H. S. Han and G. Karypis. Feature-based recommendation system. In *Proceedings of the 14th ACM international conference on Information and knowledge management*, pages 446–452. ACM, 2005.

[6] Y. Hu, Y. Koren, and C. Volinsky. Collaborative filtering for implicit feedback datasets. In *Data Mining, 2008. ICDM'08. Eighth IEEE International Conference on*, pages 263–272. IEEE, 2008.

[7] D. Kluver and J. A. Konstan. Evaluating recommender behavior for new users. In *Proceedings of the 8th ACM Conference on Recommender Systems*, pages 121–128. ACM, 2014.

[8] Y. Koren. Factorization meets the neighborhood: a multifaceted collaborative filtering model. In *Proceedings of the 14th ACM SIGKDD international conference on Knowledge discovery and data mining*, pages 426–434. ACM, 2008.

[9] Y. Koren, R. Bell, and C. Volinsky. Matrix factorization techniques for recommender systems. *Computer*, (8):30–37, 2009.

[10] Y. Li, J. Hu, C. Zhai, and Y. Chen. Improving one-class collaborative filtering by incorporating rich user information. In *Proceedings of the 19th ACM international conference on Information and knowledge management*, pages 959–968. ACM, 2010.

[11] P. Lops, M. De Gemmis, G. Semeraro, C. Musto, and F. Narducci. Content-based and collaborative techniques for tag recommendation: an empirical evaluation. *Journal of Intelligent Information Systems*, 40(1):41–61, 2013.

[12] M. Nasery, M. Elahi, and P. Cremonesi. Polimovie: a feature-based dataset for recommender systems. In *ACM RecSys 2015 CrowdRec Workshop*, 2015.

[13] J. A. Nelder and R. Mead. A simplex method for function minimization. *The computer journal*, 7(4):308–313, 1965.

[14] X. Ning and G. Karypis. Sparse linear methods with side information for top-n recommendations. In *Proceedings of the sixth ACM conference on Recommender systems*, pages 155–162. ACM, 2012.

[15] R. Pan, Y. Zhou, B. Cao, N. N. Liu, R. Lukose, M. Scholz, and Q. Yang. One-class collaborative filtering. In *Data Mining, 2008. ICDM'08. Eighth IEEE International Conference on*, pages 502–511. IEEE, 2008.

[16] N. Rubens, M. Elahi, M. Sugiyama, and D. Kaplan. Active learning in recommender systems. In *Recommender systems handbook*, pages 809–846. Springer, 2015.

[17] S. Sen, J. Vig, and J. Riedl. Tagommenders: connecting users to items through tags. In *Proceedings of the 18th international conference on World Wide Web*, pages 671–680. ACM, 2009.

[18] C.-N. Ziegler, S. M. McNee, J. A. Konstan, and G. Lausen. Improving recommendation lists through topic diversification. In *Proceedings of the 14th international conference on World Wide Web*, pages 22–32. ACM, 2005.

Moodplay: Interactive Mood-based Music Discovery and Recommendation

Ivana Andjelkovic
Media Arts and Technology
University of California, Santa
Barbara
ivana@mat.ucsb.edu

Denis Parra
CS Department
Pontificia Universidad Catolica
de Chile
dparra@ing.puc.cl

John O'Donovan
Dept. of Computer Science
University of California, Santa
Barbara
jod@cs.ucsb.edu

ABSTRACT

A large body of research in recommender systems focuses on optimizing prediction and ranking. However, recent work has highlighted the importance of other aspects of the recommendations, including transparency, control and user experience in general. Building on these aspects, we introduce *MoodPlay*, a hybrid recommender system music which integrates content and mood-based filtering in an interactive interface. We show how *MoodPlay* allows the user to explore a music collection by latent affective dimensions, and we explain how to integrate user input at recommendation time with predictions based on a pre-existing user profile. Results of a user study (N=240) are discussed, with four conditions being evaluated with varying degrees of visualization, interaction and control. Results show that visualization and interaction in a latent space improve acceptance and understanding of both metadata and item recommendations. However, too much of either can result in cognitive overload and a negative impact on user experience.

1. INTRODUCTION

Recommender systems have become invaluable tools for helping users find useful information online. There are well established algorithms, such as Collaborative and Content-Based Filters and Matrix Factorization, used across a variety of domains to recommend digital content or merchandise. Due to its unique consumption characteristics, music falls into a domain where alternative approaches to the traditional recommendation problem can help. For instance, we can listen to the same track several times without decreasing satisfaction. Compared to other domains (e.g. movies), the consumption of music is fast and more context dependent. In this paper, we focus on building an interactive recommender system that suggests music artists based on contextual information. We present interaction mechanisms that allow the user to guide the system based on affective state, which in turn adapts to changes of listening context. There are several music recommender systems that employ different types of context (daily activity [48], time of the day [3], music genre [25], etc.). However, no previous work has integrated affective context for music discovery into a visual and interactive recommendation system. Throughout the paper, we use a broad term *affect* to refer to both mood and emotion. Moods, being more permanent and less intense than emotions, are commonly used in recommendation research as tags to describe music. On the other hand, most psychology models, including the one used in our system, focus on emotions. Experimental evidence shows a strong relation between emotion and music [22] and previous research in affect-based recommender systems produced improvements over their non-contextual alternatives [13, 44]. Furthermore, the importance of building interactive recommender interfaces that go beyond the static ranked list paradigm to improve user satisfaction with a system has been studied in the past [12, 16, 5, 21, 47, 34, 29] and it is supported by results showing that small improvements in accuracy do not always correlate with better user satisfaction [28, 23]. Our goal is to build a recommender system with an interactive interface that supports discovery of unknown, interesting items via interaction in an affective space. We frame our work around the following research questions: How can metadata such as affective information be visually represented for a recommender system? How can interaction, explanation and control be supported over such a visualization? What are the effects of such interactive visualizations on the user experience with a recommender system, and what is the right amount of interaction? In our effort to answer these questions, we have produced the following key contributions:

- **A novel visual interface for recommendation.** A visualization that maps moods and music artists in the same latent space, supporting item exploration and user control.
- **Affect-based recommendation method.** A novel, hybrid recommendation algorithm for affect-based and audio content-based music recommendation.
- **Enhanced interaction techniques.** We introduce several new interaction mechanisms for hybrid recommendation in a latent space. For instance, trail-based and radius-based techniques.
- **Structural model for interaction tasks.** We present an evaluation of the system through an online experiment (N=240). Empirical results show interesting relations between user interaction, trust, and user perception, summarized in a structural model. We propose further research on interface design for exploratory tasks in recommender systems.

2. RELATED WORK

Visual Approaches to Recommendations. MacNee *et al.* [28] and Konstan *et al.* [23], highlight the need for more user-centric research in recommendations, since small improvements in recommender accuracy do not necessarily improve users' satisfaction. However, research on visual and interactive interfaces has started to grow only in recent years. Examples include visualizations of music and work-related online communities – SFViz [15], [52], collaborative filtering recommenders with rich user interactions such

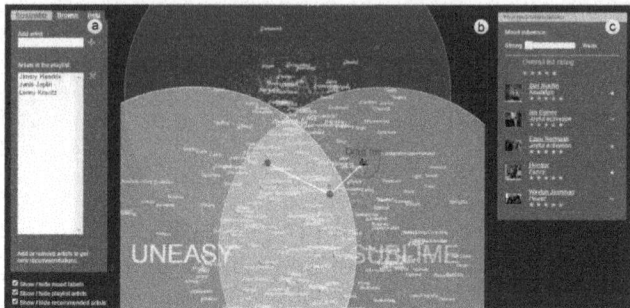

Figure 1: Screenshot of the MoodPlay interface, divided into three sections: (a) pane for entering artist names, (b) latent mood space visualization, (c) recommendation list, along with slider for adjusting mood influence

Category	Sub-category	No. of moods	Example moods
Sublimity	Tenderness	24	Delicate, romantic, sweet
	Peacefulness	22	Pastoral, relaxed, soothing
	Wonder	24	Happy, light, springlike
	Nostalgic	9	Dreamy, rustic, yearning
	Transcendence	10	Atmospheric, spiritual, uplifting
Vitality	Power	29	Ambitious, fierce, pulsing, intense
	Joyful activation	32	Animated, fun, playful, exciting
Unease	Tension	32	Nervous, harsh, rowdy, rebellious
	Sadness	18	Austere, bittersweet, gloomy, tragic
	Fear *	10	Spooky, nihilistic, ominous
	Lethargy *	8	Languid, druggy, hypnotic
	Repulsiveness *	10	Greasy, sleazy, trashy, irreverent
Other *	Stylistic *	19	Graceful, slick, elegant, elaborate
	Cerebral *	12	Detached, street-smart, ironic
	Mechanical *	7	Crunchy, complex, knotty

Table 1: Structure and description of *MoodPlay* mood hierarchy. Categories and sub-categories marked with * are the expansions from the original GEMS model.

as PeerChooser [31] and SmallWorlds [16], and interactive visualizations for recommending conference talks – TalkExplorer [47] and SetFusion [34]. There is also a range of systems that support dynamic critiquing of an algorithm, such as Pu *et al.* [37] and Chen *et al.* [8]. For a detailed review of visual and interactive recommender systems, read Chen *et al.* survey [19]. To the best of our knowledge, *Moodplay* is the first interactive music recommender system that maps the artists in a latent, navigable, affective space.

Affect-based Recommendations. The important role of emotions in human decision-making [36, 30] has made affect an actively studied variable in context-aware recommender systems. For instance, Masthoff *et al.* [26] integrated affective state in a group recommender, while González *et al.* [14] incorporated the emotional context in a recommender for a large e-commerce learning guide. More relevant to our work, Park *et al.* [32] developed a music recommender that uses mood inferred from context information. More recently, Tkalcic *et al.* [45, 17] introduced a framework to identify the stages where emotion can be used for recommendation. *MoodPlay* models the user profile based on a set of artists, represents it in an affective latent space derived from GEMS model [51] and uses it to recommend new artists.

Recommendation of music artists. Recommendations in the music domain include approaches to recommend tracks [7, 24], albums [33], playlists [25, 2, 18] and artists [5, 20]. Particularly relevant to our aim at recommonding artists, Hijikata *et al.* [20] used a Naive Bayes recommender to recommend artists, while Bostandjev *et al.* [5] proposed a hybrid recommender system with a visual interactive interface – TasteWeights. Compared to the previous research in the field, we innovate by using artists' affective representation to compute similarity within a user-controllable recommendation interface.

Affect-based Visualizations of Music Collections. Russell's circumplex model of affect [39], which represents emotions and moods as a mixture of valence and arousal, is the most popular model used in affect-based visualizations. Yang *et al.* [49] incorporated it into their music retrieval method, and commercial applications such as Habu [43] and Musicovery [6] use it as a platform for music selection. However, many emotions cannot be uniquely characterized by valence and arousal values [9] and models derived from general research in psychology may not be suitable for musical emotions [50]. To address this issue, we propose a visual representation of music-specific affective dimensions, employing the hierarchical classification of emotions in the GEMS model by Zentner *et al.* [51].

3. THE MOODPLAY SYSTEM

MoodPlay is accessible via web browser and its user interface consists of three sections: input, visualization and a recommendation panel. Users construct profiles by entering names of artists via an interactive drop-down list (Figure 1a). Based on the mood information associated with profile artists, the system positions a user avatar in a precomputed latent mood space (Figure 1b) and recommends new artists (Figure 1c).

Our interface design follows Shneiderman's visual information seeking mantra [41] by providing an overview, allowing zooming and panning the visualization, allowing filtering based on mood categories and toggling the visibility of details[1]. Recommendations are displayed as a ranked list in the right panel and the corresponding artist nodes are highlighted within the visualization. Upon clicking on names of the recommended artists, users are redirected to Last.fm where they can listen to the recommended music. They can also provide feedback by clicking on the stars below artist names.

Adaptivity of music recommenders is particularly important due to the dynamic nature of the listening context [42]. Thus, we model the change of a user's preference by enabling the movement of the avatar within visualization and maintaining an editable array of trail marks, weighted by distance from the current position (Figure 1.b). Finally, our recommendation approach accounts for the fact that mood-based similarity between artists does not necessarily match audio based similarity. Therefore, we allow users to adjust the mood influence via a slider control (Figure 1c) which dynamically re-sizes a catchment area around the current avatar position. The weaker the mood influence, the more we rely on audio similarity to calculate recommendations, and vice-versa.

3.1 A Visual Model of Affect

In order to show the relation between artists and moods in a two-dimensional space, we collected and analyzed Rovi mood metadata [10] for 4,927 artists. Each artist in our dataset is characterized by between 5-20 weighted moods out of 289, and represented with a vector $X \in \mathbb{R}^{289}$. Correspondence analysis [40] was used to reduce dimensionality to the 2D layout shown in Figure 1.

For the purpose of identifying potential clusters in our mood space, we explored whether our visual map fits into the hierarchical, music-specific emotion model proposed by Zentner *et al.* [51] - GEMS. This model consists of 3 main categories (vitality, uneasiness, sublimity), 9 sub-categories and 45 music relevant emotion

---

[1]Details in public video https://youtu.be/vH9q5ku8ocM

words distributed across different sub-categories. To perform our hierarchical classification of moods, we employed a WordNet [46] similarity tool [35] to calculate similarity scores between 289 Rovi and 45 GEMS mood words. The following steps were taken to reduce the observed classification error rate: (1) we created new mood categories to accommodate moods that do not belong to any of the GEMS categories, (2) 23 of the least frequently used mood tags in Rovi were discarded. Once the moods were classified, three clusters emerged in the 2D mood space. For visual explanation, we color each mood node according to the category it belongs to - vital moods are red, uneasy are green and sublime are blue, and we overlay Venn diagrams over the clusters.

Dataset. MoodPlay relies on a static music dataset of 4,927 artists, partially obtained randomly from Million Songs Dataset [4] and expanded by popular artists from the public EchoNest database [11] using proprietary metrics *familiarity* and *hotttness*. Mood data for each artist was obtained via Rovi API and the top ten most popular songs for each artist along with corresponding audio analysis data were obtained from EchoNest. Finally, artists in the recommendation list are linked to their external profile on Last.fm, where users can listen to artist songs.

3.2 Generating Recommendations

Recommendations are generated by the following three steps:

Offline computation of artist similarity. Artists' pairwise similarity, based on mood and audio content, is calculated offline and stored in two separate data structures. Mood-based similarity between any two artists is a function of their Euclidean distance in the affective space produced by correspondence analysis. To calculate audio-based similarity, we first identify the 10 most popular songs for each artist in our database via the EchoNest API and obtain audio analysis data for the the total of 49,270 songs from the same source. Following the approach by McFee et al. [27], obtained audio analysis data contains timbre, tempo, loudness and key confidence attributes, which are used to represent each song with a vector $v_i \in \mathbb{R}^{515}$. Finally, an accelerated approach for nearest-neighbor retrieval that uses maximum-variance KD-tree data structure was used to compute similarity between songs, since it is has a good balance of accuracy, scale and efficiency.

Online recommendation. During a user session, MoodPlay recommends new artists similar to the artists the user enters into her profile. First, we determine the overall mood by calculating the centroid of profile artist positions as a mean along x and y axes, where we then place the user avatar. Artists found within the adjustable radius around the centroid are all potential candidates for recommendation because they are considered to reflect the latent moods derived from the user's input. Among the candidate artists, we select the ten most similar to the user profile based on precomputed audio similarity data, rank them by distance from user position and display first five as recommended artists.

Trail-based recommendation. In this novel, adaptive recommendation approach, users are allowed to move in the affective space while we keep track of each new position and apply a decay function to the preference trail when recommending new artists. Recommendations from the last position in the trail are assigned the greatest weight, because we presume that the most recent mood area of interest is the most relevant to user. The weights further decrease as a function of hop distance from the end of the trail. At each trail mark, we apply the recommendation algorithm described in the previous sub-sections, which produces an initial set of recommendation candidates. We then calculate adjusted distances d_a between each trail mark and corresponding recommendation candidates in the following way. First, we normalize distances between

Feature	(1)	(2)	(3)	(4)
Profile generation	x	x	x	x
Ordered list of recommendations	x	x	x	x
Display of latent mood space		x	x	x
Navigation in latent mood space			x	x
Hybridization control			x	x
Trail based recommendations				x
Number of subjects	68	60	51	61

Table 2: Availability of different features per experimental condition. Last row in the table shows the number of valid subjects in each condition.

the trail mark and artists because radius can vary among trail marks. If the distances were not normalized, many relevant artists would be falsely considered irrelevant and would not appear in the final recommendation list. Next, we adjust the normalized distances for each trail mark based on the corresponding weights using the formula $d_a = d_n + \Delta \times (|T| - 1i)$, where d_n is a normalized distance, Δ is a decay constant, $|T|$ is a total number of trail marks and i is an iterator over the trail marks. After several tests, we found that weight constant Δ performs the best when calculated as: $\Delta = r_{min}/4$, where r_{min} is the minimal recommendation radius. The larger the value of Δ, the steeper the decay function is. Finally, the recommendation candidates are sorted based on adjusted distances, and top five are recommended to user.

4. EVALUATION

Evaluating recommender systems that contain interactive components is particularly challenging because of complex and potentially diverse interplay between the human participant and the automated algorithm. A crowdsourced study of 397 users was performed to allow for analysis of different interaction patterns with the MoodPlay recommender. After filtering out users we did not deem as valid, i.e., those who incorrectly answered attention check questions, 240 valid sessions remained.

Experimental Conditions. To understand the effects of mood-based interactions with a recommendation algorithm and to independently evaluate the influence of the MoodPlay visualization from an explanatory perspective, four conditions were tested, as shown in Table 2. The conditions have increasing visual and interaction complexity. Conditions (1) and (2) are based on a preexisting user profile while conditions (3) and (4) also allow for user input to the algorithm at recommendation time through interaction with the latent affective visualization. Figure 1 shows the full system, as tested in condition 4.

Participants. MTurk participants were paid a fixed amount of $1.30 per study. Ages ranged from 18 to 65 with an average range of 25-30. 57% were male. When asked about music tastes, 80% said they listen to music frequently. Reported use of streaming services such as Pandora was normally distributed.

Procedure and Rating Collection. Participants accepted the study on MTurk and were redirected to a Qualtrics [38] pre-study with demographic and propensity related questions. Following this, they were randomly assigned a condition and performed the main task. Finally, participants gave qualitative feedback in a post study, also administered through the Qualtrics platform. During the main task, participant were asked to enter at least three profile items from a drop-down list, shown on the left in Figure 1. In all conditions, this profile was used to generate a list of 5 recommendations, that were shown on the right side of the screen. Ratings were collected for 5 items in an initial recommendation list, based on the user profile. Participants were then allowed to interact freely with the system to generate as many intermediate recommendation lists as they wished. For each of these lists, they were required to rate at least the top 2 items. Once satisfied, they again rated the full list of items for the final list. In addition to rating individual items, participants were required to provide an overall list rating for each list that was generated.

5. RESULTS AND DISCUSSION

Now that we have described the study design and setup, we present results in three areas. First, we describe a user interaction analysis, followed by a more holistic system evaluation using a structural equation model.

Limitations. During the study setup, a computational error was made during the indexing of artists and their positioning in the mood space. This resulted in a number of the artists being assigned to incorrect mood meta-data. In particular the error affected 37% of the artists significantly. The consequence of this error was that the first step in the hybrid recommendation phase –prediction of artists with similar mood, contained some noise. However, the second step, which is based on audio content features, was unaffected by the error. Accordingly, we focus our evaluation on user characteristics, interaction with the interface and experience, and place less attention on ratings-based analyses. A follow-up experiment is underway with a corrected model to assess these aspects in detail.

User Interaction. Conditions (1) to (4) in this experiment have increasing visual and interactive complexity. In order to understand the cost of observed differences in rating accuracy or user experience, an analysis of the time spent in the recommendation session was performed for each condition. In conditions (1) and (2), sessions lasted about 6 minutes on average, while in conditions (3) and (4), sessions averaged about 8 minutes. As expected, more time was spent in the interactive conditions (3 and 4). However, an interesting result was that from these two, people spent less time in the trail-based condition. While we do not have a significant result on rating accuracy, we did observe a trend towards higher ratings in condition 3. This will be examined more closely in the followup study.

Cognitive Load. Albers [1] states that learning new system interactions requires additional work and remembering, and users prefer to optimize their cognitive resources. In our study, we observed an effect relating the novel interactive features introduced and user's perception of understanding them. Condition (1) was perceived, as expected, significantly less confusing than the other three conditions ($p < 0.05$ in all 3 cases). Now, with respect to the agreement with the question *The system helped me understand and compare moods of different artists*, we conducted non-parametric Wilcoxon tests and we found that the agreement with the statement is close to significantly larger in condition (2) than in condition (1), $W = 2389$, $p = .019$, α-level= 0.0167 (we tested three hypotheses, so the original $\alpha = .05$ becomes $\frac{\alpha}{3} = .0167$). These results, although not conclusive, are indicative that the *Moodplay* visualization increases user understanding, but additional interactions (avatar, trails, etc.) might promote too much cognitive strain and they should be adjusted.

Structural Model. Since the MoodPlay system combines a recommendation algorithm, an interactive interface and subjective experiences of participants in the experiment, there are many variables that interact with each other. To study these interactions, several structural equation models [21] were tested over the personal characteristics of users from the pre-study; objective system aspects that were controlled in each condition; subjective aspects from the post study questionnaires and observed dependent variables from analysis of the system log data. Figure 2 shows the result of one such model with a reasonable fit to the data ($X^2(240) =$

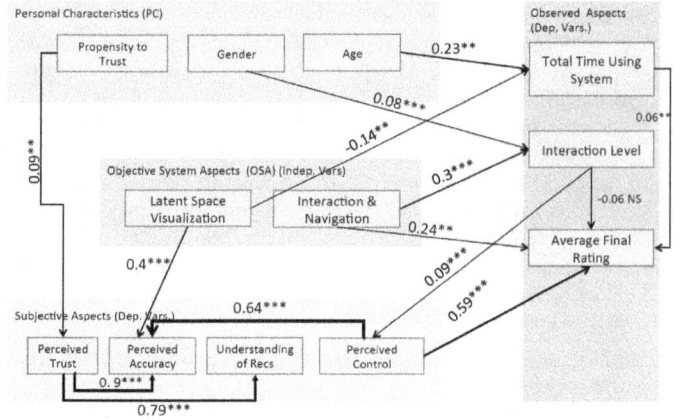

Figure 2: Structural equation model for variables in the experimental data, computed using Onyx. Significance levels are '***' p<.001, '**' p<.01, 'ns' p>.05. All factors in the model have been scaled to have a standard deviation of 1. Arrows are directed and edge values represent β co-efficients of the effect.

$190, p < 0.05$). In this representation, edge thickness highlights the stronger effect sizes and values can be positive or negative, indicating effect direction. Notably, trust (both propensity and perceptive trust) plays an important role in how users perceive and understand recommendations. Visualization of the latent space causes an improvement in perceived accuracy. Gender influences degree of interaction, while participant age was more likely to influence the total time spent in the system, with older people spending more time on their interactions.

6. CONCLUSION & FUTURE WORK

In this work we presented and evaluated *MoodPlay* –a hybrid recommender system for musical artists which introduces a novel latent space visualization based on mood tags. The system supports explanation and control of affective data through an interactive interface, and these data are applied to a user-controlled hybrid recommendation algorithm. Design and implementation of an online experiment (N=240) was presented to evaluate the *MoodPlay* system. Key findings include that participants generally liked exploring moods in the interactive latent space. Our study indicates some relation between level of interaction and cognitive strain. For example, introducing recommendation trails in the system might have produced a drop in several user experience metrics, this observed result opens an avenue for further research. In future work we will explore further the relation among personal characteristics, user perception and interaction with the ratings provided to the recommended suggestions. We will also investigate how different levels of interaction impact performance and cognitive load in information filtering tasks.

7. ACKNOWLEDGEMENTS

The author Denis Parra was supported by CONICYT, project FONDECYT 11150783. This work was partially supported by the U.S. Army Research Laboratory under Cooperative Agreement No. W911NF-09-2-0053; The views and conclusions contained in this document are those of the authors and should not be interpreted as representing the official policies, either expressed or implied, of ARL, NSF, or the U.S. Government. The U.S. Government is authorized to reproduce and distribute reprints for Government purposes notwithstanding any copyright notation here on.

8. REFERENCES

[1] M. J. Albers. Cognitive strain as a factor in effective document design. In *Proceedings of the 15th Annual International Conference on Computer Documentation*, SIGDOC '97, pages 1–6, New York, NY, USA, 1997. ACM.

[2] C. Baccigalupo and E. Plaza. Case-based sequential ordering of songs for playlist recommendation. In *Advances in Case-Based Reasoning*, pages 286–300. Springer, 2006.

[3] L. Baltrunas and X. Amatriain. Towards time-dependant recommendation based on implicit feedback. In *Workshop on context-aware recommender systems (CARSâĂŹ09)*, 2009.

[4] T. Bertin-Mahieux, D. P. Ellis, B. Whitman, and P. Lamere. The million song dataset. In *Proceedings of the 12th International Conference on Music Information Retrieval (ISMIR 2011)*, 2011.

[5] S. Bostandjiev, J. O'Donovan, and T. Höllerer. Tasteweights: a visual interactive hybrid recommender system. In *Proceedings of the sixth ACM conference on Recommender systems*, pages 35–42. ACM, 2012.

[6] V. Castaignet and F. Vavrille. About musicovery. [Online; accessed 10-May-2015].

[7] O. Celma and P. Herrera. A new approach to evaluating novel recommendations. In *Proceedings of the 2008 ACM Conference on Recommender Systems*, RecSys '08, pages 179–186, New York, NY, USA, 2008. ACM.

[8] L. Chen and P. Pu. Interaction design guidelines on critiquing-based recommender systems. *User Modeling and User-Adapted Interaction*, 19(3):167–206, 2009.

[9] G. L. Collier. Beyond valence and activity in the emotional connotations of music. *Psychology of Music*, 35(1):110–131, 2007.

[10] R. Corp. *Rovi API*. http://developer.rovicorp.com/docs.

[11] EchoNest. *EchoNest API*. http://developer.echonest.com/docs/v4.

[12] B. Faltings, P. Pu, M. Torrens, and P. Viappiani. Designing example-critiquing interaction. In *Proceedings of the 9th international conference on Intelligent user interfaces*, pages 22–29. ACM, 2004.

[13] I. Fernández-Tobías, I. Cantador, and L. Plaza. An emotion dimensional model based on social tags: Crossing folksonomies and enhancing recommendations. In *E-Commerce and Web Technologies*, pages 88–100. Springer, 2013.

[14] G. Gonzalez, J. L. De La Rosa, M. Montaner, and S. Delfin. Embedding emotional context in recommender systems. In *Data Engineering Workshop, 2007 IEEE 23rd International Conference on*, pages 845–852. IEEE, 2007.

[15] L. Gou, F. You, J. Guo, L. Wu, and X. L. Zhang. Sfviz: interest-based friends exploration and recommendation in social networks. In *Proceedings of the 2011 Visual Information Communication-International Symposium*, page 15. ACM, 2011.

[16] B. Gretarsson, J. O'Donovan, S. Bostandjiev, C. Hall, and T. Höllerer. Smallworlds: Visualizing social recommendations. In *Computer Graphics Forum*, volume 29, pages 833–842. Wiley Online Library, 2010.

[17] B.-j. Han, S. Rho, S. Jun, and E. Hwang. Music emotion classification and context-based music recommendation. *Multimedia Tools and Applications*, 47(3):433–460, 2010.

[18] N. Hariri, B. Mobasher, and R. Burke. Context-aware music recommendation based on latenttopic sequential patterns. In *Proceedings of the Sixth ACM Conference on Recommender Systems*, RecSys '12, pages 131–138, New York, NY, USA, 2012. ACM.

[19] C. He, D. Parra, and K. Verbert. Interactive recommender systems: a survey of the state of the art and future research challenges and opportunities. *Expert Systems with Applications*, 2016. in press.

[20] Y. Hijikata, Y. Kai, and S. Nishida. The relation between user intervention and user satisfaction for information recommendation. In *Proceedings of the 27th Annual ACM Symposium on Applied Computing*, pages 2002–2007. ACM, 2012.

[21] B. P. Knijnenburg, S. Bostandjiev, J. O'Donovan, and A. Kobsa. Inspectability and control in social recommenders. In *Proceedings of the sixth ACM conference on Recommender systems*, pages 43–50. ACM, 2012.

[22] S. Koelsch. A neuroscientific perspective on music therapy. *Annals of the New York Academy of Sciences*, 1169(1):374–384, 2009.

[23] J. A. Konstan and J. Riedl. Recommender systems: from algorithms to user experience. *User Modeling and User-Adapted Interaction*, 22(1-2):101–123, 2012.

[24] B. Logan. Music recommendation from song sets. In *ISMIR*, 2004.

[25] F. Maillet, D. Eck, G. Desjardins, P. Lamere, et al. Steerable playlist generation by learning song similarity from radio station playlists. In *ISMIR*, pages 345–350, 2009.

[26] J. Masthoff. The pursuit of satisfaction: affective state in group recommender systems. In *User Modeling 2005*, pages 297–306. Springer, 2005.

[27] B. McFee and G. R. G. Lanckriet. Large-scale music similarity search with spatial trees. In A. Klapuri and C. Leider, editors, *ISMIR*, pages 55–60. University of Miami, 2011.

[28] S. M. McNee, J. Riedl, and J. A. Konstan. Being accurate is not enough: how accuracy metrics have hurt recommender systems. In *CHI'06 extended abstracts on Human factors in computing systems*, pages 1097–1101. ACM, 2006.

[29] S. Nagulendra and J. Vassileva. Understanding and controlling the filter bubble through interactive visualization: A user study. In *Proceedings of the 25th ACM Conference on Hypertext and Social Media*, HT '14, pages 107–115, New York, NY, USA, 2014. ACM.

[30] K. Oatley, D. Keltner, and J. M. Jenkins. *Understanding emotions*. Blackwell publishing, 2006.

[31] J. O'Donovan, B. Smyth, B. Gretarsson, S. Bostandjiev, and T. Höllerer. Peerchooser: visual interactive recommendation. In *Proceedings of the SIGCHI Conference on Human Factors in Computing Systems*, pages 1085–1088. ACM, 2008.

[32] H.-S. Park, J.-O. Yoo, and S.-B. Cho. A context-aware music recommendation system using fuzzy bayesian networks with utility theory. In *Fuzzy systems and knowledge discovery*, pages 970–979. Springer, 2006.

[33] D. Parra and X. Amatriain. Walk the talk: Analyzing the relation between implicit and explicit feedback for preference elicitation. In *Proceedings of the 19th International Conference on User Modeling, Adaption, and Personalization*, UMAP'11, pages 255–268, Berlin, Heidelberg, 2011. Springer-Verlag.

[34] D. Parra, P. Brusilovsky, and C. Trattner. See what you want to see: Visual user-driven approach for hybrid recommendation. In *Proceedings of the 19th International Conference on Intelligent User Interfaces*, IUI '14, pages 235–240, New York, NY, USA, 2014. ACM.

[35] T. Pedersen and M. Jason. *WordNet::Similarity*. http://maraca.d.umn.edu/cgi-bin/similarity/similarity.cgi.

[36] R. W. Picard. *Affective computing*. MIT press, 2000.

[37] P. Pu, B. Faltings, L. Chen, J. Zhang, and P. Viappiani. Usability guidelines for product recommenders based on example critiquing research. In F. Ricci, L. Rokach, B. Shapira, and P. B. Kantor, editors, *Recommender Systems Handbook*, pages 511–545. Springer US, 2011.

[38] Qualtrics. *Qualtrics*. https://www.qualtrics.com.

[39] J. Russell. A circumplex model of affect. *Journal of personality and social psychology*, 39(6):1161–1178, 1980.

[40] N. J. Salkind, editor. *Encyclopedia of Research Design*. SAGE Publications, Inc., 0 edition, 2010.

[41] B. Shneiderman. The eyes have it: A task by data type taxonomy for information visualizations. In *Visual Languages, 1996. Proceedings., IEEE Symposium on*, pages 336–343. IEEE, 1996.

[42] S. Stober and A. Nürnberger. Adaptive music retrieval—a state of the art. *Multimedia Tools Appl.*, 65(3):467–494, Aug. 2013.

[43] G. Team. Habu music. [Online; accessed 10-May-2015].

[44] M. Tkalčič, U. Burnik, and A. Košir. Using affective parameters in a content-based recommender system for images. *User Modeling and User-Adapted Interaction*, 20(4):279–311, 2010.

[45] M. Tkalcic, A. Kosir, and J. Tasic. Affective recommender systems: the role of emotions in recommender systems. In *Proc. The RecSys 2011 Workshop on Human Decision Making in Recommender Systems*, pages 9–13. Citeseer, 2011.

[46] P. University. *WordNet*. https://wordnet.princeton.edu.

[47] K. Verbert, D. Parra, P. Brusilovsky, and E. Duval. Visualizing recommendations to support exploration, transparency and controllability. In *Proceedings of the 2013 international conference on Intelligent user interfaces*, IUI '13, pages 351–362, New York, NY, USA, 2013. ACM.

[48] X. Wang, D. Rosenblum, and Y. Wang. Context-aware mobile music recommendation for daily activities. In *Proceedings of the 20th ACM international conference on Multimedia*, pages 99–108. ACM, 2012.

[49] Y.-H. Yang, Y.-C. Lin, H. T. Cheng, and H. H. Chen. Mr. emo: music retrieval in the emotion plane. In A. El-Saddik, S. Vuong, C. Griwodz, A. D. Bimbo, K. S. Candan, and A. Jaimes, editors, *ACM Multimedia*, pages 1003–1004. ACM, 2008.

[50] M. Zentner and T. EEROLA. Self-report measures and models. *Handbook of Music and Emotion: Theory, Research, Applications*, 2011.

[51] M. Zentner, D. Grandjean, and K. R. Scherer. Emotions evoked by the sound of music: Characterization, classification, and measurement. *Emotion*, 8(4):494–521, 2008.

[52] S. Zhao, M. X. Zhou, X. Zhang, Q. Yuan, W. Zheng, and R. Fu. Who is doing what and when: Social map-based recommendation for content-centric social web sites. *ACM Transactions on Intelligent Systems and Technology (TIST)*, 3(1):5, 2011.

Biases in Automated Music Playlist Generation:
A Comparison of Next-Track Recommending Techniques

Dietmar Jannach
TU Dortmund, Germany
dietmar.jannach@
tu-dortmund.de

Iman Kamehkhosh
TU Dortmund, Germany
iman.kamehkhosh@
tu-dortmund.de

Geoffray Bonnin
LORIA, Nancy, France
geoffray.bonnin@
loria.fr

ABSTRACT

Playlist generation is a special form of music recommendation where the problem is to create a sequence of tracks to be played next, given a number of seed tracks. In academia, the evaluation of playlisting techniques is often done by assessing with the help of information retrieval measures if an algorithm is capable of selecting those tracks that also a human would pick next. Such approaches however cannot capture other factors, e.g., the homogeneity of the tracks that can determine the quality perception of playlists. In this work, we report the results of a multi-metric comparison of different academic approaches and a commercial playlisting service. Our results show that all tested techniques generate playlists with certain biases, e.g., towards very popular tracks, and often create playlists continuations that are quite different from those that are created by real users.

Keywords

Music Recommendation; Bias; Evaluation

1. INTRODUCTION

The automated generation of playlists is a central feature of today's music player applications and web platforms like Spotify, Deezer, or iTunes. One specific problem setting in this context often is to generate a list of next tracks to be played (a playlist), given the most recent listening history of a user. This playlist generation or playlist continuation problem can be considered as a special form of music recommendation, for which a number of algorithmic proposals were made in the research literature, see [6] or [15].

The evaluation and comparison of such playlist generation techniques is unfortunately challenging in research settings. User studies are typically expensive as the participants would have to actually listen to a number of tracks. In addition, a number of possible quality criteria – as analyzed in [13] or [22] – generally exist, among them the *homogeneity* or *diversity* of the generated playlists or the *smoothness* of track transitions [4, 17, 24, 25].

UMAP '16, July 13-17, 2016, Halifax, NS, Canada

© 2016 ACM. ISBN 978-1-4503-4370-1/16/07...$15.00

DOI: http://dx.doi.org/10.1145/2930238.2930283

One possible alternative to user studies is to use manually created ("hand-crafted" [5]) playlists as a reference point when assessing the quality of a playlister algorithm. This approach is common in the literature, e.g., [5, 7, 9, 18] to assess the capability of an algorithm of recommending those tracks that were also picked by users for the inclusion in a playlist. One of the typical evaluation methods in this context is to hide one track from a known playlist and let the algorithms predict the hidden track. *Recall* as a performance measure from the field of information retrieval can then be used to quantify the recommendation accuracy [5, 9, 21, 26]. One implicit underlying assumption of such approaches is that the user-created playlists were carefully designed which means that the tracks in the playlists are also appropriate in terms of other quality criteria like homogeneity.

Many algorithms are designed to optimize an *accuracy* criterion like the recall. However, recommendation algorithms can be quite different in terms of which items they actually recommend even when their predictive accuracy is comparable [1, 12]. Some algorithms, for example, are strongly biased to popular items whereas others have a tendency to recommend the same small set of items to everyone.

The long-term goal of our work is to better understand to which extent different playlisting techniques are capable of generating playlists that are similar to human-generated ones. In this work, we report the results of a multi-metric analysis in which we compared the playlist continuations that were generated by different algorithms with the continuations of the users. We use different accuracy, coherence, and diversity measures and assess to which extent some algorithms have biases, e.g., toward popular items. Our analysis includes both academic techniques of different types as well as the commercial playlist generation service provided by The Echo Nest, a subsidiary company of Spotify.

2. A MULTI-DIMENSIONAL COMPARISON

2.1 Experiment Setup

2.1.1 Next-Track Recommendation Algorithms

A variety of playlist generation approaches have been proposed over the last fifteen years that are, e.g., based on content similarity, collaborative filtering, Markov models, discrete optimization, and hybrid techniques [3, 7, 8, 16, 18].

In the experiments reported in this paper, we include two *collaborative filtering* methods that have shown to lead to high accuracy in terms of the recall, a *content-based* technique based on social tags, a *hybrid* method from the recent literature, and a *commercial* playlisting service. The general task of all techniques is to determine the relevance of each *target track* t^* w.r.t. a given playlist beginning or listening history h. The algorithms can be summarized as follows.

(1) Collocated Artists - Greatest Hits (CAGH): CAGH is an artist-based approach that recommends the greatest hits of artists that already appear in the playlist beginning h or are similar to the artists in h. The co-occurrence of artists in the training data is used as a similarity measure [6].

(2) kNN300: This k-Nearest-Neighbor-based method takes the playlist beginning h as an input and looks for other playlists in the training data that contain the same tracks. Different works show that this technique represents a strong baseline [6, 9, 11]. In our experiments, we set $k = 300$.

(3) Content-Based: This technique is based on social tags and ranks the tracks using the cosine similarity of the social tags assigned to the tracks. Like [11], we first compute TF-IDF vectors for each track. Given a recent history h, a tag-based similarity score is then computed as the cosine similarity of the averaged TF-IDF vector of the recent history and the TF-IDF vector of the target track t^*.

(4) kNN300PCPA: An improved version of the most accurate hybrid playlister from [11]. This playlister is based on a weighted combination of a personalized extension of the kNN-based approach with additional suitability scores.

(5) TEN: The commercial playlister of The Echo Nest[1]. Although we cannot know which algorithms are internally used or whether the recommendations are influenced by commercial considerations or constraints, the comparison can be interesting as the recommendations produced by the service result from several years of A/B-testing.

2.1.2 Evaluation Datasets

We used pools of playlist collections from three music platforms. One set was obtained from Last.fm via their public API. One was published by [19] and contains playlists created by music enthusiasts on the Art-of-The-Mix website and one collection was shared with us by 8tracks[2]. All datasets used in the experiments except the non-public one from 8tracks are available online[3].

All datasets have certain distinctive characteristics. For example, Last.fm playlists often contain only tracks of one or very few artists. This is very uncommon for playlists from AotM and forbidden for public playlists from 8tracks where each artist can only appear twice. In order to not introduce any bias, we however did not apply any heuristics-based filtering for any of the datasets to retain only playlists for which we assume that the creators invested some effort.

Table 1 shows the basic dataset statistics. Each user has at least 4 playlists, which allows us to personalize the kNN and the content-based methods used in the hybrid approach. As in [11], we retrieved additional track information (e.g., tempo, release year, social tags) using the public APIs of Last.fm, theechonest.com, and musicbrainz.org. Note that this data is incomplete and only 75% of the data points existed on average across all tracks. For all considered playlists we however ensured that certain minimum levels of the different meta-data fields were available.

---

[1]http://theechonest.com
[2]http://last.fm, http://artofthemix.org, http://8tracks.com
[3]http://ls13-www.cs.tu-dortmund.de/homepage/umap16-music/datasets.zip

Table 1: Dataset Statistics.

Measure	Last.fm	AotM	8tracks
Playlists	2,978	1,040	6,714
Users	451	142	996
Tracks	18,083	11,413	39,875
Artists	3,272	2,770	9,122
Avg. Playlists/User	6.60	7.32	6.74
Avg. Tracks/Playlist	11.68	16.98	12.97
Avg. Artists/Playlist	4.55	12.76	12.06
Avg. Genres/Playlist	16.83	39.18	38.06
Avg. Tags/Playlist	94.88	140.62	123.07

2.1.3 Measurement Method

Since our goal is to compare generated playlist continuations with those made by users, it is insufficient to hide only the last track of each playlist as done in the literature[4]. We therefore propose to split the playlists in the test set into two halves as shown in Figure 1. The *seed* half is first provided as an input to the playlister whose task is to generate a continuation that is as long as the seed half. We then compare the generated continuation with the held-out *test* half, to measure how good an algorithm is able to mimic the behavior of a human. Furthermore, we apply different other measures to assess the quality of the continuations. As usual, we split each playlist dataset into training (75%) and test sets (25%) on a per-user criterion and apply a four-fold cross-validation procedure.

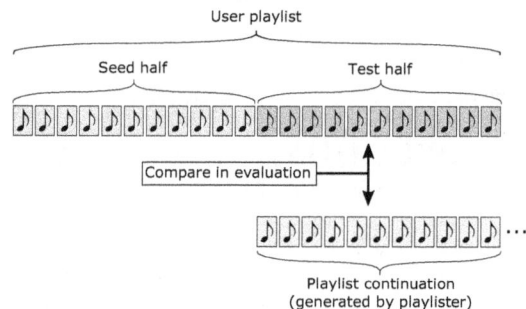

Figure 1: Proposed Evaluation Protocol

2.2 Accuracy Results

We measured four variants of precision and recall. Specifically, we determined if the algorithms recommended (a) the right tracks, (b) the relevant artists, (c) the correct genres, or (d) tracks with suitable tags. Note that we do not measure precision or recall at a predefined, static list length (e.g., precision@n), but include all recommended tracks in the measurement. Remember that the number of recommended tracks that we consider is equal to the number of seed tracks (Fig. 1). The results are shown in Fig. 2.

Tracks. The hybrid method (kNN300PCPA), as its predecessor in [11], outperformed all other techniques in terms of *track* precision and recall. The differences between this algorithms and the other algorithms are all statistically significant at $p < 0.05$ according to a Student's t-test, except for the CAGH playlister on Last.fm and AotM.

---

[4]The last tracks might in addition be non-representative for the playlist as a whole as discussed in [2].

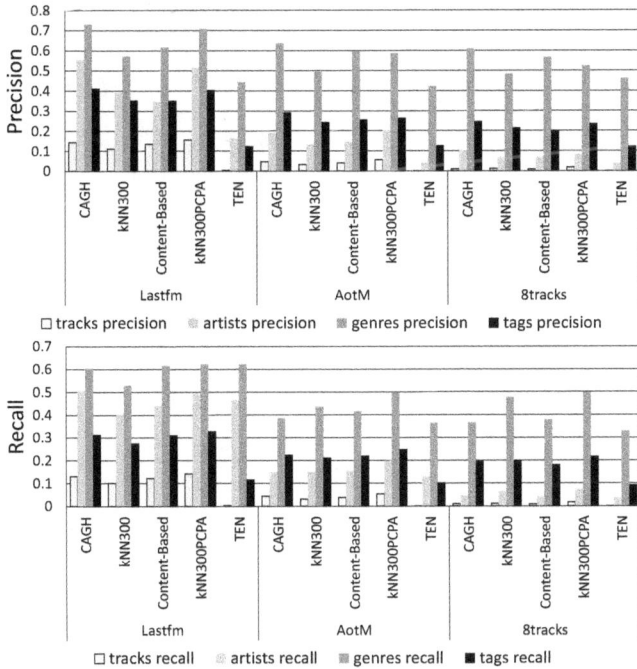

Figure 2: Precision and recall of the playlisters

Artists, Genres, and Tags. Finding exactly the hidden tracks can be challenging as is also indicated by the comparably low absolute precision and recall values. It might therefore be sufficient in practice to play music of similar artists, related genres or to find tracks that are similar in terms of their social tags. In such situations, using the comparably simple CAGH method appears to be sufficient, which for example leads to competitive precision and recall values in terms of artist, genres, and tags. Particularly on the Last.fm dataset, the effectiveness of CAGH is not surprising as these playlists often contain tracks of a few artists. The recall of CAGH on the other datasets is often a bit lower, as CAGH focuses on a too small set of artists, genres, or tags.

The Echo Nest. The commercial playlister consistently leads to the *lowest precision values* ($p < 0.05$). It also has the lowest recall values in 10 out of the 12 cases, although statistically significant differences could not always be found. This can be an indication that the playlists that are generated by the commercial service are not necessarily (exclusively) optimized for precision or recall and that also other criteria govern the track selection process. Although we cannot know the internals of The Echo Nest playlister, the analyses presented in the next sections can give us some hints about inherent biases of the commercial technique, which has assumedly been optimized over time[5].

2.3 Coherence Analysis

So far, we have focused on determining to which extent different algorithms are capable of finding the right tracks, artists, or genres to play. Analyses like [12] however show that algorithms that lead to high precision and recall values often have a popularity bias. However, recommending only

---

[5]As of 2016, The Echo Nest covers more than 35 million tracks. Nonetheless, there might be some tracks in our playlist datasets that are not known to the commercial service and could therefore not be recommended.

popular tracks as a continuation to a playlist that also contains niche tracks might lead to a limited quality perception by users. Likewise, if the user has just listened to a set of tracks with a certain "theme" and all tracks have a similar, e.g., low tempo, playing popular tracks with mixed tempos might be inappropriate.

In this section, we therefore analyze if our playlisters produce continuations that are *coherent* with the playlist beginnings in terms of two selected features, popularity and tempo. In addition, we will compare the generated continuations with those that were created by the users. We will look at the mean as well as at the distribution of the values.

2.3.1 Comparing Averaged Playlist Features

Figure 3 shows the mean tempo and popularity (playcount) values of the seed halves, test halves and generated continuations for each dataset. To make a fair comparison, we only considered those cases in the chart when each playlister could actually create a continuation. In a few cases, some playlisters could not return a playlist, which is why the first two bars (for the seed and test halves) not always have the exact same height.

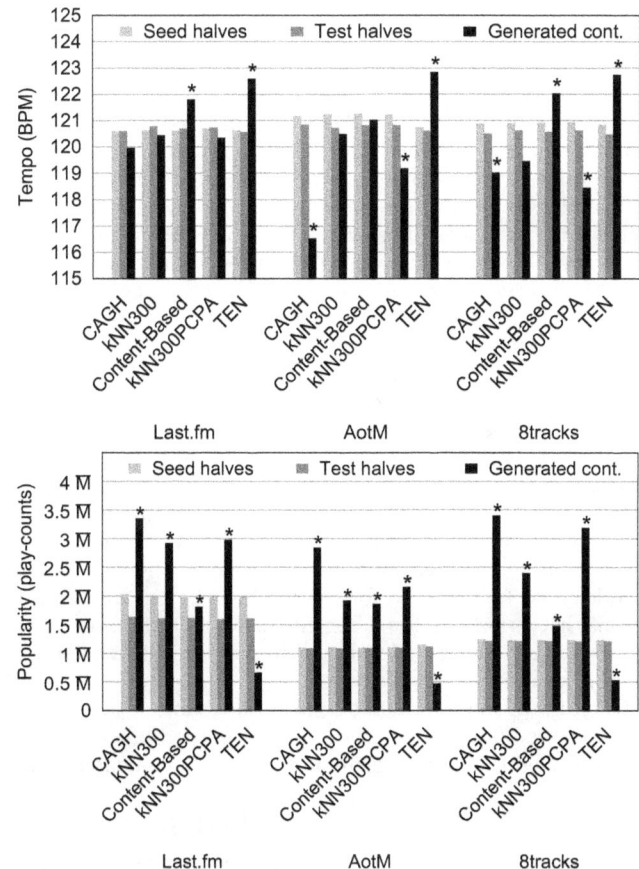

Figure 3: Comparison of average popularity and tempo values (* indicates statistical significance).

Tempo. The upper part of Fig. 3 shows that in general the tempo difference between the two halves in user-created playlists is small, as indicated by the light gray and dark gray bars. Most playlisters are successful in reproducing this behavior of users. Some playlisters (Content-Based

283

and CAGH) seem to have a slight tendency to play slower tracks and the TEN playlister seems to increase the tempo. The maximum average distance is however only 6 beats per minute, which might not be noticed by users. We repeated the measurement for the *year of release*, and found a similar trend that the playlisters could reproduce what users did.

Popularity. All academic playlisters, in particular those with high accuracy, show a strong bias toward popular tracks. For kNN300, kNN300PCPA and CAGH, this can be explained by their co-occurrence based design. The Content-Based playlister might have this bias because more social tags exist for popular tracks.

The Echo Nest, in contrast, exhibits exactly the opposite bias and tends to recommend less popular tracks than the users would have chosen. Overall, no playlister successfully reproduced the general level of popularity preferred by the users. We found similar trends for the *loudness* feature of the tracks which we do not report here due to space limitations.

Discussion. Both in terms of tempo and popularity, users seem to prefer playlist continuations (second halves) that are coherent with the first halves. The evaluated playlisters however can only reproduce this behavior for some features but also often introduce comparably strong biases.

2.3.2 Diversity (Variance) Observations

To assess whether the playlisters are capable of matching the diversity levels of user-created playlists, we determined the average tempo and popularity distance between all pairs of tracks of each playlist (Fig. 4). We report absolute distance values which allows us to interpret the results directly.

Tempo. All playlisters were more or less able to mimic the behavior of the users. The overall tempo diversity (variance) is comparably high and was reproduced by all playlisters. Similar observations were made for the *year of release*, where the variance in general was very low and playlists often only contained tracks from one single decade.

Popularity. Almost all academic playlisters not only focus on more popular tracks as seen in the previous section, the variability in terms of the popularity is also much higher than for the user-created test halves[6]. The only exception is the Content-Based playlister which is comparably successful in maintaining the diversity level preferred by the users.

The Echo Nest playlister, in contrast, tends to reduce the diversity more than users do in their continuations. Similar trends could be observed for the *loudness* of the tracks and all playlisters except the Content-Based method and TEN led to higher diversity levels when compared to the user-created continuations.

Overall, the measurements confirm that some of the playlisters exhibit biases to generate either comparably homogeneous or slightly more diverse next-track recommendations.

3. DISCUSSION AND OUTLOOK

Through the novel measurement method proposed in this paper we could see that automated algorithms sometimes create playlist continuations that are quite different from user-created ones and often exhibit certain, possibly undesired, biases. The results therefore emphasize that considering one single evaluation measure in offline experiments can

---

[6]These observations have to be put in perspective with the overall high diversity values of the seed and test halves. If we refer to Fig. 3, the mean popularity values of these halves range between a play-count of 1 and 2 million.

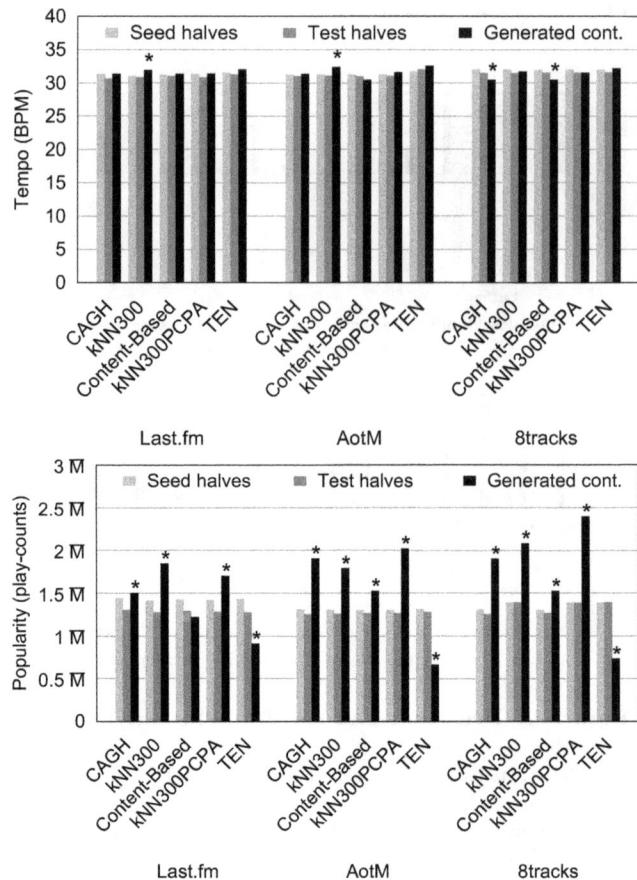

Figure 4: Comparison of Diversity Values in Terms of Tempo and Popularity (play-counts).

be insufficient also in the domain of music recommendation, which calls for multi-metric evaluation approaches as advocated, e.g., in [12] or [23]. Our work furthermore revealed that academic playlisting algorithms often produce recommendations that are largely different from those generated by a commercial service, an aspect which has not been examined in the literature before. Whether these variations can lead to measurable differences in quality perception by the users can only be answered through user studies.

A particularity of the playlist generation problem is that characteristics of the recommendation set *as a whole* (including homogeneity, diversity and track transitions) as well as the transitions between the tracks can determine the quality perception of the users [14]. So far, we have only considered a limited number of musical or meta-data features which we could obtain from public music databases.

The goal of our current work is to acquire and exploit additional information about the tracks, which shall help us better understand the underlying "theme" of a playlist (e.g., based on the lyrics) and to assess to which extent different algorithms are able to continue the playlist in this respect.

The ultimate goal is then to design new algorithmic approaches which are explicitly designed to create playlists that match one or several of the characteristics of the playlist beginnings. Specifically, one goal could be to focus on those characteristics that are particularly relevant for the individual user, as proposed in [10, 11] or [20].

4. REFERENCES

[1] P. Adamopoulos and A. Tuzhilin. On Over-specialization and Concentration Bias of Recommendations: Probabilistic Neighborhood Selection in Collaborative Filtering Systems. In *Proc. RecSys '14*, pages 153–160, 2014.

[2] A. Andric and G. Haus. Automatic Playlist Generation based on Tracking User's Listening Habits. *Multimedia Tools and Applications*, 29(2):127–151, 2006.

[3] J.-J. Aucouturier and F. Pachet. Scaling Up Music Playlist Generation. In *Proc. ICME*, volume 1, pages 105–108, 2002.

[4] W. Balkema and F. van der Heijden. Music Playlist Generation by Assimilating GMMs into SOMs. *Pattern Recognition Letters*, 31(11):1396–1402, 2010.

[5] G. Bonnin and D. Jannach. Evaluating the Quality of Playlists Based on Hand-Crafted Samples. In *Proc. ISMIR*, pages 263–268, 2013.

[6] G. Bonnin and D. Jannach. Automated Generation of Music Playlists: Survey and Experiments. *ACM Comput. Surv.*, 47(2):26:1–26:35, 2014.

[7] S. Chen, J. L. Moore, D. Turnbull, and T. Joachims. Playlist Prediction via Metric Embedding. In *Proc. KDD*, pages 714–722, 2012.

[8] C. Desrosiers and G. Karypis. A Comprehensive Survey of Neighborhood-based Recommendation Methods. In *RSs Handbook*, pages 107–144. Springer US, 2011.

[9] N. Hariri, B. Mobasher, and R. Burke. Context-Aware Music Recommendation Based on Latent Topic Sequential Patterns. In *Proc. RecSys*, pages 131–138, 2012.

[10] T. Jambor and J. Wang. Optimizing Multiple Objectives in Collaborative Filtering. In *Proc. RecSys '10*, pages 55–62, 2010.

[11] D. Jannach, L. Lerche, and I. Kamehkhosh. Beyond "Hitting the Hits": Generating Coherent Music Playlist Continuations with the Right Tracks. In *Proc. RecSys*, pages 187–194, 2015.

[12] D. Jannach, L. Lerche, I. Kamehkhosh, and M. Jugovac. What Recommenders Recommend: An Analysis of Recommendation Biases and Possible Countermeasures. *User Modeling and User-Adapted Interaction*, pages 1–65, 2015.

[13] M. Kamalzadeh, D. Baur, and T. Möller. A Survey on Music Listening and Management Behaviours. In *Proc. ISMIR*, pages 373–378, 2012.

[14] P. Lamere. I've got 10 million songs in my pocket: now what?. In Proc. RecSys 2012, pages 207–208, 2012.

[15] M. Kaminskas and F. Ricci. Contextual Music Information Retrieval and Recommendation: State of the Art and Challenges. *Computer Science Review*, 6(2-3):89–119, 2012.

[16] A. Lehtiniemi and J. Seppänen. Evaluation of Automatic Mobile Playlist Generator. In *Proc. MC*, pages 452–459, 2007.

[17] B. Logan. Content-Based Playlist Generation: Exploratory Experiments. In *Proc. ISMIR*, pages 295–296, 2002.

[18] B. McFee and G. R. G. Lanckriet. The Natural Language of Playlists. In *Proc. ISMIR*, pages 537–542, 2011.

[19] B. McFee and G. R. G. Lanckriet. Hypergraph Models of Playlist Dialects. In *Proc. ISMIR*, pages 343–348, 2012.

[20] J. Oh, S. Park, H. Yu, M. Song, and S. Park. Novel Recommendation Based on Personal Popularity Tendency. In *Proc. ICDM '11*, pages 507–516, 2011.

[21] J. C. Platt, C. J. Burges, S. Swenson, C. Weare, and A. Zheng. Learning a Gaussian Process Prior for Automatically Generating Music Playlists. In *Proc. NIPS*, pages 1425–1432, 2001.

[22] G. Reynolds, D. Barry, T. Burke, and E. Coyle. Interacting With Large Music Collections: Towards the Use of Environmental Metadata. In *Proc. ICME*, pages 989–992, 2008.

[23] A. Said, B. J. Jain, and S. Albayrak. A 3D Approach to Recommender System Evaluation. In *Proc. CSCW '13 Companion Volume*, pages 263–266, 2013.

[24] A. M. Sarroff and M. Casey. Modeling and Predicting Song Adjacencies In Commercial Albums. In *Proc. SMC*, 2012.

[25] M. Slaney and W. White. Measuring Playlist Diversity for Recommendation Systems. In *Proc. AMCMM '06*, pages 77–82, 2006.

[26] L. Xiao, L. Lu, F. Seide, and J. Zhou. Learning a Music Similarity Measure on Automatic Annotations with Application to Playlist Generation. In *Proc. ICASSP*, pages 1885–1888, 2009.

Exploring Music Diversity Needs Across Countries

Bruce Ferwerda
Johannes Kepler University
Altenberger Str. 69
A-4040 Linz, Austria
bruce.ferwerda@jku.at

Andreu Vall
Johannes Kepler University
Altenberger Str. 69
A-4040 Linz, Austria
andreu.vall@jku.at

Marko Tkalcic
Free University of Bolzano
Piazza Domenicani 3
Bolzano, Italy
marko.tkalcic@unibz.it

Markus Schedl
Johannes Kepler University
Altenberger Str. 69
A-4040 Linz, Austria
markus.schedl@jku.at

ABSTRACT

Providing diversity in recommendations has shown to positively influence the user's subjective evaluations such as satisfaction. However, it is often unknown how much diversity a recommendation set needs to consist of. In this work, we explored how music users of Last.fm apply diversity in their listening behavior. We analyzed a dataset with the music listening history of 53,309 Last.fm users capturing their *total* listening events until August 2014. We complemented this dataset with The Echo Nest features and Hofstede's cultural dimensions to explore how music diversity is applied across countries. Between 47 countries, we found distinct relationships between the cultural dimensions and music diversity variables. These results suggest that different country-based diversity measurements should be considered when applied to a recommendation set in order to maximize the user's subjective evaluations. The country-based relationships also provide opportunities for recommender systems to personalize experiences when user data is limited by being able to rely on the user's demographics.

CCS Concepts

•Human-centered computing → User models; •Social and professional topics → Cultural characteristics;

Keywords

Music Recommendations; Diversity; Cultural Differences

1. INTRODUCTION

Providing recommendation diversity to users has become an important feature for recommender systems. Recommending items with high accuracy often result in a set of recommendations that are too similar to each other, and

UMAP '16 July 13-17, 2016, Halifax, NS, Canada

© 2016 Copyright held by the owner/author(s).

ACM ISBN 978-1-4503-4370-1/16/07.

DOI: http://dx.doi.org/10.1145/2930238.2930262

thereby not covering the full spectrum of the user's interest. Giving in on accuracy by introducing diversity can positively influence the user experience, such as user satisfaction [1].

The amount of diversity that should be provided remains a debatable topic. Prior research has identified that individual characteristics (e.g., expertise) play a role in how much diversity is desired by the user [1]. The problem that persist is that often self-report measures are used to identify these influential individual characteristics. Whereas registration and login processes are becoming easier (e.g., single sign-on buttons), asking additional questions may become a bothersome process for (new) users.

The implicit acquisition (i.e., without the use of questionnaires) of individual differences remains challenging. Especially for new users there is not enough behavioral data yet to make inferences. Country information may be a useful alternative as it already consists in a standard user profile and behavior has shown te be culturally embedded. We looked at music listening behavior of Last.fm [1] users from 47 countries and explored how they apply diversity to their playlists. We computed a diversity measure based on the unique listening events (i.e., of artists and genres) of users per country. By using The Echo Nest features we were also able to look at artist characteristics (i.e., how known, familiar, or popular the artists are that have been listened to by users). This provide insights on cultural dependent diversity patterns.

2. RELATED WORK

Recommender systems intend to create a personalized set of items that are most relevant to the user. However, highly relevant items often appear too similar to each other. A set of items showing too much similarities (e.g., highly relevant items) can cause choice overload [9]. In [1] was shown that diversity has a positive effect on the attractiveness of the recommendation set, the difficulty to make a choice, and eventually on the choice satisfaction. Additionally, individual differences were found. E.g., increased expertise has positive effects on perceived item variety and attractiveness.

Besides individual characteristics, research has shown that culture consists of useful cues as well. General behavior and preferences have shown to be rooted and embodied in culture [8]; looking at behavior on a country level may provide useful information for the desired recommendation diversity.

[1] http://www.last.fm

Table 1: Correlation results.

	PDI	IDV	MAS	UAI	LTO	IND
Artist	.279*	-.373**	.155	-.020	-.259*	.080
Genre	.329*	-.265*	.074	-.051	-.108	-.113
Hot.	-.131	-.0.39	-.135	-.359*	-.641**	.557**
Fam.	-.100	-.229	.009	-.255	-.677**	.520**
Disc.	-.367**	-.294*	-.311*	-.366*	-.274*	.517**

Note. *p<.05, **p<.01

3. METHOD

A Last.fm dataset was used with 53,309 users of 47 countries and their *total* listening history until August 2014. [2] The dataset consists of users' listening (i.e., user ID, timestamp, artist name, and track name) and profile information (i.e., gender, age, country). A diversity measure was created by aggregating each user's listening history by artist and genre to identify the unique instances of each respectively. [3] E.g., a history of 90 events originating from two artists/genres means a diversity of two. Each diversity measure was normalized ($r \in [0,1]$) due to the unequal number of users between countries. The dataset was complemented with Hofstede's cultural dimensions (i.e., power distance, individualism, masculinity, uncertainty avoidance, long-term orientation, and indulgence [7]) and The Echo Nest features (i.e., genre, hotness, familiarity, and discovery).

4. RESULTS

Correlation analyses were used to explore the relationship between cultural dimensions and diversity, and report Pearson's correlation ($r \in [-1,1]$) to indicate the relationship.

Table 1 shows the correlation results between the cultural dimensions and listening characteristics. A negative correlation represents the degree of diversity, whereas a positive correlation indicates homogeneity. Positive correlations were found between a culture's power distance and artist ($r=.279$, $p=.043$) and genre ($r=.329$, $p=.027$) diversity. This indicates that users in countries scoring high on this dimension tend to apply less diversity by artist as well as by genre. Negative correlations were found between the individualism dimensions and artist ($r=-.373$, $p=.012$) and genre ($r=-.265$, $p=.048$) diversity, which indicates that users in individualistic countries tend to apply music diversity on an artist as well as genre level. Finally, a negative correlation was found between long-term orientation and artist diversity ($r=-.259$, $p=.048$). Users in countries scoring high on this dimension tend to listen to more diverse artists.

The Echo Nest features allowed us to gain more insights of the diversity characteristics of the artists. A negative correlation indicates that users of a country involve artists that score low on the respective feature of The Echo Nest when scoring high in the correlated cultural dimension (Table 1).
Hotness. Hotness was found to be negatively correlated with uncertainty avoidance ($r=-.359$, $p=.015$) and long-term orientation ($r=-.641$, $p=.000$), while a positive correlation was found with indulgence ($r=.557$, $p=.000$).
Familiarity. Familiarity was found to be negatively correlated with long-term orientation ($r=-.677$, $p=.000$), but

positively correlated with indulgence ($r=.520$, $p=.000$).
Discovery. Discovery showed a negative correlation with five out of six cultural dimensions: power distance ($r=-.367$, $p=.013$), individualism ($r=-.294$, $p=.050$), masculinity ($r=-.311$, $p=.038$), uncertainty avoidance ($r=-.366$, $p=.013$), and long-term orientation ($r=-.274$, $p=.042$). A positive correlation was found with indulgence ($r=.517$, $p=.000$).

5. CONCLUSION & IMPLICATIONS

We show with our results that different diversity patterns exist and that they are related to cultural dimensions. When looking at the relationship between listening characteristics and cultural dimensions, distinct correlations were found.

Approaching diversity on a country level enables the creation of proxy measures for personalization when data is limited . Users' personality has gained interest to make inferences for personalization (e.g., [2, 6, 11]) on an individual level. The interconnectedness of applications and social media may be exploited to implicitly acquire personality (e.g., Facebook [4], Twitter [10], Instagram [3, 5]). However, a social media connection is still needed. Our results could be used to infer diversity needs based on country information, which is often available through the user's account.

6. ACKNOWLEDGMENT

This research is supported by the Austrian Science Fund (FWF): P25655.

7. REFERENCES

[1] D. Bollen, B. P. Knijnenburg, M. C. Willemsen, and M. Graus. Understanding choice overload in recommender systems. In *RecSys*. ACM, 2010.

[2] B. Ferwerda and M. Schedl. Enhancing music recommender systems with personality information and emotional states: A proposal. In *EMPIRE*, 2014.

[3] B. Ferwerda, M. Schedl, and M. Tkalcic. Predicting personality traits with instagram pictures. In *3rd Workshop on EMPIRE*, 2015.

[4] B. Ferwerda, M. Schedl, and M. Tkalcic. Personality traits and the relationship with (non-) disclosure behavior on facebook. *WWW*, 2016.

[5] B. Ferwerda, M. Schedl, and M. Tkalcic. Using instagram picture features to predict users' personality. In *MultiMedia Modeling*, 2016.

[6] B. Ferwerda, E. Yang, M. Schedl, and M. Tkalcic. Personality traits predict music taxonomy preferences. In *CHI'15 Ext. Abstracts*, 2015.

[7] G. Hofstede, G. J. Hofstede, and M. Minkov. *Cultures and organizations: Software of the mind.* 1991.

[8] S. Kitayama and H. Park. Cultural shaping of self, emotion, and well-being: How does it work? *Soc. and Pers. Psych. Compass*, 2007.

[9] B. Scheibehenne, R. Greifeneder, and P. M. Todd. Can there ever be too many options? a meta-analytic review of choice overload. *J. of Cons. Res.*, 2010.

[10] M. Skowron, B. Ferwerda, M. Tkalcic, and M. Schedl. Fusing social media cues: Personality prediction from twitter and instagram. *WWW*, 2016.

[11] M. Tkalcic, B. Ferwerda, D. Hauger, and M. Schedl. Personality Correlates for Digital Concert Program Notes. *UMAP*, pages 1–6, 2015.

---

[2] Available at http://www.cp.jku.at/datasets/LFM-1b/
[3] Genre was obtained through The Echo Nest. To maintain a manageable dataset we do not to focus on a tracks.

An Experimental Study in Cross-Representation Mediation of User Models

Federica Cena
Università degli Studi di Torino
Dipartimento di Informatica
Torino - Italy
federica.cena@unito.it

Cristina Gena
Università degli Studi di Torino
Dipartimento di Informatica
Torino - Italy
cristina.gena@unito.it

Claudia Picardi
Università degli Studi di Torino
Dipartimento di Informatica
Torino - Italy
claudia.picardi@unito.it

ABSTRACT

The paper presents the result on cross-representation mediation of user models in the context of movie recommendation. We analyze the possibility of initializing the user models for a content-based recommender starting from movie ratings provided by users in other social applications. We focus in particular on (i) an approach for inferring user model preferences from rating and (ii) the experimentation of several methods to solve the missing value problem exploiting community-based ratings. We tested different variations of the proposed approach exploiting a subset of the MovieLens 10M Dataset, computing rating predictions, and MAE.

Keywords

Cross-representation mediation of user models, Movie recommendation, Content-based recommender systems

1. INTRODUCTION

Mediation of user models refers to the possibility of providing a user model U in a system S by exploiting other user model(s) the user may have in the same or other systems, which differ from U in one or several respects (e.g. representation, domain, or others). We focus on CF (collaborative-filtering) to CB (content-based) cross-representation mediation [1] where a CF user model (consisting in a set of user ratings) is used to extract a CB user model (expressing the user interest for the features characterizing the domain items).

This approach may offer a potential solution to mitigate the cold-start and sparsity problems in recommender systems, as well as the "paradox of the active user", who is so eager to use the system that she does not want to spend time giving the system information about herself (in our case, her interests), which could improve the system performance.

User model mediation in general, and cross-representation mediation in particular, does not *per-se* solve the problem of *missing values*: for a content-based user model as we have described, this problem consists in not knowing the user interest for a certain feature of an item to be recommended.

This may be due to the user's reticence in providing information about her, or – in case the user model the target of a mediation – to an incompleteness in the source user model, or more generally to the fact that there are too many features for the user having expressed an interest in all of them, either directly or indirectly.

One possible solution is to fill the value with community-based preferences from another source outside the target system [4]. This is in line with the idea of social information access [3], i.e., methods for exploiting users past interaction within an information system, in order to provide better access to information to the future users. Similarly, in CF recommenders, the missing ratings are filled with default values, such as the middle value of the rating range, or the average user or item rating [2, 5].

In this article, we experiment with a combination of cross-representation mediation (user model transfer from CF to CB) as a way to extract both the user model, and a default interest or preference value to cover for missing values.

2. USER MODEL EXTRACTION

We propose to extract the content-based user model from a set of movie ratings. Each movie m, is described by an *id*, a *title*, and a set of features $desc(m) = \{F_1, \ldots, F_n\}$ where each feature F_i is a pair (*category, value*). Categories are:

$$FCat = \{genre, directors, actors, production\_country, tags\}.$$

The user model UM(u) we compute consists of an **interest** function $int_u : Features \longrightarrow [0,1]$ (the interest of user u in a certain feature F) and an **action count** function $act_u : Features \longrightarrow \mathbb{N}$ (the number of actions by u involving a feature F). $act_u(F)$ is extracted as the number of movies rated by u which have F in their description ($mov(u|F)$). $int_u(F)$ is extracted as the average (normalized) rating given by u to such movies.

The interest function we extract in this way tends to be under-defined for "sparse" feature categories (such as the *actor* and *director* categories), where there are a lot of possible different feature values. We propose to tackle this problem by providing a default interest function $\overline{int}$, computed from a set of "external" ratings, provided by users not otherwise involved in the experiment. Such function is meant to be used in place of int_u whenever it is undefined.

We experimented with three ways of computing the default function.

- **Middle value:** $\overline{int} = int_{mid}$ = the global average external rating (a constant).

UMAP '16, July 13-17, 2016, Halifax, NS, Canada
ACM 978-1-4503-4370-1/16/07.
http://dx.doi.org/10.1145/2930238.2930263

- **Average user**: $\overline{int} = int_{ave}$ = the average external rating for each given feature (as if the community provinding the external ratings was a single user with its own user model).

- **Notoriety-based**: $\overline{int} = int_{ntr} = int_{mid} * ntr$ where ntr represent the notorietyof a feature F, computed as the (normalized) number of ratings given to movies with F in it.

3. EVALUATION

We evaluated our approach using the MovieLens 10M Dataset [6] and, in order to compare our results with existing work, we replicated the experimental settings by Berkovsky et al. [1]. The main difference with their settings relies on the dataset. In fact Berkovsky et al. exploited the EachMovie dataset, storing 2,811,983 ratings of 72,916 users on 1,628 movies, which is no longer available. However MovieLens was originally based on this dataset.

We first randomly selected 5000 users from the MovieLens DB, whose 701017 samples were used as "external" ratings for computing the three default interest functions int_{mid}, int_{ave}, and int_{ntr}.

We then created 10 groups of 325 users each, according to the number of ratings available for each of them.

For each group we then performed a 10-fold cross evaluation, selecting 90% of their samples as training set and the remaining 10% as evaluation set.

For each user in each group, we extracted a user model from the training set, and then run a basic content-based recommender on the evaluation set, to obtain *rating predictions*. To evaluate the approaches we computed the mean absolute error (MAE) between such predictions and the *actual* ratings provided by the user herself.

Rating predictions (for each user u and movie m in her evaluation set) according to the following formula:

$$pr_{u,m} = \frac{\sum_{c \in FCat} score_c(u,m)}{\sum_{c \in FCat} w_c}, \quad (1)$$

$score_c(u,m)$ is the score obtained by movie m according to the user model of u with respect to category c. It is computed as the average interest the user has for the features in m associated with category c.

We experimented with two variants of formula 1: *(i)* including all categories (EQ variant), and *(ii)* excluding *production_country* (FS), taking in this latter case into account the *feature selection* analysis presented in [1], which suggests to exclude this category. We tested each combination of a default interest method (*mid, ave, ntr*) and a weight set (EQ, FS) with a ten-fold cross-evaluation. We checked the resulting MAEs for each pair of combinations in order to verify the statistical significance of their differences. We obtain the following results: (i) for both EQ and FS variants the int_{ave} default function provides the best results, and int_{int} outperforms int_{ntr} (significance $\geq 99\%$); (ii) excluding the production country category does not result in significant changes in MAEs, confirming this category as irrelevant.

We also compared our best-performing combination (FS+ave) with the results in [1], which in turn compared their cross-representation mediation approach (CBFS) with a standard collaborative filtering technique (CF) applied to the same data.

In the work by Berkovsky and colleagues CBFS obtains a lower MAE than CF (about 0.16 to 0.185) for users with less than 75 samples; for more than 75 samples, CBFS worsens, stabilizing approximately at 0.20, while CF improves, decreasing to 0.17. Our approach tends to improve as the number of samples increases: its MAE is 0.17 (worse than CBFS, better than CF) for users with 1-25 samples, but then decreases to about 0.15. For more than 25 samples our approach obtains a better MAE than both CBFS and CF.

4. CONCLUSION

The results presented in this paper open the door to several further investigations. A first line of inquiry goes in the direction of combining our approach with [1], in order to benefit from the advantages of both. In fact, the two algorithms for user model inference take into account quite different aspects, and this is reflected in the different behavior they exhibit when used in recommendation. As future work, we will implement their approach using the MovieLens dataset, in order two have the two studies completely comparable.

A second study may investigate the possibility of using community ratings for fine tuning the weight of each feature category, rather than adopting the coarser approach of feature selection, where each category basically weights either 1 (selected) or 0 (discarded).

5. REFERENCES

[1] S. Berkovsky, T. Kuflik, and F. Ricci. Cross-representation mediation of user models. *User Model. User-Adapt. Interact.*, 19(1-2):35–63, 2009.

[2] J. S. Breese, D. Heckerman, and C. Kadie. Empirical analysis of predictive algorithms for collaborative filtering. In *Proceedings of the Fourteenth Conference on Uncertainty in Artificial Intelligence*, UAI'98, pages 43–52, San Francisco, CA, USA, 1998. Morgan Kaufmann Publishers Inc.

[3] P. Brusilovsky. Social information access: The other side of the social web. In V. Geffert, J. Karhumäki, A. Bertoni, B. Preneel, P. Návrat, and M. Bieliková, editors, *SOFSEM 2008: Theory and Practice of Computer Science: 34th Conference on Current Trends in Theory and Practice of Computer Science, Nový Smokovec, Slovakia, January 19-25, 2008. Proceedings*, pages 5–22, Berlin, Heidelberg, 2008. Springer Berlin Heidelberg.

[4] I. Cantador, I. Fernández-Tobías, S. Berkovsky, and P. Cremonesi. *Recommender Systems Handbook*, chapter Cross-Domain Recommender Systems, pages 919–959. Springer US, Boston, MA, 2015.

[5] M. Deshpande and G. Karypis. Item-based top-n recommendation algorithms. *ACM Trans. Inf. Syst.*, 22(1):143–177, Jan. 2004.

[6] F. M. Harper and J. A. Konstan. The movielens datasets: History and context. *ACM Transactions on Interactive Intelligent Systems*, 5(4):19, 2016.

Analyzing MOOC Entries of Professionals on LinkedIn for User Modeling and Personalized MOOC Recommendations

Guangyuan Piao
Insight Centre for Data Analytics, NUI Galway
IDA Business Park, Galway, Ireland
guangyuan.piao@insight-centre.org

John G. Breslin
Insight Centre for Data Analytics, NUI Galway
IDA Business Park, Galway, Ireland
john.breslin@nuigalway.ie

ABSTRACT

The main contribution of this work is the comparison of three user modeling strategies based on *job titles*, *educational fields* and *skills* in LinkedIn profiles, for personalized MOOC recommendations in a cold start situation. Results show that the `skill-based` user modeling strategy performs best, followed by the `job-` and `edu-based` strategies.

1. INTRODUCTION

Massive Open Online Courses (MOOCs) are an online phenomenon which has been gathering momentum over the past few years. According to a recent study [3], over half of MOOC learners (62.4%) reported themselves as being employed full-time or self-employed. This indicates that MOOCs play a significant role in educating professionals. In this work, we investigate whether information in different fields of professionals' profiles from LinkedIn[1] (e.g., job titles) allows to produce useful user profiles which can be used for personalized MOOC recommendations.

2. RELATED WORK

To provide personalized MOOC recommendations, MOOC data traces (e.g., learning history, access logs, etc.) as well as learning content information have been used in the literature [1,2]. Aher et al. [1] used data mining techniques to learn students' behaviors from data collected in a course management system for course recommendations. Apaza et al. [2] proposed recommending MOOCs based on historical grades of students in their college and inferred topics from content in course syllabus using probabilistic topic models.

Our work is different since we focus on user modeling based on user profiles and focus only on cold start situations. For instance, *does it make sense to provide MOOC recommendations based on a learner's job title(s) or skill(s)?*

[1]https://www.linkedin.com

UMAP '16 July 13-17, 2016, Halifax, NS, Canada

© 2016 Copyright held by the owner/author(s).

ACM ISBN 978-1-4503-4370-1/16/07.

DOI: http://dx.doi.org/10.1145/2930238.2930264

Table 1: Parameter estimates

Parameter	B	Exp(B)	p-value
the degree below bachelor	-0.373	0.689	0.003
bachelor's degree	-0.206	0.814	0.003
master's degree	-0.194	0.824	0.004
PhD degree	0	1	.

Dependent variable: the # of MOOCs taken by learners

3. DATA COLLECTION

We created a Google Custom Search Engine (GCSE)[2] to retrieve LinkedIn profiles with the keyword "coursera". Overall, the dataset consists of 15,744 Coursera[3] MOOC entries for 5,668 professionals from LinkedIn. 5,134 out of 5,668 profiles contain degree information. 37% of learners in our dataset have bachelor's degrees while 47% and 12% of them have master's and PhD degrees. The average number of courses taken by these learners with different degrees (from the degree below bachelor to PhD) are 2.4, 2.8, 2.9 and 3.5, respectively. Based on *Negative binomial regression* and *Poisson regression*, which are often used for modeling count variables, we can observe the "*rich get richer*" phenomenon: a "*richer*" (with a higher degree) learner tends to take more MOOCs (see Table 1). More details about the dataset is available at the supporting website of this work[4].

4. USER MODELING STRATEGIES

Users are represented by a vector of weighted keywords from a specific field in their profiles. Thus, the profile of a user $u \in U$: $P_u = \{(k, w(u, k)) \mid k \in K, u \in U\}$ consists of a set of weighted keywords where with respect to the given user u for a keyword $k \in K$ its weight $w(u, k)$ is computed by a certain function w. Here, K denotes the set of keywords from a specific field of user profiles, and U denotes users. For instance, the fields in a LinkedIn profile about a user u can be summarized as: (1) job titles: `Software Engineer`, `Java Engineer` (2) education fields: `Information Engineering`, and (3) skills: `Java, C++, Microsoft Excel`. We use the well the known TF (Term Frequency)-IDF (Inverse Document Frequency) as the weighting scheme, i.e., $w(u, k) = \log(f_{k,u}) \times \log \frac{N}{1 + |\{u \in U : k \in u\}|}$. $f_{k,c}$ denotes the number of occurrences of a keyword k in a specific field of a user u, N and $|\{u \in U : k \in u\}|$ denote the total number of

[2]https://www.google.ie/cse
[3]https://www.coursera.org
[4]http://parklize.blogspot.ie/2016/04/umap2016ea.html

users and the number of users where the keyword k appears in their user profiles. In the same way, we construct a course profile, which is represented by a vector of weighted keywords from users who have taken the course.

5. EXPERIMENTAL EVALUATION

Our main goal is to analyze and compare the applicability of different user modeling strategies in the context of MOOC recommendations. We do not aim to optimize recommendation quality, but are interested in comparing the quality achieved by the same recommendation algorithm when inputing different types of user profiles. In this regard, we apply a lightweight content-based algorithm as below.

Recommendation algorithm. Given a user profile and a set of candidate courses, the recommendation algorithm ranks the candidate courses according to their similarity to the user profile. The similarity is calculated by the *dot product* of the user and course profiles:

$$sim\,(u,c) = \frac{\vec{P_u}}{||\vec{P_u}||} \cdot \vec{P_i} \qquad (1)$$

which denotes *"how much of the course vector $\vec{P_i}$ is pointing in the same direction as the user vector $\vec{P_u}$"*. Although it is reasonable to use the cosine similarity, the dot product outperforms the cosine similarity when representing user and course profiles using the TF-IDF weight for each keyword.

Given the dataset of learners with course entries in the previous section, we filtered learners with all information about current/previous job titles, educational fields and skills in their profiles. 4,401 profiles were left after filtering. Next, we randomly divided the dataset into training (4,080) and test sets (321) for the experiment. The TF-IDF weights for each keyword were obtained based on the distribution of each keyword in the training set. The ground truth of MOOCs for 321 users, was given by MOOCs in their LinkedIn profiles. All MOOCs in the dataset were used for constructing the candidate set (442) for recommendations. The recommender system then recommends MOOCs with highest similarities to a learner profile from 442 candidate MOOCs.

We compare the quality of different user modeling strategies to that of the *top-popular* recommendation strategy as a baseline, which is a common practice for cold start situations. *Top-popular* recommendation (pop) is a non-personalized model recommends the top-N items with the highest popularity amongst learners. The performance of the recommender system was evaluated by standard evaluation methods Mean Reciprocal Rank (MRR) and Success at rank N (S@N). MRR indicates at which rank the first item relevant to the user occurs on average. S@N stands for the mean probability that a relevant item occurs within the top-N recommendations.

Results. Figure 1 shows the recommendation performance in terms of MRR and S@05. We tested the statistical significance of our results with the bootstrapped paired t-test where the significance level was set to $\alpha = 0.01$ unless otherwise noted. The results show that skill-based profiles performs best, followed by job- and edu-based profiles. All of these user modeling strategies outperform the baseline method while skill- and job-based profiles perform significantly better than the baseline method in terms of MOOC recommendations. In detail, the job-based user modeling strategy improves MRR and S@05 26% and 43% respectively,

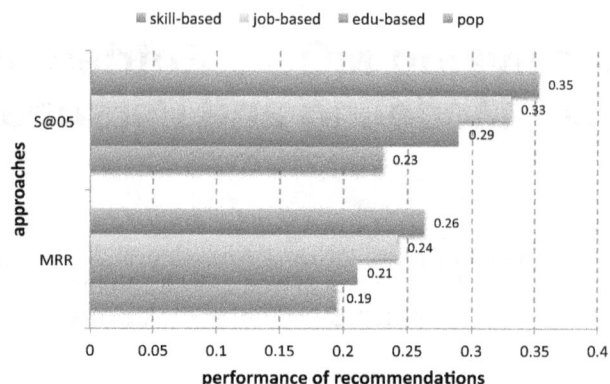

Figure 1: Results of MOOC recommendations with different user modeling strategies.

while the skill-based approach improves MRR and S@05 37% and 52% respectively compared to the non-personalized approach. edu-based user modeling strategy improves MRR and S@05 11% and 26% respectively (although the difference is not statistically significant). The results show that job titles from work experience and skills of learners are useful for user modeling in the context of MOOC recommendations. Also, it indicates that any MOOC provider that has the functionality of signing up with LinkedIn (via OAuth[5]) as well as LinkedIn itself can exploit different fields of user profiles to provide personalized MOOC recommendations, especially in a cold start situation.

6. CONCLUSIONS

In this work, we investigated three different user modeling strategies based on the collected LinkedIn dataset. The dataset showed that a *"richer"* learner tend to take a greater number of MOOCs. In terms of user modeling strategies, our experiment showed that the skill-based user modeling strategy performs better than the job- and edu-based ones in the context of MOOC recommendations.

7. ACKNOWLEDGMENTS

This publication has emanated from research conducted with the financial support of Science Foundation Ireland (SFI) under Grant Number SFI/12/RC/2289 (Insight Centre for Data Analytics).

8. REFERENCES

[1] S. B. Aher and L. Lobo. Combination of machine learning algorithms for recommendation of courses in E-Learning System based on historical data. *Knowledge-Based Systems*, 51:1–14, oct 2013.

[2] R. G. Apaza, E. V. Cervantes, L. C. Quispe, and J. O. Luna. Online Courses Recommendation based on LDA. In *SIMBig*, pages 42–48. Citeseer, 2014.

[3] G. Christensen, A. Steinmetz, B. Alcorn, A. Bennett, D. Woods, and E. J. Emanuel. The MOOC phenomenon: who takes massive open online courses and why? *Available at SSRN 2350964*, 2013.

---

[5]http://oauth.net/2/

Tell Me What You See, I Will Tell You What You Remember

Florian Marchal
LORIA - Université de Lorraine
Campus Scientifique, B.P. 239
54506 Vandœuvre - France
florian.marchal@loria.fr

Sylvain Castagnos
LORIA - Université de Lorraine
Campus Scientifique, B.P. 239
54506 Vandœuvre - France
sylvain.castagnos@loria.fr

Anne Boyer
LORIA - Université de Lorraine
Campus Scientifique, B.P. 239
54506 Vandœuvre - France
anne.boyer@loria.fr

ABSTRACT

Recommender systems usually rely on users' preferences. Nevertheless, there are many situations (e-learning, e-health) where recommendations should rather be based on their memory. So as to infer in real time and with low involvement what has been memorized by users, we propose in this paper to establish a link between gaze features and visual memory. We designed a user experiment where 24 subjects had to remember 72 images. In the meantime, we collected 18,643 fixation points. Among other metrics, our results show a strong correlation between the relative path angles and the memorized items.

Keywords

Learner modeling; Gaze data; Visual memory; Recall

1. INTRODUCTION

There are many areas where recommendations based on users' preferences are not sufficient. As an example, a recent study on Massively Open Online Courses (MOOCs)[1] shows that only 6.5% of users really achieve them. The length of the course appears to be the critical factor, since it is the same for every users. In this context, recommending resources that fit the active user's learning curve, in addition to their interests, may increase their satisfaction and the completion rate of the courses.

E-health is also a domain where it can be interesting to focus on memory. This would for instance allow to early diagnose neuro-degenerative diseases, by comparing the behavior of patients with the behavior of a healthy population. Nevertheless, modeling the memory of users in a traditional way can be very time-consuming and requires a high user involvement.

In this paper, we investigate the possibility to infer the

---

[1]Katy Jordan, University of Texas, 2013 may http://techcrunch.com/2014/03/03/study-massive-online-courses-enroll-an-average-of-43000-students-10-completion/

UMAP '16 July 13-17, 2016, Halifax, NS, Canada

© 2016 Copyright held by the owner/author(s).

ACM ISBN 978-1-4503-4370-1/16/07. . . $15.00

DOI: http://dx.doi.org/10.1145/2930238.2930265

memorized items through gaze data. Within the frame of recommenders, eye-tracking systems are mainly used to infer user preferences [6], to evaluate the accuracy of a recommender system [4], or to evaluate users' learning strategy [1]. Some works investigated the link between gaze data and memory, but most of them focus on the recognition process [5]. We propose here to use gaze features to model what has been recalled by users.

Section 2 offers a quick overview of the literature as regards eye-tracking usages to model cognitive processes. Section 3 is dedicated to the presentation of our experiment. Section 4 presents the analysis of the data and the results.

2. RELATED WORK

While most of works aim at understanding users' behavior from gaze data [8], Steichen *et al.* [9] followed eye movements to infer users' characteristics, such as perceptual speed and working memory. There are two main methods of accessing memory: recognition and recall. Recognition is the mental process which consists in comparing and associating a current and past stimuli. Recall involves to remember a stimulus which is not physically present. In cognitive neuroscience, most of works are dedicated to recognition [5]. As an example, Borkin *et al.* [2] studied the memorability of charts, using the eye-tracking to monitor how users recognize them. In this paper, we carry out an on-going research on the way to predict what is recalled by users from gaze features. Papers focusing on recall include Bondareva *et al.* [1] who estimate the quality of users' learning process from gaze data, and Steichen *et al.* [9] who explore gaze patterns through differential sequence mining. However, these papers involve the creation of predefined Areas Of Interest (AOIs), which can hardly be applied generally. Thus, we expect to extend this latter work by finding correlations between gaze features and memorized items, without the use of predefined AOIs.

3. EXPERIMENT SETUP

Our hypothesis is the following:

H1. *The analysis of gaze features can reveal which items are recalled during human-computer interactions.*

As this is a work-in-progress, our first step consists in studying if one or several of the gaze features are correlated with the memorization of items. In this section, we present the experiment we developed to validate this assumption. We took inspiration from Maxcey and Woodman [7] to show users a set of 72 images. Images were drawn from a set of 1,395 real-world objects [3], subdivided into 93 categories

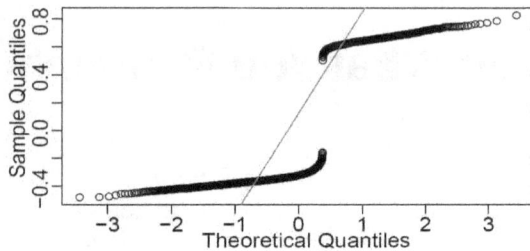

Figure 1: Difference between data and normal distribution

Table 1: Results of the permutation test

Features	R Sum Sq	Pr(Prob)	
Sum of Relative Path Angles	**0.95**	**< 2e-16**	***
Number of Fixations	**0.70**	**< 2e-16**	***
SD of Relative Path Angles	0.57	0.06209	.
Length of 1st Fixation	0.23	0.11083	
SD of Absolute Path Angles	0.21	0.51579	
SD of Saccade Length	0.33	1.00000	

Signif. codes: 0 '***' 0.001 '**' 0.01 '*' 0.05 '.' 0.1 ' ' 1
19 observations deleted due to missingness

containing 15 items. Categories were chosen for their strong salience. For each user, we randomly selected 12 categories, and 6 items per category. During a first step, images were presented one after another in a random order. Participants were instructed to study details on each picture for a later memory test. They were told that the test would require very detailed information, and that remembering only the category would not help. Each image was displayed during 5s, interleaved by a 500ms center fixation cross. After a short break, participants were instructed to describe on a sheet all the images they can remember from the first step, with no limit of time. Finally, they were asked to match their answers with memorized items by browsing the 72 images on a single page. The correct images have been categorized as "remembered", and all the others as "not remembered".

A Tobii X1 Light was used to monitor the subjects' eye movements and the software Tobii Studio was used to record the gaze data and transform them into fixations.

Twenty-four members participated in the experiment (10 females). They were between 23 and 62 years old (Mean = 32). Participants had normal or corrected-to-normal visual acuity.

4. DATA AND STATISTICAL ANALYSIS

Our data analysis proceeds in 3 steps. First, we gathered the fixation data from Tobii Studio. Then, we reconstructed the saccades from the transitions between the fixations. Finally, we dynamically built AOIs from fixation points, for each user and each image, with a simple clustering algorithm (DBSCAN). Let us notice that there were no predefined AOIs (such as specific regions of the images). Our AOIs only rely on the way users look at the images.

For all the users, a total of 18 gaze features (such as the sum, mean or standard deviation of fixation duration, or the saccade length) were computed and tested to find a potential correlation with the fact that images have been recalled or not. We first used an analysis of covariance (ANCOVA) to test data from all the images and all the users. However, the distribution of the data did not follow a normal form, as shown in Figure 1.

Thus, we chose to apply a permutation test. The latter is a non-parametric test that fits better with our non-normal distribution. The Table 1 summarizes the subset of gaze features that have a strong correlation with the fact of memorizing items. The sum of relative path angles and the number of fixations appear to be very good predictors of the memorization process, with respective residual sum of squares of 0.95 and 0.70. These results are significant at a 0.99 level, as shown in the third column of Table 1.

5. CONCLUSION AND PERSPECTIVES

Results showed that there is a direct link between some gaze features and the memorization of images. This reinforces our conviction that it will be possible to predict what the users remember, by using the gaze features. Among perspectives, we aim at building a model that can predict efficiently the memorization and adapt recommendations on these predictions.

6. REFERENCES

[1] D. Bondareva, C. Conati, R. Feyzi-Behnagh, J. M. Harley, R. Azevedo, and F. Bouchet. Inferring learning from gaze data during interaction with an environment to support self-regulated learning. In *Artificial Intelligence in Education*, pages 229–238, 2013.

[2] M. A. Borkin, Z. Bylinskii, N. W. Kim, C. M. Bainbridge, C. S. Yeh, D. Borkin, H. Pfister, and A. Oliva. Beyond Memorability: Visualization Recognition and Recall. *IEEE Transactions on Visualization and Computer Graphics*, 22(1):519–528, Jan. 2016.

[3] T. F. Brady, T. Konkle, G. A. Alvarez, and A. Oliva. Visual long-term memory has a massive storage capacity for object details. *Proceedings of the National Academy of Sciences*, 105(38):14325–14329, 2008.

[4] L. Chen and P. Pu. Eye-tracking study of user behavior in recommender interfaces. In *User Modeling, Adaptation, and Personalization*, pages 375–380. 2010.

[5] D. E. Hannula, C. L. Baym, D. E. Warren, and N. J. Cohen. The Eyes Know: Eye Movements as a Veridical Index of Memory. *Psychological Science*, 23(3):278–287, 2012.

[6] W. Lu and Y. Jia. Inferring User Preference in Good Abandonment from Eye Movements. In J. Li and Y. Sun, editors, *Web-Age Information Management*, number 9098 in Lecture Notes in Computer Science, pages 457–460. 2015.

[7] A. M. Maxcey and G. F. Woodman. Forgetting induced by recognition of visual images. *Visual Cognition*, 22(6):789–808, 2014.

[8] J. N. Sari, R. Ferdiana, P. I. Santosa, and L. E. Nugroho. An eye tracking study: exploration customer behavior on web design. pages 69–72, 2015.

[9] B. Steichen, M. M. Wu, D. Toker, C. Conati, and G. Carenini. Te, Te, Hi, Hi: Eye gaze sequence analysis for informing user-adaptive information visualizations. In *User Modeling, Adaptation, and Personalization*, pages 183–194. 2014.

Where's Your Mind At? Video-Based Mind Wandering Detection During Film Viewing

Angela Stewart, Nigel Bosch, Huili Chen, Patrick J. Donnelly, & Sidney K. D'Mello

University of Notre Dame

384 Fitzpatrick Hall, Notre Dame, IN, 46556, USA

{astewa12, pbosch1, hchen6, pdonnel4, sdmello}@nd.edu

ABSTRACT

Mind wandering (MW) is a ubiquitous phenomenon in which attention involuntarily shifts from task-related processing to task-unrelated thoughts. This study reports preliminary results of a video-based MW detector during film viewing. We collected training data in a study where participants self-reported when they caught themselves MW over the course of watching a 32.5 minute commercial film. We trained classification models on automatically extracted facial features and bodily movement and were able to detect MW with an F_1 of .30. The model was successful in reproducing the MW distribution obtained from the self-reports.

Keywords

Mind wandering, facial features, user modeling, affective computing, film viewing

1. INTRODUCTION

Most of us have had the experience of engaging in an activity, such as such as reading or watching a film, only to suddenly realize that our attention has gradually drifted away from task-related thoughts to completely unrelated thoughts like dinner or weekend plans. This shift in attention is known as mind wandering (MW). Considerable research over the last decade has documented MW's widespread incidence during a host of real-world activities. For example, in one large-scale study MW was tracked in 5,000 individuals from 83 countries working in 86 occupations with an iPhone app that prompted people to report their thoughts at random intervals throughout the day [4]. People reported MW for 46.9% of the prompts, which confirmed numerous lab studies on the pervasiveness of MW, which is estimated to occur approximately 20-50% of the time, depending on the person, task, and the environmental context [4, 5].

In addition to being quite frequent, MW is also detrimental to performance across a number of tasks, such as reading comprehension, signal detection, memory recall, and retention of learned content [7]. Further, the negative correlation between MW and performance increases in proportion to task complexity [7]. When compounded with its high frequency, MW can have serious consequences on performance and productivity. Therefore, we believe that next-generation intelligent interfaces could benefit from some mechanism to detect and address MW. Of course, an interface must first detect MW before it can respond to it. Thus,

the goal is to develop a fully-automated video-based detector of MW during film viewing.

2. METHOD

We used data from an existing study [5] in which 107 participants viewed the narrative film "The Red Balloon" (1956, Figure 1) while a video of their faces and upper bodies was recorded with a commercial webcams. Participants self-reported MW by pressing keys when they caught themselves "thinking about anything else besides the movie" or "thinking about the task itself but not the actual content of the movie."

Figure 1. Screenshot of "The Red Balloon"

MW self-reports were sparsely distributed throughout the 32.5 minute video. Our first task was to create data instances corresponding to short windows of time preceding MW reports. The procedure for creating instances was as follows:

1) Add a 3-second offset before the self-caught MW report to account for movement due to reporting (i.e., the key press).
2) For all MW reports that are within S seconds of each other, where S is the segment size, only keep the first MW report and remove any others.
3) Partition the video between consecutive MW reports into $(t_i - t_{i-1}) / S$ segments, where t_{i-1} and t_i are the timestamps of consecutive MW reports. The segment immediately preceding the MW report at t_i is a MW segment. All other segments between t_{i-1} and t_i are not MW segments.
4) Extract features from a window of data of size w, where $w < S$, from the end of each segment generated in step 3.
5) The remaining time $(S - w)$ seconds in the segment is the gap that is not analyzed.

The procedure described above is depicted in Figure 2 using a 45-second window size. In this study, we chose a 55 second segment length as it resulted in a MW rate of approximately 20% to 25%, which was consistent with previous research [1, 4, 5]. We explored various windows sizes within the 55-second segment and chose a 45-second window size for this initial analysis. We generated a total of 2,734 segments, after excluding instances in which the participants' faces could not be registered in the frame to the extent that less than 1 second of data could be extracted from the 45-second window.

UMAP '16, July 13-17, 2016, Halifax, NS, Canada

ACM 978-1-4503-4370-1/16/07.

http://dx.doi.org/10.1145/2930238.2930266

We used FACET [9], a commercialized version of the CERT computer vision software, for facial feature extraction. FACET provides likelihood estimates of the presence of 19 action units as well as head pose, face position, and face size. Features were created by aggregating FACET estimates in the window using maximum, median, and standard deviation for aggregation. In all, there were 75 facial features which were complemented by 3 features that measured gross body movement from the videos [8].

Several standard classifiers from Weka [3] were used to discriminate between MW and not MW instances. We applied SMOTE (on training data only) to account for data imbalance [2]. Feature selection was performed on a subset of participants in the training set. We evaluated the performance of our classifiers using leave-one-participant-out cross-validation.

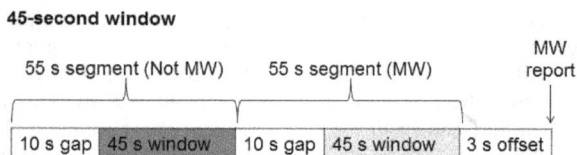

Figure 2. Example of window segmentation approach, using 45-second window sizes. Features are extracted from the dark grey (Not MW) and light grey (MW) windows.

3. RESULTS

The most accurate model was a support vector machine (SVM) classifier [6]. We compared the distribution of per participant MW rates as predicted by the model (Figure 3 - middle) to the distribution of self-reported MW rates (Figure 3 - top). We note that the model was quite accurate at predicting when participants had zero or low MW rates (compare points A and C in Figure 3) but over predicted MW in a large number of participants (compare points B and D in Figure 3). This resulted in an average predicted MW rate of double the self-reported rate.

To address this, we adjusted the model's threshold of when to predict MW. Originally, any instance that exceeded a confidence of .500 was classified as MW. We adjusted this threshold to .600, which yielded the distribution shown at the bottom of Figure 3. The resultant model no longer over predicted MW (i.e., compare points B and F in Figure 3), and correctly predicted when participants had zero or low MW rates (points A and E in in Figure 3). This model had a MW prediction precision of .30, recall of .30, and consequently a F_1 score of .30 for the MW class (minority class).

4. CONCLUSION

This present study demonstrated the feasibility of using facial features to detect MW during film viewing. Our approach used a setup that required affordable and accessible equipment to detect MW in an everyday context. We were moderately successful in advancing a fully-automated system for automatic MW detection with evidence for generalizability to new users. The ubiquity of webcams have opened up the possibility of advancing research in attentional state estimation, thereby enabling an entirely new generation of attention-aware interfaces.

5. ACKNOWLEDGEMENTS

This research was supported by the National Science Foundation (NSF) (DRL 1235958 and IIS 1523091). Any opinions, findings and conclusions, or recommendations expressed in this paper are those of the authors and do not necessarily reflect the views of the NSF.

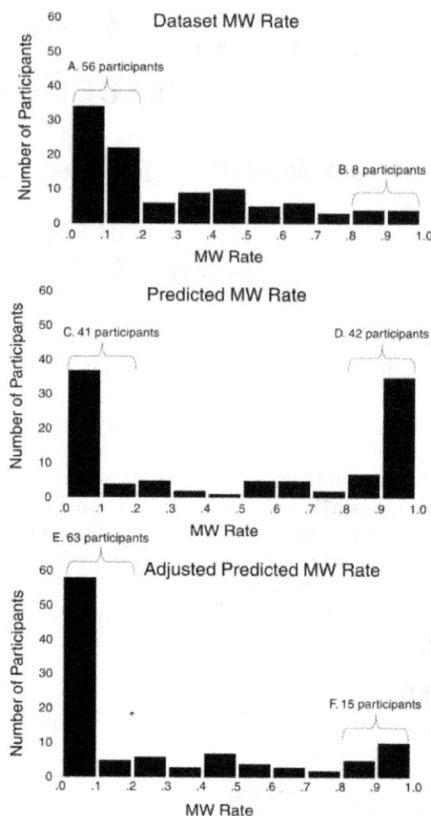

Figure 3. MW rate distributions The self-reported MW rates of the dataset (top), predicted MW rates (middle), and adjusted predicted MW rates (bottom) are shown.

6. REFERENCES

[1] Bixler, R. and D'Mello, S. 2014. Toward fully automated person-independent detection of mind wandering. *Proceedings of the 22nd International Conference on User Modeling, Adaptation, and Personalization* (Switzerland, 2014), 37–48.

[2] Chawla, N.V. et al. 2002. SMOTE: Synthetic minority over-sampling technique. *Journal of Artificial Intelligence Research.* (2002), 321–357.

[3] Holmes, G. et al. 1994. Weka: A machine learning workbench. *Intelligent Information Systems, 1994. Proceedings of the 1994 Second Australian and New Zealand Conference on* (1994), 357–361.

[4] Killingsworth, M.A. and Gilbert, D.T. 2010. A wandering mind is an unhappy mind. *Science.* 330, 6006 (2010), 932–932.

[5] Kopp, K. et al. 2015. Mind wandering during film comprehension: The role of prior knowledge and situational interest. *Psychonomic bulletin & review.* (2015), 1–7.

[6] Platt, J. 1998. Fast training of support vector machines using sequential minimal optimization. *Advances in Kernel Methods - Support Vector Learning.* MIT Press. 41 – 64.

[7] Randall, J.G. et al. 2014. Mind-Wandering, cognition, and performance: A theory-driven meta-analysis of attention regulation. *Psychological bulletin.* 140, 6 (2014), 1411.

[8] Westlund, J.K. et al. 2015. Motion Tracker: Camera-Based monitoring of bodily movements using motion silhouettes. *PloS one.* 10, 6 (2015).

[9] 2016. *Emotient module: Facial expression emotion analysis.*

User-User Relationship Migration Observed in Communication Activity

Shuhei Yamamoto
Univ. of Tsukuba, Japan
yamahei@ce.slis.tsukuba.ac.jp

Noriko Kando
NII, Tokyo, Japan
kando@nii.ac.jp

Tetsuji Satoh
Univ. of Tsukuba, Japan
satoh@ce.slis.tsukuba.ac.jp

ABSTRACT

Many Twitter users build various relationships through communication activity such as replies and retweets. For example, friends engage in conversations through replies. Fans unilaterally send many replies to celebrities. In this paper, we focus on such relationships between users. We assume that such relationships are classified into several patterns based on the feature values of communication reciprocity, and the relationships migrate to other ones as time progresses. We clarify the major relationships and transitions by analyzing the pattern frequency and transitions with high probability. From analysis results using a large amount of user pairs that we obtained over a long period, we detected several major and calm relationships.

Categories and Subject Descriptors

H.3.3 [**Information Search and Retrieval**]: Clustering

Keywords

User-User Relationship, Communication Activity, Reciprocity

1. INTRODUCTION

Many Twitter users build various relationships through communication activity such as replies and retweets. For example, friends engage in a bilateral conversation by replies (Fig. 1 (a)). Fans unilaterally send many replies to celebrities (Fig. 1 (b)). Using retweets, users frequently cite the tweets of other users who rapidly share the newest articles.

In this paper, we focus on communication reciprocity between two users. Our research observes the number of replies and retweets between two users in each time-stamp and calculates the reciprocity of replies and retweets. User pairs are classified into several patterns, and we calculate the transition probability between patterns by using a sequence of pattern numbers. We clarify the pattern frequency and transitions with high probability and detect stable and unstable

UMAP'16 July 13-17, 2016, Halifax, NS, Canada

© 2016 Copyright held by the owner/author(s).

ACM ISBN 978-1-4503-4370-1/16/07.

DOI: http://dx.doi.org/10.1145/2930238.2930268

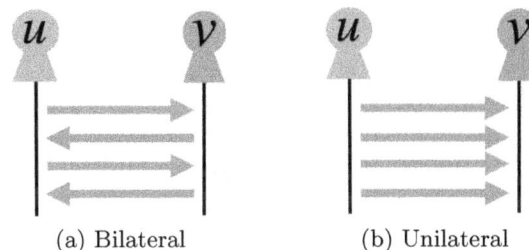

Figure 1: **Two types relationships between two users**

user pair relationships that continue to communicate over a long period.

2. RELATED WORKS

Study of network analysis on Twitter is flourishing. Myers and Leskovec [2] clarified the catalyst that increases a user's followers based on bursts of retweet diffusion. They analyzed follow networks with time-stamps and proposed a model for inferring new followers for each user. To effectively diffuse tweets, Yamaguchi et al. [3] assumed that a list name plays the role of a folksonomy tag for users included in each list, and they analyzed tagging networks by using lists on Twitter. Their analysis clarified that the number of bilaterally tagging user pairs is major in friend relationships despite the number of them being minor in Twitter. Cha et al. [1] analyzed user features with influence by comparing the number of followers, followees, replies, and retweets and clarified the user features extracted by each evaluation metric. Yang and Counts [4] compared blogs and Twitter from the viewpoint of their information diffusion structures. They concluded that users who tweeted less than 30 times a month have shorter tweet intervals than blog post-intervals, and a larger number of tweets denotes a smaller difference between the two intervals.

3. USERS RELATIONSHIP MIGRATION

To quantitatively measure the relationship between two users u and v, we define the reciprocity of replies $mrp_{u,v}$ and retweets $mrt_{u,v}$ as:

$$mrp_{u,v} = \frac{\min(rp_{u,v}, rp_{v,u})}{\max(rp_{u,v}, rp_{v,u})} , \; mrt_{u,v} = \frac{\min(rt_{u,v}, rt_{v,u})}{\max(rt_{u,v}, rt_{v,u})}, \quad (1)$$

where $rp_{u,v}$ denotes the number of replies from user u to user v. $rt_{u,v}$ denotes the number of retweets in which user u

cites v's tweets. Both $mrp_{u,v}$ and $mrt_{u,v}$ fall within 0.0 to 1.0. When user u and v bilaterally communicate, as shown in Fig. 1 (a), the values of $mrp_{u,v}$ and $mrt_{u,v}$ approach 1.0. When users u and v unilaterally communicate, as shown in Fig. 1 (b), the values of $mrp_{u,v}$ and $mrt_{u,v}$ approach 0.0.

Because the volume of communication activity is not evaluate by them, we calculate the summation of the number of replies and retweets between two users and defined the volume $com_{u,v}$ as follows: $com_{u,v} = \log(rp_{u,v} + rp_{v,u} + rt_{u,v} + rt_{v,u} + 1)$. We observe the above three feature values in each user pair and each time-stamp.

To classify user pairs into several patterns on the basis of these three feature values, we convert these into discrete values of three states $\{0, 1, 2\}$ by following formula:

$$m_{u,v} = \begin{cases} 0 & mrp = 0.0, \\ 1 & mrp < 0.5, \\ 2 & 0.5 \le mrp, \end{cases} r_{u,v} = \begin{cases} 0 & mrt = 0.0, \\ 1 & mrt < 0.5, \\ 2 & 0.5 \le mrt, \end{cases} e_{u,v} = \begin{cases} 0 & com < 2, \\ 1 & com < 4, \\ 2 & 4 \le com. \end{cases} \quad (2)$$

The number of patterns produced by such discretization is $27 (= 3^3)$. We classify each user pair into 1 of 27 patterns based on converted feature values.

To detect a major transition between patterns, we calculate the transition probability between patterns. The transition probability $p_{i,j}$ from patterns i to j is calculated as follows: $p_{i,j} = n_{i,j} / \sum_{k=1}^{K} n_{i,k}$, where $n_{i,j}$ is the frequency of the transition from patterns i to j in the transition sequences of all users and K denotes the total number of patterns, which is $K = 27$ in the case of this paper.

4. ANALYSIS RESULTS

We collected tweets from April 2012 to June 2013 (64 weeks) and set the observation time to one-week periods. We extracted user pairs where the number of active weeks exceeded 32. The number of user pairs obtained was approximate 4M.

The frequency of each pattern is shown in Table 1. We attached a label to each pattern from O to Z to simplify the transition figure. The label O denotes a pattern of feature value $(m_{u,v}^t, r_{u,v}^t, e_{u,v}^t) = (0, 0, 0)$ and was at the highest frequency of all patterns. The nine patterns of F, G, H, O, P, Q, U, V, and W have never been observed from our analysis of user pair communication activities.

We show the major transitions between patterns (Fig. 2) and drew edges that had a probability higher than 0.056 because we focus on major transition between patterns. To easily understand transition patterns, we show an edge's probability level with 5 colors: $p_{i,j} > 0.5$ as red, $0.5 \ge p_{i,j} > 0.4$ as orange, $0.4 \ge p_{i,j} > 0.3$ as yellow, $0.3 \ge p_{i,j} > 0.2$ as green, and $0.2 \ge p_{i,j} > 0.056$ as blue.

Closed transition: We can observe the closed transition between patterns A and B, which are the relationships of unilateral replying/retweeting. As an example of such user pairs, we can think of relationships between a general user and a celebrity. User pairs with a relationship of unilateral replying/retweeting almost never migrate to a bilateral one.

Stable relationship: The patterns R and S are the relationships of bilateral reply. These patterns easily stayed in their own pattern since they had a self-transition edge with high probability. This result suggests that user pairs that communicate with bilateral replies can easily maintain a stable relationship and can interact for a long of time.

Unstable relationship: The patterns L and X are an un-

Table 1: Patterns of feature occurrence and labels

	$m\ r\ e$	Freq		$m\ r\ e$	Freq		$m\ r\ e$	Freq
O	0 0 0	71M	I	1 0 0	3M	R	2 0 0	34M
A	0 0 1	13M	J	1 0 1	3M	S	2 0 1	37M
B	0 0 2	308K	K	1 0 2	124K	T	2 0 2	2M
C	0 1 0	935K	L	1 1 0	64K	U	2 1 0	0
D	0 1 1	445K	M	1 1 1	557K	V	2 1 1	0
E	0 1 2	14K	N	1 1 2	69K	W	2 1 2	0
F	0 2 0	0	O	1 2 0	0	X	2 2 0	586K
G	0 2 1	0	P	1 2 1	0	Y	2 2 1	4M
H	0 2 2	0	Q	1 2 2	0	Z	2 2 2	1M

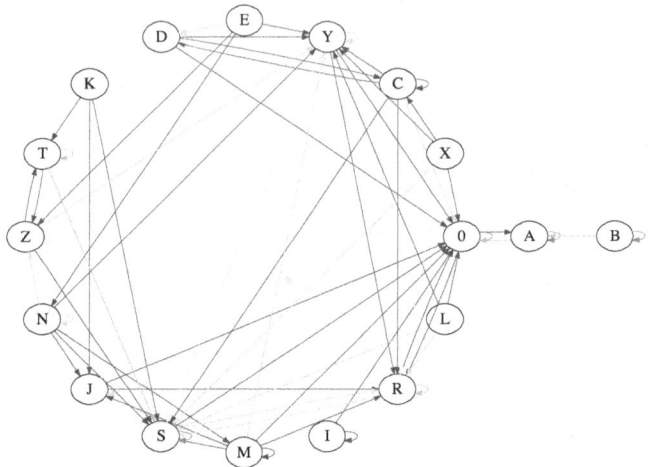

Figure 2: Major transitions between patterns

stable relationship because they do not have a self-transition edge. User pairs with slight interaction through replying and retweeting (i.e., L and X) are in an unstable relationship and immediately migrate to relationships of bilateral replying (i.e., R and S) or bilateral replying/retweeting (i.e., Y).

5. CONCLUSION

In this paper, to characterize user-user relationships, we classified user pairs into patterns on the basis of the feature values of communication activity for each week. We calculate the transition probability between patterns, draw a transition figure, and clarify stable/unstable relationships and major transitions. In the future, we will analyze user pairs using other feature values such as co-citation.

Acknowledgments: This work was supported by Grant-in-Aids for scientific Research No.25280110 and No.15J05599 and by NII's strategic open-type collaborative research.

6. REFERENCES

[1] M. Cha, H. Haddadi, F. Benevenuto, and K. Gummadi. Measuring user influence in twitter: The million follower fallacy. In *Proc. of ICWSM2010*, 2010.

[2] S. A. Myers and J. Leskovec. The bursty dynamics of the twitter information network. In *Proc. of WWW2014*, 2014.

[3] Y. Yamaguchi, M. Yoshida, C. Faloutsos, and H. Kitagawa. Patterns in interactive tagging networks. In *Proc. of ICWSM2015*, 2015.

[4] J. Yang and S. Counts. Comparing information diffusion structure in weblogs and microblogs. In *Proc. of ICWSM2010*, 2010.

Effective Recommendation with Category Hierarchy

Zhu Sun
School of Computer Science
and Engineering
Nanyang Technological
University
Singapore
sunzhu@ntu.edu.sg

Guibing Guo
Software College
Northeastern University
Shenyang, China
guogb@swc.neu.edu.cn

Jie Zhang
School of Computer Science
and Engineering
Nanyang Technological
University
Singapore
zhangj@ntu.edu.sg

ABSTRACT

Although flat item category structure where categories are independent in a same level has been well studied to enhance recommendation performance, in many real applications, item category is often organized in hierarchies to reflect the inherent correlations among categories. In this paper, we propose a novel matrix factorization model by exploiting category hierarchy from the perspectives of users and items for effective recommendation. Specifically, a user (an item) can be influenced (characterized) by her preferred categories (the categories it belongs to) in the hierarchy. We incorporate how different categories in the hierarchy co-influence a user and an item. Empirical results show the superiority of our approach against other counterparts.

Keywords

Category hierarchy, matrix factorization, recommendation

1. INTRODUCTION

In many real applications, item categories are often organized in hierarchy, which is very helpful to generate effective recommendation. For example, in Figure 1, category levels 1 to 3 and restaurants compose a hierarchical structure, where food is first divided into several generalized categories (e.g. Asian), then further classified into more localized subcategories (e.g. Thai). Suppose that a Thai greatly favors Thai food, she may possibly like Sushi to some extent. Both Thai and Sushi are Asian food, so are more or less influenced by Asian food culture. In other words, both the localized category (i.e., Thai) and the generalized category (i.e., Asian) may co-influence the user's tastes, possibly with different degrees. Thus, the hierarchy contains richer knowledge and can be adopted to boost recommendation performance.

However, most of the category-aware recommendation methods [4, 3] only focus on leveraging flat category structures, and thus fail to work with hierarchical category structures. Furthermore, several methods [1] considering category hier-

UMAP '16 July 13-17, 2016, Halifax, NS, Canada

© 2016 Copyright held by the owner/author(s).

ACM ISBN 978-1-4503-4370-1/16/07.

DOI: http://dx.doi.org/10.1145/2930238.2930269

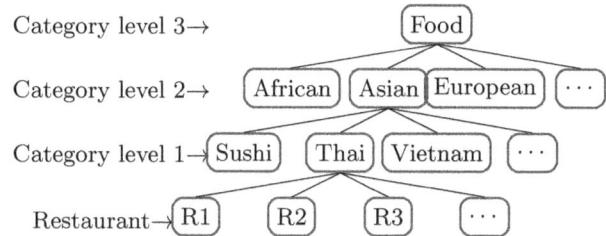

Figure 1: Category hierarchy

archy treat the categories in different hierarchical levels identically, but ignore the different effects of categories in different hierarchical levels on items that belong to them. Hence, they cannot comprehensively exploit the richer knowledge in category hierarchy for better recommendation.

In this paper, we propose a Category Hierarchy Matrix Factorization (CHMF) model to incorporate category hierarchy in terms of both users and items. Specifically, we first assume that a user's latent factor is influenced by her preferred categories in the hierarchy, and an item's latent factor is characterized by the categories it belongs to in the hierarchy. Then, by considering that categories in different hierarchical levels may generate different effects on both a user's and an item's latent factors, we automatically learn the different weights of categories in the hierarchy. Finally, empirical results demonstrate that our approach achieves superior performance over all the counterparts.

2. THE PROPOSED CHMF MODEL

Our model is built on matrix factorization [2], which factorizes the user-item rating matrix $\mathbf{R} \in \mathbb{R}^{m*n}$ into two low-rank user-feature matrix $\mathbf{U} \in \mathbb{R}^{m*d}$ and item-feature matrix $\mathbf{V} \in \mathbb{R}^{n*d}$; m, n are the number of users and items, respectively; and $d \ll min(m, n)$ is the dimension of latent features. $\mathbf{U}, \mathbf{V}$ can be learnt by solving the problem:

$$\min_{\mathbf{U}, \mathbf{V}} \frac{1}{2}\|\mathbf{O} \odot (\mathbf{U}\mathbf{V}^{\top} - \mathbf{R})\|_F^2 + \frac{\lambda}{2}(\|\mathbf{U}\|_F^2 + \|\mathbf{V}\|_F^2) \quad (1)$$

where $\mathbf{O} \in \mathbb{R}^{m*n}$ is the indicator matrix with $\mathbf{O}(i, j) = 1$ indicating user i rates item j, otherwise 0; $\odot$ is the Hadamard product; λ is the parameter to avoid over-fitting.

From bottom to top, assume we have category levels $\{0, 1, 2, \ldots, L\}$, where category level 0 refers to items, and L denotes the highest category level in the hierarchy. Based on the assumption that a user is influenced by her preferred categories in the hierarchy, we contend that the final user-feature matrix ($\overline{\mathbf{U}}$) can be reformulated by the summation of

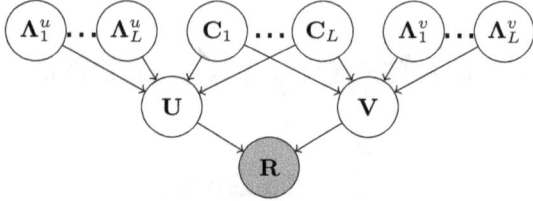

Figure 2: The framework of CHMF.

her intrinsic-feature matrix ($\mathbf{U}$) and her preferred category-feature matrix ($\mathbf{C}$) in the hierarchy[1], given by:

$$\overline{\mathbf{U}} = \mathbf{U} + \frac{1}{L}\sum_{l=1}^{L}\left(\mathbf{O}\prod_{r=1}^{l}\mathbf{A}_r\right)\cdot\mathbf{\Lambda}_l^u\cdot\mathbf{C}_l$$

where $\mathbf{A}_l \in \mathbb{R}^{|C_{(l-1)}|*|C_l|}$ is the category affiliation matrix with $\mathbf{A}_l(g,k) = 1$ indicating that subcategory g in level $(l-1)$ belongs to category k in level l, and $\mathbf{A}_l(g,k) = 0$ otherwise; $|C_l|$ is the number of categories in level l; $\mathbf{\Lambda}_l^u \in \mathbb{R}^{|C_l|*|C_l|}$ is a diagonal matrix that can be automatically learnt by our model. $\mathbf{\Lambda}_l^u(k,k) > 0$ indicates the extent to which category k in level l influences users; $\mathbf{C}_l \in \mathbb{R}^{|C_l|*d}$ denotes category-feature matrix for level l;

Similarly, based upon the assumption that an item is characterized by the categories it belongs to in the hierarchy. We posit that the final item-feature matrix ($\overline{\mathbf{V}}$) can be represented as the summation of its intrinsic-feature matrix ($\mathbf{V}$) and its corresponding category-feature matrix ($\mathbf{C}$).

$$\overline{\mathbf{V}} = \mathbf{V} + \frac{1}{L}\sum_{l=1}^{L}\left(\prod_{r=1}^{l}\mathbf{A}_r\right)\cdot\mathbf{\Lambda}_l^v\cdot\mathbf{C}_l$$

where $\mathbf{\Lambda}_l^v \in \mathbb{R}^{|C_l|*|C_l|}$ is a diagonal matrix that can also be automatically learnt by our model. $\mathbf{\Lambda}_l^v(k,k) > 0$ indicates the extent to which category k in level l influences items.

Finally, by combining the impact of the different categories in the hierarchy on both users and items, we obtain a unified category hierarchy matrix factorization (CHMF) model, with the objective function defined by:

$$\begin{aligned}\mathcal{L} = &\frac{1}{2}\|\mathbf{O}\odot(\overline{\mathbf{U}}\overline{\mathbf{V}}^\top - \mathbf{R})\|_F^2 + \frac{\lambda_1}{2}(\|\mathbf{U}\|_F^2 + \|\mathbf{V}\|_F^2)\\ &+ \frac{\lambda_2}{2}\sum_{l=1}^{L}\left(\|\mathbf{C}_l\|_F^2 + \|\mathbf{\Lambda}_l^u\|_F^2 + \|\mathbf{\Lambda}_l^v\|_F^2\right)\end{aligned}\quad(2)$$

Figure 2 illustrates the framework of CHMF model, where ratings are determined by the interaction of users and items. Users are influenced by the weighted combination of preferred categories in different levels of the hierarchy, and items are characterized by the weighted combination of categories they belong to in different levels of the hierarchy. We adopt the stochastic gradient descent (SGD) method to optimize the objective function given by Equation 2.

3. EXPERIMENTATION

We collected Foursquare check-in's data set performed over 3 weeks in 4 European capital cities (Amsterdam, London, Paris and Rome) and published on Twitter (18,552 users perform 109,790 check-in on 38,855 locations). It also contains hierarchical location category structure, where all locations are arranged within a two-level category.

We adopt the 5-fold cross validation and root mean square error (RMSE) to evaluate our proposed method, and com-

---

[1]We regard the user-/item-feature matrix $\mathbf{U}/\mathbf{V}$ in the basic MF model as the intrinsic-feature matrix for users/items.

pare with the following methods: 1) **MF** [2] the basic matrix factorization method; 2) **CMF** [4] the collective matrix factorization method; 3) **HMF** [1] the category-aware model by fusing category hierarchy; 4) **FM** [3] the category-aware model incorporating the flat item category structure. The optimal experimental settings for each method are determined either by our experiments or suggested by its authors.

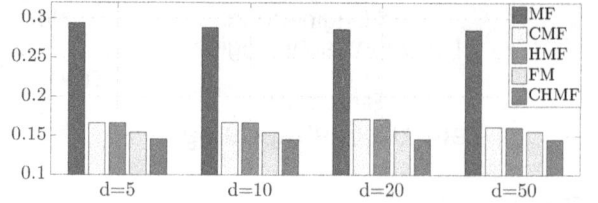

Figure 3: RMSE of comparison methods on Twitter

Figure 3 depicts the results of all comparison methods. A number of interesting observations are noted: 1) compared with category-aware methods, MF performs the worst, implying the importance of category information for better recommendation; 2) the performance of CMF is close to that of HMF, but much worse than FM. The possible reason behind is that, CMF and HMF only consider user-item and item-category interactions, but ignoring the user-category interaction, whereas FM considers the three types of interactions; 3) by incorporating category hierarchy from the perspectives of both users and items, and by automatically learning the different effects of categories in the hierarchy, CHMF significantly outperforms the other methods (p-value < 0.01), which firmly supports the importance of category hierarchy for effective recommendation.

4. CONCLUSIONS

In this paper, we proposed a novel category hierarchy matrix factorization (CHMF) approach that automatically learnt the different effects of categories in the hierarchy on both users and items. Empirical results showed that our approach gained significant improvements relative to state-of-the-art algorithms. For future work, besides rating prediction, item ranking is another interesting problem in recommender systems. Hence, we plan to incorporate category hierarchy into the study of item ranking.

5. ACKNOWLEDGEMENTS

This work is supported under the Singapore Institute of Manufacturing Technology-Nanyang Technological University (SIMTech-NTU) Joint Laboratory and Collaborative research Programme on Complex System.

6. REFERENCES

[1] N. Koenigstein, G. Dror, and Y. Koren. Yahoo! music recommendations: modeling music ratings with temporal dynamics and item taxonomy. In *RecSys*, 2011.

[2] Y. Koren, R. Bell, and C. Volinsky. Matrix factorization techniques for recommender systems. *Computer*, (8):30–37, 2009.

[3] S. Rendle. Factorization machines. In *ICDM*, 2010.

[4] A. P. Singh and G. J. Gordon. Relational learning via collective matrix factorization. In *KDD*, 2008.

Modeling User Exploration and Boundary Testing in Digital Learning Games

V. Elizabeth Owen
University of Wisconsin-Madison
225 N Mills St.
Madison, WI 53715
+16082634600
v.elizabeth.owen@gmail.com

Gabriella Anton
Northwestern University
633 Clark St.
Evanston, IL 60208
+18474913741
gabby.anton@gmail.com

Ryan Baker
Teachers College Columbia University
525 W 120th St.
New York, NY 10027
+12126783000
ryanshaunbaker@gmail.com

SUMMARY
Digital games can be potent problem solving environments which afford discovery learning through thoughtful exploration [1, 2]. As such, game microworlds facilitate self-regulated learning through sandbox elements in which students have agency in individualizing their pathways of interaction [3]. These agency-driven environments can support learning via individual discovery of problem space constraints and solutions, particularly through boundary testing and productive failure [cf. 4]. Thus, modeling of user interaction in digital learning games can provide considerable insight into emergent trajectories of discovery-based progression, in which equally engaged players may interact differently with the system. To this end, this research leverages educational data mining (EDM) [5] to investigate organic player trajectories of thoughtful exploration (around boundary testing and productive failure) in a learning gamespace. We align behavioral coding with log file data to automatically detect sequences of thoughtful exploration (TE) in play. Results include a robust predictive model of event-stream TE, with multiple trajectories of emergent student behavior—offering insight into organic learning pathways through the game-based problem space, and informing iterative design in optimization of user experience and student engagement.

Keywords
Serious games; game-based learning; microworlds; exploration; productive failure; student model; classification; behavior detection; educational data mining.

1. METHODS
This study investigates thoughtful exploration in emergent learning trajectories of students in educational games, specifically in the STEM game *Progenitor X*. *Progenitor* is a biology game developed by the Games+Learning+Society (GLS) center at UW-Madison[1]. As a regenerative biologist, the player must save infected patients from a zombie epidemic by using stem cell science to regenerate healthy tissue and organs. Key virtual lab procedures include *starting* with base cells, *treating* them, and

[1] http://www.gameslearningsociety.org/project_progenitor_x.php

UMAP '16, July 13-17, 2016, Halifax, NS, Canada
ACM 978-1-4503-4370-1/16/07.
http://dx.doi.org/10.1145/2930238.2930271

collecting the transformed cells. This core loop occurs in increasing difficulty in three systems-level biology layers: cell, tissue and organ phases. 110 middle school students played *Progenitor* at the Wisconsin Institute for Discovery as a part a public summer school program. Students completed a pre- and post- survey after an hour-long game session, which included biology items and demographic questions (e.g. grade level, gender, and gaming habits). Student choices within play were captured in the form of log file data; this was driven by ADAGE [6], an event-stream data framework designed to capture salient learning data in educational games.

1.1 Analysis Methods: Building a Detector for Thoughtful Exploration in *Progenitor X*
Prediction modeling in *Progenitor* was used to build a behavior detector, an automated model that can infer from log files whether a student is behaving in a certain way [e.g. 7]. These models can be employed to detect a variety of student behavior aspects, including affect and performance [e.g. 8, 9]. Detectors often leverage human judgment of student behavior, in a process used to train models which can then replicate that judgment. In this study, the analysis process includes: 1) distilling salient data features; 2) identifying instances of the behavior through human evaluation; and 3) predictive modeling with synchronized log file data.

1.1.1 Feature Distillation
Distilling event-stream data into salient features for analysis is vital in data mining for user modeling. In *Progenitor*, game progress markers helped guide feature distillation (including eight broad gameplay objectives, with multiple lab cycles in each). Figure 1 summarizes final features, with objectives and cycles corresponding to event-stream interaction, organized by progression (game navigation) and performance (success/failure).

	Progression	Performance
Objective	• objective added • objective starts • objective ends • UI tab: mission screen • mission screen: city selected • UI button use: view objective / add objective	• successes • UI event: complete • cycles in a finished objective • failures • restarts • attempt number
Cycle	• cycle starts / ends / quits • cycle type: cell, tissue, organ • type of cell started in cycle (type I or II) • type of cell collected in cycle (type I or II) • UI tool select / use: "start" / "move" / "treat" / "collect"	• successes • num + type of cells collected • total turns in a cycle • health remaining at end of cycle • failure (health gone) • failure (wrong cell collect) • % of health used in each cycle
Overall	• time elapsed • game starts • UI button use: "next" / "back" • UI button use: almanac • UI button use: sound off/on • Grid select: cell, tissue, organ	• game win/loss • mission success events • total objectives complete • total missions complete • mission/game quit • mission/game restart

Figure 1. Summary of base data features.

1.1.2 Coding for Thoughtful Exploration

These data enabled evaluation of the target behavior: thoughtful exploration (TE). In recent research, "exploratory behavior" has proven central to learning growth [10], in natural alignment with game-based learning environments [1, 3]. The construct of productive failure in these contexts emphasizes opportunities to explore constraints of a problem space, and test multiple solution methods [cf. 4]. Since boundary-testing and failing forward can be central to productive learning contexts [e.g. 10, 4]—and games support exploration-based discovery of problem space constraints [2]—the construct of thoughtful exploration emerges as a behavior of focus. Broadly, the target construct here entails investigating system tools, discovering constraints, and testing solutions within the game's learning space.

For TE detection, researchers observed a stream of student actions and identified instances of the behavior. For observing this stream, text replays (a text-based representation of student action during a given span of play) were utilized for their efficiency and accuracy [11]. Text replay clip size for *Progenitor X* was one objective, shown for one player at a time. Clip features displayed *sequences* of key laboratory actions, along with all UI interactions and context (time, position, etc.). Performance data was also displayed, including quit, re-start, and completion (see Figure 1).

Through the use of these text replays, player actions were observed and evaluated for the target behavior with the binary coding schema "thoughtful exploration" (TE) or "not thoughtful exploration" (no_TE). Acceptable inter-rater reliability was achieved between coders, yielding a Cohen's κ [12] of .908.

1.1.3 Behavior Prediction: the TE Detection Model

The final predictive model aligned input variables (1.1.1) with behavioral outcome variables (1.1.2). The TE detector was built using WEKA, a standard tool for data mining. Aligned to the outcome variable (number of TE instances per student), a set of algorithms were selected accordingly: RepTREE, linear regression, K*, and M5'. Models were cross-validated at the student level (the unit of analysis). A single final model was chosen based on the goodness metric of a cross-validated Pearson correlation.

```
Total collects <= 14.5: Linear Model 1 (63/55.337%)
Total collects > 14.5:
 | Total num of times type II cells collected in Obj 5 <= 0.5: LM2 (32/51.697%)
 | Total num of times type II cells collected in Obj 5 > 0.5: LM3 (15/48.256%)

Linear Model 1:                                  Linear Model 2:
total Thoughtful Exploration instances =         total Thoughtful Exploration instances =
0.0011 * duration of Obj 0 (training)            0.8926 * average % health used in Obj 0
+ 0.0282 * total cells collected in Obj 0        + 0.0322 * total optional UI buttons used in Obj 0
+ 0.7095 * average % health used in Obj 0        + 0.0008 * duration of Obj 1
+ 0.0256 * total optional UI buttons used in Obj 0  - 0.1119 * total type I cell cycles in Obj 1
+ 0.0026 * duration of Obj 1                     + 0.0033 * duration of Obj 2 (2nd half)
- 0.0178 * total type I cell cycles in Obj 1     - 0.2903 * average % health used in Obj 2 (1st half)
- 0.2307 * average % health used in Obj 2 (1st half)  + 0.0009 * duration of Obj 2 (2nd half)
+ 0.0007 * duration of Obj 2 (2nd half)          - 1.4842 * average % health used in Obj 2 (2nd half)
- 0.196 * average % health used in Obj 2 (2nd half)  + 0.321 * total times type II cells collected in Obj 5
+ 0.104 * total times type II cells collected in Obj 5  - 0.0143 * total cell collection instances in Obj 5
+ 0.0022 * total cells collected in Obj 5        + 0.0027 * total cells collected in Obj 5
+ 0.0957 * total type II cell cycles in Obj 8    + 0.2328 * total type II cell cycles in Obj 8
- 0.0033 * duration of Obj 8 (2nd half)          - 0.0041 * duration of Obj 8 (2nd half)
+ 0.1094 * total successful cycles in Obj 8 (2nd half)  + 0.1377 * total successful cycles in Obj 8 (2nd half)
- 0.0076 * total cell or tissue collection instances  - 0.0095 * total cell or tissue collection instances
- 0.1585                                         + 2.3512

Linear Model 3:
total Thoughtful Exploration instances =
- 0.196 * total type I cell cycles in Obj 1
+ 0.8926 * average % health used in Obj 0
+ 0.0322 * total optional UI buttons used in Obj 0
+ 0.0008 * duration of Obj 1
- 0.0687 * total type I cell cycles in Obj 1
- 0.0547 * total type II cell cycles in Obj 1
- 0.2903 * average % health used in Obj 2 (1st half)
+ 0.0009 * duration of Obj 2 (2nd half)
- 0.7426 * average % health used in Obj 2 (2nd half)
+ 0.4288 * total times type II cells collected in Obj 5
- 0.0224 * total cell collection instances in Obj 5
+ 0.0027 * total cells collected in Obj 5
+ 0.5849 * total type II cell cycles in Obj 8
- 0.0041 * duration of Obj 8 (2nd half)
+ 0.1377 * total successful cycles in Obj 8 (2nd half)
- 0.0095 * total cell or tissue collection instances
+ 2.7171
```

Figure 2. The *Progenitor X* detector of thoughtful exploration.

2. RESULTS

Ultimately, M5' produced the best model performance, achieving a cross-validated correlation of .627, comparable to levels in similar detector models [e.g. 9]. Output is shown below.

3. DISCUSSION AND CONCLUSION

This paper presents a predictive student model that serves as a real-time detector of thoughtful exploration in *Progenitor*, using an EDM approach to reveal organic trajectories of student behavior. The M5' detector yielded several branches of play interactions in relationship to thoughtful exploration, revealing multiple emergent user trajectories. Future research entails deeper investigation of students within each branch. Mining these emergent, varied user models also has strong design implications. These data-driven insights fuel the potential for highly effective, game-based adaptive learning systems—which can respond to the exploration and discovery-based learning inherent to games, and optimize personalized, engaging student experiences at scale.

ACKNOWLEDGMENTS

This work was made possible by a grant from the NSF (DRL-1119383), although the views expressed herein are those of the authors' and do not necessarily represent the funding agency. We also deeply thank Dr. Steinkuehler and the entire GLS team.

REFERENCES

[1] R. R. Burton and J. S. Brown, "An investigation of computer coaching for informal learning activities.," *Int. J. Man-Mach. Stud.*, vol. 11, no. 1, pp. 5–24, 1979.

[2] K. Squire, *Video Games and Learning: Teaching and Participatory Culture in the Digital Age.* Teachers College Press, 2011.

[3] L. P. Rieber, "Seriously considering play: Designing interactive learning environments based on the blending of microworlds, simulations, and games.," *Educ. Technol. Res. Dev.*, vol. 44, no. 2, pp. 43–58, 1996.

[4] M. Kapur, "Productive failure," in *Proceedings of the International Conference on the Learning Sciences*, 2006, vol. 0, pp. 307–313.

[5] R. S. Baker and K. Yacef, "The state of educational data mining in 2009: A review and future visions," *J. Educ. Data Min.*, vol. 1, no. 1, pp. 3–17, 2009.

[6] R. Halverson and V. E. Owen, "Game Based Assessment: An Integrated Model for Capturing Evidence of Learning in Play," *Int. J. Learn. Technol. Spec. Issue Game-Based Learn.*, vol. 9, no. 2, pp. 111–138, 2014.

[7] R. S. Baker, A. T. Corbett, and K. R. Koedinger, "Detecting student misuse of intelligent tutoring systems," in *Intelligent tutoring systems*, 2004, pp. 531–540.

[8] Z. A. Pardos, R. S. Baker, M. O. C. Z. San Pedro, S. M. Gowda, and S. M. Gowda, "Affective States and State Tests: Investigating How Affect and Engagement during the School Year Predict End-of-Year Learning Outcomes," *J. Learn. Anal.*, vol. 1, no. 1, pp. 107–128, 2014.

[9] R. S. Baker and J. Clarke-Midura, "Predicting Successful Inquiry Learning in a Virtual Performance Assessment for Science," in *Proceedings of the 21st International Conference on User Modeling, Adaptation, and Personalization*, 2013, pp. 203–214.

[10] D. L. Schwartz and T. Martin, "Inventing to Prepare for Future Learning: The Hidden Efficiency of Encouraging Original Student Production in Statistics Instruction," *Cogn. Instr.*, vol. 22, no. 2, pp. 129–184, 2004.

[11] R. S. Baker and A. de Carvalho, "Labeling student behavior faster and more precisely with text replays," in *Proceedings of the 1st International Conference on Educational Data Mining*, 2008, pp. 38–47.

[12] J. Cohen, "A coefficient of agreement for nominal scales.," *Educ. Psychol. Meas.*, vol. 20, no. 1, pp. 37–46, 1960.

Agent-Based Personalisation and User Modeling for Personalised Educational Games

Marieke M.M. Peeters *
Delft University of Technology
Mekelweg 4, Delft
The Netherlands
m.m.m.peeters@tudelft.nl

Karel van den Bosch
TNO
Kampweg 5, Soesterberg
The Netherlands
karel.vandenbosch@tno.nl

John-Jules Ch. Meyer
Utrecht University
Princetonplein 5, Utrecht
The Netherlands
j.j.c.meyer@uu.nl

Mark A. Neerincx
TNO
Kampweg 5, Soesterberg
and
Delft University of Technology
Mekelweg 4, Delft
The Netherlands
mark.neerincx@tno.nl

ABSTRACT

Personalisation can increase the learning efficacy of educational games by tailoring their content to the needs of the individual learner. This paper presents the *Personalised Educational Game Architecture (PEGA)*. It uses a multi-agent organisation and an ontology to offer learners personalised training in a game environment. The multi-agent organisation's flexibility enables adaptive automation; the instructor can decide to control only parts of the training, while leaving the rest to the intelligent agents.

CCS Concepts

•Human-centered computing → User models; •Computing methodologies → Intelligent agents; •Computing methodologies → Multi-agent systems; •Applied computing → Interactive learning environments;

Keywords

User Modeling; Intelligent Agents; Personalised Educational Game; Scenario-based Training; Difficulty Adjustment

1. INTRODUCTION

Many professional organisations require workers to make good decisions under risky and stressful circumstances, e.g. the fire department, army, police force, or hospital. In order to become proficient in this type of domains, learners

*Corresponding author.

UMAP '16 July 13-17, 2016, Halifax, NS, Canada

© 2016 Copyright held by the owner/author(s).

ACM ISBN 978-1-4503-4370-1/16/07.

DOI: http://dx.doi.org/10.1145/2930238.2930273

need practice and experience with situations that are critical and/or exemplary for their line of work. Yet professionals who are active in high-risk domains cannot gather experience through learning on-the-job, because in real-life situations the wrong decision may well cause life-threatening complications.

Scenario-based training (SBT) is regarded as a suitable and effective training form [1, 8]. SBT enables learners to practice exemplary situations in *'scenarios'*: interactive role-playing exercises with human actors. Traditionally, scenarios are staged in a *physical - real life -* simulated environment. SBT offers learners opportunities to experience the consequences of their decisions in a relatively safe and controlled environment.

One of the major downsides of SBT is its heavy logistic and organisational demands, e.g. the clearance and preparation of an area to stage the scenarios, the preparation of elaborate scenario scripts, the training and instruction of role players, and the simultaneous presence of all people involved (actors, trainees, instructors). Another downside is that during scenario enactment it is hard, or even impossible, to alter the course of events in the scenario, making it difficult to personalize training. Furthermore, it is often problematic to monitor and interpret events in the scenario in a structured, systematic, and non-ambiguous manner - especially in large scale scenarios involving multiple locations, it can be difficult for one person to maintain an overview of what is happening.

Development of new training technology may solve or alleviate the obstacles that prevent ample and effective use of SBT, by placing SBT in a virtual (game) environment, and controlling parts of the training with the use of artificial intelligence [1, 4, 7]. This paper introduces the *'Personalised Educational Game Architecture (PEGA)'*, which aims to provide such technology by staging SBT in a smart game environment. PEGA uses artificial intelligence to attune the behaviour of the characters and the events taking place in the scenario to the individual needs of the learner. As a result, learners can develop their competencies at their own level and pace, even in the absence of an instructor.

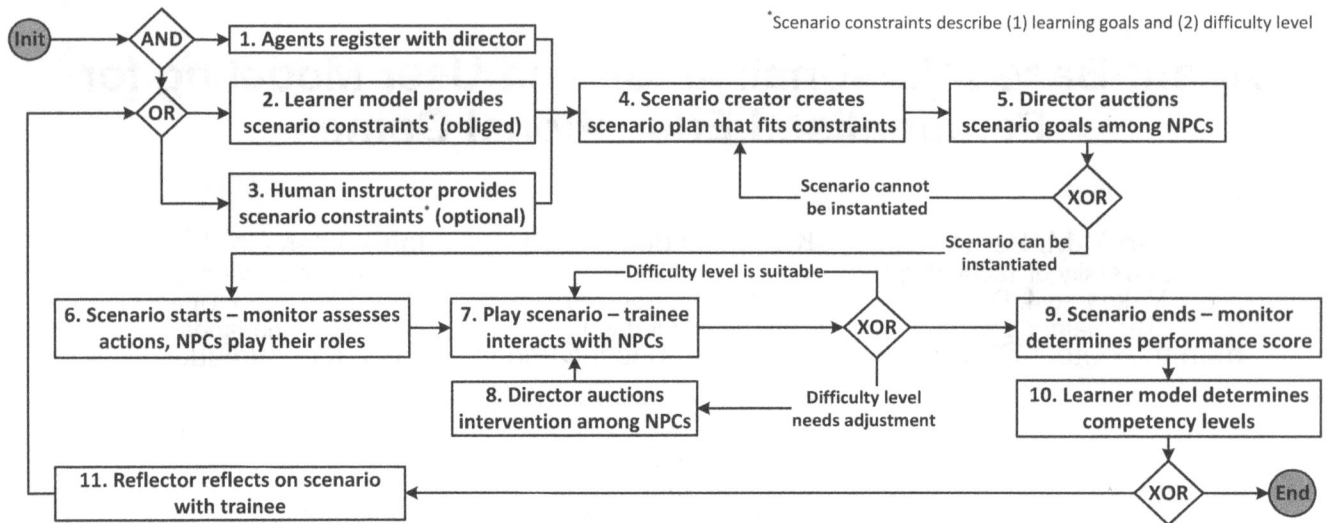

Figure 1: The behaviour of the multi-agent organisation

2. PEGA

PEGA describes an ontology and a multi-agent organisation. PEGA's *ontology* provides an explicit representation of the declarative knowledge needed for the intelligent agents to attune the game to the needs of the individual learner [6]. PEGA's *multi-agent organisation* partitions the training system into a collection of agents [2]. Scenarios are staged within a game environment inhabited by *non-player characters (NPCs)* with which the learner can interact, e.g. victims, bystanders, or friends of the victim. The *learner model* keeps track of the learner's competencies and motivation. It uses that information to determine a suitable learning goal and difficulty level. The *scenario creator* uses automated planning techniques and information in the ontology to generate a scenario that targets the learning goal - determined by the learner model - at the desired difficulty level [3, 6]. The *director* auctions the roles and goals among the NPCs. The *monitor* keeps track of the learner's actions to decide whether to adjust the scenario's difficulty level to better match the learner's competencies [5]. The *reflector* encourages the learner to reflect on the training performance after the scenario has come to an end. The behaviour of the multi-agent organisation is depicted in Figure 1.

3. DISCUSSION & CONCLUSION

PEGA's multi-agent organisation supports *adaptive automation*. The instructor decides the level of automation. The instructor can take up various roles in the training process while leaving the other roles to the agents, e.g. provide a scenario plan, monitor the learner, issue interventions, or take on the role of an NPC. The human instructor can also instruct the agents in advance of the training on how to control the environment to adapt it to the needs of the learner, enabling the learner to train in the absence of the instructor. PEGA's ontology supports coherent communication between the actors (both artificial and human) in the organisation. Future research aims to (1) develop more sophisticated agents to play their parts in PEGA, and (2) verify that learners' competency development is effectively enhanced by training with PEGA.

4. ACKNOWLEDGMENTS

The authors would like to thank Ruben de Jong and Christian van Rooij for their contributions.

5. REFERENCES

[1] J. Cannon-Bowers, J. Burns, E. Salas, and J. Pruitt. Advanced technology in scenario-based training. In J. Cannon-Bowers and E. Salas, editors, *Making Decisions Under Stress*, pages 365–374. APA, 1998.

[2] V. Dignum, F. Dignum, and J.-J. Meyer. An agent-mediated approach to the support of knowledge sharing in organizations. *The Knowledge Engineering Review*, 19(02):147–174, 2004.

[3] G. R. Ferdinandus, M. M. M. Peeters, K. van den Bosch, and J.-J. C. Meyer. Automated scenario generation - coupling planning techniques with smart objects. In *Conference for Computer Supported Education*, pages 76–81, 2013.

[4] R. L. Oser, J. A. Cannon-Bowers, E. Salas, and D. J. Dwyer. Enhancing human performance in technology-rich environments: guidelines for scenario-based training. *Human Technology Interaction in Complex Systems*, 9:175–202, 1999.

[5] M. M. M. Peeters, K. van den Bosch, J.-J. C. Meyer, and M. A. Neerincx. The Design and Effect of Automated Directions During Scenario-based Training. *Computers & Education*, 70:173–183, 2014.

[6] M. M. M. Peeters, K. van den Bosch, M. A. Neerincx, and J.-J. C. Meyer. An Ontology for Automated Scenario-based Training. *International Journal of Technology Enhanced Learning*, 6(3):195–211, 2014.

[7] M. O. Riedl and R. M. Young. Narrative planning: Balancing plot and character. *Journal of Artificial Intelligence Research*, 39(1):217–268, 2010.

[8] K. van den Bosch and J. B. J. Riemersma. Reflections on scenario-based training in tactical command. In S. Schiflett, editor, *Scaled worlds: Development, validation, and applications*, chapter 1, pages 1–21. Ashgate, 2004.

TBPR: Trinity Preference based Bayesian Personalized Ranking for Multivariate Implicit Feedback

Huihuai Qiu*
Beijing Jiaotong University
Beijing, China
huihuaiqiu@bjtu.edu.cn

Guibing Guo
Northeastern University
Shenyang, China

Jie Zhang
Nanyang Technological
University
Singapore

Zhu Sun
Nanyang Technological
University
Singapore

Hai Thanh Nguyen
Telenor Research
Oslo, Norway

Yun Liu
Beijing Jiaotong University
Beijing, China

ABSTRACT

In e-commerce systems, user preference can be inferred from multivariate implicit feedback (i.e., actions). However, most methods merely focus on homogeneous implicit feedback (i.e., *purchase*). In this paper, we adopt another two typical actions, i.e., *view* and *like*, as auxiliaries to enhance *purchase* recommendation, whereby a trinity Bayesian personalized ranking (TBPR) method is proposed. Specifically, we introduce *trinity preference* to investigate the difference of users' preference among three types of items: 1) items with purchase action; 2) items with only auxiliary actions; 3) items without any action. Empirical study on the real-world dataset demonstrates that our method significantly outperforms state-of-the-art algorithms.

Keywords

Recommendation, implicit feedback, trinity preference

1. INTRODUCTION

Personalized recommendation has become an indispensable part of e-commerce service. The study on implicit feedback (i.e., actions) based recommendation methods has received much attention nowadays since explicit feedback (i.e. ratings) may not always available. Implicit feedback is actually multivariate in real-word systems. Taking an online shopping website as an example, users may perform various actions on items such as *view* (browse the details), *like* (click the 'like' button) and *purchase* (buy the item). Although *view* and *like* are not directly related to purchase, they help model user preference as useful side information, called *auxiliary* in our study. However, existing studies [1, 3] mainly focus on homogeneous implicit feedback and merely consider *purchase*, thus to inherently suffer from the *data sparsity*

UMAP '16 July 13-17, 2016, Halifax, NS, Canada

© 2016 Copyright held by the owner/author(s).

ACM ISBN 978-1-4503-4370-1/16/07.

DOI: http://dx.doi.org/10.1145/2930238.2930272

problem. The only work integrating multivariate implicit feedback for item ranking is Adaptive Bayesian Personalized Ranking (ABPR) proposed by Pan et al. [2]. It adopts *view* as *auxiliary* but the assumption of BPR preference for homogeneous implicit feedback [3] is utilized. Moreover, too many parameters are introduced to learn the difference between user preference towards items with *purchase* and those with *view*. Besides, the generality is limited since it cannot handle more than one types of *auxiliary*.

In this paper, we propose a trinity Bayesian personalized ranking (TBPR) method which is the first approach that incorporates multiple types of *auxiliary* (i.e., *view* and *like*) with *purchase* for better recommendation. A fine-grained assumption, *trinity preference*, is utilized to investigate user preference towards three types of items: those with *purchase*, with only *auxiliary*, with no action. Furthermore, our method can automatically learn the importance of user preference difference towards items with different user actions based on the overlap of the *auxiliary* and *purchase* with few parameters. The empirical results show that our method significantly outperforms state-of-the-art algorithms by 22% in terms of AUC and 114% in terms of MAP.

2. OUR TBPR METHOD

The basic assumption of BPR preference restricts that user u prefers item i to item j if i is with *purchase* while j is not. However, user preference among items without *purchase* can be distinguished when *auxiliary* is considered. Hence, we classify items into three types as mentioned in Section 1 and define an *item trinity* for each user, $T(u) = \left\{ (i,j,k) \mid i \in I_p^u, j \in I_{oa}^u, k \in I_n^u \right\}$, I_p^u, I_{oa}^u and I_n^u are sets of items with *purchase*, with only *auxiliary* and with no action, respectively. User preference towards items in $T(u)$ should be significantly different. *Purchase*, *auxiliary* and no action indicate strong, weak and no user preference. Thus, we assume that for user u, her preference towards item j is stronger than that towards item k but weaker than that towards item i if $(i,j,k) \in T(u)$, namely *trinity preference*.

Following [3], we maximize the likelihood of preference for all users based on *trinity preference*. $\sigma(x-y) = 1/(1 + e^{-(x-y)})$ is utilized to approximate the probability $P(x > y)$, and log-likelihood is adopted to reduce the computational complexity. The objective function for TBPR model is,

$$\max f(\theta) = \sum_u \left\{ \sum_{i,j} \ln \sigma \left(\frac{\hat{x}_{uij}(\theta)}{\alpha_u} \right) + \sum_{j,k} \ln \sigma \left(\hat{x}_{ujk}(\theta) \right) \right\} - \mathcal{R}(\theta),$$

where θ is a set of model parameters to be learnt; $\mathcal{R}(\theta)$ is the regularization term to avoid overfitting; $\hat{x}_{uij}(\theta) = \hat{r}_{ui}(\theta) - \hat{r}_{uj}(\theta)$ is the estimated preference difference of u for i with *purchase* and j with *auxiliary*; α_u is a parameter which controls the contribution of the estimated preference difference $\hat{x}_{uij}$.

In fact, the smaller the preference difference between i, j, the less contributions $\hat{x}_{uij}$ should make in the objective function $f(\theta)$, which means the larger α_u should be. Smaller preference difference between i and j can be inferred from higher correlation between user u's *purchase* and *auxiliary*. In other words, α_u is positively influenced by the correlation between *purchase* and *auxiliary* of user u. Since a user can perform multiple actions on an item, there is overlap between *purchase* and *auxiliary*. More overlap indicates higher correlation, i.e., the larger α_u. Thus, we adopt the overlap to initialize α_u, based on which, α_u can be finely learnt. Let $\alpha_u^{(0)} = \omega \cdot O^u$, where $\alpha_u^{(0)}$ is the initial value of α_u; $\omega > 0$ is the coefficient controlling the importance of O^u; O^u represents the overlap percentage of *purchase* and *auxiliary* for user u. However, we find that the overlap percentage of *auxiliary* in *purchase* (O_{ap}^u) and that of *purchase* in *auxiliary* (O_{pa}^u) are asymmetric. Thus, O^u named *overlap index* should be influenced by both O_{ap}^u and O_{pa}^u, $O^u = 2 \cdot O_{pa}^u \cdot O_{ap}^u / (O_{pa}^u + O_{ap}^u)$. Since we consider two types of *auxiliary*: *view* and *like*, $O^u(view)$ (the *overlap index* for *view* and *purchase*) and $O^u(like)$ (the *overlap index* for *like* and *purchase*) is calculated respectively. Note that due to the complicated motivation for a user to click 'like', some *like* has nothing to do with *purchase*. For instance, people share something cool on their homepages and their friends would click 'like' as support. To filter out the noise in *like*, we select items with both *like* and *view* to compose the filtered *like* item set, since most users would view before they purchase. The final $\alpha_u^{(0)}$ is given by: $\alpha_u^{(0)} = \rho \cdot \alpha_u^{(0)}(view) + (1 - \rho) \cdot \alpha_u^{(0)}(like)$, where $\rho \in [0, 1]$ controls the importance of *view*. Note that if user u only performs *view/like*, then $\rho = 1/0$; Based on $\alpha_u^{(0)}$, α_u can be further finely learnt by our model.

3. EXPERIMENTS AND ANALYSIS

A dataset originated from an online fashion app, Sobazaar (4,712 users perform 18,267 *purchase*, 225,651 *view* and 100,067 *like* over 7,015 items), is used in our empirical study.

We apply the 5-fold cross validation and 6 widely used metrics, including precision@5, recall@5, area under the ROC curve (AUC), normalized discounted cumulative gain (NDCG), mean average precision (MAP) and mean reciprocal rank (MRR), to evaluate the performance of each method. Larger values of these metrics indicate better recommendation performance. We compare two baseline methods with different versions of TBPR: (1) **BPR** [3] is the classic Bayesian personalized ranking method; (2) **ABPR** [2] is the adaptive BPR method and the first work to incorporate one type of *auxiliary*, i.e., *view*; (3) **TBPR**$_{cv}$ only considers *view* and sets $\alpha_u^{(0)}$ to a same constant for all users; (4) **TBPR**$_v$ only considers *view*; (5) **TBPR**$_l$ only considers *like*; (6) **TBPR**$_{fl}$

Table 1: Recommendation performance of different methods on Sobazaar dataset.

Methods	Pre@5	Rec@5	AUC	MAP	NDCG	MRR
BPR	0.0100	0.0358	0.7299	0.0257	0.1463	0.0337
ABPR	0.0101*	0.0364*	0.7314*	0.0262*	0.1468*	0.0341*
TBPR$_{cv}$	0.0111	0.0400	0.8481	0.0302	0.1589	0.0388
TBPR$_v$	0.0146	0.0596	0.8868	0.0496	0.1860	0.0574
TBPR$_l$	0.0104	0.0378	0.7816	0.0269	0.1505	0.0348
TBPR$_{fl}$	0.0106	0.0377	0.8052	0.0297	0.1544	0.0367
TBPR$_b$	**0.0172**	**0.0682**	**0.8901**	**0.0561**	**0.1929**	**0.0654**
Improve	55%	70%	22%	114%	31%	92%

only considers filtered *like*; (7) **TBPR**$_b$ considers both *view* and filtered *like*.

Table 1 shows the performance of all comparison methods, where the best performance of our method is highlighted in bold, and the best performance of baseline methods is marked by '*'. The row 'Improve' indicates the improvements of our best performance relative to the '*' results. Some interesting observations can be noted: 1) ABPR performs better than BPR, indicating the importance of auxiliary action for better recommendation; 2) TBPR$_v$ consistently outperforms ABPR across all the metrics, which demonstrates that our fine-grained assumption is able to help model user preference more accurately; 3) The performance of TBPR$_v$ is better than that of TBPR$_{cv}$, verifying that it is more reasonable to treat each user distinctively by learning α_u. 4) TBPR$_{fl}$ outperforms TBPR$_l$ slightly. This implies that *auxiliary* having higher correlation with *purchase* are more effective to enhance recommendation performance; 5) TBPR$_b$ incorporating both *view* and *like* performs best, which suggests that the best performance can be generated by appropriately integrating both types of *auxiliary*.

4. CONCLUSIONS AND FUTURE WORK

In this paper, we proposed a *trinity preference* based Bayesian personalized ranking (TBPR) model for multivariate implicit feedback. A fine-grained assumption was presented to distinguish the user preference difference between items with *purchase* and those with *auxiliary* more accurately. Empirical study shows that our method achieves significant better recommendation performance than state-of-the-art algorithms. For future work, we plan to find ways to incorporate other types of *auxiliary*.

5. ACKNOWLEDGMENTS

This work is supported by the Telenor-NTU Joint R&D grant awarded to Dr. Jie Zhang. We also thank Jarle Snertingdalen, Markus Kruger and Atif Hakeem who provide Sobazaar data.

6. REFERENCES

[1] W. Pan and L. Chen. Gbpr: Group preference based bayesian personalized ranking for one-class collaborative filtering. In *IJCAI*, 2013.

[2] W. Pan, H. Zhong, C. Xu, and Z. Ming. Adaptive bayesian personalized ranking for heterogeneous implicit feedbacks. *KBS*, 73:173–180, 2015.

[3] S. Rendle, C. Freudenthaler, Z. Gantner, and L. Schmidt-Thieme. Bpr: Bayesian personalized ranking from implicit feedback. In *UAI*, 2009.

Modeling Community Behavior through Semantic Analysis of Social Data: the Italian Hate Map Experience

Cataldo Musto, Giovanni Semeraro, Marco de Gemmis, Pasquale Lops
Dept. of Computer Science
University of Bari 'Aldo Moro', Italy
name.surname@uniba.it

ABSTRACT

This paper presents the results of THE ITALIAN HATE MAP, a research project aiming to monitor the level of *intolerance* of the Italian country by mining the content posted on social networks. Within the project, a pipeline of algorithms for data extraction, semantic processing, sentiment analysis and content classification has been defined to process huge amounts of Tweets and to build a map of the most at-risk areas, thus identifying the Italian communities tending to have a more intolerant behavior.

The outcomes resulting from the analysis of the maps confirmed the insight that the adoption of semantic content analysis techniques can be very useful to *create value* from the rough content available on the Web, and to go one step further in understanding very complex phenomena by modeling *offline* behavior of the communities on the ground of their *online* behavior on social networks.

Keywords

Semantics; Community Behavior; Urban Informatics; Social Media; Sentiment Analysis; Content Processing

1. BACKGROUND AND CONTRIBUTIONS

Recent statistics show that episodes of *intolerance* are commonplace around the world. As an example, 179 Italian women were killed[1] in 2013, 17% of british gay citizens have been victimized within the past three years[2] and 51% of Americans expressed anti-black sentiments in a poll of 2012[3]. These data clearly show that problems as racism, violence against women and homophobia are far away from being resolved.

However, the recent and huge availability of data coming from social networks let tackle these issues in a totally new way. As an example, mining micro-blogs content is drawing more and more attention since latent information about people sentiment, thinking and opinions can be automatically extracted from textual content, and this paves the way to the development of intelligent services relying on content analytics of *human-generated* streams. Specifically, content produced on social networks can be analyzed to identify the areas where intolerant behaviors (expressed through the use of an intolerant *lexicon*) more frequently occur, and this information can be used to guide the definition of specific interventions (recovery and prevention) on the territory.

According to this insight, The Italian Hate Map project aimed to model and identify intolerant individuals on the ground of the content they posted on social networks and to aggregate these users on a geographical basis (by exploiting information about geo-localization) in order to identify the most at-risk areas of the Italian territory. In other terms, the project had the ambitious goal of modeling *offline behavior* of Italian communities on the ground of *online* one, by exploiting the use of an intolerant language on social media as an indicator of tendency towards intolerant behaviors. This non-trivial task of community modeling led to several interesting applications, since the identification of the most at-risk areas was used by public administrations to guide the definition of specific interventions (recovery and prevention) on the territory. The project was clearly inspired by the Hate Map built by Humboldt University[4], but, differently from the USA Hate Map, we automatically labeled intolerant content by exploiting a pipeline a techniques for semantic processing and sentiment analysis of extracted data.

Generally speaking, our project falls in the research line of social (or participatory) sensing [1], which is based on the insight that the mash-up of crowd-based data can lead to the development of novel services and applications. In the follows, we will describe the methodology that was designed to reach the goals of the project and we will show some quantitative preliminary result of the research.

[1]http://bit.ly/1AHNO6b
[2]http://bit.ly/1CwZtXL
[3]http://bit.ly/1k20Kev

UMAP '16, July 13–17, 2016, Halifax, Nova Scotia, Canada.

© 2016 Copyright held by the owner/author(s).

ACM ISBN 978-1-4503-4370-1/16/07...$15.00

DOI: http://dx.doi.org/10.1145/2930238.2930274

2. BUILDING THE ITALIAN HATE MAPS

We exploited a domain-agnostic framework for semantic analysis of social streams called CrowdPulse [3]. The framework is based on the concept of *processing graphs*. Each *processing graph* consists of a set of *nodes* and a set of *edges* connecting these nodes. The general workflow is depicted in Figure 1. First, the SOCIAL EXTRACTOR was launched

[4]http://users.humboldt.edu/mstephens/hate/hate_map.html

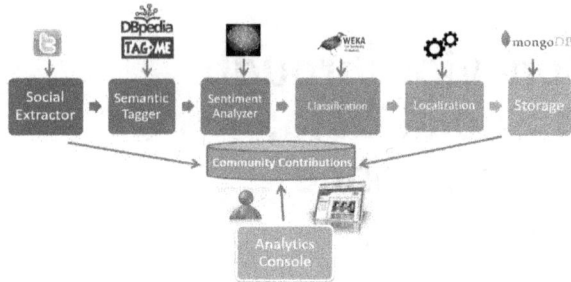

Figure 1: General Workflow

by defining a set of *sensible terms* for each intolerance dimension. The definition of the lexicons associated to each dimension was performed by psychologists with specific experience in this domain. The final list contained 47 Italian terms.

Dimension	#Tweets	#GeoTweets	%GeoTweets
Homophobia	110,774	8,501	7,66%
Racism	154,170	1,940	1,24%
Violence	1,102,494	28,886	2,62%
Disability	479,654	3,410	0,75%
Anti-Semitism	965	174	18,03%

Table 1: Statistics about extracted content

Next, semantic processing and sentiment analysis were exploited to remove ambiguous and non-intolerant Tweets. Indeed, the retrieval process performed by the SOCIAL EXTRACTOR relies on a simple keyword-based search, thus a lot of noisy Tweets (especially when *polysemous* terms are used as sensible terms) are returned. To this end, all the content has been processed by a SEMANTIC TAGGER which exploits entity linking algorithms as Tag.me[5] and DBpedia Spotlight[6] to disambiguate the terms occurring in the Tweets. Due to space reasons it is not possible to come into details of the strategy, but the insight is that entity linking algorithm can automatically identify the meaning of the terms occurring in the Tweet, thus they can be used to filter out Tweets containing polysemous terms (as the Italian term *finocchio*, which is both a translation of *fennel* and *queer*). After, disambiguated Tweets are processed through a SENTIMENT ANALYZER. In this case we followed the insight that a Tweet with a *neutral* or *positive* sentiment score doesn't convey any intolerant message, thus it can be removed from the maps. As regards sentiment analysis, we implemented the lexicon-based approach described in [2]. Given such a representation, we trained a classification model by asking domain experts to manually annotate a sample 1000 extracted Tweets as *intolerant* or *not intolerant*. We used these Tweets to build a classification model able to identify new *intolerant* Tweet. Finally, the remaining Tweets have been localized in order to produce an *heat map* as that shown in the figure. Beyond the Tweets containing an explicit geo-localization, we introduced some heuristics to increase the amount of geo-localized Tweets: as an example, all the Tweets posted by a users having with an explicit *location* attribute inherited that location.

---

[5]http://tagme.di.unipi.it/

[6]https://github.com/dbpedia-spotlight/dbpedia-spotlight/wiki

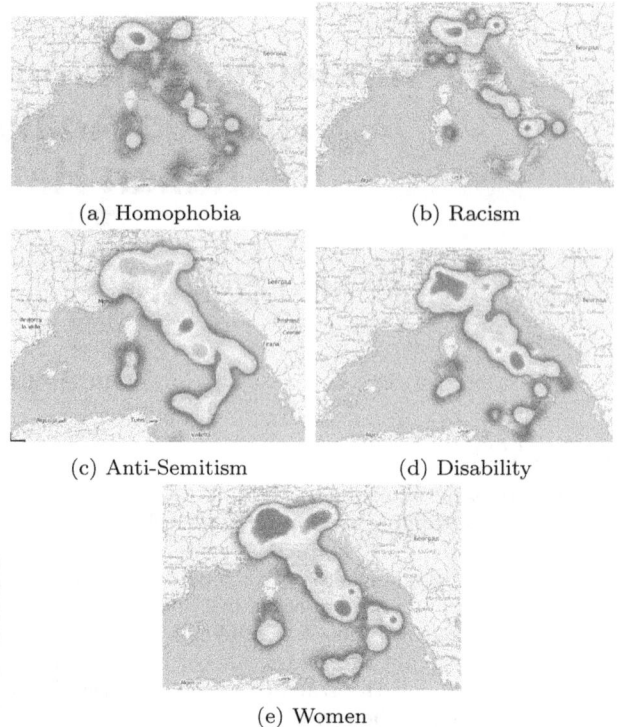

(a) Homophobia   (b) Racism

(c) Anti-Semitism   (d) Disability

(e) Women

Figure 2: The Italian Hate Maps

As reported in Table 1, in a time window of 10 months we extracted more than 1,600,000 intolerant Tweets, and the resulting Hate Maps are shown in Figure 2. Clearly, the qualitative discussion of the outcomes of this research is out of the scope of the paper, but the project gave the evidence of the potential of strategies for monitoring and mining textual data for social goods. Indeed, in this specific scenario, we aggregated single *people-based* information to build an aggregated map providing psychologists with complex *community-based* findings. Thanks to state-of-the-art techniques for content analysis and machine learning, the outcomes of the project unveiled several hidden and latent reading keys to better explain such phenomena. In the future we will study the *temporal trends* of the content extracted from social networks, in order to assess whether some peaks observed *online* led to some *offline* intolerant act in that area. The vision we tried to carry on is that content analytics techniques can act as a *bridge* to connect offline and online worlds, extending the comprehension of several complex phenomena on the ground of the information which is continuously spread on the Web.

3. REFERENCES

[1] C. Aggarwal and T. Abdelzaher. Social sensing. In *Managing and Mining Sensor Data*, pages 237–297. Springer, 2013.

[2] P. Basile and N. Novielli. Uniba: Sentiment analysis of english tweets combining micro-blogging, lexicon and semantic features. *Proceedings of SemEval 2015*, pages 595–600, 2015.

[3] C. Musto, G. Semeraro, P. Lops, and M. de Gemmis. CrowdPulse: A framework for real-time semantic analysis of social streams. *Information Systems*, 54:127–146, 2015.

From More-Like-This to Better-Than-This: Hotel Recommendations from User Generated Reviews

Ruihai Dong
Insight Centre for Data Analytics
University College Dublin
Belfield, Dublin 4, Ireland
ruihai.dong@insight-centre.org

Barry Smyth
Insight Centre for Data Analytics
University College Dublin
Belfield, Dublin 4, Ireland
barry.smyth@insight-centre.org

ABSTRACT

To help users discover relevant products and items recommender systems must learn about the likes and dislikes of users and the pros and cons of items. In this paper we present a novel approach to building rich feature-based user profiles and item descriptions by mining user-generated reviews. We show how this information can be integrated into recommender systems to deliver better recommendations and an improved user experience.

Keywords

Sentimental Product Recommendation; Crowdsourcing

1. INTRODUCTION

Recommender systems help to provide users with the right information at the right time. They do this by learning about a user's interests and preferences over time and use this profile information to select and/or rank items for recommendation, preferring those that are similar to those the user has liked in the past. Traditional recommendation approaches, such as collaborative filtering and content-based techniques, rely on product ratings or meta-data. Recently however researchers have considered user-generated review content as a new type of recommendation knowledge [1].

Today's e-commerce sites are awash with user-generated reviews and sites like Amazon and TripAdvisor routinely list hundreds or even thousands of reviews alongside their products. The features mentioned in these reviews, and the sentiment expressed by real-users, represent a powerful source of objective evaluation data. Dong et al. [2] proposed using this opinion information as the basis for item profiling and recommendation. Intuitively, if a feature is frequently mentioned by a user then it likely indicates that it is important to the user. Likewise, Musat et al. [4] built a user interest profile for each user based on the topics mentioned in reviews.

In this paper we focus on a form of *personalised opinionated* recommendation by suggesting items that are not only *similar* to those a user has liked in the past, but that are *better* based on features that matter to the user. We focus on one particular use-case for this in the context of a hotel recommendation site: consider a user u_q who

is traveling to a new city and wishes to book a hotel that is *like* some query hotel h_q that she has stayed in previously. The main contribution of this work is to show how we can combine similarity and sentiment to produce better personalized recommendations than could be generated using similarity alone.

2. ITEM AND USER DESCRIPTIONS

This paper builds on recent work on mining features and opinions from user reviews for recommender system [2]. In this section, we will outline how to use this information to build rich feature-based user and item descriptions based on the features that users mention in their reviews and the polarity of their opinions.

Each item/hotel (h_i) is associated with a set of customer reviews $reviews(h_i) = \{r_1, \ldots, r_n\}$ and the opinion mining process extracts a set of features, $f_1, \ldots, f_m$, from these reviews, based on the techniques [2]. Each feature, f_j associated with an *importance* score and a *sentiment* score as per Equations 2 and 3. An item description consist of these features and scores as per Equation 1.

$$item(h_i) = \{(f_j, i(f_j, h_i), s(f_j, h_i)) : f_j \in reviews(h_i)\} \quad (1)$$

The importance score of f_j, $i(f_j, h_i)$, is the relative number of times that f_j is mentioned in the reviews of hotel h_i.

$$i(f_j, h_i) = \frac{count(f_j, h_i)}{|reviews(h_i)|} \quad (2)$$

The sentiment score of f_j, $s(f_j, h_i)$, is the degree to which f_j is mentioned positively or negatively in $reviews(h_i)$. Note, $pos(f_j, h_i)$ and $neg(f_j, h_i)$ denote the number of mentions of f_j labeled as positive or negative during the sentiment analysis phase.

$$s(f_j, h_i) = \frac{pos(f_j, h_i) - neg(f_j, h_i)}{pos(f_j, h_i) + neg(f_j, h_i)} \quad (3)$$

Similarly, we can generate a profile of a user u_q based on the reviews that they have written, by extracting features and importance information from these reviews as in Equation 4.

$$user(u_q) = \{(f_j, i(f_j, u_q)) : f_j \in reviews(u_q)\} \quad (4)$$

3. RECOMMENDATION RANKING

To begin with we implement a standard *more-like-this* approach in which we consider a query user u_q looking at some hotel h_q and requesting similar items $h_1, ..., h_c$. We use h_q as the query and compare this to candidate items $h_1, ...h_c$, computing a similarity score for each as the basis for ranking. Equation 5 demonstrates this for h_q and h_c, using the importance scores of shared features as the feature values.

$$Sim_h(h_q, h_c) = \frac{\sum\limits_{f_i \in F(h_q) \cap F(h_c)} i(f_i, h_q) \times i(f_i, h_c)}{\sqrt{\sum\limits_{f_i \in F(h_q)} i(f_i, h_q)^2} \times \sqrt{\sum\limits_{f_i \in F(h_c)} i(f_i, h_c)^2}} \quad (5)$$

The above is a non-personalized similarity metric: the user's profile has no bearing on the computation. We also implement a personalized version in which we use the importance weights from the query user u_q instead of the weights from h_q as in Equation 6.

$$Sim_u(u_q, h_c) = \frac{\sum\limits_{f_i \in F(u_q) \cap F(h_c)} i(f_i, u_q) \times i(f_i, h_c)}{\sqrt{\sum\limits_{f_i \in F(u_q)} i(f_i, u_q)^2} \times \sqrt{\sum\limits_{f_i \in F(h_c)} i(f_i, h_c)^2}} \quad (6)$$

Next we implement a *better-than-this* approach in which we incorporate information. As mentioned earlier, sentiment information is unusual in a recommendation context but it's availability makes it possible to consider not only how similar an item is to some query but also whether it enjoys a better sentiment value; we want to recommend items that are not similar to the query and have also been (more) positively reviewed. We do this based on a feature-by-feature sentiment comparison as per Equation 7. We can say that f_i is *better* in a candiate item h_c than the query item h_q ($better(f_i, h_q, h_c) > 0$) if f_i in h_c has a higher sentiment score than it does in h_q. Then we can calculate the sentiment score, $Sent(h_q, h_c)$ from the sum of these better scores for the features that are common to h_q and h_c as per Equation 8.

$$better(f_i, h_q, h_c) = s(f_i, h_c) - s(f_i, h_q) \quad (7)$$

$$Sent(h_q, h_c) = \frac{\sum_{f_i \in F(h_q) \cap F(h_c)} better(f_i, h_q, h_c) * i(f_i, h_c)}{|F(h_q) \cap F(h_c)|} \quad (8)$$

Accordingly we can implement two scoring functions based on the above as per Equation 9: (1) a non-personalized version combining Sim_h and $Sent$; and (2) a personalized version combining Sim_u and $Sent$. We can adjust the relative influence of similarity and sentiment by using the parameter w.

$$Score(q, i) = (1 - w) \times Sim(q, i) + w \times Sent(q, i) \quad (9)$$

4. EVALUATION

The dataset used in this work is based on the TripAdvisor dataset [3] which covers 148,575 users and 1,701 hotels. For the purpose of this work we start with a subset of 1,000 users with at least 5 hotel reviews to collect a total of 11,993 reviews for 10,162 hotels. For each of these hotels, we collected their top 100 reviews to produce a larger set of 867,644 hotel reviews.

For each of these users and hotels we apply opinion mining to generate feature-based descriptions. On average our test users have written 12 reviews resulting in profiles containing an average of 91 different features. Likewise the hotels are associated with an average of 89 reviews each, with 189 features per review.

To evaluate our recommendation approaches we produce 888 *test triples* of the form (u_q, h_q, h_t) corresponding to a query user u_q, a query hotel from u_q's profile, and a target hotel visited and rated as

5-star by u_q. For each triple we use h_q (or h_q and u_q depending on approach) as an input and rank-order the other hotels in the same city as h_t, using one of the two scoring variations, varying w to adjust the mix of similarity and sentiment. We compute how often h_t is within the top-20 of these ranked hotels.

The results presented in Figure 1 show that as we increase w (that is, increase the influence of sentiment over similarity) the hit-rate of both the personalized and non-personalized versions improves. For example, at $w = 0$ sentiment is not included in the recommendation scoring and we can see that the hit-rate falls between 0.26 and 0.30; meaning that the target hotel is found in the top-20 recommendations 26%-30% of the time. As we increase w up to about 0.5-0.6 then this hit-rate increases to between 0.35 and 0.38. Beyond this value of w the hit-rate begins to fall again. This tells us that the introduction of sentiment has a positive impact on recommendation quality, up to a point. Furthermore, we can clearly see how the personalized variation outperforms the non-personalized variations, by about 20%, particularly for values of $w < 0.6$.

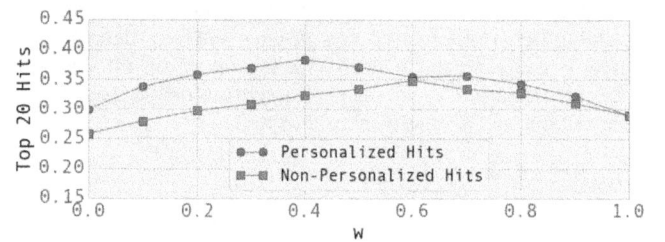

Figure 1: Recommendation hits for top 20 ranked items.

5. CONCLUSIONS

In this short paper we have outlined an approach to recommendation based on user profiles and item descriptions that are mined from user-generated reviews. We have described how this approach allows us to mix similarity and sentiment during recommendation to demonstrate the value of both factors during recommendation. Furthermore, we have shown how this approach can also be used in a personalized recommendation setting.

6. ACKNOWLEDGEMENTS

This work is supported by Science Foundation Ireland under Grant Number SFI/12/RC/2289.

7. REFERENCES

[1] Chen, L., Chen, G., and Wang, F. Recommender systems based on user reviews: the state of the art. *User Modeling and User-Adapted Interaction 25*, 2 (2015), 99–154.

[2] Dong, R., O'Mahony, M. P., Schaal, M., McCarthy, K., and Smyth, B. Combining similarity and sentiment in opinion mining for product recommendation. *Journal of Intelligent Information Systems* (2015), 1–28.

[3] Dong, R., O'Mahony, M. P., and Smyth, B. Further Experiments in Opinionated Product Recommendation. In *Proceedings of The 22nd International Conference on Case-Based Reasoning* (Cork, Ireland, Sept. 2014), 110–124.

[4] Musat, C.-C., Liang, Y., and Faltings, B. Recommendation using textual opinions. In *IJCAI International Joint Conference on Artificial Intelligence*, IJCAI '13, AAAI Press (2013), 2684–2690.

Internal & External Attributions for Emotions Within an ITS

Naomi Wixon
Worcester Polytechnic Institute
100 Institute Road
Worcester, Massachusetts
mwixon@wpi.edu

Sarah Schultz
Worcester Polytechnic Institute
100 Institute Road
Worcester, Massachusetts
seschultz@wpi.edu

Kasia Muldner
Carleton University
1125 Colonel By Drive
Ottawa, Ontario
kasia.muldner@carleton.ca

Danielle Allessio
University of Massachusetts-Amherst
140 Governors' Drive
Amherst, Massachusetts
allessio@educ.umass.edu

Winslow Burleson
New York University
665 Broadway, 11th Floor
New York, NY
wb50@nyu.edu

Beverly Woolf
University of Massachusetts-Amherst
140 Governors' Drive
Amherst, Massachusetts
bev@cs.umass.edu

Ivon Arroyo
Worcester Polytechnic Institute
100 Institute Road
Worcester, Massachusetts
iarroyo@wpi.edu

ABSTRACT
Students self-reported not only their emotional state, but also the causal attributions of their emotions. After coding emotions with internal references to self, and external references to the environment or domain, we examined how sub-groups of students based on internal/external attributions and above or below median performance differ in terms of their emotional state, perceptions of item difficulty, and gender.

Keywords
Keywords: emotion; attribution; education; mathematics; ITS

1. INTRODUCTION
In our previous work [1], we explored the overall relationships between students' reports of affect and their attributions of those reports, i.e. their statement about the cause of that emotion. We noticed that two of the most common tags of attribution were "internal," and "external." In this work, we explore these attributions in greater depth.

Here, we use data from MathSpring (formerly Wayang Outpost), an Intelligent Tutoring System, to examine the internal vs. external attributions. By using tags from student reports in concert with student success and failure, as well as self-reports of affective state our aim is to gain a richer way to measure affect that will be incorporated into the design of a student model.

An understanding of whether students attribute their successes or failures to internal or external causes may provide indication of their emotional state. For example, students may take pride if they give an internal cause for success, which may be attributed to their performance in a difficult task. However if they succeed at what they perceive to be an easy task they may feel a lower degree of pride for doing work they consider to be beneath them [2].

> Please tell us how you are feeling.
> Based on the last few problems tell us about your level of
> Confidence in solving math problems
>
> ○ Not at all Confident
> ○ A little Confident
> ○ Somewhat Confident
> ○ Quite a bit Confident
> ○ Extremely Confident
>
> Why is that?

Figure 1. Self-Report Window with Likert Scale for Emotion (Confidence) and Open Response for Attribution

2. METHODS
2.1 Sample & Prior Data Preparation
The data for this study came from N=123 7th and 8th graders working with MathSpring. MathSpring prompted students at regular intervals asking about four affective states: confidence, excitement, frustration, and interest. Students responded using a Likert-scale self-report, meant to rate their emotional state on a scale from 1 being least, up to 5 being most, see Figure 1. In

addition, students were asked to explain why they felt the way that they had reported. As part of a larger study to determine common attributions across multiple reports, a tagging protocol, partially based on qualitative methods, was developed [1] to find common attributes across multiple reports. "Internal" tags achieved a kappa of 0.84, while "external" tags achieved a kappa of 0.69. We also included tags of "easy" and "hard" which referred to whether or not the self-report contained attributions of high or low item difficulty. "Easy" tags achieved a kappa of 0.90, while "Hard" tags achieved a kappa of 0.78.

2.2 Data Analysis

The data were analyzed at the report level, where a report corresponds to an instance of a student reporting their emotional state and associated causal attributions.(see Figure 1). Typically, a single student contributed several reports. Our goal was to compare Internal vs External attributions and student performance in terms of "High performing" and "Low performing". Thus, we needed a measure of student performance, and attempted to do it in the simplest way possible. Since students were able to make several successive attempts at a problem, a measurement of percent correct was less meaningful. Instead we calculated the percentage of times a student solved a problem on their first attempt out of the total problems they had solved prior to reporting. The percent solved on first was then taken and used to split responses between the "High performing" and "Low performing" categories based on the median of percent solved on first. Instances where the percent solved on first was below the median (<89%) were categorized "Low performing" while the instances at or above 89% were categorized "High performing". After splitting responses into groups different affect self-reports and attributions were compared against the remaining groups with an independent-samples t-test to determine significant differences.

3. RESULTS

Unfortunately, due to the overall high performance of the students (median percent solved on first attempt at time of report was 89%) we may have a comparison between students experiencing a ceiling effect in the "High performing" case and engaged in actual learning in the "Low performing" case. The results may say more about how they attribute their feelings when either confronted with a series of successes or more uncertain progress.

Internal attributions had the fewest references to item difficulty, while external attributions had the most. Students in the External & High performing category showed the highest portion of "Easy" attributions and the lowest mean reported confidence suggesting that while students may experience a ceiling effect in performance, they attributed their feelings to external causes such as the material being too easy, thus reducing confidence. Meanwhile, the Internal & High performing category reported relatively few attributions of "Easy" and the second highest degrees of confidence, frustration, and interest. While these students may have experienced challenge as evidenced by their reported frustration, their degree of confidence and interest suggest they also believed in their abilities. Interestingly, this group represents significantly the highest proportion of female students reporting of any group at 69% as opposed to the total sample at 55%.

4. DISCUSSION

The data seem to suggest that the externalizing group is experiencing reduced confidence and interest due to low item difficulty, while the same seems less true of the internalizing group. Similarly, the lower performing groups seem to associate different internal and external attributions given their differing emotions. The external group may hold more performance based goals expressed through high degrees of both confidence and frustration. As such they may be more highly invested in their successful status and frustrated by any missteps. The internalizing lower performing group reports the highest degree of interest by a fairly wide margin. This finding yields at least two future directions for research: First, simply testing this hypothesis to see if these groups can be well described by performance vs learning goals. Second, to tailor pedagogy and scaffolding to the two groups based on how they approach the ITS with different outlooks, preferences, and perhaps even goals.

Table 2. Results for Internal/External Attributions

		Confidence	Interest	Frustration	Hard	Easy	Female
Internal & Low	M	2.85	2.08**	3.36	.03*	.05*	.55
	SD	1.67	1.2	1.79	.17	.23	.500
	N	25	25	20	101	101	101
Internal & High	M	2.99	1.65	4.20	.01**	.06	.69**
	SD	1.39	1.15	1.41	.09	.23	.47
	N	18	18	19	86	86	86
External & Low	M	3.49*	1.28**	4.36**	.12**	.07	.49
	SD	1.49	.59	1.0	.32	.26	.50
	N	21	22	24	107	107	107
External & High	M	2.36*	1.37*	3.59	.07	.16**	.49
	SD	1.82	.83	1.68	.26	.37	.50
	N	20	34	29	115	115	115
Total	M	2.99	1.58	3.87	.06	.09	.55
	SD	1.61	1.0	1.54	.24	.29	.50
	N	84	99	92	409	409	409

As compared to total remaining sample by t-test: M=Mean, **sig. different by p<0.05, *marginally sig. different by p<0.10

5. ACKNOWLEDGMENTS

Our thanks to Ryan Baker & Jaclyn Ocumpaugh for their helpful suggestions and criticisms for this work. This research was funded by the National Science Foundation, #1324385, Cyberlearning DIP, Impact of Adaptive Interventions on Student Affect, Performance, and Learning; Burleson, Arroyo and Woolf (PIs). Any opinions, findings, conclusions or recommendations expressed in this paper are those of the authors and do not necessarily reflect the views of the funding agencies.

6. REFERENCES

[1] Schultz, S., Wixon, N., Allessio, D., Muldner, K., Burleson, W., Woolf, B., & Arroyo, I., (in press). Blinded by Science?: Exploring Affective Meaning in Students' Own Words. *Proceedings of the 16th International Conference on Intelligent Tutoring Systems.*

[2] Weiner, B. (2010). The Development of an Attribution-Based Theory of Motivation: A History of Ideas. *Educational Psychologist*, 45:1, 28-36.

Adaptive Exercise Selection
for an Intelligent Tutoring System

Juliet Okpo*
Computing Science
University of Aberdeen
Aberdeen, United Kingdom
r02jao15@abdn.ac.uk

ABSTRACT

This PhD project investigates how an Intelligent Tutoring System can adapt exercise selection to the personality of a learner. This paper provides an overview of the research area, research questions and work to date.

Keywords

Learning, Exercise selection, Intelligent Tutoring Systems, Personality, Adaptation

1. INTRODUCTION

Modern educational advances aim at adapting learning tasks to the needs of individual learners instead of using one predefined and fixed pattern of learning tasks [27]. Learners differ in many characteristics such as their past performance, mental capacity and particularly in their personalities. Taking these differences into account is essential for the adaptive selection of learning tasks for individual learners. Ideally, good tutoring should take into consideration individual differences among a heterogeneous group of learners. Also learning systems such as Computer Assisted Instruction (CAI) systems and Intelligent Tutoring Systems (ITS) are used to achieve this learning objective. ITSs are designed to be adaptive solution environments and aid in improving learning.

Learning tasks are concrete, authentic, whole-task experiences that are organized sequentially from easy to difficult [4]. Learning tasks depict work in a learning environment such as a classroom or any other place involving learning. This therefore implies that for a learning task, there are resources available to accomplish the task, there are set objectives to accomplish and also some form of operations to accomplish the set objectives. One of the major operations is task selection for learners, as determining the best task is key to achieving the best learning objective. Learning

*Supervisors: Prof. Judith Masthoff, Dr Nigel Beacham & Dr Matt Dennis, University of Aberdeen

UMAP '16, July 13-17, 2016, Halifax, NS, Canada
ACM 978-1-4503-4370-1/16/07.
http://dx.doi.org/10.1145/2930238.2930369

tasks administered by tutors should be selected effectively and therefore must adhere to several conditions that should be favourable to the learner. Each task must be at the right cognitive level of the learner [28, 13], meaning that the tasks must neither be too easy, as this will bore the learner due to the lack of challenge in the learning content, nor too difficult, as this could overwhelm the learner due to excessive cognitive load. Therefore there is a need to decide whether subsequent tasks given to learners should be equally difficult, less difficult or more difficult than the previous task.

Performance, mental efficiency and cognitive load have been used as learner characteristics in Intelligent Tutoring Systems (ITS) for task selection (e.g. [2, 6, 7]). Although there have been a number of adaptations to learner personality [8, 17], learner personality has not been considered as a learner characteristic in task selection so far.

This PhD project investigates how Intelligent Tutoring Systems can adapt teaching and learning to individual students based on their personality. We will develop algorithms which will enable intelligent tutoring systems to adapt exercise selection to learner personality and learner performance. In particular, we will investigate how exercises can be selected and optimized to individual learner characteristics such as self-esteem and other personality traits. Self-esteem is seen as an important component of personality [18]. Significant associations can be found between self-esteem and all personality traits such as openness, conscientiousness, extraversion, agreeableness and neuroticism [11]. Self-esteem is defined as how favourably a person regards oneself [23]. It was thus decided that self-esteem was a good characteristic to investigate first. The research will consider student motivation and attainment. An empirical computer science approach will be followed. A series of experiments will be run to test hypotheses of what will work best.

2. RELATED WORK

From our literature review, it has been observed that there have been many works on adapting learning content to different learner characteristics. In the area of task selection, the focus has been on the design of intelligent tutors that select learning tasks for the learner based on the learner's past performance, available learning support and recently, cognitive load (e.g., [2, 15, 24, 25, 6, 5]). Very little work has focused on the area of selecting learning tasks based on learner personality.

Other studies on exercise selection have provided empirical evidence that students often do not have sufficiently developed self-directed learning skills to select suitable tasks

[14]. Furthermore, exercise selection is also regarded as a self-directed learning skill which enables learners to select a task themselves that best fits their learning needs as provided by self-assessment [26]. In this particular study, a learner needs to determine if the subsequent task should contain less support, equal support, or more support, or if it should be less difficult, equally difficult or more difficult than the previous task. The differences in self-assessment and task-selection processes between effective and ineffective learners studying in a learner-controlled instructional environment have also been investigated, and results indicated that they used the same task aspects to select learning tasks [15].

There is prior research on adaptation to personality in e-learning systems. Feedback was adapted to learner personality to increase motivation [9]. This work investigated how a conversational agent, taking the role of a virtual tutor, could deliver personalised feedback on performance to learners. It also investigates the most effective emotional support to incorporate in this feedback in order to maintain learner motivation. [17] adapted linguistic style to personality. They showed how they could systematically apply results from psycholinguistic studies that document the linguistic reflexes of personality, in order to develop models to control personage's parameters, and produce utterances matching particular personality profiles [17]. There has also been substantial work on Self-Efficacy in Learners. [21, 22, 20] demonstrated that dynamic models enriched with physiological data can more accurately predict student's self-efficacy during problem-solving and evaluation results suggest that self-efficacy can be modelled in an intelligent tutoring system. [30] also found that mild changes in the performance content of students have been influence through self-efficacy beliefs to cooperate with learning processes.

There is also evidence that certain personality characteristics strengthen or reduce the effect of interest [1]. For example, initiative and persistence (two aspects of action control) independently affect effort expenditure. Disengagement interacts with interest. Students who have the skill to uncouple a learning intention from an action plan are more affected by low interest than students who lack this skill [1]. Investigation reports also show that an individual's learning orientation, and therefore their approach to learning, is partially determined by their personality. A deep approach to learning was positively associated with extraversion and openness to experience. A surface approach was positively related to neuroticism and agreeableness. A strategic approach correlated positively with extraversion and conscientiousness and negatively with neuroticism [10]. Therefore personality should be taken into account when implementing Intelligent Tutoring Systems (ITS) for task selection and not just performance and cognitive load alone to produce better learning outcomes.

The unique aspect of my PhD will investigate how exercises can be selected and optimized to individual learner personality (as well as to performance).

3. RESEARCH QUESTIONS

In this thesis, we investigate how a computer can adapt learning to learner personality in the way a human would do, using the User-as-Wizard method [19]. We will investigate this by observing how humans would select exercises for students with different levels of personality traits in controlled situations. These considerations have led us to a series of questions on how this major objective can be achieved:

1. How can we model learner personality such as self-esteem?

2. Which exercises should be selected based on learner's personality?

3. Which adaptations are possible with exercise selection and what exercises are best to use to investigate this?

4. What algorithm can effectively adapt exercise selection to learner performance and personality?

5. How can we evaluate our algorithms and how effective is the algorithm?

4. METHODOLOGY

We will use the user-as-wizard approach [19] for the methodology of this thesis. This will be used by asking participants playing the role of the system in different experiments to select the next exercise for learners with different learner characteristics in controlled situations. Exercises to be selected would have different task characteristics also as illustrated in the poster attached. We use the User-as-Wizard methodology as it generates empirical data in a controlled manner compared to other methods. For example, adaptations arising from the observation of teachers in a classroom setting could be influenced by several compounding factors, such as learner affect, current health status of either the pupil or the teacher. As most humans can teach and also empathise with others, the user-as-wizard approach seems appropriate. Our research plan includes many qualitative studies with teachers to gather their inputs and all adaptations arising from empirical studies will be checked by real teachers and learners after our algorithms have been developed. The process we shall be using to answer our research questions is as follows.

4.1 Phase 1A

The first step in the process is to establish which personality traits are important for exercise selection. Thus, the personality of the learner needs to be expressed to participants in future studies. To provide a sense of learner personality, we could make participants interact with real people in order to know what kind of personality the target learner has. However, if we were to use this method, it would not only be very difficult to know the current affective state of the learner, a lot of time need to be spent by the participant in order to fully understand their personality. Alternatively, we could task the imagination of the participant and tell them outright what type of personality a learner has. This approach is unlikely to elicit empathy from participants and is likely to be disregarded when placed with other data because it does not provide much context about the learner. So it is of great importance to provide enough evidence of the personality of the learner for the participants to pinpoint and empathise with them.

In prior work, [8] addressed this problem by developing *personality trait stories* which expressed traits from the Five-Factor Model [11] at high and low levels. We will use these existing stories, and following a similar methodology, create new stories for other personality traits. For example, to create stories for Self-Esteem, we used the well-established State Self-Esteem scale [12]. The SSES consists of 20 items that measure momentary fluctuations in self-esteem. For each story, we changed a selection of the Individual Current Thought questionnaire items into the third person, inverting them where necessary. In trying to make the story real, we linked it with a character, a student called Kate. We decided to pick the name Kate because of its universality.

4.2 Phase 1B

In this phase we shall be running experiments to determine and validate the difficulty levels of exercises. For this investigation we shall be using a parameter-based strategy. For example, participants in an experiment will be shown a set of balls of varying weights, and a number of baskets (the number of balls and number of baskets are parameters that are likely to influence the difficulty of the exercise). Participants will be asked to distribute the balls into the baskets so that the sum of the weights in each basket will be equal. Participants will also be asked to rate the difficulty of these exercises. Based on our findings, we will determine the difficulty levels of the exercises. Our findings will be used to investigate the effect of personality on task selection following the methodology below.

4.3 Phase 2

In this phase we will conduct qualitative research (namely focus groups and interviews) to find out how an e-learning system can automatically adapt exercise selection to different types of learners. This will involve the exploration of different personality traits of learners, and will also provide insights in the other characteristics of learners and exercises students and teachers find important for exercise selection.

4.4 Phase 3

This phase investigates whether participants will select exercises of different difficulties for learners depending on prior performance and learner personality. In a series of experiments, participants will be shown a story about a learner depicting the learner's personality from the previously validated stories (e.g. depicting high or low self-esteem) and the performance of the learner on previous exercises (perfect, good, just passing, or fail). Participants playing the role of a teacher will select the next exercise for this learner from a range (each with a different validated difficulty level). We will conduct multiple studies for different personality traits. With the data we collect from phase 3, we will create algorithms that can adapt exercise selection to personality and past performance.

4.5 Phase 4

In this phase, we will construct different algorithms inspired by the data from Phase 3 that adapt exercise selection to different personality traits and past performance.

4.6 Phase 5

We evaluate our algorithms by testing with teachers and learners, using controlled studies and qualitative studies.

4.7 Phase 6

Based on the results of Phase 5, we shall thoroughly refine our algorithms.

5. WORK TO DATE

So far we have designed an experiment to investigate the role of self-esteem and performance in task selection for learners. This involved the creation and validation of stories to express self-esteem.

We also implemented two experiments which asked participants, playing the role of a teacher, to select the next exercise for fictional learners with varying self-esteem levels and performance. Participants selected one from a range of multiplication exercises which vary in difficulty and method (a similar exercise using a different approach) in the first experiment, and three levels of difficulty in the second experiment, for the student to attempt next. We expressed the self-esteem of the fictional learner to our participants using short stories (developed as described in Phase 1A). We found that performance is important for exercise selection, as expected, but we did not find any robust evidence for SE being taken into account by participants. There may be a trend for low SE learners who "just passed" to receive an exercise of the same difficulty more frequently than high SE learners. It could be that the exercise difficulty we chose was too coarse-grained. To investigate SE again where more gradual changes in difficulty are possible, we have designed materials to establish a validated set of task difficulties.

We have also conducted six focus groups involving undergraduate and postgraduate students from the department of Computing Science. For the focus groups, we used consent forms, information sheets, trait stories, exercise cards and performance cards. We collected information about how learners felt that an e-learning system should adapt exercise selection to different types of learners and what learner characteristics would be important.

6. FUTURE WORK

The research plan for the next few months is to investigate exercise difficulty where more gradual changes in difficulty are possible. Difficulty levels have been investigated in the past using various strategies. Similarity measures were used by [16] to evaluate quiz difficulty levels. This work introduced a mechanism for controlling the difficulty level of the generated quizzes based on a semantic similarity measure. Also, a graph based strategy for difficulty level estimation for chemistry was used by [29]. Following a similar approach by [3], we shall be using the parameter based strategy for our difficulty level estimation. This strategy makes use of parameters which would be defined to control the number of questions to be generated. We shall be viewing a parameter as a quantity that influences the output of a mathematical object. This is due to the fact that we shall be using mathematics questions for our difficulty level estimation.

We shall be investigating the effect of personality as a learner characteristic to be considered in the selection of the next exercise for a learner. We are trying to establish what influence personality has in the selection of the next task for learners. We are of the opinion that past performance or other learner characteristics alone is insufficient for the optimal selection of the next exercise for learners. Subsequently, the differences found would then be encapsulated into an algorithm to allow an Intelligent Tutoring System to utilize these adaptations. These adaptions can then be evaluated in future studies.

7. ACKNOWLEDGMENTS

This work is partially funded by the Niger Delta Development Commission, Nigeria.

8. REFERENCES

[1] M. Boekaerts. Personality and the psychology of learning. *Eur. J. Pers.*, 10(5):377–404, 1996.

[2] G. Camp, F. Paas, R. Rikers, and J. van Merrienboer. Dynamic problem selection in air traffic control training: A comparison between performance, mental effort and mental efficiency. *Comput Hum Behav*, 17(5):575–595, 2001.

[3] I. Cheng, R. Shen, and A. Basu. An algorithm for automatic difficulty level estimation of multimedia mathematical test items. In *Advanced Learning Technologies, ICALT'08*, pages 175–179. IEEE, 2008.

[4] R. E. Clark, D. Feldon, J. J. van Merriënboer, K. Yates, and S. Early. Cognitive task analysis. *Handbook of research on educational communications and technology*, 3:577–593, 2008.

[5] G. Corbalan, L. Kester, and J. J. Van Merriënboer. Towards a personalized task selection model with shared instructional control. *Instructional Science*, 34(5):399–422, 2006.

[6] G. Corbalan, L. Kester, and J. J. van Merriënboer. Selecting learning tasks: Effects of adaptation and shared control on learning efficiency and task involvement. *CEP*, 33(4):733–756, 2008.

[7] G. Corbalan, L. Kester, and J. J. Van Merriënboer. Learner-controlled selection of tasks with different surface and structural features: Effects on transfer and efficiency. *Comput Hum Behav*, 27(1):76–81, 2011.

[8] M. Dennis, J. Masthoff, and C. Mellish. The quest for validated personality trait stories. In *Proceedings of IUI 2012*, pages 273–276. ACM, 2012.

[9] M. Dennis, J. Masthoff, and C. Mellish. Adapting progress feedback and emotional support to learner personality. *IJAIED*, pages 1–55, 2015.

[10] A. Duff, E. Boyle, K. Dunleavy, and J. Ferguson. The relationship between personality, approach to learning and academic performance. *Personality and individual differences*, 36(8):1907–1920, 2004.

[11] L. Goldberg. Some ruminations about the structure of individual differences: Developing a common lexicon for the major characteristics of human personality. In *Invited paper, Convention of the Western Psychological Association, Honolulu, Hawaii*, 1980.

[12] T. F. Heatherton and J. Polivy. Development and validation of a scale for measuring state self-esteem. *Journal of Personality and Social psychology*, 60(6):895, 1991.

[13] M. Henningsen and M. K. Stein. Mathematical tasks and student cognition: Classroom-based factors that support and inhibit high-level mathematical thinking and reasoning. *Journal for Research in Mathematics Education*, pages 524–549, 1997.

[14] W. Kicken, S. Brand-Gruwel, and J. J. van Merriënboer. Scaffolding advice on task selection: a safe path toward self-directed learning in on-demand education. *Int. J. Voc. Tech. Educ.*, 60(3):223–239, 2008.

[15] D. Kostons, T. van Gog, and F. Paas. Self-assessment and task selection in learner-controlled instruction: Differences between effective and ineffective learners. *Computers & Education*, 54(4):932–940, 2010.

[16] C. Lin, D. Liu, W. Pang, and Z. Wang. Sherlock: A semi-automatic framework for quiz generation using a hybrid semantic similarity measure. *Cognitive computation*, 7(6):667–679, 2015.

[17] F. Mairesse and M. A. Walker. Towards personality-based user adaptation: psychologically informed stylistic language generation. *UMUAI*, 20(3):227–278, 2010.

[18] A. H. Maslow. *On dominance, self-esteem, and self-actualization*. Maurice Bassett, 1973.

[19] J. Masthoff. The user as wizard: A method for early involvement in the design and evaluation of adaptive systems. In *5th Workshop on User-centred Design and Adaptive Systems*, pages 460–469, 2006.

[20] S. W. McQuiggan and J. C. Lester. Diagnosing self-efficacy in intelligent tutoring systems: an empirical study. In *Intelligent Tutoring Systems*, pages 565–574. Springer, 2006.

[21] S. W. McQuiggan and J. C. Lester. Modeling and evaluating empathy in embodied companion agents. *International Journal of Human-Computer Studies*, 65(4):348–360, 2007.

[22] S. W. Mcquiggan, B. W. Mott, and J. C. Lester. Modeling self-efficacy in intelligent tutoring systems: An inductive approach. *User modeling and user-adapted interaction*, 18(1-2):81–123, 2008.

[23] M. Rosenberg. *Conceiving the self*. RE Krieger, 1986.

[24] R. J. Salden, F. Paas, and J. J. Van Merriënboer. Personalised adaptive task selection in air traffic control: Effects on training efficiency and transfer. *Learning and Instruction*, 16(4):350–362, 2006.

[25] A. C. Stephens, E. J. Knuth, M. L. Blanton, I. Isler, A. M. Gardiner, and T. Marum. Equation structure and the meaning of the equal sign: The impact of task selection in eliciting elementary studentsâĂŹ understandings. *JMB*, 32(2):173–182, 2013.

[26] E. Taminiau, L. Kester, G. Corbalan, J. M. Spector, P. A. Kirschner, and J. Van Merriënboer. Designing on-demand education for simultaneous development of domain-specific and self-directed learning skills. *JCAL*, 31(5):405–421, 2015.

[27] B. W. Tuckman. A tripartite model of motivation for achievement: Attitude/drive/strategy. In *annual meeting of the American Psychological Association, Boston, MA*, 1999.

[28] T. Van Gog, L. Kester, and F. Paas. Effects of concurrent monitoring on cognitive load and performance as a function of task complexity. *Applied Cognitive Psychology*, 25(4):584–587, 2011.

[29] G. Wu and I. Cheng. An interactive 3d environment for computer based education. In *Multimedia and Expo, 2007 IEEE International Conference on*, pages 1834–1837. IEEE, 2007.

[30] B. J. Zimmerman. Self-efficacy: An essential motive to learn. *Contemporary educational psychology*, 25(1):82–91, 2000.

Detecting Student Engagement: Human Versus Machine

Nigel Bosch
University of Notre Dame
384 Fitzpatrick Hall
Notre Dame, IN 46556, USA
pbosch1@nd.edu

ABSTRACT

Engagement is complex and multifaceted, but crucial to learning. Computerized learning environments can provide a superior learning experience for students by automatically detecting student engagement (and, thus also disengagement) and adapting to it. This paper describes results from several previous studies that utilized facial features to automatically detect student engagement, and proposes new methods to expand and improve results. Videos of students will be annotated by third-party observers as mind wandering (disengaged) or not mind wandering (engaged). Automatic detectors will also be trained to classify the same videos based on students' facial features, and compared to the machine predictions. These detectors will then be improved by engineering features to capture facial expressions noted by observers and more heavily weighting training instances that were exceptionally-well classified by observers. Finally, implications of previous results and proposed work are discussed.

Keywords

Affective computing; engagement detection; facial expressions

1. INTRODUCTION

Most people can relate to the experience of becoming disengaged from almost any task where distractions occur or daydreams happen. For example, a student might spend nearly as much time in a lecture text messaging or plumbing the depths of Wikipedia as they do actually listening to the teacher. Similarly, while reading a textbook you might go through the motions of reading but soon find yourself thinking about something else entirely. This lack of engagement (in other words, disengagement) can be detrimental to performance in tasks such as learning [17].

Unsurprisingly, previous research has shown that engagement is positively related to learning [15]. Educational software can utilize this relationship to improve the learning experience for students and promote learning by adapting to a student's level of engagement and redirecting them toward the learning goal if necessary (intervening). Such interventions can be triggered by automated engagement detection systems. For example, in a fully automated learning environment a hint could be given to a student if the system detects that the student is confused or frustrated by the learning material and may soon become disengaged [9].

UMAP '16, July 13-17, 2016, Halifax, NS, Canada
ACM 978-1-4503-4370-1/16/07.
http://dx.doi.org/10.1145/2930238.2930371

Accurate engagement detection is thus key to developing such learning systems and strategies. Many techniques have been employed to detect engagement and related constructs, including interaction log-files, eye gaze, physiological measurements, facial features, and others [7,16]. Each of these channels of data has their own advantages and disadvantages. For example, interaction log-files require no sensors, but are often highly context dependent. Gaze trackers measure the locus of attention precisely, but are not common in learning environments. Physiological sensors are increasingly popular in fitness trackers and related hardware, and can be used easily throughout the day. However, they are less accurate than other methods for detecting some components of engagement. Facial features are widely available via inexpensive and commonplace webcams, but are sensitive to various factors like lighting, occlusions, and movement. This paper focuses on face-based engagement detection methods, because it is potentially superior to other methods in terms of availability in various domains and potentially complementary to other modalities by focusing on visible features.

There are several facets to engagement that must also be discussed to properly situate the proposed work within the body of related work. This paper examines three components of engagement: affective, cognitive, and behavioral. Examples of these might be a student who is interested in a topic and enjoying learning about it (affective engagement), a student who is reading a book and thinking about how the material integrates with their previous knowledge of the topic (cognitive), or a student diligently typing an essay (behavioral). Various affective states play a role in engagement as well. For example, frustration can lead to boredom [9], which in turn indicates a lack of affective and cognitive engagement. Figure 1 illustrates the model of affective states and engagement that will be considered in this paper.

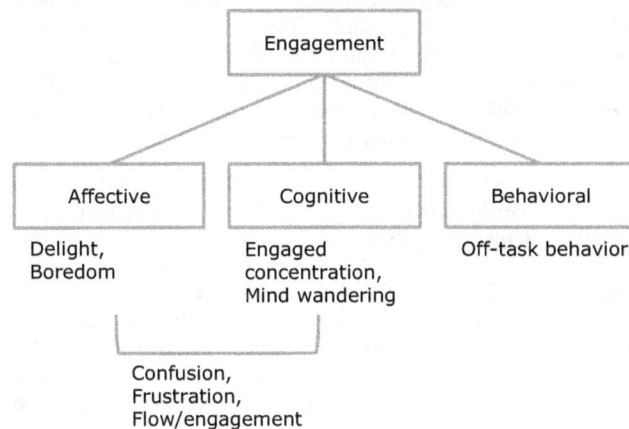

Figure 1. Conceptualized breakdown of engagement

The focus of proposed research in this paper is on mind wandering (MW), a type of cognitive disengagement. Students mind wander when they shift their focus from thinking about the learning task at hand toward unrelated thoughts [17]. For example, a student might mind wander thinking about a television show they recently saw. Such students are no longer cognitively engaged in the task at hand, though they may not immediately realize it. Hence, it might be useful to detect MW and refocus students' attention. MW detection has been the subject of research efforts utilizing eye gaze and physiology [3,16], but face-based techniques are not yet well explored. Furthermore, it is not clear how well different techniques work for annotating MW.

There are various methods of engagement annotation, which typically fall into two broad categories: self-reports or third-party observations. One of the primary advantages of self-reported emotions is that the student making a self-report has access to their own internal state of mind, which an observer does not. On the other hand, observations made by a third party do not require interrupting students at all. However, observers lack access to the internal state of students, and must make their judgments based on external cues alone (which more closely matches the method an automatic detector must use).

This paper briefly reviews progress made toward the goal of automatic face-based engagement detection, including components of engagement and the affective states that manifest in relation to engagement (Figure 1). Both self-reported and observer labels of engagement have been employed for training the detectors as well. Proposed enhancements to engagement detection are then presented, focusing on a new study designed to capture cognitive disengagement and improve engagement detection via human knowledge.

Both self-reports and observations are also considered in related work, since the approaches have complementary strengths and weaknesses. Face-based approaches to automatic detection are discussed for various aspect of engagement mentioned (Figure 1), including affective states that manifest as a part of engagement.

2. RELATED WORK
Many methods have been used to detect engagements and its components [7]. Primarily face-based approaches are reviewed here, as the proposed work focuses on facial features.

2.1 Affective and cognitive state detection
Kapoor et al. [12] developed one of the first systems for detecting frustration in an automated learning environment. They used multimodal data channels including facial features (from video), a posture-sensing chair, a pressure-sensitive mouse, a skin conductance sensor, and interaction data to predict frustration. They were able to predict when a user would self-report frustration with 79% accuracy (chance being 58%).

Hoque et al. [11] used facial features and temporal information in videos to classify smiles as either frustrated or delighted – two states that are related to engagement and learning. They accurately distinguished between frustrated and delighted smiles correctly in 92% of cases. They also found differences between acted facial expressions and naturalistic facial expressions. In acted data only 10% of frustrated cases included a smile, whereas in naturally occurring frustration smiles were present in 90% of cases. These results illustrate that there can be large differences between naturalistic and posed data.

The Computer Expression Recognition Toolbox (CERT) [13] is a computer vision tool used to automatically detect AUs as well as head pose and head position information. CERT uses features extracted from Gabor filters as inputs to SVMs to provide likelihood estimates for the presence of 19 different AUs in any given frame of a video stream. It also supplies measures of unilateral (one side of the face only) AUs for three action units, as well as "Fear Brow" and "Distress Brow," which indicate the presence of combinations of AU1 (Inner Brow Raiser), AU2 (Outer Brow Raiser), and AU4 (Brow Lowerer). CERT has been tested with databases of both posed facial expressions and spontaneous facial expressions, achieving accuracy of 90.1% and 79.9%, respectively, when discriminating between instances of the AU present vs. absent [13].

Grafsgaard et al. [10] used CERT to recognize the level of frustration (self-reported on a Likert scale) in a learning session and achieved modest results ($R^2 = .24$). Additionally, they found good agreement between the output of CERT AU recognition and human-coded ground truth measurements of AUs. After correcting for individual differences in facial feature movements they achieved Cohen's kappa >= .68 for several key AUs. They did not perform detection at a fine-grained level (i.e. specific affective episodes), instead detecting the presence of affect in the entire learning session. However, their work does provide evidence of the validity of CERT for automated AU detection.

2.2 Behavioral engagement detection
In a recent engagement detection effort, Whitehill et al. [18] used Gabor features (appearance-based features capturing textures of various parts of the face) with a support vector machine (SVM) classifier to detect engagement as students interacted with cognitive skills training software. Labels used in their study were obtained from retrospective annotation of videos by third-party observers. Four levels of engagement were annotated, ranging from complete disengagement (not even looking at the material) to strong engagement. This type of engagement annotation primarily captures behavioral engagement. They were able to detect engagement with an Area Under the ROC Curve (AUC, averaged across all four levels of engagement) of .729 where AUC = .5 is chance level detection.

Finally, off-task behavior detection in learning environments is perhaps the most clearly behavioral type of engagement detection. Off-task behavior has been detected with interaction log-file clickstream data [1]. However, face-based approaches in learning contexts are not yet well established.

3. CURRENT RESULTS
The results described briefly in this paper extend the related work to demonstrate the feasibility of automatic face-based detection of components of engagement.

Some of the completed results used texture-based facial features and heart rate detected from changes in skin color to detect behavioral engagement [14]. Students wrote essays and self-reported engagement (i.e., if they were working on the essay) both during the writing task and afterword. Engagement was detected with accuracy of AUC = .758 (versus chance = .5), using a fusion of both types of features extracted.

Completed work also included detection of components of cognitive and affective engagement using facial features. In one study confusion and frustration were detected at 22.1% and 23.2% above chance respectively [4]. In another study, both confusion (AUC = .637) and frustration (AUC = .609) were detected above chance levels. Importantly, engagement detectors fit to specific learning scenarios were more effective (average AUC = .595) than general detectors (average AUC = .554), indicating that the learning task can have an appreciable effect on detector accuracy.

Finally, research so far also explored some engagement detection aspects in the wild, using facial features extracted from face videos in a computer-enabled classroom. Boredom (AUC = .610), confusion (.649), delight (.867), engaged concentration (.679), frustration (.631), and off-task behavior (.816) were all detected at levels above chance. These results demonstrated the feasibility of detecting various facets of engagement in the wild, despite the noisy nature of data collected in a classroom environment.

4. PROPOSED WORK

Completed work has primarily focused on affective, behavioral, and related facets of engagement. As discussed previously, MW is a cognitive component of engagement that has not been well researched in terms of facial features or automatic face-based detection. The proposed work (not yet completed) focuses on answering questions about human observer perception of MW, automated MW detection, and if observers can improve detection.

Data collection will consist of obtaining observer ratings of face videos of humans MW or not MW. These video clips come from a study in which 98 participants read an instructional text and self-reported MW whenever they realized they had been MW. Video clips for observer annotation will then be extracted in 12-second windows leading up to MW self-reports. 12 seconds was chosen to correspond to the average MW report time within a page, as a compromise between shorter windows (less data to use) and longer windows (fewer windows can be extracted because they won't fit between page start and MW report). Non-MW video clips will be similarly extracted from periods of time where there were no MW self-reports, with windows ending at the average MW report position. In total, there are 3,272 such clips available from the original dataset collected for proposed work.

Clips will be rated by observers on Amazon Mechanical Turk, which has been used in many previous studies (e.g., [6]). Observers will be shown a sequence of 10 clips asked to judge each clip as MW or non-MW and provide a confidence rating regarding their observation. Additionally, observers will be asked to describe the reason for each of their observations in a text box. They will be provided with detailed descriptions of MW to aid them in determining what constitutes MW and what does not.

After all videos have been coded by observers, the text responses will be examined to identify common themes (e.g., selected MW because participant yawned). The most frequent themes will then be made into checkboxes in the observation interface, and the text response will be removed. Clips will then be rated on Mechanical Turk repeatedly to improve reliability of ratings.

4.1 Observer-based MW classification

Maximum Likelihood Estimation (MLE) will be used to calculate the set of clip labels that is most consistent with the observer ratings. Observers who tend to disagree with other observers are likely less reliable and thus will have all of their ratings weighted lower, and vice versa. In the event of ties the clip label will be randomly assigned. This analysis will be the first measure of how well third-party observers can detect MW from facial expressions.

4.2 Automatic MW classification

One third of students (33 students) will be randomly chosen and their clips will be reserved as the evaluation set. The rest of the clips (roughly 2,200) will compose the development set which will be used to create automatic MW detectors.

A unique set of high- and low- level facial features will be extracted for MW classification. High level features will be based on action units extracted using EmotientSDK for each video frame. AUs will then be aggregated across the duration of each 12 second clip to obtain the mean and standard deviation of each AU. Prior work has shown that various time scales are effective for different classification tasks [5]. Thus, AUs will also be aggregated for 3, 6, and 9 second subsections of each clip to create a set of multiscale features. Relationships between AUs will be captured by features measuring the Jensen-Shannon divergence (JSD) of AU pairs. Finally, temporal features of AUs will be encoded by applying 1-dimensional Gabor filters to each detected AU signal and measuring the patterns of presence and absence of each AU within the clip [2].

Low-level facial features will be extracted using Local Binary Patterns in Three Orthogonal Planes (LBP-TOP) and 2-dimensional Gabor filters. These features have been shown to be effective for engagement classification [14,18]. LBP-TOP features capture texture patterns, which can be indicative of facial expression changes. For example, if a student smiles the texture pattern near the mouth will change from ordinary skin texture to a lip texture as the mouth widens. Gabor filters are particularly well suited for detecting edges, which can capture not only the edges of facial features such as eyes and eyebrows, but also skin wrinkles that occur in some facial expressions (e.g., on the nose when the brow is furrowed).

Support vector machine (SVM) classifiers will be trained using leave-one-student-out cross validation on the development data. SVMs will be used because they have been used successfully in previous engagement detection research [18], and because they lend themselves to modification for improving predictions using human observations of MW (section 4.3). Individual SVMs will be trained for each group of related features (e.g., LBP-TOP features) and combined with a logistic regression. The feature set will be reduced using feature selection.

This analysis will provide a baseline for improvement of MW classification. It is also novel in that student MW during reading has not been well studied before. Additionally, timescale-invariant features have not been explored for MW detection.

4.3 Improving automatic predictions

Knowledge gained from observer ratings may be useful for improving the accuracy of automatic detectors. The first step will be to compare the accuracies of observer and automatic predictions. This will be done on the evaluation dataset. F1 score of MW will be the primary accuracy metric, area under the receiver operating characteristic curve (AUROC) and area under the precision-recall curve (AUPRC) will also be considered as they are common metrics.

There are several potential avenues for improving the automatic detectors by integrating observer knowledge. Even if humans prove less accurate than computers at classifying MW, their input could prove valuable if they are able to classify different instances well than the automatic methods. First, instances in the development set that were poorly classified by the detectors but classified well by observers will be isolated. Then, the observers justifications for their ratings (both text responses and check boxes) will be examined to determine if there are facial cues that should be added as features. For example, LBP-TOP features could be engineered to capture features from a very specific part of the face, or more heavily weight features from that part of the face. Second, weights will be assigned to instances during training so this set of important isolated instances will be more influential in training, and thus influence the position of the SVM hyperplane. Similarly, instances that cannot be well classified by either humans or computers will be weighted lower as they are likely unhelpful for classification. Third, examples from this set of isolated instances will be annotated by researchers to determine if there are additional clues observers may have used to accurately classify these instances. All of these methods will utilize the development training set only, to avoid overfitting to characteristics of the evaluation dataset.

Finally, observer judgments will be augmented with the automatic predictions by training a model using observer judgments and automatic predictions as features. This model will serve as a further comparison to determine if observers are utilizing important features that are not captured by automatic detectors.

This analysis will be the first to compare third-party observations with automatic face-based predictions of MW. It will also be the first to explore the possibility of improving face-based MW detection using knowledge gleaned from human observers.

5. CONCLUSIONS

Engagement is important for learning [8,17]. Engagement detection thus offers opportunities for improving learning through automated engagement evaluation and targeted interventions. This paper describes prior work laying the ground for automatic face-based detection of various aspects of engagement. Face-based detection is particularly attractive for practical applications due to its potential for context generalizability. MW is a relatively unexplored facet of engagement detection, especially with face-based approaches. This paper proposed work to address questions of how well third-party observers can detect MW and what can be done to improve automatic detection. The proposed work, if effective, will provide a powerful addition to computerized learning environments in the future by automatically detecting MW from faces and improving detection by incorporating observer annotations of MW.

6. ACKNOWLEDGEMENTS

I would like to thank my advisor, Sidney D'Mello, for his guidance on this research. This research was supported by the National Science Foundation (NSF) (DRL 1235958 and IIS 1523091). Any opinions, findings and conclusions, or recommendations expressed in this paper are those of the author(s) and do not necessarily reflect the views of the NSF.

7. REFERENCES

1. Ryan Shaun Baker, Albert T. Corbett, Kenneth R. Koedinger, and Angela Z. Wagner. 2004. Off-task behavior in the cognitive tutor classroom: When students "game the system." *Proceedings of the SIGCHI Conference on Human Factors in Computing Systems*, ACM, 383–390.
2. Marian Stewart Bartlett, Gwen C. Littlewort, Mark G. Frank, and Kang Lee. 2014. Automatic decoding of facial movements reveals deceptive pain expressions. *Current biology: CB* 24, 7: 738–743.
3. Nathaniel Blanchard, Robert Bixler, Tera Joyce, and Sidney D'Mello. 2014. Automated physiological-based detection of mind wandering during learning. *Proceedings of the 12th International Conference on Intelligent Tutoring Systems (ITS 2014)*, Switzerland: Springer International Publishing, 55–60.
4. Nigel Bosch, Yuxuan Chen, and Sidney D'Mello. 2014. It's written on your face: Detecting affective states from facial expressions while learning computer programming. *Proceedings of the 12th International Conference on Intelligent Tutoring Systems (ITS 2014)*, Switzerland: Springer International Publishing, 39–44.
5. Nigel Bosch, Sidney D'Mello, Ryan Baker, et al. 2015. Automatic detection of learning-centered affective states in the wild. *Proceedings of the 2015 International Conference on Intelligent User Interfaces (IUI 2015)*, New York, NY: ACM, 379–388.
6. Michael Buhrmester, Tracy Kwang, and Samuel D. Gosling. 2011. Amazon's mechanical turk a new source of inexpensive, yet high-quality, data? *Perspectives on Psychological Science* 6, 1: 3–5.
7. Rafael A. Calvo and Sidney D'Mello. 2010. Affect detection: An interdisciplinary review of models, methods, and their applications. *IEEE Transactions on Affective Computing* 1, 1: 18–37.
8. Sidney D'Mello. 2013. A selective meta-analysis on the relative incidence of discrete affective states during learning with technology. *Journal of Educational Psychology* 105, 4: 1082–1099.
9. Sidney D'Mello and Art Graesser. 2012. Dynamics of affective states during complex learning. *Learning and Instruction* 22, 2: 145–157.
10. Joseph F. Grafsgaard, Joseph B. Wiggins, Kristy Elizabeth Boyer, Eric N. Wiebe, and James C. Lester. 2013. Automatically recognizing facial expression: Predicting engagement and frustration. *Proceedings of the 6th International Conference on Educational Data Mining*.
11. Mohammed (Ehsan) Hoque, Daniel McDuff, and Rosalind W. Picard. 2012. Exploring temporal patterns in classifying frustrated and delighted smiles. *IEEE Transactions on Affective Computing* 3, 3: 323–334.
12. Ashish Kapoor, Winslow Burleson, and Rosalind W. Picard. 2007. Automatic prediction of frustration. *International Journal of Human-Computer Studies* 65, 8: 724–736.
13. Gwen Littlewort, J. Whitehill, Tingfan Wu, et al. 2011. The computer expression recognition toolbox (CERT). *2011 IEEE International Conference on Automatic Face Gesture Recognition and Workshops (FG 2011)*, 298–305.
14. Hamed Monkaresi, Nigel Bosch, Rafael A. Calvo, and Sidney K. D'Mello. in press. Automated detection of engagement using video-based estimation of facial expressions and heart rate. *IEEE Transactions on Affective Computing*.
15. Zachary A. Pardos, Ryan S. J. D. Baker, Maria O. C. Z. San Pedro, Sujith M. Gowda, and Supreeth M. Gowda. 2013. Affective states and state tests: Investigating how affect throughout the school year predicts end of year learning outcomes. *Proceedings of the Third International Conference on Learning Analytics and Knowledge*, ACM, 117–124.
16. Erik D. Reichle, Andrew E. Reineberg, and Jonathan W. Schooler. 2010. Eye movements during mindless reading. *Psychological Science* 21, 9: 1300–1310.
17. Jonathan Smallwood, Daniel J. Fishman, and Jonathan W. Schooler. 2007. Counting the cost of an absent mind: Mind wandering as an underrecognized influence on educational performance. *Psychonomic Bulletin & Review* 14, 2: 230–236.
18. J. Whitehill, Z. Serpell, Yi-Ching Lin, A Foster, and J.R. Movellan. 2014. The faces of engagement: Automatic recognition of student engagement from facial expressions. *IEEE Transactions on Affective Computing* 5, 1: 86–98.

Designing Culture-based Persuasive Technology to Promote Physical Activity among University Students

Kiemute Oyibo
University of Saskatchewan
Saskatoon, Canada
kiemute.oyibo@usask.ca

ABSTRACT

Overweight and obesity are taking a huge toll on nations' financial and health resources annually. Student populations are at risk due to their sedentary lifestyles and the high demands of academic scholarship, leaving them with little or no time to exercise. Recently, persuasive technology, promoting physical activity, has been proposed. However, the traditional "one-size-fits-all" approach has not been effective among the student population. This calls for a newer and more effective approach, which leverages the available recreational and technological resources in the university at personal, social and cultural levels. In an effort to address students' sedentary behaviors, I aim to combine user behavior models, persuasive technology design and cultural strategies from Health Sciences for a more personalized and effective intervention. This paper presents the approach and the preliminary results of two user studies among 218 and 292 subjects from a Canadian and a Nigerian university respectively.

Keywords
Physical activity; persuasive technology; user model; university.

1. INTRODUCTION
The global prevalence of obesity and overweight and the associated chronic diseases due to sedentary lifestyle, occasioned by technological advancement, is worrisome. Overweight and obesity are among the major risk factors that account for global mortality [32]. They cut across ages, genders, cultures, and affect all income-level countries [32]. In Canada, *"one in four adults"* (p. 9) are obese [15]. Between 1981 and 2009, the prevalence of obesity nearly doubled . Over the years, obesity has become more severe with physical fitness levels declining. According to to [7], *"the more Canadians settle into a life of physical inactivity, the more they exert a toll on the country's healthcare system"*. In 2009, for example, the cost due to sedentary lifestyle stood at $6.8 billion, amounting to 3.7% of all healthcare costs [7]. In China, the obesity prevalence is alarming as well, with 63 million obese people living in China in 2014 [1]. The rapid growth in Chinese economy, coupled with the fast-changing lifestyle, has led to China witnessing an unprecedented increase in the prevalence of obesity and overweight in the last decade, costing her 2.4% of her national healthcare expenditure annually [23]. Further, in Africa, overweight and obesity, due to rapidly changing diets and patterns of physical activity (PA) [32], are on the rise, with the possibility of becoming an epidemic in the near future [21].

UMAP '16, July 13-17, 2016, Halifax, NS, Canada
ACM 978-1-4503-4370-1/16/07.
http://dx.doi.org/10.1145/2930238.2930372

The student populations in Canada and other nations are also affected by the obesity "epidemic". The typically sedentary manner of studying, coupled with the high demands of academic success, has resulted in long hours of sitting in front of computer screens and books, leading to higher risk of overweight, obesity and cardiovascular diseases [13]. For example, research [14] has shown most university students fall short of the recommended level of weekly PA required to maintain optimal health. As a result, there is need for a systematically tailored intervention to change students' sedentary behaviors towards a physically active lifestyle. Universities hold a great potential to effect beneficial changes in students' lifestyles in this regard. Research has shown that one of the most effective ways to cut down the related healthcare costs is to prevent the associated chronic diseases as early as possible by adopting an active lifestyle [32]. However, research has shown that even though humans generally want to adopt a healthy lifestyle, they find it very difficult to motivate themselves to engage in or sustain the target behavior, even when they are aware of the health benefits [22]. This calls for a new, more personalized, refined and effective behavioral change approach, informed by a theoretical behavioral framework, which leverages the personal, social, cultural, environmental and the available technological resources of the target population to tackle sedentary behaviors [32]. Information technology, which has so far mostly increased the prevalence of sedentary behaviors and obesity, can be mobilized to tackle the problem through persuasive applications. The university, as a citadel of learning, offers a unique opportunity for the cultivation, acquisition and entrenchment of life-long healthy lifestyles and habits. It provides a transformation environment for young people to adult life. By leveraging the socio-cultural background, the wide availability of recreational and technological and mobile devices, e.g., clothing-embedded sensors, step-counters, smartphones, etc., which are becoming less expensive and ubiquitous over time, my thesis aims to address the following overarching research question:

How can the university's technological resources, recreational facilities, the geographical proximity and the similarity in the rhythm of students' day-to-day activities be leveraged in designing a persuasive technology intervention to promote an active lifestyle among university students by taking the culture of the target users into consideration?

Moreover, I have carried out user studies among 218 students from a Canadian university and 292 students from a Nigerian university to model the PA of students using Social Cognitive Theory (SCT) [3]. My findings show that self-efficacy and self-regulation are the strongest determinants of PA among the Canadian group (CG), while social support and body image are the strongest determinants of PA among the Nigerian group (NG).

The rest of this paper is organized as follows. Sections 2 focuses on related work and Section 3 on research method. Section 4 and Section 5 focus on preliminary result and discussion respectively. Finally, Section 6 dwells on conclusion and future work.

2. RELATED WORK

A number of PTs have been used to promote PA. UbiFit is a mobile PT that uses on-body sensing and activity inference to encourage people to track their PA and incorporate it into their daily lives [10]. Chick Clique is a preventive cell phone app that encourages teenage girls to exercise by leveraging their social desire to engage with their peers [29]. Flowie is a context-aware app that uses a virtual coach to motivate older adults to walk more [2]. Interactive technologies have also be used in promoting PA. Dance Dance Revolution is an interactive video game on the console, which uses music and dancing to engage young people in a PA that feels like fun, not hard work. This has led to positive health outcomes, such as higher heart rate and energy expenditure. Other interactive video games with positive health outcomes include Wii Sports, Wii Fit, etc. [11]. Although numerous PT interventions exist (e.g., those discussed above) for self-tracking and promoting PA, very few have been specifically targeted at the university student population and designed based on a behavioral model or cultural strategies. Most often adopt the one-size-fits-all design approach. How one PT design principle was chosen over another has been unclear [20]. However, research [19] has shown that theory-informed PT interventions, targeted at specific users and individuals, are more likely to succeed. Thus, our approach is to combine user behavior model, PT design and cultural strategies for a more effective intervention.

3. METHOD

As we age (especially after the age of 30), the human muscle mass and strength start declining gradually [12]. Due to the sedentary lifestyle of studying, students stand a great risk. To reduce the atrophying of the skeletal muscles and prevent chronic diseases caused by sedentary lifestyle, medical doctors and researchers have recommended that people engage in regular exercise [12]. My research sets out to find a theory-and-culture informed strategy and method to design tailorable persuasive applications to effectively promote PA among university students. To answer the research question, posed in the introduction, I adopted the Design Science Research (DSR) framework shown in Figure 1. The DSR framework illustrates a five-stage approach, which alternates between stages directly involving and those not involving the target users. The stars denote the progress so far.

Stage 1: This stage comprises: 1) problem identification and motivation; and 2) objective of a solution. The first phase is discussed in Sections 1 and 2. The second phase (my research goal) is to design PT guidelines and personalized interactive apps [28] to motivate students to engage in PA. To realize this, I aim to consider three broad categories of PA in which students can participate at both personal and social levels. I termed (codenamed) these categories the "S-Cube of Physical Activity". They include *Step*, *Stretch* and *Squeeze*. Table 1 describes the S-Cube and gives some example micro-exercises. Regarding *Step*, research has shown that many people fall below the minimum 10000 steps a day required to be optimally healthy [13]. Thus, my proposed PT app (PPA) will be equipped with context awareness to prompt users at the right time and place to take some steps, e.g., to use the staircase instead of the lift. Regarding *Stretch*, research [4] has shown that most people sit for more than 300 min/day. To increase students' PA during screen time, my PPA will help motivate them to engage in beneficial micro-exercises from time to time, e.g., stretching the body. Finally, regarding *Squeeze*, "*the facial muscles are rarely exercised to any significant extent,*" and "*from a physiological point of view... the effects of weight training stop at the neck*" [12]. However, research has shown that

Table 1. The S-Cube of physical activity

Activity	Description	Micro-Exercises
Step	Exercising the legs (from the waist downward).	Mobile app prompting a user to use the staircase instead of the lift or a desktop app prompting a user to stand up and take some walk after a long screen time.
Stretch	Exercising the middle part of the body (from the shoulder to the waist).	Mobile app prompting a user to do some body stretches (e.g., sideways) after using the washroom or spending a while in front of the computer screen.
Squeeze	Exercising the face (from the neck upward).	Desktop app prompting a user in front of the screen to do facial exercise (e.g., squeezes).

facial movement has the potential of maintaining the elastic fiber content of the facial skin, making it firmer, more elastic and reducing facial wrinkles [12]. My PPA will help motivate students to take advantage of exercising their face and neck muscles while in front of the screen. It will help them visualize and keep track of their facial movements, set goals and compete.

Stage 2: This stage focuses on user research. It answers the question, "who will *use* the intervention?" [8]. In this stage (aka the theory stage), evidence is gathered to develop a model that would serve as a theoretical basis for an intervention in Stages 3 and 4 (aka experimental stage). Research has shown that interventions based on behavioral theories and models are more likely to succeed [19]. So far, I have carried out two user studies (approved by the University of Saskatchewan research ethics board) to model PA determinants among 218 and 292 students of a Canadian university (online) and a Nigerian university (paper-based) respectively. To motivate participants, in the former, they were given a chance to enter for a draw to win $50, while in the latter they were each given a phone credit card of $0.5. The results are presented and discussed in Sections 4 and 5 respectively.

Stage 3: This stage comprises: 1) design and development of the PPA based on the user models from Stage 2; and 2) demonstration of the PPA through technical testing to ensure it meets the research objective. For tailoring, I shall combine cultural strategies (peripheral, evidential, linguistic, constitute-involving and socio-cultural) from Health Science [18] with PT design strategies (e.g., Fogg's eight-step design process and Persuasive System Design (PSD) framework [17] for a more effective PPA. The PPA shall be implemented on selected computing devices, e.g., desktops, mobiles, wearables, watches, etc. It will integrate students' academic activities, possess goal-setting and self-tracking features and apply personalized visualization and gamification techniques within a social context to motivate students to engage actively in PA. In visualization, the app will have the ability to monitor and display users' PA (e.g., performance, progress and fitness levels) by using culturally oriented metaphors. It is expected that such metaphorical visualization would elicit exciting discussions among peers and motivate others in a social context to engage more in PA. Further, the app will have the capability to recommend and match-make users with similar psychosocial characteristics and preferences. This will allow users to form peer support groups to motivate one another to exercise in the gym and engage in sporting activities. In gamification, users would have the ability to earn virtual reward (e.g. points, badges, etc.) upon completing planned PA tasks on individual and collective basis. They would also have the opportunity to cooperate and compete as teams on certain tasks.

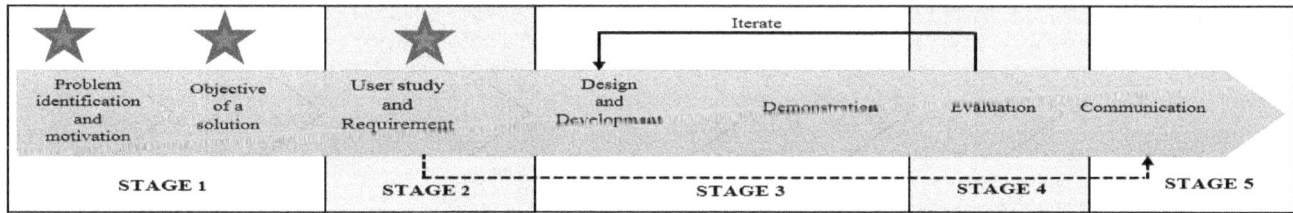

Figure 1. Design Science Research framework (adapted from Reinecke and Bernstein [24])

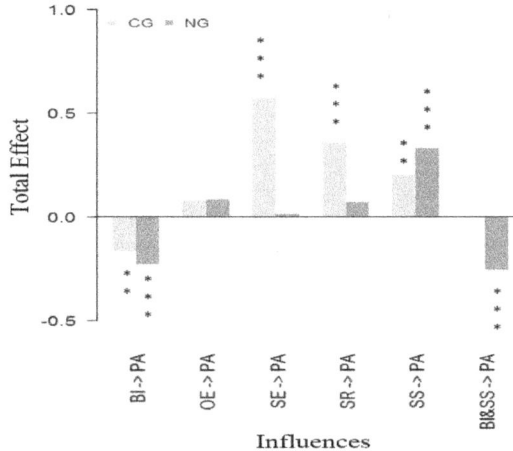

Figure 2. Total effects of driver constructs on target construct

Theories and concepts in complex adaptive systems (such as autonomy, adaptation, synchronization and cost-benefit ratio) towards self-organization and evolution shall be used to drive behavioral change. For example, positive feedback loops within the context of gamification shall be used to motivate or influence team mates and opponents to perform simple tasks at the micro-level to realize greater goals at the macro-level.

Stage 4: This stage, user testing, answers the question, "how *effective* is the intervention?" [8]. Here, we will evaluate the initial implemented PT app versions both through a mockup crowdsourced study that measures the intention, attitude and self-efficacy, which are shown to be direct predictors for engaging in the targeted behavior [22] and with groups of students in different countries (e.g., by using pervasive technology acceptance model (PTAM) [9]) and getting user feedback. The user comments and suggestions will be fed back into the design and development phase of Stage 3 towards developing an improved version of the app.

Stage 5: Stage 5 focuses on writing and disseminating the findings, which arise from the user studies and evaluation of the PT application in a field study with the target user population.

4. CURRENT PROGRESS AND RESULT

In a practical context, according to [28], it is important for designers of an interactive persuasive system to have a clear model of the desired effects on the target users and the way in which the system's features should be designed to realize them. Such a model will both guide design and help in planning the evaluation of the system. As such, using the SCT for health promotion [3], I carried out a user study in order to model the PA determinants among my target populations. I conducted the study in two different countries because 1) research [20] has shown that culture influences PA; 2) Canada and Nigeria belong to different cultures (*individualist* and *collectivist* respectively [16]), which may differ in PA determinant models. In the path analysis, six SCT constructs, measured using prior validated instruments (see Table 2 with example items) were

Table 2. SCT physical activity constructs and examples

Construct	Examples of Instrument's Item
Self-Efficacy (SE) [25]	*How confident are you right now that you can exercise three times per week for 20 minutes if:* 1) *You felt tired.* 2) *You had to exercise alone?*
Self-Regulation (SR) [26]	1) *I often set exercise goals.* 2) *I never seem to have enough time to exercise.* 3) *I schedule all events in my life around my exercise routine.*
Outcome Expectation (OE) [31]	1) *Exercise will strengthen my bones.* 2) *Exercise will give me a sense of personal accomplishment.* 3) *Exercise will improve my social standing.*
Social Support (SS) [27]	1) *During the past 3 months, my family offered to exercise with me.* 2) *During the past 3 months, my friend(s) offered to exercise with me.*
Body Image (BI) [30]	*Have you been particularly self-conscious about your shape when in the company of other people?*
Physical Activity (PA) [6]	*During the last 7 days, on how many days did you do vigorous physical activities like heavy lifting, digging, aerobics, or fast bicycling?*

considered. Figure 2 summarizes the two group's models: the total effect of the driver constructs on *PA*. First, *SE* and *SR* have positive total effects (0.573 and 0.354 respectively at p<0.001) on *PA* for the CG only, with *SR* mediating the effect of *SE* on *PA*. Second, *SS* and *BI* have positive and negative total effects respectively on *PA* for both groups, with the NG (0.329 and -0.231, p<0.001) having a stronger effect than the CG (0.198 and -0.167, p<0.01). However, *BI* and *SS* interact to impact *PA* of the NG (-0.258, p<0.001) only.

5. DISCUSSION

The path analysis in Section 4 shows the CG and NG possess some similarities and differences as well. Regarding similarities, the *PA* of both groups is influenced by *BI* and *SS*, but not by *OE*. This suggests that while *BI* and *SS* motivate both groups to participate in PA, the awareness of the health benefits of *PA* alone does not, as other motivators are also essential [3]. One can speculate that this is due to the ubiquity of health promotion information, to which young people have become desensitized. Regarding differences, *SE* and *SR* influence *PA* of the CG only, while *SS* and *BI* influence PA of the NG much more. A possible explanation for these differences can be found in Hofstede's dimensional classification of culture [16]. Based on the classification, Canada belongs to an *individualist* culture where people tend to be independent, self-determined and self-motivated towards realizing *personal* goals. Thus, *SE* and *SR*, which are intrinsic determinants, tend to have stronger effect on the *PA* of the CG. On the other hand, Nigeria belongs to a *collectivist* culture, where people tend to do things in social groups to realize *collective* goals and aspirations. Thus, *SS*, an extrinsic determinant, has stronger effect than *SE* on the *PA* of the NG. In addition, *SS* (an extrinsic determinant) interacts with *BI* (an intrinsic determinant) to influence *PA*, with the former moderating. The moderation of *BI* by *SS* can be explained as follows. People often worry about their body image in the company of others. For example, those who have negative *BI* may not like to engage in PA in a social space such as the gym, as they feel others are always evaluating their physique [5]. Our findings indicate that for those who have higher *SS* from their family or friends in the NG, their *BI* is more likely to influence their *PA* than would those who are not given such support, with positive *BI* increasing their *PA* and negative *BI* decreasing their *PA*. This indicates that, for the NG, if their *BI* is amenable to improvement as outlined by [5], there is a chance of increasing their *PA* in a social context, which is the hallmark of a collectivist culture. The implication of these findings is that, given the total effects, tailored PT apps with features that promote *SE* and *SR* would be more effective for the CG, while those with features that promote *SS* and positive *BI* would be more effective for the NG.

6. CONCLUSION AND FUTURE WORK

I presented a DSR approach aimed at designing PT to promote PA among university students in order to tackle the sedentary behaviors due to technological advancement. I discussed two SCT models of 218 Canadian and 292 Nigerian students' PA, which will inform a tailored intervention. The models show that *SE* and *SR* are the strongest drivers of *PA* among the Canadian group, while *BI* and *SS* are the strongest drivers of *PA* among the Nigerian group. In the future, I intend to conduct focus group sessions to determine cultural and PT strategies that will inform the intervention design, and evaluate them by crowdsourced and field studies.

REFERENCES

[1]   62 million people in China obese, sparking fears of "alarming" financial burden: 2014. *http://www.scmp.com/lifestyle*. Accessed: 2016-03-18.

[2]   Albaina, I.M. et al. 2009. Flowie: A persuasive virtual coach to motivate elderly individuals to walk. *International ICST Conference on Pervasive Computing Technologies for Healthcare* (2009), 1–7.

[3]   Bandura, A. 2004. Health promotion by social cognitive means. *Health Educ. & Behav.* 31, 2 (2004), 143–164.

[4]   Bauman, A. et al. 2011. The descriptive epidemiology of sitting: A 20-country comparison using the international physical activity questionnaire (IPAQ). *American Journal of Preventive Medicine*. 41, 2 (2011), 228–235.

[5]   Body Image and Physical Activity: 2016. *http://appliedsportpsych.org*. Accessed: 2016-02-11.

[6]   C. Craig et al. 2003. International physical activity questionnaire: 12-country reliability and validity. *Med and Sci in Sports and Exerc*. 35, 8 (2003), 1381–1395.

[7]   CBCNews 2012. Physical inactivity costs taxpayers 6.8B a year. *The Canadian Press*. (2012).

[8]   Complete Beginner's Guide to Design Research: 2010. *http://www.uxbooth.com/articles/complete-beginners-guide-to-design-research/*. Accessed: 2016-03-20.

[9]   Connelly, K. 2007. On developing a technology acceptance model for pervasive computing. *Ubiquitous System Evaluation (USE) - a workshop at the 9th Intl Conf on Ubiquitous Computing (UBICOMP)* (2007).

[10]   Consolvo, S. et al. 2008. Activity sensing in the wild: a field trial of ubifit garden. *Proc. of the SIGCHI Conf on Hum Factors in Comp Sys (CHI '08)*. (2008), 1797–1806.

[11]   Dominic, D. et al. 2013. Promoting physical activity through persuasive technology. *International Journal of Inventive Engineering and Sciences* (2013), 16–22.

[12]   FlexEffect Facialbuilding: 1997. *http://flexeffect.com/research*. Accessed: 2016-03-01.

[13]   Fountaine, C.J. et al. 2008. Physical activity and screen time sedentary behaviors in college students. *International Journal of Exercise Science*. 4, 1 (2008), 102–112.

[14]   Gómez-López, M. et al. 2010. Perceived barriers by university students in the practice of physical activities. *Journal of Sports Sci and Med*. 9, 3 (2010), 374–381.

[15]   Hodgson, C. et al. 2011. Obesity in Canada: A joint report from the Public Health Agency of Canada and the Canadian Institute for Health Information. *Canadian Institute for Health Information*. (2011), 62.

[16]   Hofstede, G. and Hofstede, G.J. 1991. *Cultures and Organizations: Software of the Mind*. McGraw-Hill.

[17]   Kegel, R.H.P. and Wieringa, R.J. 2014. Persuasive Technologies : A Systematic Literature Review and Application to PISA. (2014).

[18]   Kreuter, M.W. et al. 2003. Achieving cultural appropriateness in health promotion programs: targeted and tailored approaches. *Health Education and Behavior*. 30, 2 (2003), 133–146.

[19]   Michie, S. et al. 2008. From theory to intervention: mapping theoretically derived behavioural determinants to behaviour change techniques. *Applied psychology*. 57, 4 (2008), 660–680.

[20]   Mohd Mohadis, H. and Mohamad Ali, N. 2015. Using Socio-ecological Model to Inform the Design of Persuasive Applications. *Proc. of 33rd Ann ACM Conf Ext Abst on Hum Factors in Comp Sys* (2015), 1905–1910.

[21]   Obesity: Africa's new crisis: 2014. *http://www.theguardian.com/society/2014/sep/21/obesity-africas-new-crisis*. Accessed: 2015-11-25.

[22]   Orji, R. 2014. *Design for Behaviour Change: A Model-driven Approach for Tailoring Persuasive Technologies*. University of Saskatchewan, Canada.

[23]   Qin, X. and Pan, J. 2015. The Medical Cost Attributable to Obesity and Overweight in China: Estimation Based on Longitudinal Surveys. *Health Econ*. (2015).

[24]   Reinecke, K. and Bernstein, A. 2013. Knowing What a User Likes: A Design Science Approach to Interfaces that Adapt to Culture. *MIS Quarterly*. 37, 2 (2013), 427–453.

[25]   Resnick, B. and Jenkins, L.S. 2000. Testing the Reliability and Validity of the Self-Efficacy for Exercise Scale. *Nursing Research*. 49, 3 (2000), 154–159.

[26]   Rovniak, L.S. et al. 2002. Social cognitive determinants of physical activity in young adults: a prospective structural equation analysis. *Ann Behav Med*. 24, 2 (2002), 149–156.

[27]   Social support and exercise survey: 1986. *http://sallis.ucsd.edu/Documents/Measures_documents/SocialSupport_exercise.pdf*. Accessed: 2015-09-05.

[28]   Spagnolli, A. et al. 2016. Interactive persuasive systems : A perspective on theory and evaluation. *Intl Journal of Human-Computer Interaction*. 32, 3 (2016), 177–189.

[29]   Toscos, T. et al. 2006. Chick clique: persuasive technology to motivate teenage girls to exercise. *CHI '06 Extended Abstracts on Human Factors in Computing Systems* (2006), 1873–1878.

[30]   Welch, E. et al. 2012. Body Shape Questionnaire: Psychometric properties of the short version (BSQ-8C) and norms from the general Swedish population. *Body Image*. 9, (2012), 547–550.

[31]   Wójcicki, T.R. et al. 2009. Assessing outcome expectations in older adults : the multidimensional outcome expectations for exercise scale. *J of Gerontol. Ser B, Psychol Sci & Soc Sci*. 64, 1 (2009), 33–40.

[32]   World Health Organization 2004. *Global Strategy on Diet, Physical Activity and Health*.

Deeper Knowledge Tracing by Modeling Skill Application Context for Better Personalized Learning

Yun Huang[*]
Intelligent Systems Program
University of Pittsburgh
210 S. Bouquet Street
Pittsburgh, PA, USA
yuh43@pitt.edu

ABSTRACT

Traditional Knowledge Tracing, which traces students' knowledge of each decomposed individual skill, has been a popular learner model for adaptive tutoring. Typically, a student is guided to the next skill when the student's knowledge on current skill is inferred as mastery. Unfortunately, this traditional approach no longer suffices to model complex skill practices where simple decompositions can not capture potential additional skills underlying the context as a whole. In such cases, mastery should only be granted when a student not only understands the basic of a skill but also can fluently apply a skill in varied application contexts. In this thesis, we aim to propose a data-driven approach to construct learner models considering different skill application contexts for tracing deeper knowledge, primarily based on Bayesian Networks. We aim to conduct novel, comprehensive, "deep" evaluations, including internal data-drive evaluations, and external end-user evaluations examining the real world impact for students' personalized learning.

Keywords

complex skill, multiple skills, deep learning, Knowledge Tracing, Bayesian Network

1. INTRODUCTION

Knowledge Tracing (KT) [3] has established itself as an efficient approach to model student skill acquisition in intelligent tutoring systems. To apply KT, one needs to decompose domain knowledge into elementary skills and map each problem-solving step to an individual skill. KT has demonstrated its ability to track student knowledge for different domains, and may now be considered the most popular learner modeling approach. However, a known limitation

[*]Advisor: Peter Brusilovsky, School of Information Sciences, University of Pittsburgh

UMAP '16 July 13-17, 2016, Halifax, NS, Canada

© 2016 Copyright held by the owner/author(s).

ACM ISBN 978-1-4503-4370-1/16/07.

DOI: http://dx.doi.org/10.1145/2930238.2930373

on KT is the assumption of skill independence in problems that involve multiple (complex) skills. Recent research on KT has challenged this assumption, and has demonstrated that there is additional knowledge related to specific skill combinations; in other words, the knowledge about a set of skills is more than the "sum" of the knowledge of individual skills [8], some skills must be integrated (or connected) with other skills to produce the desired behavior [11]. Also, recent research that has applied a difficulty factor assessment [12] demonstrated that some factors underlying the context, when combined with a students' original skills, can raise the difficulty of the material being learned and should be included in the skill model representation. Here are two examples of just such a situation:

- Students were found to be significantly worse at translating two-step algebra story problems into expressions (e.g., 800-40x) than they were at translating two closely matched one-step problems (with answers 800-y and 40x) [8].
- "16-30" can be more difficult than "20-16" since it involves the difficulty factor of "Negative Result" [12].

This illustrates that in some domains, we need to pay specific attention to *the context of skill application*. One of these domains is arguably computer programming. Research on computer science education has long argued that knowledge of a programming language cannot be reduced to a sum of knowledge about different programming constructs, since there are many stable combinations (patterns or plans) that must be taught and practiced [14]. To generalize these findings to other domains, we argue that skill application context can represent "chunks", general problem-solving patterns that are critical in acquiring expertise in a domain.

Meanwhile, complex skill knowledge modeling has been a challenge and has attracted increasing attention. Starting from [4] constructing simple variants based on traditional Knowledge Tracing, more advanced models have been put forward to address the multiple skill credit and blame assignment issue [13, 6, 15]. However, these student models use a "flat" knowledge structure that overlooks any potential interactions among skills and any interactions between skills and difficulty factors. Essentially, these models don't provide the requisite formalism of considering the "context" for a skill's mastery. Works that consider the relationships among skills mostly focus on prerequisite relationships [2, 1] or a granular hierarchy [7].

Regarding the data-driven evaluations of learner models, prior studies mostly use student problem-solving performance prediction [3, 6], which raises some concerns. For example, [5] has shown that highly predictive models may be useless for adaptive tutoring, and [9] has shown that they can have low parameter plausibility or consistency. While some attempts have been made to evaluate models in terms of their effects on tutoring [13], a recent learner outcome-effort paradigm [5] offers a promising way to empirically evaluate student models for adaptive tutoring, which we plan to extend. We believe that a good learner model should demonstrate significant impact for real-world personalized learning, so we also plan to design classroom studies to investigate the impact of such a model on actual diagnosis accuracy, student awareness of mastery, recommendation quality, and content creation.

2. EXPECTED CONTRIBUTIONS

We expect to achieve the following major contributions:

- **A novel perspective and data-driven approach to building skill and learner models considering skill application context.** Our work will be the first to introduce the variability of application context to model students' deeper knowledge using data-driven techniques. We propose to categorize the "context" by the combinations among skills, between skills and difficulty factors. Mastery of a skill can only be granted when a student demonstrates the ability to apply this skill in varied contexts.

- **A novel multifaceted evaluation framework for learner models that considers the practically important aspects.** We propose to use a new, comprehensive internal data-driven evaluation (such as parameter plausibility, mastery prediction quality), and external evaluation to examine end-user values.

- **A novel learner model that more accurately diagnoses and increases students' awareness of pursuing deeper learning.** We expect that our new learner model can more accurately differentiate shallow learning from deep learning. We also expect that the open learner model implementation can increase students' awareness of pursuing real mastery, rather than simply increasing a performance score by attempting simple problems.

- **A novel learner model that enables better recommendation.** We expect that under our new learner model, recommendation can more accurately target specific applications or aspects of a skill, which would save time on simple cases.

- **A novel skill model representation that encourages better content creation to address different skill application contexts.** We expect that our extracted skill model (used by the learner model) would be able to guide content authors to find content that addresses a variety of skill application contexts.

Also, we expect to contribute to addressing the following important issues in building learner models:

- **Model complexity.** This is a common concern when applying Bayesian networks to build learner models. We will explore proper representations for the skill and learner model, heuristics to search within the space of representations, and efficient implementations and advanced techniques to reduce the overall complexity.

- **Model interpretability.** We expect that the extracted "context" representation units could be interpreted by learners or teachers. However, data-driven methods can be sensitive to the size or characteristics of the data, the information type (such as performance information or domain knowledge). We will explore the effect of such factors and will consider the application of automatic text analysis, combined with affordable expert effort, to achieve our goal without the loss of model predictive performance.

3. PROPOSED APPROACH AND EVALUATION

3.1 Model Construction

3.1.1 Overview

We plan to construct a Bayesian network (BN) which we call *conjunctive knowledge modeling with hierarchical skill-context units (CKM-HC)* to model the context of skill application. Figure 1 shows the structure of our model. The O nodes (shaded) represent binary observed student performance, K nodes represent binary latent skill knowledge level, and M nodes represent the aggregated binary latent skill knowledge level, which we call *Mastery*. Edges denote causal relations. This model has three main functionalities that derive from three main parts: performance prediction (*Prediction*), dynamic knowledge estimation (*Knowledge*), and mastery decision (*Mastery*). To save space, we will mainly describe how we represent the skill application context, learn the network, and obtain the mastery decision.

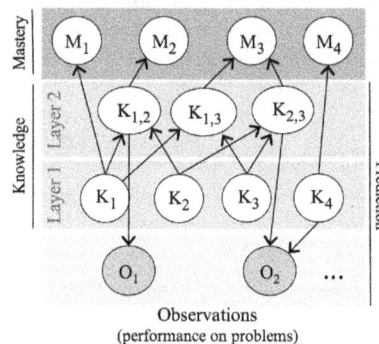

Figure 1: The BN structure of a simplified instantiation of CKM-HC with pairwise combinations for skill application contexts in one practice time slice.

- **Skill Application Context Representation.** We represent application contexts by units arranged hierarchically in both the Knowledge and Mastery Parts:

  - The first layer models the basic understanding of each individual skill (Figure 1 Layer 1). It also contains individual difficulty factors (if any).
  - The intermediate layers (e.g., Figure 1 Layer 2) model the skill application contexts by *context units*. Nodes from upper layers can be derived from lower layers with smaller units. A skill context unit can be constructed from skill combinations or from skill and difficulty factor combinations.

326

- The last layer models the mastery of each individual skill, where the nodes are fed from skill context units or single skills in the first layer. To avoid repeated computation, skill context units only connect to a single Mastery node, with the one representing the latter basic skill in the temporal order in which the skills appear in the course.

- **Network Structure and Parameter Learning.** The final structure of the network depends on the skill context units that it incorporates. If we do not limit the search space of units, the network's complexity will grow exponentially. Also, since the network involves latent variables, we use the Expectation Maximization algorithm, which requires time-consuming posterior computation. We propose a greedy search algorithm for learning the network structure. It requires a pre-ordering of the skill context units of the candidates. During each iteration, it compares the cost function value (e.g., data log likelihood) of the network incorporating a new skill context unit with the optimal one from previous iterations. To rank the context units, we can use the following general information:

  - *Original problem to skill qmatrix.* This provides basic frequency information for skill context units – those with higher frequencies can be considered to be more stable "patterns" to be modeled.
  - *Students' performance data.* We can employ strategies such as extracting context units when the difference of difficulties between the combined skill unit and its hardest constituent skill (unit) is large.
  - *Natural language processing on the problem text.* We can employ strategies such as extracting context units that have enough proximity to one another in the text.

  We can also consider using domain knowledge or resources to help extract more meaningful or more typical skill context units. For example, in programming, we can use an abstract syntax tree (AST).

  Another aspect we find challenging is to consider the *temporal learning effect* in such a "complex" network. As a first step, we ignore this effect during the model learning process, while maintaining the dynamic knowledge estimation during the application phase, just as [2]. We leave this issue for further exploration.

- **Mastery Decision.** CKM-HC aggregates knowledge estimates from skill context units assigned to the current skill, and gives a final knowledge estimate of the skill, based on which mastery is decided. We now aggregate knowledge levels by computing the joint probability of all required skill units being in a known state.

3.2 Model Evaluation

We plan to conduct both internal data-driven and external end-user evaluations to compare our proposed skill and learner model with different alternatives, including:

- Traditional Knowledge Tracing with original coarse-grained individual skills, where each observation maps to a single skill.
- Weakest Knowledge Tracing [4] with original individual skills, where each observation maps to multiple skills with a minimization function over skills.

- Conjunctive knowledge modeling [13, 15] with original individual skills, where each observation maps to multiple skills with a conjunctive relation among skills.
- Conjunctive knowledge modeling with hierarchical skill-context units where each observation maps to multiple skills with a conjunctive relation among skills.

3.2.1 Internal Data-Driven Evaluation

We first conduct an internal data-drive evaluation based on extending a recent learner effort-outcome paradigm (LEOPARD) [5] and a multifaceted evaluation framework [9]:

- **Mastery accuracy.** Once a learner model asserts mastery of an item's required skills, the student should be unlikely to fail in the actual performance.
- **Mastery effort.** This metric empirically quantifies the number of practices needed to reach mastery of a set of skills by the estimations of a learner model.
- **Parameter plausibility.** The metric investigates the consistency of the fitted parameters with the models' assumptions and with users' intuition.
- **Predictive accuracy on student answers.** We will evaluate how well the new model predicts the correctness of a student's answer, or the content of a student's solution, based on the problem type.

We can also consider external data-driven evaluations, such as predicting external test performance in cases where such data is available, as in [3].

3.2.2 External End-User Evaluation

We will conduct classroom and user studies based on a personalized learning system, based on our learner model. This system should contain the following components:

- **Open learner model.** Our proposed learner model intrinsically empowers new visualizations, and we intend to investigate possible open learner model implementations. Figure 2 demonstrates one example.
- **Recommendation.** We plan to implement new recommendations based on the new learner model. For example, in Figure 2, each cell that corresponds to a specific context unit will link to the recommended materials for its application context unit, so that students can be guided to more focused practice materials.
- **Learning content creation.** Once we construct a skill model that has all of the important application context units, we can build a tool to help identify "missing" learning content, in order to cover the context of some important skill application.

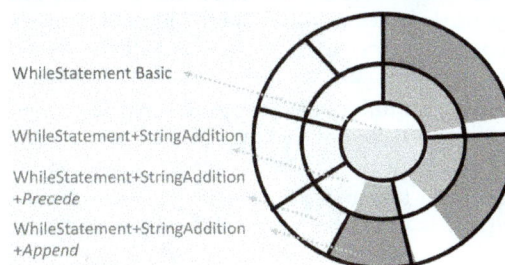

Figure 2: An example of the open learner model implementation of our proposed learner model in the Java programming domain.

Based on the new personalized learning system, we will compare the following aspects of the different models:

1. Do students agree more with the knowledge and mastery estimation or diagnosis from the new learner model?

2. Does the new learner model increase students' awareness of pursuing true mastery rather than performance?

3. Does the new learner model enable more helpful recommendation or remediation?

4. Does the new learner model enable students to achieve a deeper understanding evaluated by certain specifically designed intermediate and final tests?

5. Does the new learner model encourage better learning content creation?

4. PROGRESS

We have conducted preliminary studies with the simplest form of skill application context units, which are *pairwise skill combinations* constructed by grouping two original individual skills together, as in Figure 1, and we evaluated the new model by using some proposed internal data-driven metrics. The results seem to be promising, but more effort is required for further improvement. We used a Java programming comprehension dataset and a SQL generation dataset collected across two years from University of Pittsburgh classes. Due to the runtime limitation, we employed a heuristic approach to choose skill combinations (without a complete search procedural), and conducted internal data-driven evaluations (by a 10-fold cross validation). We found that incorporating pairwise skill combinations can significantly increase mastery accuracy and more reasonably direct students' practice efforts, as compared to traditional knowledge tracing models and their non-hierarchical counterparts. Meanwhile, the predicted performance of all models were similar. On the Java dataset, we also explored the effects of considering textual proximity (in a simple way) or of adding experts' examination for skill combination extraction, and achieved some interesting results. Our preliminary results are summarized in [10]. As the next steps in our study, we aim to achieve the following goals:

- Consider and collect datasets with higher complexity and a greater variety of skill application contexts.

- Explore efficient implementations and advanced techniques to reduce the complexity and to include the temporal learning effect of the Bayesian network.

- Incorporate higher order skill combinations and difficulty factors by intensively applying natural language processing techniques.

- Explore the necessity and effects of including external domain knowledge or resources in skill context unit extraction, particularly on how to balance the model's accuracy and make its results easier to interpret.

- Conduct an affordable user study and use expert engineering to explore the significance, nature, and categorization of the skill application context units.

- Implement the new learner model into an adaptive system and conduct both user and classroom studies.

5. REFERENCES

[1] C. Carmona, E. Millán, J.-L. Pérez-de-la Cruz, M. Trella, and R. Conejo. Introducing prerequisite relations in a multi-layered bayesian student model. In *User Modeling*, pages 347–356. Springer, 2005.

[2] C. Conati, A. Gertner, and K. Vanlehn. Using bayesian networks to manage uncertainty in student modeling. *User Modeling and User-Adapted Interaction*, 12(4):371–417, 2002.

[3] A. T. Corbett and J. R. Anderson. Knowledge tracing: Modelling the acquisition of procedural knowledge. *User Modeling and User-Adapted Interaction*, 4(4):253–278, 1995.

[4] Y. Gong, J. E. Beck, and N. T. Heffernan. Comparing knowledge tracing and performance factor analysis by using multiple model fitting procedures. In *Intelligent Tutoring Systems*, pages 35–44. Springer, 2010.

[5] J. P. González-Brenes and Y. Huang. Your model is predictive but is it useful? theoretical and empirical considerations of a new paradigm for adaptive tutoring evaluation. In *Proc. of the 8th Intl. Conf. on Educational Data Mining*, pages 187–194, 2015.

[6] J. P. González-Brenes, Y. Huang, and P. Brusilovsky. General features in knowledge tracing: Applications to multiple subskills, temporal item response theory, and expert knowledge. In *Proc. of the 7th Intl. Conf. on Educational Data Mining*, pages 84–91, 2014.

[7] J. E. Greer and G. I. McCalla. A computational framework for granularity and its application to educational diagnosis. In *Intl. Joint Conf. on Artificial Intelligence*, pages 477–482, 1989.

[8] N. T. Heffernan and K. R. Koedinger. The composition effect in symbolizing: The role of symbol production vs. text comprehension. In *Proceedings of the Nineteenth Annual Conference of the Cognitive Science Society*, pages 307–312. Lawrence Erlbaum Associates.

[9] Y. Huang, J. P. González-Brenes, R. Kumar, and P. Brusilovsky. A framework for multifaceted evaluation of student models. In *Proceedings of the 8th International Conference on Educational Data Mining*, pages 203–210, 2015.

[10] Y. Huang, J. Guerra, and P. Brusilovsky. A data-driven framework of modeling skill combinations for deeper knowledge tracing. In *Proc. of the 9th Intl. Conf. on Educational Data Mining (Accepted)*.

[11] K. R. Koedinger, A. T. Corbett, and C. Perfetti. The knowledge-learning-instruction framework: Bridging the science-practice chasm to enhance robust student learning. *Cognitive science*, 36(5):757–798, 2012.

[12] K. R. Koedinger, E. A. McLaughlin, and J. C. Stamper. Automated student model improvement. *Proc. of the 8th Intl. Conf. on Educational Data Mining*, pages 17–24, 2012.

[13] K. R. Koedinger, P. I. Pavlik Jr, J. C. Stamper, T. Nixon, and S. Ritter. Avoiding problem selection thrashing with conjunctive knowledge tracing. In *Proc. of the 7th Intl. Conf. on Educational Data Mining*, pages 91–100, 2011.

[14] E. Soloway and K. Ehrlich. Empirical studies of programming knowledge. *IEEE Trans. Software Engineering*, SE-10(5):595–609, 1984.

[15] Y. Xu and J. Mostow. A unified 5-dimensional framework for student models. In *Workshop on Approaching Twenty Years of Knowledge Tracing at the 7th Intl. Conf. on Educational Data Mining*, pages 122–129. Citeseer, 2014.

Open Social Learner Models for Self-Regulated Learning and Learning Motivation

Julio Guerra*
School of Information Sciences
University of Pittsburgh
jdg60@pitt.edu

ABSTRACT

Open Learner Models (OLM) have demonstrated a multitude of benefits supporting metacognition and engaging learners. Although researchers have study different representations of OLM, a broader view that situates OLM in Self-Regulated Learning (SRL) is missing. An important element in SRL that can bring a better understanding of these tools and their effects concerns to learning motivation theories. In this work I connect these aspects and propose to study the effects of OLM and motivational factors drawn from learning motivation theories. To account for a broader spectrum of OLM representations, I proposed to explore the addition of social information and different levels of granularity in the OLM. I propose to evaluate different designs and then to evaluate the resulting interface in field studies. With the proposed work I expect to gain a deeper understanding of the effects of OLM tools which can be used to guide the development of better tools, better personalization and adaptive mechanisms, better use of such tools in supporting Self-Regulated Learning, and ultimately impact positively in learning.

CCS Concepts

•**Human-centered computing** → *Empirical studies in visualization;*

Keywords

Open Learner Model, Learning Motivation

1. INTRODUCTION

Open learner models (OLMs) are learning tools that take an internal model of the learner maintained by a computer-based adaptive or tutoring system and shows it to the learner. According to [7], OLMs can support a variety of aspects, including metacognitive processes such as awareness and

---

*Advisor: Peter Brusilovsky, School of Information Sciences, University of Pittsburgh

UMAP '16 July 13-17, 2016, Halifax, NS, Canada
© 2016 Copyright held by the owner/author(s).
ACM ISBN 978-1-4503-4370-1/16/07.
DOI: http://dx.doi.org/10.1145/2930238.2930375

learning control, and collaboration and trust in the system, among others. Previous work on open learner models (OLMs) and our previous work on open social learner models (OSLMs) [6, 13] show interesting effects on engagement with the learning content and the system, and sometimes contradictory guidance effects. For example [22, 17] showed that OLM helps learners to select better problems and [14] shows that OSLMs produce a "conservative guidance" effect that makes students advance more sequentially through the course content. Moreover, few articles report on the effects of OLMs on learning [18, 22], but those that do note that they are usually buffered by metacognitive aspects [9]. I believe that the effects of OLMs are hidden behind individual differences. For example, [22] found that OLMs produced significant positive differences between pretest and posttest only for "less able" students. In our own work, we have found evidence that OSLMs produce different effects across gender [6]. On the other hand, research on learning theories connects the engagement found in self-regulated learning with different aspects, which range from metacognitive skills [2], to learner beliefs [11], to goal orientation [28], among others. For example, literature on learning motivation connects to self-regulated learning and finds evidence to suggest that motivational factors explain the engagement in SRL processes [29, 28]; this suggests that learning motivation should be considered in the study of SRL environments, such as OLMs. However, no study to date has explored the effects of OLMs, OSLMs, and learning motivation together, and an overall study of the relationships between engagement in using OLMs and SRLs is missing. Achieving a better understanding of the effects that OLM tools produce in learners is important, because it can guide the development of better tools, better personalization, and adaptive mechanisms, which will allow us to make better use of such tools in supporting self-regulated learning processes.

In this work, I propose to study the effects of using an OLM in conjunction with a variety of motivational factors, as defined by different learning motivation theories and frameworks, including the achievement-goal orientation framework [12], self-theories [11], and learning activation [23]. An OSLM system already deployed in our previous studies will be used [13] (see Figure 1). This system incorporates social comparison features that have demonstrated engagement effects in previous studies [6, 13]. To better study the effects of this system and the effect of the OLM, I propose to implement and evaluate different visualizations that complement the information displayed by the system, with the addition of a fine-grained learner model. A fine-grained learner model represents the level of inferred knowledge of the learner in the multitude of conceptual units of the domain and their relationships, which gives the learner a potential powerful metacognitive tool [9], and enables my work to study the effects of granularity and structure on the OLM.

2. RELATED WORK

In traditional adaptive and personalized computed-based learning environments, a user model captures individual aspects, preferences, and general aspects of the learning progress of a student, which allows the system to perform both adaptation and personalization tasks [5]. Open learner models (or open student models), OLMs, release a representation of the user model to the learner with the goal of promoting reflection and encouraging self-regulated processes [7].

Different types of OLMs have been explored, and [8] offers a review of these. Researchers have explored different representations that range from overall knowledge states *skill-meters* [22] to structured representations such as treemaps [4] and concept-maps [18]. Some works present systems with different alternative or complementary representations of their users, such as prerequisite-based concept-maps, hierarchical representation of concept details, and hierarchical representation of the overall course organization [20].

The review of [8] also distinguish different approaches that incorporate a social dimension into an OLM. There have been studies on group interaction modeling, where the learners' interactions are represented to support collaboration and assessment of collaborative work [27]. Another approach explores awareness, social navigational support, and social-comparison effects as a result of showing the models of other learners or aggregated knowledge/progress states of groups of learners [3, 6], which has been called an Open Social Learner Model (OSLM), or an Open Social Student Model (OSSM). OSLM has been demonstrated to produce different effects in both engagement and navigational patterns. For example [15, 16] in different studies consistently found that by showing the models of peer learners, students covered more topics in the system, reached higher success rates in self-assessment problems, and that strong students lead in system exploration. Our later work confirms these findings and reveals some other effects. For example, in [6], we showed how the treatment group, which was exposed to social comparison visualizations, presents higher rates of system usage, learning effectiveness (see [25] for a detailed description of learning or instructional effectiveness), and interaction effects with gender. While we have repeatedly demonstrated the positive uses of an OSLM in classroom studies, our past work in OSLM explores a relatively simple visualization of the learner progress in a coarse-grained representation that is based on topics (see Figure 1). My work focuses on taking this exploration further, and to study the effects of an OSLM that combines both coarse and fine-grained representations.

3. WHY LEARNING MOTIVATION?

Self-regulated learning (SRL) defines an active learner who monitors and controls their own learning process cognitively, meta-cognitively, and emotionally [29]. Zimmerman summarizes three dimensions of SRL: (i) the dual focus in self-regulation process and strategies that target those processes; (ii) the key role of continuing feedback that enables SRL to

Figure 1: Mastery Grids with added social comparison features. the first row represents the progress of the learner (each cell is a topic), the third row represents the average progress of the active students, and the second row represents the difference between the learner and the rest of the class.

happen; and (iii) the interdependence between motivation and self-regulating processes [29]. This interdependence has been broadly studied. For example, the social cognitive view of SRL focuses in self-efficacy, a measure of self-regulation, as the force behind motivation [2]. Other authors have confirmed the positive relation between self-efficacy and other motivational elements, like goal-setting [26]. Moreover, self-regulated learners "who proactively seek out information when needed and take the necessary steps to master it" [29], are closely related to the Mastery-Approach orientation defined by the achievement-goal orientation framework [12]. This framework contains four goal orientations: Mastery-Approach, Mastery-Avoidance, Performance-Approach, and Performance-Avoidance. Mastery-Approach oriented students pursue learning, while Performance-oriented students pursue the demonstration of performance and are usually more sensitive to comparison and scores. Mastery-Avoidance students avoid achieving the minimum, and Performance-Avoidance students avoid performing worse than others or receiving the lowest scores. The implications of these orientations in regulatory learning processes have been well reported in existing literature. For example, according to [28], the goal orientation adopted by the learner is a positive predictor of adaptive behaviors: mastery-oriented students present higher levels of SRL elements, including higher self-efficacy and the use of self-regulatory strategies. Researchers have studied the factors that can foster different achievement-goal orientations. Self-theories [11] reveal how the learners' beliefs in their own intelligence as a fixed or growable resource impact in engagement in adaptive behaviors and learning success. When facing challenging tasks, students who consider intelligence to be a fixed capacity tend to feel threatened, become especially sensitive to external judgment, and usually embrace performance goals. On the other hand, growth-minded students who believe that intelligence can always grow tend to take learning challenges positively, expend more effort, and assume mastery-oriented goals [21]. External factors also impact a student's orientation. For example, mastery-oriented environmental factors, such as an environment that supports autonomous work, can foster the adoption of a Mastery orientation [10], while performance-oriented elements can account for the adoption of performance goals [24]. Research has also established relationships between the different goal orientations. For example, a student can present high levels of performance and mastery orientation goals at the same time [1]. These elements are important to my work because they provide a basis for the idea of incorporating performance and mastery oriented features together in the system, such as social comparison and a fine-grained representation of the OLM, and also suggests that such features can support the simultaneous adoption of both mastery and performance orientations.

4. PROPOSED RESEARCH

I propose to study the relationship between the effects of using an OLM and the learning motivation profile of the learners. This relationship has two major aspects. On one hand, the motivational profile, as defined by different motivational theories and frameworks, is hypothesized to explain different engagement approaches. On the other hand, the motivational profile is not static and can be influenced by the learning experience. By knowing how the motivational profile expresses itself in the patterns of usage of the system, we can see if these patterns change by using different representations of OLM and OSLM with different levels of granularity, and the ways in which these variants might affect overall changes in motivation. My work seeks to answer the following research questions.

- How do students with different motivational profiles engage in using a learning system that provides an OLM?
- What are the effects of social comparison features?
- What are the effects of the granularity of the OLM?
- How does an OLM influence motivation?

To answer these questions, I have organized the proposed work in two parts. Part 1 explores and assesses alternatives to represent an OLM. The goal is to reduce the design space of a OLM and to inform the development of a definitive interface, which I call the Rich-OLM. We foresee that a Rich-OLM will involve both a coarse-grained and a fine-grained view of the learner model, along with the inclusion of aggregated information from other learners. The fine-grained view will visualize concepts, as well as the structure of relationships between concepts and the coarse elements (topics). We think that all of this information can support students with different goals and motivations when using the system. A design study is proposed to carry the evaluation of different design alternatives. The resulting Rich-OLM is evaluated in Part 2 through term-long classroom (field) studies to assess its overall effect on the learning experience, which includes a variety of aspects: system usage, navigational and activity patterns, changes in motivational factors, and learning outcomes.

The motivational profile is measured in Part 2. The factors included in the motivational profile are distilled from different learning motivation theories, including the Learning Activation Questionnaire [23]. the Achievement Goal Revised questionnaire [12] and the Mindset questionnaire [11]. Learning Activation measures the factors of Fascination, Values, and Competency-Beliefs with 14 items, all of them being domain-dependent, and using 4 and 5 points of ordinal scales. The Achievement Goal questionnaire contains 12 questions, 3 for each factor: Mastery-Approach, Mastery-Avoidance, Performance-Approach, and Performance-Avoidance. All questions use a 7-point Likert scale. The Mindset questionnaire contains 12 questions using a 6-point Likert scale with 6 for each of the opposite factors: an Incremental mindset (the intelligence is growable) and an Entity mindset (the intelligence is fixed). The motivation questionnaires will be given at both the beginning and at the end of the classroom studies, which wil allow for the measure of any change in the motivational profile of the students.

Table 1: Number of active students (those who used the system) in previous classroom studies.

Domain	Active Users	Questionnaires collected
Java	217	162
SQL	86	80
Python	490	426

5. CURRENT PROGRESS

To this date, we have conducted several classroom studies using Mastery Grids OSLM (Figure 1); the results of some of these are reported in different articles [19, 6, 13]. As a result, a considerable amount of data on the usage of the system has been collected, including questionnaires measuring the motivational profile. Data has been collected in three domains: Java programming, SQL programming, and Python programming, in different class groups using Mastery Grids with varied material that includes assessment exercises, code examples, and code animations. Table 1 shows the number of active students and students who have answered the questionnaires in previous studies. Current classroom studies are being conducted in a "pure" baseline mode, without the use of the OLM interface. New term-long classroom studies in the 3 domains (Java, SQL, and Python programming) are planned for the second part of 2016, where an extended version of Mastery Grids, including fine-grained OSLM features, will be tested.

In parallel, Part 1 is being executed. We are exploring different alternatives of complementing Mastery Grids with a view of the fine-grained learner model; namely, the concept space representation of the learner model. A set of interviews were conducted with students who used Mastery Grids in previous terms with the goal of verifying the extent to which students use the system differently and the extent to which they think that a detailed OLM, including a fine-grained view (concept space), and the exposure of the models of other learners are valuable information to support their learning and influences their motivation to use the system. Results confirm these views: students have differing opinions about what information is helpful and how they would eventually use that information. In general, students would like to be able to see the concept space (which concepts are in each topic) and how they are doing in learning those concepts. Second, they would like to know how others are doing, but they also expressed some concerns about this information: *What does it mean for a student to be in the average of the class? What if other students who do a lot of activities are advanced students that need to expend only a little effort to excel?* Addressing these concerns is necessary in order to generate a visualization that can support a variety of students.

6. EXPECTED CONTRIBUTIONS

We expect to achieve the following main contributions:

- Role of motivational factors in engagement with SRL learning tool.
- Design guidelines for OLM that consider different motivational profiles.
- Understanding role of the different features in an OLM, including granularity and social comparison features.
- The effects of using OLMs on a change of motivation.

- Adaptation guidelines for adaptive navigational support systems, based on OLMs.

7. REFERENCES

[1] C. Ames. Classrooms: Goals, structures, and student motivation. *Journal of educational psychology*, 84(3):261, 1992.

[2] A. Bandura. *Social foundations of thought and action: A social cognitive theory*. Prentice-Hall, Inc, 1986.

[3] P. Brusilovsky, G. Chavan, and R. Farzan. Social adaptive navigation support for open corpus electronic textbooks. In *Adaptive Hypermedia and Adaptive Web-Based Systems*, pages 24–33. Springer, 2004.

[4] P. Brusilovsky, I.-H. Hsiao, and Y. Folajimi. Quizmap: open social student modeling and adaptive navigation support with treemaps. In *Towards Ubiquitous Learning*, pages 71–82. Springer, 2011.

[5] P. Brusilovsky and E. Millán. User models for adaptive hypermedia and adaptive educational systems. In *The adaptive web*, pages 3–53. Springer-Verlag, 2007.

[6] P. Brusilovsky, S. Somyurek, J. Guerra, R. Hosseini, V. Zadorozhny, and P. Durlach. Open social student modeling for personalized learning. *IEEE Transactions on Emerging Topics in Computing*, PP(99):1–1, 2015.

[7] S. Bull and J. Kay. Student models that invite the learner in: The smili:() open learner modelling framework. *International Journal of Artificial Intelligence in Education*, 17(2):89–120, 2007.

[8] S. Bull and J. Kay. Open learner models. In *Advances in intelligent tutoring systems*, pages 301–322. Springer, 2010.

[9] S. Bull and J. Kay. Open learner models as drivers for metacognitive processes. In *International Handbook of Metacognition and Learning Technologies*, pages 349–365. Springer, 2013.

[10] K. D. Ciani, M. J. Middleton, J. J. Summers, and K. M. Sheldon. Buffering against performance classroom goal structures: The importance of autonomy support and classroom community. *Contemporary Educational Psychology*, 35(1):88–99, 2010.

[11] C. S. Dweck. *Self-theories: Their role in motivation, personality, and development*. Psychology Press, 2000.

[12] A. J. Elliot and K. Murayama. On the measurement of achievement goals: Critique, illustration, and application. *Journal of Educational Psychology*, 100(3):613, 2008.

[13] J. Guerra, R. Hosseini, S. Somyürek, and P. Brusilovsky. An intelligent interface for learning content: Combining an open learner model and social comparison to support self-regulated learning and engagement. IUI, 2016.

[14] R. Hosseini, I.-H. Hsiao, J. Guerra, and P. Brusilovsky. What should i do next? adaptive sequencing in the context of open social student modeling. In *Design for Teaching and Learning in a Networked World*, pages 155–168. Springer, 2015.

[15] I.-H. Hsiao, F. Bakalov, P. Brusilovsky, and B. König-Ries. Progressor: social navigation support through open social student modeling. *New Review of Hypermedia and Multimedia*, 19(2):112–131, 2013.

[16] I.-H. Hsiao and P. Brusilovsky. Motivational social visualizations for personalized e-learning. In *21st Century Learning for 21st Century Skills*, pages 153–165. Springer, 2012.

[17] I.-H. Hsiao, S. Sosnovsky, and P. Brusilovsky. Guiding students to the right questions: adaptive navigation support in an e-learning system for java programming. *Journal of Computer Assisted Learning*, 26(4):270–283, 2010.

[18] A. Kumar and A. Maries. The effect of open student model on learning: A study. *FRONTIERS IN ARTIFICIAL INTELLIGENCE AND APPLICATIONS*, 158:596, 2007.

[19] T. D. Loboda, J. Guerra, R. Hosseini, and P. Brusilovsky. Mastery grids: An open source social educational progress visualization. In *Open Learning and Teaching in Educational Communities*, pages 235–248. Springer, 2014.

[20] A. Mabbott and S. Bull. Student preferences for editing, persuading, and negotiating the open learner model. In *Intelligent tutoring systems*, pages 481–490. Springer, 2006.

[21] J. A. Mangels, B. Butterfield, J. Lamb, C. Good, and C. S. Dweck. Why do beliefs about intelligence influence learning success? a social cognitive neuroscience model. *Social cognitive and affective neuroscience*, 1(2):75–86, 2006.

[22] A. Mitrovic. Evaluating the effect of open student models on self-assessment. In *International Journal of Artificial Intelligence in Education*. Citeseer, 2007.

[23] D. W. Moore, M. E. Bathgate, J. Chung, and M. A. Cannady. Technical report: Measuring activation and engagement. Technical report, Activation Lab, Learning Research and Development Center, University of Pittsburgh, Pittsburgh, PA (USA), 2011.

[24] P. A. O'Keefe, A. Ben-Eliyahu, and L. Linnenbrink-Garcia. Shaping achievement goal orientations in a mastery-structured environment and concomitant changes in related contingencies of self-worth. *Motivation and Emotion*, 37(1):50–64, 2013.

[25] F. G. Paas and J. J. Van Merriënboer. The efficiency of instructional conditions: An approach to combine mental effort and performance measures. *Human Factors: The Journal of the Human Factors and Ergonomics Society*, 35(4):737–743, 1993.

[26] D. H. Schunk. Goal setting and self-efficacy during self-regulated learning. *Educational psychologist*, 25(1):71–86, 1990.

[27] K. Upton and J. Kay. Narcissus: group and individual models to support small group work. In *User Modeling, Adaptation, and Personalization*, pages 54–65. Springer, 2009.

[28] C. A. Wolters, L. Y. Shirley, and P. R. Pintrich. The relation between goal orientation and students' motivational beliefs and self-regulated learning. *Learning and individual differences*, 8(3):211–238, 1996.

[29] B. J. Zimmerman. Self-regulated learning and academic achievement: An overview. *Educational psychologist*, 25(1):3–17, 1990.

Towards Comprehensive User Modeling on the Social Web for Personalized Link Recommendations

Guangyuan Piao
Insight Centre for Data Analytics, NUI Galway
IDA Business Park, Galway, Ireland
guangyuan.piao@insight-centre.org

ABSTRACT

User modeling for individual users on the Social Web plays a significant role and is a fundamental step for personalization as well as recommendations. Previous studies have proposed various user modeling strategies in different dimensions such as (1) *interest representation*, (2) *interest propagation*, (3) *content enrichment* and (4) *temporal dynamics of user interests*. This research mainly focuses on the first two dimensions *interest representation* and *propagation*. In addition, we also investigate the combination of these four dimensions and their synergistic effect on the quality of user modeling. Different user modeling strategies will then be evaluated in the context of personalized link recommender systems using standard evaluation methodologies such as Mean Reciprocal Rank (MRR), recall (R@N) and success (S@N) at rank N.

1. INTRODUCTION AND MOTIVATIONS

With the advent of Web 2.0, users participate more and more in the evolution of the Web and become big contributors to data on the Web. The term "Social Web" indicates a paradigm shift from a machine-centered view of the Web towards a more user- or community-centered view [1]. In this context, a better understanding of user interactions and then using this to extract, analyze and represent the information about users on the Web is crucial for systems providing personalized services as well as recommendations. One of the challenges for service providers is to provide accurate recommendations and personalization without having to explicitly ask for users' feedback or make users wait for reliable recommendations only after a long initial training period on the system (the so-called *cold start* problem). To overcome these challenges, it is important to create qualitative and quantitative user models on the Social Web.

Interest representation. The representation of user interests is a major dimension for user modeling on the Social Web. Previous work either used *bag-of-words*, *topic model* or *bag-of-concepts* approach to represent user interests. Bag-of-concepts approach uses concepts for representing user

UMAP '16 July 13-17, 2016, Halifax, NS, Canada

© 2016 Copyright held by the owner/author(s).

ACM ISBN 978-1-4503-4370-1/16/07.

DOI: http://dx.doi.org/10.1145/2930238.2930367

My Top 3 #lastfm Artists: Eagles of Death Metal (14), The Black Keys (6) & The Wombats (6) #mm bit.ly/dcwe7t

Figure 1: A sample tweet

interests. For example, given a tweet posted by a user in Figure 1, we know that the user is interested in entities such as `dbpedia`[1]`:The_Wombats` and `dbpedia:The_Black_Keys`. Recently, studies have been using *bag-of-concepts* approach as background knowledge of concepts from a Knowledge Base (KB) (defined as the combination of an ontology and instances of the classes in the ontology [19]) can be leveraged for extending user interests. By a *concept* we mean an *entity*, *category* or *class* from a KB (e.g., DBpedia[2]) for representing user interests.

Interest propagation with background knowledge. A Knowledge Base provides cross-domain background knowledge about concepts. For instance, DBpedia is the semantic representation of Wikipedia[3] and is a KB consisting of a large amount of facts about concepts. Compared to traditional taxonomies or lexical databases (e.g. WordNet [13]) it provides a larger set of concepts and the relationships among these concepts, continuously updated by the Wikipedia community. Therefore, DBpedia is helpful for extending user interest profiles to provide more semantic information about users. For instance, in the example in Figure 1, we can further infer that the user is interested in `dbpedia:Indie_rock` as both `dbpedia:The_Wombats` and `dbpedia:The_Black_Keys` are pointing to `dbpedia:Indie_rock` via the property `dbpedia-owl`[4]`:genre`.

Enrichment. One of the problems in user modeling on the Social Web is short posts (e.g., 140 characters for tweets) generated by users. To better understand the semantic meaning of short posts, enriching the posts with different sources (e.g., embedded links in the posts [4,10]) is important.

Dynamics. The interests of users might change over time. Previous studies showed that considering the time decay of user interests improves the quality of user modeling.

---

[1] The prefix `dbpedia` denotes http://dbpedia.org/resource/
[2] http://wiki.dbpedia.org
[3] https://en.wikipedia.org/wiki/Main_Page
[4] The prefix `dbpedia-owl` denotes http://dbpedia.org/ontology/

In this thesis, we propose using synsets from WordNet and concepts from DBpedia for representing user interests. In addition, we investigate different methods using background knowledge from WordNet as well as DBpedia for extending user interests. On top of that, we look at whether the quality of user modeling can be improved by considering temporal dynamics and enrichment using existing approaches. Our hypothesis is that the final extended user interest profiles, which are based on enriched user profiles considering temporal dynamics, can represent current user interests better and improve the quality of link recommendations.

2. RELATED WORK

Representation of user interests. A line of work has been proposed to use *concept-based* representation of user interests using a KB from Linked Data (e.g., Freebase, DBpedia) [4, 5, 15] or an encyclopedia such as Wikipedia [9, 11, 12]. This line of work goes beyond other approaches, such as *bag-of-words* [14] and *topic modeling* [8] which focus on words and cannot provide semantic information and relationships among these words. Thus, we start with *concept-based* user profiles in our work, and mainly focus on related work with respect to the *concept-based* user profiles here.

Semantics-enabled user modeling. On top of the *concept-based* user profiles, researchers have proposed using rich semantic information from a KB to extend the interests of users. Abel et al. [5] proposed using DBpedia to extend user profiles with respect to point of interests (POI) and showed that the extended POI profiles outperform the original user profiles without any extension in the context of POI recommendations. Orlandi et al. [15] proposed *category-based* user profiles based on the category information of entities from DBpedia. Besides a straightforward extension that gives equal weight to each extended category with respect to an entity, they also proposed a discounting strategy for those extended categories. The results based on a user study showed that *category-based* user profiles have similar performance to the *entity-based* ones. Even so, *category-based* profiles revealed much more information about user interests and the authors claimed that the *category-based* profiles might be helpful in the context of recommender systems [15]. However, they did not further evaluate those user modeling strategies in the context of recommendations.

Enrichment for short messages. The length of User-Generated Content (UGC) on Online Social Networks (OSNs) such as Twitter[5] is usually short. For example, Twitter messages (tweets) are limited to 140 characters which makes it difficult to detect the semantics of these messages. Researchers [4, 10] have been exploring embedded links in short messages to enrich the content. For example, Abel et al. [4] exploited URLs shared via tweets and devised a methodology to link tweets to news articles in their monitored news pool so as to use the content of news articles to enrich the user interest profiles.

Dynamics of user interests. Based on the hypothesis that the interests of users change over time, previous work considered the temporal dynamics of interests for user modeling in OSNs [2, 3, 6, 15]. In [3], the authors evaluated short-term and long-term user profiles in the context of news recommendations on Twitter. Short-term user profiles extract user interests within a short-term period (e.g., the last

---

[5]https://www.twitter.com

two weeks) while the long-term user profiles extract user interests using their entire historical UGC. Instead of extracting user profiles within a certain period, researchers have proposed using a decay function for the interests of users. In this case, the weights of user interests were discounted by time, i.e., the interests appearing a long time ago would decay heavily. However, every work proposed its own evaluation method for its measure and there was no study provides a comparison of different methods proposed in the literature.

3. PROBLEM STATEMENT AND RESEARCH GOALS

While related work reveals several insights regarding the user modeling process on the Social Web, there are limitations with respect to the representation of user interests and the interest propagation using a KB such as DBpedia.

Interest representation. Although a KB provides a great amount of semantic information about concepts, not everything (which is a concept in KB) is covered by a KB. This is problematic especially in the case of the Social Web where new concepts/topics emerge everyday. In this regard, user interests might not be fully extracted and covered using concepts in a KB. In addition, Knowledge Bases such as DBpedia lack full coverage for the lexicographic senses of lemmas, which can be provided by a lexical database such as WordNet.

Interest propagation using DBpedia. Despite the focus on leveraging category information for entities from DBpedia in the literature, background knowledge of concepts in DBpedia is provided through different types of information. For example, category information in DBpedia relies on the category system of Wikipedia to capture the idea of a "theme", i.e., a subject of an entity while class information about entities uses classification from YAGO [20]. In addition, there are many semantically related entities which are connected via various properties. Thus, different types of information (e.g., *categories*, *classes* and *connected entities via different properties*) should be considered all together for extending user interest profiles.

Comprehensive user modeling. In addition, there is a need to study comprehensive user modeling strategies considering different dimensions together to investigate whether the quality of user interest profiles can be improved further due to any synergetic effect of the combination. For instance, user interests extracted through the embedded links within UGC can also further extended using background knowledge from DBpedia to reveal more information about users.

Research questions to address these research gaps are summarized as follows:

RQ 1. (How) can we exploit different aspects (e.g., categories, classes, connected entities via different properties) of background knowledge from DBpedia for extending user interest profiles?

RQ 2. Does the use of the lexical database and knowledge base for the representation of user interests improve the quality of user modeling?

RQ 3. Is there any synergetic effect on user modeling by combining different dimensions? In other words, does the extended user interest profiles, which are based on enriched user profiles considering temporal dynamics, improve the quality of user modeling?

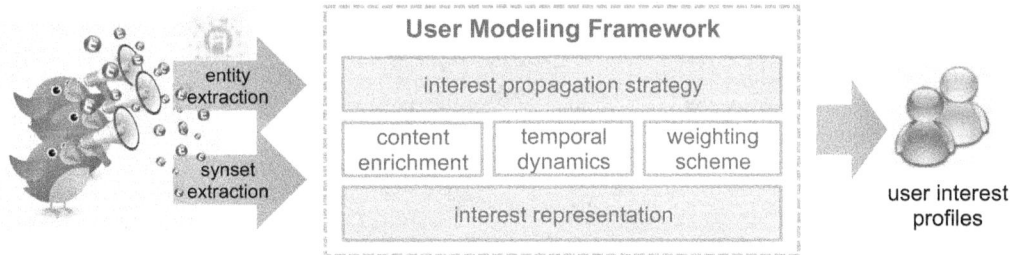

Figure 2: The process of generating user interest profiles using our user modeling framework

4. EVALUATION SETUP

Dataset. To evaluate different user modeling strategies, we need to collect a dataset of OSN users. Based on the about.me[6] dataset collected from our previous studies, we further extracted UGC of users from Twitter and Google+. about.me offers registered users a simple platform from which to link multiple online identities of them including popular OSNs such as Twitter, Google+[7] etc. We crawled a large number of OSN accounts of users from about.me, which consist of 247,630 public profile pages of users and their OSN account information. Furthermore, we randomly selected 480 users from about.me dataset who had been using Twitter and Google+, and collected all the UGC of those 480 users from these two OSNs for our study.

Evaluation Methodology. The quality of different user modeling strategies can be evaluated by investigating how these strategies affect the performance of an application which works on the basis of user interests. In the same way from previous studies [5], we evaluate different user modeling strategies in the context of a personalized recommender system where the recommended items are links. The ground truth and a set of candidate links are built by the links shared by users via their UGC. The recommender system then recommends links based on a recommendation algorithm with different user profiles generated by different user modeling strategies as input. The quality of the top-N recommendations is measured via standard evaluation metrics such as MRR (Mean Reciprocal Rank), success rate (S@N), precision and recall (P@N and R@N).

One thing to note is that our main goal is to analyze and compare the applicability of the different user modeling strategies in the context of recommendations. We do not aim to optimize recommendation quality, but are interested in comparing the quality achieved by the same recommendation algorithm when inputing different types of user profiles. Therefore, we apply a lightweight content-based algorithm, like the one used in [5], that recommends items according to their *cosine* similarity with a given user profile.

5. APPROACH AND PROGRESS TO DATE

In this work, we use synsets from WordNet or concepts from DBpedia for representing the interests of users. Synsets in WordNet are unordered sets of synonyms - words that denote the same concept and are interchangeable in many contexts. The generic model for interest profiles representing users is specified in Definition 1.

Definition 1. The interest profile of a user $u \in U$ is a set of weighted WordNet synsets or DBpedia concepts where with respect to the given user u for an interest $i \in I$ its weight $w(u, i)$ is computed by a certain function w.

Here, I denotes the set of synsets in WordNet and concepts in DBpedia, and U denotes users, respectively.

The general process of generating user interest profiles is presented in Figure 2. Entities in UGC are extracted using the Aylien API[8] and synsets can be extracted by adopting a previous method for generating WordNet-based user profiles [7]. On top of the representation of user interest profiles, our user modeling framework is able to adhere to different strategies with respect to a specific interest propagation strategy as well as other existing strategies regarding enrichment and dynamics of user interests.

Progress to date. Until now, we have focused on extending strategies using DBpedia for concept-based user profiles. Preliminary results of the extending strategies were published in [16]. In that work, we evaluated two *category-based* user modeling strategies with DBpedia from [15]; one is *category-based* user profiles *replacing* the corresponding *entity-based* user profiles, and the other one is *category-based* user profiles with a discounting strategy for the weight of each category based on its specificity within DBpedia graph. In addition, we investigated a mixed approach that combines the *entity-* and *category-based* user profiles. Results showed that the combined user profiles with the discounting strategy for extended categories provide the best performance in terms of link recommendations. In contrast, both *category-based* user modeling strategies with/without a discounting strategy did not outperform *entity-based* user profiles.

In terms of $w(u, c)$ in Definition 1, previous studies have been applying $CF_u(c)$ (frequency of c in u's UGC, e.g., tweets) as the weighting scheme $w(u, c)$. However, our recent experiment using $CF_u(c) \times IDF_u(c)$ as the weighting scheme showed significant improvement over using $CF_u(c)$ where $IDF_u(c) = \log[\# \ of \ all \ users]/[\# \ of \ users \ interested \ in \ c]$.

6. FUTURE PLAN AND CONTRIBUTIONS

Although we leveraged DBpedia categories for user modeling with a discounting strategy, there is much more information about entities in DBpedia via various properties. As a discounting strategy for extended entities from DBpedia plays a significant role, we need to derive a discounting strategy for extending user profiles with various properties in DBpedia. For instance, we can apply discounting strategies based on the lessons learned from similarity-based Linked

---

[6]http://about.me
[7]https://plus.google.com

[8]http://aylien.com

Data-enabled recommender systems [17] as the normalizations of properties in this research area play the same role as ours. As a further step, we plan to adopt the spreading activation theory [18] for interest propagation by leveraging different types of information from DBpedia.

In the near future, we would investigate and evaluate the proposed interest representation model, which is using WordNet synsets and DBpedia concepts together for representing user interests, in the context of link recommendations using our collected Twitter and Google+ dataset.

Finally, we aim to study combined user modeling strategies considering different dimensions mentioned in the related work to derive more sophisticated user interest profiles in the context of personalized link recommendations.

The main contributions of this research can be summarized as follows.

- We propose a method exploiting different types of information from DBpedia for extending user profiles.

- We investigate and evaluate the representation of user interests by using synsets from WordNet and concepts from DBpedia for user modeling.

- Importantly, this research study will provide a comprehensive user modeling framework combining aforementioned different dimensions to retrieve extended user interest profiles, which are based on enriched user profiles considering temporal dynamics.

7. ACKNOWLEDGMENTS

This publication has emanated from research conducted with the financial support of Science Foundation Ireland (SFI) under Grant Number SFI/12/RC/2289 (Insight Centre for Data Analytics). In addition, I would like to thank my supervisor Dr. John G. Breslin for his support and feedback.

8. REFERENCES

[1] F. Abel. *Contextualization, User Modeling and Personalization in the Social Web–From Social Tagging via Context to Cross-System User Modeling and Personalization.* PhD thesis, Leibniz University of Hanover, 2011.

[2] F. Abel, Q. Gao, G.-J. Houben, and K. Tao. Analyzing temporal dynamics in twitter profiles for personalized recommendations in the social web. In *Proceedings of the 3rd International Web Science Conference*, page 2. ACM, 2011.

[3] F. Abel, Q. Gao, G.-J. Houben, and K. Tao. Analyzing user modeling on twitter for personalized news recommendations. In *User Modeling, Adaption and Personalization*, pages 1–12. Springer, 2011.

[4] F. Abel, Q. Gao, G.-J. Houben, and K. Tao. Semantic enrichment of twitter posts for user profile construction on the social web. In *The Semantic Web: Research and Applications*, pages 375–389. Springer, 2011.

[5] F. Abel, C. Hauff, G.-J. Houben, and K. Tao. Leveraging User Modeling on the Social Web with Linked Data. In *Web Engineering SE - 31*, pages 378–385. Springer, 2012.

[6] C. Budak, A. Kannan, R. Agrawal, and J. Pedersen. Inferring user interests from microblogs. Technical report, 2014.

[7] M. Degemmis, P. Lops, and G. Semeraro. A content-collaborative recommender that exploits WordNet-based user profiles for neighborhood formation. *User Modeling and User-Adapted Interaction*, 17(3):217–255, 2007.

[8] M. Harvey, F. Crestani, and M. J. Carman. Building User Profiles from Topic Models for Personalised Search. *Cikm*, pages 2309–2314, 2013.

[9] P. Kapanipathi, P. Jain, C. Venkataramani, and A. Sheth. User Interests Identification on Twitter Using a Hierarchical Knowledge Base. In *The Semantic Web: Trends and Challenges*, pages 99–113. Springer, 2014.

[10] S. Kinsella, M. Wang, J. G. Breslin, and C. Hayes. Improving categorisation in social media using hyperlinks to structured data sources. In *The Semantic Web: Research and Applications*, pages 390–404. Springer, 2011.

[11] C. Lu, W. Lam, and Y. Zhang. Twitter user modeling and tweets recommendation based on wikipedia concept graph. In *Workshops at the Twenty-Sixth AAAI Conference on Artificial Intelligence*, 2012.

[12] M. Michelson and S. A. Macskassy. Discovering users' topics of interest on twitter: a first look. In *Proceedings of the fourth workshop on Analytics for noisy unstructured text data*, pages 73–80. ACM, 2010.

[13] G. A. Miller. WordNet: a lexical database for English. *Communications of the ACM*, 38(11):39–41, 1995.

[14] A. Mislove, B. Viswanath, K. P. Gummadi, and P. Druschel. You are who you know: inferring user profiles in online social networks. In *Proceedings of the third ACM international conference on Web search and data mining*, pages 251–260. ACM, 2010.

[15] F. Orlandi, J. Breslin, and A. Passant. Aggregated, interoperable and multi-domain user profiles for the social web. In *Proceedings of the 8th International Conference on Semantic Systems*, pages 41–48. ACM, 2012.

[16] G. Piao and J. G. Breslin. Analyzing Aggregated Semantics-enabled User Modeling on Google+ and Twitter for Personalized Link Recommendations. In *User Modeling, Adaptation, and Personalization*. ACM, 2016.

[17] G. Piao and J. G. Breslin. Measuring Semantic Distance for Linked Open Data-enabled Recommender Systems. In *Proceedings of the 31st Annual ACM Symposium on Applied Computing*, pages 315–320. ACM, 2016.

[18] G. Salton and C. Buckley. On the use of spreading activation methods in automatic information. In *Proceedings of the 11th annual international ACM SIGIR conference on Research and development in information retrieval - SIGIR '88*, pages 147–160, New York, New York, USA, 1988. ACM Press.

[19] S. Staab and R. Studer. *Handbook on Ontologies.* Springer Publishing Company, Incorporated, 2nd edition, 2009.

[20] F. M. Suchanek, G. Kasneci, and G. Weikum. Yago: a core of semantic knowledge. In *Proceedings of the 16th international conference on World Wide Web*, pages 697–706. ACM, 2007.

Picture-based Approach to Group Recommender Systems in the E-Tourism Domain

Amra Delic
E-Commerce Group
TU Wien
Vienna, Austria
amra.delic@tuwien.ac.at *

ABSTRACT

This PhD research aims to integrate group decision making into a personality based recommender systems in a domain with complex and emotional products i.e., e-tourism domain. In this domain, decisions, especially in groups, are often non rational. Based on the ongoing research on picture-based recommender systems at the e-commerce group, TU Wien and the software of Pixtri OG, the research will develop new methods to model group recommendations and support emotion-aware group decision processes, based on and evaluated by a world-wide study.

Keywords

Group recommender systems; Observational study; Preference aggregation; Group decision processes; Group dynamics

1. INTRODUCTION

The travel and tourism domain is one of the leading industries regarding the e-commerce presence with the constant growth of online transactions [20], products and services [5]. As the number of alternatives (i.e., tourism products) offered online has increased it has become a tedious challenge for consumers to find what fits their preferences. As a consequence, among the most influential and most challenging topics are personalization and recommender systems. Recommending tourism product is riskier than recommending other types of products (e.g., books, movies, etc.), for several reasons: 1) The tourism product is more complex (i.e., a combination of products and services) and in the same time less tangible [20]; 2) It is an emotional experience and explicit preference characterization is problematic especially in the early phase of the travel decision-making process; 3) The lack of the user-item ratings in the tourism recommender systems which directly affects recommendation quality of

---

*PhD candidate's supervisor: Hannes Werthner, TU Wien and co-supervisor: Julia Neidhardt, TU Wien

UMAP '16 July 13-17, 2016, Halifax, NS, Canada
© 2016 Copyright held by the owner/author(s).
ACM ISBN 978-1-4503-4370-1/16/07.
DOI: http://dx.doi.org/10.1145/2930238.2930368

approaches like collaborative filtering; 4) Traveling is a social activity. When delivering recommendations therefore, all these aspects should be considered.

With respect to the emotional aspects of tourism products and also due to the deficit of the user-item ratings there are novel approaches to user preference elicitation such as the picture-based approach, serving as a starting point for this PhD research. The key concept of this approach is to enable a user to express emotional and sometimes even "unaware" travel preferences implicitly with the help of pictures. Based on 17 well-established tourist roles [2] and the "Big Five" personality traits, the authors of [10] and [11] identified seven factors to represent different travel behavioral patterns (i.e., *Sun & Chill-out, Knowledge & Travel, Independence & History, Culture & Indulgence, Social & Sport, Action & Fun, Nature & Recreation*). For each of these travel behavioral patterns, appropriate pictures were identified. Then, user preferences are captured by prompting the user to select pictures from this predefined set. Thus, the user profile is a point in the seven-dimensional space where each dimension corresponds to one of the seven factors (i.e., travel behavioral pattern). Since POIs (Points Of Interest) can be represented with respect to the same seven factors, i.e., in the same seven-dimensional space, the recommendations for a user can be simply calculated as Euclidean distance between the user profile and the POIs.

2. PROBLEM DESCRIPTION

The goal of this PhD research is to develop methods to generalize the picture based approach to group recommender systems. To realize this goal, following challenges have to be addressed:

Aggregating individual travel behavioral patterns.
One of the core components of each recommender system is the user model that captures individual preferences and dislikes. When considering group recommendations, a strategy to capture preferences of the entire group has to be defined. Usually the group model is obtained as an aggregation of the individual models. The objective is that the group model preserves relevant, individual preferences in order to ensure members' satisfaction with the recommendation. Often, the user model contains preferences in the form of the rating history of a user. Opposed to this, in the picture based approach the user model is given by the previously described travel behavioral patterns. The user-centric representation makes the picture based approach quite unique. As a consequence, however, standard aggregation techniques

might not be applicable in a straightforward manner. Thus, a thorough evaluation of existing aggregation approaches will be required. Furthermore, if necessary, new aggregation approaches will be proposed.

Aggregating individual travel preferences.

Travel preferences are travel features that are explicitly given by a user like preferred climate, planned activities, maximum price, etc. In order to deliver group recommendations, the individual travel preferences have to be aggregated. Sometimes it might make sense to favor the preferences of certain group members (e.g., to favor the needs of children over the parents' preferences). In these cases weights can be assigned to the individual preferences. However, again it depends strongly on the user model, how the aggregation of travel preferences at group level can be accomplished. The group profile is obtained as a combination of the group travel behavioral patterns and the group preferences.

Group decision support.

Clearly, the proposed recommendation approach includes aggregation methods for both, travel behavioral patterns and travel preferences but it should also include decision/ negotiation support. Travel behavioral patterns are more stable and enduring since they impersonate not only travel attitude, but also personality traits. Opposed to the travel preferences, these patterns are not negotiable. Furthermore, two negotiation approaches are possible and they are related to the: 1) Early stage information disclosure and 2) Late stage information disclosure. Both refer to the moment in the process when the group members get to know individual travel preferences of other group members. In the first case, the group decision support enables the group members to decide altogether on certain travel preferences, while in the second case the group decision support helps the group members to decide after the recommendations were created. In general, analyzing the differences between the preferences of the group and the recommendations that are implied by those preferences before the negotiation process and after it will lead to valuable insights into the group behavior and group dynamics regarding joint traveling. Furthermore, in the group negotiation phase of the recommendation process a very important aspect to be considered is the emotion contagion phenomenon - the emotions transfer between group members. Summing up, the focus of this research is to generalize the picture-based approach to the group recommender systems and to support the group decision making process in the presented context. The recommendations will be based on a group profile: the aggregation of the individual travel behavioral patterns and the aggregation of individual travel preferences.

3. STATE OF THE ART

In recent years, research focuses increasingly on models, algorithms and applications in the recommender systems domain. In the following the state of the art of the group recommenders and emotion-aware recommenders is shortly discussed.

Group recommender systems.

Many of the products and activities that are typically in the focus of the recommender systems also have social dimensions, i.e., they are consumed or experienced by a group of people rather than by an individual user, e.g., movies, restaurants, travel destinations, etc. Thus, research is more and more dealing with group recommender systems. An overview on the state of the art of the group recommender systems is presented in [8].

Challenges and aggregation approaches: Major challenges for the group recommender systems are outlined in [4]. In the existing research, the most attention was devoted to the challenge two, i.e., aggregation of the individual preferences into a group model and in general three approaches were identified [4]: 1) Aggregation of the calculated individuals' recommendations; 2) Aggregation of individuals' ratings; 3) Building a group preference model. The main difference in these approaches is the moment in which individual profiles are aggregated. Our approach concentrates on building a group preference model before creating the recommendation.

Aggregation strategies: Aggregation methods motivated by the Social Choice Theory were analyzed in [7]. In [16] applications of so-called Power Balance Maps (PBM) as aggregation strategies were studied. PBMs store the rating history of each group member. Group preferences are captured in the group model, i.e., the aggregation of the individuals' PBMs. Also, the Analytic Hierarchy Process (AHP) was studied as an aggregation strategy in the group recommender systems. It synthesizes all the judgments to obtain the overall priority of the alternatives (items) [13].

Evaluation and enhancement of group recommendations: Recommender systems for social content and social activities were empirically evaluated using concrete implementations [7]. Different satisfaction functions that ensure a certain satisfaction level for each group member were studied in [9]. Furthermore, influence among group members such as the impact of conflict modes (i.e., behavior tendencies of an individual in a conflict situation) on the recommendations accuracy were analyzed in [14]. The authors concluded that the accuracy can be particularly improved when one movie is recommended and especially when conflict modes of group members are highly diverse. Obviously, in groups individuals express different behavior, some act as initiators of activities, while others act as followers. The impact of these different behaviors on accuracy of recommendations was studied in [21]. Also, in [3] a group recommendation engine takes into consideration three types of features: 1) Collective features; 2) Member features; and 3) Individual features.

Group decision making.

Negotiation processes in recommender systems were analyzed in [6], and the authors of [4] discussed the advantages and disadvantages of early preference information disclosure in group recommendation processes. In [1], group decision making processes were analyzed in detail. Groups are more likely to make better decisions if they follow a certain structure during the decision making process. The situation and the importance of the decision determine the structure and the approach that should be undertaken. Although in [1], group decisions in general were discussed, the theory and insights can be applied to group recommenders and will be applied in the context of this PhD research.

Emotion-aware recommender systems.

In [18], the authors gave an overview of affective recommender systems, explaining the importance of different roles of user emotions in different stages of human interaction with recommender systems. The embodiment of personality traits as lasting factors and emotions as constantly changing factors into recommender systems were studied in [19]. In [12] [17], the authors emphasized the importance of personality in recommender systems and decision making processes. Furthermore, they stated that the incorporation of personality into recommender systems could help to understand how user preferences are determined in the first place. A prominent method to model and elicit user preferences in the context of emotion-aware recommenders is the picture-based approach described in the section 1.

4. MAIN CONTRIBUTIONS

This PhD research aims to broaden the knowledge base in the context that has been described in the previous sections. Group recommender systems are extremely hard to evaluate due to the lack of appropriate data sets and the ground truth in general. "What is the best for the group of people with different or even conflicting preferences?" is a widely researched question in many social disciplines (e.g. hundreds of different voting systems in different countries exist and not one of them is perfect and could not be perfect according to Arrow's paradox). Analysis of the group dynamics is crucial in this work, but also raises many questions. This research will be focused on answering research questions provided in the section 5. Moreover, it should provide new insights into the groups' behavior and decision making processes with respect to emotional and less tangible tourism products in the field of group recommender systems.

5. METHODOLOGICAL APPROACH AND PROGRESS

This PhD research is guided by the following research questions: **RQ1** (Aggregating travel behavioral patterns): What are good/ reasonable ways to aggregate the individual travel behavioral patterns to obtain a meaningful aggregation at the group level that can be represented in the multi-dimensional model space? **RQ2** (Aggregating travel preferences and group profile): What are good/ reasonable ways to aggregate the preferences and dislikes of the individual users to obtain travel preferences at the group level, and how to combine these preferences with the aggregated travel behavioral patterns? **RQ3** (Information disclosure and negotiation support): How to support the decision process and define the best moment during the group recommendation process to disclose the individual travel preferences to the other group members, and to enable a negotiation on these travel preferences at the group level? To achieve this, an iterative approach will be undertaken, starting with 1) Offline group decision making study; 2) Model building; 3) Implementation and evaluation.

Short overview.

The ongoing research of the e-commerce group at the TU Wien and the software of Pixtri OG (http://www.pixtri. com/) in the field of picture-based recommenders for individual users serve as the starting point. The group model for the group recommendation system will be an extension of the existing model - an aggregation of the group members' profiles, combining both, travel behavioral patterns and travel preferences. To define appropriate aggregation strategy an extensive study about the group decision processes in the travel domain will be carried out. The respective insights should also support the design of the decision/ negotiation approach. An important part of the study is the evaluation of the formal model. For evaluation purposes a user-centric approach should be used. The PhD research is currently in the first phase which is described in details in the following section.

Major research phases.

1. Group decision making study: In cooperation with the International Federation for Information Technologies in Travel and Tourism (IFITT, http://www.ifitt.org/), eleven universities worldwide will conduct a study with students on group decision processes in the travel and tourism context. The study was first implemented at three universities (i.e., University of Klagenfurt, Delft University of Technology and University of Leiden), followed by an extended study at the Vienna University of Technology. In Vienna, all together 47 students participated that were divided in groups. Each group selected two observers, while other group members acted as decision makers. The study was carried out through three phases. In the first phase decision makers filled in a pre-study questionnaire which captured their individual profiles, preferences and dislikes. The questionnaire was matched with the travel behavioral patterns and travel preferences of the picture-based approach. Furthermore, a short training for observers took place. In the second phase, students organized a meeting. The task for the decision makers was to jointly choose a destination that they as a group would like to visit. Also, they were asked for their second choice in case that their first choice is no longer available. Observers audio-recorded and documented behavior of the decision makers. In the third, final phase, decision makers filled in the post-study questionnaire: first and second group choice, group choice satisfaction, perceived group similarity and identification, decision process difficulty and organization of the study. Currently, this rich data is analyzed quantitatively and qualitatively. Implemented studies serve not only as an exploratory starting point for other participating universities, but also, firstly as a hypothesis construction phase and secondly as a source of insights for the next phases of this PhD research.

2. Model building

2.1 Aggregating individual travel behavioral patterns: A variety of approaches mentioned in the state of the art section will be analyzed as aggregation mechanisms for building the group profile as a composition of the group members' profiles. However, the existing approaches are based on completely different initial user profiles, consisting of user ratings on previously experienced items, while our user model is defined through personality based factors (i.e., travel behavioral patterns). Due to this major distinction, the applicability of existing approaches is not clear, and neither are the results of those approaches.

2.2 Aggregating individual travel preferences and group profile: The appropriateness of aggregation methods for travel preferences depends on the respective representation approach. Travel preferences, i.e., features of a planned trip such as budget, time constraints or preferred activities might be represented by different types of features. In order to treat this heterogeneity and to represent them in a "uniform" way (e.g., as a vector) a metrics with different distance function is needed (see [15]). Thus, the distance measure would allow the combination of both aspects, i.e., travel behavioral patterns and travel preferences. An issue to be considered is the weighting of the different attributes, i.e., are they equally important and/or negotiable. The group decision making study (i.e., the first research phase) can provide answers regarding this particular topic. The main goal of the aggregation methods is to ensure that each group member is satisfied. Thus, the choice of an appropriate aggregation method is crucial.

2.3 Group decision/ negotiation support: The decision/ negotiation support approach should follow a certain structure in the decision making process, as it is argued in the state of the art section. This process also depends on the moment of information disclosure. If the preferences of each group member are disclosed to the rest of the group in an early phase, then the group travel preferences can be negotiated, while, in the late phase of preferences disclosure, the group can be supported to negotiate given recommendations. The analysis of the differences in the two approaches would allow us to gain knowledge about group decision making processes regarding traveling in general. A further important aspect to be taken into consideration is the structure of the group, i.e., are all members equally important or are there "dominant" players. The group decision making study will provide the basis for this phase and also it will allow us to understand if some particular information from the user/ group model can be used to ease and enhance the decision/ negotiation support.

3. Implementation and evaluation: The goal of this phase is to estimate methods and model developed in previously described phases. As it is already stated, group recommender systems require user-centric evaluation since appropriate data sets do not exist and the ground truth is unknown. To evaluate the developed theoretical framework a software artifact should be implemented. The evaluation of the recommender system should also provide the input for refinement of the theoretical framework. The research and evaluation will follow the design science methodology.

6. REFERENCES

[1] D. Forsyth. *Group Dynamics*. Wadsworth Cengage Learning, 6th edition, 2014.

[2] H. Gibson and A. Yiannakis. Tourist roles: Needs and the lifecourse. *Annals of tourism research*, 29(2):358–383, 2002.

[3] L. Hu, J. Cao, G. Xu, L. Cao, Z. Gu, and W. Cao. Deep modeling of group preferences for group-based recommendation. In *AAAI*, pages 1861–1867. 2014.

[4] A. Jameson. More than the sum of its members: challenges for group recommender systems. In *Proceedings of the working conference on Advanced visual interfaces*, pages 48–54, 2004.

[5] K. Kabassi. Personalizing recommendations for tourists. *Telematics and Informatics*, 27(1):51–66, 2010.

[6] D. Kudenko, M. Bauer, and D. Dengler. Group decision making through mediated discussions. In *User Modeling 2003*, pages 238–247. Springer, 2003.

[7] J. Masthoff. Group modeling: Selecting a sequence of television items to suit a group of viewers. In *Personalized Digital Television*, pages 93–141. Springer, 2004.

[8] J. Masthoff. Group recommender systems: aggregation, satisfaction and group attributes. In F. Ricci, L. Rokach, and B. Shapira, editors, *Recommender Systems Handbook*, pages 743–776. Springer, 2015.

[9] J. Masthoff and A. Gatt. In pursuit of satisfaction and the prevention of embarrassment: affective state in group recommender systems. In *User Modeling and User-Adapted Interaction*, volume 16, pages 281–319. Springer, 2006.

[10] J. Neidhardt, R. Schuster, L. Seyfang, and H. Werthner. Eliciting the users' unknown preferences. In *Proceedings of the 8th ACM Conference on Recommender systems*, pages 309–312, 2645767, 2014. ACM.

[11] J. Neidhardt, L. Seyfang, R. Schuster, and H. Werthner. A picture-based approach to recommender systems. *Information Technology & Tourism*, 15(1):49–69, 2015.

[12] M. A. S. Nunes and R. Hu. Personality-based recommender systems: an overview. In *Proceedings of the sixth ACM conference on Recommender systems*, pages 5–6. ACM, 2012.

[13] M.-H. Park, H.-S. Park, and S.-B. Cho. Restaurant recommendation for group of people in mobile environments using probabilistic multi-criteria decision making. In *Computer-Human Interaction*, pages 114–122. Springer, 2008.

[14] J. A. Recio-Garcia, G. Jimenez-Diaz, A. A. Sanchez-Ruiz, and B. Diaz-Agudo. Personality aware recommendations to groups. In *Proceedings of the third ACM conference on Recommender systems*, pages 325–328. ACM, 2009.

[15] F. Ricci and H. Werthner. Case base querying for travel planning recommendation. *Information Technology & Tourism*, 4(3-4):215–226, 2001.

[16] S. Seko, T. Yagi, M. Motegi, and S. Muto. Group recommendation using feature space representing behavioral tendency and power balance among members. In *Proceedings of the fifth ACM conference on Recommender systems*, pages 101–108. ACM, 2011.

[17] M. Tkalcic and L. Chen. Personality and recommender systems. pages 715–739. Springer, 2nd edition, 2015.

[18] M. Tkalcic, A. Kosir, and J. Tasic. Affective recommender systems: the role of emotions in recommender systems. In *Proc. The RecSys 2011 Workshop on Human Decision Making in Recommender Systems*, pages 9–13. Citeseer, 2011.

[19] M. Tkalcic, G. Semeraro, and M. de Gemmis. Personality and emotions in decision making and recommender systems. In *DMRS*, pages 14–18, 2014.

[20] H. Werthner and F. Ricci. E-commerce and tourism. *Communications of the ACM*, 47(12):101–105, 2004.

[21] M. Ye, X. Liu, and W.-C. Lee. Exploring social influence for recommendation: a generative model approach. In *Proceedings of the 35th international ACM SIGIR conference on Research and development in information retrieval*, pages 671–680. ACM, 2012.

The New Challenges when Modeling Context through Diversity over Time in Recommender Systems

Amaury L'Huillier *
KIWI Team, LORIA -
University of Lorraine
Campus Scientifique, B.P. 239
54506 Vandœuvre - France
amaury.lhuillier@loria.fr

ABSTRACT

The main goal of recommender systems is to help users to filter all the information available by suggesting items they may like without they had to find them by themselves. Although the rating prediction is a pretty well controlled topic, being able to make a recommendation at the right moment still remain a challenging task. To this end, most researches try to integrate contextual information (weather, mood, location of users, etc.) in the recommendation process. Even if this process increases users satisfaction, using personal information faces with users' privacy issues. In a different way, our approach is only giving credits to the evolution of diversity within the recent history of consultations, allowing us to automatically detect implicit contexts. In this paper, we will discuss the scientific challenges to be overcome to take maximum advantage of those implicit contexts in the recommendation process.

Keywords

Diversity, Context, Recommendation, User Privacy

1. INTRODUCTION AND MOTIVATIONS

Recommender systems (RS) have been studied for the last two decades. Although significant progresses were achieved to date, many challenges remain. We know from many user studies that proposing items to users solely based on the rating prediction is not enough [9]. Precision is not self sufficient to provide good recommendations and other human factors have to be integrated in the recommendation process. In our case, we will focus on the relationship between two human factors which are the context [5] and the diversity [10]. We will present why and how the notion of context has become an important part of the recommendation process and what are its limitations. Then, we will present the

*This PhD thesis, along with the results presented in this paper, are made under the supervision of Sylvain Castagnos and Anne Boyer (KIWI Team, LORIA - University of Lorraine).

UMAP '16 July 13-17, 2016, Halifax, NS, Canada

© 2016 Copyright held by the owner/author(s).

ACM ISBN 978-1-4503-4370-1/16/07.

DOI: http://dx.doi.org/10.1145/2930238.2930370

notion of diversity and explain the reasons why monitoring its evolution over time could be promising to overcome the limitations faced by the contextual recommender systems. The goal of a context-aware recommender system (CARS) is to adapt the recommendation to the current characteristics of the user situation, also called his context. As an example, a recommendation should not be the same either a user is alone or with some friends even if the model of preferences used is the same in both cases. In their state-of-the-art on CARS, Adomavicius and Tuzhilin [1] present several ways to include contextual information (like the weather, the time of the day, or the user mood) into the recommendation process. All the user studies reported in their paper highlighted an improvement in term of user satisfaction, regardless the domain used (restaurant, music, movies). By integrating additional information about context, the recommendations proposed are closer to users' current needs comparatively to traditional RS. However, an important drawback of all CARS is their reliance on the collect and the exploitation of this contextual information making them intrusive. While we live in a time when user privacy is more and more debated, it seems primordial to focus on non-intrusive and privacy-preserving systems. Developing such a respectful recommender system which has identical performances (in term of user satisfaction) in comparison with the models relying on contextual factors is one of the long-term goal we intend to achieve.

Rather than using personal information to detect the context, we believe that an in-depth analysis of the evolution in the user consultation path could be a promising way to understand the user needs. In other words, to preserve privacy, we argue that we do not need to know the characteristics of the context. We should instead detect the break points within a sequence of consultations (corresponding to changes of context), and then exploit meta-data about items consulted within a context since contend-based techniques are known to be less intrusive [4].

We will now present some examples of use of the diversity to explain why the dimension could be related to the context. Presenting diverse recommendations to users is very useful in some cases as it offers alternatives to users [8]. However, being able to automatically detect and adjust the diversity level over time still remains a difficult task. Even if such a model did not exists yet, the possibilities offered have already been discussed [2]. The authors explain in the case of an e-commerce website that the diversity level to use in the recommendations should be high in the beginning of a navigation session and should decrease gradually as the session ends. The main idea of our works is to extend this idea, by analysing the evolution of diversity over time in the path of the users to infer their needs by detecting ends of session, but also changes of context. Hence, it is not the awareness of characteristics of the user situation (begin or end of session) which is used to adapt recommendations and diversity level, it is the evolution of diversity itself which gives to the system the clues to make the most appropriate recommendations. Currently, we have developed a model to monitor in real time the evolution of diversity that we will present and discuss in the next part.

2. FROM DIVERSITY TO CONTEXT

As explain in the previous section, we have developed a model to monitor and exploit the evolution of diversity over time that we called DANCE [6].

2.1 General Principle

DANCE can be used to compute at each time step (each consultation) the diversity brought by an item (the target) according to the previous consulted items (the history). The size of the history used to compute the diversity is fixed by a parameter of our model. So, with the diversity value obtained, it is possible to quantify how an item is similar or different compared to the previous consulted items. All we need is the set of attributes for each type of item (webpages, music, books, ...) and the associated values. The diversity can be then computed for any type of attribute (numerical, binary, string, interval, ...) as long as it is possible to compute the similarity[1] existing between two values of this attributes. It is possible to model the evolution of diversity for one attribute in particular, for a subset of attributes, or for all the attributes available by averaging the values of diversity obtained. The full mathematical formalism of our model is available in [3].

2.2 Utility and Application Domains

DANCE can model the evolution of diversity over time and then it is possible to detect some important variations of diversity. Detecting those important variations is very useful as it means that the user is changing his interests, he does not want similar items anymore. Hence, the recommender system must quickly adapt its strategy in order to fit the recommendation to these new interests. In [7], we defined the notion of implicit context as the common characteristics shared by the consulted items during a certain time lapse. The notion of implicit context was created in opposition with explicit context, which is defined as a situation for which the contextual factors are known. An implicit context only refers to a sequence of items while an explicit context includes additional information about the users (ip address, gender, age, ...). In term of privacy, implicit contexts are clearly less intrusive, as all pieces of information are extracted from the items and not from the user. Then, our model DANCE is able to detect changes of context within users' sequences of consultations, and each subsequence of items consulted between two changes of context corresponds to an implicit context. We then aim to use these implicit contexts so as to provide relevant recommendations to users.

We tested and validated the ability of our model to split sequences of consultations into implicit contexts with a large musical dataset (more than 200,000 consultations). We computed the diversity based on the musical attributes extracted from TheEchonest[2]. We gather 7 artist-related attributes, and 6 song-related attributes. We have therefore developed diversity formulas according to the nature of those attributes: interval (band years of activities), numerical (duration, tempo), binary (mode), list of words (genre), location (coordinates of artist). We have demonstrated that there exists a strong overlap between implicit contexts and existing sessions [6]. This overlap confirms that we can give meaning to the changes of context detected by our model, and by extension that implicit contexts are good alternatives to explicit contexts. Indeed, when a user starts a new session, his explicit context changes (he was at the office and now he starts to listen some music at home). As most of changes of implicit contexts also correspond to ends of sessions, this supports that implicit contexts can be used to provide contextual recommendations. In addition to the overlap between implicit contexts and sessions, we have noticed that it could exist several implicit contexts inside a single session.

Despite the fact that we validated our approach with a musical dataset, DANCE is a generic model and can be used in many application domains. The only specific parts which have to be adapted are the diversity formulas per attribute which, in our case, were related to songs and artists.

2.3 Strengths and Limitations

Our model is highly reactive, as computing the diversity evolution and detecting changes of implicit context can be done in real time. The small size of the history used to do so both preserves user privacy as we do not retain all the user history, and ensures a linear complexity. As the diversity is computed by using several attributes, the model can easily be parameterized by adjusting the weight of each attribute according to the user characteristics. As an example, if the variation of an attribute seems important to a user, this attribute must have more impact in the value of the diversity computed. In the next section, we explain more precisely how such a parameterization could be carried out. In [3], we demonstrated that DANCE is robust up to 60% of missing data and provides good performances even if users are consulting different types of items. Those results support the genericity of our model and will allow us to deploy it in real conditions without significant modifications. Only the formulas used to compute diversity must be adapted to the attributes that characterize available items.

One limitation of our model is that it only fits to situations and application domains where we have contiguous sequences of consultations, with items consulted in relatively short time laps (at least few items must be consulted per hour). Music, news, e-commerce or professional social networks like LinkedIn[3] or Yupeek[4] are domains for which our model can then be used. For all those domains, users consult many items and can provide feedbacks within just a few minutes (maybe less). Our model can then try to capture the current implicit context of users by analysing diversity evolution. Conversely, if there are not enough consultations

---

[1] The similarity is the opposite value of the diversity.

[2] http://the.echonest.com/
[3] https://www.linkedin.com/
[4] https://my.yupeek.com/

or if the gaps of time between the consultations are too long, the model will fail at providing contextualized recommendations. As an example, users rarely watch several movies in a row.

3. SCIENTIFIC CHALLENGES

As stated in the previous section, we proposed a model to detect changes of implicit context. Our long-term goal is to rely on this model to provide recommendations of items in accordance with the user context, while preserving his privacy. The following subsection will introduce the scientific challenges to address on the road to such a system.

3.1 Parameterization of the model

DANCE is a generic model and can be easily parameterized. The parameterization occurs in the computation of the diversity, and while defining the detection conditions of a change of context. As the diversity is computed on the basis of a set of attributes, it is possible to weight these attributes in order to give them more impact on the value of the global diversity (which is the value actually used to detect the changes of implicit context). In [7], we used a genetic algorithm to adjust some parameters of the model. Genetic algorithms are often used to find a solution to a problem for which state spaces are too large to be explored in a reasonable time. In our case, we aim at finding the most appropriate weight for each attribute, according to a fitness function. The latter allows us to specialize our model, and to train it to favour the detection of certain types of context changes (ends of session, skipped items, thematic changes, strong or slight variations, ...). The results showed that by adapting the weight of some attributes, the percentage of overlap between changes of implicit context and ends of session can be increased. In some cases, the distribution of the weights can give meaning to the changes of context. As an example, the tempo and the energy of songs were often highly weighted when applying our model to our music dataset, while the weight of the location of artist was low. The weights are computed for each user, since we all have different habits of consultations (even if they could also be computed for all the users put together). However, if some attributes are always lowly weighted for almost all users, it can indicate that these attributes are not relevant for the type of context changes we aim to detect or for this application domain. On the opposite, if they are always highly weighted, they are mandatory when modelling usages. We also proved that the parameterization of our model was stable because the configurations of the weights obtained were very similar from one execution of our genetic algorithm to another.

One difficulty remains for this parameterization process. We should provide a way to dynamically adapt the fitness function to match user's feedback and expectations all over their consultations so as to improve the performances of our model. This could lead the model to recompute the weights of attributes for each user periodically or at some specific moments/situations. We can also imagine that user behaviors varies from an explicit context to another. Recomputing weights will thus allow us to build a map of relations between implicit and explicit contexts (assuming that we have the information about the contextual factors, even if collected *a posteriori*).

3.2 Context-based recommendations

Currently, DANCE can be used to split a sequence of consultations into implicit contexts on the basis of the evolution of diversity. All the items contained in a same implicit context share common characteristics that we could use to provide recommendations. Previously, we have explained that using contextual information leads to better recommendations and we want to use our implicit contexts to achieve the same goal. We will now present the different required steps so as to use implicit context:

- detect in real time and as soon as possible the current context (CC). The faster the system identify the implicit context, the better the recommendations will fit to the context. For the moment, we validated our approach *a posteriori* on an offline dataset. In real situation, the model will have to analyse sequences while they are not over;
- use the history of the active user, or all the users to find all the implicit similar contexts to CC;
- mine those similar contexts to find the most relevant items to recommend. The goal here is to predict the user interest for the items found in the similar contexts. As the number of items to be recommended is limited, all the items found previously have to be ranked according to their relevance to CC. The relevance can be estimated from the history of the user. For instance, if a user usually consults several times some items, he might have few tolerance toward novelty and serendipity. Otherwise, we can find relevant items from other users' history. Analysing the way the attributes of the current context evolves could be another solution to rank the items. For example, in a context where the price of the consulted items is always within a fixed interval, selecting items that respect that condition could be an efficient way to find relevant items.

This process of recommendation offers a major advantage: only the items directly related to the active user's short-term needs are used in the recommendation process. Indeed, unlike traditional systems which use all the items of the current session to provide recommendations, our approach ensures to select relevant items.

DANCE could also be used to predict the end of an explicit context and even to anticipate the next one. The history of a user, or of all the users, can be used as a train set and several rules can be extracted and used to improve the recommendation. Pattern mining techniques or association rules algorithms could be used to increase the prediction of transitions between contexts.

3.3 Characterization of implicit contexts

Providing recommendations adapted to the current context is very important but not self sufficient. Whatever how well a recommendation fits to the context according to the system, if the user does not accept it, this recommendation is a failure. That is why an important part of the recommendation process is to ensure that the user will understand the reasons why the system proposes those items in particular. To maximize the acceptance rate of the recommendations based on the implicit contexts, we have to find ways to automatically characterize the current context. Such a characterization could be used to explain to a user both how the system perceives his current context and why the recommendations made are adapted to it.

Extracting the characteristics could be done by analysing the differences of diversity between attributes. As we currently do not know what is the best way to characterise an implicit context, we aim at developing an automatic machine learning model able to detect and extract the representative characteristics of each implicit context. Such a model could determine the subset of attributes for which the evolution of diversity is remarkable: very low or very high variations, significant correlation between several attributes... The goal is not to find a unique characterisation for each context, which would not only make the calculations of similar contexts difficult, but would complicate the user explanation task. The system must find the best compromise between the mathematical identification of principal components within the context and the understanding/acceptance by users, as the optimal classification of the characteristics can be different from users' perception. As an example, there could exist some contexts for which the diversity of all the attributes is pretty low. Conversely, there can exist some contexts for which the user expects a high specialisation for some attributes and a high diversity for all the others. For instance, in a professional social network, a possible explanation of an implicit context detected in a consultation sequence of job offers could be: "According to your previous consultations we realized that you are looking for a job in the health informatics domain with a minimum wage of 2000 Euros per month but the location seems regardless to you. That is why we recommend you those items".

The characterization task we want to develop is close to the task performed by a critique-based recommender. Indeed, after each cycle of recommendation, a critique-based recommender tries to discover the right combinations of attributes in order to help the user to filter the items.

3.4 User perception of implicit contexts

Our model DANCE has been evaluated offline and our recommendation systems based on implicit contexts will be evaluated as well. However, conducting user studies and confronting our model to real users in a real situation of recommendation is necessary in order to evaluate the user satisfaction, the acceptance and the adoption rates [2].

In a first time, we want to measure the perception of the notion of implicit context. We would like to ask users to split contiguous sequences of consultation into shorter sequences and ask them to explain why they split them in this manner. The main idea is to compare the contexts determined by the users with the implicit contexts computed by our model. By comparing these two kinds of contexts, 4 possibilities could be considered:

- Users' contexts are the same, or closely similar in comparison to the implicit contexts;
- Users' contexts are partially the same compared to implicit contexts;
- Users' contexts are different from implicit contexts, but users would also agree with the implicit contexts;
- Users' contexts are different from implicit contexts and users do not understand them.

In the first case, the implicit contexts are perceived by users and this supports the relevance of the notion of implicit context. In the second case, since there is a an overlap between the implicit contexts and the contexts given by the users, we can suppose that a parameterization of our model could reduce this difference. The explanations of the users

could be used to set the fitness function. The third case could mean that there are different relevant ways to split a sequence into implicit contexts. Furthermore, the two approaches may potentially be both relevant and could be used to provide recommendations. In the fourth case, it would be necessary to adapt the explanations of the recommendations as the user will not understand the implicit context used to provide the recommendations.

In a second time, we want to test our approach of recommendation according to the user satisfaction. To achieve this goal, we are developing an online music service in order to monitor the whole recommendation process. With such a tool, we will be able to collect user feedback with satisfaction survey, to test different parameterizations and ways to compute our implicit contexts (either by our current split process or by using the users' one), to make A/B testing to compare our method with several recommendation approaches.

4. CONCLUSION

As a conclusion, we had promising results to model users' context from the observation of diversity over time. We are expecting this approach to be the cornerstone of an all new privacy-preserving recommendation framework.

5. REFERENCES

[1] G. Adomavicius and A. Tuzhilin. Context–aware recommender systems. *Recommender Systems Handbook*, pages 217–253, 2011.

[2] S. Castagnos, A. Brun, and A. Boyer. When diversity is needed... but not expected! In *IMMM*, pages 44–50, 2013.

[3] S. Castagnos, A. L 'huillier, and A. Boyer. Toward a Robust Diversity-Based Model to Detect Changes of Context. In *27th IEEE International Conference on Tools with Artificial Intelligence (ICTAI 2015)*, Vietri sul Mare, Italy, Nov. 2015.

[4] L. F. Cranor. Hey, that's personal! In L. Ardissono, P. Bruna, and A. Mitrovic, editors, *User Modeling 2005*, volume 3538 of *Lecture Notes in Computer Science*, pages 4–4. Springer Berlin Heidelberg, 2005.

[5] A. K. Dey, G. D. Abowd, and D. Salber. A conceptual framework and a toolkit for supporting the rapid prototyping of context-aware applications. *Hum.-Comput. Interact.*, 16(2):97–166, Dec. 2001.

[6] A. L'Huillier, S. Castagnos, and A. Boyer. Understanding Usages by Modeling Diversity over Time. volume 1181 of *UMAP 2014 Extended Proceedings*, Aalborg, Denmark, July 2014.

[7] A. L'Huillier, S. Castagnos, and A. Boyer. Modéliser la diversité au cours du temps pour détecter le contexte dans un service de musique en ligne. *Revue des Sciences et Technologies de l'Information*, 2016.

[8] L. McGinty and B. Smyth. On the role of diversity in conversational recommender systems. In *Proceedings of the Fifth International Conference on Case–Based Reasoning*, pages 276–290. Springer, 2003.

[9] S. M. McNee, J. Riedl, and J. A. Konstan. Being accurate is not enough: how accuracy metrics have hurt recommender systems. pages 1097–1101, 2006.

[10] B. Smyth and P. McClave. Similarity vs. diversity. ICCBR '01, pages 347–361, London, UK, UK, 2001.

Enhancing Personalized Document Ranking using Social Information

Nawal OULD AMER
Universite de Grenoble
LIG laboratory, MRIM Group Grenoble, France
nawal.ould-amer@imag.fr

CCS Concepts

•Information systems → Personalization; Information retrieval; Retrieval models and ranking; Document topic models;

Keywords

User model, Personalized search, Social search, Profile filtering

1. RESEARCH OVERVIEW

Social networks (like Facebook[1] and MySpace[2]), collaborative bookmarking systems (like Bibsonomy[3], Delicious[4], and CiteULike[5]) and Microblog systems like twitter[6], offer services such as sharing, commenting, tagging, publishing, rating, retweeting and discussing, that make users increasingly active. Hence, users are more and more connected. Given the tremendous amount of information, witch is generated by these platforms, there is a need to an Information Retrieval (IR) system to automatically answer user's queries. However, IR system, in this case should take into account additional criteria, such as user's social networks, user's interests, user's preferences, etc. In other words, the classical IR systems should be personalized.

In personalized information retrieval, the search process considers a user's model that covers user's interest, behavior and history. Commonly, users models are build trough user's query logs [10], user's posts (such as tweets, blogs and comments) [15], user's tags and bookmarking [1, 12, 16]. Consequently, a user is represented by a profile. The user profile is then used in IR system in two main scenarios, *"query expansion"* [3, 4, 7], or document *"re-ranking"*[6, 8, 9,

---

[1]https://www.facebook.com/
[2]https://myspace.com/
[3]http://www.bibsonomy.org/
[4]http://delicious.com/
[5]http://www.citeulike.org/
[6]https://twitter.com/

UMAP '16 July 13-17, 2016, Halifax, NS, Canada

© 2016 Copyright held by the owner/author(s).

ACM ISBN 978-1-4503-4370-1/16/07.

DOI: http://dx.doi.org/10.1145/2930238.2930374

15]. In this work, I focus on documents re-ranking within the framework of social bookmaking systems.

Several studies have been interested in improving personalized documents ranking by using both: user's information (such as his interests, preferences, ...) and other social information [1, 8, 11, 14, 15, 20]. The re-ranking function, within the approaches that are based on bookmarking systems, is based user's tags that are derived from their bookmarks [8, 14, 17, 20]. In [8, 18], the ranking model considers both the matching score between a query and the social annotations of the document, and the matching between the user profile and the document. In [20], the authors propose a probabilistic model based on Latent Dirichlet Allocation (LDA), where the model incorporates user interests that are represented by topics, and are based on their social annotations.

Other works personalize the search process using the user's social network. Several ways are introduced for choosing these users from the social network of a particular user. For example, selecting users that have an explicit relationship as *"follower"* [15] or *"friend"* [11] with the query issuer, selecting users that have annotated the considered document [8], or selecting users that have similar interests with the query issuer [18]. For example, [15] propose a collaborative personalized search model based on topic models, which exploits the user's social relations. Each user and his "friends" have two-level representation: a topic level and a word level. The goal of these two levels is to disambiguate the query.

In [9], the personalized social search is based on the user's social relations. In this approach, the documents are re-ranked according to their relations with others users in the user's social network. These other users are weighted by their similarity to the query issuer. Similarly, [8] strengthens the document score by considering other users from the social network that have annotated the document, and integrate similarity scores with the query issuer.

In the above mentioned approaches, the two major facets used are: (1) integrating the user profile into search process, where the user profile is used to compute the matching score of the document, and (2) selecting other users from the social networks of the query issuer, which are weighted by their similarity with the query issuer. However, a user could be interested in several topics. Therefore, using the whole profile could degrade the effectiveness of the personalized search. Furthermore, similarity criteria for weighting users from the social network can be strengthened by an *"expertise weight"* according to the query.

The research questions on which I focus are:

- How to model user and which strategy of user profile filtering can be used to improve the results ?

- Which criteria for selecting users from the social networks can be used to enhance the results ?

2. RESEARCH FOCUS

2.1 Profile Filtering

The user profile reflect user's interests. Using the whole profile may become noisy. Therefore, I need to filter the user profile according to his query. I conduct preliminary quantitative analysis on Bibsonomy [7] dataset to study user profiles: for each user I calculate the number of topics in which the user is interested through his tags. To achieve this, I first use Latent Dirichlet Allocation (LDA) [5], using Mallet[8], to discover a set of K topics from the document collection. Afterward, I consider each user as a document to determine the topics that describe the user, leading to one topic distribution θ_u per user u. For example, $\theta_u = \{topic_1 : 0.13,\ topic_2 : 0.09,\ topic_3 : 0.05, ...\}$. Then, I fix a threshold to determine the topics of a user. I analyzed the topic distribution for all users in Bibsonomy, the mean of distribution is 0.05. Thus, I use two threshold values $threshold_1 = 0.05$ (5%, a conservative value that keeps most of the topics) and $threshold_2 = 0.1$ (10%, a stricter version of the profile topics). Further to have significant analysis, I selected 2 classes of users. The first class considers all users that have more than 100 tags (i.e. active users), and the second class keeps all users. Figure 1, presents the percentage of users of the collection (y-axis), that have $\leq 1, \leq 2, ..., \leq K$ topics (x-axis). The figure shows that for the two classes more than 50% of the users have 4 topics or more. These results encourage me to do some filtering to user profiles.

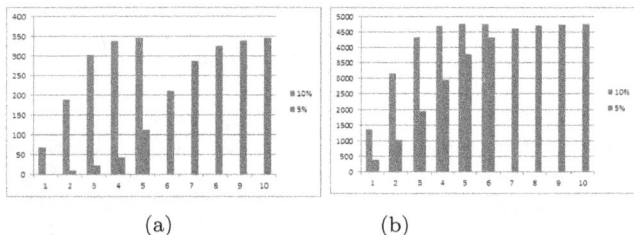

(a)   (b)

Figure 1: (a): All users, (b): users with >= 100 tags

To sum up, the analysis shows that a user could be interested in several topics. The next step, is to find a strategy to select the right part of the user profile which improves the results. To achieve this goal, I use also topic modeling to extract query's topics.

2.2 Users Selection

The user social connections provide a good information about the user's preferences. Using this information is not trivial. In fact, relying on similar users of the query issuer, friends of the query issuer, or both, is not enough. The criteria on which I focus is user expertise. Which users are

[7]http://www.bibsonomy.org/
[8]http://mallet.cs.umass.edu/

expert in query topics. The topical expertise selecting involves the task of finding users with the good profile for q given query need.

2.3 Preliminary Results

I conducted some preliminary experiments to study the profile filtering approach. I used Bibsonomy dataset, which is described in [2]. Table 1 presents some statistics about this dataset.

Table 1: Bibsonomy dataset statistics

Dataset	Web pages	Users	Tags	unique Tag
Bibsonomy	308 906	4750	1 500 000	59 886

Evaluating the personalized IR systems is a real problem. In fact, the evaluation requires personalized relevance judgments. To alleviate this problem, some works proposed an alternative approach is based on this assumption: *"The document d is relevant if this document is tagged by user u with a tag t, and this tag t is used as query issued by the user u"*. For my experiments, I used the same protocol. As results, I select 200 queries and their relevance judgments . For evaluation, the performances is reported with the Mean Average Precision (MAP) and the Mean Reciprocal Rank (MRR) measures.

As preliminary experiments, I have compared a classical model for a personalized social search [17] and my extended classical model (i.e, profile filtered). The classical model is described with the following formula:

$$Score(d, q, u) = \alpha Score(q, d) + (1 - \alpha) Score(u, d) \quad (1)$$

where $Score(q, d)$ represents the matching score between document d and the query q, $Score(u, d)$ represents the matching score between the profile of u and the document d, and α is a parameter to determines the importance of each part of the document ranking formula.

The extended model is based on using the filtered profile of user. For that, I used a naive method to model the user with the filtered profile based on the query. First, I detected a topics of the query using LDA. After that, I model the user with topics and I select the terms within the topics of queries which are detected. The extended model is described with this formula:

$$Score(d, q, u) = \beta Score(q, d) + (1 - \beta) Score(u_{fil}, d) \quad (2)$$

where $Score(q, d)$ represents the matching score between document d and the query q, $Score(u_{fil}, d)$ represents the matching score between the filtered-profile of u and the document d, and β is a parameter that determines the importance of each part of the document ranking formula.

All matching scores in the above formulas (i.e, Eq 1 and Eq 2) are computing using the Language Model with Dirichlet smoothing [19] implemented in Terrier search engine [13]. Note that I fixed β and α to 0.5. The experimental results are shown in Table 2. The table shows that he extended model outperforms the classical model. This is due to the fact that a classical approach fail to determine the relevant part of user profile. In fact, the whole profile is used, which generates some noise. This shows that the user profile should

Table 2: Preliminary

Model	MAP	MRR
Classical Model	0.0415	0.2165
Extended Model	0.0771	0.2658

be filtered to keep the relevant parts that enhance the results.

3. FUTURE WORKS

As future works, I would like to achieve the following goals:

- **New Evaluation Protocol**
  Evaluation of personalized information retrieval systems requires personalized relevance judgments. Hence, some work proposed a protocol for the personalized evaluation [17]. The main assumption is: *"The document d is relevant if this document is tagged by user u with a tag t, and this tag t is used as query issued by the user u"*. In fact, a query generated by this protocol consists of one term (i.e, tag) and the document tagged by the user using this term is relevant. I would like to test the approaches with queries that have more than 1 term. Therefore, it is indispensable to create a new evaluation protocol that permits to achieve this purpose. Furthermore, I plane to conduct a user study to have a real queries and relevance-judgments to conduct a real experiments.

- **New Public Dataset**
  The method used by most of studies is based on streaming data from social platforms such as Delicious, Bibsonomy, and Twitter, by using their API. Some of these datasets are available such as Bibsonomy [2], and Delicious [17]. To use these datasets, we should download the web pages, and in most of the time some pages are not available or are changed. Then, it make difficult to compare with a state-of-the-art approaches which are tested on these datasets. Another problem is that some of the available datasets do not provide a relations between users, which make difficult to test all approaches based on explicit relations between users. To alleviate these problems, I am working on elaborating a new dataset that covers all necessary information and make it available.

- **Personalized Model**
  I am now focusing on an extension to the classical topic model to consider user layer and social information (i.e other users) layer. Furthermore, I plane to work on a new approach for selecting users in the social networks that based on social and topical criteria.

4. REFERENCES

[1] S. Bao, G. Xue, X. Wu, Y. Yu, B. Fei, and Z. Su. Optimizing web search using social annotations. In *Proceedings of the 16th International Conference on World Wide Web*, WWW '07, pages 501–510, New York, NY, USA, 2007. ACM.

[2] D. Benz, A. Hotho, R. Jäschke, B. Krause, F. Mitzlaff, C. Schmitz, and G. Stumme. The social bookmark and publication management system bibsonomy. *The VLDB Journal*, 19(6):849–875, Dec. 2010.

[3] C. Biancalana, F. Gasparetti, A. Micarelli, and G. Sansonetti. Social semantic query expansion. *ACM Trans. Intell. Syst. Technol.*, 4(4):60:1–60:43, Oct. 2013.

[4] C. Biancalana, A. Micarelli, and C. Squarcella. Nereau: A social approach to query expansion. In *Proceedings of the 10th ACM Workshop on Web Information and Data Management*, WIDM '08, pages 95–102, New York, NY, USA, 2008. ACM.

[5] D. M. Blei, A. Y. Ng, and M. I. Jordan. Latent dirichlet allocation. *J. Mach. Learn. Res.*, 3:993–1022, Mar. 2003.

[6] M. R. Bouadjenek, H. Hacid, and M. Bouzeghoub. Sopra: A new social personalized ranking function for improving web search. In *Proceedings of the 36th International ACM SIGIR Conference on Research and Development in Information Retrieval*, SIGIR '13, pages 861–864, New York, NY, USA, 2013. ACM.

[7] M. R. Bouadjenek, H. Hacid, M. Bouzeghoub, and J. Daigremont. Personalized social query expansion using social bookmarking systems. In *Proceedings of the 34th International ACM SIGIR Conference on Research and Development in Information Retrieval*, SIGIR '11, pages 1113–1114, New York, NY, USA, 2011. ACM.

[8] M. R. Bouadjenek, H. Hacid, M. Bouzeghoub, and A. Vakali. Using social annotations to enhance document representation for personalized search. In *Proceedings of the 36th International ACM SIGIR Conference on Research and Development in Information Retrieval*, SIGIR '13, pages 1049–1052, New York, NY, USA, 2013. ACM.

[9] D. Carmel, N. Zwerdling, I. Guy, S. Ofek-Koifman, N. Har'el, I. Ronen, E. Uziel, S. Yogev, and S. Chernov. Personalized social search based on the user's social network. In *Proceedings of the 18th ACM Conference on Information and Knowledge Management*, CIKM '09, pages 1227–1236, New York, NY, USA, 2009. ACM.

[10] Z. Dou, R. Song, and J.-R. Wen. A large-scale evaluation and analysis of personalized search strategies. In *Proceedings of the 16th International Conference on World Wide Web*, WWW '07, pages 581–590, New York, NY, USA, 2007. ACM.

[11] A. Khodaei, S. Sohangir, and C. Shahabi. *Recommendation and Search in Social Networks*, chapter Personalization of Web Search Using Social Signals, pages 139–163. Springer International Publishing, Cham, 2015.

[12] M. G. Noll and C. Meinel. Web search personalization via social bookmarking and tagging. In *Proceedings of the 6th International The Semantic Web and 2Nd Asian Conference on Asian Semantic Web Conference*, ISWC'07/ASWC'07, pages 367–380, Berlin, Heidelberg, 2007. Springer-Verlag.

[13] I. Ounis, G. Amati, V. Plachouras, B. He, C. Macdonald, and C. Lioma. Terrier: A High Performance and Scalable Information Retrieval Platform. In *Proceedings of ACM SIGIR'06 Workshop*

on *Open Source Information Retrieval (OSIR 2006)*, 2006.

[14] D. Vallet, I. Cantador, and J. M. Jose. Personalizing web search with folksonomy-based user and document profiles. In *Proceedings of the 32Nd European Conference on Advances in Information Retrieval*, ECIR'2010, pages 420–431, Berlin, Heidelberg, 2010. Springer-Verlag.

[15] J. Vosecky, K. W.-T. Leung, and W. Ng. Collaborative personalized twitter search with topic-language models. In *Proceedings of the 37th International ACM SIGIR Conference on Research & Development in Information Retrieval*, SIGIR '14, pages 53–62, New York, NY, USA, 2014. ACM.

[16] X. Wu, L. Zhang, and Y. Yu. Exploring social annotations for the semantic web. In *Proceedings of the 15th International Conference on World Wide Web*, WWW '06, pages 417–426, New York, NY, USA, 2006. ACM.

[17] S. Xu, S. Bao, B. Fei, Z. Su, and Y. Yu. Exploring folksonomy for personalized search. In *Proceedings of the 31st Annual International ACM SIGIR Conference on Research and Development in Information Retrieval*, SIGIR '08, pages 155–162, New York, NY, USA, 2008. ACM.

[18] Z. Xu, T. Lukasiewicz, and O. Tifrea-Marciuska. Improving personalized search on the social web based on similarities between users. In *Proceedings of the 8th International Conference on Scalable Uncertainty Management - Volume 8720*, SUM 2014, pages 306–319, New York, NY, USA, 2014. Springer-Verlag New York, Inc.

[19] C. Zhai and J. Lafferty. A study of smoothing methods for language models applied to information retrieval. *ACM Trans. Inf. Syst.*, 22(2):179–214, Apr. 2004.

[20] D. Zhou, J. Bian, S. Zheng, H. Zha, and C. L. Giles. Exploring social annotations for information retrieval. In *Proceedings of the 17th International Conference on World Wide Web*, WWW '08, pages 715–724, New York, NY, USA, 2008. ACM.

Author Index

www.ingramcontent.com/pod-product-compliance
Lightning Source LLC
Chambersburg PA
CBHW080902220326
41598CB00034B/5446